MARXISM IN THE POSTMODERN AGE

CRITICAL PERSPECTIVES
A Guilford Series

Edited by
DOUGLAS KELLNER
University of Texas, Austin

Postmodern Theory: Critical Interrogations
Steven Best and Douglas Kellner

A Theory of Human Need
Len Doyal and Ian Gough

Psychoanalytic Politics, Second Edition:
Jacques Lacan and Freud's French Revolution
Sherry Turkle

Postnational Identity:
Critical Theory and Existential Philosophy
in Habermas, Kierkegaard, and Havel
Martin J. Matuštík

Theory as Resistance:
Politics and Culture after (Post)structuralism
Mas'ud Zavarzadeh and Donald Morton

Postmodernism and Social Inquiry
David R. Dickens and Andrea Fontana, Editors

Marxism in the Postmodern Age:
Confronting the New World Order
Antonio Callari, Stephen Cullenberg, and
Carole Biewener, Editors

Forthcoming

After Marxism
Ronald Aronson

MARXISM IN THE POSTMODERN AGE
Confronting the New World Order

Antonio Callari
Stephen Cullenberg
Carole Biewener
Editors

THE GUILFORD PRESS
New York   London

"Always Just over the Horizon: The East German Intellectual
and the Elusive Public Sphere" © 1992 Inez Hedges

"Waiting for the Revolution, or How to Smash Capitalism
While Working at Home in Your Spare Time" © 1993 the
Association for Economic and Social Analysis

"Intimations of Mortality: On Historical Communism and the
'End of History'" © 1993 Gregory Elliot

"Clintonism, Welfare, and the Antisocial Wage: The
Emergence of a Neoliberal Political Imaginary" © 1993 the
Association for Economic and Social Analysis

Library of Congress Cataloging-in-Publication Data

Marxism in the postmodern age : confronting the new world order /
    edited by Antonio Callari, Stephen Cullenberg, Carole Biewener.
        p.   cm. — (Critical perspectives)
    Includes bibliographical references and index.
    ISBN 0-89862-423-1
        1. Socialism.   2. Communism.   3. Communism and society.   4. Post-
communism.   5. World politics—1989-   6. Postmodernism—Social
aspects.   7. Feminist theory.   I. Callari, Antonio.
II. Cullenberg, Stephen.   III. Biewener, Carole.   IV. Series:
Critical perspectives (New York, N.Y.)
HX44.5.M383   1995
335.43—dc20   93-49636
                                                                           CIP

Contributors

JACK AMARIGLIO teaches Economics at Merrimack College and is the editor of *Rethinking* MARXISM. He is the author of many articles on the history and philosophy of economic thought and Marxian theory. He is coeditor of a forthcoming book entitled *Postmodernism, Economics, and Knowledge.*

CATHERINE ANDERSON lives in the Boston area. Her book, *In the Mother Tongue,* was published by Alicejamesbooks in Cambridge, MA.

ETIENNE BALIBAR teaches courses in Epistemology and in Political Philosophy at the University of Paris I in the Department of Philosophy. He has written extensively on Marxism and on political theory. His current work explores forms of subjectivity constructed in and through relationships between citizenship and nationalism. He is the author, with Immanuel Wallerstein, of *Race, Nation, Class: Ambiguous Identities.* His most recent books are: *Masses, Classes, Ideas: Studies on Politics and Philosophy before and after Marx* and *Lieux et Noms de la vérité* (The Places and Names of Truth).

DAVID BARKIN is Professor of Economics at the Xochimilco Campus of the Universidad Autonoma Metropolitana in Mexico City. He was awarded the National Prize in Political Economy in Mexico and is a fellow of the Academy of Scientific Research. He is a member of the National Research Council and has published widely on problems of development and international economic integration. He is presently on leave as a Senior Fellow at the Lincoln Institute of Land Policy in Cambridge, Massachusetts.

ROSALYN BAXANDALL is Professor of American Studies at the State University of New York at Old Westbury. She is the author of *Words on Fire, the Life and Writing of Elizabeth Gurley Flynn,* coauthor of *The Rise and Fall of the Suburban Dream, 1945-2000,* and coeditor of *America's Working Women, an Anthology of Women's Work, 1620-1970.* She has written extensively on working women, day care, sexuality, reproductive rights, and race and gender in suburbia. She has also been a feminist activitist for more than 25 years, active on many boards and coalitions.

CAROLE BIEWENER teaches Economics at Simmons College, Boston, and is an editor of *Rethinking* MARXISM. She has written on contemporary French socialism and is currently researching the European Monetary System.

THEODORE BURCZAK currently teaches Economics at Williams College in Williamstown, MA. He is interested in developing a radical, subjectivist economics.

ANTONIO CALLARI is Professor of Economics at Franklin and Marshall College in Lancaster, PA. An editor of *Rethinking* MARXISM, he has written on Marxian economics, politics, and philosophy. He is currently working on a history of economics from a postmodernist perspective. He is also active as a community organizer.

STEPHEN CULLENBERG is Associate Professor of Economics at the University of California, Riverside and an editor of *Rethinking* MARXISM. He is the author of *The Falling Rate of Profit: Recasting the Marxian Debate* and articles on Marxian theory, political economy, and socialist alternatives, and is coeditor with Bernd Magnus of *Whither Marxism: Global Crises in International Perspective*.

THOMAS DELGIUDICE is Assistant Professor in the Politics, Economics, and Society Program at the State University of New York at Old Westbury. His primary interest is in the relationships between international trade and class relations.

GEORGE DEMARTINO teaches at the School of International Studies, University of Denver, Colorado. He has served as a union organizer, negotiator, and consultant and has written on labor issues. He is an editor of *Rethinking* MARXISM.

JONATHAN DISKIN teaches in the departments of Economics and Peace and Global Studies at Earlham College in Richmond, IN.

GREGORY ELLIOTT was educated at Balliol College, Oxford, England. A member of the Radical Philosophy Collective, he is the author of *Althusser: The Detour of Theory* and *Labourism and the English Genius: The Strange Death of Labour England?* and editor of *Althusser: A Critical Reader*.

MARY A. ENGELMEYER is currently a graduate student in the Department of Economics at the University of Notre Dame. She is doing research on the concept of family farming in order to understand its class and gender aspects, and plans to continue research in farming in order to add the dimension of race and to expand research beyond the arena of family farming in the Midwest to other areas such as the Northeast, the South, and the West.

BARBARA EPSTEIN teaches in the History of Consciousness Board at the University of California, Santa Cruz. She is working on a book on the political culture of post-World War II United States.

HARRIET FRAAD is a psychoanalytic psychotherapist and a Marxian feminist activist. Her articles appear in *Rethinking* MARXISM and *The Journal of Psychohistory*. She recently published, with Stephen Resnick and Richard D. Wolff, *Bringing It All Back Home: Class, Gender, and Power in the Household*. She is also an editor of *Rethinking* MARXISM.

NANCY FRASER is Professor of Philosophy at Northwestern University, where she is also a Fellow of the Center for Urban Affairs and Policy Research and an affiliate of the Women's Studies Program. She is the author of *Unruly Practices: Power, Discourse, and Gender in Contemporary Social Theory*, the coauthor of *Streit Zum Differenz*, and the coeditor of *Revaluing French Feminism: Critical Essays on Difference, Agency, and Culture*.

J. K. GIBSON-GRAHAM is the pen name of Katherine Gibson and Julie Graham, industrial geographers who write about conceptions of industrial society and their implications for gender and class politics. Gibson is Director of Women's Studies at Monash University in Melbourne, Australia. Graham teaches in the Department of Geography at the University of Massachusetts–Amherst and is a member of the editorial board of *Rethinking* MARXISM.

MARTHA E. GIMENEZ, Associate Professor of Sociology at the University of Colorado at Boulder, has written on the political economy of population, Marxist feminist theory, poverty, and the political constructions of race, ethnicity, and gender. Her work has appeared in *Science and Society*, *The Review of Radical Political Economics*, *The International Journal of Health Services*, *Gender and Society*, and *Latin American Perspectives*. Together with Jane Collins, she edited *Work Without Wages*.

MICHAEL HARDT is Visiting Assistant Professor in the Literature Program at Duke University. He is coauthor (with Antonio Negri) of *Labor of Dionysus: A Critique of the State-form* and author of *Gilles Deleuze: An Apprenticeship in Philosophy*.

BARBARA HARLOW teaches English and Comparative Literature at the University of Texas at Austin. She is the author of *Resistance Literature* and *Barred: Women, Writing, and Political Detention*. Currently she is working on projects on the "cultural politics of partition" and "writers, martyrs, revolutionaries."

LAURENCE HARRIS is Professor of Economics at the School of Oriental and African Studies, University of London. His publications cover Marxist theory (including *Rereading Capital* and the *Dictionary of Marxist Thought*), money and finance (including *Monetary Theory* and *New Perspectives on the Financial System*), and the economics of southern Africa. He has advised the African National Congress for many years and, in 1993, was coauthor of the ANC–Congress of South African Trade Unions' economic policy framework, *Making Democracy Work*.

INEZ HEDGES is Professor of French, German, and Cinema Studies at Northeastern University, Boston. She is the author of *Breaking the Frame: Film Language and the Experience of Limits* and *Languages of Revolt: Dada and Surrealist Literature and Film*.

ROSEMARY HENNESSY teaches postmodern critical cultural studies and feminist, lesbian, and gay theory in the English Department at the University of Albany, State University of New York, where she is also affiliated with Women's Studies. Her book, *Materialist Feminism and the Politics of Discourse*, shows how the resources of the Marxist tradition can contribute to contemporary efforts to rethink the subject of feminism; her current work addresses the rearticulation of sexual identities under advanced capitalism.

M. C. HOWARD is Professor of Economics at the University of Waterloo, Ontario. Coauthor with J. E. King of *A History of Marxian Economics* and author of other books and articles in the areas of economic theory and intellectual history, Howard is presently engaged in the analysis of economic systems within the context of the world economy and globalization.

SUSAN EVE JAHODA is currently Associate Professor in the Art Department at the University of Massachusetts–Amherst. Art editor of *Rethinking* MARXISM, she has been the recipient of grants from the National Endowment for the Arts and the New York Foundation of the Arts. Her work has been exhibited in Europe and the United States and has appeared in journals such as *Afterimage, Heresies*, and *Arts Magazine*.

JOY JAMES is Assistant Professor of Women's Studies at the University of Massachusetts–Amherst and coeditor of *Spirit, Space, and Survival: African American Women in (White) Academe*.

SUT JHALLY is Professor of Communication at the University of Massachusetts–Amherst and founder and Executive Director of *Mediated, the Media Education Foundation*. He has written broadly on the media, advertising, and popular culture.

CINDI KATZ, a geographer, is on the faculty of the Graduate School of the City University of New York and teaches Environmental Psychology, Cultural Studies, and Women's Studies. Her work concerns the production of place, space, and nature in everyday life. She is the editor, with Janice Monk, of *Full Circles: Geographies of Women over the Life Course*.

DOUGLAS KELLNER is Professor of Philosophy at the University of Texas at Austin and is author of *Herbert Marcuse and the Crisis of Marxism; Critical Theory, Marxism, and Modernity; Jean Baudrillard: From Marxism to Postmodernism and Beyond*; and *Postmodern Theory*, as well as other books and articles on social theory, culture, and politics. His forthcoming book is *Between Modernity and Postmodernism*.

J. E. KING is Reader in Economics at LaTrobe University, Australia. Coauthor with M. C. Howard of *A History of Marxian Economics* and author of other books and articles in the areas of labour economics and intellectual history, King is presently engaged in research on the historical development of post-Keynesian economics.

JOEL KOVEL is Alger Hiss Professor of Social Studies at Bard College. His most recent books are *History and Spirit* and *Red Hunting in the Promised Land*.

AMITAVA KUMAR teaches in the English Department at the University of Florida, Gainesville. He is a member of Impact Visuals, a New York-based progressive photo co-op. His photojournalism and poetry have appeared in publications in both India and the United States, including *The Times of India, Indian Express, The Guardian, Z Magazine*, Rethinking MARXISM, and *Artpaper*.

MICHAEL A. LEBOWITZ teaches Marxian Economics at Simon Fraser University in Burnaby, B.C. In addition to his recent book, *Beyond Capital*, his interests and writings revolve around crisis theory, methodology, and the theory of socialist economy.

RICHARD LEVINS, a Marxist ecologist, is active in the radical science, alternative agriculture, Puerto Rican independence, and Latin America Solidarity movements. He serves on the Board of OXFAM America and teaches at the Harvard School of Public Health, Cambridge, MA.

JUSTIN LEWIS is Associate Professor in the Department of Communication, University of Massachusetts–Amherst. He has written several books on a range of media, cultural, and cultural policy issues.

RICHARD LICHTMAN has taught Philosophy at the University of California, Berkeley, and Social Theory and Therapy at the Wright Institute for the past

20 years. He is the author of *The Production of Desire* and the recently published *Essays in Critical Social Theory: Towards a Marxist Critique of Liberal Ideology*.

ANDREA LISS is a Visiting Faculty member in the Art and Photography programs at the California Institute of the Arts. She is a doctoral candidate in the Department of Art History at the University of California, Los Angeles, where she is writing her dissertation, entitled *Trespassing Shadows: History, Mourning and Photography in Contemporary Representations of Holocaust Memory*. She was awarded the American Association of University Women Educational Fellowship for 1993–1994.

ERNEST MANDEL received his Ph.D. from the Free University of Berlin. He was a member of the economic studies commission of the Belgian Trade Union Federation FGTB from 1954 to 1963, Professor at Vrije Universitieit in Brussels from 1972 to 1991, and, until his retirement, a member of the leadership of the Fourth International and its Belgian section. He is the author of numerous books: *Marxist Economic Theory, Late Capitalism, Long Waves of Capitalist Development, Power and Money,* and *Trotsky as Alternative*.

RICHARD MCINTYRE is Associate Professor of Economics at the University of Rhode Island. He has published in a variety of journals including *Review of Radical Political Economics, Review of Social Economy, Journal of Economic Issues,* and *Rethinking* MARXISM. He is currently editing a collection of critical essays on post-Fordism, researching the contribution of the slave trade to primitive accumulation in New England, and, with Michael Hillard, writing a critique of recent neo-institutionalist and neo-Marxian labor economics. He is an editor of *Rethinking* MARXISM.

ELLEN MESSER-DAVIDOW, an Associate Professor at the University of Minnesota, teaches in the departments of English, Women's Studies, and Cultural Studies. She has recently edited, with David R. Shumway and David J. Sylvan, *Knowledges: Historical and Critical Studies in Disciplinarity*, and is now completing *Disciplining Feminism: Episodes in the Discursive Production of Social Change*, a study of how academic feminism was produced.

RALPH MILIBAND (deceased) taught for many years at the London School of Economics. He was Professor of Politics at Leeds University from 1972 to 1977. He subsequently taught at Brandeis University, Boston; York University, Toronto; and the Graduate School of the City University of New York. Among his books are *The State in Capitalist Society, Marxism and Politics,* and *Divided Societies*.

WARREN MONTAG currently teaches Restoration and Eighteenth-Century English Literature at Occidental College, Los Angeles. His book *The Unthinkable Swift: The Spontaneous Philosophy of a Church-of-England Man* will be published in the Fall of 1994. He is editing a collection of contemporary essays on Spinoza to be published by the University of Minnesota Press.

BRUCE NORTON is currently a Visiting Assistant Professor of Economics at Connecticut College. He has written various articles on patterns of reasoning in Marxian and radical accumulation theories. He also edits the "New Directions/Rethinking Marxism" book series for the Association for Economic and Social Analysis.

STEPHEN RESNICK teaches Economics at the University of Massachusetts–Amherst. He has written extensively on Marxian theory. He is currently working with Richard D. Wolff on a class analysis of the USSR. He is an editor of *Rethinking* MARXISM. With Richard D. Wolff, he coauthored *Economics: Marxian versus Neoclassical* and *Knowledge and Class: A Marxian Critique of Political Economy.*

FRANK ROSENGARTEN is Professor Emeritus of Italian and Comparative Literature at Queens College, New York, and the Graduate School of the City University of New York. He has published three books on Italian political and cultural history and is editor of two recently published books, *New Studies in the Politics and Culture of U.S. Communism* and *Antonio Gramsci: Letters from Prison.* He is co-chair, with Randy Martin and Michael Brown, of the Research Group on Socialism and Democracy.

MARTHA ROSLER is an artist whose projects take a number of forms, including photography with text, video, and installation. Her work has been widely exhibited on several continents and her videotapes have been shown internationally on television and in museum exhibitions. Much of her work concerns information, power, and social mythologies. In addition to the work documented in this volume, she has recently produced projects on housing and homelessness in Missouri, on toxic flows in working-class Greenpoint, Brooklyn, and on a Jewish graveyard in a working-class community of Hamburg, Germany, that had been razed by the Nazis and is now a contested site of gentrification. Rosler writes about art and culture and is Director of Graduate Studies in Art at Rutgers University.

SHEILA ROWBOTHAM is currently a Simon Senior Research Fellow in the Sociology Department at the Manchester University. From her early work on, she has consistently been interested in the relationship between feminism and socialism and the forms taken by women's popular action, both historically and in the present. Her recent publications include *Women in Movement* and, with Swatsi Mitter, *Dignity and Daily Bread: New Forms of Economic Organizing among Poor Women in the Third World and the First.* She is currently writing a history of women in Britain and the United States during the twentieth century.

DAVID F. RUCCIO teaches economics at the University of Notre Dame. He has published essays on Latin American development, socialist planning, and postmodernism in economics. He is an editor of *Rethinking* MARXISM.

DEAN J. SAITTA is an Assistant Professor of Anthropology at the University of Denver. He is currently writing a book about the political economy of ancient North America.

BLAIR SANDLER is a graduate student in Economics at the University of Massachusetts–Amherst, whose Ph.D. dissertation is a class analysis of corporate responses to environmentalism. He currently lives in the San Francisco Bay Area.

JOHN SINISI teaches Economics at the Pennsylvania State University Schuylkill Campus. He is currently working on a comparative study of Hobbesian and Marxian understandings of the intertwining of economic and political processes.

GAYATRI CHAKRAVORTY SPIVAK, Avalon Foundation Professor in the Humanities at Columbia University, teaches English and Cultural Politics. Among her publications are a translation of and critical introduction to Derrida's *Of Grammatology; In Other Worlds: Essays in Cultural Politics; The Post-Colonial Critic; Outside in the Teaching Machine;* and numerous articles in her fields of interest: critical theory, feminism, and neocolonial discourse studies.

CAROL A. STABILE is a Visiting Teaching Associate at the Institute of Communications Research, University of Illinois, Urbana–Champaign. She is the author of *Selling Futures: Feminism, Postmodernism and the Technological Fix.*

KEVIN ST. MARTIN is currently a student in the Graduate School of Geography at Clark University. He is working toward a doctorate in Industrial Geography and has a strong second interest in cartography and geographic information systems.

IMMANUEL WALLERSTEIN is Director of the Fernand Braudel Center for the Study of Economies, Historical Systems, and Civilizations, and is Distinguished Professor of Sociology at Binghamton University. He is author of *The Modern World System, Historical Capitalism,* and more recently of *Unthinking Social Science: The Limits of Nineteenth-Century Paradigms.*

KATHI WEEKS teaches Political Theory at Fairfield University, Connecticut. She is currently preparing a manuscript on feminist standpoint theory.

GORDON WHITE is a Professorial Fellow at the Institute of Development Studies, University of Sussex, Brighton, England. While his research is mainly focused on contemporary China, he is now exploring critical political economy perspectives on the effects of globalization on employment and social welfare systems in both the industrialized and the industrializing countries and the implications of increasing international economic integration for domestic governance and accountability.

RHONDA M. WILLIAMS is a political economist and Assistant Professor in the Afro-American Studies Program at the University of Maryland, College Park. Her recent explorations of the race and gender dimensions of economic restructuring will appear in Adler and Bernstein's (eds.) *Understanding American Economic Decline.* Williams is also studying economic conceptualizations of families and poverty in this era of structural transformation.

RICHARD D. WOLFF is a Professor of Economics at the University of Massachusetts–Amherst. With his colleague, Stephen Resnick, he is preparing a class analysis of the USSR, 1917–1990. It is an application of the new interpretation of Marxian political economy contained in their book *Knowledge and Class: A Marxian Critique of Political Economy.* He is an editor of *Rethinking* MARXISM.

Preface

This book contains a selection of papers presented at the international conference, "Marxism in the New World Order: Crises and Possibilities," held at the University of Massachusetts at Amherst on November 12–14, 1992. This was the second international conference organized by the journal *Rethinking* MARXISM and the Association for Economic and Social Analysis.[1] The book is therefore part of an ongoing project of theoretical explorations designed to facilitate the development of Marxism and Marxist theory. Due to space constraints, the volume can only offer an exemplary mix of the some 375 papers presented at the 1992 conference (grouped in 140 panels and 3 plenaries).[2]

The conference had several dimensions that went beyond the usual boundaries of an academic conference. The nontraditional character of the conference reflects how Marxism has itself developed and changed over the course of the last two decades, and the conference certainly went beyond the borders one would imagine of a Marxist conference of twenty years ago, in which there would have been a greater focus on economics and politics (themselves more narrowly conceived then than they are today) and less on the cultural, artistic, emotional, ethical, and psychological dimensions of social life. Not only did the conference include papers that addressed these varied dimensions of social life, it also incorporated directly into its program artistic events, alternative forms of expression, and nontraditional productions of meaning. There were photographs (by Sutapa Biswas and Amitava Kumar), films (by Prathiba Parmar, Tony Buba, and Steffie Domike), videos (on Marx and, contemporaneously produced, on the conference itself), theater (by Zone West, Sarah White, and Leonard Lehrman and Karen Ruoff Kramer), poetry (by Catherine Anderson), and cartoons (by Tuli Kupferberg). Integrated as a central element of the conference's overall personality was a major art exhibition, "This Is My Body, This Is My Blood," curated by Susan Jahoda and May Stevens. In this exhibition the "body" was isolated and constructed as a site of struggle depicting the material, bodily effects of patterns of oppression and control on subjected identities.[3] Along with the art exhibition there was an art installation at a nearby shopping mall, "Resituations: A Detour into the Heart of the Mall," by Stashu Kybartas, Jackie Hayden, Sherry Millner, and James Mumford. The artistic aspect of the conference is represented in this book with poetry by Catherine Anderson; commentaries on artistic exhibitions by Andrea Liss and Martha Rosler; and photographic representations of forms of oppression and resistance by Amitava Kumar. Such artistic expressions are one of the important characteristics of the nature of the Marxism(s) taking shape in the world today.

This conference also differed from its imagined counterpart of decades past in its incorporation of papers and artistic expressions reflecting issues, identities, and forms of struggle that would not have been given as central a place in the bordered (economistic) constructions of the Marxism we used to know. Considerations on sexuality, race, gender, desire, spirituality, childhood, utopian images of socialism, and ecology all found an equal place at the table, along with considerations on class, economics, and class politics. That is why many of the papers and much of the art selected for this volume address these other-than-class issues, themes, and identities. Indeed, in many respects the 1992 conference was a forum for conversations, considerations, and negotiations about the contradictory interplay of class and other-than-class dimensions of social life. It offered a space to reconsider and extend the complicated, creative, and often fraught relationships among varying types of Marxism and between Marxism and other progressive socialist traditions or cultures.

The conference, of course, contained many contributions on economic and class processes and on well-established issues in Marxian theory: economic crises, imperialism, socialism, class politics, hegemony, alienation, and so on. But, recognizing that Marxian theory is itself a developing field and that much of the impetus for development has come from the interaction between its analyses and visions and those of other social struggles, the organizers of the conference wanted to create a space for discussions not only within Marxism and its different traditions but also between Marxism(s) and other critical traditions. By integrating artistic elements into the conference format, we hoped to announce a reopening of a deep concern by Marxists with the nonanalytical dimensions of being (aesthetic, emotional, libidinal, cultural, ideological) that the scientism and economism of the cold war era too often neglected. By integrating into the conference the nonclass issues and identities of new social movements and others, we hoped to announce a project of cooperation between Marxism and other critical and "struggling" traditions to search for and describe the identities of and strategies for a fresh imaginary of alternatives to capitalism. We think that, in addressing the contradictions and tensions of the competing, conflicting, and over-determining aspects of social existence—be they cultural, political, psychological, natural, or economic—the conference broke new ground.

There is no suggestion here that the contributions included in the conference and documented to some extent in this volume represent a completed, formal, official map of the relationship between Marxism and its focus on class and other centers of political, theoretical, and cultural expression—anything but. Yet, these contributions do explore many of the cultural, political, natural, and psychological aspects of social life that intersect with class relations to produce patterns of social being and forms of oppression and of resistance. What has been called orthodox or official Marxism—what we could call "cold war Marxism"—operated with a deductive, determinist scheme that subsumed the other-than-class dimensions of social being to a more or less singular class logic, with the consequence that this Marxism's culture and politics were also lean and singular, not strong in relation to multifarious effects of bourgeois hegemony, not strong in terms of contributing to viable and dynamic radical social movements for change. If Marxism is now entering a new phase of consciousness and development, this is because for many there is a new season of open inquiry into the dimensions of social being that cold war Marxism neglected or deterministically subsumed to class. The links between these dimensions and the class dimension remains an open question that needs to be explored without prefigured solutions. We believe that such exploration opens new avenues for furthering future Marxisms and future socialist struggles for radical change. Indeed, as we already noted, the conference and this book are a part of this open process of exploration, which recognizes that a decentering of class offers important contributions to the vitality of Marxism.[4]

The project of developing the nondeterminist traditions of Marxism is in some important ways a scholarly, intellectual project, but it is not solely a scholarly project. There was a decidedly political dimension to the conferences that *Rethinking* MARXISM organized, as the organizers were repeatedly told by many of the conference participants. The conferences provided necessary institutional shells for a rejuvenation and recuperation of Marxism. Remarking on this fact, Frigga Haug (1993) recently summarized her experience of the second conference thus:

> It was also a pleasure suddenly to meet and talk with all those real people who before had just been references in the literature. They were all there: the classical feminists as well as the well-known male international Marxists. Especially encouraging was the overwhelming good feeling brought

on by the sense of participation in a common project. This was understood by the fact that almost none of the speakers left for home after addressing their panels. Instead, they could be met everywhere and each day of the conference, in discussions as well as listening. All the events were overcrowded. One felt an air of a new awakening. Perhaps it was the effort to integrate postmodernism into Marxism, making it less threatening, that stimulated the liberated feeling that there is still a possibility for doing things that make sense. Perhaps it was the sense of progress in the future, because so many young students, male and female, were undertaking the discovery of Marx for themselves.

The conference and this book owe much of their success to the concerns, questions, and conversations of the hundreds of people who have participated in these "events." We are greatly indebted to the support, work, commitment, and creative energy of a great number of individuals and organizations. We gratefully acknowledge the financial contributions of The Guilford Press; the University of Massachusetts–Amherst (Chancellor Richard O'Brien, Provost Glen Gordon, Dean Samuel F. Conti, Dean Seymour Berger, and Dean Lee Edwards; the Departments of Economics, Art, English, and Women's Studies; and the Interdepartmental Program in Film Studies, the University of Massachusetts Arts Council, the Student Enrichment Cultural Fund, and the Herter Art Gallery); Franklin and Marshall College (Economics); the Five College Consortium; Amherst College (English, Political Science, Russian/Slavic Studies, and Music); Mount Holyoke College (Political Science, Women's Studies, and African-American Studies); Hampshire College (Cultural Studies, Social Sciences, and the Office of the President); and Smith College (Government Studies and Comparative Literature).

The debate and character of the conference were wonderfully enhanced by panels cosponsored by the following organizations and journals: the Radical Philosophy Association, *Social Text*, *Boundary 2*, the Marxist Literary Group, *Science and Society*, *Studies in Political Economy*, the International Gramsci Society, *Actuel Marx*, *Antipode*, and *Capitalism, Nature, Socialism*.

We also wish to thank especially the following individuals who contributed in uncounted ways to making the conference a great success: Jack Amariglio, Masato Aoki, Enid Arvidson, Suzanne Bergeron, Robert Blake, Joan Braderman, Ted Burczak, S. Charusheela, Norman Cowie, Fred Curtis, Thomas DelGiudice, George DeMartino, Harriet Fraad, Satyanada Gabriel, Rob Garnett, Julie Graham, Karen Graubart, DeeDee Halleck, Marlene Housner, Elizabeth Hynes, Susan Jahoda, Denise Johnson, Ann Rosalind Jones, Karen Ruoff Kramer, Mary Lasota, Leonard Lehrman, Lee Levin, Lucy Lippard, Allan MacNeil, Tekla McInerney, Claude Misukiewicz, William Olson, Andrew Parker, Stephen Resnick,

John Roche, David Ruccio, Mary Russo, Tracy Schucker, Amy Silverstein, May Stevens, Judith Wilson, Richard Wolff, the administrative staff in the University of Massachusetts Economics Department, and the administrative staff, faculty, and graduate students in the University of Massachusetts Art Department.

We also thank Peter Wissoker, our editor at The Guilford Press, for working with us to publish this volume. His insight, skill, and patience have been greatly appreciated.

Finally, we sadly note the death of Ralph Miliband, a contributor to this volume and a speaker at a plenary session of the conference. Ralph Miliband died in London on May 22, 1994, while this volume was in press. We will miss his scholarship.

Antonio Callari
Stephen Cullenberg
Carole Biewener

NOTES

1. The chair of the organizing committee for this second conference was Antonio Callari. Stephen Cullenberg chaired the organizing committee for the first conference, "Marxism Now: Traditions and Difference," held in November 1989.

2. We have had to count on the cooperation of the contributors to the volume, who agreed to revise and reduce their papers—sometimes omitting parts of arguments, sometimes condensing them, sometimes removing bibliographical references—in order to fit a large number of contributions within our page constraints.

3. Elizabeth Hynes, Susan Jahoda, and May Stevens edited a catalog of this exhibit, which can be ordered from Susan Jahoda, Department of Art, University of Massachusetts at Amherst, Amherst, MA, 01003.

4. The Introduction to the inaugural issue of *Rethinking* MARXISM stated: "While serving as a conduit for all attempts to reformulate Marxism, *Rethinking* MARXISM will stress one of the many traditions in Marxism. We are especially committed to a non-determinist Marxism: a Marxism that does not claim to have found the essence of social life in one or another social activity or grouping. In our view, this non-determinist position is one tradition that has been greatly under-represented in the debates among Marxists and between Marxists and other serious thinkers" (*Rethinking* MARXISM, *1* [Spring 1988]: 8).

REFERENCES

Haug, F. 1993. "Marxism in the New World Order: Crises and Possibilities." *Rethinking Marxism*, 6 (Summer): 126.

Contents

Part Two. IMAGES AS SITES OF STRUGGLES

Part Three. THE STATE, DEMOCRACY, SOCIALISM, AND REVOLUTION

Part Four. FEMINISM, RACE, SEXUALITY, AND NATURE: INTERSECTIONS WITH MARXISM

Part Five. SOCIALISMS/CAPITALISMS

Part Six. DIMENSIONS OF CLASS ANALYSIS

Part Seven. BORDERS OF THE NEW WORLD

Part Eight. POLITICAL STRUGGLE OVER THE NORTH AMERICAN ORDER

Introduction
Marxism in the New World Order: Crises and Possibilities

ANTONIO CALLARI
STEPHEN CULLENBERG
CAROLE BIEWENER

The end of the cold war era has brought with it the dissolution of many established political and theoretical certainties. Yet, in this time of decomposition and recomposition of global relations, the "new world order" is not as defined or as definitive as the major media might lead one to believe. Indeed, the phrase "new world order" carries a sense of closure that is not warranted by the wide array of events currently shaping our lives. Some of the transformations seem full of nightmarish possibilities. One need only to think of the territorial and ethnic struggles that are engulfing major populations, or of the further weakening of democratic and/or community control over resources and capital that is prefigured in treaties such as the North American Free Trade Agreement and the GATT.

The dynamics that used to fit neatly into a system of binary oppositions (East/West, socialist/capitalist, center/periphery) are, like a deck of cards, being reshuffled and recomposed into new patterns and alliances. We would like to consider this dissolution of established polarities along the following three axes: the East/West divide, the singular class politics of domestic relations, and the North/South polarity. The transformation and/or dissolution of each of these axes brings new challenges and opportunities for the masses of struggling peoples, and for

Marxism. In this changing and often threatening world it is important for the Left and for Marxism to find new ways of struggling to shape the new world in emancipatory ways. With the dissolution of long-held certainties, Marxists are challenged to offer democratic and liberatory inspirations, to develop an alternative progressive analysis and imaginary.

THE EAST/WEST DIVIDE

Today Marxism finds itself in a changing context, a transformed world that is shaped in part by the demise of the East/West opposition. The "collapse" of Communism in 1989 has both encouraged and depressed those working within the Marxist tradition. For many who have been highly critical of socialism as actually practiced in the former Soviet Union and Eastern Europe, the collapse of this form of socialism is seen as a welcome opening to rethink socialism's future without the albatross of central planning or authoritarian regimes. The uncertainties of the new world are seen as enabling new possibilities for radical social change that had been stymied, in part, by the inflexible certainties of the East/West divide.

At the same time, the collapse of Communism in 1989 presents a political problem for Marxists: how to respond to the liberal proclamation that the end of history comes with capitalism and not with socialism. This political challenge adds urgency to the need to build progressive alternatives to capitalism that are rooted in popular struggles. From this perspective, the insecurities of the new "capitalist" world order, with its mass unemployment, economic stagnation, racially motivated attacks on immigrants and others, heightened exploitation, and intensified violence can be sharply contrasted with the economic and political securities and certainties of the socialist alternative that, for some, were associated with the former Soviet Union.

Thus, this aspect of the changing world—the collapse of the regimes in Eastern Europe—has reshaped and repositioned internal theoretical tensions and struggles within the Left in general and within Marxism in particular. In confronting these changes Marxists need to recognize the authoritarian aspects of these regimes and to understand the economic stagnation, ethnic and nationalist tensions, environmental devastation, and gendered differences they fostered, while also considering the economic security they created via full employment policies, extensive social welfare programs, relatively equitable income distribution, and worker participation. In confronting these changes Marxists also need to come to terms with the relationship of Marxism to such societies, to understand the ways in which Marxist traditions contributed to both the progressive and repressive aspects of the Soviet and Eastern European experience.

Marxism—at least orthodox Marxism—has been essentially connected with the world order of cold war dimensions. Deterministic, orthodox Marxism, the "official" Marxism that reigned supreme in the Soviet Union and elsewhere, participated in the theoretical construction of "the world" by using systemic, essentialist, totalizing, and hierarchical conceptual categories. Such a Marxism too often reduced complex social formations to expressions of articulated modes of production, and subordinated struggles and resistance of all sorts to the economistic primacy of "class struggle." It is the task of much new thinking in Marxism to disconnect the imaginary of socialism from this form of orthodoxy and to generate a new and different analysis of social processes and thus of a socialist vision.

That orthodox Marxism continues to be simply and unproblematically equated with Marxism *tout court* can certainly be understood given the cynical political motives of many conservatives and liberals who wish to banish Marxism from the intellectual and political landscape altogether. Thus, in addition to the challenges within Marxism posed by the collapse of the old world order, there are renewed "external" hardships that are shaping the political circumstances of the Left. It is indeed ironic that while the concrete walls of the cold war have come down, other walls, no less real for being intellectual, have been erected to keep Marxism from the table of authoritative discourses.

Yet, despite attacks from the Right and others, and despite the conservative and free-market ideologies that seem so dominant today after the end of the cold war, Marxism retains formidable critical powers. Its historical method of investigation enables Marxists to understand the contextualized and contradictory character of socially constituted subjects and social processes. This provides Marxists with a dynamic, textured, and even sensual ontological "sense" of the world, and enables us to carve out compelling radical imaginaries of nonexploitative ways of (re)producing this world. Indeed, Marxism's vitality in large part derives from its profound allegiance to struggles for social justice.

Even a casual familiarity with the Marxian tradition makes it quite clear that the universe of Marxism was never as unimodal as the tradition of orthodoxy implied, either as spoken by the official organs of the Eastern regimes or as conveyed by anti-Marxists in the West. Some Marxian (or Marxian-inspired) challenges to orthodoxy have, for example, led to the development of a distinct tradition of Western Marxism. Gramsci's reinstatement of the concept of hegemony and Althusser's critique of essentialist Marxism, the critical work of the Frankfurt school, and the development of nontraditional forms of struggle around the world (e.g.,

liberation theology), as well as the development of nonorthodox paths of
theoretical research into the global social formation (e.g., world systems
theory), have all taken Marxism in profoundly different directions in recent years.

For some, these theoretical developments and the "academization"
of Marxism have been a sign of the crisis of its regeneration. Western
Marxism, some argue, is detached from the labor movement and other
forms of class struggle that have traditionally animated its theoretical and
political interventions. Yet, for others, the creation of a diverse Marxian
intellectual culture is an important political act in itself, with far-reaching
consequences—although we doubt that any Marxist would deny that connections between struggles of various kinds, whether they be traditional
forms of class struggle, other progressive struggles, or struggles within
Marxian theory, are of vital importance. Given the current conjuncture,
especially in the United States, the creation of a vibrant and sophisticated
body of Marxian theory is no minor political achievement, measured in
terms of both accomplishment and effect. Perhaps Fredric Jameson put
it best in his comment on the role of Marxist intellectuals today: "To create
a Marxist culture in this country, to make Marxism an unavoidable presence and a distinct, original, and unmistakable voice in American social,
cultural, and intellectual life, in short, to form a Marxist intelligentsia
for the struggles of the future—this seems to me the supreme mission of
a Marxist pedagogy and radical intellectual life today" (1979/80, 33).
Marxists have long recognized that intellectual work has political consequences; and the development of new and creative directions in Marxian
theory is of fundamental importance as we confront the new world order.

Yet, once we get past the political cynicism that refuses to recognize
the vitality of and diversity within Marxism, we must acknowledge that
Marxism has suffered from a kind of "realist tyranny." By this we mean
that for a long time the hard and fast lines of cold war rhetoric and reality made orthodox Marxism into the official position of the tradition.
The newer and challenging traditions, their insights, issues, and concerns
could all too easily be labeled as dissenting—thus implicitly affirming
orthodoxy as "the center."

Therefore, when the gathering storms of social transformations in
the East and the West finally broke, they did produce a very real crisis
for the theory that had constructed social systems as more or less centered
unities. In the East, the economistic constructions of "real socialism"
proved unable to withstand the cold war escalation of military expenditures, or to negotiate popular demands for cultural and political liberties that went beyond the logic of economic necessity—and, as it turned
out, even this logic was woefully constructed. In the West, as the social
order increasingly felt the stress of its capitalist contradictions, the class

analyses of orthodox Marxism seemed capable of understanding these contradictions, but much less capable of negotiating a political vision that could make the socialist project come to terms convincingly with the struggles of new social movements. The analytics of Marxism, many argued, were too economistic to be able to understand and respond to these new developments, to yield new satisfactory imaginaries. And the politics of this orthodox Marxism, which could be twisted to serve authoritarian and repressive regimes, was often anathema to democratically inspired progressives.

THE DOMESTIC POLITICS OF CLASS

The age of the cold war had national dimensions as well, and these dimensions have also been undergoing critical transformations that pose new challenges for Marxists. For the Left, as well as for ruling circles, the binary oppositions of global dynamics often found a domestic counterpart in the structuring of politics around a singular divide, that of a class politics too often constructed in economistic and hegemonic terms. The dissolution of the singular construction of class politics in national social formations began earlier than the dissolution of the old East/West international order. The emergence of new subjects, identities, and social movements constructed in terms of race, ethnicity, gender, sexuality, and religion, and the development of new areas of political concern—as with the Greens, the peace movement, and "internationalist" or anti-imperialist movements—are powerful sources of struggle and resistance that have both complemented and challenged older forms of class-based politics.

The patterns of domestic politics have therefore also been reshuffled, which poses additional challenges for the Marxian tradition. There has been a long-perceived need to rethink the nature, sources, and consequences of social struggles in ways that do not fit the old boundaries of class, those boundaries handed down by the traditions of older forms of struggle. Marxism found itself ill-equipped to handle the new movements and struggles that did not fit neatly with the production-based forms of the class struggle it had so long enunciated. Yet these new movements have also contributed to the long process of Marxism's theoretical regeneration that occurred through the 1970s and 1980s.

By the mid-1970s the best thinkers in the tradition realized that orthodox Marxism had entered a period of crisis. They set about, in many different ways, to revolutionize Marxian thought, to transform the structure of its concepts, to alter its epistemological grounds, to change the terms of its relationship to the political practices connected with it, to move it beyond its crisis. Of course, the fostering of new ideas and new directions in a body of discourse has more or less lengthy gestation periods. The work of rethinking Marxism has proceeded by stages, focusing first on recognizing its inadequacies, its problem areas, its empty spaces, and then moving to address them. It also takes time for those who participate in the process of theoretical transformations from different angles and with different understandings to coalesce around new shared meanings and projects; and it takes time for this coalescing to take new institutional forms.

We are now some time removed from the mid-1970s, when the crisis of Marxism first emerged. But this has been a time of gestation and of maturation, so that by now most Marxian thinkers by and large have coalesced in an intellectual project that we could label as "anti-economism." Insights from poststructuralist and postmodern thought have been woven into Marxian discourse in ways that have both challenged and extended traditional Marxism. The work of Michel Foucault, Jacques Derrida, and Jean-Francois Lyotard, among many others, have raised profound questions about the centrality of the master narratives of unidirectional progress that can be traced back to the Enlightenment. Questions about the nature and character of historical development, causality, knowledge, power, subjectivity, and desire have been put on the Marxist table in new and provocative ways, fundamentally challenging orthodox Marxism, whose philosophical roots are embedded in modernist discourse.

Alongside postmodern and poststructuralist theories, and at times together with them, feminist theory has also presented fundamental challenges to Marxism. Traditional Marxian concerns with the division of labor, the reproduction of class relations, and the commodification of social life have all been "engendered" by feminist theory. Feminist insights about the situatedness of subjectivity and discourse have pushed the Marxian appreciation for the historical and contextual character of "meanings" in new directions. Notions of gendered and decentered subjects are now no longer peripheral to Marxism, but are being incorporated into the basic approaches of different Marxist traditions. Moreover, feminist issues such as reproductive rights and its abuses, unpaid household labor, adequate child care, and comparable worth are now the object of theoretical analysis and political struggle by Marxists and feminists. As a result, a deeper understanding is developing of how issues of class and gender are implicated in Marxist–feminist discourse and practice.

Indeed, critiques of determinist modes of reasoning have forced Marxists to reconsider their political, economic, and cultural analyses in order to understand subjects and political groups formed around a wide set of interests and identities—including gender, race, nationality, and sexuality, as well as class. In this work of reconstructing Marxism along antieconomistic lines, Marxists have been challenged to find new ways of locating "class" in diverse social spaces.

Thus, for Marxists, the new world brings, in part, a decentering of class. To confront this aspect of the changing world, Marxists are developing new ways of situating class in the new arenas of social struggle and identity. We are understanding how "traditional" class politics are also gendered and racialized politics, and conversely that new social movements may have potentially radical class effects. Here then the challenge for Marxists is to develop the ways in which the loss of class as a universal or hegemonic project provides new areas of strength and vitality within Marxism, and opens new horizons for progressive political action. However, the one-sidedness of traditional Marxist class struggles should not be replaced by new social movements that displace the presence and effectivity of class altogether. With the decentering of class, Marxists can continue to highlight the class aspects and consequences of social life, while showing how class affects but does not necessarily predominate in a variety of ostensibly nonclass struggles. Marxism is developing traditions that are able to show the class effects of what have been regarded as nonclass struggles, without reinscribing class as the central force of these struggles. For example, Marxists have contributed to struggles over reproductive rights by showing the links between feminist concerns about gender subordination and the rights of women and class issues about who does the work of child care and under what conditions, or about who has access to reproductive technology and medical services and for what reasons. In organizing to stop the spread of the HIV virus, Marxists need to highlight the class aspects of this crisis, emphasizing the links between joblessness and drug use or between the lack of economic development and prostitution, while also recognizing how the racialized, gendered, and sexualized aspects of the spread of HIV reinforce and help (re)produce these class aspects.

In this regard, the rethinking of Marxism in nondeterministic directions has meant not only resituating class in new social spaces and movements, but also appreciating and exploring the character and import of the other-than-class aspects of social life. Such rethinking depends upon respecting and seeking out the insights and contributions of feminists, civil rights activists, artists, liberation theologists, queer theorists, environmental activists, "nativists," and anti-imperialists. In recognizing that new identities and social movements cannot be reduced to class, Marxists can consider how the other-than-class aspects of social life and the new forms of identity, representation, and social struggle have implications for reforming and potentially transforming exploitative class processes. This awareness motivates discussion of how the emergence of new identities and the politics of new social movements may contribute to radical changes that threaten or undermine class exploitation. And, we are able to recognize how the expansion of reproductive rights, the eradication of HIV, the establishment of security in communities of color, the end of environmental degradation, and the elimination of child abuse and the battering of women are necessary conditions for the kinds of progressive social change and justice that Marxists have always struggled for.

In this manner, confronting the new world order requires Marxists to recognize decentered and decentralized strategies for political action, while reemphasizing the importance and significance of class. It means confronting the binary polarizations between "class" and "other-than-class" politics in order to open up new ways of struggling over class and furthering socialist change.

THE NORTH/SOUTH POLARITY

It is also all too clear that another of the binary oppositions characteristic of the cold war age, the North/South divide, is undergoing fundamental transformation. It could not be otherwise, since this divide has been critically inserted in the geopolitics of East/West oppositions. But the transformations of North/South issues and politics has also been shaped by the transnational character of new social movements and struggles over racial, ethnic, environmental, and gender issues that have transformed the terrain and character of national politics.

The transformation of the North/South divide is perhaps *least* structured by the international and domestic changes occasioned or allowed by the collapse of the East/West global bipolarity. For example, it is a more open-ended question of how the dynamics of the formation of economic blocs (European, Asian, North American)—which remind us of pre-World War II patterns of imperialistic oppositions—will be integrated with the economies of the South in the age of transnational corporations. Indeed, the political, cultural, and economic diversity among Southern nations is increasingly more imposing than the shared circumstances captured by the term "third world."

Marxists have contributed to recognizing the construction and contours of the North/South divide, particularly in work that has focused on the center/periphery polarity. Thus, the reshaping of the world order challenges Marxists to examine this "old" polarity, both because of the decentering of the Soviet Union and the multicentering of the economic blocs, and because of the uneven development of "peripheral" nations. The reshaping and redefinition of the North/South or the center/

periphery divide will be a crucial arena for the emergence of new institutional patterns of power and new forms of struggle and resistance.

Will the reperipheralization of Eastern Europe contribute to newly peripheralized African, South American, and South Asian nations? Or will it instead open up new spaces for development that are less structured by the former East/West and North/South polarities? Are there circumstances under which nationalist movements can provide viable strategies for furthering liberation and community empowerment, along with radical challenges to capitalist exploitation? Under what circumstances does the spread of commodification, of markets, provide conditions for reproducing and intensifying capitalist exploitation? Are there circumstances in which markets might foster noncapitalist forms of producing and appropriating an economic surplus? In what ways can markets be emancipatory? Does the construction of new identities and social movements along religious, ethnic, racial, or gender lines offer avenues for furthering emancipatory changes that threaten the seeming hegemony of capitalist relations? What does the reinvention and reinsertion of "native" cultures and values mean for modern Western traditions? Do they offer new venues for rethinking and remaking communities in a postmodern, post-Western fashion? And, how will segments of the working class in the North respond to the loss of wages and job security that seems to be accompanying the supranational character of capital today?

These and other questions are ones that the Left in general, and Marxists in particular, will have to confront and come to terms with as a number of intersecting struggles reshape a new order.

*   *   *

The papers in this volume—as did all the papers at the conference "Marxism in the New World Order: Crises and Possibilities"—begin to confront these compelling questions and enormous challenges. They also clear the path for their confrontation and exploration by working both to reassert the importance of class analysis (but not as the essentialist cause) and to expand the reach of Marxian theory to areas and sites for theoretical, cultural, and political alliances that the Marxism of the cold war age had neglected.

This book thus contributes to Marxism's theoretical renewal and transformation. Each of the papers allows us to see, in varying mixtures, the old and the new: the continued privileging that Marxism affords to the historical method of investigation; the continued commitment of Marxian analysis to bring to the fore the class dimensions of all struggles of liberation, thus enriching these struggles; and the new directions in

Marxian theory and in class analysis that begin to build bridges between class identities and the identities of subjects not reducible to a unimodal class dimension.

Some of the papers focus on analogies between class processes of exploitation and other forms of oppression. Others offer noneconomistic reconstructions of the categories of Marxian analysis. Many of the papers find a way out of the economism of orthodox readings of Marx by focusing on the incompleteness of Marx's work. Some accomplish this by offering an alternative epistemological stance. Other papers identify new forms of struggle that populate the new world order and argue for a rethinking of the strategies of reform and/or revolution that have long been the staple of Marxist thought. Some of them extend Marxism into novel areas of investigation, such as queer theory and childhood. Some offer new readings on the history of the Soviet Union. Despite their differences in approach and focus, all contribute to the continual regeneration of vital Marxist traditions in the post-cold war era, traditions whose existence the pundits and politicians deny.

The urgent political, economic, and cultural issues facing the world today require open debate among the rich diversity of Marxist traditions. In turn, Marxists in their diversity and in their shared commitment to a just and democratic future have a crucial role to play in recognizing, opposing, and overcoming the many forms of oppression and exploitation that are being reconstituted as the new world order takes shape.

REFERENCE

Jameson, F. 1979/80. "Marxism and Teaching." *New Political Science* 1 (2/3): 31–36.

PART ONE

THE SUBJECTS
OF MARXIAN THEORY

Postmodernism, Marxism, and the Critique of Modern Economic Thought

JACK AMARIGLIO
DAVID F. RUCCIO

f postmodernism as critique has exhausted itself in cultural and literary circles, this result stands in direct opposition to the situation within contemporary economics. The destabilizing effects of postmodernism are only beginning to be noticed in the area of economics, and the resistance of economic philosophers and historians to the critical currents of postmodern theory is precisely because they have understood (correctly, we think) the mostly nihilistic implications of adopting epistemologically "relativist" and antiscientistic stances. Add to this the fact that most economists remain firmly committed to the modernist premises of their enterprise—to the unified rationality of the intentional economic subject/agent, to determinism in causal explanations, to a notion of economic knowledge (for both subjects and economic scientists) that treats cognition as a "mirror of nature"—and what emerges is a picture of a discipline in which the transition from high modernism (if it has even reached that stage) to postmodernism has largely been arrested.

This characterization is not only true of mainstream, especially neoclassical and Keynesian, economic theories; to different degrees it holds as well for most Marxian approaches, from orthodox and classical versions to the more recent analytical Marxism and others. Thus, while it is

A longer version of this paper forthcoming in *Rethinking* MARXISM (Fall 1994) develops in more detail the arguments summarized here.

13

now increasingly fashionable to declare postmodern thought to have been merely a passing fad (one wonders from what tried-but-true point of view), it remains the case that the challenges unleashed by postmodernism to the unified, rational subject, to all forms of determinism, and to traditional epistemology have hardly been met—let alone overturned—in the field of economics.

This situation may now be changing. A "new" philosophy of economics—one that is not wedded to repetitious and stale renegotiations of logical positivism but, instead, is pursuing the alternative paths created by postmodern approaches to science and language—has developed in recent years with great vigor and scope. This new philosophy is evident in projects that range from Stephen Resnick and Richard Wolff's antideterministic reconfiguration of Marxian epistemology and methodology, Donald McCloskey's focus on economic "rhetoric," and Arjo Klamer's antimodernist anthropological investigations of economic "conversations," to Philip Mirowski's revelation of contemporary neoclassical economic theory's ill-fated reliance on the metaphors and methods of nineteenth-century physical science, Diana Strassmann's and Julie Nelson's depictions of the gendered writing strategies of most economic theory, and finally to our own attempts to unearth the "postmodern moments" of twentieth-century economic thought. It cannot be said that these departures from traditional economic philosophy all acknowledge the progenitors of postmodern theory (and here we include the works of Nietzsche, Foucault, Derrida, and Lyotard, among others); indeed, some of them explicitly refuse the connection to postmodernism, and to poststructuralism and deconstruction. Nevertheless, it is our view that the discursive forms and timing of their critiques have been made possible mostly as a result of the spread of postmodern theory and culture in the West during the past twenty-five years. Certainly, the marked shift that each of these projects exemplifies away from the debates about the "growth of scientific knowledge" and the meaning of "falsifiability," and toward the investigation of the discursive elements of the production of economic theories and the social conditions implied in "reading" economic writings, has been stimulated by postmodern concerns for textuality and power, as well as by a fundamental disbelief in the self-professed disinterestedness of positive economic analysis.

In writing about the development of these postmodern projects, we wish to make clear our strong difference with those (most often non-economists) who unwittingly collapse the issue of the nature of contemporary economic processes and the issue of the quality and character of current economic theory. In this paper, we do not treat postmodernism as a surrogate for discussing something called "late capitalism." Aside from our skepticism about such a term, we do not regard the changes that are now occurring in cultural and social theory as a corollary or a reflection of the emergence of "consumerism" or some other fetishized sign under which all postmodern theory is supposed to exist. We do not deny the influence of economic processes on postmodern discursivity (or vice versa); what we do reject is the simplistic (and, we believe, mistaken) way in which the theory of late capitalism—or, what is often taken to be the same, postindustrial or consumer society—has been read. We also reject the even more facile way in which this theory has been used to support the view that there can be a more-or-less simple transposition to the cultural and theoretical level of the economic processes that are said to underlie this phase of capitalist development. Deducing a ubiquitous "consumerism" (and then postmodernism) from the idea that the realization of surplus-value is decidedly problematic in the present world (but when has it been otherwise in the history of capitalism?) simply will not do.

In any event, we do not attempt in this chapter to characterize the "modes of production" that can be said to exist at present. And, certainly, no implications about economic processes should be derived from our discussion of the postmodern moments of contemporary economics. Here, we concentrate our efforts on economic thought, on depicting and evaluating the postmodern moments of first mainstream and then Marxian modes of theorizing about the economy. In doing so, we note immediately that there is good reason to see all contemporary economic thought as comprising exemplars of what has been called economic modernism. Although neoclassical, Keynesian, and Marxian economic theories (to name just three) differ from one another—in some places considerably—we also think that there are conceptual contrasts that serve as the foundational axes around which these discourses are composed. Together, these contrasts or distinctions partly constitute the common modernity of these otherwise different theoretical frameworks. We will concentrate on only three of these here: (1) order and disorder (i.e., the related questions of ontological structural patterns and causal determinism); (2) centering and decentering (here we limit our attention to the composition and nature of the economic subject); and (3) certainty and uncertainty (both as epistemological discursive norms and as descriptions of an ontological reality).

Our view is that economic modernism both constitutes these contrasts, which are fundamental to any discourse permitted to be viewed as economic theory, and emphasizes one side of each contrast in preference to the other. In general, the modernist preference is for order, centering, and certainty. The reasons for this are not hard to fathom. Many economists, both mainstream and radical, regard as impossible, "nihilistic," and ultimately inappropriate as theory or science most attempts to complicate economic thinking along the lines of disorder, decentering, and uncertainty. That is, even when these latter elements are allowed in, as objects of analysis—but not, of course, as epistemological norms—they are always mastered or brought under control by the ordering of disorder (discovering the pattern underlying seemingly anarchic economic events), by the centering of decentering (showing that the chaos of desire and the individuation of society do find their limit in some original and intentional subjectivity), and by making certain, or at least probable, uncertainty (demonstrating both that there are reasonable, if not absolute, grounds for knowledge and the action based on it, and that most degrees of uncertainty can be calculated by agents and economists alike). Thus, while modern economic thought may not discard—and may even relish the challenge of theorizing—disorder, decentering, and uncertainty, it also does so in the conceit that these elements are, in the last analysis, superseded by the discursive ordering and analysis that presumably make up modern scientific activity.

MAINSTREAM ECONOMICS

Neoclassical economic thought, while constituted by the tension implicit in these dualities, does tell at least one compelling story, which demonstrates effectively the robust connections among the preferences for order, centering, and certainty in economic modernism. Often told by employing the trope of irony (perhaps modernism's characteristic literary strategy), the story of the "invisible hand" emerges as the result of initially positing disorder, decentering, and uncertainty and then deriving a set of consequences that seems to be remote—an unlikely possibility—from the stipulation of the initial conditions.

Drawing upon Adam Smith, neoclassical economists begin with the premise that civil society, rather than being governed by an overarching religious authority or state, is fractured into a plethora of individuated and competing human atoms. These "atoms" take actions on their own behalf without knowing in advance either the actions of others or, for that matter, the potential consequences of their own actions. Of course, the initial ferment and disorder that are suggested by the interaction of the teeming mass of individual actors is shown to converge toward a well-ordered, "general equilibrium" solution—in which all individuals maximize their utility, and economy-wide optimality is achieved—by virtue of decentralized markets. Thus, the modernist paradox is solved by first positing a new, human centering (self-interested, rational subjects), and then showing how the intentional actions of such individuals have the unintended consequences of achieving social order—since market transactions are shown to be mostly orderly processes—and eliminating uncertainty as agents come to "know" the consequences of their self-directed, rational actions. Here, then, the initial premise of apparent anarchy and fragmentation is overcome by the order, centering, and certainty that are both essential attributes and effects of market processes. The unfolding of this story gives rise to the characteristic optimism and progressivism—the utopian vision—of modernism, since it confirms post-Enlightenment beliefs in the efficacy and social beneficence of rationally directed, free, and individual choice.

Within the confines of mainstream economic theories, however, the dualities that are, in our view, representative of such modernist stories are in fact unstable and often begin to unravel and/or deconstruct themselves. Thus, in the ceaseless pursuit to update the kind of market story we have just presented, economists in this century have frequently embraced indeterminism, disequilibria, and chaos, "partly" rational or even rule-driven subjects, and radical uncertainty that they perceive as part and parcel of modern market processes. But these elements also constitute the postmodern moments whose nihilistic potential, if and when pursued, calls into question the coherence and consistency of such narratives. While, to date, these postmodern moments have been mostly domesticated and contained by the modernizing aspects of economic theory,[1] they are often picked up and pushed toward their postmodern limits by opponents and critics of the mainstream.

For example, within Post Keynesian and feminist economics (to name just two), concepts of disorder or decentering or uncertainty often play a key role in criticisms of neoclassical and mainstream Keynesian theories. For Post Keynesians influenced by the work of G. L. S. Shackle, "true uncertainty," seen as diametrically opposed to certain or even probable knowledge, is touted as the basis for a thoroughgoing reconsideration of economic theory. While Shackle's work is embedded in a form of subjectivism, and therefore preserves the humanist centering characteristic of economic modernism, the radicality of his view of the impossibility of economic knowledge and thus of knowledge-based choice is sufficient to summon up the charge of nihilism. Other Post Keynesians court similar charges in pursuing the ever-present disequilibria that arise in market situations. The entire apparatus of general equilibrium is called into question by the claim that transactions made outside equilibrium are not only common but constitute the norm. In this Post Keynesian view, the mostly disorderly nature of decentralized markets is stressed, although it is true that explanations are often given in which some order is indeed uncovered to explain the ever-present tendencies toward disequilibrium.

Feminist economics, though in its initial stages, also draws out some of the more postmodern aspects of traditional theory and adds to them a concern with gendering. In fact, the very pluralizing of economic subjectivity implicit in some recent feminist work, and the displacing of the autonomous subject by structural forces that are said to "socially construct" all economic subjects, uses gender as a means of fracturing the totalizing (and male) edifice of traditional neoclassical and Keynesian theory. By bringing to the fore gendered subjectivities and knowledges, feminist economists have begun to construct new theoretical perspectives, tending more toward decentered (and therefore more disorderly) economic totalities and a sort of "uncertainty" regarding the nature and effects of rationality and knowledge on economic processes. It is no accident, then, that defenders of the traditional neoclassical and Keynesian faith have had the most difficulty in the fragmenting of economic theory that the introduction of such gendered notions of subjectivity and knowledge represent. We should also add that other feminist economists, aware of the possible disintegration of the dominant economic frameworks, have reasserted the importance of retaining the centered economic subject as the founding moment of economic theory, and have moved to halt the disorderliness that more postmodern feminists in economics have introduced.

MARXIAN ECONOMICS

While we are indebted to the elucidation and deployment by some Post Keynesians and feminists of the postmodern moments of mainstream theory, we have found that the pull of modernism on those theoretical frameworks has been strong enough to blunt the edge of their critique. We have also found that the modernist cast of much Marxian theory has had a similar effect, restraining Marxian criticisms of the mainstream economics tradition and of the economic system that tradition so often celebrates. In the remainder of this paper, therefore, we turn our attention to identifying and criticizing modernism within Marxism, and to posing a postmodern Marxian alternative. In so doing, we point out how the contrasts we identified above help to constitute modernist Marxian economic and social thought and show as well how, "in the last instance," the preference or emphasis is on forms of order, centering, and certainty. Likewise, however, we argue that the postmodern moments of Marxian economics can also be exploited and developed in order to accomplish a veritable "rupture" with key elements of modernist Marxian discourse.

The dialectical tensions in the order/disorder, centering/decentering, certainty/uncertainty oppositions get played out in many ways in the Marxist tradition. To name just a few here, these tensions constitute the differentiations and contrasts between the realms of production and circulation, between markets and planning, and ultimately between capitalism and socialism. The distinction between production and circulation is elaborated by modernist Marxism as the difference between the production of value, on one hand, and the realization of that value on the other. In many versions, production is seen as structured and stable, at least to the extent that the production of value is organized and controlled—ordered in a despotic fashion—by capitalists. Markets, however, are considered to be unplanned and thus anarchic: because of the absence of foreknowledge of demand, and because demand is decentralized and is attendant upon the myriad individual decisions of workers and other firms, capitalists face considerable uncertainty in attempting to recover the profits embodied in the commodities when they enter the realm of circulation. The crisis of accumulation caused by the inability of some capitalists to realize the surplus value appropriated from their workers is therefore predicated on the original distinction between production and circulation under capitalism, insofar as the disorder of the market is blamed for eventually and persistently disrupting production and throwing the entire economic system into a temporary if not permanent crisis.

The diagnosis suggests the cure: planned production and coordination among firms. This solution, so the story goes, can be practiced only within the bounds of socialism, since the elimination of competitive market forces and private property serve as the necessary conditions for the emergence of coordination and planning. A more orderly sphere of production is possible in socialism as long as a central planning board is able to calculate accurately the needed balance between inputs and outputs, levels of consumption and accumulation, within and across different industries and branches of production. Hence, the superiority of socialist production lies precisely in the elimination of the disorder and uncertainty that characterize capitalist exchange.

Of course, there are many other ways in which Marxian analyses have privileged socialism in preference to capitalism, but many of these are based, we think, on the general preference for order, centering, and certainty. The centrality of subjectivity in constructing an ethics of system choice, associated with the modernist reading of Marx's discussion of commodity fetishism, also serves the distinction between capitalism and socialism. The typical conception is that general commodity relations distort subjects and their consciousness to the degree that they come to attribute the qualitative relations among themselves to the commodities that they possess and exchange. This "false consciousness" is a misperception, but it is also the "true expression" of the one-sidedness and alienation that is the lot of subjects in a totally commodified system. The consequences for the economy of this fetishism of commodities are several: capital is treated as a "thing" and not a social relation; money is seen as the source of self-expanding value; surplus is viewed as arising in exchange; and much else. The overthrow of capitalism, once again, promises a solution to all of this. In socialism commodity fetishism is banished, since production is no longer for exchange but for use, thus eliminating the crucial condition for fetishism to arise. In the modernist Marxian tradition, then, socialism is additionally preferred to capitalism in that the crippling and distorting forms of subjectivity that reflect general market relations under capitalism are replaced by those forms of subjectivity in which agents are now able to "see" clearly (since these relations are now transparent) the social relations behind their interdependent links.

We have no interest in diminishing the significant achievements associated with the utopian imaginary created by the oppositions characteristic of modernist Marxism which, at the least, keep alive the idea that alternatives both to mainstream economic theory and to the economic and social systems it so often ends up celebrating can and should be explored. We do not, however, think that modernism has served Marxism well since, to our mind, it has built up a theoretical edifice with dubious political consequences. For example, we think that the modernist tendency has overemphasized the existence of disorder in capitalism and the negative consequences of the types of disorder that arise within the capitalist system. Likewise, it has exaggerated the orderly nature of socialism, and especially of planning, and has viewed as unduly positive the consequences of such order. Therefore, we are interested in elucidating and developing those elements of Marxian discourse that emphasize disorder, decentering, and uncertainty, which for us constitute the postmodern moments of Marxian theory.

The distinctiveness of this postmodern Marxian discourse can be envisaged by rethinking such oppositions as that between capitalism and socialism with this emphasis in mind. For example, Marx's historical analysis of a capitalist economy can be read more in terms of the idea of historical conjuncture and contingency than "laws of motion" and necessity. It is just this reading that Althusser and his school have contributed to the Marxian tradition with the concepts of overdetermination and process without a subject. Such concepts, if taken seriously, imply a radical contingency and uncertainty about social and economic processes. One implication for the contrast between capitalism and socialism is that postmodern Marxism sees all outcomes in either social formation as always and everywhere contingent. Thus, it cannot be taken for granted nor understood as the necessary effects of the concept that, for example, socialist planning will mean more or less certainty, more or less order, in comparison to capitalist markets. Likewise, capitalist markets imply nothing in particular about the possibility for economic crises, the meeting of individual needs, and so forth. The effects of markets and planning depend crucially on the concrete conditions of existence of each and are not given in advance in the form of their respective concepts.

Similarly, a postmodern reading of commodity fetishism creates the possibility of conceiving of a subject that is constantly being constructed anew (and in multiple and contradictory ways), the resulting construction of which has no "center." This notion of the "open" subject serves to challenge the difference between capitalism and socialism that modernist Marxism tends to draw between the "really" fractured and alienated subject of capitalism and the potentially holistic and unalienated "socialist man". For postmodern Marxism, the difference between subjects in the two social formations is a matter of the different elements of their overdetermination (e.g., by capitalist class processes in one and by collective or communal class processes in the other), and not of the absence or presence of subjective unity and true consciousness in either formation.

Finally, as Althusser, Hindess and Hirst, Resnick and Wolff, and others have argued, there is a distinct Marxian conceptualization of knowledge that eschews the presuppositions and logical consequences of modernist (empiricist and rationalist) epistemologies. We call this conceptualization postmodern because, in our view, it arises from rejecting notions of certainty and replacing them with forms of cognition that tend toward uncertainty (at least in the sense of indeterminism), forms based on the plurality of and often incommensurable differences between knowledges. Distinguishing between capitalism and socialism based on possible differences in forms of knowledge (or the lack thereof) is modernist in its basic premises. For modernist Marxism, the relativism that characterizes capitalism is attributed to the fact that it tends to fracture and segregate individuals and groups by a division of labor and class distinctions. Socialism, in this view, marks the moment of the historical transcendence of such fragmented knowledge and allows all of its members to see the whole. Thus, for example, planning can succeed where markets cannot in discerning the needs underlying the plan and in calculating the effects of instituting it. The indeterminism and uncertainty of capitalism is overcome by rational planning whose objective basis—the victory of the proletariat with its full appreciation of the totality—guarantees in advance the superiority of its knowledge and practice.

Postmodern Marxian discourse regards this view as unhelpful and ultimately damaging as a distinction between capitalism and socialism. It is clear, to us at least, that socialism has been and will be beset with the radical uncertainty that goes along with the contingency of events and the multiplicity of knowledges. Moreover, considerable harm has been done to peoples living under (modernist) socialist regimes—and to the very concept of socialism—as a result of the claim by the party or state to have privileged (and not partisan) objective knowledge. For us, socialist planning will always be marked by the mediation of different knowledges and subjectivities, and the resulting plan, a contingent act if there ever was one, may need to declare itself as partisan, provisional, and uncertain of its effects if it is to avoid the disasters that have befallen planning mechanisms inculcated with modernist explanations and ideals, utopian though they may be. The totalizing promise of rational centralized planning is a modernist one. The declared partiality, relativism, and uncertainty of such planning is, in contrast, postmodern.

ACKNOWLEDGMENTS

We wish to thank Joseph Buttigieg, Julie Graham, Sandra Harding, Arjo Klamer, Ellen Messer-Davidow, and Bruce Norton for their helpful comments and suggestions.

NOTE

1. For example, uncertainty is shown to be about degrees of either objective or subjective rational belief, thus keeping alive empiricist notions of objective reality beyond the subject or, alternatively, the inherent wholeness and rationality of the subject.

REFERENCES

Althusser, L. 1970. *For Marx*, trans. B. Brewster. New York: Vintage Books.

Althusser, L. and Balibar, E. 1975. *Reading Capital*, trans. B. Brewster. London: New Left Books.

Amariglio, J. 1990. "Economics as a Postmodern Discourse." In *Economics as Discourse*, ed. W. Samuels, 15–46. Boston: Kluwer Academic Press.

Amariglio, J. and Callari, A. 1993. "Marxian Value Theory and the Problem of the Subject: The Role of Commodity Fetishism." In *Fetishism as Cultural Discourse*, eds. E. Apter and W. Pietz, 186–216. Ithaca: Cornell University Press.

Amariglio, J.; Resnick, S.; and Wolff, R. 1990, Autumn. "Division and Difference in the 'Discipline' of Economics." *Critical Inquiry* 17: 108–137.

Derrida, J. 1978. *Writing and Difference*, trans. A Bass. Chicago: University of Chicago Press.

Foucault, M. 1973. *The Order of Things*. New York: Vintage Books.

Hindess, B. and Hirst, P. Q. 1975. *Pre-capitalist Modes of Production*. London: Routledge & Kegan Paul.

Klamer, A. 1990. "Toward the Native's Point of View: The Difficulty of Changing the Conversation." In *Economics and Hermeneutics*, ed. D. Lavoie, 19–33. London: Routledge.

Lyotard, J.-F. 1984. *The Postmodern Condition: A Report on Knowledge*, trans. G. Bennington and B. Massumi. Minneapolis: University of Minnesota Press.

McCloskey, D. 1985. *The Rhetoric of Economics*. Madison: University of Wisconsin Press.

Mirowski, P. 1991. *More Heat Than Light*. Cambridge, England: Cambridge University Press.

Nelson, J. A. 1992. "Gender, Metaphor, and the Definition of Economics." *Economics and Philosophy* 8 (1): 103–125.

——. 1993. "The Study of Choice or the Study of Provisioning? Gender and the Definition of Economics." In *Beyond Economic Man*, eds. M. A. Ferber and J. A. Nelson, 23–36. Chicago: University of Chicago Press.

Nietzsche, F. 1967. *The Will to Power*. New York: Random House.

Resnick, S. and Wolff, R. 1987. *Knowledge and Class*. Chicago: University of Chicago Press.

Ruccio, D. F. 1986. "Essentialism and Socialist Economic Planning: A Methodological Critique of Optimal Planning Theory." In *Research in the History of Economic Thought and Methodology*, Vol. 4, 85–108. Greenwich: JAI Press.

——. 1991, Summer. "Postmodernism and Economics." *Journal of Post Keynesian Economics* 13: 495–510.

——. 1992, Summer. "Failure of Socialism, Future of Socialists?" *Rethinking Marxism* 5 (2): 7–22.

Shackle, G. L. S. 1955. *Uncertainty in Economics*. Cambridge, England: Cambridge University Press.

——. 1966. *The Nature of Economic Thought: Selected Papers, 1955–1964*. Cambridge, England: Cambridge University Press.

——. 1972. *Epistemics and Economics*. Cambridge, England: Cambridge University Press.

Strassmann, D. 1993. "Not a Free Market: The Rhetoric of Disciplinary Authority in Economics." In *Beyond Economic Man*, eds. M. A. Ferber and J. A. Nelson, 54–68. Chicago: University of Chicago Press.

——. 1993. "The Stories of Economics and the Power of the Storyteller." *History of Political Economy* 25 (1): 147–165.

Wolff, R. and Resnick, S. 1987. *Economics: Marxian Versus Neoclassical*. Baltimore: Johns Hopkins University Press.

Spinoza's Democracy: The Passions of Social Assemblages

MICHAEL HARDT

pinoza's *Political Treatise* is, according to Antonio Negri (1992, 17), the work that founds modern democratic political thinking in Europe. As opposed to the ancient notion of democracy, which regarded the freedoms and participation of citizenship as limited to the *polis*, Spinoza's democracy extends equally across a universal plane. This is the sense in which Spinoza proposes democracy as the "completely absolute" form of government, *omnino absolutum imperium* (*Political Treatise*, Chapter XI, paragraph 1). If it is true that Spinoza's notion of democracy holds a central position in modern political thought, however, it cannot be said that his conception corresponds to our political reality, or even that it has been adopted by the major currents of modern political theory. Rather, Spinoza's democracy can be considered central in the sense that it remains continually present as an enigma and as a rigorous model against which our political forms and theories are measured. In contrast to the majority of modern propositions of democracy, which pose democratic government as functioning indirectly through the establishment of contracts and the transfer of the rights of the citizens, Spinoza's democracy requires the immediate and direct expression or participation of the entire social field. This Spinozian notion is fundamental to our contemporary political thinking, but not in the sense that it has been fully accepted and realized; it functions instead as an anomaly or a pressure that forces us continually to rethink and critique our own

notions of democratic government. Spinoza remains present throughout modern political thinking as a subversive force.

We can appreciate the force of this enigma or aporia by examining one of Spinoza's central democratic propositions, that the "natural right" of a subject can never be transferred to another, a proposition that demonstrates the rigor and radicality of Spinozian democracy. Let us consider just two related examples of this position. "With regard to politics, the difference between Hobbes and me . . . consists of this: that I continually preserve the natural right intact so that the supreme Power in a State has no more right over the subject than is proportionate to the power by which it is superior to the subject. This is what always takes place in the state of nature" (*Letter 50* to Jarig Jelles). Spinoza's refusal of the transfer or alienation of rights, of course, implies a refusal of the power of contracts, or rather a constant subordination of the contract to the changeable will of the subject. "When a person gives a pledge to someone else . . . this pledge remains valid only as long as his or her will does not change. . . . If the person judges that the pledge is causing him or her more loss than gain . . . then, since it is the decision of his or her own judgement that the pact should be broken, it will be done by the right of nature" (*Political Treatise*, Chapter II, paragraph 12).[1] The desire of the subject is thus given priority over any transfer or representation of authority, any external forces of order.

From the perspective of the major currents of modern democratic thinking this set of propositions, which refer the civil state back to the state of nature, seems open to two possibilities and two dangers for politics. On the one hand, the refusal of the transfer of right and hence of social contracts seems to make impossible most of the modern strategies for the construction and maintenance of social order, and hence leave the civil state vulnerable to the chaos of nature that Hobbes and others feared. On the other hand, if Spinoza's use of nature does not refer to irrational and disorganized competition but rather to a state of order, then his "natural right" seems to refer us to a preconstituted, theological notion of the natural order that would dictate in some sense the relationship of social subjects and thereby limit our freedom.

Neither of these alternatives, however, gives us an adequate interpretation of Spinoza's position. When Spinoza refers to natural right he is not invoking either a fixed and eternal social order or a state of chaos and destruction; he is pointing to a process of organization and formation that transforms nature itself. "Spinozian naturalism," explains Etienne Balibar (1985, 48), "does not deprive the notion of history of its meaning; on the contrary, nature is nothing but a new way of thinking history." Spinoza unhinges nature from any ontological fixity and fills it with a productive dynamic. The question of right, then, should be referred back to the plasticity and constitution of nature, to the genealogy of nature itself and the forces that compose it. The refusal of contracts and any other transfer of right further underlines the centrality of this process of constitution to Spinozian democracy. From the perspective of the majority of modern theorists, such as Hobbes, Rousseau, Hegel, and Kant, the refusal to give priority to the validity of contracts seems to leave a hole in the center of Spinozian social theory, making the social order vulnerable to the vicissitudes of irrational popular sentiment. Spinozian democracy, in other words, should be recognized first in terms of what it denies, what it lacks. From a Spinozian perspective, however, this "void" left by the lack of rational State authority is filled by the practices of the masses. These are the forces that make it possible to conceive of a radical and direct democracy, and this, it seems to me, is what needs to be grasped in order to appreciate the enigma of Spinoza's politics.

Antonio Negri is perhaps the contemporary theorist who has developed most fully the radically democratic possibilities of Spinoza's thought. Negri explains that the void left in Spinozian social theory by the refusal of fixed moral or normative structures is the space occupied by the ethical practice of the multitude.[2] In contrast to the mob (*vulgus*), which without external guidance can only act haphazardly and destructively, the multitude (*multitudo*) is capable of acting in accordance with its own desires, transforming itself and its world. In this sense the multitude is the subject of Spinozian democracy, the subject that acts in the void where other modern theories would pose mechanisms of contract, representation, or State control. The terminological distinction between mob and multitude, however, should not be understood as an opposition between irrational and rational social forces; the practices of the multitude cannot be properly understood as either rational or irrational, but should be understood primarily in terms of a logic of desire and passions. Spinozian political thought, in this sense, is really a genealogy of the passions of the social body. In order to understand democracy as the practice of the multitude, then, we have to look deeper into the immanent forces of organization, forces that construct and form nature itself, and that support a radical and direct democracy outside of any framework of contractual, representational, or moral order. In order to understand Spinozian democracy, in other words, we have to recognize first the ontological and political process that Negri calls constitution: the productive and organizational motor that drives the multitude.

The development of this political theory in Spinoza's texts, of course, remains unfinished. The chapter of the *Political Treatise* on democracy was never completed.[3] When we recognize the pressures that Negri puts on the notion of democracy, however, and understand the constitutive functions the multitude must fulfill, we have a key to discovering the existing elements of this democracy elsewhere in Spinoza's texts. In this light, in fact, we can recognize how Gilles Deleuze's work on Spinoza, although it does not primarily address directly political issues, is fundamental for an adequate understanding of Spinoza's politics. Deleuze's investigation of the powers of bodies and the logic of their interactions defines an internal mechanics and elaborates on the corporeal and passional logic that sustains the multitude as the subject of democracy. This is the field of forces that fills what from a traditional perspective appears as the "void" of Spinozian democracy.

At the heart of Deleuze's interpretation is his understanding of Spinoza's ontological practice: the notion of a corporeal and intellectual practice capable of intervening in and constituting nature itself.[4] Deleuze does not look for the mechanisms of this practice immediately in grand social constructs, but focuses rather on the micro level and the elemental interaction among bodies driven by desire. Ethical questions of practice at this level must be posed in terms of the affects: passive affections and active affections. Spinoza defines passive affections, or passions, as those caused by forces outside us and, since their production is outside our control, they remain contingent in relation to us and may bring about either sadness or joy. Active affections, or actions, are caused by us ourselves and thus are both joyful and necessary—necessary in the sense that the joy they produce is not haphazard but continually returns. Deleuze insists, however, that we must grasp the logic of this productive dynamic at the most local level, the level at which the forces surrounding us greatly surpass our own power; here our bodies and minds are dominated not only by passive rather than active affections, but also by sad rather than joyful passions. This is the point of departure for the ethical path to be followed. Joy, in Spinozian terms, is nothing but the process of the increase of our power, and thus it is the guiding thread of any ethical and political project. "The ethical question falls then," Deleuze explains, "into two parts: How can we come to produce active affections? But first of all: How can we come to experience a maximum of joyful passions?" (1991, 246). How can we begin a practice of joy? This ethical tension toward joy is in fact, we will soon see, the motor that drives the collective constitution of the multitude.

Deleuze suggests that we begin our investigation of this constitutive dynamic by looking more closely at Spinoza's physics of bodies. The structure of the body, Deleuze explains, should be understood as a system of relations between the parts of a body. "By inquiring how these relations vary from one body to another, we have a way of directly determining the resemblances between two bodies, however disparate they may be" (278). In other words, our investigation of the structures or relationships that constitute the body allows us to recognize common relationships that exist between our body and another body. An encounter between our body and this other body will necessarily be joyful because the common relationship guarantees a compatibility and the opportunity to compose a new relationship, a new body, thereby increasing our power. Precisely in this way the analysis of bodies allows us to begin a practical project. By recognizing similar compositions or relationships among bodies we have the criteria necessary for a first ethical selection of joy: We are able to favor compatible encounters (that is, joyful passions) and avoid incompatible encounters (that is, sad passions). When we make this selection we begin the process of producing common notions. "A common notion," Deleuze explains, "is always an idea of a similarity of composition in existing modes" (275). The formation of the common notion constitutes the first step of an ethical practice.

The first adequate idea we can have, that is, the first active idea that contains or envelops its own cause, is the recognition of something in common between two bodies; this adequate idea immediately leads to another adequate idea; in this way we can proceed in our constructive project to become active rather than passive. The experience of joy is the spark that sets the ethical progression in motion. "When we encounter a body that agrees with our own," according to Deleuze, "when we experience a joyful passive affection, we are induced to form the idea of what is common to that body and our own" (282). The process begins with the experience of joy. This chance encounter with a compatible body allows us or induces us to recognize a common relationship, to form a common notion. There are two processes going on here, however, that Deleuze insists must be kept distinct. In the first moment, we strive both to avoid the sad passions that diminish our power and to accumulate joyful passions. This effort of selection does increase our power, but never to the point of becoming active: Joyful passions are always the result of an external cause, and they always indicate an inadequate idea. "We must then," Deleuze insists, "by the aid of joyful passions, form the idea of what is common to some external body and our own. For this idea alone, this common notion, is adequate" (283). The first moment, the accumulation of joyful passions, prepares the condition for this leap that provides us with an adequate idea, and hence an action rather than a passion—a joy that we bring about ourselves, a joy that is no longer the fruit of hazard but necessary, a joy that returns eternally.

With this practical construction of common notions Spinoza has given a radically new vision of ontology and nature. Being can no longer be considered a given arrangement or order; here being is the assemblage of "composable" relationships. We should keep in mind, however, that the essential element for ontological constitution remains the

Spinozian focus on causality, on the "productivity" and "producibility" of being. The common notion is the assemblage of two composable relationships to create a new, more powerful relationship—a new, more powerful body. This assemblage, however, is not merely a chance composition but an ontological constitution, because the process envelops the cause within the new body itself. The practical strategy of the formation of common notions, of ontological assemblages, has forged the ontological investigation into an ethical project: Become active, become adequate, become being. Spinoza's constitutive practice defines the productive series: from joyful passive affections to common notions and finally to active affections. The composition that is brought about in this sequence is the constitution of being itself.[5]

If we turn our focus now to the political terrain, we find that this ontological logic of assemblage presented in the formation of common notions is the same logic that plays a central role in the formation of the multitude. The multitude, in other words, is not a fixed or given element of the political scene, but it is continually made and unmade according the composition and decomposition of its relationships. The theory of power and bodies we have examined thus far is translated into terms of political practice in Spinoza's theory of right. "All that a body can do (its power)," Deleuze writes, "is also its 'natural right'" (257). To understand this proposition of natural right we have to recognize how Spinoza's internal logic of assemblage and constitution guides the reasoning here. Political constitution follows the logic of the affects.

As we have seen in terms of the body, Spinoza insists that we begin our political thought from the lowest level of our power, from the lowest point of social organization. Just as no one is born active, so too no one is born citizen. Every element of Spinozian society must be constituted internally with the elements at hand, by the constituent subjects (be they ignorant or learned), on the basis of the existing affections (be they passions or actions). We know that the human condition is characterized predominantly by our weakness, that the forces surrounding us in nature greatly surpass our own strength, and hence that our power to be affected is filled largely by passive rather than active affections. This devaluation, however, is also an affirmation of our freedom. When Spinoza insists that our natural right is coextensive with our power, this means that no social order can be imposed by any transcendent elements, by anything outside of the immanent field of forces. Thus, any conception of duty or obligation or any mechanism of contract or representation must be secondary to and dependent on the assertion of our power. The expression of power free from any moral order is the primary ethical principle of society. "Pushing to the utmost what one can do," Deleuze explains, "is the properly ethical task. It is here that Spinoza's ethics takes the body as model; for every body extends its power as far as it can. In a sense every being, each moment, pushes to the utmost what it can do" (1991, 269). This ethical formulation does not primarily place the accent on the limitation of our power, but rather poses a dynamic between the limit and what we can do: Each time we reach an extreme point, what we can do rises up to move beyond that point. The ethical task highlights our material striving (*conatus*) moving in the world to express our power beyond the given limits of the present arrangement, the present order. This ethical striving is the open expression of multiplicity. Spinoza's conception of natural right, then, presents the freedom from order, the freedom of multiplicity, the freedom of society in anarchy.

The society described by this initial state of nature, however, presents us with an unlivable condition—or, more accurately, it presents us with the minimum point of our power. In the state of nature thus conceived, I experience chance encounters with other bodies that, have very little in common with my own, since we are predominantly determined by passions. In this condition not only is my power to be affected filled predominantly by passive affections, but also those passive affections are mostly sad. Just as previously we have moved from passive affections to active affections, here we must discover a passage for the increase of our power from natural right to civil right. "There could be only one way to make the state of nature livable," Deleuze claims, "by striving to *organize its encounters*" (260–261). The civil state is the state of nature made livable; or more precisely, it is the state of nature infused with the project of the increase of our power. As we have seen before, the increase of our power involves the organization of composable relationships and, consequently, the constitution of a second nature. "If two come together and unite their strength," Spinoza says, "they have jointly more power, and consequently more right against other forces in nature, than either of them alone; and the more there be that join in alliance, the more right they will collectively possess" (*Political Treatise*, Chapter II, paragraph 13). The heart of Spinozian politics, then, is oriented toward the organization of social encounters, in order to encourage useful and composable relationships. Natural right is not negated in the passage to civil right, as it is in dialectical conceptions of society, but rather is preserved and intensified.

In this transformation the multiplicity of society is forged into a multitude. The multitude remains contingent in that it is always open to antagonism and conflict, but through its dynamic of increasing power it attains a plane of consistency; it has the capacity to pose social normativity as civil right. The multitude is multiplicity made powerful. Spinoza's conception of civil right, then, complements the first notion of freedom with a second: from the freedom from order to the freedom of organization. The freedom of multiplicity thus becomes the freedom of the multitude, and Spinoza defines the rule of the multitude as democracy. In the passage of freedom from multiplicity to multitude, Spinoza composes and intensifies anarchy in democracy. Spinozian democracy, the absolute rule of the multitude through the equality of its constituent members, is founded on what Deleuze calls the "art of organizing encounters" (262). The corporeal common notion, the adequate social body, is given material form in the multitude.

This interpretation of Spinoza's politics poses a rigorously corporeal and passional logic of assemblage oriented toward collective joy. The multitude thus conceived removes democratic thinking from any idealist or rationalist schema, any forms of representation or mediation, and any contractual processes of abstraction from the material desires of existing collective social subjects. This logic of constitution and assemblage fills in the gap left by his refusal of contractual and representational mechanisms with a productive social dynamic. The corporeality and passion of the multitude, and the immanence and openness of its horizon serve not only to subvert the major currents of modern political thought but also to propose an alternative notion of democracy. Spinoza shows us just how revolutionary democracy can be. "Spinoza's innovation is in fact a philosophy of communism; Spinozian ontology is nothing but a genealogy of communism" (Negri 1992, 163). If indeed, as Antonio Negri claims, history has in certain ways caught up with Spinoza's vision, then soon perhaps his revolutionary democracy can cease to be an enigma and begin to be a reality.

NOTES

1. We should note that this refusal of contracts in the *Political Treatise* is at odds with Spinoza's discourse on contracts in the *Theologico-Political Treatise*, written some ten years earlier. My discussion here will focus on the later work considering it for our purposes here a more mature expression of Spinoza's political thought.

2. For analyses of the term "*multitudo*" in Spinoza's work, see Negri (1991, 187–190; 1992, 71–83) and Balibar (1985, 84–87; 1989, 104–128).

3. For a hypothetical construction of the unwritten chapter of Spinoza's *Political Treatise* on democracy, see Negri's "Reliqua Desiderantur: Congettura per una definizione del concetto di democrazia nell'ultimo Spinoza," now included in Negri (1992). "My conjecture," Negri (1992, 84; my translation) writes, "is that Spinozian democracy . . . must be conceived as a social practice of singularities that are woven together in a mass process, or better, as *pietas* that forms and constitutes the single reciprocal relationships that extend among the multiplicity of subjects that constitute the multitude."

4. I examine Deleuze's reading of Spinoza at length in Hardt (1993), Chapter 3, in particular pp. 87–111.

5. For a brief summary of this notion of ontological constitution, see Hardt (1993, 112–122).

REFERENCES

Balibar, E. 1989. "Spinoza, the Anti-Orwell: The Fear of the Masses." *Rethinking Marxism* 2 (3): 104–139.

———. 1985. *Spinoza et la politique*. Paris: Presses Universitaires de France.

Deleuze, G. 1991. *Expressionism in Philosophy: Spinoza*, trans. M. Joughin. New York: Zone Books.

Hardt, M. 1993. *Gilles Deleuze: An Apprenticeship in Philosophy*. Minneapolis: University of Minnesota Press.

Negri, A. 1991. *The Savage Anomaly: The Power of Spinoza's Metaphysics and Politics*, trans. M. Hardt. Minneapolis: University of Minnesota Press.

———. 1992. *Spinoza sovversivo*. Rome: Antonio Pellicani Editore.

The End of Orthodox Marxism

DOUGLAS KELLNER

Crises of Marxism have erupted regularly throughout the century. The concept of "crisis" within Marxian theory has its origins in theories of the "crisis of capitalism," which were linked to notions of the collapse of capitalism and triumph of socialism. The term "crisis" in Marxian discourse thus suggests the possibility of cata-clysmic collapse and, as Habermas suggests (1975, 1), a terminal illness that could bring death to its patient.[1] The term "crisis" was applied to Marxism itself by Sorel, Korsch, and others earlier in the century (see Gouldner 1980). In recent years, there have been many claims that with the collapse of the Soviet Union, the era of Marxism is over and the theory is now obsolete. Consequently, it is claimed that the crisis of Marxism has terminated in its collapse and that Marxism is no longer a viable theory or politics for the present age.[2]

During World War I, the failure of the Second International and Marxian parties and individuals to stop the war put in question the political force of Marxism as an organized movement. The failure to carry through European revolutions after the war produced new crises of Marxism and the triumph of fascism threatened to eliminate Marxist governments, parties, and militants. After World War II, the integration of the working class and stabilization of capitalism in the so-called democratic capitalist countries seemed to portend the obsolescence of Marxism.[3] Thus Marxism, like capitalism, its object and other, has been in crisis throughout the century.

However, just as capitalism has survived many crises, so has Marxism. Just as various crises of capitalism have elicited new survival strategies that in certain ways have strengthened the capitalist system (i.e., imperialism, organized capitalism, state capitalism, the welfare state, the consumer society, transnational capitalism, technocapitalism, etc.), so too crises of Marxism have periodically led to the development and improvement of Marx and Engel's original theory. Indeed, historical materialism is intrinsically a historical theory; its categories thus demand revision and development as new historical conditions and situations emerge. Revision is the very life of the Marxian dialectic, and the theory itself demands development, reconstruction, and even abandonment of obsolete or inadequate features as conditions emerge that put tenets of the original theory in question.

Against those who proclaim the obsolescence of Marxism in the contemporary era, I argue that Marxism continues to provide theoretical resources to explain contemporary developments in capitalist societies, and contains political resources that can continue to help us work toward their transformation. Thus, it is my contention that Marxism continues to possess resources to theorize and criticize the present age and that Marxian politics remains at least a part of a progressive or radical politics in the current era. I do, however, believe that the collapse of the Soviet Union points to the end of a certain version of orthodox Marxism, if not of Marxism itself.

CRISES OF MARXISM

Throughout the twentieth century Marxism has been in crisis, as new events emerge that require revision and development of the theory. Marx and Engels and then subsequent Marxists were always revising and reconstructing the theory to take account of historical developments and to fill in deficiencies in the original theory. In this sense, "crises of Marxism" are not so much signs of the obsolescence of Marxian theory as a typical situation for a social theory that faces anomalies or events that challenge its theories. Such crises require revision and modification of the theory in the light of new historical conditions and experiences, and since the death of Marx, many Marxists have periodically revised, updated, and thus strengthened Marxian theory.[4]

Nevertheless, the collapse of Soviet Communism is such an epochal event that perhaps one can say that a certain version of Marxism is now at its end. I am speaking of that version of "orthodox Marxism" that claimed that it was theorizing the very movement of history, that history guaranteed the triumph of socialism, and that the collapse of capitalism and the transition to socialism and communism were inevitable. Such a Marxism claimed to be grounded in a "scientific" analysis of history and exhibited features of certainty, dogmatism, and orthodoxy. Orthodox Marxism was systematized in the Soviet Union and transmitted in different versions all over the world. It was rooted in doctrines concerning the revolutionary vocation of the proletariat and the certainty that capitalism would be overthrown by a revolutionary proletariat. Orthodox Marxism claimed that such socialism was being produced in the Soviet Union and that the triumph of socialism on a world scale was guaranteed by the success of Soviet Communism.[5]

This version of orthodox Marxism had harmful consequences for the construction of socialism. Belief that history itself was leading to socialism, that one was part of the flow of history, led to submission to historical trends and the dictates of party leaders who could claim to read the direction and flow of history. It created arrogance and dogmatism, and produced a version of Marxism that could be used to legitimate oppressive societies. This version of orthodox Marxism is obviously totally discredited and obsolete; in turn, it discredits the Marxism–Leninism and "scientific Marxism" that was associated with it. Yet I would argue that a critical Marxism that remains open, nondogmatic, and more modest continues to provide theoretical and political resources to develop a critical theory and radical politics for the present age. (On the difference between scientific and critical Marxism, see Gouldner 1980.)

The particular challenge and opportunity today for critical Marxism is to provide an account of the restructuring of capitalism and the new system of technocapitalism that is now emerging. I would argue that Marxian theory provides the best perspectives and resources for this monumental task, and that Marxian theory continues to provide powerful resources to develop a social theory and radical politics for the present age. For Marxian theory is at bottom a theory of capitalism, rooted in the political economy of the existing social system. If the economy is undergoing changes, and if economic factors continue to play a key role in all aspects of social life, then a theory of capitalism is a necessary component of radical social theory. Since no competing economic theory or critique of capitalism has emerged to replace Marxism, it still is an indispensable part of radical social theory.

It is, however, necessary for Marxian theory to develop new categories and analyses in order to theorize the current restructuring and crises of capitalism. Although this process has appeared to signify a disorganized capitalism for some theorists (i.e., Offe 1985; Lash and Urry 1987), it also involves a reorganization of capitalism, sometimes described as "post-Fordism," which requires new analyses (Harvey 1989). Many Marxists are in fact providing these analyses, thus updating Marxian political economy. In addition, it has been well documented in the past decades that there have been tremendous advances in Marxian social theory, cultural theory, philosophy, and within every conceivable academic discipline, providing new Marxian analyses of all domains of social life. These efforts provide indispensable components of a reconstructed Marxism for the present age.

Indeed, from this perspective we can see the limitations of the fashionable postmodern theories that have accumulated a certain degree of cultural capital and influence by critiquing Marxism and other modern theories. Such theories proclaim "the end of history" at the very moment that Communism is collapsing, the capitalist system is restructuring itself, and new possibilities and problems are appearing on the historical scene with increased acceleration and urgency. To say that "history" has ended in such a situation is totally ludicrous. Baudrillard's (1976) concept of "the end of political economy" is an equally absurd event to proclaim at a time when capitalism is restructuring itself on a global level. Indeed, the attack on macro and systemic theories is also disabling at the very time in which we need new theories and politics to conceptualize the new socioeconomic, political, and cultural configurations of the moment, and to seek solutions to the political problems of the present age that are increasingly global in nature (i.e., global debt crisis, global ecological crisis, the globalization of local political conflicts as in the Gulf War and the present crises in the former Yugoslavia and elsewhere). Thus I would argue that Marxism contains the resources to develop a critical theory of the present age, and that renouncing it because of the political collapse of Soviet Communism, which arguably was a distortion of the theory in the first place, is simplistic and unproductive.

RETHINKING SOCIALISM

Only the most extreme ideological enemy of Marxism, or the uninformed pseudointellectual, could seriously maintain that Marxian theory is obsolete. But what of Marxian politics? As a theory, while Marxism is arguably alive and well, Marxian politics seem nonetheless to be floundering. It is a curiosity of the fate of Marxism today that in the past decades, while there has been a tremendous development of theory, there has been a steady decline in Marxian politics, as well as a declining role for Marxian discourse and practice in contemporary political movements. Some Marxian radicals have urged that the discourse of socialism be abandoned in the present context, while socialist parties in the Western capitalist countries seem to be rapidly declining in power and influence. Labor struggles and the sort of class politics classically associated with Marxian theory also seem to be in decline, so that the question arises as to whether the very discourse of socialism and revolution should be abandoned.

In the following discussion, I concede that socialism and social change need to be reconsidered, but I argue for the continued relevance of Marxian political theory. In part, its continuing political relevance is due to its intense and resolute focus on class. The class theory of politics, I believe, constitutes both an enduring contribution of Marxian theory and an obdurate limitation. During the past 12 years in the United States and more or less elsewhere throughout the world, there have been growing class divisions between rich and poor, between the haves and the have-nots. To proclaim the obsolescence of social classes and class struggle seems absolutely wrong in the face of the palatable reality of class.

Yet the class privileged by the classical Marxian theory of revolution, the proletariat, the industrial working class, is a declining class sector in the Western industrial countries, although this is not in the developing world, where industrial labor is increasingly exported. Beginning with the Frankfurt School, Marxian theorists questioned whether the proletariat could serve as a revolutionary subject, as it did in the original revolutionary theory of Marx. It is also a widely accepted tenet that classical Marxism exaggerates the primacy of class and downplays the salience of gender and race. Clearly, oppression takes place in many more spheres than just those of the economy and the workplace, so that a radical politics of the future should take account of gender and race as well as class.

Although it would be wrong to ignore the centrality of class and the importance of class politics, a radical politics today should be more multicultural, race and gender focused, and broad-based than the original Marxian theory. Thus, a form of Marxism seems to have come to an end: the Marxism of the industrial working class, of proletarian revolution. Marxism was identified since its beginnings with working-class revolution, and Marxian-inspired revolutions legitimated themselves as working class revolutions. No doubt a future Marxism will have to distance itself from its concept of the proletariat and from its privileging of the industrial working class as the subject of revolution and of the construction of socialism. As new technologies expand and the industrial proletariat shrinks, new agents of social change must be sought. (This was the dilemma of the Frankfurt School. For discussion of the political implications of this impasse, see Kellner 1989.)

On the negative side, the collapse of the Soviet Union has generated an ideological celebration of capitalism and market economy as the best economic system, as well as producing the actual dismantling of state Communist societies and the implementation of market economies in the former Soviet empire. Thus the economic and political counterweight to capitalism and an alternative world system disappeared, leaving capitalist political economy triumphant. But the passing away of a social system that fundamentally distorted Marxian theory has opened the way for a new type of socialism that could enhance freedom, democracy, and human happiness. In this context, it seems to me premature to jettison the concept of socialism when existing capitalist societies are in need of such profound transformation. I would argue that one can still use the concept of socialism as a practical guide to inform policies in democratic capitalist societies and to make specific policy demands: full employment; health care; shortening the work week; democratizing the workplace, the media, and other domains of society. One can also use socialist ideas to call for more radical democratization, yet one should perhaps argue that with a genuinely democratic socialism, all classes of society will participate in self-management Thus, there should be no privileging of the working class or any other class, as occurs in some versions of classical Marxism.

Further, Marxian concepts can be used to demonstrate the problems with an unrestrained capitalism and to justify regulation and social control of capitalism. During an era in which "free markets" are being touted as the source of economic prosperity and human freedom alike, the Marxian critique of market capitalism shows their limitations. Since capitalism has produced incredible suffering all over the world, such critiques should emphasize its limitations, the need for regulation, and ultimately a better organization of society. Putting the imperative to maximize the accumulation of capital over the needs of people is one of the structural limitations of capitalism. Radical discourse should attack this weakness in legitimating social change, especially since such an attack could win the favor of large amounts of people.

Perhaps most importantly, the Marxian vision of emancipation should continue to animate struggles for a freer and more democratic society. The Marxian demand for shortening the workday and increasing the realm of leisure seems especially relevant during an era when technology makes possible less work, yet capitalism continues to impose more work (see Schorr 1992). Marx's vision of emancipation and full development of the individual seems appropriate to the present level of technological development and can provide a critical standpoint to denounce continued societal oppression. Its emphasis on the democratization of social life is appropriate when the democratic revolution seems to have triumphed, or to be at least possible, on a worldwide scale.

The Marxian vision of democracy and freedom, I would argue, is preferable to the liberal version in that it has a more comprehensive vision of democracy, which encompasses all realms of social life. The popular sovereignty exercised in the Paris Commune, and celebrated by Marx and Engels as a model for the self-management of society, would involve genuine popular sovereignty on the social and political level, as well as economic democracy. While the existing socialist societies never developed social democracy, there existed at the least a modicum of workplace democracy. In the liberal capitalist countries, by contrast, democracy is effectively curtailed to periodic voting, and there is little real popular sovereignty in the social realm or democracy in the workplace.

Thus, classical liberalism's notion of representative democracy—its equation of democracy with voting—severely restricts the conception of democracy, yielding only a weak democracy that conservative forces easily manipulate by using their wealth and power to control electoral processes. The classical liberal concept of freedom is also truncated, often limiting freedom to individual freedom of choice in the market and political popularity contests. The question also arises as to whether the vast majority of the population are really free in capitalist societies that do not provide the economic basis to live a free life. How can one be said to be "free" when one is suffering constant anxiety about employment, homelessness, health care, the environment, and the possibility of economic collapse? Adorno's demand for a life without anxiety is relevant as a critical marker against really existing capitalist insecurity and anxiety.

Yet it must be admitted that "really existing communist societies" (see Bahro 1978) never incorporated the bourgeois tradition of rights, individual liberties, and democracy to the extent stressed by some of the Marxian classics. Failure to adequately appropriate the progressive heritage of liberalism into Marxian political theory rendered it vulnerable to liberal critiques and the belief that only liberalism provided genuine freedom and democracy. Marxism should have established itself as the champion of these political values, but an underdeveloped Marxian political philosophy and really existing political oppression of the socialist regimes created an identification of Marxism with oppression and liberalism with freedom and democracy.

Finally, against liberalism's individualism—as well as some so-called postmodern politics that stress micropolitics—one could argue that Marxian concepts of mass politics, that call for mass struggle, radical systemic change, and fundamental restructuring of the system were exemplified by the very struggles in Eastern Europe and the former Soviet Union that were previously claimed to have invalidated Marxian theory. The dramatic mass struggles and upheavals in these regions caused fundamental social change (which may, however, turn out to be regressive in many ways). Thus, whereas micropolitics may contribute to such a process, it seems premature to claim that the era of mass politics, associated in part with Marxism, is over.

Indeed, Marxian political theory articulates and grounds those values that can unify disparate political movements. Mindless champions of "new social movements" per se as the contemporary agents of change obscure the fact that some of these movements are reactionary, some are at best liberal, and some are genuinely progressive. We need broad political perspectives to judge between contending political movements and to provide values and ideals that might unite specific movements for specific goals. As Jesse Jackson reminds us, coalition politics requires discovering the common ground that might unite progressive movements, who then together can move to the higher ground of democratic political transformation.

Whither, then, Marxism? Certainly it can no longer be regarded as the master theory and narrative it appeared to be in its classical forms, but it remains an important perspective for critical theory today. We continue to live in a capitalist society and as long as we do, Marxism will continue to be relevant. A reconstructed Marxism, a Marxism without guarantees, teleology, and foundations will be more open, tolerant, skeptical, and modest than previous versions. A Marxism for the twenty-first century could help promote democracy, freedom, justice, and equality, and counterattack conservative ideologies that merely promote the interests of the rich and powerful. As long as tremendous class inequality, human suffering, and oppression exists there is the need for critical theories like Marxism and visions of radical social change that the tradition has inspired. Marxism will disappear either when the nightmare of capitalism is finally over or when a democratic and free society emerges that will produce its own philosophy and way of life. If Marxism has inspired such a project, then the doctrine can pass on to a happy obsolescence and the sufferings and struggles of those in the Marxian tradition will be redeemed.

NOTES

1. Habermas notes that the term "crisis" in the medical sense "refers to the phase of an illness in which it is decided whether or not the organism's self-healing powers are sufficient for recovery" (1975, 1). A crisis in this sense thus threatens the survival of a phenomenon and suggests that if it does not survive the crisis, it will cease to exist.

2. U.S. State Department neo-Hegelian Francis Fukujama has proclaimed the "end of history" after the fall of the Berlin Wall and the collapse of the Soviet Empire. He declared "the ultimate triumph of Western liberal democracy" and "the unabashed victory of economic and political liberalism" (1989, 3). As Derrida reminds us (1993), such claims have been made regularly from the 1950s throughout the cold war. The question arises, however, whether the collapse of Communism in the Soviet Union portends the obsolescence of Marxism.

3. For descriptions of these crises of Marxism and the ways that Western Marxian theorists responded to the crises, see my book on Herbert Marcuse (1984) who attempted to reconstruct the Marxian theory in response to a series of crises of Marxism.

4. This was the life work of Herbert Marcuse, and many other Marxists have also responded to crises of Marxism with important, sometimes spectacular, developments of the theory. For examples, see my books on Marcuse (1984) and on the critical theory of the Frankfurt School (1989).

5. See Marcuse (1958) for analysis of the specific features of orthodox Marxism produced in the Soviet Union and disseminated throughout the world.

REFERENCES

Bahro, R. 1978. *The Alternative in Eastern Europe*. London: New Left Books.

Baudrillard, J. 1976. *L'echange symbolique et la mort*. Paris: Gallimard.

Derrida, J. 1993, April. "Spectre of Marx: The State of the Debt, the Work of Mourning and the New International." Paper presented at the "Whither Marxism?" conference, University of California at Riverside.

Fukuyama, F. 1991, Summer. "The End of History?" *The National Interest*. 16: 3–18.

——. 1992. *The End of History*. New York: The Free Press.

Gouldner, A. 1980. *The Two Marxisms*. New York: Seabury Press.

Habermas, J. 1975. *Legitimation Crisis*. Boston: Beacon Press.

Harvey, D. 1989. *The Condition of Postmodernity*. Oxford: Blackwell.

Kellner, D. 1984. *Herbert Marcuse and the Crisis of Marxism*. London: Macmillan.

——. 1989. *Critical Theory, Marxism, and Modernity*. Cambridge, England: Polity and Johns Hopkins University Press.

Lash, S. and Urry, J. 1987. *The End of Organized Capitalism*. Cambridge, England: Polity Press.

Marcuse, H. 1958/1985. *Soviet Marxism*. New York: Columbia University Press.

Offe, C. 1985. *Disorganized Capitalism*. Oxford: Basil Blackwell.

Schorr, J. 1992. *The Overworked American*. New York: Basic Books.

Marxism and Spirituality

JOEL KOVEL

arxism is recognized to be a synthesis between German philosophy, French political theory, and English economics. I would argue that the observation is true but incomplete, because it leaves out the fourth, indispensable source of the Marxist synthesis: radical spirituality.

The reason for the omission is not hard to find. Marxism's vaunted materialism seems to dissolve any connection with the notoriously "idealistic" realm of spirit. From this standpoint, for Marxism to claim a spirituality would amount to an association with traditional religious obscurantism and reaction, as well as with the mushy, easily commodified and incipiently right-wing contemporary spiritual movements known as "New Age." Indeed, the notion of spirit had already retreated in the Hegelian philosophy that Marx incorporated and superseded. Spirit (*Geist*) is doubtless the leading term of Hegel's thought; however, Hegel moves the category away from the otherworldly religious domain, and toward an idealism that, being objective, was also inherently mediated by the material world. From this point of view, Marx merely moved one decisive step further into the material dimension, retaining Hegel's dialectic but now locating it firmly on the ground of history and nature. Thus Hegel turned religion into philosophy, which Marx turned into historical materialism under the impact of political economy and revolutionary politics, wringing out the category of Spirit as he went.

So it would seem. But how, then, do we account for the fact that the young Marx, in one of his most fully articulated efforts to go beyond Hegel, wrote of religion as "the soul of soulless conditions"? There is no doubt that the intent of this famous passage, set off as it was against the still more famous notion of religion as "the opium of the people," was to criticize religion for its inadequacy while recognizing its value and merit in respect to the rest of the bourgeois order. Thus Marx (1975, 244) also refers to religion as "the heart of a heartless world." Now, since no one would deny in respect to this last phrase that Marx is for "heart" in the world—that is, for a world filled with compassion and human sympathy— how can it be denied that he is also for "soul" in the world? And since to affirm soul is to affirm the spiritual dimension, it must be that Marx regards spiritual realization as in some sense a goal of revolution.

Were this a marginal passage, we would need take the argument no further. But it is anything but marginal: These lines from the Introduction to his "Contribution to the Critique of Hegel's Philosophy of Right" are famous not because they are a curiosity within Marx's thought, but because they are an example of the revolutionary ardor and humanism that belongs to Marxism at its best. Wherever Marxism has gone wrong— whether by becoming reformist, economistic, rigid, and/or authoritarian—it betrays its roots by violating insights such as these. And since these insights are spiritual ones, we can claim that a fully realized Marxism should embody them as fully realized spirituality, and that a failed Marxism either bypasses the spiritual dimension or perverts it. It was in this respect an antispiritual, economistic Marxism that lost the German working class to the perverted spirituality of Nazism; and it was a perversely spiritual Marxism that turned into the quasi-religion of Stalinism.

Now if spirit is somehow necessary for a fully realized Marxism, it should be a component of Marxian discourse. For Marx, moral passion cannot be severed from "scientific" insight; what distinguishes authentic Marxism is the synthesis between value and theory. And if this synthesis leads Marx to use the term "spirit" to describe what is missing from the bourgeois world and needs to be restored by revolutionary practice, then that same "spirit" has to be included in our understanding of the world.

But what does this mean? We can translate reasonably well the metaphorical "heart" that Marx claims to be missing from capitalist society into concrete terms. But spirit? Is this merely a metaphor for some kind of exalted feeling or morality? And if it is more than a metaphor, how do we talk about spirit without religious or New Age language? Theoretically it should be possible to do so, because spirit is prior to religion. A religion consists of a kind of incorporation of the spirit dimension into a historical project according to the needs and imagination of a particular group. Religion is a way of realizing spirit, but also binds spirit. In the process, religion captures the language of spirit. It becomes a kind of veil, interposing its theology—the "word of God"—the apprehension of spirit. Critical reflection on the prevailing theology is necessary if religion is to move toward its spiritual realization. This follows along the lines of Marx's intent, when he sought, in the same youthful essay, to tear away the veil of religious illusion in order to pluck "the imaginary flowers from the chain . . . so that [humanity] shall throw off the chain and pluck the living flower" (1975, 244)—that is, to find in communism the true content of spirit. It needs to be added, however, that he did not succeed in doing so. Whether he was too distracted or too ambivalent, the fact remains that Marx never pursued his insight into the role of spirituality. He did not reject the attitude noted above, but, like much else in his early thought, it was put aside. Spirit terms appear in the later work, but there is no exploration of what spirit would mean for Marxism.

This goal lays before us, and remains so with this essay. However, it may be possible to sharpen the question, or at least to make some dent in the prevailing skepticism about spiritual matters. Most contemporary Marxists and radicals simply reject any notion of spirit beyond a casual figure of speech. If pressed, many would say that the notion of spirit is philosophically disreputable. To the demythologizing post-Enlightenment mentality, to affirm spirit amounts to postulating a kind of metaphysic, an ahistorical essence that eventually requires smuggling back the notion of a god.

We cannot deal adequately with the philosophical issues within the bounds of this brief essay. But it might be useful to remind ourselves that spirit is prior to religion and that it is religion which constructs god out of spirit. Further, there is nothing inherently ahistorical about spirit. To the contrary, spirit may be regarded as specifically historical. Religions are but one kind of spiritual outcome, and there is no *a priori* reason why they should be the only kind, nor why the god of monotheism need be the end product of spirituality. In view of this, it might be argued that the world religions were neither more nor less than phase-specific manifestations of spirit for their time, while another, nontheistic manifestation of spirit is required for our time. All of which brings us once again to the definition of spirit.

It is no easy matter to define what "spirit" means, given the inherent ineffability of spiritual phenomena and the ever-changing history of spirituality. At the least, we can distinguish five major senses of the term:

- Spirit as a vital power, as in the sense of being *inspired* (i.e., in-spirited)

- Spirit as a kind of occult being, as in the sense of *spirits of the ancestors*—more generally, we might call this the notion of "spirit being" as Other
- Spirit as a kind of authentic meaning, as in the *spirit of the agreement*
- Spirit as a relation to the body, especially having to do with desire, as in *the spirit was willing but the flesh was weak*
- Spirit as a kind of godlike entity, as in the *Holy Spirit* of Catholic theology

Clearly, there is no obvious common denominator here, and to find some ground shared by all these propositions one has to undertake a considerable degree of abstraction. Doing so, we arrive at the common property of spiritual phenomena as *that which surpasses the immediate given properties of the self*; that is, the relation of the self to the expanded kind of being encountered as its boundaries give way. To be inspired means, accordingly, to be lifted out of the ordinary limits of energy available to the self; to encounter a "spirit being" means to go past what psychology calls the "ego-boundary"; to get at spiritual meaning entails going beyond the obvious, given meanings of things to get at their truth; to relate spirit to flesh means to surpass the limits of desire; finally, the relation to godhead provides the most explicit sense that spirit is somehow outside the self yet related to the self.

Perhaps the most important property of spiritual experience so far as we are concerned is that it cannot leave the self unchanged. To encounter spirit must be a more radical experience than sticking one's toe in the water and pulling it out again. The encounter with what is beyond the self must actually change the self. Perhaps the best-known instance of this is Christianity's notion of being "born again." Given an expanded view of spirit, however, we can say that all phenomena that radically change the self are inherently spiritual; and since Marxism is nothing if not a program for radical change, then it, too, must be inherently spiritual.

Spirit is an answer to the ontological question, What does the verb, "to be" mean when applied to "human being"? A moment's reflection will convince us that there is no ready answer to this question, and perhaps no positive answer at all. Here an academic philosopher might break off, snug in the belief that propositions not operationally frameable are not worth pursuing. But in life as contrasted to the academy, we cannot get along without this verb, and we had might as well learn to give it shape and relationship. This entails seeing various social formations from the standpoint of their relation to being. Capitalism in this regard is not just an economic arrangement but a form of being, and in Marx's view, a deformation. Thus Marx (1978) in the *Manuscripts* observes that under the conditions of alienated labor, the verb, "to have," replaces "to be" at the center of social relations. What goes for the worker, however, goes for the whole mode of production. Indeed, what is capitalism if not the ascendancy of having over being throughout all aspects of society? Such an ontological definition of capitalism is a necessary complement to the critique of political economy—necessary, that is, if the boundaries of economism are to be surpassed. How else can Marxism escape the confines of a narrow restructuring of the economy unless it addresses itself to all forms of social being: the ways people love and hate each other, the ways parents are with children, the ways people play and make culture as well as work, the ways self-experience is constructed, and, necessarily, the ways self-experience is transcended in spirit? In this respect, spiritual transformation is the integral of all aspects of being into a new state of development. The release of being from having is the liberation from capitalist egoism and possessiveness into what the *Communist Manifesto* calls "an association, in which the free development of each is the condition for the free development of all," that is, solidarity and unalienated labor (Marx and Engels 1992, 43).Therefore, spiritual transformation and socialist transformation are fundamentally one.

We may summarize. Spirit as an answer to the ontological question is a statement that a human being most fully "is" when it surpasses itself. This is integral to the philosophical roots of Marxism, for the core of Marx's notion of human being is creative power through the labor process, a creativity that includes the capacity for self- as well as social transformation. The subject creates itself through object making. We "are" as we produce—not by the alienated production under conditions of domination, but through the free association and development of creativity. And we are ourselves as spirit when we produce new self-relations to being.

These reflections notwithstanding, in the real world the gulf between people who define themselves as spiritual and those who are Marxist remains wide. If Marxists have rejected spirituality for its idealistic and metaphysical character, spiritually inclined people, whether of traditional religion or the New Age, have been almost uniformly hostile to Marxism on the grounds of its alleged "materialism." Actually, there are two oppositions here, depending upon the nature of Marxist materialism. One is between spirituality and Stalinist Marxism, whose "materialism" is not much more than a mimickry of the worst features of capitalism's reduction of the world to brute matter. To the extent that a spiritual critique of Stalinism may reinforce the latter's demise, so much the better. But there is another, deeper kind of opposition. For authentic Marxism remains materialist as well, and this materialism, which is historical rather than mechanical in character, also challenges traditional spirituality.

Here the tension is between disembodied notions of spirit and Marx's insistence that human activity be approached as "sensuous activity." From another angle Marx demands that spirituality, like all forms of human activity, be critiqued from the standpoint of praxis—conscious, purposive, historically situated action. Spirit might be the fulfillment of being, but this comes from within material transformation and not via the heavens. Since Marxism is historical materialism, it calls for nothing less than a *historical materialism of the spirit*. One condition of this is that spirituality be seen from the standpoint of class and the relations of production. Here traditional religious as well as New Age spirituality are themselves put to a severe test, which includes looking at uncomfortable subjects like the politics of the church, or the class position of New Age acolytes. It also means regarding spirituality from the standpoint of its role in the struggle against domination and exploitation. Finally, it means a radical re-visioning of the relations between spirit and nature. For if spirit emerges out of praxis, and praxis is the conscious transforming of nature, then spirit and nature are not to be split from each other. Spirit does not come out of an abstract, empty space; it is immanent in nature and released through emancipatory action. This would apply as well—indeed, with particular insistence—to that part of nature which is our bodily flesh, with its various desires. From this standpoint, human being is nature becoming conscious of itself, the consciousness subjected to all the vicissitudes of alienation in patriarchy, racism, and class domination. And spirit emerges from the direct, sensuous encounter with matter, rather than being split-off from matter.

A historical materialism of the spirit indicates how Marxism can become truly spiritual and what would constitute the spirituality appropriate to a Marxian social transformation. The models for this are fragmentary and full of contradiction. They consist of flashes in the bleak history of domination, defeated revolutionary movements, the insights of spiritual geniuses. Like any real spiritual path, this is to be made by hard, uncertain work. I do not think, in any case, that a spirituality appropriate to Marxism's potentials would match the pattern of traditional religion. The great world religions, it has already been observed, all belong to class society. They project the dream of an emancipated existence, whether through Judaism's god of justice, Christianity's god of love or Buddhism's compassionate self. Thus they become the soul of soulless conditions. But religions look at this beyond from here, and carry a fallen earth into their heaven. With the exception of Buddhism, the world religions—especially in the dominant line extending from Judaism through Christianity and into Islam—reproduce patriarchal domination in their ideal realm. The gods of power are male, and the female figures, Eve and Mary being the two most important representations, remain defined through the Father, in relation to whom they either rebel futilely or passively submit.

The figure of Jesus is the great exception to this rule, and stands in the most direct relation to the spiritual potentialities of Marxism. This association is anchored in the emancipatory passages of the Gospels and the works of the radical Reformation, of which Marx and Engels were great admirers. It has been carried forward by countless lay and clerical believers, most inspiringly in the Central American revolutions. The reflex in thought of this practice has been liberation theology, a movement which has produced literally scores of works attempting a Christian–Marxian synthesis. Though liberation theology has been in considerable retreat, thanks largely to the reactionary Pope John Paul II, the logic of its "special option for the poor" continues to link Marxism and Christianity.

However, I see no synthesis emerging from this association. There is no possibility, in my view, that any institutional church hierarchy will preside over its own revolutionizing. Christian radicals have to choose between a Jesus who is the "Son of God," and one so detached from the traditional religious structures as to require a fundamentally different spiritual realization. But a Jesus who is not the divine Son of God (or the product of a virgin birth) is only a man with great spiritual powers, a man who awakens in all people the dream of spiritual transformation: the "Kingdom of Heaven," to revert to yet another patriarchal remnant within Christianity. Under the pressure of this dilemma, great numbers of religious Christians have left the church. But if this is the option before the radically religious, how can a spiritually inclined Marxist find a path within the established religious field?

Buddhism, in contrast, seeks an unmediated encounter with being itself. As a religion not tied to god-building, Buddhism would seem particularly suited for appropriation by the spiritually inclined Marxist. Buddhism *ablates* the self, which it regards as an illusion, and offers a message of compassion, thus surpassing capitalist egoism. And yet, although many Buddhists have been politically active, especially in movements of nonviolence, nothing approaching a Buddhist–Marxist dialogue exists. One reason for this may be that Buddhist praxis, grounded in meditation, focuses on individual transformation and cedes decisions on social issues to the prevailing structure of power. In practice, Buddhism requires a withdrawal from the world as a condition for meditation. It is the religion of contemplation; and while this is surely not the bourgeois contemplation Marx warns against, Buddhism seems to confine itself to redirecting the individual to paths of compassion and nonharmful occupation, in the hope that this essentially voluntarist pathway will some-how spread and transform society. This tends to lead Buddhism to sim-ply short-circuit the hard facts of class injustice, patriarchy or the state—a defect that, it may be added, often leads Buddhist groups to reproduce some of the authoritarian aspects of the larger society. (However, see Jones 1989 for a sign of a different approach).

The dialogue has also been closed off from the side of Marxism, which has until now proven unable to confront the radical insight of Buddhism; namely, that there is a kind of inner world of unbounded being which is in some way a firmament of our existence. In this insight, being opens up into us. To appreciate this aspect of existence, however, one has to become receptive to it. Generally speaking, Marxists from Karl Marx to the present day have shown themselves unwilling to undertake such receptivity. However we rationalize this attitude, it comes down to being so preoccupied with the "struggle" as to be shut off to any con-templative practice through which one would become spiritually open to the full possibilities of being. It is this, I suspect, more than any theory of materialism which constitutes the real barrier to a spiritual develop-ment within Marxism.

In sum, a historical materialism of the spirit expands both the scope of traditional historical materialism and the conception of praxis. It nei-ther privileges the inner world as in religious states of withdrawal, nor marginalizes it as in the despiritualized political traditions. It adds to the emphasis on external struggle a dimension of receptivity and openness to being. This receptivity should not be confused with passivity or iner-tia, any more than activity should be confused with violence. A person silently meditating is actively struggling with ego in order to become more open to being.

It may be that the best models for the spirituality appropriate to Marxism are not to be found in the world religions at all but in the spiri-tuality of indigenous people. For here, in this communism, conditions were not soulless. Native Americans, for example, had no church or priesthood, because they had no class system or state. They did not bur-den themselves with a singular Father god demanding obedience, but saw a spirit in each thing, integrated into a kind of Great Spirit in every-thing. Because they were not subjected to a commodity system in which exchange value leaches out use value, they were able to sacralize each thing and give it being, nor did they hold themselves over the rest of nature. They felt, as William Blake (1956, 193) said, that "every thing that lives is Holy." Blake, by the way, shows that one can live this kind of spiri-tuality even in the midst of class society, although, as might be expected, he was an uncompromising revolutionary and by the standards of his world, a madman. He also reminds us that spiritual realization requires the integration of art and politics, along with the lessons of religious experience. Perhaps Marxism, now that it has undergone its greatest defeat and been forced to return to basics, will learn this as well.

REFERENCES

Blake, W. 1956. "The Marriage of Heaven and Hell." In *Poetry and Prose of William Blake*, ed. G. Keynes. London: The Nonesuch Library.

Jones, K. 1989. *The Social Face of Buddhism*. London: Wisdom Publications.

Marx, K. 1975. "A Contribution to the Critique of Hegel's Philosophy of Right. Introduction." In *Karl Marx Early Writings*, trans. R. Livingstone and G. Benton, 243–257. New York: Vintage Books.

——. 1978. "Economic and Philosophic Manuscripts of 1844." In *The Marx-Engels Reader*, ed. R. Tucker, 66–142. New York: W. W. Norton.

Marx, K. and Engels, F. 1992. *The Communist Manifesto*. New York: Bantam.

A Process Without a Subject or Goal(s): How to Read Althusser's Autobiography

WARREN MONTAG

hen I was recently invited to present a paper on Althusser's contribution to Marxism, I first thought I would discuss Althusser's relation to seventeenth-century political philosophy, especially that of Hobbes and Spinoza. But then it occurred to me that I was at that very moment reading with great interest Althusser's autobiography *L'avenir dure longtemps*, which had recently appeared in France amid tremendous publicity. I wondered why it did not occur to me to discuss this extremely controversial work, a work in which Althusser explains or attempts to explain how and why he murdered his wife by recapitulating the findings of his long psychoanalysis, as well as how he became a Marxist and a materialist and remained so to the end of his days. Part of the answer lies in the fact that it is difficult to know how to situate this work, which often seems more literary than philosophical or political, and it is not clear how the autobiography directly concerns Althusser's contributions to Marxism. But more than that, Althusser's autobiography is painful and disturbing to read, at least for anyone for whom Althusser is an important reference point. I know that a number of people who were close to Althusser and who had read the manuscript felt that it would be a mistake to publish it. They asked if it were appropriate to publish this very detailed autobiography, which was sure to appeal to the most lurid interests, before publishing Althusser's many unpublished theoretical works. Would not the very notoriety of his autobiography once again push into the background Althusser's philosophi-

cal writing, which had remained all but invisible in France since the events of 1980, especially at a time when *la pensée 68* was so under attack and Marxism itself was dismissed as utterly irrelevant? I thought they were right then, and to some extent, I still do. But here we are: the work is published and appeared in English translation in 1994. The autobiography is now a public fact, and as Althusser would say, it is an objective reality; as such, it will produce effects that will shape how and perhaps even if Althusser's philosophical work will be read. And so, although Althusser's autobiography will certainly not alter the course of Marxist theory, if we take seriously Althusser's project, we must confront the inescapable reality of this text and its effects.

But there is another possible objection to a discussion of Althusser's autobiography that must be answered. Certainly there is a distinction to be made between literature and philosophy, between an autobiography and a work on the Marxist concept of contradiction. Few would argue that Hobbes' verse autobiography, or even Rousseau's *Confessions* are necessary to an understanding of *Leviathan* or *The Discourse on the Origins of Inequality*. If we found, say, a detective novel written by Althusser, would that also pertain to a discussion of his contribution to Marxism? There is a temptation to ask with Foucault what an author is anyway except for a theoretical device that allows us to posit a unity between otherwise disparate and divergent works, a device exemplary of the myth of the originary subject, the very myth that Althusser's work permitted us to analyze.

In a certain sense, this objection is perfectly valid. Even leaving to the side the critique of the originary subject that I agree is vital, it is far from clear to me that Althusser's observations on his parents or the long narrative of his relationship to his wife, Hélène Legotien, are directly connected to his philosophical work, unless we are content with the crudest kind of psychoanalytic criticism. But I have become highly suspicious of the function of this distinction applied to Althusser in our historical conjuncture. I am beginning to suspect that those of us who have regarded Althusser as a major reference point and who have been influenced by him in different ways and to varying degrees have collectively employed what might be called discursive defense mechanisms in the face not only of the tragedy of the single act by which he destroyed Hélène Legotien (and in another sense himself), but also in the face of the disturbing, and tragic, parts of his character: the manic, the depressive, the destructive, and the self-destructive. We reacted by collectively splitting Althusser into good and bad objects: Althusser the philosopher, and Althusser the madman and murderer. And we saw this split in terms of a succession. The good Althusser of the 1960s and 1970s was simply replaced by the madman of the 1980s. Bad objects are devalued and cast out, excommunicated. Of course, the Althusser of the 1960s and 1970s continued to be spoken of, but most commonly in the past tense. In fact, by the mid-1980s it was often said, even occasionally in print, that Althusser had died some years before. In France, the work that announced itself as the definitive postmortem on the antihumanism of the 1960s, *La pensée 68* by Luc Ferry and Alain Renault, which appeared in 1985, declared Pierre Bourdieu the major figure of French Marxism of the 1960s, and dismissed Althusser in a few lines. I myself participated in a conference in 1988 (two years before his death) called "The Legacy of Althusser" in which the unstated assumption shared by the participants (except Etienne Balibar who brought this contradiction to our attention) was that Althusser, at least the Althusser that mattered to us, was dead— a body of work was completed and nothing could be added to it even by the man named Althusser, who was no longer capable of producing anything that could be, in the strictest sense, considered Althusserian.

Of course we could employ this defense precisely because Althusser remained silent for nearly ten years. Or at least we thought he remained silent: in fact, in 1988, two years before his death, there appeared, in Spanish translation only, an interview with Althusser conducted by a Mexican philosopher, Fernanda Navarro, in Paris in 1986. This interview, which was extensive enough to be published as a book, *Filosofía y marxismo*, showed clearly that Althusser was still Althusser, a Marxist and a materialist, who continued to defend the essentials of his work (the notions of the theoretical break, philosophy as class struggle in theory, and the Ideological State Apparatuses), but who even more importantly had broken new ground. There is a valuable discussion of ancient materialism, of the relation of chance and necessity in Epicurus, as well as interesting commentary on Derrida and Foucault. But is it not symptomatic that this work only appeared in Spanish translation and not in the original French or even in English? The explanation in part lies in the fact that Althusser saw Latin America as the political and cultural environment in which his work produced the greatest effects. But *Filosofía y marxismo* went nearly unheralded in Latin American and Spanish intellectual circles. Even more striking is the fact that although the work was automatically acquired and catalogued by many of the major research libraries in the United States, there is no mention of it even in supposedly comprehensive studies of Althusser published several years after its appearance. Now, apart from Balibar's reference to it in 1990 in his *Écrits pour Althusser*, it lies still enveloped in the inner darkness of exclusion, invisible even in its visibility, illegible even though nothing prevents us from reading it. Why is this the case?

The answer lies at the heart of Althusser's autobiography, in the conflict that animates it and that brought it into being. It was as if having been found incapable of assuming responsibility for the murder he committed, Althusser ceased to be a legal subject, and, more fundamentally, and entirely in accordance with his theory, ceased by that fact to be a speaking subject at all. To be placed outside the system in which innocence or guilt is determined is to be condemned to a juridical death. In fact, Althusser the philosopher, insofar as to be a philosopher means to occupy an institutional position and to publish works, ceased to exist. Having been declared not responsible for his actions (according to French law, not even required to stand trial and therefore neither required nor permitted to explain himself, to confess or even to express regret,) he became a *non-lieu*, destined to live, as he put it, "under a tombstone of silence," never again to be called upon to speak. Paradoxically, only death retroactively conferred upon the post-1980 Althusser the status of a speaking subject. Although the editors of the autobiography tell us that Althusser intended to publish it during his lifetime, this seems unimaginable to me. Althusser wrote *L'avenir dure longtemps* as if he were already dead, intervening from beyond the grave to undo (or perhaps to complete—that is the question) the effects of the seemingly irrevocable act by which he destroyed not only the life of another person but his own life and works.

I bring this point up because it defines the conflict proper to his autobiography. There is a key passage in which Althusser describes the moment in 1965 when both *For Marx* and *Reading Capital* appeared: "When my books appeared in October, I was seized by such a panic that I could only speak of destroying them (but how?), and finally the ultimate, but radical solution of destroying myself"(p. 141). He then recounts the lengthy hospitalization that followed. His conflict was never resolved and only became more acute with further publications and interventions. He finally found a way far more thorough than suicide to destroy himself. For suicide would leave his works intact to be rediscovered or rehabilitated by succeeding generations. The very fact of his death might give rise to a wave of sympathy, at least in the academic public, that might in turn lead to a resurgence of interest in Althusser—the very thing that he feared. By committing murder he succeeded in securing his own excommunication, to be neither spoken to nor spoken of, out of sight, out of hearing, made inaudible, invisible, illegible. But by the mid-1980s, faced with the prospect of his own death, Althusser had to endure the thought that his unpublished writings would finally be published, and again he would become the object of public interest. He might well have destroyed all of his unpublished manuscripts; in fact, he did destroy a number of them. But he had already given copies of almost everything to friends, who in turn had made copies for others, so that there would be no preventing their publication or at least diffusion after his death. All he could

do then was to write this autobiography, which displays all the ambivalence of Althusser himself: It not only describes but itself embodies
Althusser's most self-destructive impulses. The question now for all of
us who agree on the vital importance of Althusser's work and who feel
that the publication, translation and discussion of his previously unpublished texts is a priority, is whether or not we will allow him posthumously
to destroy his work.

Althusser, especially in his later writings, discussed the need to analyze the fantasy that underlies the rationalist problematic, the fantasy of
the omnipotence of thought. His autobiography shows his appreciation
of the function of such fantasies in his own life, not least in his desire to
control the destiny of his own writing, even to the extent of destroying
it, annulling it, withdrawing millions of copies of his works from circulation. Fortunately, these remained fantasies, and even the desire to destroy his work will never be realized. But, of course, the autobiography
itself is the (attempted) enactment of an omnipotent fantasy, the fantasy
that one can know what one is and that one is master of oneself and even
master of the way one is seen by others.

On the face of it, there is something paradoxical about the idea of
Althusser as autobiographer; it was he who deemed as the golden rule
of materialism Marx's dictum that one does not judge an individual by
what he thinks about himself. It was Althusser who denounced the notion of consciousness as the faculty of unification that might gather together in one totality the thoughts, perceptions, and memories that are
supposedly "its own." But in one sense this is exactly what *L'avenir* is:
the narrative of a life. Far from fleeing his subjectivity, as one critic has
charged, Althusser has tried meticulously to reconstruct it without trying to justify or exculpate himself. He seeks to follow the temporal order
"of the affects from which I have been constituted" (1992, 25). Thus in a
sense Althusser writes of his life as a completed whole of which he is
outside, a whole that, as in the Aristotelian prescription, consists of a
beginning, a middle, and an end—an end which he not only brought about
himself but which he survived in order to observe. But it would be a grave
mistake to judge Althusser by what he thinks about himself.

How do we judge—that is, understand—*L'avenir*? First, by its effects:
No work is innocent of its effects. One of its effects has certainly been to
reopen the case of Althusser, to recreate interest in a body of work (much
of which remains unpublished) that has already become the stake in a
new struggle. Some of the reviews have been empathic toward the man
and respectful of the body of work. But these are not its most significant
or symptomatic effects. More revealing are the attacks that have entered
into a silent and disavowed complicity with Althusser's self-destructive
parts and have used the autobiography as a pretext to attack Althusser

and everything he has written. I refer in particular to Althusser's insistence throughout *L'avenir* that he was an intellectual fraud from the beginning to the end of his career. As a secondary student, he tells us, he learned the art of writing elegant and impressive sounding essays on themes of which he knew virtually nothing. As a philosophy professor he writes:

> Obviously my knowledge of philosophical texts was very limited. I knew Descartes and Malebranche, a little Spinoza, Aristotle, the Sophists, the Stoics not at all, Plato fairly well, Pascal and Kant not at all, a little Hegel and finally certain closely read passages from Marx. I became a legend on the basis of my way of learning and finally of knowing philosophy, as I like to repeat, by hearsay (the first form of knowledge according to Spinoza) from . . . my friends, by gathering information from them in passing, and finally from my own students in their essays and dissertations. (157–158)

He goes on to say, "it is a curiosity (which has a meaning but one which perhaps still escapes me), I was never able to understand, despite my psychoanalytic efforts and all my experience (as an analysand) any of Freud's texts, nor any of his commentators' texts! I am completely deaf to them" (159–160).

We might be tempted to laugh at these "confessions," especially given the fact that Althusser seems to have forgotten that his "little" knowledge of Hegel allowed him to write a 200 page *mémoire* (thesis) in 1947 under the supervision of Gaston Bachelard on the notion of content in the philosophy of Hegel, which examines in some detail Hegel's *Phenomenology*, as well as the *Philosophy of Right* and the *Philosophy of History*. He also slipped when he reported to Fernanda Navarro in 1986 (and therefore after writing the autobiography) that Pascal's was the only philosophical text that he possessed during his five-year sojourn in a German prisoner of war camp, and that he knew it by heart when he was repatriated in 1945. Indeed, this is confirmed by Althusser's recently published *Journal de captivité* (1993), written during his stay in the camp, which is filled with passages copied from the *Pensées*, together with frequent meditations on the meaning of these passages. We might be tempted to laugh when the author of "Freud and Lacan"—which remains, far more than anything by Reich or Marcuse, the definitive Marxist account of Freud and psychoanalysis—tells us he does not understand Freud. It is difficult to comprehend what the word "understand" could even mean in this context. It is not a question here of low self-esteem on Althusser's part or even the severe dissociation to which he was certainly prone; it is rather a question of a deliberate strategy of self-annihilation, a way of destroying his books after all. And he has successfully manipulated reviewers into judgments such as the following from the journal *Lingua Franca*

(September/October, 1992: 15): "The man who taught philosophy to generations of students at the École Normale admits to having read 'little' Hegel, 'scarcely any' Spinoza, Heidegger or Husserl and 'not to have understood Freud.' The brilliant author of *For Marx* and *Reading Capital* . . . was an 'imaginary marxist . . . full of artifice and fakery.'" At the extreme, Mark Lilla in the *Times Literary Supplement* (September 25, 1992: 3) is moved by Althusser's autobiography to ask "whether anything can be learned by picking over the bones of a relatively minor thinker who was, by all accounts, sick and dangerous." The madman who vacillated between delusional grandiosity and suicidal depression, who suffered a psychotic episode after his first sexual experience, and who shoplifted compulsively in London in the 1970s: these are the images that Althusser invites us to take away from his work.

I was struck by a passage that occurs at the end of the first part of *L'avenir*. In some of the most beautiful and moving pages of the text, Althusser recalls Hélène, and remembers that he saw in her face "the extreme anxiety of not existing, of being already dead and buried under a tombstone of incomprehension" (150). Of course, Althusser is speaking of himself: He begins his autobiography in exactly the same words; the tombstone of silence—the tombstone of incomprehension under which he lay buried neither dead nor alive—is cited as the very reason for his writing it in the first place. What is truly striking about *L'avenir* is not so much the fear of death as this sense of already being dead, of having always already been dead or having never been born. Althusser moved from his family, to the prisoner of war camp, to the school that he only left after 1980, and then to enter a hospital—remaining or hoping to remain, despite outward appearances, unborn, undifferentiated. He even heard in his name, Louis, the impersonal pronoun *lui*, "him."

We can see the compromises through which Althusser could convince himself that he did not exist: His work was not his, he had read nothing, he knew nothing, not only was he an imaginary Marxist but an imaginary human being as well. But this compromise allowed him to live in one important way, in his writing. His writing, which he would have preferred, as he tells us, to have published anonymously or to have kept confined—as he in fact did with so many works—to the family of colleagues and friends without ever exposing it to the world. Caught in the delusion of his own omnipotence, Althusser finally became, to borrow a phrase from Beckett, "a dupe of not being a dupe," and tells us more than he ought to if he is effectively to destroy himself. For there are signs of active and joyous passions in this autobiography, the kind Spinoza spoke of as the only true good—Spinoza, whose work Althusser knew "only a little." Althusser has fooled himself because there is in him that which seeks to live, to participate in the world, and even to change it.

And although he often could not bear to think of it, this "relatively minor thinker" left an indelible mark on philosophy and on Marxism. I am sure that publication of his writing on Machiavelli, Spinoza, Locke, and Epicurus, among others, will only confirm this mark. At a time when so many have left their Marxism behind and sought to bury everything that they said or did as Marxists, Althusser has shown everything but renounced nothing. Against the grain of his personality, and amidst all the temptations to self-destruction, Althusser firmly maintains his theoretical and political positions. He writes that at a time when

> marxism is declared dead and buried . . . on the basis of an unbelievable eclecticism and theoretical poverty, with the pretext of a so-called postmodernity, or, once again, based on the notion that matter has disappeared, having given way to the immaterialities of communication. . . . I remain profoundly attached, not to the letter—to which I have never held— but to the materialist inspiration of Marx. I am an optimist: I believe that this inspiration will cross all deserts and even if it takes new forms—which is inevitable in a world of change—it will live. (1992, 216)

I believe that he must be right, for this materialist inspiration, which is nothing other than the theory immanent in the practice of the oppressed and exploited, and which neither began nor will end with Althusser, has crossed the deserts, the silent spaces of Althusser's own solitude, the unspeakable pain of a life lived in the interstices of death, to give his existence the significance that he both desired and feared. Whatever the unconscious meaning of this work for Althusser, we can hear in it the voice of this materialist inspiration as it speaks through him, despite him. *L'avenir dure longtemps* can be for us—if we will listen to it fully and genuinely, and permit ourselves to hear all its voices—a work of great beauty and finally of great optimism, the incomplete and unmastered narrative of Althusser's "long march in solitude and against death."

REFERENCES

Althusser, L. 1971. "Freud and Lacan." In *Lenin and Philosophy*. New York: Monthly Review Press.
——. 1992. *L'avenir dure longtemps, suivi de les faits*. Paris: Stock/IMEC.
——. 1993. *Stalag XA 1940–1945, Journal de captivité de Louis Althusser*. Paris: Stock/IMEC.
Balibar, E. 1991. *Écrits pour Althusser*. Paris: Editions la Découverte.
Ferry, L. and Renault, A. 1985. *La Pensée 68: Essai sur l'anti-humanisme contemporain*. Paris: Gallimard.
Navarro, F. 1988. *Filosofía y marxismo: Entrevista a Louis Althusser*. Mexico, D.F.: Siglo Veintiuno Editores.

Late Capitalism and Postmodernism: Jameson/Mandel

BRUCE NORTON

The postmodern cultural epoch theorized by Fredric Jameson has been analyzed from many angles. In the literature on postmodernism, his *New Left Review* formulation (1984) is indeed, as Douglas Kellner has noted, "probably the most quoted, discussed, and debated article of the past decade" (1989, 2). And that is appropriate, in Kellner's view, for not only are Jameson's critical powers formidable by any standard, but one of the stakes at issue in his work is "no less than the status of Marxism and the radical political project to which it is committed" (1989, 2). In a discussion primarily carried on by cultural theorists, art critics, and philosophers, Jameson's efforts are sometimes seen as a referendum on the contemporary relevance of "Marxism" itself.

In a peculiar and polarizing dynamic, the Marxism in question—the framework Jameson develops to explain and situate postmodernism—is a starkly modernist one. It stands in part on theses of a sort traditional to several teleological strands of twentieth-century analysis. Societies incorporating capitalist economic processes are said to take their overall shape from a logic of capitalist development. This logic, moreover, unfolds via successive historical epochs, each of which is marked by certain dominating economic and noneconomic traits. Marxism is then a theory that begins by positing the singular transformative power of "capital," its laws, and the unfolding epochs these produce; within that context it takes up the manifold, complexly interrelated—indeed in some manner and some respects "overdetermined"—cultural and other processes that

59

make up a particular era.[1] With Jameson's intervention a twentieth-century classical sort of Marxism looks in the face of the cacophony of postmodernist and poststructuralist themes—fragmentation, the death of foundational knowledge, incommensurability, and so on—and, rather than flinching, offers a grand narrative to make sense of it all.

As one consequence Jameson's postmodernity is unambiguously epochal and irreversible. Beginning perhaps in the 1960s, as he suggests, much of the globe began to undergo a set of changes describable as entering into the postmodern. These amount to the emergence of a new cultural "force field," or "cultural dominant," in which older forms of art, cultural production, and subjectivity have been displaced by newer forms.[2] Namely, in both aesthetic and subjective realms the depth models that helped to constitute modernism have collapsed, leaving a flat terrain, a play of images, rather than a configuration of outer appearances covering inner "meanings." Where, for example, modernist works of art had to be reconstructed and interpreted by the viewer if their meaning was to be approached, postmodern art plays with images in a way that prohibits consistent reconstruction. And where people once had inner, authentic selves beneath their surface appearances, we are now not repressed/expressed, authentic/inauthentic, but subject to the permanently planar fate of fragmentation. Lacking unique inner visions, artists need no longer develop distinctly personal styles, such as Faulkner's long sentences; instead they borrow at will from any number of voices and positions. Regarding politics, the reign of the depthless has a more disturbing implication. Adrift in a world of constantly shifting and seemingly random images, people have lost the ability to situate themselves with respect to history and the "redemptive human projects" by which, in modernist conditions, history was sometimes changed (Jameson 1984).

These cultural changes, as noted, are fed by an economic shift. As the title of Jameson's article and book (1991) suggests, postmodernism is the "cultural 'logic' of late capitalism," the third major long wave period theorized by Ernest Mandel (1975). Jameson's linkage here is easy to summarize, for his own work does not venture much past summary at this point (about which see below). As he construes it, Mandel's post-World War II stage involves a vast expansion of capital's powers. Around the globe previously noncapitalist spheres in agriculture, services, and elsewhere fell rapidly to capital's onslaught. At the same time computer and information/entertainment revolutions enormously intensified the daily life role of commodities within capitalism's domain. Postmodernism is then ultimately the "logic," or cultural outcome, of the vastly expanded commodification of human affairs that these developments produced. Or, as Jameson suggests, it results from the death of the extracapitalist space from which, in its friction with the capitalist, the critical sensibilities and aesthetic and political endeavors of the modernist period once found nourishment. In extending its sway, capital has destroyed the relative autonomy of culture, hitching cultural processes now firmly to its own needs (1984, 86–87). Thus, far from the "postindustrialist" qua postcapitalist phenomenon that recent changes in the economy and culture have sometimes been construed as, Jameson's postmodernity results from the emergence—in line with the expectations of Marxian theory as he understands it—of a moment of capital "purer" and more encompassing than ever (1984, 55, 77).

Rather than pursue Jameson's rich depiction of postmodernist culture per se, the following discussion focuses on the narrower question of economic epochs and their source, "capital" construed as a totality structured by an abstract logic. Although not all commentators have registered the fact, these ideas are not in fact presuppositions at the core of any Marxian economic analysis. The subject of controversy, both are fundamentally incompatible, for example, with one important wing in Marxian thought today, the post-Althusserian. The kind of analysis these ideas support is also more generally under attack in what would seem to be one of its home camps, radical economic thought.[3] Yet, due no doubt in part to Jameson's unusual abilities as critic and writer, in the unexpected and unusually prominent arena of postmodernist theory this approach to Marxian theory has staged a very large comeback[4]—and, as we have seen, has done so to some extent as the representative of "Marxism" pure and simple.

If the focus is on epochalization below, the analysis will not be a general one. Rather, this paper seeks to highlight and play off a particular problem with Jameson's epochal construction that prior critics have not noted. The problem concerns a disjuncture between the structure of the epoch Jameson ascribes to Mandel and Mandel's own conception of the workings of "late capitalism."

JAMESON/MANDEL

As Kellner instructively outlines, since the late 1960s Jameson has striven for a historical approach to literary criticism, by which he understands an analysis that places evolving subjectivities and literary forms and themes within evolving periods or stages of economic development (Kellner 1989, 6–18; see also Best and Kellner 1991, 183, 189). Under attack for "totalistic" thought since his work on postmodernism began to appear, Jameson has not hesitated to put his analytical principles in clear terms. It is not, as he argues, his own peculiar taste for totalizing theory (or his belief in Hegel's Absolute Spirit) that binds him to his epochalizing approach. Rather, capitalism presents itself as a "unifying or totalizing force" (1988a, 348). That is an understanding on which, in his view, both Marxian theory and socialist political hopes hinge (1989, 373–374).[5]

Jameson also suggests that critics may fail to understand abstraction, for totalistic thought is simply an effort in that direction (1991, 400). The kind of abstraction in question is more precisely the only approach possible to the sort of *historical* understanding of human affairs, which is, after all, a fundamental necessity of any Marxian project—especially if the present epoch's very systematicity is fragmentation. "Historical reconstruction," Jameson argues, is equivalent to "the positing of global characterizations and hypotheses, the abstraction from the 'blooming, buzzing confusion' of immediacy" (1991, 400).

Jameson's attraction to Mandel's theory of the third great stage of capitalist development may be readily understood given these general perspectives. Moreover, Mandel provided not just a fresh epochal option, but, as Jameson later noted, one well suited to the challenge he had come to feel most pressing: to respond to Baudrillard's and Bell's visions of a world irretrievably transformed by media invasion and cultural shift (1989, 370–371). Outflanked on the right by Bell's postindustrial society analysis, leftist thinkers had found themselves disarmed on these issues.

"Late Capitalism," Jameson reports,

> changed all that . . . and for the first time theorized a third stage of capitalism from a usably Marxian perspective. This is what made my own thoughts on "postmodernism" possible, which are therefore to be understood as an attempt to theorize the specific logic of the cultural production of that third stage, and not as yet another disembodied culture critique or diagnosis of the spirit of the age. (1989, 370–371)

It is indeed not hard to scan *Late Capitalism* and find all manner of support for Jameson's conception of contemporary affairs. Mandel's expansionary post-World War II capitalism, like Jameson's, is an expanding totality drawing ever more of life as a whole within its domain. Mandel also sounds a variety of Jameson's more particular themes: the increasing mechanization of all spheres of the economy, including unprecedented commodity expansion in commerce, transport and services sectors; the dynamic explosion of computer technologies; capitalist penetration of agriculture and raw materials production around the globe; a radically accelerated pace of technological change. And for Mandel as for Jameson all such basic features of the contemporary economy are "derived from the laws of motion of capital" (Mandel 1975, 193) and shaped more particularly by spread of new electronic technologies.[6]

Yet there is a wrenching problem in Jameson's claim to have situated his cultural analysis firmly on the basis of Mandel's work: he represses as much as he takes from *Late Capitalism*'s depiction of the third stage of capitalist development.[7] Several of Jameson's critics have perhaps signalled this problem by noting a vagueness in Jameson's treatment of Mandel. Thus David Shumway charges Jameson with relying on "an empty signifier" when he refers to the economic backdrop of his analysis, "rather than on systematic reference to specific aspects of late capitalism" (Shumway 1989, 190). Kellner's introduction to the volume in which Shumway's paper appears repeats the general criticism, terming the treatment of specific relations between the new economy and the new culture, "arguably, the weakest part of Jameson's analysis" (1989, 28).

The problem is more than this, however, and it speaks to the question of the innocence of the abstractions, the "global characterizations and hypotheses" that Jameson deploys in his quest for historical theory. Jameson *cannot* take from Mandel what Mandel himself presents as the heart of his analysis. Whatever their overlaps, the theories of contemporary capitalism which Jameson and Mandel present are quite different, and necessarily so: they are components of two different grand accounts of the logic of capitalist development, and the two head in quite different directions. In several fundamental respects they proceed in entirely incompatible ways.

It is not simply "history" that stage theories of capitalist development have pursued: It is the *telos* of progressively dysfunctional and irrational capitalist functioning. In this respect Mandel's work follows the vein of all Marxian falling rate of profit theories. Accordingly, his late capitalism is a totality wracked by contradiction at every seam, expressing, indeed, the *ever-sharpening* contradictions between the forces and relations of production that capitalism is, in this tradition, doomed to express. It is a totality on a mission.[8]

Mandel's project in *Late Capitalism* can be summarized as an effort to show that (1) capitalism is a totality driven by a set of interacting and in some respects relatively flexible inner "laws of motion" (see esp. Chapter 1); (2) the laws of motion are flexible in the particular sense that they are influenced at certain points by profit-raising extraeconomic forces such as wars and shifts in class forces (see Chapter 5 and the related work *Long Waves in Capitalist Development*); (3) this combined laws of motion/extraeconomic effects analysis is perfectly capable of accounting for and understanding the several long wave upturns that the world economy has experienced since the early nineteenth century, in particular the period lasting several decades after World War II (see Chapter 4); (4) nevertheless these expansive periods in no way undercut general Marxian theses of progressively destructive capitalist development, as Mandel understands them (*passim*, esp. Chapters 17 and 18; see also, e.g., 221–222). Contradictions, as he never ceases to emphasize, continue to sharpen even in the periods of rapid growth.[9] In any case the profit- and accumulation-dampening laws of motion of capitalist development inevitably express themselves eventually. In all these ways, the end is visible. As the final chapter of *Late Capitalism* begins,

> Late capitalism is the epoch in history of the development of the capitalist mode of production in which the contradiction between the growth of the forces of production and the survival of the capitalist relations of production assumes an explosive form. This contradiction leads to a spreading crisis of these relations of production. (1975, 562)

Yet Jameson reports from Mandel only the section of the argument that treats capital in terms of infinite commodity expansion, the subtext roughly corresponding with part (3) of the outline above. He presents as Mandel's story the subsection of *Late Capitalism* that seeks to show that falling rate of profit, laws-of-motion-style Marxian economic theories can indeed account for what might appear to *contradict* these theories: long periods of expansion like the post-World War II boom. Thus he takes Mandel's counterpoint and makes it the melody.

Moreover, as we have seen, Jameson uses this partial appropriation to make a move no falling rate of profit theorist—and certainly not Ernest Mandel—could contemplate: He enfolds subjectivity within the capitalist totality. By doing so he destroys one pole of the duality that constitutes twentieth century falling rate of profit theory. In that tradition the iron necessities of capitalist economic processes fit and function with an odd but absolutely necessary complement: an entirely different sort of sphere of human affairs, the more spontaneous political and cultural space in which workers react to capitalism's craziness and rebel. From Grossman (1992) and Rosdolsky (1977) to Mattick (1969), Yaffe (1973), Shaikh (1978), and Mandel (1975), Marxist economics has been thought to have this dominating purpose: to mobilize, sustain, and enforce worker resistance. These authors have sought to warn of the inevitable, to strip away illusions that "state capitalism" is more stable than capitalism of old, and to furnish the vision that might guide working people to a third path, away from both social democracy and the encased historicism of official Soviet thought.[10] Thus the capitalist "totalities" that falling rate of profit theorists have envisioned have been self-structuring and self-regulating, to be sure, but of necessity they have not been thought to cannibalize life as a whole. Working people are the victims of the irrationality and disfunctionality of the system, *and they simultaneously stand outside it in some way*, so that their perceptions and reactions have meaning. Otherwise there is no point in the project—or no point that these theorists, forged for the most part in the blaze of twentieth-century European politics, would recognize.

By transforming falling rate of profit theorists' "capital" in these ways, Jameson does not just undermine their vision. Because he sets the capitalist totality off in a different direction, his modifications loosely speaking *reverse* the vision. His capitalism is not doomed: it is seemingly all powerful. His totality, unleashed, not only escapes the liberating role that its creators envisioned for it, it turns and engulfs us all.[11]

CONCLUSION

The "abstractions" that Jameson deploys to envision capital as an internally determinate system are not innocent. They are not simply humans' only shot at understanding "history" and thus constructing meaning. Neither are they merely the transparent legacy of Marx himself. Presented as "transcendental" knowledge, as Warren Montag (1988) so eloquently writes, they are instead and unavoidably social products—constructs, the product of a variety of visions, the emergence of which was shaped and molded during the last century by a multiplicity of social forces and theoretical dilemmas.

We can be more precise. The conception of "capital" as an epochally unfolding totality, which Jameson presents as the transcendental legacy of Marxian theory as a whole, carries out a well-defined political/theoretical role: a demonstration of necessity, a marking of capitalism's limits. Whatever the specificities of the Lukacsian and critical theory traditions within which Jameson first found his epochal footing, when he takes Mandel's "late capitalism" as the context for his work he embraces a proudly essentialist tradition devoted to demonstrating that capitalism has a *telos*. Marxism is thought to posit that as capitalism develops, this *telos*, enforced by the essential contradiction between the forces and relations of production, has its way. Capitalism must therefore be construed in a way that allows that to happen: It has to be an expressive totality—a system structured and driven by an abstractly fixed logic. This tradition (like its competitor, monopoly capital theory) has therefore provided as one legacy a complex vision of the process of capital accumulation as a self-enclosed and self-determining system.[12]

It is perhaps just this expectation of internally determinate systematicity that is then Jameson's general appropriation from Mandel. In this view a Marxian position proposes the unifying and systematizing centrality of the economic through the notion of an *epoch*: a fixed set of dominant relations that are thought supported by capital's inner nature at a certain stage of its unfolding. To be able to analyze phenomena in those terms is, one suspects, a victory in itself for Jameson, since for him it means to deploy Marxism.

From a political economy standpoint, however, this particular victory is devastating in implication. While it is equally central to a variety of other Marxian traditions, the primeval given that shapes Jameson's system—the notion of capital as an innately expansive substance—has always before served as the origin of a *telos* that is its negation, progressive capitalist dysfunction. This occurs when firms' incessant reinvestment ultimately raises the organic composition of capital, creates investment-retarding market concentration, or in some other way produces a barrier to its own continuation. Now it stands on its own. Capitalist commodity expansion spreads chemically, encountering no particular resistance produced by its own structure, overcoming without limit, rewriting according to its own will.

Jameson's Marxism contains postmodernism within a modernist narrative, at a price. Like other Marxian stage theories of capitalist development, it links concepts of the basic nature of "capital" to certain necessities (DeMartino 1993). These are now not barriers signalling capitalism's approaching end, however, but the opposite, marks of the system's all-pervasive, subject-redefining power. A theoretical tradition devoted to demonstrating the need for complete political resistance—the need to smash the "system" in all its manifestations—now purportedly demonstrates the reverse, a systemic power so strong as to smother any visible tendency toward resistance.

Lost in all this are the fragmentations, inconsistencies, and contradictions that mark both "capitalism" and the subject in other postmodernist and Marxist perspectives. For Marxian thinkers seeking escape from the unifying visions of traditional epochal theory, it is precisely these fragmentations, inconsistencies, and contradictions that nourish new possibilities for change. To begin to see and value such possibilities, one needs to release the economic from the hermetic casing that enables it, as "capital," to function as the bearer of necessity. One needs to dismantle, in other words, the self-constituting and self-determining economic logic that traditional epochal and falling rate of profit analyses have been so concerned to nurture. Then one might begin anew, this time in a way that recognizes the complex mutual constitution of economic, cultural, and other aspects of social life, and the partial, rather than transcendental, nature of social theory.

ACKNOWLEDGMENTS

For discussions helpful to this chapter the author is indebted to Jack Amariglio, David Ruccio, and Stephen Cullenberg. Julie Graham's suggestions were especially helpful in revising it as well.

NOTES

1. Jameson's use of "overdetermination" and other Althusserian terms sometimes leads people to regard his work as "Althusserian" in important respects. Best and Kellner, for example, write that Jameson "polemicizes against the randomizing effects of poststructuralist acausal theories of society and history and adopts an Althusserian model of overdetermination of the social totality" (1991, 185). Compare Best (1989, 347), which, perhaps influenced by Jameson's self-description (in Kellner 1989, 52) presents the latter as offering, in part, a "decentered and discontinuous perspective toward a non-reductionist and non-essentialist rehabilitation of totality." In the current view such descriptions are seriously misleading, given the overall framework in question.

2. Jameson sometimes suggests that by leaving room for subsidiary tendencies via his "cultural dominant" and "cultural hegemony" terminology he has avoided Hegelian-style reductionism in his cultural analysis. Davis (1988) disagrees.

3. Space prevents citation of post-Althusserian writings here. On accumulation theories, see, however, Resnick and Wolff (1987), Arvidsen (1992), Graham (1991, 1992a), Cullenberg (1994), Norton (1988, 1992), Ruccio (1989) and the 1992 interchange between Richard Peet, Resnick and Wolff, and Graham in *Antipode* for an introductory sample. From a quite different perspective, James O'Connor (1987) develops a critique of the "scientism" of what he calls "economic crisis theory."

4. One index: Jameson's book won the 1990 James Russell Lowell Prize awarded by the Modern Language Association. To my knowledge, no work positing capitalism as the product of a logic of capital has ever achieved similar recognition in general academic circles in the United States.

5. Jameson addresses these issues in most directly political terms in (1988a, esp. 354–356). A lucid and moving recent writing on the role of totality in Marxian analysis is Jameson (1988b).

6. See especially the passage on p. 387 of *Late Capitalism*, which launches several of Jameson's primary themes in precise terms.

7. This disjuncture was first pointed out to me in a conversation with Jack Amariglio, Julie Graham, and David Ruccio. I am particularly indebted to Jack Amariglio for directing my attention toward the issue.

8. Norton (1988) criticizes Mandel at length. Ruccio (1992) lucidly summarizes some effects the forces/relations vision of capitalism has had on understandings of capitalism's assumed successor, socialism.

9. When it turns to Jameson's particular interest, subjectivity, Mandel's

chapter "Ideology in Late Capitalism" argues accordingly that, however dispirited people become in the face of all-penetrating commodification, the system's increasing irrationality precisely blocks it from "'integration' of the working class" (see Chapter 16 and p. 506).

10. Mandel places himself in closest relation to the work of Rosdolsky (Mandel 1975, 11). Norton (1992) discusses the political vision of falling rate of profit theorists, from Grossman to Shaikh, in relation to their theories. See also Jacoby (1975).

11. Jameson's theoretical strategy parallels Baran and Sweezy's (1966) in this respect. Perhaps drawing in part from common inspiration in critical theory, both attack contemporary capitalism by arguing that we ourselves have been infected by the logic of capital in its current stage. Baran and Sweezy argue that we are debilitated by capitalism's progressive dysfunction and irrationality, Jameson that meaning is undermined by capitalism's success. In both cases the critiques are powerful. They are, however, difficult to move beyond, since no one is left outside the system's logic (a problem that Jameson himself speaks of, although he presents it in rosy light as the problem of being "dialectical"; see 1984, 57, 86). Moreover, how does one smash a totality, without bringing on apocalypse, anyway?

12. Graham (1991) traces the legacy of teleological frameworks in a contemporary school, Regulation theory. Cullenberg (1994) develops the critical role which Hegelian notions of totality have played in various Marxist economic theories; it also lucidly dissects the misunderstandings of respective positions which have marked arguments over falling rate of profit theories held between Hegelians and proponents of Cartesian approaches to economic analysis. Norton (1986, in press) analyzes concepts of the endogenous self-determination of capital in the theory of monopoly capitalism.

REFERENCES

Arvidson, E. 1992. "Essentialism and Postmodernism in Urban Theory." Presented at the conference "Marxism in the New World Order: Crises and Possibilities," Amherst, MA.

Baran, P. and Sweezy, P. 1966. *Monopoly Capital: An Essay on the American Economic and Social Order*. New York: Monthly Review.

Best, S. 1989. "Jameson, Totality, and the Poststructuralist Critique." In Kellner, 1989, 333–368.

Best, S. and Kellner, D. 1991. *Postmodern Theory: Critical Interrogations*. New York: Guilford Press.

Cullenberg, S. E. 1994. *The Falling Rate of Profit: Recasting the Marxian Debate*. London: Pluto.

Davis, M. 1988. "Urban Renaissance and the Spirit of Postmodernism." In *Postmodernism and Its Discontents*, ed. E. A. Kaplan, 79–87. London: Verso.

DeMartino, G. 1993. "The Necessity/Contingency Dualism in Marxian Crisis Theory: The Case of Long-Wave Theory." *Review of Radical Political Economics* 25 (3): 68–74.

Graham, J. 1991, Spring. "Fordism/Post-Fordism, Marxism/Post-Marxism: The Second Cultural Divide." *Rethinking Marxism* 4: 39–58.

———. 1992a. "Post-Fordism as Politics: the Political Consequences of Narratives on the Left." *Environment and Planning: D. Society and Space* 10: 393–410.

———. 1992b. "Anti-Essentialism and Overdetermination—A Response to Dick Peet." *Antipode* 24 (2): 141–156.

Grossman, H. 1992. *The Law of Accumulation and Breakdown of the Capitalist System*. London: Pluto.

Jacoby, R. 1975. "The Politics of the Crisis Theory: Toward the Critique of Automatic Marxism II." *Telos* 23: 2–52.

Jameson, F. 1984, July–August. "Postmodernism, or the Cultural Logic of Late Capitalism." *New Left Review* 146: 53–92.

———. 1988a. "Cognitive Mapping." In *Marxism and the Interpretation of Culture*, eds. C. Nelson and L. Grossberg, 347–360. Urbana and Chicago: University of Illinois.

———. 1988b, Spring. "History and Class Consciousness as an Unfinished Project." *Rethinking Marxism* 1: 49–72

———. 1989. "Afterword—Marxism and Postmodernism." In Kellner 1989, 369–387.

———. 1991. *Postmodernism, or the Cultural Logic of Late Capitalism*. Durham: Duke University Press.

Kellner, D., ed. 1989. *Postmodernism/Jameson/Critique*. Washington, DC: Maisonneuve.

Mandel, E. 1975. *Late Capitalism*. London: Verso (1978 ed.).

———. 1980. *Long Waves of Capitalist Development: The Marxist Interpretation*. Cambridge, England: Cambridge University Press.

Mattick, P. 1969. *Marx and Keynes: The Limits of the Mixed Economy*. Boston: Porter Sargent.

Montag, W. 1988. "What Is At Stake in the Debate on Postmodernism?" In Kaplan 1989, 88–103.

Norton, B. 1986, December. "Steindl, Levine, and the Inner Logic of Accumulation: A Marxian Critique." *Social Concept* 3: 43–66.

———. 1988. "Epochs and Essences: A Review of Marxist Long-Wave and Stagnation Theories." *Cambridge Journal of Economics* 12: 203–224.

———. 1992. "Radical Theories of Accumulation and Crisis: Developments and Directions." In *Radical Economics*, eds. B. B. Roberts and S. Feiner, 155–198. Boston: Kluwer Academic Press.

———. in press. "The Theory of Monopoly Capitalism and Classical Economics." *History of Political Economy* 27 (4).

O'Connor, J. 1987. *The Meaning of Crisis: A Theoretical Introduction*. Oxford: Basil Blackwell.

Peet, R. 1992. "Some Critical Questions for Anti-Essentialism." *Antipode* 24 (2): 113–130.

Resnick, S. A. and Wolff, R. D. 1987. *Knowledge and Class: A Marxian Critique of Political Economy*. Chicago: University of Chicago.

———. 1992. "Reply to Richard Peet." *Antipode* 24 (2): 131–140.

Rosdolsky, R. 1977. *The Making of Marx's "Capital,"* trans. P. Burgess. London: Pluto.

Ruccio, D. F. 1989, Fall. "Fordism on a World Scale: International Dimensions of Regulation." *Review of Radical Political Economics* 21: 33–53.

——. 1992, Summer. "Failure of Socialism, Future of Socialists?" *Rethinking Marxism* 5: 7–22.

Shaikh, A. 1978. "Political Economy and Capitalism: Notes on Dobb's Theory of Crisis." *Cambridge Journal of Economics* 2: 233–251.

Shumway, D. 1989. "Jameson/Hermeneutics/Postmodernism." In Kellner 1989, 172–202.

Yaffe, D. 1973. "The Marxian Theory of Crisis, Capital and the State." *Economy and Society* 2: 186–232.

Retrieval and Renewal

SHEILA ROWBOTHAM

nly the awkward, obstinate, and ornery would be ready to praise Marx in 1993. Perhaps because my first encounter with Marxist ideas occurred in the late 1950s and early 1960s, a period when Marxism was not at all fashionable, I am unwilling to abandon an attachment I developed as a student when first reading his works seriously. My initial encounter had been puzzling. Ill with scarlet fever at a Methodist boarding school in the East Yorkshire countryside, I became friendly with a Finnish girl two years older than I. She told me about Jack Kerouac's *On the Road* and "The Communist Manifesto." I confess to liking *On the Road* at fifteen rather more than Marx's "Manifesto." Eventually, it was sheer curiosity that brought me to Marxism. A medieval history lecturer sneered about a Marxist, Gordon Leff, writing on the Pelagian heresy. Heresy appealed, and this was to be my first Marxian work. My friendship with Bob Rowthorn and Gareth Stedman Jones brought me away from mysticism and the beats toward Marxism a year later, while the best intellectual advice I received came from my tutor Beryl Smalley. An Aristotelian by theoretical inclination, influenced by Catholicism and Marxism, she was a historian of early humanist thought. "Read Marx," she said, "not people on Marx." This time I read in earnest and was overwhelmed by the gigantic canvasses, the political passion, the ironic humor, and the extraordinary depth of understanding for the processes of historical transformation.

It was a moment in the interpretation of Marx when the interaction between the individual and society was being emphasized. The Marx I read was certainly aware of the individual as a potential, but he also constantly placed human beings within a web of social relationships partly formed by the legacy of the human past. During the 1960s, there was a growing body of historical work in the Marxist tradition that used and developed Marx's concepts but also showed the way toward a rethinking of Marxism. In the work of E. P. Thompson and Christopher Hill, questions about the material and social character of culture, the development of political and social consciousness, and the interconnection between explicitly articulated theory and implicit know-how were being shaped.

The idea that Marxism was being constantly created was an intellectual heritage that derived from the upheaval in Hungary during 1956. There was not then a single Marxism, a fossilized Stalinist version, but a Marxism that could inspire and be applied in an open and nondogmatic spirit. I think such a reading of Marx is still valuable. However, many questions have been raised by the feminist movement about Marxism's assumptions. These and the criticisms of other social movements are important indicators of problems that have emerged from attempts to make socialism. If a new kind of socialist movement is to arise, it would need to work through the weak points revealed by new movements.

I want to focus on one area that has been a continuing source of contestation between feminists and Marxists: the relationship between social emancipation and self-emancipation. This conflict has emerged within several different contexts. There has been the effort to link personal life with public politics summed up in the slogan "the personal is political." There has also been an assertion of the individual, both in liberal feminism's emphasis on equal opportunities, and in cultural feminism's interest in spiritual growth. The women's liberation movement, as it emerged in the late 1960s and early 1970s, emphasized self-realization through activity and insisted, against the canons of Marxism, that women must be agents of their own liberation. The modern women's movement has also tended to stress a personal morality against a strategic readiness within some forms of Marxism to subordinate means to ends.

The reasons for this emphasis were partly the political influence of civil rights and the New Left on the early women's liberation movement. Both civil rights and New Left movements in the United States were preoccupied with the process of self-emancipation and social emancipation, and concerned to break with the prevailing forms of politics in which the end justified the means. Both movements were utopian in the sense that they envisaged individuals changing and social relationships between people being transformed by the political action of human beings. Modern feminism was to extend such concepts of the social and political to more personal aspects of culture.

As it became evident that many of the modern movements' preoccupations were not unique, more work came to be done on the history of feminism. Some of these themes about the public/private domains recur so frequently that it could appear that there have been certain issues that have divided women politically from men. Indeed, some forms of feminism, now and in the past, have argued for an essentially female political and social perspective and culture.

In *Three Guineas* (1938, 297) Virginia Woolf made the famous observation:

> For such will be our ruin if you, in the immensity of your public abstractions, forget the private figure, or if we in the intensity of our private emotions, forget the public world. Both houses will be ruined, the public and the private, the material and the spiritual.

She was addressing a young male socialist. However, it would be too simple to think that she means simply to oppose an essentially feminine perspective to a masculine public politics, for in a footnote (1984, 309–310), she quotes Whitman, Coleridge, Rousseau, and George Sand—the French utopian socialist and writer—saying that the realization of the individual woman is linked to wider social relations. The argument really is about how politics are to be approached and defined within the whole culture. Virginia Woolf was writing against the prevailing assumptions about politics, for in the late 1930s, personal concerns were secondary to the strategic goals of both the social democratic and communist approaches to emancipation.

Rather than enclosing woman in abstractions of difference, it can be argued nonetheless that the specific social circumstances of gender can affect one's values and priorities. The experience of being a woman has thus been a basis for a series of critiques of traditional Marxism's emphasis upon the economic sphere, upon production and the exclusive agency of the working class. Not only feminists but also socialist and anarchist women have levelled such criticisms and there has been a persistent pressure from working-class women to redefine class to include community needs and power relations in the family. Marxism's powerful focus on one aspect of subordination, the worker's exploitation, tended to eclipse or make others secondary. The repeated tendency for conflict to arise between feminism and Marxism has not only been then because of the personal behavior and attitudes of men, but because Marxism took certain theoretical positions that denied aspects of women's experience. In contrast to the insights of earlier forms of socialism, for example, it discarded important understandings about the integral connection between psychological and cultural experience and material and social existence.

If we examine alternative strands within radicalism, it is possible to find differing emphases upon this relationship between self- and social emancipation, which give a more equal weight to the individual and society rather than detaching or subordinating the individual. Also, daily life was seen as changing along side production. Recent feminist historical inquiry has reexamined the significance of this early socialism. For example, Barbara Taylor in *Eve and the New Jerusalem*, shows how early radicals like William Thompson, author of *Appeal on Behalf of One Half the Human Race* in 1825, was very aware of internalized forms of subordination and control through culture. Similarly, writers on the French utopian socialist/feminists like Claire Goldberg Moses in *French Feminism in the Nineteenth Century* have shown that French pioneers in the early 1830s were demanding liberty for women and the people through a new organization of both industry and the household. When the concept of emancipation exploded in action during the 1830s, it was assumed that self-emancipation, freeing oneself through participation, would combine with social emancipation. Emancipation, then, was not a demand to enter simply into what existed, but a process of changing the external world and oneself. In the 1830s, utopian socialists tended to simply assume that emancipation of the working class and of women were linked, without demonstrating how.

By 1848, debates within the labor movement had become concerned not simply with what might be desirable, but with finding a necessary cause for social transformation. French working women grappled with the problem of agency. The necessity that Marx was to find in the proletariat had begun to appear in arguments about women's agency. For example, a self-educated seamstress, Jeanne Deroin, argued that women brought to politics a uniquely different experience from men's because of their lives as mothers (Riot-Sarcey 1989). However, she envisaged both politics and mothering changing in the process of transformation—Hers was a radical approach to women's difference, not the conservative invocation of motherhood which assumed it was a bulwark against radical reform.

A problem faced by the women of 1848 was how to validate existing aspects of working-class women's experience that, while not theoretically conscious, could still be a source for an alternative vision of social and economic transformation. This awareness of differing forms of knowledge and the tension between existing qualities within a subordinated group and the projected future were both crucial elements in the transition to society as it might be. Both presented themselves as unresolved problems in later attempts to create socialism. Another connected concern debated by working-class women in 1848 was to be neglected within the Marxist tradition until Gramsci. That was how everyday understandings, the tacit forms of knowledge embedded in activity, could be generalized and coordinated into a wider social knowledge. The working women of 1848 knew very well that part of subordination was the feeling, "we know nothing" (Mies 1981, 76). In an early women's journal, *La Politique des Femmes*, a character called "The Socialist Woman" refuses this interpretation of self: "How come? You don't know how you feed your children, care for your husbands, how you work, think, observe, and you don't have enough commonsense to distinguish between right and wrong?" (Mies 1981, 77).

The Socialist Woman declares that this is "all that is needed." By socializing personal class and gender-based experience, a new household, a new family, a new association of producers might become possible. When these hopes were dashed, the ambitious combination of self- and social emancipation splintered. Defeat meant the traces were to be buried and thus many of the trails were to be lost. When socialism revived in the late nineteenth century, some of the concerns were to reappear, but there were to be important differences. Firstly, capitalist society was no longer in its newly creative phase, as it had been when early industry came into being. It was established; part of the structure of everyday life. In countries like Britain, by the late nineteenth century, it is possible to see the actual separation of production and household appearing as an assumption accepted as common sense. Secondly, liberalism, which had itself been influenced by utopian socialism and discarded some of its ideas, had gained ascendancy. Socialists, consequently, defined themselves in opposition to the *limits* of liberalism. In the process, socialists emphasized collectivism, community, fellowship, and sometimes the state as an alternative rather than a complement to individual emancipation. Certain strands like William Morris' socialism retained links to 1848 and to the Commune; during the 1880s, Morris wrote and spoke about the transformation of human desire in the process of the making of socialism. But the socialists of the late nineteenth century were inclined to dismiss the individual rights and the self-emancipation that were liberalism's strengths.

By the 1890s, splits between a Marxist-influenced socialism and anarchism further fragmented the connection between self- and social emancipation. Emma Goldman in the early twentieth century struggled to transcend both the individualist anarchist emphasis on self-development and the more collectivist anarchist communism of Alexander Berkman. She said the essential problem was "how to be one's self and yet in oneness with others, to feel deeply with all human beings and still retain one's own characteristic polities" (in Sochen 1973, 63). Emma Goldman was remarkably aware of the need for such a balance. However, other women in the anarchist and anarcho-syndicalist milieu also sought practically and theoretically to combine the personal and the political. Traces of the earlier endeavor to assert self-emancipation and the role of women as agents of change appear in the ideas of women like Elizabeth Gurley Flynn, a member of the syndicalist Industrial Workers of the World (IWW) and a supporter of birth control and the transformation of the household, and the young Margaret Sanger, a socialist advocate of birth control.

In France, Hélène Brion and Madeleine Pelletier were among a small group of feminists close to anarcho-syndicalism. They faced, however, not simply male prejudices but theoretical difficulties in unifying a vision of self- and social emancipation. This was partly because despite its stress on agency and direct action, syndicalism reduced the terrain of politics. As Hélène Brion pointed out, syndicalist emphasis on class struggle around production dismissed sexual and cultural oppression. She reminded French syndicalists that Flora Tristan, Jeanne Deroin, and many women in the past had sought freedom not only from wage slavery but from gender subordination (Rowbotham 1992, 174–175).

The effort to combine sexual freedom with working-class emancipation in the syndicalist milieu tended to result in a dualism. Margaret Sanger coined the phrase "birth control," and in the early years of the twentieth century, linked this to workers' control. However, this assigned to women control over reproduction and left production to men. The integrated vision of 1848 was difficult, even though there was clearly a conscious memory of some connection.

In the early 1920s, a small group of Left Communist women, which included Alexandra Kollontai in the Soviet Union and Henrietta Roland Holst in Holland, were still attempting to link transformation of personal culture in the household and in sexual relations with Marxism. There was also enthusiasm for personal liberation among women in the early Chinese and Indian radical Nationalist movements. However, this effort was to be overwhelmed under the combined pressures of right-wing Nationalism, Stalinism, and Fascism.

Non-Marxian traditions of socialism retained utopian elements into the 1920s. After the collapse of William Morris's Socialist League in Britain, the Independent Labour Party, which was formed in 1893, had emphasized personal connections between everyday life and the political struggle against social inequality. Many women participated in the Independent Labour Party. Among them was Isabella Ford, a middle-class woman from a radical Quaker family in Leeds. In the period before World War I, she was active both in the organization of working-class women and in an attempt to forge a labor–feminist alliance for suffrage. Isabella Ford always emphasized the need for middle-class women to learn from the first-hand experience of working women, while the stress she placed on democratic process resembled the politics of Jeanne Deroin and other socialist women of 1848, a connection of which she was conscious (Rowbotham 1992, 132–136 and 167–173).

A later generation of younger feminists, like birth control reformers Stella Browne and Dora Russell, turned to the Independent Labour Party (ILP) as a more open organization, which did not push a coherent line on issues around sexual liberation, as the Bolshevized Communist party did. This is not to say that they did not have to struggle against male prejudice, but the ethical socialism of the ILP did implicitly allow for some discussion of personal life and relationships, a concern that was to become increasingly subordinate by the late 1920s within Communism. By the time Virginia Woolf was writing in the late 1930s, the ILP was in decline and a new generation was eagerly embracing "scientific" socialism.

Perhaps what we can glean from examining other forms of radicalism is a process of retrieval. Marx possessed significant insights, yet he also dismissed understandings that were especially relevant to women, because of the particular nature of gender subordination. The tendency for feminism to connect self- and social emancipation in many differing historical manifestations arises partly because the power to define what is personal and what is political has been predominantly a male prerogative. This demarcation has determined the contours of what is possible for women in such vital ways that the very assertion of a claim to freedom has always confronted boundary marks. Thus those forms of radical culture that have been more aware than mainstream Marxism of the interrelationship between self and the social have enabled women to make a forcible intervention.

Reconsidering these intellectual currents and political cultures is not only significant for women. While it would be foolish to blame Marx or even Lenin for all the iniquities of state socialism, it is worth remembering that their dismissal of the individual and the personal contributed to a vision of socialism that subordinated individual freedom and development and neglected to find a balance between self-emancipation and social emancipation. The collapse of state socialism in Eastern Europe and in the former Soviet Union has inclined the intelligentsia in these countries and in Western capitalism to focus on self-emancipation. However, a denial of the interaction between self and society involves an ostrich-like submergence in the sand. This denial negates all responsibility to challenge the social inequalities and forms of subordination which have proliferated tragically in the last decade. If socialists are to find a means of making individual human beings more happy in their association with one another, I believe we need to go back to earlier thinking and recover connections between self- and social emancipation that were too carelessly abandoned. Some of the preoccupations of modern feminism, and work inspired by feminism that has asked new questions of the past, also provide valuable clues for reassessing Marx. It should be possible to respect his strengths and be honest about his deficiencies. For me, rethinking Marxism means openness then to diverse currents in radicalism, as well as to the critiques presented by modern feminism. The basis for a recreation of socialism must, I believe, be neither the submergence of the individual within collectivity nor an exclusive focus on the individual apart from social relationships, but a new balance between the individual and the social (Bashkar, Outhwalte, and Soper 1991).

REFERENCES

Bhaskar, R., Outhwalte, W., and Soper, K., eds. 1991. *A Meeting of Minds, Socialists Discuss Philosophy–Towards A New Symposim?* London: The Socialist Society.

Mies, M. 1981. "Utopian Socialism and Women's Emancipation." In *Feminism in Europe: Liberal and Socialist Strategies 1789–1919*, ed. M. Mies and K. Jayawardena. The Hague: Institute of Social Studies.

Moses, C. G. 1984. *French Feminism in the Nineteenth Century*. Albany: State University of New York Press.

Riot-Sarcey, M. 1989. "Une vie publique privée d'histoire: Jeanne Deroin ou l'oubli de soi." In *Silence emancipation des femmes entre privé et public*, Cahiers du Cedref, Université Paris VII.

Rowbotham, S. 1992. *Women in Movement*. New York and London: Routledge.

Sochen, J. 1973. *Movers and Shakers. American Women Thinkers and Activists 1900–1970*. New York: Quadrangle.

Taylor, B. 1983. *Eve and the New Jerusalem, Socialism and Feminism in the Nineteenth Century*. London: Virago.

Thompson, W. 1983. *Appeal on Behalf of One Half the Human Race, Women, against the Pretensions of the Other Half, Men, to Retain Them in Political and Thence in Civil and Domestic Slavery; in Reply to a Paragraph of Mr. Mill's Celebrated "Article on Government."* London: Virago.

Woolf, V. 1984. *A Room of One's Own and Three Guineas*. London: Chatto and Windus.

Marxism in the Shadow of Hobbes

JOHN SINISI

It is often said that most people are selfish and will do almost anything to further their own interests. The depressing social implications of this view of human nature find their most thorough articulation in the dour logic of the great seventeenth-century thinker Thomas Hobbes. In this paper I produce a Marxian reading of the influence and relevance of the ideas of Hobbes on and for modern economic and social theory. First, I develop a reading of Adam Smith's classic explanation and defense of capitalism as (in part) a response to the ideas of Hobbes. I then sketch a powerful neo-Hobbesian critique of the economics of Smith and of mainstream economics after Smith. Finally, I comment on some surprising affinities between neo-Hobbesian and Marxian approaches to economic and social analysis.

THE HOBBESIAN CONTEXT OF ADAM SMITH'S DEFENSE OF CAPITALISM

The most influential argument used to defend capitalism as an economic system is the "invisible hand" argument, first elaborated by Adam Smith in *The Wealth of Nations*. This argument is developed within the individualist tradition of social thought, which begins with the premise that the key to understanding society is the realistic recognition that self-interested striving is the dominant and irresistible driving force in human

79

nature. At its core, the individualist science of society is an inquiry into how self-interested individuals will respond to different social conditions and an inquiry into the social consequences of those responses.

The individualist doctrine that self-interest is the essence of human nature (and ethical and political arguments based on it) has a very long history, dating back to the Sophists in ancient Greece, but for most of that history it existed as a repressed and feared undercurrent of philosophical and political thought. For 2000 years in the Western world, states (with the aid of mainstream religion and philosophy) applied Plato's recommended medicine of repression to individualist ideas, but never managed to extirpate them. Eventually, these ideas erupted into prominence at the dawn of the modern age in the works of Machiavelli (1970) and Hobbes (1968); and, as recast by John Locke (1960) and Adam Smith (1937), individualist ideas became not merely socially acceptable but the new orthodoxy, the philosophical underpinnings of the emerging social structures of representative democracy and capitalist economies.

Hobbes had reflected long and deeply on the causes of the civil war that tore English society apart in the mid-seventeenth century. He concluded that the disasters of the civil war were caused in large part by the various demands for liberty (religious, political, and economic) that had grown stronger and stronger in Europe over the preceding century. In *Leviathan*, Hobbes argued that because self-interested striving is the dominant force in human nature, granting the demands for liberty is a recipe for social disaster. Liberty leads to conflicts; conflicts escalate as neither side is willing to accept defeat and each resorts to more and more extreme tactics in the effort to avoid defeat and gain victory. Liberty creates a situation "where every man is enemy to every man. . . . In such condition, there is no place for industry because the fruit thereof is uncertain; . . . and which is worst of all, continuall feare, and danger of violent death; And the life of man, solitary, poore, nasty, brutish and short" (Hobbes 1968, 186).

Hobbes argued that the only way to avoid the disasters of the anarchic war of every man against every man is to give unlimited power to the state. The sovereign of this powerful state would, in his own self-interest, issue and enforce laws against attacking others and these laws would be obeyed, since it would be obvious to each person that disobedience would be futile and lead only to punishment or death at the hands of the powerful sovereign.

But most thinkers in the individualist tradition rejected this Hobbesian solution, arguing that it would merely replace anarchy ("the war of every man against every man") with tyranny (the war of an all-powerful sovereign against the hapless individuals under his power). The problem with the Hobbesian solution is not that it would create a state apparatus to prevent anarchy. Such an apparatus is necessary. The problem is that it would leave the power of the individuals who control that apparatus unchecked and uncontrolled.

The individualist tradition, beginning with Locke, developed a style of political analysis in which social and political problems are solved (or, even better, avoided) by arranging social institutions in such a way as to create a system of checks and balances, a system in which the self-interest and power of each group always runs up against the self-interest and power of other groups. It was Smith who extended this style of argument from a discussion of political problems to a discussion of economic problems (Sinisi 1992).

Thus the starting point of Smith's analysis of economic problems is his neo-Hobbesian conception of human nature: a conception of human beings as rational and self-interested, as seekers of pleasure and avoiders of pain. Economically human nature manifests itself as the desire to have and consume the necessaries and conveniences of life while avoiding as much as possible the labor necessary to produce them. In all economic systems, economic decisions are made by individuals more concerned about the effect of their decisions on themselves than they are about the effect of their decisions on the economic and political well-being of the society in which they live.

Smith saw the dominance of self-interested striving in human nature as creating two major obstacles to economic development:

1. It leads to unending struggles over who is to control a society's economic resources and who will be forced to do the hard labor on which every economy depends.
2. Those who win the struggles tend to use the resources and the surplus product that they thereby control to protect their privileged positions and to lead a life of luxury.

These struggles and tendencies result in a great waste of human resources and of the surplus product (since they are diverted from economically useful to economically useless deployments), a waste that severely inhibits economic development.

Smith accepted the Hobbesian view that human nature is invariant. Hence all efforts to solve these problems by changing human nature are doomed to failure. The solution must be to change social conditions, to create conditions within which the best way for individuals to promote their self-interest is by doing what needs to be done to promote economic development.

Smith conceptualized these problems and their solutions in terms of the economic dynamics of different systems of property rights. In the absence of state-recognized and -enforced property rights, the anarchy of the Hobbesian state of nature would assert itself. Smith also recognized that property rights can be defined and divided in many different ways, leading to many different economic and social results.

Smith claimed that economic development presupposes that property rights be privately held and very unevenly divided. He argued that an important condition of existence of economic development is the emergence in various industries of large-scale production based on a detailed division of labor. This will lead to a significantly larger surplus product and hence to a faster pace of economic development. But a detailed division of labor and large-scale production will not occur in an economy where property is evenly divided. An even division leads to small-scale production (with the bulk of the population self-employed). And this leads to a small surplus product, insufficient to finance the necessary projects of capital accumulation on which economic development depends. Hence, Smith concluded, the unequal distribution of property is a necessary condition of economic development.

But, Smith recognized, it is not a sufficient condition. Traditional societies achieve and maintain this uneven distribution of property rights through a very uneven distribution of political power. In these societies becoming or remaining wealthy depends on achieving and maintaining positions of political (or religious or cultural) power. It does not depend on running estates and enterprises efficiently, nor on innovating more efficient ways of producing products, nor on using the surplus productively. Hence in these societies economic development does not occur.

But, Smith argued, mankind has step-by-step discovered the one system of property rights that leads to general prosperity and economic development. With a rhetorical flourish he dubs it "the system of natural liberty." In terms of the economy, it has three important aspects.

1. State recognition and enforcement of private property rights in all economic resources and consumer goods. Violent conflict over control of these resources will be averted by the protection of these property rights by a powerful judicial and police apparatus.

2. State recognition and enforcement of economic liberty for all individuals. This means the freedom of each individual to use their property as they choose. It also means freedom of contract, the right of each individual to sell or rent their property to anyone for mutually agreeable compensation.

3. State recognition and enforcement of the inalienable property rights of each individual to their own body and person.

From an economic point of view, this means that slavery and serfdom are illegal. However, when combined with the other elements of the legal system, it also means that each individual is free to sell his or her labor (power) to others for specified periods of time. Hence wage labor is legal.

Smith argued that in a society with this system of property rights, most individuals acting out of self-interest will form and enter into a market economy. Instead of trying to be economically self-sufficient, most individuals will tend to specialize. They will then sell their specialized output in one market and purchase the many other use values they need or desire in other markets.

Because of the self-interested striving of the individuals participating in these markets, and their liberty to pursue their self-interest as they choose, these markets will be intensely competitive. In this competition, some will be successful and grow rich, while others will be unsuccessful and eventually lose the ability to be self-employed. To survive they will then sell their labor (power) to the winners of the market competition who are intent on growing richer by expanding the size of their business operations.

Thus the old economy of self-employed independent producers will gradually disappear and be replaced by an economy of capitalist enterprises employing wage laborers. This does not end the market competition, but transforms it: The formerly self-employed now are forced to compete for jobs against each other in labor markets, and the newly arisen capitalist enterprises begin to compete against each other.

Competitive markets are understood as transmission belts through which individuals, enterprises, and nations can be harmed by or benefit from changes occurring elsewhere in the economic system. Self-interest leads individuals to do what is necessary to avoid being harmed, and if possible to benefit.

Smith had very emphatic views on the keys to success in these competitive markets. For workers competing against each other in labor markets, the keys to success are the willingness and ability to work hard and efficiently. And for capitalist enterprises competing against each other, the keys to success are: (1) efficiency, the ability to produce goods as cheaply as possible; (2) innovation and flexibility, the ability to innovate new products and/or better ways of producing old products, as well as the ability to respond rapidly and effectively to the innovations of others; and (3) a willingness and ability to reinvest profits in the enterprise in order to finance expansion and/or modernization.

Since these are the keys to success in competitive markets, these are the behaviors that will be adopted by self-interested individuals in competitive markets. And since these forms of behavior lead to economic development, it follows that competitive markets induce individuals, in the rational pursuit of what is best for themselves, to behave in ways that lead to the social good of economic development. In short, according to Smith, market pressure is the basic mechanism, the invisible hand, through which capitalism, "the system of natural liberty," overcomes the obstacles to economic development created by the selfishness of human nature.

THE NEO-HOBBESIAN CRITIQUE OF ADAM SMITH'S DEFENSE OF CAPITALISM

Variations on Smith's "invisible hand" argument remain central to both theoretical and popular explanations and defenses of capitalism. The most striking development of the argument has occurred in the recent work of a group of political economists, often referred to as "neo-Hobbesians." The most innovative and influential member of this group is James Buchanan, winner of the Nobel Prize in economics in 1986.

The neo-Hobbesian movement represents an attempt to return the individualist tradition of social theory to its Hobbesian roots. This means accepting in full seriousness the thesis that self-interested striving is the essence of human nature. And this means recognizing that individuals will do whatever must or can be done to promote their self-interest, including breaking the rules by which the economic and other social games are being played, and struggling to change the rules in ways favorable to their interests (Buchanan 1975).

In general, neo-Hobbesians argue that Smith did a brilliant job in conceptualizing the economic problems created by the selfishness of human nature and in explaining why the solution to these problems can best be achieved within the framework of a capitalist economy. But in his economic texts (though not in some of his noneconomic texts), Smith ignores the complex set of problems involving the rules of the game that the selfishness of human nature poses to the effective functioning of all economies, including capitalist ones.

Smith, and the mainstream economic tradition that later followed him, simply assume in their economic analyses that once the rules of an economic game are established and a state apparatus is in place to enforce them, these rules (laws, government regulations, contracts) will be obeyed.

But playing by the rules of the game cannot be assumed. Individuals will always break or bend the rules when it is in their self-interest to do so. This has profound economic consequences. Not only does rule violation in itself waste resources and weaken an economy, the diversion of resources from economic uses to efforts to enforce the rules is another major drain on the economy. Hence an important measuring rod of the economic efficiency of any economy is the sum of the losses of economic resources from rule violation and from enforcement of the rules.

Smith also recognized that the rules under which the economic game is played in any society can be changed, and that different sets of rules lead to different economic results. Indeed, the basic thesis of Smith is that the rules that define a capitalist economy produce better results than any other set of rules. But in conducting economic analyses, Smith implicitly assumes the existing set of rules as a background given and ignores the possibility that part of the strategy of economic agents might be to change those rules in ways favorable to their self-interest.

This amounts to an implicit assumption that a rigid wall can be erected between the economic and political spheres and that economic power (the power that arises from control of great economic resources) and political power (the power that arises from high positions in the state apparatus) do not intertwine, do not mold and shape each other. In other words, the implicit assumptions are that the wealthy will not use their wealth to try to control the state apparatus, and that those who control the state apparatus will neither use their political power to gain control of economic resources nor attempt to establish, interpret, or enforce laws and regulations in ways favorable to their own economic self-interest.

But given the self-interested character of human nature, these assumptions are invalid and cannot be sustained. And if these assumptions about the rigid wall between the economic and political spheres of society are dropped, a very different portrait of the functioning of the economy in a capitalist society will emerge. Since self-interested individuals will use economic resources to achieve political ends and political power to achieve economic ends, we must study these interactions if we are to understand either the economy of a nation or its politics.

Hence, neo-Hobbesians conclude, the proper task of economic theory after Adam Smith must be to investigate those aspects of capitalist and noncapitalist economies that Smith ignored, the tendency for individuals to violate the rules, the costs of enforcing the rules, and struggles to change the rules. It must then explore how these aspects will effect and change the functioning of an economy. The academic barriers between the different branches of social theory must be destroyed and a new unified approach to social theory developed, beginning with and guided by the assumption that individuals will do whatever must and can be done to promote their self-interest.

Unfortunately, economic theory after Smith moved in a very different direction. The basic tendency in the mainstream, culminating in neoclassical economics, was to interpret the dominance of self-interest in a prettified, non-Hobbesian way, to assume that rules would be obeyed, and to take the political–legal system within which economic activity occurs as a fundamental given. On this basis neoclassical economic theory developed ever more sophisticated analyses of the decision procedures of self-interested economic agents and of the different economic results produced by self-interested decisions in various market and nonmarket structures.

Neoclassical theory did a brilliant job in what it attempted to do, which was to explore the logic of a given set of rules, assuming that those rules would be obeyed. But it ignored the more serious "Hobbesian" problems posed by the selfishness of human nature to any economy: the tendency of individuals to violate the rules and to struggle to change the rules in ways favorable to themselves.

NEO-HOBBESIAN AND MARXIAN THOUGHT

At first glance, neo-Hobbesian thought seems as distant and as hostile to Marxian thought as possible. The disagreements and differences are real and profound. But, I would argue, there are also profoundly positive connections between neo-Hobbesian and Marxian thought that open up the possibility for real dialogue and useful debate. I outline below three main points of intersection.

1. The dominant attitude in social theory since the mid-nineteenth century insists that for methodological and epistemological reasons the different aspects of social life—economic, political, cultural, and psychological—can and must be studied separately. But both neo-Hobbesian and Marxian theorists share the more ambitious goal of building a unified social science, covering all aspects of social life. In each case this goal flows from their recognition that economic, political, and cultural processes mold and shape each other, and hence must be studied in their relation to each other. However, it must be noted and emphasized that the two groups arrive at this belief in very different ways. For neo-Hobbesians, this complex intertwining of all things social arises from a belief in self-interested striving as the immutable essence of human nature, combined with the belief that all things social comprise both the environment within which individuals act and the means at their disposal for pursuing their ends. For Marxists, human nature is not the given around which all change whirls, but is itself an ever-changing aspect of the changing social complexity. Thus, whereas neo-Hobbesians strive to

understand how the pursuit of self-interest by individuals shapes and changes their social environment, Marxists also strive to understand how individuals in changing their social environment also change their human nature. For Marxists, the dominance of self-interested striving on which neoclassical and neo-Hobbesian theorists base their defense of capitalism is not an immutable given but itself an aspect of the ever changing historical flux.

2. It has always been an important aspect of the Marxian project to paint a vivid and convincing portrait of the dark side of capitalism—to argue that the rise and spread of capitalism may have triggered modern economic development, but that this development was rooted in and arises from the exploitation and misery of much of the world's population. This portrait of the dark side of capitalism is remarkably Hobbesian in structure. For what Hobbesians claim is true in general, that human behavior is dominated by the ruthless pursuit of self-interest, Marxists claim is true under capitalism, since under capitalism those not exhibiting such ruthless self-concern will be defeated and swallowed up by those who do.

3. In attempting to understand the dynamics of capitalist societies, both Marxists and neo-Hobbesians emphasize the significant conflicts of interest between individuals in different social positions and between different social groups, and hence they also both emphasize the struggles for power and advantage to which these conflicts give rise. This is in marked contrast to mainstream economic theory, in particular to neo-classical economics, which understands capitalist economies as systems of voluntary exchanges which are mutually advantageous.

Certainly there are significant differences between Marxists and neo-Hobbesians with respect to the understanding of social conflicts and struggles. Neo-Hobbesians emphasize struggles over violations and enforcements of existing rules and struggles to change the rules. Marxists emphasize class struggles over the exploitation of workers and over the distribution and use of the surplus extracted from workers. These are two very different ways of understanding social struggles. But, I would suggest, they are complementary, and certainly not mutually exclusive.

Although these and other differences between neo-Hobbesian and Marxian theory are profound, they share a remarkably large base of assumptions and attitudes about how to analyze social processes and social struggles. Hence, communication and dialogue is possible, the recognition of which constitutes a major advance over the total incomprehension that has always existed between neoclassical economists and Marxists.

REFERENCES

Buchanan, J. 1975. *The Limits of Liberty: Between Anarchy and Leviathan*. Chicago: University of Chicago Press.

Hobbes, T. 1968. *Leviathan*. Baltimore: Penguin Books.

Locke, J. 1960. *Two Treatises of Government*. Cambridge, England: Cambridge University Press.

Machiavelli, N. 1970. *The Discourses*, trans. L. Walker. Baltimore: Penguin Books.

Sinisi, J. 1992. "Economic Struggles and Economic Development." Ph.D. dissertation, University of Massachusetts—Amherst.

Smith, A. 1937. *The Wealth of Nations*. New York: Modern Library.

In the New World Order: A Speech

GAYATRI CHAKRAVORTY SPIVAK

We are all aware that the "new world order" after the implosion of the Bolshevik experiment requires a proliferation of military aggression for the reshuffling of recolonization without the Soviet presence—guaranteeing a so-called favorable climate for free enterprise. We are also aware that it means a broad-stroke change in the global economic pattern, or what is referred to as a new attempt to impose unification on the world by and through the "market." But what does it look like from the point of view of the new or developing states, the newly decolonizing or the old decolonized nations—South Africa, say, or India? It is impossible for these states to escape the orthodox constraints of a "neoliberal" world economic system that, in the name of development, and now "sustainable development," removes all barriers between itself and fragile national economies, so that any possibility of social redistribution is severely damaged. The debates within the African National Congress as to the degree of nationalization to be implemented within the new state are, to some extent, wishful thinking.

As recently as 1991, Samir Amin characterized "the Indian bourgeoisie" as an "ally, but not a lackey," of "the U.S. government" (32). Let us now read the words of Praful Bidwai, a Delhi-based journalist:

> A radical change is being quietly but resolutely wrought in India's relations with the United States. The change represents a clean break with India's independent, non-aligned foreign policy and heralds a new "partnership,"

possibly a "strategic consensus," even an alliance between the two countries. . . . India—erstwhile leader of the Non-Aligned Movement, . . . is all set to enter into close political, strategic and economic "co-operation" with America under her tutelage. These recent developments include radical right-wing changes in India's economic policies. (Bidwai 1992, 47–48)

Orthodox economic constraints strangle the possibility of social redistribution. We should not overlook the additional fact that the ruling bourgeoisies in many of these developing countries share a common interest with dominant global capital. To quote *Frontier*, a Calcutta-based journal:

The increasing oppression of Indian labor is so pervasive that a token strike by the organized can hardly reveal the horrible plight of the unorganized. The way the new economic policies are affecting the unorganized sector, not to speak of [the] peasant economy, in isolation, is yet to be assessed. Even if central trade unions succeed in summoning energy to resort to sustained agitation, they cannot gain much in terms of solidarity and economic concessions from the IMF-World Bank boys [the local bourgeoisie] by systematically excluding the unorganized. (Editorial 1992, 2)

When I delivered this chapter as a speech, there had recently been presidential elections in the United States, and we were hoping that there would be a relaxation of interventionist militarism and a greater concern for domestic issues, particularly regarding social redistribution. But the U.S. domestic economy cannot simply be shored up by a regulated dance step between fiscal policy and the Federal Reserve. Indeed, the Clinton administration's survival depends upon containing this dance. The new world order economic policies can hardly be relaxed in this context. Apart from the many concessions given for the final passage of an attenuated economic program, the details of the establishment of free trade with Mexico bear us out. And if we consider the policies of the World Bank, the International Monetary Fund, and the myriad aid and consulting agencies—not to mention the contracting and subcontracting transnationals—no change is noticeable with a change in administration. I remain, alas, a vulgar Marxist in many respects—convinced, for example, that when there is no extraeconomic coercion abroad and our private or domestic or national economy may be improving, we do not notice things as much. Although the removal of George Bush is an unquestioned good, I have to remind myself that the binary opposition between domestic and international is as spurious as that between isolationist and universalist U.S. positions.

It is in this new and uneven context, the helplessness of the new and developing states, that I want to reopen the question of new social movements: specifically, feminism and ecology. The other two important tendencies are, of course, nationalisms and subnationalisms, not identical though related. In the states that have been subjected to the greatest recent economic restructuring in the new world order, the always loose hyphens between nation and state have come almost undone. In this breach, violent fundamentalisms are trying to renegotiate fascist theocratic states in the name of nations. I will not touch upon them, not because I have nothing to say about them, but because our approach to them must be so different, in kind, that I cannot do justice to them in the time given to us.

In a piece published in *Rethinking* MARXISM, Immanuel Wallerstein comments:

> The anti-systemic movements are in search of a new strategy, to replace the one they have used for 125 years—taking state power. But will they find an alternative strategy? . . . The so-called new social movements (Greens, women, minorities, etc.) have found themselves in the dilemma of the socialist movement in the late nineteenth century. . . . The path that such movements will take . . . will determine whether we make the transition to something better or something worse. The problem is that no one today knows what path they will take, not even these movements themselves. (Wallerstein 1992, 99–100)

Much of what is said here is just, and I certainly do not have the teleological vision or inclination to make predictions. Yet it must be said that this is too Eurocentric a view. The non-Eurocentric ecology movement is not identified with the Green Party or the Green movement, and is on occasion opposed to them, in spite of all the much-publicized rock concerts. However fragile, in this movement lies our hope against the devastation of the developing state in the new world order; even if, in areas where the very possibility of the state is threatened, the role of an ecological vision seems remote. Global nationalisms and subnationalisms are not to be identified with minorities, although the lines intersect. And just as poverty and class, and race and color are not identical, so also women and feminists are not identical. Further, while non-Eurocentric feminism and ecology *can* be a cohesive force, nationalism and subnationalism cannot. Their strength lies elsewhere. And finally, in the context of the predicament of the new and developing state in the new world economic order, the non-Eurocentric feminist and ecological movements, with a Marxist economic analysis of necessity incorporated, are largely uninterested in *state* power. They are looking to form a new inter-nationality, which can both resist and support these states in their collaboration and powerlessness in the field of social redistribution. These tendencies were clearly visible in counter-Rio, the alternative conference consolidating resistance to the so-called Earth Summit.

In feminism the two clearest arenas are homeworking as an international phenomenon and population control. Homeworkers are women who work at home under conditions of "sweating," where the wage per piece can be indefinitely lowered if necessary (Allen and Walkowitz 1987). This type of woman's labor dates from before capitalism, but under international subcontracting and now post-fordist capitalism it extends from Aran Islands sweaters to high-tech computer terminal work at home. Now women all over the world are absorbing many of the costs of management, the costs of health care, of workplace safety and the like, by working at home. Against the needs of international and local capital, state regulations for equity in homeworking, if they exist at all, are not implemented. Capital is here helped by patriarchy. Many women accept homeworking, some unwillingly, through internalized gendering that tells them that they are freely choosing to work in the home.

State power is here irrelevant as a direct goal. The phenomenon is global, yet the organizing initiative must be local. And in this sphere, the women's movement has to acknowledge and face two difficult truths. First, we must learn not to treat homeworking as a peripheral phenomenon, as if it were no more than a continuation of unpaid service in the home. We must deconstruct the breach between home and work in the ideology of our global struggle, in order to reach this female bottom layer that holds up contemporary global capital (Mitter 1986; Allen and Walkowitz 1987). Secondly, we have to face the possibility that internalized gendering by women, perceived as ethical choice, accepts exploitation as it accepts sexism in the name of a willing conviction that this is how a woman is good as a woman, even ethical as a woman. How on earth are you, am I, going to say to this woman: "This is not the way to be good! Become like me! Think of yourself, not the other!" Here the limits, not only of state power, but of organizing itself, are revealed. Of course, one must fight to pass laws. And of course there must be vigilance that they are implemented. But the real force of the struggle must come from the actual players contemplating the possibility that to organize against homeworking is not to stop being a good woman, a responsible woman, a real woman with husband and home, a woman. The recognition of male exploitation must be supplemented with this acknowledgement, and the only way to help bring it forth is by establishing an ethical singularity with the woman in question. This is itself a necessary supplement to a collective action to which the woman might offer resistance, passive or active. This is what a non-Eurocentric *new* social movement looks like.

That population control relates to the regulation of migrancy is demonstrable. In the new world order, U.S. Marxist–feminists cannot afford to isolate a concern for reproductive rights from the phenomenon of population control. I am quite aware that rage against the struggle for reproductive rights is on the rise in the United States, that Catholic fundamentalism has consolidated its antifeminist stand through the Pope's call to U.S. youth in August 1993. I am also aware that it is not possible to answer the question, why do people act? Yet, through narratives accounting for collective and singular motives, the world is run and runs itself. What narrative might a woman in a developed country offer herself in order to plan a family, through birth control and, one hopes, legal abortion?

Not the narrative of ethical universalism or ecological sanity. Health and personal pain, certainly, but also the fact that children are expensive. How, then, in the underclass of developing societies, where there is little access to consumerism, or among the rural subaltern, where there is no such access, can we expect women to behave with a counterintuitive ecological sanity or concern for consumption? Akhter (1992, 62) has pointed out that "the consumption explosion in the West, specially in the United States, is much more dangerous than the population 'explosion' in terms of putting pressure on natural resources . . . [and yet] the poor of the developing countries . . . are now being blamed for the destruction of the environment." But quite apart from this, a question can be asked about the two kinds of subject being assumed here: the subject of duty and the subject of rights. Why must the women of the developing world behave with a responsibility imposed from above, when the fight is on (and should be) to make it possible for women in the developed world to claim rights? This is not a position against family planning, but a demand for subject management of planning. In the event, what the woman in a developed country, poor or rich, wants at least notionally to claim as a right, the woman in the developing country undergoes, as mutilation for money. And beyond such questions, in the context of the consolidation of the new world order, we must note that the imposition of population control measures upon the women of developing nations has invariably been tied to so-called international aid since the early 1970s.

Since my reading audience is mostly students and academics, the question I ask is in fact more practical than the hope of "organizing the masses": If the new world order demands that women in developed countries rethink their universal narratives of freedom in less restrictive terms, and that subaltern women in developing countries are not simply moved from patriarchal to transnational duty, how, from our classrooms and our focuses of local involvement, can we get a handle on this?

(When we bring in psychoanalysis of one sort or another or the psychological dimension to feminize the Marxist story, we hardly ever think of these broader ethico-economic storylines that mark the North–South divide).

In the context of a short life span, for instance, and a high rate of infant mortality, there is a certain acceptance of death as a natural event in postcolonial subalternity. This is being regularly taught as an attitude in thanatology courses in the United States, in the face of moral dilemmas raised by medical science and an unexamined concept of infinite rights. What can one learn or unlearn by this unreal contact between the subject of rights in the North and the subject of (insertion into) responsibility in the South? That something must be lost in order that something be gained? That the Northern subject contradicts what the best believe the Southern subject should be taught about freedom as a right and therefore an end? Beyond the mode of production narrative and its structuralist revision, beyond the surplus labor narrative and its post-Marxist fabulation, it is these types of question as well that should be made accessible to as many students as possible.

My general argument has concerned itself with the changing space of the developing state under the economic restructuring in the new world order, and the error in assuming that the internationalist impulse in the new social movements emerging from the South had a primary interest in acquiring state power. In the field of feminism, I will offer the example of FINRRAGE (Feminist International Network of Resistance to Reproductive and Genetic Engineering). This is "an international network of feminists with contacts in 34 countries."[1] One of the many aims of the organization is "to develop a global movement of feminist resistance." Far from consolidating via structures of state power,

> as a network, FINRRAGE does not have a formal membership status but rather provides links between individual women, as well as different kinds of local, national or international women's organizations who share common concerns and viewpoints. FINRRAGE affiliates work within their countries in choosing priorities for issues and activities suited to their specific situation. This may involve critical grassroots investigation or academic research, information to women and the general public, outreach to groups and individuals, lobbying, cultural or political forms of expressing opposition, or the establishment of alternatives for women.[2]

I address briefly below the nature of the resistance to "sustainable development" as the latter is recoded by the World Bank, an initiative that must, once again, incorporate Marxist economic analysis.

The World Bank uses "sustainable development" as an excuse—it is after all a bank, and therefore in the final instance "more interested in lending money than looking after [the possible] victims" of the consequences of its policies—to intervene in the ecobiomes of subaltern groups in postcolonial states (Vandana Shiva 1991). Investigative work by the alternative ecological movement repeatedly shows that these interventions displace and destroy small and large groups who have lived close to the soil for centuries. Thus postcolonial development continues the work that colonial racism began. There is no question here of a refusal of development within a scene of pervasive exploitation and corruption. It is a question of sustaining genuine development through local self-management. Because any local initiative runs interference with transnational capitalism and is therefore, in potential collectivity, of global impact, it is not possible for the postcolonial state in the new world order to take or support such initiatives extensively. Therefore the so-called new social movements must build up an alternative inter-nationality that will stand behind the state. Here again, we see a difference between claiming rights as an end and valuing the right to the insertion into responsibility to the eco-biome—to nature. For the subaltern of the South, the issue today is not conservation and recycling, it is ecological survival through popular movements claiming responsibility to a nature saved from dominant capital.

To emphasize our role as educators in this alternative world order, I point at the death of Bandung. The Bandung era is generally considered to be 1955–1975. The Bandung Conference was certainly held in the hope that there would be a third way for developing nations in the new world order seemingly established after World War II. Its ghost was finally laid to rest in the so-called negotiations of the Uruguay Round of the General Agreement of Tariffs and Trade as the Soviet Union was dissolving, the possibility of nonalignment was disappearing, and its appropriation, for the moment, by the United States was to be fought out in future by the Industrial Countries.[3] A memorial service was held at the meeting of the nonaligned nations in Djakarta in early September 1992, with the notable absence of Saddam Hussein and Hosni Mubarak. Fidel Castro sent a representative.

What I am about to say is not just academic but also personal hindsight. I entered college in Calcutta the year of the Bandung Conference. The story of that failed attempt at a third or exorbitant position, still embracing the world system with the desire for a different slot in its structural functioning, can now be traced in the rift between the cultural and intellectual production of the so-called third world and its economic program and aspirations. And, as a university teacher of nearly thirty years' experience, I would suggest that there was no sustained academic effort in the human sciences to constitute, through education, a subject for this already compromised "third world" vision. The humanist academy remained within the world system, cut off from the social sciences, class-locked in various ways with no access to an informed or instructed awareness of the system that it inhabited, that operated it as it in turn operated the system, of which it was the condition as well as the effect, at the same time. And the academy, as well as the economic dreams of an alternate *third* world, with a center different rather than beyond a first world center, remained entirely alien to the subaltern layer in these places now called "developing." One of the most terrifying consequences of this alienation was the appropriation of the label "third world" by first world minorities. I am no stranger to migrant activism, but a global look at the possibility of an alternative world order must acknowledge that the migrant, although often from below, has also—potential and thwarted though it may be—a common interest with dominant global capital. As I say to my self-selected Third-World students at Columbia (who are therefore of course already routed through certain circuits of privilege): "One doesn't get off on being Third World in the Third World; there is a difference between 'get off our backs' and 'we want in.'" We must continue to want in, honorably, but we must honor the difference. And as Jack Amariglio pointed out to me correctly, one speaks differently to the old immigrant white working class.

I have published detailed suggestions for working with these aporias in the context of the U.S. multicultural literature classroom (Spivak in press). But the multicultural scene in the North must become aware that the two important new social movements in the South—these specific kinds of feminist and ecological networks—are crucially interested in building inter-nationality through mainstreaming in education in the so-called developed countries. Whatever the currents of nationalisms and subnationalisms and fundamentalisms, these challengers of the new world order are determined that, this time around, the error of Bandung, the widening rift between the cultural lobby—consolidating ideologies—and the politico-economic strategies, will not be repeated.

I want to end on a deliberately cryptic note. I want to present my own agenda of teaching for the new world order. Over the years, I have painstakingly learned from deconstruction the trick of not honoring its master's credentials. At the same time, I have tried to keep in mind that I earn my living in the United States, and that students who come to deconstruction in the academy also traverse pathways of privilege. The agenda is so cryptic because its training time is the labor of the classroom, and its testing space outside the academy.

1. *For feminism.* Marx understood labor power and commodity as each other's *différance*. Reification theory, with a necessarily fetishized notion of the proletariat as agent, in effect moralizes it as an opposition between the fatalism of capitalist economics and the "conscious[ness] of the immanent meanings of these contradictions for the total development" (Lukacs 1985, 197). Resistance in the body politics of global feminism can be advanced by de-moralizing the opposition and charting the mechanics of how the *différance* is made to operate.

2. *For democracy*. Academic freedom, conceptualized by way of the European Enlightenment, keeps itself confined to the university. The subject of university education in the South is colonial, even in its resistance. It must respond to the call of the other, the subject of rural literacy. State literacy programs are insufficient in the new world order.

3. *For ecology*. Liberation theologies are narratives of individual transcendence in sacrifice. The "sacredness" of animist space must be learned as a name for alterity, rather than museumized from above. I have already indicated the limits of the "nation-state" in this arena, as it is exacerbated in the new world order.

NOTES

1. This quotation and the two following it are taken from the descriptive flier about FINRRAGE obtainable in the West from FINRRAGE International Coordination, P.O. Box 201903, D-2000 Hamburg 20, Germany.

2. See note 1.

3. To get a sense of this from a non-Marxist and a Marxist point of view, respectively, see Bhagwati 1990 and Raghavan 1990.

REFERENCES

Allen, S. and Walkowitz, C. 1987. *Homeworking: Myth and Reality*. New York: Macmillan.

Amin, S. et al. 1991, January. "Four Comments on Kerala." *Monthly Review* 42 (8): 24–39.

Bhagwati, J. 1990. *The World Trading System at Risk*. Princeton: Princeton University Press.

Bidwai, P. 1992. "India's Passage to Washington." *The Nation* v. 254 (January 20).

Editorial. 1992. *Frontier* 25 (8): 1–2.

Lukacs, G. 1985. *History and Class Consciousness: Studies in Marxist Dialectics*, trans. R. Livingstone. Cambridge, MA: MIT Press.

Mitter, S. 1986. *Common Fate Common Bond*. London: Pluto Press.

Raghavan, C. 1990. *Recolonization: GATT, the Uruguay Round and the Third World*. London: Zed Books.

Spivak, G. C. in press. "Teaching for the Times." In *Decolonizing the Imagination*, ed. Jan Nederveen Pieterse. London: Zed Books.

Vandana Shiva. 1991. *Ecology and the Politics of Survival*. London: Sage.

Wallerstein, I. 1992, Spring. "Post-America and the Collapse of Leninism." *Rethinking Marxism* 5 (1): 93–99.

PART TWO

IMAGES AS
SITES OF STRUGGLES

Three Poems

CATHERINE ANDERSON

A PHOTOGRAPH OF FARMWORKERS

I
Thirty miles from Delano
that sun can bring cups of sweat
over the face, streams of it rolling
from the hairline.
The old mother wraps and unwraps
her swollen fingers to work the rows.
In a field of ripening lettuce
they are resting for this image
made of graphite and cut silver,
as light as hen feathers.
How much of nothing hair and clothes tell us.
But the sun is imaginable,
a daily weight a person bears
lowered first on haunches, then
rising a thousand times
from the small of the back.

II
The others are faces in still shots,
blurred half smiles,
shadowed and grave above the eyes.

Angelos Sanchez and his mother, wife,
and three tanned daughters.
Last summer they all traveled over the border
with high, fluish fevers.
For miles the oldest girl had to fan
her sister's skin
in the back of a pickup.
It was night-time, and they held their faces
close to the cooling metal floor,
hearing the cracked road bottom,
and the beat of stones
against the truck axle.

III
Now the sky above them is a blue,
tight line.
They would like to laugh,
but they must be serious.
Some of them are shirtless, a few in straw hats.
The women are wearing loose cotton blouses.
All June they have picked lettuce
and tomorrow they will drive to New Mexico
and then toward Oklahoma,
where the land becomes one flat blade,
and the sun is an animal of hair and teeth.
It grasps the flesh on your back,
then claws out of your hand until darkness,
when it hides to sleep.

HOUSE, WEEDS, AND TREES

All my longer dreams, the ones with color
and voices, winding plots and denouement
take place in my childhood house,
inside its small rooms,
the kitchen, my bedroom.

Hours before sleep, I used to watch
our bare, almost branchless maples
flicker in the porchlight next door.

If I saw a low, bright star in the sky,
Venus, or the North Star, I stared longer,
thinking how light as age,
how it takes a thousand years
for a shaky blaze of gas to reach us
and gleam, calmly.

And once, up early, I found my parents
asleep in the living room;
my mother folded up in the lap of the couch,
my father sitting in a chair, taking giant breaths
through his shirt.
For a while, I watched their heavy sleep
in a room full of light.
Then I took down our plaid blankets
and covered them up,
even though I couldn't imagine
my parents cold, or dreaming.

*   *   *

The people next door made extra money
selling dirt from their backyard.
White conch shells lined their driveway
and I wanted to go live them:
six rowdy children, a tall mother with a diaper
on her head, and a mammoth father emerging
every morning like Ahab, growly and bearded,
so unlike my small father with a ball-point pen in his shirt.
In summertime, they had a rock garden
and a billygoat tied to a plum tree.
Our yards shared wild crabapple trees flowering
in thorns and big rosettes,
and a crop of magnificent weeds our neighbors loved—
dandelions, Queen Anne's lace, Gall of the Earth—
until my mother mowed everything down one morning,
a white storm of heads and stems
blowing behind her.
The people next door didn't mind,
knowing seeds and flowers would return.
They moved their dump trucks down the lot,
digging for rich bottom soil.

When they found a large rock,
I watched them haul up it like a treasure,
roll it to the garden,
hose it down until it shined.

In autumn, they nailed sheets of plastic to the windows,
gave up the dirt business for the winter,
and sold orthopedic shoes by catalogue.
The kids, like us, passed on scarves and sweaters,
but they walked through ice puddles without boots,
flung snowballs with their bare hands.
And once, after their porch light
had been burning till morning,
my mother told me how the oldest boy
had been hit by a truck
as he was rounding a highway curve
on his handbuilt cycle, head bent
to the side, his fingers holding together
two wires of the engine.

*   *   *

Tract homes went up fast in the 1950s,
dream homes they were called
by the magazines—dreams I heard
my father tell as he planned a new
patio or heated breezeway.
And racing my bicycle up hills
no higher than a knuckle
on a man's hand, I dreamed,
soloing between an edge of sky
and edge of road.
When their son was hit,
the family next door moved away;
and soon after, our troubles came thick,
too, like weeds.
There was no girl my age in their family,
yet our houses were exactly alike,
five rooms with rectangular windows
cut from a carpenter's template.
Late at night, I'm sure they heard what I did—
the TV droning, pots banging in the sink
and later, when our houses were dark and listening,

the same diesels humming on a steel bridge far away,
a tune riding over the creek, over the pines.

THE NAME OF A TREE

Right here on Ash Street, Ana says, she used to stagger
up the stairs like a drunk.
There was no light, so she patted the wall,
following hardened gum and kick marks.
Those were crazy days she tells me—

two kids, no money, no job—
when English made the sound of click, swish,
money gliding from a cash drawer,
and the only words she knew were numbers—
seventy-five cents ringing down the throat
of a soda machine, her soapy fingers counting quarters
to feed the dryer.

Some days I am Ana's teacher, some days she is mine.
This morning we look through her kitchen window,
the one she can't get clean, cobwebs massed
between sash and pane. The sky is blue-gold, almost
the color of home. Ana, I say, each winter
I get more lonely. Both of us would like the sun
to linger, be that round fruit in June, but Ana says
it's better to forget what you used to know:
the taste of fish cooked in banana leaves,
the rose color of sea waves at dusk,
the names for clouds and wild storms, and a tree
that grows, she says, as full
as a flame in the heart of all warm countries,
south of here.

Always Just over the Horizon: The East German Intellectual and the Elusive Public Sphere

INEZ HEDGES

icture the following scenes, taken from three films made in the German Democratic Republic (GDR).

Karla, a young schoolteacher, is having an argument with her principal about pedagogical methods: "I want them to learn to think. And to confide in me. It has something to do with democracy. And if I achieve that, I'll gladly give up all my authority." The principal reacts with pain and rage: "What wonderful ideals! Truth, thinking, democracy. Everybody learns from everybody else. Everybody likes and confides in everyone. Great! We're all just human. I'm the only inhuman one—an ancient communist, who's still harping about class struggle. . . . But the facts of school life are that there is a kind of battlefront between students and teachers. And if you don't know that, you won't get very far" (Plenzdorf 1980, 53–54).

At a meeting of the top echelon of a large factory, Kati, a young woman engineer who is pregnant but unmarried, is questioned about the identity of the child's father. The person doing the grilling is

This is a shortened version of an article that appeared in *Socialism and Democracy* 1992, 8 (2–3): 59–75. Copyright 1992 by Inez Hedges. Adapted by permission. Parts of this text were given as the keynote address at the conference (*Re)Fusing the Frame* at Lehigh University in February 1992.

the party secretary assigned to the factory. It is he, in fact, who is the father; but both he and the engineer know that revelation of the scandal would result in a change in factory management—one that would impair its hard-won efficient functioning. Besides, the woman believes that the man "only needs a little more time" to decide to leave his wife. She refuses to name him in front of the others.

Maria, a college-age woman from Berlin, is having an affair with the judge who, years before, sentenced her brother to prison for "slander against the state." At that time the harsh prison sentence he meted out was helpful to his career; now he wants to lighten the sentence to show that he is a part of the power elite that favors a loosening of restrictions. Even though she has been pressing him to arrange for her brother's release, she becomes disgusted when she realizes that he just uses other human beings for his own career ends.

From 1965 to 1966, the entire production of the Deutsche Film Aktien Gesellschaft (DEFA), the government-financed film studio of the GDR, was banned. The dozen or so films in various stages of completion—from which these three scenes were taken—were swept off the drawing board and pulled out of the theaters in a massive cultural clean-up introduced by party spokesman Erich Honecker at the Eleventh Plenary of the ruling party, the Sozialistische Einheitspartei Deutschland (SED), in December of 1965. Attacking not only the DEFA films, but selected plays, poetry collections, and television programs as well, Honecker accused their creators of seeking to "awaken doubts about the politics of the GDR and to disseminate an ideology of skepticism" (Gregor et al. 1990, Section 15, 2).

Made during the short-lived cultural thaw that immediately followed upon the building of the Berlin Wall, these DEFA films air some of the problems that came up during the GDR's transition to socialism. As cultural products intended for the general population, they offered the possibility for wide discussion of social problems in what would effectively have been a nonbourgeois public sphere—a discussion about the future possibilities of socialism that was brutally cut off. As East German film historian Rolf Richter writes, "The 11th Plenary was not just a sign of cultural politics—it legislated the end of critical self-examination about the opportunities and methods of socialism" (Richter 1990). To reconsider these films leads us naturally to wonder, as Barton Byg has put it, "what might have been" (Byg 1990). But the interest of the films does not end there. As a body of work, the films also reflect new narrative emphases that constitute a valid contribution to film history and cultural theory.

This contribution has to do with the positioning of women and working-class people in narrative—particularly in three of the banned films: Herman Zschoche's *Karla*, Frank Beyer's *Spur der Steine* (*Traces of the Stones*), and Kurt Maetzig's *Das Kaninchen bin ich* (*The Rabbit Is Me*), from which the scenes I have cited were respectively taken. In each of these films, the situation of the woman protagonist stands as a metaphor for the problematic relations between the worker and the state in what the East German ruling elite defensively called "real existing socialism." The values and ideals of the woman/worker are as ignored as her physical and psychological needs; she is only valued as a contributor to productivity, successively defined in the different films as an efficiently functioning factory, a rigid educational curriculum consisting of pre-established "facts," and an ideological conformity that preempts family relations.

The revolutionary cultural change that would accompany and contribute to the creation of a society not governed by bourgeois values, as Oskar Negt and Alexander Kluge have argued, would require a different definition of productivity, one characterized by new *habits* governing personal relations, social relations, and public life (Negt and Kluge 1972, 270). Ironically, the spirit of the Eleventh Plenary was to reinforce those very disenfranchising attributes of worker experience under capitalism that Negt and Kluge describe: isolation, divisiveness, repression, suppression, and assimilation (66).

Despite subsequent partial "thaws" (such as the cultural thaw announced by Honecker in 1971 at the Eighth Party Congress after he had become president), 1965 marked a decisive turning point in the development of East Germany. Here the State carved out huge areas of arbitrary power for itself, limiting the form and content of public discussion. As ex-SED member Michael Schumann has pointed out, the controls instituted by the government effectively prevented the creative engagement of the people in the construction of a new society—a society, paradoxically, that was supposedly engineered with the happiness of the people in mind (Schumann 1992, 26–27). Citizens of the GDR, from schoolchildren to adults, learned to negotiate several "codes" of speech and behaviour appropriate to different social situations; some beliefs were professed at school or in the workplace, others at home. The divided consciousness that was a feature of this system reproduced the conditions of working people under capitalism.

I have mentioned these three films in which women play major roles in order to highlight, additionally, the "double burden" borne by women in the SED regime. It is no accident that, at the end of each film, the women are displaced: Karla rides out of town toward the new job she's been transferred to; Kati suddenly packs up and leaves the factory without taking leave of anyone; Maria's brother beats her up when he gets out of prison, and she too leaves home to look for a better future. While none of the endings is without hope—each protagonist can count on a job or an education—all show women bravely departing from the battlefield where they have suffered a defeat. Once again, the films function as a metaphor for the special situation of the woman worker in the GDR: promised equality in jobs and education in the GDR constitution, she nevertheless found that self-fulfillment was left out of the picture. The liberal child care support and maternity leave meant economic independence from a male partner and served as an ally to the state encouragement of childbearing, yet it also helped to keep women in subservient jobs (where their services could be more easily dispensed with during maternity leaves), and made it easy for men to avoid the burden of childrearing entirely (Nickel 1991–1992). Significantly, there were no women directors at the DEFA who could count on annual funding of their film projects in the way that the male directors could.

The critical look at the real problems in the GDR's transition to socialism offered by the dozen or so films that came to be known as the "rabbit" films (after the one singled out in Honecker's speech, *The Rabbit Is Me*) was too much for the ruling party. The political turn of events signalled by the Eleventh Plenary led to the dismissal of the head of the DEFA, Klaus Wischnewski, and of the minister for film, Günter Witt. Frank Beyer, the director of *Traces of the Stones*, was unable to work in film for years. Hermann Zschoche, whose film *Karla* represented his first serious effort as a director, withdrew into children's films, comedies, and modern fairy tales. Kurt Maetzig (1966, 4), who had directed *The Rabbit Is Me*, apologized for his film in a letter to *Neues Deutschland*. Ulbricht (1966, 3) answered a few days later, saying that writers and artists had the greatest freedom to create anything that would be "useful" for the state. They were to be discouraged, however, from demanding freedoms that would work against the state, the party, and Germany. As Richter (1990, 42) later wrote, "the category of usefulness was thus elevated to a central category of aesthetics, whereas we can say today that it was a matter of what was useful to a small group and its conception of a social experiment that it called 'socialism.'" After 1966, in the absence of a public sphere where political and artistic matters could be openly discussed, works of art themselves became a kind of alternative forum. Strategies of resistance were developed that enabled artists to portray social problems in a somewhat encoded fashion.

In 1974 Frank Beyer was finally allowed to make another film. This was *Jakob der Lügner* (*Jacob the Liar*), which came out in 1974 and was nominated for an Academy Award. My claim that the progressive phalanx of the East German intelligentsia was not deluded or "bought off" by the establishment rests in part on this film. Ostensibly it is a film about a German-Jewish ghetto in 1944. Jacob is on his way home one night when a guard accuses him of being out after the curfew hour and sends him to a police station where he is to ask for his "just punishment." At the station, he overhears a radio broadcast that suggests the Russian "liberators" are fighting at Bezanika, within a few hundred kilometers of the ghetto. But the next day, when he tries to tell a young man the news, he is not believed. In a moment of crisis (the young man is about to get himself shot by stealing some food), Jacob tells his first lie: "I have a radio."

From then on, Jacob cannot escape this lie. News of the "radio" spreads through the ghetto, and people are always coming up to him to ask what's new. So Jacob keeps on lying—with the positive effect that suicides stop in the ghetto. People begin to have hope again. Lovers make plans to marry. There will be life after the ghetto after all.

Is this just a film about the historical past? Looking back through public statements made by Beyer upon the film's release, it appears that it is much more. In an interview in *Neues Deutschland*, Beyer (1974, 5) said: "The primary purpose of the film is not to draw a picture of Jewish suffering during fascism or to set up a memorial to antifascist resistors. . . . Our purpose is to reflect, together with the spectator, about truth and lies in life, about dream and reality . . . The idea that human dignity cannot be destroyed is defended until the end."

In Beyer's work, truth and lies emerge as the most important issue. Without equating fascism with Stalinism—the realism of the film anchors it securely in the fascist past—Beyer shows that in practical terms they had structural similarities. He was much freer to say so, of course, after the fall of the Berlin Wall:

> People recognized that Stalinism had many similarities with fascism: the same structures of command, the loud self-praise, the same strutting and showing-off, and above all the mental terrorization of dissidents. But because of their bad conscience they didn't dare say anything. (Beyer 1990)

In 1975, in an interview in the GDR publication *Film and Fernsehen*, he could only leave clues: "Some people think that a story that contains more than is told directly and straightforwardly might be a code for something else that is itself straightforward and direct. On the contrary: it's not that the story means something else, but that it contains more, that it refers to larger issues, to life and the conditions of human existence in general" (Wischnewski 1975).

Jakob der Lügner, he goes on to say, is about people living in a condition of hopelessness. The people in the film are living in such harsh conditions that they need illusions as much as bread. In one of the film's most memorable scenes, Jakob is confronted by a little girl, Lina, who begs him to let her hear the radio. He takes her down to the coal cellar, where, hiding behind a partition, he simulates a radio interview with Winston Churchill, a brass band, and a narrated fairy tale. Lina does peek, but she goes back to her seat and enjoys the rest of the show. Indeed, she asks for more.

If we see this film as a metaphor for Beyer's own assessment of the state of the GDR in 1974, the figure of Jacob becomes a self-portrait, or at least the portrait of the GDR intellectual. We then experience an almost convulsive reframing, not just of the film but of our understanding of the GDR dissident writers and artists from 1965 onward. Lina, who peeks and sees that the "radio" is a fiction, also knows how to understand the false radio's true message of hope. She represents the East German readers, the theater audience and the filmgoers who can read between the lines, find the truth among the lies.

In one of the more bizarre manifestations of state control, the unabated suppression of public discussion included the secret encouragement of an alternative cultural scene (e.g., in Berlin's Prenzlauer Berg district) that was, at the same time, riddled with informers from the Ministry of State Security (*Der Spiegel* 1991). These were strategies intended to counterpoise the real and vital opposition to the regime that flourished in small oppositional groups. As Jürgen Habermas (1991a, 19) notes, "The pacesetters of . . . revolution were voluntary associations in the churches, the human rights groups, the oppositional circles pursuing ecological and feminist goals, against whose latent influence the totalitarian public sphere could from the beginning be stabilized only through reliance on force."

In November 1989, TV stations all over the world transmitted the euphoric image of East meeting West as the Berlin Wall was opened. A few months later, the "rabbit" films were pulled out the archives and shown at the Berlinale film festival. Films whose production had been interrupted were now completed. After the Berlinale, the films were shown on German television, along with a documentary by Christa Maerker (1990, 3), which made the statement that the GDR regime would not have fallen as soon as 1989 if, instead of deciding in 1965 to ban the films and drive writers, artists, and intellectuals out of the country, it had sought to build a consensus within the society.

The thirst of GDR intellectuals for democratic participation in their society continues to be thwarted, however. Both Peter Marcuse (1990; 1991) and Dorothy Rosenberg (1991) have described East–West relations as a colonization of East Germany by West Germany. In his assessment of the current situation, Habermas (1991b, 19) writes that "the political self-consciousness of a nation of citizens can only constitute itself within the medium of open communication. And this, in turn, is dependent on a cultural infrastructure that, in the new German states, is being allowed to disintegrate." Habermas is at pains to point out that once the intellectual capacities of a society have been interrupted for a few years, it is likely that they will be destroyed for good. This is precisely what is happening with the reorganization of the universities, the closing down of the East Berlin Academy of Arts, and the redirection of theaters, publishing houses, and other cultural institutions toward a market economy.

As euphoria retreats from the German stage, those who were part of an oppositional culture on both sides of the Wall are likely to find themselves in the counterculture once more. More generally, thoughtful people on both sides will benefit from asking what the West stands to learn from the East. A preliminary list might include the following:

1. We can be inspired by the ability of some leading GDR intellectuals to distinguish socialist ideals from the bureaucratic forms of state power. Up until the last minute, Frank Beyer, Christa Wolf, Volker Braun, Stefan Heym and others were urging that the fall of the government should not mean the abandonment of socialism (Beyer et al. 1989).
2. We should seriously consider the negative impact that generous day care and maternity leave had on women's ability to assume positions of responsibility in the workplace.
3. We can learn from the multiple strategies of resistance developed and refined by GDR writers, filmmakers, and artists in the face of censorship.
4. We should study the grassroots movements (churches, human rights groups, ecology groups, etc.) that were ultimately so influential in toppling an intolerable, though apparently unassailable, regime.

As can be seen from this list, there are both negative and positive things to be learned. Most importantly, however, the example of the GDR counters the argument against socialism that purports to base itself on "human nature"—the claim that socialism can't work because people are by nature competitive and greedy. This is best exemplified in the psychological dimension of GDR artistic productions.

Traces of the Stones—a novel of over 700 pages by Erik Neutsch before it was made into a banned play by Heiner Müller and a banned film by Frank Beyer—is more than the story of the woman engineer I outlined at the beginning. It is also the story of the fight for the mind of Hans Balla, the skeptical work brigade leader who champions individualism over socialism. When he is finally won over, he brings the brigade with him. His decision is not a capitulation to authority but a change of commitment—one that overcomes the divisiveness and alienation that previously characterized his relation to his superiors. A crucial moment of that transformation shows Balla, at a congress of party officials where he has been invited to speak for the common worker, throwing aside his prepared script and speaking his mind about the problems at the factory. In real life, unfortunately, the GDR power elite dammed up that energy and consequently never experienced what that commitment could have wrought.

ACKNOWLEDGMENTS

My thanks to the organizers of the conference (Re)Fusing the Frame, Simon Morgan-Russell and Paul E. Winters. My research was funded by a DAAD Study Visit in 1991. In Berlin, filmmaker Christa Maerker, Dr. Prof. Karl Prümm, Dr. Rolf Richter, and Dr. Erika Richter provided invaluable assistance.

REFERENCES

Beyer, F. 1974. "Traum vom besseren Leben" [Dream of a Better Life]. *Neues Deutschland* (17 December): 5.

——. 1990. "Interview." In *EPD Film* 1: 1.

Beyer, F. et al. 1989. "Für unser Land" [For Our Land]. *Neues Deutschland* (26 November): 4.

Byg, B. 1990. "What Might Have Been: DEFA Films of the Past and the Future of German Cinema." In *Cineaste* 4: 9–15.

Der Spiegel. 1991. "Pegasus an der Stasi-Leine" [Pegasus on a Stasi Leash]. *Der Spiegel* 27: 276–280.

Gregor, E. et al. eds. 1990. *20. internationales forum des jungen films berlin 1990* [Twentieth International Forum of Young Films]. Berlin: 40. internationale filmfestspiele.

Habermas, J. 1991a. "Further Reflections on the Public Sphere." In *Habermas and the Public Sphere*, ed. Craig Calhoun. Cambridge, MA: MIT Press.

——. 1991b. "Die andere Zerstörung der Vernunft" [The Other Destruction of Reason]. *Die Zeit* (17 May): 19.

Maerker, C. 1990. *Verbannte Bilder* [Exiled Images]. Unpublished screenplay.

Maetzig, K. 1966. "Der Künstler steht nicht ausserhalb des Kampfes" [The Artist Does Not Stand Outside of the Struggle]. *Neues Deutschland* (5 January): 4.

Marcuse, P. 1990. "East German Requiem." *The Nation* (22 October): 449–450.

——. 1991. "Brainwashing in East Germany: 'De-Stalinization' as Ideological Colonization." *Monthly Review Newsletter* (Fall): 1–2.

Negt, O. and Kluge, A. 1972. *Öffentlichkeit und Erfahrung. Zur Organisationsanalyse von bürgerlicher und proletarischer Öffentlichkeit* [Public Sphere and Experience: Toward an Analysis of the Bourgeois and the Proletarian Public Sphere]. Frankfurt am Main: Suhrkamp.

Nickel, H. M. 1991–1992. "Women in the German Democratic Republic and in the New Federal States: Looking Backwards and Forwards." In *German Politics and Society* 24/25 (Winter): 34–52.

Plenzdorf, U. 1980. *Karla*. Frankfurt am Main: Suhrkamp.

Richter, R. 1981. "Herman Zschoche." In *DEFA Spielfilmregisseure und ihre Kritiker* [DEFA Feature Film Directors and Their Critics]. Vol. I, 224–241. Berlin: Henschel.

——. 1990. "Weder Willkür noch Zufall" [Neither Arbitrariness nor Chance]. In *Film und Fernsehen* 6: 41–44.

Rosenberg, D. 1991. "The Colonization of East Germany." *Monthly Review* 4 (September): 14–33.

Schumann, M. 1992. *Zweigeteilt. Über den Umgang mit der SED-Vergangenheit* [Divided in Two. On the Treatment of the SED Past]. Hamburg: VSA Verlag.

Ulbricht, W. 1966. "Brief des Genossen Walter Ulbricht an Genossen Prof. Dr. Kurt Maetzig" [Letter from Comrade Walter Ulbricht to Comrade Professor Kurt Maetzig]. *Neues Deutschland* (23 January): 3.

Wischnewski, K. 1975. "Über Jakob und Andere" [On Jakob and Others]. *Film und Fernsehen*. (Reprinted in Behn, M. and Bock, H. 1988. *Film und Gesellschaft in der DDR* [Film and Society in the GDR], Vol. I. Hamburg.)

Racism, Genocide, and Resistance: The Politics of Language and International Law

JOY JAMES

GENOCIDE IN THE WAR ZONES

> Racism killed Malice Green, and if racism itself is not
> destroyed, it will destroy our nation. It got Malice Green
> at night. It will get you in the morning.
> —*Rev. Adams' 1992 funeral eulogy for Malice Green,*
> *who was beaten to death by Detroit police*

Outside of a few communities, people rarely speak about racist state murders in a language that allows one to understand and mourn our losses. Atrocities can inspire a truth-telling competent to critique and condemn racist violence. This truth-telling most often happens in eulogies at funerals and memorials. The rest of the time, we usually hear and speak the semi-illiteracy of conventional rhetoric shaping the dominant discourse on "race." This semi-illiteracy arises from severing racism from its logical culmination in genocide, and restricting the referent for human atrocities to holocaust(s) commodified for mass consumption. Resisting racist destruction and genocide requires demystifying contemporary racism, genocide, and fascism, and organizing to implement international human rights conventions in the United States.

This chapter is dedicated to the memory of: Fred Hampton, Anna Mae Aquash, Eleanor Bumpers, Yvonne Smallwood, Malice Green, Michael Stewart, Dulce September, Chris Hani, and the countless remembered and forgotten who died fighting racist violence.

African and Native American activists have long organized against genocide and human rights violations in U.S. domestic and foreign policy. In 1951, the African-American-led Civil Rights Congress petitioned the United Nations. With its document, *We Charge Genocide: The Crime of Government against the Negro People*, it interpreted and promoted the language and implementation of the 1948 *U.N. Convention on the Prevention and Elimination of Genocide*:

> It is sometimes incorrectly thought that genocide means the complete and definitive destruction of a race or people. The Genocide Convention, however, adopted by the General Assembly of the United Nations on December 9, 1948, defines genocide as any killings on the basis of race, or in its specific words, as "killing members of the group." Any intent to destroy, *in whole or in part*, a national, racial, ethnic or religious group is genocide, according to the Convention. Thus, the Convention states, "causing serious bodily or mental harm to members of the group" is genocide as well as "killing members of the group."
>
> We maintain, therefore, that the oppressed Negro citizens of the United States, segregated, discriminated against, and long the target of violence suffer from genocide as the result of the consistent, conscious, unified policies of every branch of government. (Patterson 1951, xi)

U.S. domestic genocidal policies, mirroring foreign policies of racial imperialism, have historically focused on Native and African Americans. The Senate delayed ratification of the Genocide Convention to 1986 because Congress feared Native and African Americans' use of the Convention against the United States in international courts (Boyle 1989). Currently, the International Indian Treaty Council and the Freedom Now Party use the U.N. Convention on Genocide to petition the U.N. and educate communities about U.S. domestic repression: upwards of one hundred U.S. political prisoners, the disproportionate imprisonment of African, Latin, and Native Americans, and the torture in U.S. prisons. Activists and writers also argue for the enforcement of the Convention, which prohibits involuntary sterilization of a targeted population. This occurs under the guise of "population control," as sexism and racism shape U.S. genocide to focus on Puerto Rican, African, and Native American women: For example, the U.S. Indian Health Service (IHS) of the Bureau of Indian Affairs has involuntarily sterilized approximately 40% of all Native American women. Children are not exempt from state racist policies: in 1990, the IHS inoculated Inuit children with HIV-correlated hepatitis-B vaccine which the World Health Organization had banned; in 1993, the HIV-correlated hepatitis-A vaccine was tested on Native Americans of the northern plains reservations (Churchill 1993, 24).

Implemented into law in 1988 with restrictive amendments, the Convention on Genocide *theoretically* criminalizes and outlaws such policies creating or inciting genocide. *In practice*, the United States has consistently positioned itself as an outlaw state; its crimes against humanity, targeting African and Native Americans for the most severe repression, shape the daily life of these populations. With African American infant mortality doubled that of whites, by the mid-1980s, life expectancy for whites had increased (from 75.3 years to 75.4), while life expectancy for African Americans had decreased (from 69.7 to 69.4 years) (National Urban League 1988). Native American life expectancy on reservations is 45 and 48 years for men and women, respectively (Churchill 1993, 46). Manning Marable's grim assessment of the possible impact of state policies on city residents applies to those who live on reservations:

> The direction of America's political economy and social hierarchy is veering toward a kind of subtle apocalypse which promises to obliterate the lowest stratum of the Black and Latino poor. For the Right will not be satisfied with institutionalization of bureaucratic walls that surround and maintain the ghetto. The genocidal logic of the situation could demand, in the not too distant future, the rejection of the ghetto's right to survival in the new capitalist order. (Marable 1982, 253)

Conventional language's catchall term, "racism," which is virtually meaningless when severed from genocide, is more obscurantist than analytical. Most language mystifies racism to disconnect it from institutional white supremacy and genocide and privatize it as personal behavior and speech. Dismembered language distracts from the impact of racist state policies, since how we talk about racism determines what we do about genocide.

RACIST DISCOURSE, "WHITE RIGHTS," AND WHITE SUPREMACY

> How do you get to be the sort of victor who claims to be the vanquished also.
> —*Jamaica Kincaid,* Lucy

The race discourses of various ideologies distance racism from genocide. The result of this distancing is that issues of identity replace institutional analysis. Racialized identity and speech are endemic to the United States. Yet, a focus on these alone deflects from the political and economic aspects of structural racism and white supremacy: Whether or not anything is publicly said, policies perpetuate dominance and genocide.

Racism has come to be understood as "a form of discourse . . . that can be effectively blocked by means of linguistic taboos" (Freedman 1992,

26). Perversely, as racial epithets become taboo, so does antiracist terminology: "race" supplants "racist"; "multiculturalism" and "race relations" supplants "antiracism" in the language of conservatives and
progressives alike; reformist policies such as affirmative action ("quotas")
are denounced as "polarizing" and "antidemocratic."

The absence of racial epithets notwithstanding, supremacist language and racial mythology inspired the electoral campaigns of neo-Nazi
David Duke and former presidents Ronald Reagan and George Bush.
All shared the rhetoric of European neofascist movements, that is, the
language of "white rights" and the redress of "white victimization."
Neofascists' denunciation of "white victimization," allegedly stemming
from "black racism" and equity programs, proves frighteningly compatible with the language of conservatives, moderates, and progressives.
"White rights" provides the ideological ground for neoconservatives
to advocate, and neoliberals to ignore, genocidal policies. The ascent
from rightist racism to leftist racism is not as steep as one would like to
imagine.

For example, in the "Whiteness" issue of the liberal national weekly,
The Village Voice, Slavoj Zizek has a particular interpretation of Malcolm
X that allows him to argue that the idea that whites should accept responsibility for white supremacy is a form of "racism": "Only by acknowledging that, ultimately, they can do nothing, that the emancipation of
African Americans must be their own deed, only by renouncing the false
self-blame of whites, which conceals its exact opposite, patronizing arrogance, can whites actually do something for African American emancipation" (Zizek 1993, 31). With no one (i.e., no white) to blame for truly
horrific conditions, the overthrow of white supremacy is now a black
thing, a struggle for which African Americans become solely responsible.
Zizek's argument would move African Americans from a position of structural inferiority to one of equality, investing them with a special ability/
power to effect social change. But the effect of this Horatio Alger man-
date is that all genocide is reduced to autogenocide.

Tikkun's editor Michael Lerner wrote "Jews Are Not White" for the
same issue of the *Voice*, which is a much more circumspect but nonetheless real exculpation of the power structure. Without differentiating
between Ashkenazi, Sephardic, or Ethiopian Jews, or referring to the
complicity of non-Wasps in white supremacy, Lerner argues that to
achieve "the liberatory potential of multiculturalism" we must

> reject the fantasized concept of "whiteness" and instead recognize the com-
> plex stories of each cultural tradition, not privileging one group over an-
> other. . . . [Today, however, multiculturalism] is merely the tool of an elite
> of minority intellectuals seeking to establish themselves inside an intellec-

tual world that has too long excluded them. And in that context, Jews must respond with an equally determined insistence that we are not white, and that those who claim we are and exclude our history and literature from the newly emerging multicultural canon are our oppressors. (Lerner 1993, 34)

Here, few other than Aryans qualify as members of a mythic construction of "whiteness." (Ironically, propaganda of European Jews as "deficient" in whiteness has fueled and still fuels antisemitic persecution.) However, the reality is that white supremacy accommodates non-Aryan "whites" in Israel and Palestine, Southern Africa, and throughout the Americas. Both Zizek's and Lerner's writings are indicative of the mystification of contemporary racism, institutional antisemitism and racialized state elites, promoting a conventional language that, with increasing aggressiveness, argues for white rights under white supremacy. The fundamental state and white right is to be not responsible for oppression. The ultimate white right is to claim to be victimized by those targeted for genocide who engage in resistance. Instructing that "minorities" oppress each other and *majorities*, conventional race language erases the role of state institutions and confuses ignorance and abusive chauvinism with systems of oppression.

That ethnic "minorities" lack institutional or state power to dominate dominant ethnic groups becomes irrelevant when racism is crassly reduced to all (real and alleged) ethnic chauvinism (that of European descent is universalized as the norm, and so conventionally does not appear chauvinistic). If oppressive state hierarchies are real, the critical distinction between chauvinism and racism must be maintained. Transforming odious ethnic chauvinism into a colorized version of white supremacy—which is the only racialized oppression we have known for half a millennium—trivializes white supremacy. (The different forms of ethnic pride and revolutionary nationalism among the newly colonized have often been reduced to the conservative ideologies of ethnic chauvinism in media representations.)

Colonized groups are granted the equal opportunity of being labeled "ethnic oppressors" or "reverse racists" when a false equality projects illusions of domination that deflect from real structures of oppression. This false illusion of domination, by fictionalizing state racism and complicitous populations, rationalizes an otherwise illogical concept: red, black, brown, or yellow "racists" or racial oppressors within a white supremacist state. Only when racism is severed from genocide does one argue that oppressed ethnic groups can implement policies creating racism and antisemitism. Here, denigrating structural critiques elevates debates of ethnic identity and innocence to degrade struggles against domestic genocide.

MEMORY AND MEANING

> The present political chaos is connected with the decay of language.
>
> —*George Orwell*, Politics and the English Language

However impossible it is to talk about racism meaningfully without discussing genocide, it is equally impossible to speak with moral opprobrium of genocide without reference to fascism. Genocide's meaning stems from the tribunals following the Nazi atrocities of World War II. Constructed as the antithesis and anathema to Western democracy and civilization, the concept has great political and ethical weight, which has rarely been brought to bear on the United States. The label "fascist" is even more infrequently applied to U.S. policies. Like most states, the U.S. denies that its policies are racist, with genocidal or neofascist consequences. However, it uses both terms in interventionist rhetoric to mobilize civilian support (e.g., for the bombings of Panama and Iraq, George Bush referred to Manuel Noriega and Saddam Hussein as Hitler-like personas or "fascists").

The term "fascism" is usually limited to specific historical events in Europe, leaving unexamined the phenomenon of fascism and neofascist aspects in state racism. Describing "fascism" as "a system of political, economic, social and cultural organization," Noam Chomsky rejects conventional restrictions:

> If we want to talk about [fascism] reasonably we have to disassociate it from concentration camps and gas chambers. There was a fascism before there were extermination camps. . . . From a socio-cultural point of view, fascism meant an attack on the ideals of the Enlightenment. . . . on the idea that people had natural rights, that they were fundamentally equal, that it was an infringement of essential human rights if systems of authority subordinated some to others. (Barsamian 1993, 32)

Chomsky's argument demystifies fascism as a distant evil; yet it does not acknowledge that the Enlightenment ideals of the civilized, rational mind were (are) themselves premised on racism. The European Enlightenment's construction of the Western liberal individual as the standard for civilized humanity concurred with its reconstructing those enslaved or colonized by Europeans with an essentialist inferiority. This worldview placed and places "the colonized beyond the liberal equation of universal freedom and equality by rendering them in racist terms as qualitatively different. . . . Racism was, in short, basic to the creation of liberalism and the identity of the European" (Fitzpatrick 1990, 249). The Enlightenment legacy dulls recognition of the pervasiveness of racism's influence, just as the language of denial and rhetorical opposition hinder radical resistance to racism.

Given the racialization of the value of human life as an Enlightenment legacy in Europe and European settler states, and the narcissism
of white supremacy, the presence of humanity, and abhorrence over its
loss, is based on "whiteness," constructed as European. (This is reflected
in Western European and U.S. indifference to the genocide of Bosnian
Muslims as the "Other" Europeans.) It is difficult then to assess the conventional meanings of genocide within the context of state and social
constructions of Nazi Germany's genocidal policies as *the* referent for
memory and meaning concerning racist atrocities.

The 1993 dedication of the U.S. Holocaust Memorial Museum in
Washington, D.C. legitimizes the historical reality of Nazi Germany's
genocidal policies against Jews, which an estimated one fifth of the U.S.
population denies (Solomon 1993). Yet, the Museum, the state, and corporate donors promote a consciousness in which this tragedy, abstracted
from historical, concurrent, and contemporary genocides, manifests as
the only real expression of genocide. No national poll is likely to be conducted to see what percentage believes indigenous and African holocausts
happen(ed) in the Americas. The national museum, dedicated to preventing future holocausts, with no mention of American genocides or
U.S. national racism and antisemitism, valorizes the U.S. government and
ignores its genocidal policies. It calls us to awaken to, or to be anesthe-
tized by, the horrors of holocausts as past "events," occurring outside of
this nation, which is now reconstructed as the protector against genocide. The contradictions of the U.S. national museum suggest that the
spectator was never intended to be an actor:

> [The museum narrative] suggests an outcome that isn't really possible. . . .
> It strains toward completeness and closure and understanding; these dra-
> matic reassurances are evoked, but never satisfied. Except to the extent
> that the museum hints at a moral to the story: American democracy. Press
> materials explain, "the charter of the Museum is to remind visitors of the
> importance of democratic values and to underscore our national commit-
> ment to human rights." On the way out of the exhibit one practically walks
> into a wall bearing the seal of the United States. Arched over the eagle
> and "E Pluribus Unum" are the words "For the dead and the living we must
> bear witness." (Solomon 1993, 35)

Bear witness to what? The German holocaust is presented as "a discourse,
a representation forever being deconstructed, a spectacle, an industry"
that promises comforting closure to and containment of human barbarism and tragedy: "The Nazis came to power, committed atrocities, and
were defeated. The end" (Solomon 1993, 36). Whoever tells this particular
story omits information on collaborators and contemporaneous European genocides (Solomon 1993, 36). Collective memory of selective holo-

causts, remembered in fragmented fashion, reveal the depoliticizing aspects of race language: The language of the horrified spectator is not necessarily the language of the antiracist activist. "Identification" through viewing a spectacle, no matter how horrific, does not necessarily lead to analysis, moral commitment, or political organizing. Ongoing genocidal practices diminish before the symbolic, as national memory is shaped more by marketing than by regret for racist policies and philosophies that (inevitably) culminate in genocide.

State-constructed memory and meaning obstruct confronting racism as genocide. Calls to consciousness, relying on mystified and Eurocentric constructions of humanity and suffering, are conditioned by the surrealism and hypocrisy of regret. With the loss of European life as the only common and binding referent for atrocities, no conventional language denounces the genocide of Native and African Americans as inherently meaningful and significant, with its own moral and political value. To the extent that resistance is tied to this language, Native, African, and European American writers use the German Nazi atrocities (as the recognized referents for "holocaust" and "fascism") to make U.S. genocidal practices "meaningful."

LAW AND RESISTANCE

> First the law dies and then people die.
> —*1993 sign in Solingen, Germany, protesting the neo-Nazi arson murders of five Turkish girls and women and parliament's amending the German constitution to restrict asylum for foreigners.*

To prevent atrocities, we are told, we have law. U.S. constitutional law gave us slavery, broken indigenous treaties, suppression of political dissent, codified sexism and homophobia, and opened doors for monopoly capitalism. In addition, constitutional law, as an Enlightenment project, exists within a worldview that posits "law's innocence," as law first "marks out the areas" within which racism is allowed to operate legally, and then rationalizes its operation (Fitzpatrick 1990, 250–251).

The limitations of constitutional law stem from its malleability by dominant elites and structures that define rights and their enforcement, and a universalizing Western worldview excluding the contributions to law of traditional Native American and African cosmologies. These limitations also shape the frailties of international law. However, the language of U.N. conventions provides specific norms to address the classism, racism, and sexism of U.S. constitutional law, oppressive policies, and obscurantist language. Understanding that law in itself is insufficient for political change, activists organize for the implementation of international human rights conventions, working for the language of the conventions as an educational and political strategy to resist genocidal policies, by expanding and redefining the conventional concept of rights and entitlements within the United States.

Although the conservative nature of the U.S. Supreme Court makes the enforcement of conventions unlikely, according to the U.S. Constitution's "supremacy clause," treaties are part of the "supreme law of the land," and preempt national law (just as federal law prevails over state laws). Calling for the enactment of treaties challenges U.S. foreign and domestic policies. For example, the Convention on the Suppression and Punishment of the Crime of Apartheid supersedes the weak Congressional bills and prevents further U.S. support for the destabilization of Southern Africa. The Geneva Conventions (1949) and Nuremberg Principles war crimes or "crimes against humanity," covering the treatment of military, civilians, and political prisoners during times of war, would criminalize CIA-directed/U.S.-funded contra wars and internal, domestic wars waged against U.S. activists.

These conventions are also supported by the U.N. Charter. When the United States signed the U.N. Charter it agreed to uphold: "equal rights and self-determination of peoples . . . higher standards of living, full employment . . . universal respect for, and observance of human rights and fundamental freedoms for all without distinction as to race, sex, language, or religion" (Article 55, United Nations Charter). If accountable to that Charter, the United States would discontinue in the 1990s its policies of the 1980s, during which it spent approximately $1 billion a year on the Pentagon and engaged in covert operations to destabilize governments and liberation movements. Also, if international law prevailed, there would be a conventional understanding of the criminality of the U.S.-dominated financial institutions, which structure economic exploitation so that, for example, each year African, Caribbean, and Latin American nations transfer $20 billion or more to their historic colonizers, more than they receive in aid and loans; 14% of the world's population consume 70% of its resources; and an estimated half million young children die (UNICEF 1988). The Charter would remand domestic "austerity" programs in which millions live below a whimsically set poverty line, and over one million are estimated to be homeless; African Americans are poorer today than a generation ago; two out of three adults in poverty are women; and women of color are twice as likely to be poor than white women. The enforcement of human rights law would decrease the number of war zones.

The Charter and other conventions also prohibit state repression, illegal surveillance and imprisonment, increasing police powers through the U.S. preventive detention law, the 1984 Bail Reform Act, and the criminalization of radical political dissent. It also makes illegal "The Federal Violence Initiative," which criminalizes an entire population. Approved by the National Mental Health Advisory Council, the "Initiative" is federally funded "to identify at least 100,000 inner city children whose alleged biochemical and genetic defects will make them violent in later life. . . . Treatment will consist of behavior modification in the family, special 'day camps,' and drugs" (Center for the Study of Psychiatry 1992).

Various organizations seek the enforcement of the U.N. conventions and Charter as *the* language of rights in the United States. At the 1985 U.N. Conference on the Decade on Women in Kenya, the Women's Coalition for Nairobi, organized by U.S. Women for Racial and Economic Equality, obtained over 2,000 U.S. delegates' signatures on a petition calling for the U.S. government to obey the U.N. conventions and Charter. The petition demanded nuclear disarmament; equal pay and full employment; full rights for undocumented workers; "quality of life measures" to eliminate economic, racial, and sexual violence and discrimination; quality reproductive choice and child care; and aid to women in independence struggles in Southern Africa and the Middle East. In 1986, Marcia Walker, Mayor Pro-Tem, and Kathleen P. Salisbury, City Clerk, signed ordinance No. 2807 of the Burlington, Iowa City Council to bring the city's human rights ordinance into compliance with the *U.N. Convention on the Elimination of All Forms of Racial Discrimination* (Boyle 1989). In 1993, New York Assemblyman's Roger Greene formed an independent party, "The Children First Party," based on the U.N. conventions on the rights of children, to focus on legislation dealing with children's needs and rights. Also, in 1993 the New York-based Center for Constitutional Rights used international law in arguing its case for Diana Ortiz, the U.S. nun tortured and raped by U.S.-funded death squads in Guatemala.

CONCLUSION

Racism in U.S. foreign and domestic policy culminates in genocide. The inability of conventional language to confront the devaluing and destruction of human life based on white supremacy creates a silence around U.S. "race wars" and struggles for survival and liberation. The reduction of "racism" to speech, social manners, or the incivility of aberrational minorities ignores state racist violence and the massive increase in white supremacist hate group activities. Rendering racism an abstraction and its attendants, genocide and fascism, social fictions, racialized language's obscurantism transcends ideology and ethnic, class, and gender identity.

By rejecting this language, activists create, with international human rights conventions, a literacy in political and moral language adequate to convey and confront the devastation of genocidal policies. Demystifying racialized speech and organizing to implement human rights treaties as "law," simultaneously enforceable for national and international communities, might be our most important forms of resistance to racism as genocide.

REFERENCES

Barsamian, D. 1993. "Information Control and the State: An Interview with Noam Chomsky," *Radical America* 22 (2–3): 27–39.

Boyle, F. 1989. "The Hypocrisy and Racism Behind the Formulation of U.S. Human Rights Foreign Policy." *Social Justice* 16 (1): 71–93.

Center for the Study of Psychiatry. 1992, September 23. "Report from the Center for the Study of Psychiatry. *The Federal Violence Initiative*. Bethesda, MD: Author.

Churchill, W. 1993, March. "Crimes Against Humanity." *Z Magazine* 6 (3).

Fitzpatrick, P. 1990. "Racism and the Innocence of Law." In *Anatomy of Racism*, ed. D. Goldberg. Minneapolis: University of Minnesota Press.

Freedman, C. 1992, Spring. "Louisiana *Duce*: Notes Toward a Systematic Analysis of Postmodern Fascism in America." *Rethinking Marxism* 5 (1): 19–31.

Lerner, M. 1993. "Jews Are Not White." *Village Voice* 20.

Marable, M. 1982. *How Capitalism Underdeveloped Black America*. Boston: South End Press.

National Urban League. 1988. *1998 State of Black America*. New York: National Urban League.

Patterson, W. 1951. *We Charge Genocide: The Crime of Government against the Negro People. A Petition to the United Nations*. New York: Civil Rights Congress.

Simpson, C. 1988. *Blowback: The First Full Account of America's Recruitment of Nazis, and Its Disastrous Effect on Our Domestic and Foreign Policy*. New York: Weidenfeld and Nicholson.

Solomon, A. 1993. "An American Tragedy?: The Holocaust Museum Shapes Up for Domestic Consumption." *Village Voice* 19.

UNICEF. 1988. *State of the World*. New York: United Nations.

Zizek, S. 1993. "The 'Theft of Enjoyment.'" *Village Voice* 20.

The Twentieth World: Images of Power and Resistance

AMITAVA KUMAR

The Latin American activist–writer, Eduardo Galeano has written of Sebastiao Salgado's photographs: "These images that seem torn from the pages of the Old Testament are actually portraits of the human condition in the twentieth century, symbols of our one world, which is not a first, a third, or a twentieth world. From their mighty silence, these images, these portraits, question the hypocritical frontiers that safeguard the bourgeois order and protect its right to power and inheritance." In giving my exhibition (these photographs were exhibited at the conference) the somewhat "absurd" title "The Twentieth World," I wanted the viewers of these photographs to think not only about the invisible worlds within the world they live in, but also about the connections between these worlds. As images of the singular and unequal world we live in, these pictures seemed, to me at least, to challenge the easy assumptions about the separateness of the "first" and the "third" worlds.

I have looked at the faces of some of the men and women in India, the land of my birth, and found only evacuation zones, abandoned, cleared even of memories. The starving woman with a garland of dry marigolds wrapped around her neck is not a nameless site, however; we have to begin recognizing in her appearance the political geography of postcolonial histories and countless, well-remembered struggles. The T-shirt worn by an African American in a protest march following the Rodney King trial and verdict declares the importance of a concrete sense of the community over the abstract and absent notion of justice. The tattoo on the hand of the New York-based, activist-diva Diamanda Galas is a similar proclamation, shattering the catatonia of impassivity around AIDS and linking us in a community bound by insurgent compassion. The pockmarked, stone faces of the founding fathers are all that remain outside the crumbling walls of a small-town college in eastern India. And in that postnationalist space, resistance is more clearly evident in the raised fist of the woman from Bhopal who presents herself not as a victim but rather as a combatant in the fight against multinational capitalism. Her allies will—or should—include the woman in the American Midwest holding a sign that says "I will work for food." The forging of those alliances is the task that lies outside the frame of these few, selected photographs.

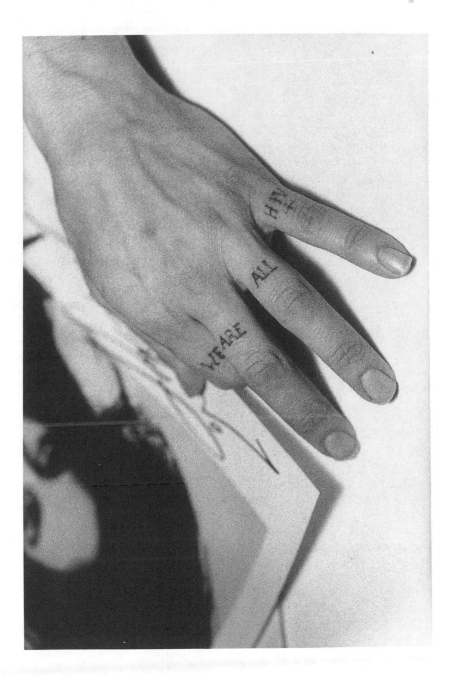

Affirming Inaction: Television and the New Politics of Race

JUSTIN LEWIS
SUT JHALLY

To deal with race and racial inequality has been an abiding concern in contemporary North American culture. Since racism is often understood as a perception dependent upon negative or stereotypical images, debates about race have often centered around the issue of representation, with analytical eyes increasingly inclined toward the main image maker in our culture—television.

In order to make sense of the many competing claims about the way black people are represented on television, we carried out extensive research based upon a content analysis of prime-time television together with a series of fifty-two focus group interviews, made up of twenty-six white, twenty-three black, and three Latino groups, from a range of class backgrounds. The interviews were designed to probe attitudes to race and the media representation thereof. To facilitate these discussions, each interview began with the viewing of an episode of *The Cosby Show*.

The Cosby Show was chosen because it has, in many ways, changed the way television thinks about portraying black people. As *The Cosby Show* has gone from being innovative to institutional, African Americans have become a fairly common sight on network television in the United States. And not just any African Americans: Our content analysis confirmed that we now see a plethora of middle- and upper-middle-class black charac-

For an elaboration of the ideas presented in this paper, see Jhally and Lewis (1992).

ters populating our screens. Bill Cosby can be credited with spurring a move towards racial equality on television. Television characters on U.S. television have always inclined to be middle or upper middle-class—now, in the 1990s, black people have become an equal and everyday part of this upwardly mobile world.

The Cosby Show is, in this sense, more than just another sitcom. It has become a symbol of a new age in popular culture, an age where black actors no longer have to suffer the indignities of playing a crude and limited array of black stereotypes, an age where white audiences can accept television programs with more than just a "token" black character, an age where black people appear increasingly confident in mastering the art of the possible. There is, it seems, much to thank Bill Cosby for.

For these reasons, we began our research genuinely well disposed towards the trend *The Cosby Show* represented. Some of the criticisms of the show seemed, to us, a little churlish, chiding the show with a set of standards by which nearly *everything* on network television falls well short. For all its flaws, we were inclined to think that Bill Cosby's show had pushed popular culture ever so gently in a positive direction. Our journey through a detailed and sometimes exhaustive piece of qualitative audience research dramatically changed this sanguine view.

Without wishing to damn with faint praise, the show is full of good intentions. It would appear to promote an attitude of racial tolerance among white viewers, and to generate a feeling of pride among black viewers. But the show is caught up in a set of cultural assumptions that go well beyond the scope of any one program maker—no matter how influential. What we discovered, in essence, was that the social and cultural context that gives the show its meaning turns its good intentions upside down.

The social success of black television characters in the wake of *The Cosby Show* does not reflect a trend toward black prosperity in the world beyond television. On the contrary, the Cosby era has witnessed a comparative decline in the fortunes of most African Americans in the United States. The racial inequalities that scarred the United States before the civil rights movement could only be rectified by instituting major structural changes in the nation's social, political, and economic life. From 1980 to 1992, the White House withdrew from any notion of intervention in an iniquitous system, committing itself instead to promoting a freewheeling capitalist economy. This laissez-faire approach was responsible for the gradual erosion of advances made by black people during the 1960s. For all the gains made in the fictional world of television, the United States remains a racially divided society.

Maintaining these divisions is a class system that keeps most people in their place. The "American Dream" is a fantasy that few can or will ever realize. It is an idea sustained by anecdotes that focus on the exceptions, not on the rules. If we are to begin any kind of serious analysis of racial divisions in the United States, we must acknowledge the existence of the class barriers that ensnare the majority of black people.

The economic laws of free-market capitalism keep these class barriers in place with a cavalier efficiency. Our society has declared itself officially nonracist, and invited its black citizens to compete alongside everyone else. The game of monopoly is instructive here. If three white people begin a game of monopoly, a black player who is invited to join them halfway through enters at a serious disadvantage. Unless blessed by an unlikely combination of good luck and good sense, the black player will be unable to overcome these economic disadvantages and compete on equal terms. This is how the United States has treated most of its black citizens: It offers the promise of equal opportunity without providing the means to fulfill it.

There is a wealth of evidence about the operation of these structural inequalities. What is remarkable about our culture is that it refuses to acknowledge the existence of class structures, let alone understand how they influence racial inequalities. And yet, at certain moments, we *do* accept these things as obvious. We expect rich white children to do better than poor black children. We expect it, because we know that they will go to better schools, be brought up in more comfortable surroundings and be offered more opportunities. And our expectations would often be proved right. The children who succeed in spite of these odds are glamorous figures in our culture *precisely because* they defy these expectations. Unfortunately, our culture teaches us to ignore these social structures in a naive obsession with individual endeavor. U.S. television is directly culpable for this mass incomprehension. It has created a world that shifts the class boundaries upward, so that the definition of what is normal no longer includes the working class. It then behaves as if nothing has happened, and the class barriers that divide working-class viewers from upper-middle-class television characters simply melt away. These pictures from the "American Dream" are paraded in front of us in sitcoms and drama series night after night. In television land, everybody, or everybody with an ounce of merit, is making it.

But surely, it's only television, isn't it? Most people realize that the real world is different, don't they? Well, yes and no. Our study suggests that the line the television world and the world beyond the screen has, for most people, become exceedingly hazy. We watch, at one moment with credulity, and at another with disbelief. We mix skepticism with an extraordinary faith in the television's capacity to tell us the truth. We know that the Huxtables are not real, yet we continually think about them as if they were. We learn to live in the dreams of network executives.

Characters like *Roseanne*, as the viewers in our study repeatedly confirmed, become noticeable because they defy this norm. Simply by being working class, she stands out. In the United States there are nearly twice as many janitors as all the lawyers and doctors put together, and yet, on television, the legal or medical professions are run of the mill, while to portray a major character as a janitor seems ostentatiously class conscious. The negative response to *thirtysomething* was, in this context, extremely revealing. Here was a show that dealt, fairly intimately, with the lives of a group of middle- and upper-middle-class people. In sociodemographic terms, these characters were run-of-the-mill for network television, where most characters of any importance are middle or upper middle class. Why, then, was this show in particular invariably described, often pejoratively, as a *yuppie* drama?

The answer tells us a great deal about the way class is represented on television. *Thirtysomething* was unusual *not* because it was about young professionals, but because it was *self-consciously* about young professionals. It was difficult to watch an episode without being aware that this was a group of people that were, in class terms, fairly privileged. Here was a show that was conspicuously and unapologetically class conscious. When most television characters display a liberal concern for the poor or the homeless, we are invited to applaud their altruism. When characters on *thirtysomething* did so, we were more likely to cringe with embarrassment at the class contradictions thrown up by such philanthropic gestures. *Thirtysomething*'s principal sin was not that it showed us yuppies, but that it made them appear part of an exclusive world that many people will never inhabit. With its coy realism, *thirtysomething* was killjoy television, puncturing the myth of the American Dream.

The prosperous, comfortable world in which most television characters live is much more welcoming, and it is this less disconcerting world that *The Cosby Show* fits like the proverbial glove. In order to be "normal" on television, the show's characters *had* to be middle or upper middle class—what, after all, could be more routine than a lawyer and a doctor, two of television's favorite occupations? It also had to *look* normal, to portray these wealthy professionals as a "regular," "everyday" family. The show has succeeded in absorbing this contradiction quite brilliantly; its popularity depends upon this combination of accessibility and affluence. Professionals and blue-collar workers can both watch the show and see themselves reflected in it. Social barriers, like class or race, are absent from this world. They have to be. To acknowledge the presence of such things would make too many viewers uncomfortable. Television has thereby imposed a set of cultural rules upon us that give us certain expectations about the way the television world should be.

This makes it very difficult for people schooled in the evasive language of North American television to comprehend the world around them seriously. Any analysis of class structures is simply absent from our popular vocabulary. When our respondents tried to make sense of class issues thrown up by a discussion of *The Cosby Show*, many were forced to displace the idea of class onto a set of racial categories. This was often the case for our black respondents, who got enmeshed in the debate about whether the show was "too white." Yet what is portrayed is not "white" culture (whatever that is), but *upper-middle-class culture*. In the stilted discourse of U.S. television, many respondents found it difficult to make this distinction.

We cannot blame Bill Cosby for playing by the rules of network television. Indeed, our study makes clear that it is only by conforming to these cultural limitations that he was able to make a black family so widely acceptable to white television viewers. The consequence of including black people in this television world, however, is the fostering of damaging delusions. Television, having confused people about class, becomes incomprehensible about race.

Among white people, the admission of black characters to television's upwardly mobile world gives credence to the idea that racial divisions, whether perpetuated by class barriers or by racism, do not exist. Most white people are extremely receptive to such a message. It allows them to feel good about themselves and about the society they are part of. The Cosby/Huxtable persona (along with the many other black professionals it has brought forth into the television world) tells people that, as one of our respondents put it, "there really is room in the United States for minorities to get ahead, without affirmative action."

Affirmative action has become a hot issue in contemporary politics. Conservatives in both parties are able to use their opposition to it as a way of mobilizing white votes. Indeed, our study reveals that the opposition to affirmative action among white people is overwhelming. What was particularly notable was that while most white people are prepared to acknowledge that such a policy was *once* necessary, the prevailing feeling was that this was no longer so.

There are, of course, circumstances in which a well-qualified black person will receive a warm reception from employers concerned to promote an "equal opportunities" image. Any cursory glance at social statistics, however, demonstrates that this is because employers are so embarrassed by current levels of inequality in the workplace. Almost any social index you look at will tell you that we live in a society in which black and white people are not equal. They are not equal in terms of education, health, housing, employment, or wealth. So why is affirmative action suddenly no longer necessary? Partly, we would suggest, because our popular culture tells us so.

During our content analysis of the three main networks, we came across only one program that offered a glimpse of these racial divisions. What was significant about this program, however, was that it did not take place in the present, but in the *past*, during the early days of the civil rights movement. Television was only able to show us racial divisions in the United States by traveling back in time to the "bad old days." Most of the black characters in television's here and now seemed blissfully free of such things. Recent attempts by Hollywood to deal with racial inequality adopt the same strategy. Racism, whether on *Driving Miss Daisy* or *The Long Walk Home*, is confined to the safe distance of history. While there are some notable exceptions, the general impression is clear: Racial inequality is behind us.

Television, despite—and in some ways because of—the liberal intentions of many who write its stories, has pushed our culture backwards. White people are not prepared to deal with the problem of racial inequality because they are no longer sure why there *is* a problem. *The Cosby Show*, our study made increasingly clear, is an intrinsic part of this process of public disenlightenment. Television becomes Dr. Feelgood, indulging its white audience so that their response to racial inequality becomes a guilt-free self-righteous inactivity.

This has saddled us with a new, repressed form of racism. For, while television now portrays a world of equal opportunity, most white people know enough about the world to see that black people achieve less, on the whole, than white people. They know that black people are disproportionately likely to live in poor neighborhoods or drop out of school. How can this knowledge be reconciled with the the smiling faces of the Huxtables, whose success has been achieved so effortlessly? If we are blind to the roots of the racial inequality embedded in our society's class structure, then there *is* only one way to reconcile this paradoxical state of affairs. If white people are disproportionately successful, then they must be disproportionately smarter or hard-working. While few of our respondents were prepared to be this explicit (although a number came very close), their failure to acknowledge class or racial barriers means that this is the only other explanation available. What we end up with, in the apparently enlightened welcome white viewers extend to the Huxtable household, is a new, sophisticated form of racism. The Huxtables' success casts a shadow of failure across the majority of black people who have, by these standards, failed. Television, which tells us nothing about the structures behind success or failure, leaves white viewers to assume that the black people who do not match up to their television counterparts have only themselves to blame.

In a rather different way, the effect of *The Cosby Show* on its black audience is also one of deceptive flattery. The dominant reaction of our black viewers to the show was "for this relief, much thanks." After suffering years of negative media stereotyping, most black viewers were delighted by a show that portrayed African Americans as intelligent, sensitive, and *successful*. The problem with this response is that it embraces the assumption that, on television, a positive image is a prosperous image. This dubious equation means that African Americans are trapped into a position where any reflection of more typical black experience—which is certainly *not* upper middle class—is "stereotypical." As one of our black respondents said, even though he was painfully aware that *The Cosby Show* presented a misleading picture of what life was like for most black Americans, "There's part of me that says, in a way, I don't want white America to see us, you know, struggling or whatever." On television there is no dignity in struggling unless you win.

This analysis of stereotyping dominates contemporary thought. It is the consequence of a television world that has told us that to be working class is to be marginal. To be "normal" on network television in the United States, our popular culture tells us, you have to be middle or upper middle class. Thus it is that viewers are able to see the Huxtable family as both "regular," "average," and "everyday" *and* as successful, well-heeled professionals. This may be Orwellian doublethink, but it is what television encourages us to think.

For black viewers, this deceit amounts to a form of cultural blackmail. It leaves two choices. Either to be complicit partners in an image system that masks the deep racial divisions in the United States, or else be forced to buy into the fiction that, as one respondent put it, "there are black millionaires all over the place," thereby justifying *The Cosby Show* as a legitimate portrayal of average African American life. As we have suggested, it doesn't have to be this way. There is no reason why television characters cannot be working class and dignified and admirable— or even just plain *normal*. Other television cultures have managed to avoid distorting and suppressing the class structure of their societies; why can't we manage it in the United States? There are, we suggest, two main obstacles: the first is ideological, the second economic.

The American Dream is much more than a gentle fantasy; it is the dominant discourse in the United States for understanding (or misunderstanding) class. It is a cultural doctrine that encompasses vast tracts of American life. No politician would dare to question our belief in it. Although politicians of many different persuasions pay lip service to it, this Dream is not politically neutral: It favors those on the political Right that say that anyone, regardless of circumstance, can make it if he or she tries. In such an egalitarian world, the free market can remain untamed.

For government to intervene to eradicate the enormous social problems in the United States would imply that the world is not naturally fair, and that opportunity is not universal, thus defying the logic of the dream.

The ideological dominance of the American Dream is sustained by its massive presence in popular culture. The television and film industries churn out fables, reducing us to a mental state of spellbound passivity. The success we are encouraged to strive for is always linked to the acquisition of goods, a notion fueled by the ubiquitous language of advertising, in which consumers do not usually see *themselves* in commercials, they see a vision of a glamorous and affluent world to which they aspire. Underlying the preponderance of middle- and upper-middle-class characters on display is the relentless message that this is what the world of happiness and contentment looks like. In this context, ordinary settings seem humdrum or even depressing. Not only do we expect television to be more dramatic than everyday life, but, in the United States, we *also* expect it to be more affluent. We don't just want a good story, we want a "classy" setting. This is the language of advertising. It is also, now, the discourse of the American Dream. This language is now so important in our culture that these attitudes seem perfectly natural; it is only when we look at other television cultures that we can see that they are not.

Few other industrial nations leave their cultural industries as dependent upon advertising revenue as they are in the United States, where very little happens in popular culture without a commercial sponsor. This takes place in a lightly regulated free-market economy where cultural industries are not accountable to a notion of public service, but to the bottom line of profitability. Apart from tiny grants to public broadcasting, the survival of radio and television stations depends almost entirely on their ability to sell consumers (viewers or listeners) to advertisers. Moreover, broadcasters are required to do little in the way of public service, and no regulations exist that encourage quality, diversity, innovation, or educational value in programming. This means that not only does advertising create a cultural climate that influences the form and style of programs, it also commits television to the production of formulaic programming: Once cultural patterns are established, it is difficult to deviate from them without losing the ratings that bring in the station's revenue.

Which brings us back to *The Cosby Show* and its many offshoots. In order to be successful and to stay on the air, *The Cosby Show* had to meet certain viewers expectations. This, as we have seen, meant seducing viewers with the vision of comfortable affluence that the Huxtables epitomize. Once television has succumbed to the discourse of the American Dream, where a positive image is a prosperous one, it cannot afford the drop in ratings that will accompany a redefinition of viewers' expectations. Television programs that deviate from the norm (e.g., *Frank's Place, Cop Rock*, or *Twin Peaks*) are short-lived. In such a system, *The Cosby Show*'s survival depends upon meeting the demands of a formula that pleases as many people as possible, something that it does with consummate success, pleasing black and white people, blue-collar workers and professionals, all in slightly different ways, playing with an ambiguity that maximizes its audience. If the *The Cosby Show* had to undo a set of associations built up by the years of television that preceded it, it would have had to rethink the pervasive discourse of the American Dream. This, in turn, would have meant rethinking the whole way television is funded and regulated in the United States. The problems we have identified go far beyond the harmonious world inside the Huxtables' New York brownstone.

What we are suggesting is that we reconsider not only the whole notion of media stereotyping but also the ideological and economic conditions that underpin it. If we do not, we place our culture on a never-ending rollercoaster ride of images and attitudes without ever giving ourselves, as a society, the time to think about the consequences of those images. Discussions about television's influence tends to be limited to the effect of sex or violence. But, if our study tells us anything, it is that we need to be more attentive to the attitudes cultivated by "normal" everyday television. In the case of the *Cosby* phenomenon, these attitudes can affect the way we think about "issues" like race and class and, in so doing, even influence the results of elections. Our culture is much too important to be left to the lowest common denominator laws of the free market. We must begin to think qualitatively as well as quantitatively: Choice means lots of different programs, not lots of different channels.

REFERENCE

Jhally, S. and Lewis, J. 1992. *Enlightened Racism: The Cosby Show, Audiences, and the Myth of the American Dream.* Boulder, CO: Westview Press.

Uncanny Signs of History:
The Unstable Subject

ANDREA LISS
with artwork by **SUSAN EVE JAHODA**

s I was reading the catalogue of the exhibition *This Is My Body, This Is My Blood*, (Hynes, Jahoda, and Stevens 1992, 1) that accompanied the conference "Marxism in the New World Order: Crises and Possibilities" (November, 1992), the editors' words called out eloquently and touched me:

> The continuing crises of the body have their metaphoric and real expressions in the sexual division of labor. . . . The body has been part of a personal sphere associated with women who care intimately for the bodies of their family members. This caring labor is complex. It is intertwined, among other things, with love and the constructions of all that is personal and private. The labor involved in and the knowledge concerned with maintaining human bodies are the most unrecognized and unappreciated aspects of female domestic labor. As Marxists we recognize that the crisis of the body often manifests itself as a denial of the body and the labor that maintains it, thus keeping us blind to the domain of household exploitation. This denial enables cheap sentimentality to substitute for the long overdue celebration of the profound human learning achieved by women as they have confronted their own and other's bodies inside and outside the household.

The editors' promising proclamation ushers in much more, however, than a "long overdue celebration." Their acknowledgment of women's silent labor—a labor that is by no means naturally restricted to women or the home—implies a radical shift in a Marxist conception of history. It recognizes that the assigning of "proper places" is not a neutral activity, but a process deeply embedded in political, economic, and psychic patriarchal structures. We are working here on an ideological register vastly removed from Kaplan's (1992) representation of Marx as a man who forgot his mother and, by implication, a Marxism that blithely ignores and categorizes women's work.[1] The editors' move to recognize women's intimate spheres both as loving places and as sites where violence often occurs and political redress is justified, has long been ushered in by the variously inflected and often conflicting aspects of feminist thinking. In the crucial thinking that informed *This Is My Body, This Is My Blood*, the metaphor and the reality of the wounded body is explicit. Catalogue essayist Robert Blake writes that the artists' transgression of silence "charts wounds, differences, openings, breaks, refusals, recollections, collective and individual sites of resistance" (Hynes et al. 1992, 19).

Tantamount to any breach with history and its attendant legal binds is a feminist understanding of the political microlevel of the private that is not restricted to women's lives alone. In this sense, a reconfigured Marxist approach to the body recognizes the monumental task of redressing the debilitating effects caused by whitewashing the embedded connections between the intimate and the public spheres. Feminist psychotherapist Laura S. Brown proposes a revolutionary way of rethinking the silenced everyday realm and its intersection with history by upturning the conventional definition of trauma. Defined by the American Psychiatric Association as "an event that is outside the range of human experience" (Brown 1991, 121), trauma has been used as a recourse to represent clients who encounter damage in wars or natural disasters. Brown (1991, 121) points out that victims of such events are rarely blamed for what befalls them. She adds, "Nor do those who wage war or go down to the sea in ships that sink come under the sort of scrutiny we find given to battered women, or survivors of rape or incest." Brown recounts the familiar litany in the courts in which legal defendants working against her clients perversely frame the definition of trauma in order to argue that rape and incest occur too frequently and are thus too normal to be considered "outside the range of human experience." She (1991, 122 and 132) directs challenges to her own profession in an effort to redirect the discourse and its damaging effects:

> We must ask questions about how we have understood that which constitutes a traumatic event, and how some experiences have been excluded and turned inward upon their victims. . . . Do we, as did Freud a century ago, betray the truth of what we know of the immediacy and frequency of traumatic events in daily life; or do we follow the radical potential of psycho-

analysis which opened the doors to the unconscious and the irrational, to the next stage in which we re-tell the lost truths of pain among us?

Susan Eve Jahoda's contribution to *This Is My Body, This Is My Blood*, the video installation *The Unstable Subject*, participates fiercely and with subdued passion in the task of telling pain through the infinite dislodgements of her own identity formation under the oppressive family shadow of Holocaust traces. Her labors are indeed doubled. Doubled silences. Riddled mandates. To represent, to give form to, to give voice to, to hear and obscure an other's voice. Speaking and writing history are actions at the core of a feminist perspective on representation. Between the near-impossibility of telling and the trauma to remember, to ritualize, and to politicize, there are approaches. There must be.

In the space we have here I want to consider how *The Unstable Subject* negotiates the dilemmas of representing its subject matter through Jahoda's feminist autobiographical strategy and the interrelated status of representation itself in the work. The piece is based on nine "diaristic" texts, as the artist describes them, of which three are reproduced here. For me, these texts create an open-ended relay between document, fiction, and the uncanny precision of dream. They are the organizing matrix of the videotape, which is played on three monitors that can be viewed simultaneously. In the installation setting, the central monitor sits on a desk that is covered with an intricately embroidered tablecloth and a hospital sheet. The desk is further embellished with a tea set and papers that document various kinds of women's diseases. Two of the four filing cabinets in the installation double as pedestals for the other two monitors. The file drawers are labeled with designations such as Business Management and Industry, Concentration Camps and Domestic Economy, Needle Trades, Eating Disorders, and Fashion. Knitting needles, manila folders, dollhouse furniture, and family snapshots spill out of the drawers. The installation pointedly simulates a space that is at once bureaucratic, clinical, and domestic in order to analyze the social construct of false and debilitating categorizations. The videotape imagery insinuates the ways that mergings between the political and the intimate spheres always occur in the subtexts of women's lives. It highlights a woman carrying out familiar chores in the aura of ghostly unfamiliarity. Appearing in all the sequences, this woman prepares a cake, rips out the seams of a child's dress, pours milk into a stainless steel bowl, and watches herself in a mirror surgically applying makeup to one eye. These somber and eloquent sequences approach a state of being that could gingerly be called the real, especially in their juxtaposition with industrial advertising film clips from the 1950s to the 1980s that cruelly play on stereotypes of women's domestic roles.

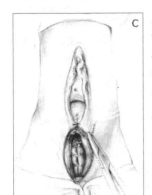

I feel ill. My nerves are raw and I have pains in my groin. I sit with my head down. The shadows in the room are creating faces, intestines and petals. She is staring at me. An image on the wall. Pain(t)ed face— yellow, green, pink flesh.

I am aging. My body is changing shape. I crawl into myself, into my mother. If only I could sever the root. Starve the egg. Murder the connection. Imago.

I saw my newly born daughter encased in a tall, transparent body. Half female. Half male. She wandered out of her room, across the hallway and disappeared. I breathed a sigh of relief. A sharp pain traversed my chest. My breasts filled with salt water. I expressed it into a watering can. I fed it to a dying jade plant in the living room. My daughter re-appeared and asked me for some milk. I explained that I

to help you transform a tense, irritable, depressed patient into a woman who is receptive to your counsel and adjusted to her environment

didn't have any. I said it had turned to blood. I suggested she ask her father. I said he might be able to produce some.

We visited my parents last week. As I un-packed the children's clothing I suddenly remembered a remark the doctor made to my husband after the birth of our daughter. "Congratulations" he said "and oh, by the way, I put in an extra stitch for you."

Text and video stills from *The Unstable Subject*, S. E. Jahoda, 1992.

Within this surreal tale that investigates the interplay between the self, the family, and the state, the "I" of the self elusively dislocates itself. In fact, Jahoda's use of the "I" occurs in only one text-and-image sequence, reproduced here, a sequence that distances the writer from the "she" of the teenage girl in the other sequences. The autobiographical place of the author's presence, whether it is oscillating in the "I" or the distanced "she," resists being situated as a singular, and thus isolated, self. In this sense, Jahoda's work reiterates the 1960s' and 1970s' feminist warning that the personal is political. Thinking about women's acts of autobiography in 1978, Cohen (1978, vi) wrote, "Subjectivity and introspection, which in the past were inappropriately labeled as shallow, narcissistic, or 'feminine,' have suddenly become valued, even celebrated." In 1992, however, Jahoda is acutely aware of the past and current dangers of the female "I" being named, ostracized, and quarantined, literally and figuratively. Her autobiographical strategy both exposes and veils, without claiming a unilaterally personalized or victimized voice. *The Unstable Subject* works within a highly mediated field of cultural representations that intersect with the personal and the institutional. Jahoda's location and dislocation of selves within the piece are in tune with the 1990s' rethinkings of feminist representation. As Braidotti (1989, 97) has refigured the terms:

> The "body" in question is the threshold of subjectivity: as such it is neither the sum of its organs—a fixed biological essence—nor the result of social conditioning—a historical entity. The "body" is rather to be thought of as the point of intersection, as the interface between the biological and the social, that is to say between the socio-political field of the microphysics of power and the subjective dimension.

The Unstable Subject overlaps the asymmetries between "the microphysics of power and the subjective dimension" through a series of pauses and passages in the videotape that invoke experience and the pathos of its representation.[2] It opens with the text, reproduced here, that begins "She used to hear her parents making love at night." In the videotape, no images accompany this text. As it is read, the screen fills with potent darkness. The tone shifts soon after, and an "instructional film" takes the viewer carefully and cruelly through the reasons that "Margie" failed at her first attempt to make a chocolate cake for her new husband. Jahoda directs the ironic humor of the film to a more somber and analytic place through the juxtaposition of images she has created. The actress that passes between sequences throughout the tape appears in relation to the cake scene counting pills at a dining room table. She places the sedatives in a cooking bowl and proceeds to mash them with measuring spoons. Later in the videotape, Jahoda cuts in a sequence from the film *Dead*

She used to hear her parents making love at night. She imagined her father thrusting the memory of death into her mother. They were all born with a taste of torture. Once a teacher instructed her

to wash her mouth out with soap. Once her mother told her that jews were pro- cessed into soap. Last weekend was Pass- over. The five of them spent two days together. Her parents fought constantly. She nibbled away at a walnut cake her mother had baked and burnt. By Sunday she had consumed the whole cake. Her father often mentioned that he had starved during the war. The only thing he had to eat was stale rye bread. He believed in the family. He always talked about his grandchildren at the dinner table. She suspected she'd never provide him with any. She suspected her older sister preferred women. The youngest was too young. She noticed a gold ring on her elder sister's finger. She asked if it was a present from someone. The response came hesitantly. "My friend Sonia paid for half of it and ..." "Does Sonia have one?" he interrupted before she had time to finish the sentence. That night when they were all in bed she heard her sister crying. She entered her room. She entered her bed. She held her in her arms, close to her body.

Text and video still from *The Unstable Subject*, S. E. Jahoda, 1992.

Ringers in which the gynecologist is chastised by his identical twin, also a gynecologist, for using the wrong tool on his patient. He replies, "There's nothing the matter with the instrument, it's the body. The woman's body was all wrong." By employing images and voices from mass-market films and instructional media, Jahoda is relieved of telling stories about women's oppression solely through the personal voice. When her voice is audible through the spoken texts, it reaches us through an eerily disembodied address. In the spirit of warning and teaching, the stories document relationships with uncanny poetic precision. The author does not blame the viewer/reader; she asks him or her to be aware of how women respond to the contradictory cultural messages they receive.

Since Jahoda posits the subject as itself in flux, the dilemma of authenticity becomes all the more doubled as the mediated personal is recounted through the remnants of historical events. The sequence in the videotape where the Holocaust is brought to the surface underscores these dilemmas. There is an absence here of mediated imagery, and no attempt at cutting irony. A sequence opens without an image as we hear a woman's voice speaking Hebrew underneath the translator's English. She recounts how her family was shot before her eyes and her daughter was grabbed from her arms. The woman was shot, too, but did not feel anything while she lay beneath corpses.[3] After we hear this woman's account, Jahoda reintroduces images: the eye watching, family snapshots of women sitting in a row, archival footage from the Lodz ghetto, plans of the Auschwitz crematorium and, then, more family photos showing a wedding and her father with two of his daughters. Working through the development of this sequence, Jahoda had at first relied too heavily on mediated images—excerpts from George Stevens' 1959 film, *The Story of Anne Frank*—and on too many Holocaust photographs that had been interspersed with family photographs. The intimate images had functioned as documents standing in for the artist's familial relationships and her unresolved sense of self-formation. Although seemingly unrelated to the archival images, the family photographs paradoxically and perversely returned a semblance of humanity to the otherwise nameless and faceless corpses that figure so prominently in the documentary photographs. Jahoda's use of the Holocaust photographs was an attempt to go beyond family dynamics and to invoke the irresolvable conditions and material surfaces of the most senseless dissolution and extermination of bodies and selves; but the photographs still functioned as obscene screens onto her own self-identity. Now, in the final version, allowing in both family imagery and a sparer use of documentary photography, Jahoda has found more effective ways to employ the material as obscured windows onto the realities. This is perhaps one of the most delicate and difficult sequences in the work because it represents a space where filtered autobiography is overwhelmed by history at the passage between self, family, and event. Rather than attempting to recount the complete horrific history, or account for it, Jahoda suggests detours from the concept of a comprehensible history and works in the realm of documentation and her own memories, suggesting that history and memory are active processes in the present. That is, the legacy of the Holocaust cannot be safely guarded, or safeguarded within the museologized boundaries of the past. Indeed, Benjamin (1980, 1242) warned against setting the past into a mold denuded of contemporary provocations. "The way in which the past is honored as 'heritage,'" he wrote, "is more disastrous than its simple disappearance could ever be."

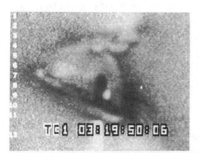

After the shock-treatments he didn't recognize her. Her mother said it was because her skirt was too short. He was hospitalized for three weeks. She left school every day after lunch. She told her teachers she was having ultra-violet treatments for an acne condition on her back and shoulders. She changed out of her school uniform in the ladies-room at the bus station. She always took the number forty-two bus. She considered it to be her lucky number. It was the year her grandparents were gassed at Auschwitz. She always went to the same place. The cafeteria in the basement of the Eye Hospital. She'd been in

the children's room was six. Her parents mother had slammed The glass shattered right eye. Blood always drank one cup package of custard- going home. Two home he cut her She found them

for ten days when she had been fighting. Her a cupboard door shut. and fell into her was everywhere. She of milky tea and ate a cream biscuits before days after he returned skirts into triangles.

stuffed underneath her bed. She stopped going to the Eye Hospital. She stopped going to school. She rode the number forty-two bus for five hours every day. He waited for her to come home. He hated comings and goings. She could see his face pressed up against the window. It looked grey and distorted. He always assumed she'd had an accident. He always assumed they'd all had acci- dents. He was never specific. They were forbidden to take trains. Two weeks after he returned home he poured her perfumes down the toilet and smashed the bottles. She found her lipsticks and mascara in the kitchen trash. Her allowance stopped. He stopped

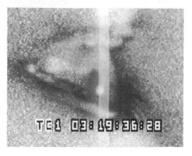

shaving. He cut his pin-striped trousers off at the knees. He forbade her to go out at night. One night she defied him. He chased her down the street. He was sobbing. The next day he was hospitalized. He didn't recognize her after the shock-treatments. Her mother said it was because her skirt was too short.

Text and video stills from *The Unstable Subject*, S. E. Jahoda, 1992.

If we move both toward and away from Benjamin's warning, we must add the caveat that the Holocaust as past is a complex of events that can hardly be embraced as heritage, but remains as a devastating and sometimes inspiring legacy. In the absence—or rather, in the passing—of survivors and direct witnesses we are confronted with the inevitable dilemma about who can legitimately voice and recount the events. The dilemmas of legitimacy and the transference of memory are, indeed, the very problems that underlie the formation of the discipline of history. We hear today urgent and understandable concern about the impropriety of anyone speaking for the events beyond the voices of direct witnesses. Yet adherence to this modernist obsession with authenticity resigns the telling of the events to yet another realm of silence.

With *The Unstable Subject*, however, the question becomes "Whose memories?" In a related project, the allegorical comic book tales of Art Spiegelman (1986 and 1991), *Maus I* and *Maus II*, we may remember that the artist's translation of the Holocaust through his father/witness is simultaneously an attempt to retrieve his mother's lost body through her diaries and photographs.[4] As a boy, his story recounts, Art imagined saving his mother rather than his father from the ovens. *Maus* relives this psychic performance and thus buries the artist's father alive through his vain search for Anja's memories. As Miller (1992, 43) points out, if women's autobiographies have been traditionally characterized by the presence of another "by way of alterity," *Maus* would figure into the genre and at the same time would redefine the gendered polarization of autobiographical representation. However, if Jahoda's investment in alterity is not as nameable as that employed by Spiegelman, this should not usher in a postfeminist backlash that returns us to earlier brandings of women's autobiography as "narcissistic" (Cohen 1978). In *The Unstable Subject* Jahoda is primarily concerned with retrieving women's bodies in their multiple senses. The artist's stories cannot be neatly separated from the "heritage" of the Holocaust; they unevenly conflate with her father's history and pathology. She tries to find spaces to think through the dilemmas in order to represent how the monstrous events have reached her and have become her legacy through localized family relations.

The subjective activity in *The Unstable Subject* overwhelmingly exceeds the privatized notion of self. Its mediated multiple voices are never in one place. They are dispersed, somehow never touchable. Lippard (1992, 11) writes, "Jahoda's subject is variously personalized and depersonalized, enabled and disabled." Jahoda's feminist deconstructive mode of approach often becomes disembodied as a mediation between the autobiographical, the palpable spaces of women's lives, and institutionalized bodies. Any artist breaching the imminently fragile territory of someone else's trauma and its doubling in their own lives may risk

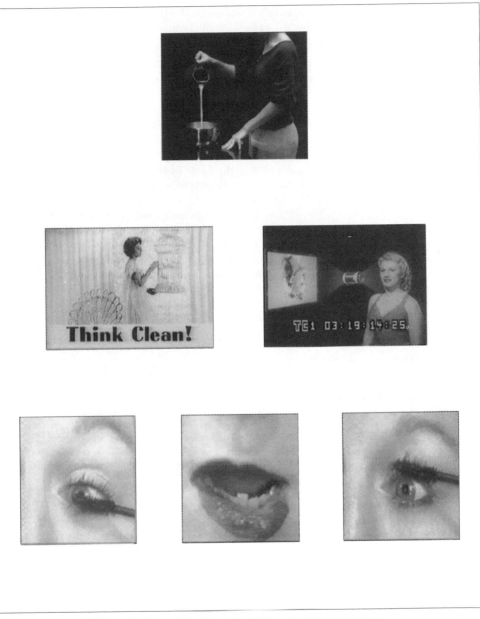

Video stills from *The Unstable Subject*, S. E. Jahoda, 1992.

going too far out of history's confines. Despite Jahoda's risks and conflations (her "excesses"), or because of them, she expands the boundaries of history and representation by confronting her selves and others.

NOTES

1. Kaplan analyzes motherhood discourses in nineteenth- and twentieth-century Western culture. She writes, "Freud's ideas, like those of Marx and Darwin, can be seen as themselves phallocentric: even where women are implicated, there is rarely treatment of the specificity of their situations, least of all specific attention to the mother, who is simply (so significantly) absent, per se, from all these narratives" (1992, 25).

2. Scott (1992) contests the easy equation that some "historians of difference" make between lived experience and historical evidence. She argues that these historians decontextualize resistance and difference: "Questions about the constructed nature of experience, about how subjects are constituted as different in the first place, about how one's vision is structured—about language (or discourse) and history—are left aside" (1992, 25). I am struck by Jahoda's postmodern handling of these questions—a methodology that does not find experience and analysis mutually exclusive. In fact, Scott concludes her essay by acknowledging,

> Experience is not a word we can do without, although it is tempting, given its usage to essentialize identity and reify the subject, to abandon it altogether. But experience is so much a part of everyday language, so imbricated in our narratives that it seems futile to argue for its expulsion. . . . The study of experience, therefore, must call into question its originary status in historical explanation. . . . Experience is, in this approach, not the origin of our explanation, but that which we want to explain. This kind of approach does not undercut politics by denying the existence of subjects, it instead interrogates the processes of their creation, and, in so doing, refigures history and the role of the historian, and opens new ways for thinking about change. (1992, 37–38)

3. This material is excerpted from the television series *The World at War*, Thames Television (1982).

4. For a discussion attentive to the use of autobiography, gender, and absence, see Miller (1992). For an analysis attune to the employment of photographs, see Hirsch (1992–1993).

REFERENCES

Benjamin, W. 1980. *Gesammelte Schriften*, Vol. I. Frankfurt/Main: Suhrkamp.
Braidotti, R. 1989. "The Politics of Ontological Difference." In *Between Feminism and Psychoanalysis*, ed. T. Brennan, 89–105. London: Routledge.

Brown, L. S. 1991, Spring. "Not Outside the Range: One Feminist Perspective on Psychic Trauma." *American Imago* 48 (1): 119–133.

Cohen, J. T. 1978. *In/Sights: Self-Portraits by Women*. Boston: David R. Godine.

Hirsch, M. 1992–1993, Winter. "Family Pictures: *Maus*, Mourning, and Post-Memory." *Discourse* 15(2): 3–29.

Hynes, E.; Jahoda, S.; and Stevens, M., eds. 1992. *This is my body, this is my blood*. University of Massachusetts at Amherst.

Kaplan, E. A. 1992. *Motherhood and Representation: The Mother in Popular Culture and Melodrama*. London: Routledge.

Lippard, L. 1992. "Here's Where It Hurts." In E. Hynes et al. (1992, 9–13).

Miller, N. K. 1992, November. "Cartoons of the Self: Portrait of the Artist as a Young Murderer, Art Spiegelman's *Maus*." *M/E/A/N/I/N/G* 12: 43–54.

Scott, J. W. 1992. "'Experience.'" In *Feminists Theorize the Political*, eds. J. Butler and J. W. Scott, 22–40. London: Routledge.

Spiegelman, A. 1986. *Maus: A Survivor's Tale. I: My Father Bleeds History*. New York: Pantheon Books.

——. 1991. *Maus: A Survivor's Tale, II: And Here My Troubles Began*. New York: Pantheon Books.

Thames Television. 1982. *The World At War: Vol. 20. Genocide*.

"If You Lived Here . . ."

MARTHA ROSLER

Walk through any city these days—here or indeed in most of the world—and you are likely to see people living in the streets. No matter how clean, stylish, or well-swept the city, it is likely to have a street population. My dismay at the way in which people adapted to this new presence of people on the street was weighing heavily in 1988, when I was offered a six-month art show in New York City for the following year. I decided on an installation on urban displacement and homelessness—but I soon realized that the theme was too complex, and the time too short, to allow me to generate a meaningful work alone. My premise was that homelessness required a treatment far more analytic and critical than that usually offered by liberal humanist documentary photography or worse, expressionist laments. Seeing homelessness as an outcome rather than a condition of being, I wanted to show how various social forces endanger the stability of people's living conditions and eventually push many onto the street. I also wanted to bring forward larger issues of social manipulation and urban planning, and to suggest a role for utopian visions.

It seemed a good strategy to assemble the work of many different people in many different media, and with varying perspectives on urban life. The final format of three exhibitions included well over 200 partici-

The exhibitions and forums that I discuss in this essay were held in New York from January through June of 1989. For a further elaboration of the ideas presented here, see Rosler (1991).

Mad Houser hut and other works, from *Homeless: The Street and Other Venues*. The slogan on the wall reads, "Homelessness exists not because the housing system is not working but because this is the way it works" (Peter Marcuse, urbanist). (Photograph: Oren Slor)

pants. Urged by my sponsor, the Dia Art Foundation, to hold public meetings, I arranged forums at which invited speakers made brief presentations, followed by discussion open to everyone present. The project was titled "If You Lived Here . . . ," after a real-estate come-on: "If You Lived Here, You'd Be Home Now." Through every phase of the project, I was fortunate to work with the astute, highly knowledgeable young artist and student of urban planning Dan Wiley.

What argument, in its broad outlines, did I mean to put forward? I'll briefly outline the thinking that drove the project. By the mid-twentieth century, chronic displacement had largely disappeared from the United States, thanks to federal building programs and economic booms. Many of the displaced were housed in accommodations subsidized by the state (albeit sometimes meager, confining, or otherwise problematic). Over the past decade or so, however, changes in political economy, and the results of state policy, created so many displaced persons that "the problem of homelessness" entered social discourse. To understand the great expansion in the number of people living on the streets, in suburbs as well as center cities, one must of course look beyond rising rents and the deinstitutionalization of mentally ill people. One must take into account runaway shops and the larger shift of the economy from productive industry to nonproductive financial and real-estate industries, as well as government policy and the growing income gap between rich and poor. Throughout, ideological shifts in notions of public responsibility and of "the public" itself—not to mention of "the city"—make all the more difficult attempts to understand the failure of present housing policies and to devise solutions.

Irrespective of public and corporate commissions, artists have always been capable of mobilizing around elements of social life; the city is art's habitat. For artists the image of the city's mean streets may feed a certain romantic bohemianism. Because artists often share urban spaces with the poor and underhoused, they have been positioned as both perpetrators and victims in the pernicious processes of urban displacement. They have been represented as a pivotal group, easing the middle-class return to center cities. Ironically, artists themselves are often displaced by the same wealthy professionals—their clientele—who follow them into now-chic neighborhoods. Although my project's main task was a consideration of an underreported, underdescribed, multidetermined set of conditions producing the bald results of homelessness and sadly inadequate housing, it was simultaneously intended to provoke a rethinking of artists' role in urban processes and, further, to suggest how art communities (might) take on such issues. How can artists represent a city's "buried" life, the lives in fact of most city residents? How are artists implicated in forming the image and living model of the city? Many artists engage in direct activism; some work with homeless people in or outside institutional structures; some produce posters and street works; some rehabilitate houses. But there are also many other approaches.

Each exhibition in the three-show cycle embodied a line of argument about the grounding of urban life. Although homelessness was at the project's center, it was the entire focus only in the middle exhibition, *Homeless: The Street and Other Venues*. This was the show covering issues that people surely expected: homeless people, whether visibly living on the streets or in the subways and terminals, or invisibly, in "welfare hotels" or doubled up with relatives. The first exhibition, *Home Front*, was conceived as a set of representations of contested neighborhoods. The last exhibition, *City: Visions and Revisions*, was meant to be "proactive," outlining visions, actual and fanciful, of city life.

There were three routes of address in this project. First were the art works and installations: videotapes, films, and photo works, paintings and drawings, billboards, comics, montages, poems, pamphlets, posters, and so on. Next, statistical graphs and charts were arrayed above eye level, in the gallery equivalent of "waste space." Finally, trying to provide a resource led to the idea of the reading room, a wooden structure reconfigured for each show. Books and journals, photo books, historical and critical studies, and project plans could be read there and a variety of material taken home, from flyers for demonstrations to organizational brochures.

I hoped to establish an ambiance quite different from that of the usual art gallery offering. There was an effort to blur "inside" and "outside," fudging the distinction between the gallery space as a large room and as a world apart, a zone of aestheticism. Because of the reputation and exhibition history (white male, high modernist) of the sponsoring foundation, I thought it crucial to transgress the pristine qualities of the perfect white-walled box. Billboards, street posters, and other exterior works were hung inside. Large maps bristling with flags located the sites of the works shown. There were a couple of "living room" spaces, with couches, rugs, and tables, in which to sit while viewing tapes or reading. The Mad Housers, activist designers from Atlanta, came up and built three huts for homeless people; one was left in the gallery for the duration and the others were erected with and for people in Manhattan and Brooklyn.

The gray-painted gallery front, with its frosted windows, was so self-effacing that even I often walked right on by. We painted a sign saying "Come On In—We're Home" in large red letters on the glass door, and ACT-UP (AIDS Coalition to Unleash Power) pasted posters on AIDS and homelessness on the front portals. A sidewalk text by activist–artist Stuart Nicholson compared shelters for the homeless with Middle East refugee camps. (This "graffito" reportedly ignited a furor among the artists owning condos in the SoHo building housing the gallery.)

Each show had a motto or slogan prominently painted on the wall. For *Home Front*, the truculence of official responses to the housing crisis was indicated by the remark attributed to New York mayor Ed Koch: "If you can't afford to live here, mo-o-ve!" Homeless had a quotation from urbanist Peter Marcuse: "Homelessness exists not because the system is not working but because this is the way it works." For *City: Visions*, the line was from the French uprising of May 1968: "Under the cobblestones, the street," suggesting suppressed links between pleasure, the body, and the city.

The project's public forums provided an opportunity for direct speech, for conversation and exchange between artists, community people, and others—activists, squatters, academics, journalists, politicians.

Works from *Home Front*: Tony Masso, "New Brunswick: Decade Update"; Mel Rosenthal, "The South Bronx, USA"; and Juan Sánchez, "Banderas." (Photograph: Oren Slor)

Home Front's forum was "Housing: Gentrification, Dislocation, and Fighting Back"; *Homeless's*, "Homelessness: Causes, Conditions, Cures"; and for *City: Visions*, "Planning: Power, Politics, and People." During *Home Front* an additional forum, on artists' housing, aroused bitter exchanges. Forum speakers included grass-roots organizers, representatives of groups helping low-income tenants seeking judicial redress, advocates for the homeless, homeless activists, and people in sponsored-scale residences, ACORN organizers and squatters, a New York City councilman and cultural representatives; artists' housing developers; journalists, writers, and scholars, including Marshall Berman, Peter Marcuse, Frances Fox Piven, and Neil Smith; artists and filmmakers, including Cenén, Jamelie Hassan, Adrienne Leban, Bienvenida Matias, Marilyn Nance, and Lori-Jean Saigh; and many participants from the floor.

In the first show, *Home Front*, housing statistics were interspersed with real-estate ads touting luxurious living in pretentiously named Manhattan high-rises, the prose and the poetry of profit—and loss. The term "home front" suggests a war zone, after all, and one outcome of a loss on that front is homelessness. The show also offered help to embattled tenants, directing them to militant neighborhood groups and advocacy organizations. Chinatown History Project members Sam Sue and Andrea Callard constructed a tenement kitchen providing a detailed examination of the narratives of life—historical and contemporary—in Chinatown, through wall texts, a hand-out, and a slide-and-tape show on the area's changing ethnic composition and current (multiracial) tenant organizing.

Puerto Rican artist and *independentista* Juan Sánchez displayed his Bandera paintings, incorporating poems and photographs about "Nuyorican" life. Willie Birch's paintings featured African American and Latino life in Williamsburg, Brooklyn. Marie-Annick Brown's complex installation used official documents and artifacts to follow the history of a Harlem building from its nineteenth-century construction until its recent conversion into condominiums. Tony Masso's photo-text work traced the razing of historic downtown New Brunswick, N.J., by a consortium established by Johnson & Johnson and Rutgers University. Max Becher's photos showed television abodes from *Star Trek* to *Dallas* to *The Jeffersons*. Janet Koenig exhibited imaginary colonizations of city neighborhoods by museum "satellites," while Cindy Feldman's humorous altered postcards showed where homeless people might be housed. Dan Wiley's *Two Waterfronts* carefully documented the differential development by city and state of the East River (poor) and Hudson River (rich) waterfronts of Manhattan.

The activist *Clinton Coalition of Concern* documented some efforts to save their homes in the New York district historically called Hell's Kitchen, about to fall to the monolithic Times Square redevelopment (now stalled by the real-estate crash). It exhibited a paper trail on a building whose residents faced eviction for nonpayment of utility bills, a trail leading to the owner hiding behind a dummy corporation: the utility company itself, Con Edison. Detroit's Urban Center for Photography showed street posters consisting of enlarged photos of decayed or burned-out buildings that they'd nailed onto buildings there, with the stenciled slogan "Demolished by Neglect." *Home Front* set the stage for a consideration of homelessness in the next exhibition.

For this middle show, *Homeless: The Street and Other Venues*, it was critical not to reproduce the dichotomy informing most discussions of homelessness: "us and them." The self-organized group of homeless people, Homeward Bound Community Services, participated in the

Tenement installation by the Chinatown History Project and works by the Urban Center for Photography (Detroit), Dina Bursztyn, and others, from *Home Front*. (Photograph: Oren Slor)

show's conception and maintained an office in the gallery for its duration. They also participated in the forum and held workshops advertised through flyers in the homeless community. Their organizing efforts include both substantive movements toward bettering members' lives and advocacy with municipal agencies. Members of Bullet Space, a Lower East Side artists' squatter building housing a gallery, exhibited paintings and sculpture. There were works by homeless and poor, unprofessionalized artists. New York school classes—organized by teacher–members of Artists/Teachers Concerned—showed works on home and homelessness. The Mad Housers built their three shelters. Bus-bench posters by Robbie Conal and his students at Otis/Parsons offered ironic visions of the nonexistent "L.A.'s official housing project for the homeless." Emmaus House, a Harlem shelter whose residents had work in the exhibition, also sent singers to the opening and speakers to the forum. Residents of New York's Third Street Men's Shelter, organized by painter Rachael Romero,

Works by New York City school children and others, from *Homeless: The Street and Other Venues*. (Photograph: Oren Slor)

contributed a complex collage of drawn and painted elements. In *Homeless* the reading room structure was opened out into a straight wall dividing the gallery. On one side was the library and Homeward Bound's office; on the other, a "shelter" whose beds could only stand unused, symbolic, because of fire laws and the sponsors' wishes. Homeward Bound held public meetings there.

In the third exhibition, *City: Visions and Revisions*, the production of urban space was conceived as a matter of economic and social decisions and as a complex "metasignification." Architects and planners in this exhibition offered some solutions to urban problems—from new designs for urban in-fill housing, to housing for people with AIDS and for homeless families, to utopic visions of cities. Among the architects, David Stainback showed ironic condo plans for the Statue of Liberty and the Washington Monument. Christine Benglia Bevington and Troy West's contributions addressed housing for homeless women and children;

Bevington's in-fill housing plans ranged from private to fully communal and West's plans were for a free-standing group residence. West also collaborated with Jacqueline Leavitt on a high-rise garden plan for Times Square. Gustavo Bonevardi and Lee Ledbetter exhibited plans for AIDS housing in the South Bronx. Part of the ambitious exhibition "Reweaving the Urban Fabric," organized by the New York State Council on the Arts with Richard Plunz and others, offered examples of moderate-income housing from the United States and Western Europe.

Another large-scale photo work, Camilo Vergara and Kenneth Jackson's "Ruins and Revival," indicated how planning choices, architectural designs, and government neglect speed neighborhood decay. London's Docklands Community Poster Project, founded by Loraine Leeson and Peter Dunn, exhibited street works developed with and for residents of London's working-class East End, about to be routed by Canary Wharf, Europe's largest development project (now wounded by the recession along with its mega-developer, Canada's Olympia & York). The Embassy Hotel in London, Ontario, a "skid row" hotel for single men, showed photos of its rooms: environments (not instances of interior decor) done by artists in conjunction with the residents. The Embassy's project organizer, Jamelie Hassan, spoke at the forum.

Community activist William Price's slide-and-tape show described a mid-1970s effort to occupy a group of abandoned Manhattan buildings and obtain city assistance in rehabilitating them. Artist Betti-Sue Hertz, drawing on the work of urban anthropologists and photographers, produced an interpretive installation on *casitas*, small structures resembling Caribbean villas built by Puerto Ricans and Dominicans on empty lots. (The third Mad Houser hut, built in the gallery and moved to a Brooklyn *casita* location, is still in use there.) In *City: Visions* the reading room was a desk on the outside of the hut; inside was a darkened installation by the San Diego–Tijuana Border Art Workshop/Taller de Arte Fronterizo (BAW/TAF) about the eviction of Latino workers, including twenty-year residents from San Diego county's brushy canyons as tract towns spring up—the waste space of displacement under the suburban street.

A number of the project's works were photographic, often documentary. From the start, however, I'd decided not to show works depicting people lying in public places, reasoning that, among other things, if one wished to see homeless people one could step outside. Representing homeless people as abject victims of social circumstance would be to sell them out as surely as do the public policies that put them on the street in the first place. Nevertheless, two wall texts argued for and against photographing the homeless. The "anti" position was mine. The other, by photographer Mel Rosenthal, expressed the hope of thawing people's

Casita project by Betti-Sue Hertz, from *City: Visions and Revisions*. (Photograph: Oren Slor)

numbness. Rosenthal's own works in the project were not of homeless people but of South Bronx residents and of a squatter village in Puerto Rico named Villa Sin Miedo (Town without Fear).

It is worth considering how the makers of more traditional documentaries positioned themselves in relation to the "documentary question." Many were intended as contributions to political struggles; they weren't produced by people who subscribe to the kind of professionalism that measures itself by its distance from its subject. Some hardly question their own means of (re)production. In videotapes like Julia Keydel's *St. Francis Residence* and Arlyn Gajilan's *Not Just a Number*, the interview format is well-adapted to having the unheard speak about their lives. Other films and videotapes were directly activist. For embattled tenants, *Don't Move, Fight Back* (made in conjunction with the upper Manhattan Strycker's Bay tenants' group); *How to Pull a Rent Strike* and *Techos y Derechos* (both by Tami Gold and Steve Krinsky for East Orange, N.J.'s Shelterforce); and *Clinton Coalition of Concern* (by videomaker–member Brian Connell) are rallying tapes, showing people fighting for their homes and providing a blueprint.

Edgar Anstey's *Housing Problems*, made in 1935, shows why London's worst slums had to be razed to make way for public (council) housing. Videomaker Nettie Wild in Vancouver and filmmaker Bienvenida Matias in New York's Lower East Side showed tenants united to save or rehabilitate their homes. (Both women later moved into the projects they studied.) Several tapes, such as Charles Koppelman's *Squatters: The Other Philadelphia Story*, showed successful squatters. Unlike *Techos y Derechos* ("Roofs and Rights"), whose exultant tenants won a court battle, some works followed failures in the making—but even failures can be instructive. Curtis Choy's film *Fall of the I-Hotel* showed the hard-fought but unsuccessful effort to save the International Hotel, which housed aged Filipinos in San Francisco. Filmmakers Nancy Salzer and Pablo Frasconi, in *South Norwalk: Survival of a Small City*, showed poor and working-class residents, primarily Latino and black, being cleared out of a former mill town rehabilitated for white yuppies. In George Corsetti's film *Poletown Lives!*, the city of Detroit tears down a thriving Polish neighborhood to make way for an auto plant. In Jeff Gates's photo work *In Our Path*, a Los Angeles community is razed for a future freeway; and in Erik Davis's videotape *Where Can I Live?* the gentrification of Park Slope, Brooklyn, displaces poor Latino residents. Clayton Patterson's four-hour tape of the 1988 Tompkins Square police riot provides an unprecedented look at one aspect of the gentrification struggle.

Some photo works are strategically skewed. In Dan Higgins' humorous *Onion Portraits*, groups of residents of the Vermont town Winooski ("onion" in the local Indian language), from the fire company to the church to the local bar, hold onions in ones, twos, and bunches. The work suggests the tight bonds in working-class Winooski, a former mill town under severe gentrification stress from nearby Burlington. Problematizing documentary's historic reliance on physiognomy, Mark Berghash puts huge closeups of people's faces together with first-person texts or tapes. Some are people in terrible circumstances, such as homelessness, and others are rich, but who's who?

Some photographers reject "humanist" documentary, with its multiplicity of buried texts about powerlessness. Rhonda Wilson, of Birmingham, England, wittily staged images for her poster series on women and homelessness in England. Directly interrogating the voyeurism and "imperialism" of documentary photography, Greg Sholette incorporated Jacob Riis's photo *Police Station Lodgers . . . in the West 47th Street Police Station* into a sculptural relief whose conceit centers on the interpretation of a woman's smile. In many cases, subjects made works about their lives. *2371 Second Avenue* (East Harlem) and *Life in the G: Gowanus Gentrified* (Brooklyn) were videotapes made by Latino teenagers and the Educational Video Center, while the photos and documents that African American photographer Marilyn Nance made of her city-owned Brooklyn building were used as evidence in the tenants' successful court case to manage their own building. These artists, like many in the three shows, were conscious of the need to rethink the means of representation and to speak from positions different from the usual ones.

Who saw these shows? Many people, including artists and students, come to SoHo; many visited the Dia gallery and saw the shows. Some visitors saw the show and its library as a resource; teachers also brought their classes. The static presuppositions some critics applied to these shows surprised me; they seemed to forget that art-world audiences aren't born but constructed, laboriously, like any constituency. Each element— shows, forums, poetry readings, screenings, workshops—was separately advertised. Some project fliers and mainstream news articles didn't mention the art connection. The diverse people making up the project brought people from their own professions and social circles, as well as politicians, church workers, and friends. It is likely that Dia and I had differing aims in producing this project. They saw it as furthering their publication series on timely social and artistic topics. I intended to open the gallery to those who might not normally visit a SoHo show and to look at homelessness without sentimentality or reductiveness; I hoped that the project and its accompanying book might be part of the discourses of a wider activism that includes artists and draws on complex analyses of the spaces and conditions of modern life and identity.

For the project's book, published in 1991, I chose a cover photo showing the demolition of the Pruitt-Igoe housing project in St. Louis— an act marking the moment of postmodernism, according to architectural historian Charles Jencks. Coincidentally, in 1992 I was invited by the Washington University Art Gallery in St. Louis to mount an installation on homelessness. Conditions in this hypersegregated city are very different from those in New York. Virtually all the homeless are African American, and city services are routed through the Catholic Church. Providers are highly paternalistic or evangelistic, and there are no self-organized homeless activists or advocates. The housing groups I worked with were Habitat for Humanity, church-run groups, and the grass-roots group ACORN—the only activist group I could find. In St. Louis, ACORN organizes for tenants' rights, acting through demonstrations, agitation, and law suits. Art works were exhibited by clients of a women's self-help center (outside the church ambit) and residents of homes run by the Salvation Army, the Catholic Church, mainstream Protestant churches, and evangelical groups, black and white. Emerging from the back wall was half of a low-cost home for single people designed by the School of Architecture faculty member Tom Thompson, built there by his students.

During the research for this exhibition I conducted a video interview of a university gallery employee who'd grown up in Pruitt-Igoe; he'd witnessed its demolition from the window of his elementary school classroom. His story of Pruitt-Igoe is very different from the usual narrative of misplaced civic liberal schema lost on the unruly, poor, black population. (I'm currently in the process of editing this video interview.) Reworking or reframing images of homeless or precariously housed people takes place in a larger social context, in which the image of marginalization itself must constantly be challenged. Changing social reality requires simultaneously challenging simplifying overlaid images and the routes to representation.

REFERENCE

Rosler, M. 1991. *If You Lived Here . . .: The City in Art, Theory, and Social Activism,* ed. Brian Wallis. Seattle: Bay Press.

PART THREE

THE STATE, DEMOCRACY, SOCIALISM, AND REVOLUTION

Subjectivism and Democratic Firms: A Response to Hayek's Critique of Socialism

THEODORE BURCZAK

Throughout his life, the Austrian economist Friedrich Hayek was a harsh critic of socialism and an advocate of classical liberalism. Whether he was writing in economics, political theory, philosophy, or legal theory, his motive was partly to show that the idea of socialism rested on faulty intellectual foundations. Hayek identified socialism with two ideas: that the state can coordinate the economy more rationally than spontaneous market forces, and that a socialist state can be a catalyst for social justice. He believed that socialism was virtually defined by both of these ideas, and he argued that if these two ideas were invalid, socialism was invalid as well. For Hayek, who wrote from a subjectivist perspective that emphasized the impossibility of objective knowledge and the limits of reason, both social justice and central planning were "mirages" and "fatal conceits" that provided weak grounds for a socialist project.

My aim is to address Hayek's critique of socialism and to explore whether a defense of socialism can be constructed that remains broadly consistent with his subjectivism. This task seems especially important for the Left, given the new prominence Hayek's thought has assumed. For instance, the crisis of 1989 is taken by many to be a vindication of Hayek's life-long project to discredit the idea of socialism. Many Eastern European economists are increasingly turning to Hayek's writings for direction, and George Bush awarded him the Medal of Freedom in 1991. Hayek, it seems, has become one of the new heroes of the capitalist reaction. I believe, however, that if socialism is conceived as the collective, democratic appropriation of surplus labor, rather than as a centrally planned economy that is a mechanism for social justice, socialism can survive on Hayek's subjectivist intellectual terrain.

HAYEK'S CRITIQUE OF SOCIALISM

The heart of Hayek's critique of socialism is epistemological: Socialists, he tells us, overestimate, and perhaps more significantly, misunderstand human reason. He maintains that socialism rests on the possibility of obtaining and centralizing objective knowledge, knowledge of resource scarcities, costs, technology, preferences, and the "social good." According to Hayek, socialism is inseparable from the idea that the state can centralize this objective knowledge in order to coordinate and distribute economic resources more rationally and justly than spontaneous and anarchic market forces.

Against the modernist belief in the power of human reason to attain objective knowledge, Hayek poses the notion of subjectivism and the related concept of the market as a discovery process. In brief, subjectivism entails the view that *all* perception is irreducibly subjective; that is, it is impossible to obtain an isomorphism between human perception and the "real" world. Thus, in Hayek's thought, not only are consumer preferences subjective—a point readily accepted by most contemporary economists—but so too is the perception of costs, profit, and technology—a point not often considered. To emphasize the centrality of subjectivism, he claims that the economic problem is how to coordinate what he calls dispersed knowledge, that is, scattered individual's subjective perceptions of economic opportunity (Hayek 1948). What marks this thought as particularly unique is his attempt to build a theory of the market and a defense of laissez faire on subjectivist principles. Subjectivism, he insists, knocks to the ground what he identifies as the two key pillars of socialist thought: the state's superiority at economic coordination and the state's ability to achieve social justice.

The benefit of the market, according to Hayek (1978), is that it facilitates a competitive process that allows individuals to discover whether their subjective perceptions of economic opportunity are warranted, given others' subjective preferences and perceptions. For instance, the pressures of competition test the compatibility of entrepreneurs' perceptions of profit with others' subjective tastes. The competitive market process is thus a process of discovery of consumer demands and new, more efficient methods of production. And it is precisely this competitive discovery process that produces the unintended consequence of coordinating dispersed and subjectively held knowledge. The market discovery process coordinates economic activity in ways that central planning cannot replicate. A plan can only express planners' limited perceptions of preferences, scarcities, and technologies, thereby neglecting much of the economic knowledge that necessarily exists only as the subjective knowledge of diverse individuals.

To reinforce his critique of central planning, Hayek also draws a distinction between "knowledge how" and "knowledge that" in order to explain why much subjective knowledge guiding human action cannot be communicated to state officials (1988, 78). People may "know how" to perform a certain action without being able to articulate how or why they "know that" an action might produce a particular result. "Knowledge how" encompasses rule-guided, intuitive knowledge, which Hayek believes guides much human conduct in all spheres of activity, including the economic. Because "knowledge how" is intrinsically individual and inarticulate, planning boards cannot incorporate this knowledge in their instructions. Thus, in a planned economy the subjective knowledge of most individuals would not be utilized because it cannot be expressed to a central agency. In order for "knowledge how" to be socially useful, individuals must be free to act upon it. For Hayek (1973, 55–56), freedom is "a state in which each can use his knowledge for his purposes," a state that he presumes private property and the freedom of contract uniquely enables.

The second important aspect of Hayek's critique of socialism is also connected with his subjectivism. He describes socialist theory as infected with a brand of animism that conceives the economy as if it were directed by a single, rational mind. "Imagining that all order is the result of design," Hayek writes, "socialists conclude that order must be improvable by better design of some superior mind" (1988, 108). Socialist thinkers, Hayek maintains, are propelled by the belief that the outcomes of the market process serve particular group interests, thereby giving socialists the goal of using state power to make the economy serve the common interest by rationally designing economic outcomes to achieve a truly common good, or social justice. But the market, counters Hayek, does not serve any group or general interest. He depicts a market economy as an ever-evolving order under the direction of no one. Since he understands evolutionary processes to be neither just nor unjust, Hayek believes it is an intellectual error to suppose that the market process is biased towards the interests of any particular group. Moreover, the idea that government can implement some objectively definable common interest cannot stand if we acknowledge that it is impossible for government to discover the nature of this supposed common interest, since individuals have subjective and diverse notions of what constitutes a just society.

SOCIALISM AS DEMOCRATIC APPROPRIATION

Although many economists understand Hayek's critique of socialism to have been refuted during the 1930s and 1940s by various proposals for market socialism, it is becoming increasingly understood that Hayek's subjectivism was not appreciated and that the market socialists did not meet his charges. For example, Oscar Lange's famous blueprint for market socialism preserves a central planning board that possesses the ability to acquire objective knowledge of costs, technology, and resource availability, enabling it to monitor the productive activities of socialist firms (Lippincott 1972). But as Robin Blackburn (1991, 38) points out, Hayek's critique of the market socialists "could only really have been met by a case for socialist self-management and public enterprise that based itself on the dispersed character of economic knowledge." And as far as I am aware, there has yet to appear a systematic defense of socialism that takes seriously Hayek's notion of dispersed and subjectively held knowledge. The rest of this paper sketches such a defense by advocating the collective, democratic appropriation of surplus labor.

To start, we should note that it is possible to define socialism independently of both social justice and central planning. Marx (1978, 532), for instance, dismissed socialist projects centered on government redistribution of income because such projects left intact capitalist relations of production. For Marx, socialism did not involve redistributing income generated in capitalist firms, or some other potentially worthy goal, but rather transforming class relations (i.e., the abolition of capitalist exploitation and the implementation of collective production and appropriation of surplus labor). Marx is often interpreted as supporting the replacement of the market by central planning in order to end the capitalist production and appropriation of surplus labor. But strictly speaking, Marxian exploitation does not occur in exchange; it occurs in production, so that central planning may or may not be associated with collective production and appropriation. If we are willing to grant Hayek's subjectivist arguments against central planning, we must turn to other institutional forms consistent with collective production and appropriation. One direction we might turn is to the many proposals for cooperatives or worker-managed firms.

One such proposal is Stephen Cullenberg's "thin" definition of socialism. Cullenberg (1992, 76) defines socialism as a form of society in which surplus labor is appropriated collectively, by which he means that at the initial site of surplus labor production, "all individuals employed at that site share equally (one person, one vote) in the appropriation of the surplus labor." In other words, collective appropriation could take place in democratic firms that operate in an unregulated market economy. This definition of socialism as the collective, democratic appropriation of surplus labor is "thin" in the sense that it does not necessarily imply anything about income distribution, the form of property ownership, environmental conservation, the end of gender and racial oppression—in short, social justice. It does, however, require workers to have an equal voice in determining how surplus labor is appropriated.

I do not mean to suggest that the goals often associated with social justice are unworthy. But to identify socialism with social justice—a "thick" definition of socialism that contains a laundry list of items often identified as constituting the common good—establishes an unreachable goal and exposes it to Hayek's critique of socialism as a rationalist utopia. The spirit of a "thin" definition, on the other hand, seems consistent with Hayek's subjectivist rejection of the attempt to institute a broad-based social agenda founded on the idea of a collective purpose that the state can realize. In addition, the definition of socialism as the collective appropriation of surplus labor in democratic firms does not fall prey to Hayek's criticisms of central planning.

Hayek's writings contain a few hints about how he might have responded to a socialist project aiming at the democratic appropriation of surplus labor. For instance, he contends, "It is by no means obvious that a person who finds it in his interest to sell his services should thereby also acquire a voice in its conduct or in determining the purposes towards which this organization is to be directed" (Hayek 1979, 39). But surely we could just as well ask whether it is by any means obvious that a person who sells the services of capital should thereby acquire a voice in the conduct or in determining the goals of the firm. Whether a firm is run in the interests of capital or labor is a question that must be decided on either moral or efficiency grounds, and I believe that on both of these grounds a stronger argument can be made for labor's interests rather than capital's.

First, as Cullenberg (1992, 78) points out, there is no reason why firms should not be run in the interests of workers: "If one rejects collective appropriation one also rejects the right of individuals to participate on an equal footing in making decisions concerning issues that are of central importance to their lives." However, if there is no objective standard by which some individuals are able to judge others' interests, it is difficult not to allow individuals to participate as equals in decisions affecting their well-being. This argument strikes Hayek in a vulnerable area. Part of his stance against central planning is that markets allow individuals to pursue courses of action that they believe might be in their best interests; central planning, in Hayek's view, necessarily thwarts at least some individuals' attempts to test their perceptions of self-interest. Yet when Hayek defends economic freedom, he regards individuals only as consumers or entrepreneurs; he neglects the fact that many people spend a considerable part of their lives as workers in a hierarchical structure in which they are frequently told what is good for them.

It seems, then, that Hayek implicitly adopts the position that workers can be told what is in their best interests. If so, there is a tension in Hayek's liberalism in his attempt to distinguish between individuals in their role as consumers, who are allowed to participate in determining what is in their interests, and individuals in their role as workers, who are not allowed to participate in decisions regarding their well-being. Unlike capitalist appropriation, democratic appropriation facilitates worker involvement in workplace decisions that have important consequences for their lives. This argument is consonant with Hayek's opposition to planning because it limits individuals' exploration of their interests. Democratic appropriation enables people to explore their interests at work in the same way that Hayek argues they are able to explore their interests in the market.

Of course, defenders of free-market capitalism, including Hayek, typically assume full employment, so that if workers do not like the way they are treated on the job, they are free to cross the street and find another source of employment. In this way, classical liberals suppose that workers can choose what is in their self-interest. But a consistent subjectivist economics, an economics that extends subjectivism to the treatment of expectations, calls into question Hayek's assumption that a market economy is a full-employment, spontaneous order. John Maynard Keynes' most revolutionary insight was that objective knowledge of the future is impossible, which forces economic actors, particularly investors, to base their decisions on highly subjective and unstable expectations of the likely outcomes of events. From this Keynes (1937, 218) concluded, "It is not surprising that the volume of investment," and the level of employment, "should fluctuate widely from time to time." For Keynes, full employment occurred in a market economy only by accident. Thus, by extending subjectivism to the theory of expectations, Keynes' economics denies the legitimacy of Hayek's full employment assumption. If we use subjectivism to invalidate the assumption of full employment, the categories of Hayek's own thought suggest that capital owners can exercise illegitimate coercive power over workers, since capitalists monopolize and restrict access to the means of production.

In *The Constitution of Liberty*, Hayek (1960, 133) argues that a liberal society strives to minimize coercion because coercion restricts people's ability to explore their interests. He defines coercion as occurring "when one man's actions are made to serve another man's will, not for his own but for the other's purpose." Significantly, he believes monopolists can wield this illegitimate power "whenever they are in a position to withhold an indispensable supply," like a monopolist of spring water in the middle of a desert (1960, 136). But from this perspective, in a market economy populated by people with subjective expectations, individual capital owners can wield coercive power over their workers because normally jobs are not necessarily available for all those seeking employment. Capital owners possess an indispensable supply of the means of production, and they are not always willing to make this supply available. Consequently, the authority to direct production and the threat of firing wielded by capital owners are coercive in the same sense as is the threat to withhold water made by the monopolist of a spring. One implication of a subjectivist macroeconomic theory that extends subjectivism to expectations and rejects the full-employment assumption is that capitalist appropriation involves coercion.

Along with his belief that capitalists do not coerce workers, Hayek also advances an instrumental defense of capitalist appropriation. According to Hayek (1967, 303), the democratic appropriation of surplus labor is inefficient because it restricts managers' ability to discipline workers and because it discourages efficient risk-taking. Let us take each of these arguments in turn.

Bowles and Gintis (1993) contest the claim that capitalist firms are necessarily the most efficient institutions of production. They argue that it is quite conceivable that firms in which workers democratically appropriate surplus labor would actually utilize resources more efficiently than capitalist firms.[1] Bowles and Gintis reach this conclusion by pointing out that capitalist firms must expend tremendous resources monitoring the productive activities of workers. They show that firms can reap efficiency gains by transferring claims to the surplus to inputs that are hard to monitor, for instance labor. When workers appropriate surplus labor, they have less incentive to shirk and to act uncooperatively, since they rather than capital owners receive the benefits of their efforts.

Bowles and Gintis also discuss the assertion that firms that democratically appropriate surplus labor would discourage risk-taking. They acknowledge Hayek's argument that risk-taking, or what they call entrepreneurship, is a difficult-to-monitor input that might be promoted only by giving external owners at least some control of the firm and a partial claim to surplus labor. From Bowles and Gintis's perspective, there is a trade-off between the democratic appropriation of surplus labor and innovation. To minimize this trade-off, Ellerman (1990, 202–205) proposes that democratic firms issue "profit-sharing securities" that do not give the holder any control rights but do promise a mandatory, variable return tied to the firm's performance. In this way, risk could be shared with external "owners" without workers ceding control over the firm.

There might be other beneficial, unintended consequences of democratic appropriation to consider, as well. For instance, workers might be more apt to address local externalities created by their firms than would absentee capital owners, since workers generally live near their places of employment. In addition, from a Hayekian perspective we might view democratic appropriation as a means of institutionalizing a setting in which workers could report their subjective perceptions of economic opportunity, for instance, their perception of a more efficient technology. Insofar as capitalist firms frequently do not utilize workers' perceptions of potential technological or marketing improvements, firms in which surplus labor is democratically appropriated might be more innovative than capitalist firms. Finally, there is an extensive literature criticizing capitalism for undermining communities that are necessary to sustain an individual's sense of self and belonging. Firms in which surplus labor is democratically appropriated might alleviate the sense of alienation that communitarians believe capitalism encourages.

Despite assertions to the contrary, I believe socialism can survive on Hayek's subjectivist terrain. If we accept Hayek's subjectivism, the identification of socialism with central planning and proposals for market socialism like Lange's, in which the state instructs and supervises enterprises about how to produce, are called into question. In addition, if we accept Hayek's subjectivism, an objective notion of social justice seems to be an altogether slippery concept, a concept requiring considerable work to rehabilitate on subjectivist grounds. However, the definition of socialism as the democratic appropriation of surplus labor disentangles socialism from the belief that the state should plan production and promote social justice, thereby sidestepping Hayek's critique. Thus, if socialism is conceived as involving collective, democratic forms of the class process, the recent announcements of the death of the socialist ideal at Hayek's hands are premature.

NOTE

1. To be precise, Bowles and Gintis do not use a notion of surplus labor. They speak of the democratic firm as making workers "residual claimants."

REFERENCES

Blackburn, R. 1991, January–February. "Fin de Siècle: Socialism after the Crash." *New Left Review* 185: 5–66.
Bowles, S. and Gintis, H. 1993. "The Democratic Firm: An Agency Theoretic Evaluation." In *Markets and Democracy: Participation, Accountability and*

Efficiency, eds. S. Bowles, H. Gintis, and B. Gustafsson. Cambridge, England: Cambridge University Press.

Cullenberg, S. 1992, Summer. "Socialism's Burden: Toward a 'Thin' Definition of Socialism." *Rethinking Marxism* 5: 64–83.

Ellerman, D. P. 1990. *The Democratic Worker-Owned Firm*. Boston: Unwin Hyman.

Hayek, F. A. 1948. "The Use of Knowledge in Society." In *Individualism and Economic Order*, F. A. Hayek, 77–91. Chicago: University of Chicago Press.

——. 1960. *The Constitution of Liberty*. Chicago: University of Chicago Press.

——. 1967. "The Corporation in a Democratic Society." In *Studies in Philosophy, Politics and Economics*, F. A. Hayek, 300–312. Chicago: University of Chicago Press.

——. 1973. *Law, Legislation and Liberty*, Vol. I. *Rules and Order*. Chicago: University of Chicago Press.

——. 1978. "Competition as a Discovery Procedure." In *New Studies in Politics, Economics and the History of Ideas*, F. A. Hayek, 179–190. Chicago: University of Chicago Press.

——. 1979. *Law, Legislation and Liberty*, Vol. III. *The Political Order of a Free People*. Chicago: University of Chicago Press.

——. 1988. *The Fatal Conceit. The Errors of Socialism*. Chicago: University of Chicago Press.

Keynes, J. M. 1937, February. "The General Theory of Employment." *Quarterly Journal of Economics* 51: 209–223.

Lippincott, B., ed. 1972. *On the Economic Theory of Socialism*. Minneapolis: University of Minnesota Press.

Marx, K. 1978. "Critique of the Gotha Program." In *The Marx-Engels Reader*, 2nd edition, ed. R. C. Tucker, 525–541. New York: W. W. Norton.

Post-Marxism and Class

BLAIR SANDLER
JONATHAN DISKIN

In contemporary radical social theory, concepts of radical democracy have been used to level a critique against classical Marxism. This critique and reorientation, labeled post-Marxism by Laclau and Mouffe, in their important book, *Hegemony and Socialist Strategy* (1985), draws upon resources in the Marxist *tradition*, but challenges the logic of Marxian *theory*. The latter, Laclau and Mouffe argue, has imposed limits on the liberatory potential of movements for social change by reducing political movements and historical subjects to a closed logic of necessary economic laws. This closed Marxism mapped out a space for necessity that failed to theorize politics adequately as a moment of instability and openness in which an "objectified" notion of the social, as a space defined by its laws of motion, is subject to radical dislocation and overdetermination by "subversive exteriors," which are not themselves determined by the logic of necessity. As Laclau argues, "'Politics' is an ontological category: there is politics because there is subversion and dislocation of the social" (1990, 61).

While classical Marxism is certainly replete with any number of reductions and instances of "theoretical closure," the post-Marxist critique of this closure (and the work of Laclau and Mouffe in particular), produces its own peculiar reductions and omissions that it is our aim to elucidate. Unlike other critics of Laclau and Mouffe, however, we strongly endorse the anti-essentialism of their work and their focus on the importance of the constructed and discursive nature of social relationships and identities.[1] In the present essay we presume this shared commitment, and focus our attention on their failure to extend their anti-essentialist, reconstructive gaze to the economy itself.[2]

We argue that Laclau and Mouffe conflate the tradition of methodological essentialism in Marxism with the concepts of Marxian class analysis themselves, especially the commodity status of labor power and class exploitation. In their analysis of labor power as a commodity, Laclau and Mouffe (and Bowles and Gintis 1981, on whom they draw) attempt to demonstrate the closure of Marxist theory and point the way toward their radical democratic alternative. They refer to the concept of labor power as a commodity (LPAC) as a "fiction" and argue that through this concept Marx reduced subjects to the necessity of economic laws. However, Laclau and Mouffe's brilliant analysis of economism in the classical Marxist tradition leads to an unfortunate rejection of Marxism *tout court*, and a needless repudiation of the Marxian concepts of class and exploitation. They displace Marxian economic analyses of capitalism that utilize notions of class exploitation, in favor of a schematic and empiricist political economic history of capitalism. This latter—surprisingly, given the detailed and careful effort at extending and reconstructing concepts such as hegemony—simply assumes the obviousness of key concepts, such as commodification, indicating the lack of a well-specified economic dimension to their post-Marxist project.[3]

But, as we argue, the concept of LPAC and the class notions of exploitation with which it is associated, are neither essentialist nor nonessentialist in themselves. The concepts of LPAC and class exploitation may be transformed through their rearticulation in nonessentialist logics. However, this possibility appears to be ruled out by design in the emerging post-Marxist tradition. At stake is what it means to conceptualize capitalism as we move beyond essentialist conceptions throughout many realms of theory and practice.

MARXISM AND CLOSURE

Laclau and Mouffe argue that classical Marxism developed into a closed theoretical space in which the laws of motion of the economy were thought to exert necessary effects. A teleology of history was produced in which political development and the emergence of class actors followed directly from the development of the capitalist economy itself. Importantly, it is the conceptual terrain of class analysis which, for Laclau and Mouffe, closes the space of Marxism. For class refers us to both the "objective" structure of capitalism and the "subjective" identity of agents. Class essentialism thus binds these two elements together.

The terrain of Marxian theory, at least through Gramsci, according to Laclau and Mouffe, can be seen as an attempt to maintain the validity of this *logic of necessity* in the face of an increasing number of special cases, contingent events, setbacks, workers acting against their "class interests," and so on. The logic of necessity was supported by a variety of *logics of contingency* that sought to show how such contingent events could be understood as temporary deviations, national variations, or epiphenomenal side events, and thus did not fundamentally alter the logic of necessity. They present a genealogy of Marxism as a series of strategies designed to reconcile political movements and identities with economic developments that increasingly seemed inadequate to insure a socialist sentiment. In particular, Marxism needed continually to link the formation of a revolutionary agent, class subjects, to economic developments in order to produce a closed discursive space in which politics and economics were converging on a socialist future.

First, Kautskian simplicity created a social space of "*pure relations of interiority.* We can pass from working class to capitalists, from the economic sphere to the political sphere, from manufacture to monopoly capitalism, without having to depart for one instant from the internal rationality and intelligibility of a closed paradigm" (Laclau and Mouffe 1985, 16, emphasis in original).

A second strategy was dualism, which sought to identify important logics of contingency and to show how they might relate to the interior logic of necessary development. However, logics of contingency are either reduced to manifestations of necessity (as different tempos, rhythms, and national variations, which will converge back to necessity), or these other logics disappear "into the general terrain of contingent variation, or [are] referred to entities escaping all theoretical determination, such as will or ethical decision" (1985, 48). In short, "economic fragmentation was unable to constitute class unity and referred us on to political recomposition; yet political recomposition was unable to found the *necessary* class character of social agents" (48).

Finally, Gramsci's concept of hegemony "fills a space left vacant by a crisis of what should have been a normal historical development. For that reason, the hegemonization of a task or an ensemble of political forces belongs to the terrain of historical contingency" (1985, 48). Yet, even in Gramsci's focus on the constitutive role of ideology and the formation of class consciousness, the identity of agents is "constituted in a terrain different from that in which the hegemonic practices operate." This is the "inner essentialist core which continues to be present in Gramsci's thought, setting a limit to the deconstructive logic of hegemony"(1985, 70). In order to remove these limits, and thereby move beyond essentialism, Laclau and Mouffe turn their attention to that which stands as the anchor of this discourse, the economy itself.

THE ECONOMY: THE LAST REDOUBT OF ESSENTIALISM

At the root of this persistent class essentialism in the Marxist tradition, they argue, is an economistic concept of the economy itself. The economy is a discursive space that imparts a direction to history: "If history has a sense and a rational substratum, it is due to the general law of development of the productive forces" (Laclau and Mouffe 1985, 77). But if this law is to have full validity, "it is necessary that all the elements intervening in the productive process be submitted to its determinations" (1985, 78). That is, if the economy is to structure the space of the social as necessity, then the elements of the economy itself must not introduce new and unforeseen determination into this closed space. In particular, agents, as economic forces, must have a unified identity rooted in "the economic level" and its "laws of motion." In order for this proposition to follow, human labor power must be understood as an internal moment of the objective process of economic development; that is, labor power must be brought within the logic of necessity. "To ensure this, Marxism had to resort to a fiction: it conceived of labour-power as a commodity" (1985, 78). Thus, LPAC operates to submit workers to the determination of the forces of production—and closes a space in the field of the economic where the subversive "exterior" power of human subjects might have intervened. Here, in a nutshell, is the pivotal role that LPAC plays in the post-Marxist "proof" of Marxist closure: LPAC is the keystone of economism because it is the *economic* concept that reduces the "subjective" to "objective" forces. Let us examine how Laclau and Mouffe "demonstrate" the reductive closure of the economic space in Marxism before we turn to some implications for their social analysis of capitalism.

THE SPECIFICITY OF LABOR POWER

Why, for Laclau and Mouffe, is labor power *not* a commodity? Consider the *differentia specifica* of labor power:

> Labour-power differs from the other necessary elements of production in that the capitalist must do more than simply purchase it; he must also make it produce labour. This essential aspect, however, escapes the conception

of labour-power as a commodity whose use-value is labour. For if it were merely a commodity like the others, its use-value could obviously be made automatically effective from the very moment of its purchase. "The designation of labour as the use-value of labour-power to capital obscures the absolutely fundamental distinction between productive inputs embodied in people capable of social practices and all those remaining inputs for whom ownership by capital is sufficient to secure the 'consumption' of their productive services." (1985, 78)[4]

When the post-Marxists claim that labor power is "embodied in people capable of social practices," we can only agree. The problem we have is not with their conception of labor power as an active, socially overdetermined process, but with their conception of the commodity form. Implicitly, Laclau and Mouffe have defined the concept "commodity" through their insistence that, in contrast to noncommodities such as labor power, the use value of a commodity can "be made automatically effective from the very moment of its purchase." Such a formulation suggests that commodities, through the ownership relation and the very passivity of the commodity, are fully subject to the logic of capital. In the realm of capitalist production, ownership confers power onto a logic that has not itself been constructed. With this conception, ironically, the logic of capital is not eliminated from the post-Marxist conception of the economy, but merely denied one of its objects: labor power.

We argue, in contrast, that there are *no* commodities whose use-value is automatically effective from the moment of purchase, that ownership by capital is *never* sufficient to secure the consumption of a commodity's productive services. The post-Marxist argument suggests that because workers can change the circumstances of their "consumption" through negotiation and strategic behavior, political practices subvert any pure logic of capital. Politics is taken to be an "exterior," which overdetermines production and therefore undermines the closed space of the logic of capital. Again, we can only agree with the notion of an exterior that shatters the seamless unity of an expressive totality. However, the post-Marxist focus on the exercise of power and the claims of property rights required to consume labor power should not blind us to the "openness" of production and the creation of value in general, to the force not only of power but of many constitutive "exteriors."

The ability of a commodity-owning capitalist to "productively consume" inputs is overdetermined by a host of conditions of existence, including the natural, political, and cultural. The consumption of steel, for example (and the transfer of its value to different capitalist commodities), depends upon the legal framework that may protect domestic markets; consumer preferences for imports versus domestic goods;

changing technologies of production and transport; cultural movements, such as environmentalism, which may result in subsidies, taxes, boycotts; and so on. Ownership of steel, in other words, is *not* sufficient to insure the use-value of steel.

If we truly wish to break with the determinism and essentialism noted by Laclau and Mouffe, we should not reject the commodity status of labor power on logical grounds. Rather, we must reject the notion of an internal logic of capital (as they do in the case of labor power), and assert that *no* object or process (including, of course, labor power) exists only as an expression of such a logic. When attention is restricted to the political processes of agency, then labor power appears to be radically different from all other inputs. But when such political relationships are conceived as only one of the many conditions of existence and "exteriors" for the consumption of commodities, then labor power is like all other commodities in the sense that they are overdetermined by non-economic processes of all sorts.

Throughout their "genealogy of hegemony" Laclau and Mouffe argue against "class essentialism," as they do all essentialisms. But their deconstruction of economism does more than simply displace essentialist logic: The rejection of LPAC undercuts the specifically Marxist conception of capitalist exploitation: the appropriation of surplus value created by workers who sell their labor power as a commodity. The post-Marxists' rejection of the commodity status of labor power leads them to reject Marx's approach to value analysis and class as the production, appropriation, and distribution of surplus labor time, and leaves no concept of economic exploitation in its place.

THE ECONOMIC DISCOURSE OF POST-MARXISM

The post-Marxist theoretical treatment of the concepts LPAC and commodity illustrates a general weakness of post-Marxism: Economic discourse tends to suffer from "an essentialism of the elements" (1985, 103). Rather than recognizing that economic concepts are overdetermined by their discursive conditions of existence, Laclau and Mouffe treat them as essentialist "things in themselves." For with the post-Marxist rejection of classical Marxist notions of LPAC, class, and exploitation, there reappears a stage theory of capitalism, based on other classical Marxist economic concepts, invoked later in *Hegemony and Socialist Strategy* as the "empirical" context in which subject positions are arrayed. Now, the post-Marxist use of Marxian concepts is not in itself a contradiction, as Laclau and Mouffe themselves write after their rejection of essentialist logics of necessity:

> This is the point at which many of the concepts of classical analysis—"cen-
> tre", "power", "autonomy", etc.—can be reintroduced, if their status is re-
> defined: all of them are contingent social logics which, as such, acquire
> their meaning in precise conjunctural and relational contexts, where they
> will always be limited by other—frequently contradictory—logics; but none
> of them has absolute validity, in the sense of defining a space or structural
> moment which could not in its turn be subverted. (1985, 142)

Yet their language belies the "subversion" and limitation of "logics"
they profess. Following Aglietta's description of Fordism, for example,
Laclau and Mouffe note the "spread of capitalist relations of production
to the whole set of social relations, and the subordination of the latter to
the logic of production for profit." This "logic of production for profit,"
named later in the same paragraph the "logic of capitalist accumulation"
(1985, 161), in turn gives rise to the trajectory of contemporary capitalism itself: "the commodification, bureaucratization and increasing
homogenization of social life" (164). This analysis is further underscored
by the claim that the "'commodification' of social life destroyed previous social relations, replacing them with commodity relations through
which the logic of capitalist accumulation penetrated into increasingly
numerous spheres"(161). To us, it is not clear how such statements differ from notions about the laws of motion of capitalism that Laclau and
Mouffe have spent so much time deconstructing. Either the logic of commodification is the logic of capital (clearly a conflation), or else there is
no reason—certainly none given—why the former should imply the latter. Historical processes are not obvious empirical facts to be taken as
given, but require explicit theoretical elaboration.

Laclau and Mouffe portray capitalism as a total historical force field,
a homogeneous space that serves as the context within which overdetermined subjects are constituted.[5] There is a tension between this
capitalism, and the careful deconstruction in *Hegemony and Socialist Strategy* of logics of necessity. By the very logic of hegemony, articulation and
overdetermination, which must refer to concepts as they do to subjects,
the Marxist economic categories on which Laclau and Mouffe depend
could not simply be taken over and given a new logic without going
through an entire process of conceptual rearticulation. The meaning of
these economic concepts was originally constructed precisely within an
essentialist discourse. But Laclau and Mouffe have *disintegrated* that discourse: "A conception which denies any essentialist approach to social
relations, must also state the precarious character of every identity and
the impossibility of fixing the sense of the 'elements' in any ultimate literality" (1985, 96). Laclau notes that "adding heterogeneous elements
and concepts is not enough to build a unified theoretical framework; it

is the logical articulation between [the concepts] that must be shown" (1990, 223). Unfortunately, Laclau and Mouffe have failed to produce the "logical articulation" among economic concepts that is necessary to formulate a properly nonessentialist economic sphere. Thus, those Marxist economic concepts that appear in Laclau and Mouffe's analysis act as abstract place holders, so many "empirical referents" (1985, 143), which without explicit articulation to the new discourse of *Hegemony and Socialist Strategy* (which these concepts never receive), have no theoretical content. As Althusser once noted, "ideology rushes in to fill the vacuum produced when the obviousness of empirical description replaces theory (1979, 110).

For us, the appearance of untheorized economic concepts in the second half of *Hegemony and Socialist Strategy* represents a major consequence of the failure to extend the nonessentialist reconceptualization to the categories of political economy, and points to the terrain of politics on which these concepts are now situated: "The space of the economy is itself structured as a political space" (1985, 77). Concepts once Marxist now buttress an economic discourse dominated by concepts of power, inequality, and ownership. In Marxism, too, of course, there is power, inequality, and ownership, but there these concepts are articulated in a discourse with class exploitation as mutual conditions of existence. In *Hegemony and Socialist Strategy*, they replace that discourse: Class is subsumed into an unspecified form of unequal economic power, but the how and why of this power, its conditions of existence, are not theorized. Class exploitation is certainly one condition of existence of power; just as certainly, power is only one among many conditions of existence of class exploitation. From Marx's specification of capitalism as a particular form of production and distribution of surplus labor (presumably with its own particular "overdetermination of effects"), we have in the post-Marxist space of the economy a theoretical retreat into a generalized "economic inequality."

Overall there is a threefold recomposition of the economic space at work in *Hegemony and Socialist Strategy*. Firstly, Laclau and Mouffe abandon particular concepts (LPAC, class processes, and exploitation) as essentialist things in themselves. Secondly, they reintroduce other traditional Marxist economic concepts (commodification, the logic of accumulation) through a narrative of capitalism that is not itself the product of theoretical construction. Thirdly, they rename capitalist relations of production as political concepts (domination and oppression). The effect of this recomposition is not merely to displace essentialist class concepts from their unique and privileged ontological position (the rightful and necessary come-uppance due every essentialism), but to collapse the theoretical structure of the economic space itself.

Laclau and Mouffe raise the following question: What can we utilize from the Marxist tradition to analyze capitalism today? Accepting the need to move beyond essentialism, we can follow Althusser, Laclau and Mouffe, and Resnick and Wolff (1987) down a path marked "overdetermination." Yet this path, "opened" by deconstructing the erstwhile centrality of economic processes, branches in many possible directions. Laclau and Mouffe take a "political" path. But others are possible.[6] One is the extension of antiessentialist logics to the basic concepts of Marxian class analysis. Rather than collapsing economic notions into their cultural and political conditions of existence, we must both rethink the specificity of class processes as they are constituted by subjectivity and political practices, and take seriously the constitutive power of exploitation.

NOTES

1. See, e.g., Geras (1987), as well as Laclau and Mouffe's 1987 reply to his critique (in Laclau 1990).

2. See our recent essay (Diskin and Sandler 1993) in which we discuss Laclau and Mouffe's anti-essentialism in more detail, and develop at greater length some arguments presented here.

3. In a closely related variant of post-Marxism, Bowles and Gintis elaborate a form of economic analysis in which the exercise of power replaces exploitation as the dominant theme. See Bowles and Gintis (1987, especially Chapter 3).

4. The internal quote is from Bowles and Gintis (1981, 8).

5. For a related critique of totalizing narratives of capitalism see Gibson-Graham in Part Three of this volume.

6. The rejection of the economic and its displacement by the political is in no way inherent in a turn toward issues of subjectivity. See Amariglio and Callari (1989) for a persuasive re-reading of Marxian economic categories in light of more complex notions of subjectivity.

REFERENCES

Althusser, L. 1979. *Reading Capital*, trans. B. Brewster. London: Verso Press.

Amariglio, J. and Callari, A. 1989, Fall. "Marxian Value Theory and the Problem of the Subject: The Role of Commodity Fetishism." *Rethinking Marxism* 2 (3): 31–60.

Bowles, S. and Gintis, H. 1987. *Capitalism and Democracy*. New York: Basic Books.

——. 1981. "Structure and Practice in the Labour Theory of Value." *Review of Radical Political Economics* 12 (4): 12–26.

Diskin, J. and Sandler, B. 1993, Fall. "Essentialism and the Economy in the Post-Marxist Imaginary: Re-opening the Sutures." *Rethinking Marxism* 6 (3): 28–48.

Geras, N. 1987, May–June. "Post-Marxism?" *New Left Review* 163: 40–82.

Laclau, E. 1990. *New Reflections on the Revolutions of Our Time*, trans. J. Barnes et. al. London: Verso Press.

Laclau E. and Mouffe, C. 1985. *Hegemony and Socialist Strategy: Towards a Radical Democratic Politics*, trans. W. Moore and P. Cammack. London: Verso Press.

Resnick, S. and Wolff, R. 1987. *Knowledge and Class*. Chicago: University of Chicago Press.

Waiting for the Revolution, or How to Smash Capitalism While Working at Home in Your Spare Time

J. K. GIBSON-GRAHAM

Sometimes I ask myself why it is that feminists can have revolution now, while Marxists have to wait. I find this question thought provoking, despite its flippancy and falsifications. The question points to the proximity of social transformation for certain feminisms—that conception of gender as always being renegotiated, that vision of social transformation taking place at the interpersonal level as well as at the larger social scale. My feminism reshapes the terrain of my existence on a daily basis. Why can't my Marxism generate a lived project of socialist construction?

This question of the socialist "absence" has led me to a number of answers, but one has recently been uppermost in my mind. It seems to me that what Marxism has been called upon to transform is something that cannot be transformed—something I will call Capitalism. Let me say this more clearly. Marxism has produced a discourse of Capitalism that ostensibly delineates an object of transformative class politics, but that operates more powerfully to discourage projects of class transformation. In a sense, Marxism has contributed to the socialist absence through the very way in which it has theorized the capitalist presence.

In the context of poststructuralist theory both the political subject and the social totality have been rent apart and retheorized as continu-

A longer version of this paper was published as Gibson-Graham (1993). Copyright 1993 by the Association for Economic and Social Analysis. Adapted by permission.

ally under construction, decentered, constituted by antagonisms, fragmented, plural, discursively as well as socially constructed; but Capitalism has been relatively immune to radical reconceptualization. Indeed, there seems to be a sense that—within Marxism at least—a single meaning can be associated with the word. Thus when we call the United States a capitalist country, we do so without fear of contradiction. This is not because we all have the same understanding of what capitalism is (for there are many capitalisms in the Marxist community), but because the meaning of capitalism is not a focus of widespread rethinking and reformulation.

Without defining Capitalism at this point, I wish to identify some of the characteristics that give it the power to deflect socialist (and other progressive) transformations. In the theories of capitalism put forward by economic theorists such as David Harvey, Michel Aglietta, Ernest Mandel, and Immanuel Wallerstein, and drawn upon by a wide range of social and cultural analysts, we see that Capitalism takes a number of prominent discursive forms. I call these discursive features of Capitalism "unity," "singularity," and "totality." Taken together (as they seldom are in particular textual settings) these features constitute Capitalism as *an object of transformation that cannot be transformed*.

UNITY

The birth of the concept of Capitalism as we know it coincided in time with the birth of "the economy" as an autonomous social sphere. Not surprisingly, then, Capitalism shares with its more abstract sibling the qualities of an integrated system and the capability of reproducing itself (or of being reproduced). Represented as an organism through which flows of social labor circulate in various forms, Capitalism regulates itself according to logics or laws,[1] propelled by a life force along a preordained (though not untroubled) trajectory of growth.

Often the unity of Capitalism is represented in more architectural terms. Capitalism (or capitalist society) becomes a structure in which parts are related to one another, linked to functions, and arranged "in accordance with an architecture that is . . . no less invisible than visible" (Foucault 1973, 231). The architectural/structural metaphor confers upon Capitalism qualities of durability and persistence as well as unity and coherence, giving it greater purchase on social reality than more ephemeral phenomena. While Marxist conceptions usually emphasize the contradictory and crisis-ridden nature of capitalist development, capitalist crisis may itself be seen as a unifying process. Crises are commonly presented as originating at the organic center of a capitalist society—the relationship between capital and labor, for example, or the process of capital accumulation—and as radiating outward to destabilize the entire economic and social formation.

What is important here is not the different metaphors and images of economy and society but the fact that they all confer integrity upon Capitalism. Through its architectural or organismic representation as an edifice or body, Capitalism becomes not an uncentered aggregate of practices but a structural and systemic unity, potentially coextensive with the (national or global) economy as a whole. Understood as a unified system or structure, Capitalism is not ultimately vulnerable to local and partial efforts at transformation. Any such efforts can always be subverted by Capitalism at another scale or in another dimension. Attempts, for example, to transform production may be seen as hopeless without control of the financial system; and socialisms in one city or in one country may be seen as undermined by Capitalism at the international scale. Capitalism cannot be gradually replaced or removed piecemeal; it must be transformed in its entirety or not at all. Thus one of the effects of the unity of Capitalism is to confront the Left with the task of systemic transformation.

SINGULARITY

Capitalism presents itself as a singularity in the sense of having no peer or equivalent and also in the sense that, when it appears fully developed within a particular social formation, it tends to be dominant or alone. As a *sui generis* economic form, Capitalism has no true analogues. Slavery, independent commodity production, feudalism, socialism, and primitive communism all lack the systemic properties of Capitalism and the ability to reproduce and expand themselves according to internal laws. Unlike socialism, which is always struggling to be born, which needs the protection and fostering of the state, which is fragile and easily deformed, Capitalism takes on its full form as a natural outcome of an internally driven growth process.

Its organic unity gives Capitalism the peculiar power to regenerate itself, and even to subsume its moments of crisis as requirements of its continued growth and development. Socialism has never been endowed with that mythic capability of feeding on its own crises; its reproduction was never driven from within by a life force, but always from without; it could never reproduce itself but always had to be reproduced, often an arduous if not impossible process. Other modes of production that lack the organic unity of Capitalism are more capable of being instituted or replaced incrementally and more likely to coexist with other economic forms. Capitalism, by contrast, tends to appear by itself. Thus, in the

United States, if feudal or ancient classes exist, they exist as residual forms; if slavery exists, it exists as a marginal form; if socialism or communism exists, it exists as a prefigurative form. None of these forms truly and fully coexists with Capitalism. Where Capitalism does coexist with other forms, those places (the so-called third world, for example) are seen as not fully "developed." Rather than signaling the real possibility of Capitalism's coexistence with noncapitalist economic forms, the simultaneous presence of Capitalism and noncapitalism marks the third world as insufficient and incomplete.

One impact of the notion of capitalist exclusivity is a monolithic conception of class, at least in the context of "advanced capitalist" countries. The term "class" usually refers to a social cleavage along the axis of capital and labor, since Capitalism cannot coexist with any but residual or prefigurative noncapitalist relations. The presence and fullness of the capitalist monolith not only denies the possibility of economic or class diversity in the present but also prefigures a monolithic socialism—where everyone is a comrade and class diversity does not exist. Capitalism's singularity operates to discourage projects to create alternative economic institutions and class relations, since these will necessarily be marginal in the context of Capitalism's exclusivity. The inability of Capitalism to coexist thus produces not only the present impossibility of alternatives but their future unlikelihood, pushing socialist projects to the distant and unrealizable future.

TOTALITY

The third characteristic of Capitalism is its tendency to present itself as the social totality. This is most obvious in images of containment and subsumption. Noncapitalist forms of production such as commodity production by self-employed workers, or the production of household goods and services, are seen as somehow taking place *within* Capitalism. Household production becomes subsumed to Capitalism as capitalist "reproduction." Even oppressions experienced along entirely different lines of social antagonism are convened within Capitalism's social embrace.

Capitalism not only casts a wider net than other things, it also constitutes us more fully. Our lives are saturated with Capitalism. We cannot get outside Capitalism—it has no outside. It becomes that which has no outside by swallowing up its conditions of existence. The banking system, the national state, domestic production, the built environment, nature as a product, media culture—all are conditions of Capitalism's existence that seem to lose their autonomy, their contradictory capability to be read as conditions of its nonexistence. Even socialism functions as the double or place-holder of Capitalism, rather than as its active and contradictory constituent. Socialism is just Capitalism's opposite, a great emptiness on the other side of a membrane, a social space where the fullness of Capitalism is negated. When the socialist bubble in Eastern Europe burst, Capitalism flooded in like a miasma.

It seems we have banished economic determinism and the economistic conception of class as the major axis of social transformation, but we have enshrined the economy once again—this time in a vast metonymic emplacement. Capitalism, which is a name for a form of economy, is invoked in every social dimension; our wealthy industrial societies are summarily characterized as capitalist social formations. On the one hand, we have taken back social life from the economy while, on the other, we have allowed Capitalism to colonize the entire social space.

This means that the Left is not only presented with the revolutionary task of transforming the whole economy; it must replace the entire society as well. It is not surprising that there seems to be no room for a thriving and powerful noncapitalist economy, politics, and culture—though it is heartening to consider that these may nevertheless exist.

ALTERNATIVES TO CAPITALISM

I have characterized Marxism as producing a discourse of Capitalism that represents capitalism as unified, singular, and total rather than as dispersed, plural, and partial in relation to the economy and society as a whole. I do not mean to present Marxism itself as noncontradictory; clearly Marxism has produced discourses with different and, in fact, opposite characteristics. But I detect the presence and potency of the discourse I call Capitalism in what it makes unimaginable: a currently existing socialism in places like the United States. What strikes me as an inability among Marxists to view our activities as "socialist construction" is produced in part by a Marxist discourse, one in which Capitalism is constituted as necessarily hegemonic by virtue of its internal characteristics.

As Marxists we often struggle to define the discursive features of Capitalism as errors or illusions. We undermine images of Capitalism's structural or systemic unity; we criticize the ways in which it is allowed to spill over into noneconomic social domains. Yet even so the hegemony of Capitalism reasserts itself. It is visible, for example, in each new analysis that presents an economy as predominantly or monolithically capitalist. We may deprive Capitalism of self-generating capacities and structural integrity; we may rob it of the power to confer upon our societies a fictive and fantastic wholeness; but Capitalism still appears essentially alone. As the ultimate container within which we live, Capitalism is unable to coexist.

For all its variety, the discourse of Capitalism is so pervasive that it leaves us almost incapable of producing alternative conceptions. Perhaps, then, the way to begin to break free of Capitalism is to turn its prevalent representations on their heads. What if we theorized capitalism not as something large and embracing but as one social component among others? What if we expelled those conditions of existence—for example, property law—that have become absorbed within the conception of capitalism and allowed them their contradictory autonomy, to become conditions of existence not only of capitalism but of noncapitalism, to become conditions of capitalism's nonexistence? What if capitalism were not an entire system of economy or a macrostructure or a mode of production but simply one form of exploitation among many? What if the economy were not single but plural, not homogeneous but heterogeneous, not unified but fragmented? What if capitalism were a set of practices scattered over the landscape that are (for convenience and in violation of difference) lumped under one category? If "subjectivity" and "society" can undergo a radical rethinking, producing a crisis of individual and social identity where a presumed fixity previously existed, can't we give Capitalism an identity crisis as well? If we did, how might the "socialist project" itself be transformed?

The question is, how do we begin to see this monolithic and homogeneous Capitalism not as our "reality" but as a fantasy of wholeness, one that operates to obscure diversity and disunity in the economy and society alike? In order to begin to do this we may need to get closer to redefining Capitalism for ourselves. Yet this is a very difficult thing to do.[2] If we divorce Capitalism from unity, from singularity, from totality, we are left with "capitalism"—and what might that be? Let us start where most people are starting today. One of the things that has produced the sense of capitalism's ubiquity is its identification with the market, a prevalent identification outside Marxism and within Marxism, one that is surprisingly not uncommon. And yet of course so many economic transactions are non-market transactions that it is apparent once we begin to think about it that to define capitalism as coextensive with the market is to define much economic activity as noncapitalist.

In this regard, what have for me cast the greatest light upon the discourse of Capitalism (and on the ways in which I have been confined within it without seeing its confines) are studies of the household "economy" produced by Nancy Folbre (1994), Harriet Fraad et al. (1989), and other feminist theorists. These theorists argue convincingly that the household in so-called advanced capitalist societies is a major locus of production and that, in terms of both value of output and numbers of people involved, the household sector can hardly be called marginal. In fact, it can arguably be seen as equivalent to or more important than the capitalist sector. We must therefore seek to understand the discursive marginalization of the household sector as a complex effect, one that is not produced as a simple reflection of the marginal and residual status of the household economy itself.

If we can grant that nonmarket transactions (both within and outside the household) account for a substantial portion of transactions, and that therefore what we have blithely called a capitalist economy in the United States is certainly not wholly or even predominantly a market economy, perhaps we can also look within and behind the market to see the differences concealed there. The market, which has existed throughout time and over vast geographies, can hardly be invoked in any but the most general economic characterization; if we pull back this blanket term, it would not be surprising to see a huge variety of things wriggling beneath it. The question then becomes not whether "the market" obscures differences but how we want to characterize the differences under the blanket. As Marxists we might be interested in something other than the ways in which goods and services are transacted. We might instead consider Marx's delineation of economic difference in terms of forms of exploitation, in other words, the specific forms in which surplus labor is produced, appropriated, and distributed—which was indeed what Marx was concerned to know and transform.

In any particular society we may find a great variety of forms of exploitation associated with production for a market: independent forms in which a self-employed producer appropriates her own surplus labor, capitalist forms in which surplus value is appropriated from wage labor, collective or communal forms in which producers jointly appropriate surplus labor, slave forms in which surplus labor is appropriated from workers who do not have freedom of contract. None of these forms of class exploitation can be presumed to be marginal before we have even looked under the blanket.

Calling the economy "capitalist" denies the existence of these diverse economic and class processes, precluding economic diversity in the present, and thereby making it unlikely in the proximate future. But what if we could force Capitalism to withdraw from defining the economy as a whole? We might then see feudalisms, primitive communisms, socialisms, independent commodity production, slaveries, and of course capitalisms, as well as hitherto unspecified forms of exploitation. Defined in terms of the ways in which surplus labor is produced and appropriated, these diverse exploitations introduce diversity into the dimension of class, and at the same time make thinkable (i.e., apparently reasonable and realistic) the possibility of socialist class transformation.

None of this is to deny the power or even the prevalence of capitalism. It is, however, to question the presumption of both.

CONCLUSION

One of our goals as Marxists has been to produce a knowledge of capitalism. But as "that which is known," Capitalism has become the intimate enemy. We have uncloaked the ideologically clothed, obscure monster but we have installed a naked and visible monster in its place. In return for our labors of creation, the monster has robbed us of all force. We hear—and find it easy to believe—that the Left is in disarray.

I am arguing that part of what produces the disarray of the Left is the vision of what the Left is arrayed against. When capitalism is represented as a unified system coextensive with the nation or even the world, when it is portrayed as crowding out all other economic forms, when it is allowed to define entire societies, it becomes something that can only be defeated and replaced by a massive collective movement (or by a process of systemic dissolution that such a movement might assist). In the face of such an opponent, the Left will always be in disarray.

The new world order is often represented as political fragmentation founded upon economic unification. In a world of diversity and plurality, the economy appears as the last stronghold of unity and singularity. But why can't the economy be fragmented too? If we theorized it as fragmented in the United States, we could begin to see a huge state sector (incorporating a variety of forms of appropriation of surplus labor), a very large sector of self-employed and family-based producers (most noncapitalist), a huge household sector (again, quite various in terms of forms of exploitation, with some households moving towards communal or collective appropriation and others operating in a traditional mode in which a man appropriates surplus labor from a woman). None of these diverse forms of exploitation is easy to see or to theorize as consequential in so-called capitalist social formations.

If Capitalism takes up the available social space, there's no room for anything else. If Capitalism cannot coexist, there's no possibility of anything else. If Capitalism is large, other things appear small and inconsequential. If Capitalism functions as a unity, it cannot be partially or locally replaced. My project (in which again I am not alone) is to help create the discursive conditions under which socialist construction becomes a "realistic" present activity rather than a ludicrous or utopian future goal. To achieve this I must smash Capitalism and see it in a thousand pieces. I must make its unity a fantasy, visible as a denial of diversity and change.

In the absence of Capitalism, I might suggest a different object of socialist politics. Perhaps we might be able to focus some of our transformative energies on exploitation, on the production and appropriation of surplus labor that goes on around us in so many forms, and in which we participate in various ways. In the household, in the so-called workplace, in the community, surplus labor is produced and appropriated every day by ourselves and by others. Marx made these processes visible, but they have been obscured by the discourse of Capitalism, with its vision of two great classes locked in millennial struggle. This discourse, despite its authority and power, cannot account for much of our experience of exploitation and for the diversity of class positions and consciousnesses that exploitation participates in creating.

If we can divorce our ideas of class from systemic social conceptions, and simultaneously divorce our ideas of class transformation from projects of systemic transformation, we may be able to envision local and proximate socialisms. Defining socialism as the communal production and appropriation of surplus labor, we could encounter and construct it at home, at work, at large. These "thinly defined" socialisms wouldn't remake our societies overnight in some total and millennial fashion (see Cullenberg 1992), but they could participate in constituting and reconstituting them on a daily basis. They wouldn't be a panacea for all the ills that we love to heap on the doorstep of Capitalism, but they could be visible and replicable now.[3]

To step outside the discourse of Capitalism, to abjure its powers and transcend the limits it has placed on socialist activity, is not to step outside Marxism as I understand it. Rather it is to divorce Marxism from one of its many and problematic marriages—the marriage to "the economy" in its holistic and self-sustaining form. This marriage has spawned a healthy lineage within the Marxist tradition and has contributed to a wide range of political movements and successes. Now I am suggesting that the marriage is no longer fruitful or, more precisely, that its recent offspring are monstrous and frail. Without delineating the innumerable grounds for bringing the marriage to an end, I would like to hail its passing, and to ask myself and others not to confuse its passing with the passing of Marxism itself. For Marxism directs us to consider exploitation, and that is something that has not passed away.

ACKNOWLEDGMENTS

I gratefully acknowledge the helpful comments of Jack Amariglio and Will Milberg on the first draft of this paper.

NOTES

1. Many theorists do not wish to accord the economy the capacity to author its own causation, recognizing in this theoretical move one of the major buttresses of economic determinist social thought. The regulatory mechanisms allowing for the reproduction of Capitalism may be transported outside the economy itself, so that social conditions and institutions external and contingent, rather than internal and necessary, to the capitalist economy are responsible for its maintenance and stability (Graham 1992).

2. Fortunately I am not the only one trying to do it. See, for example, Resnick and Wolff (1987).

3. It is interesting to think about what the conditions promoting such socialisms might be, including forms of communal and collective subjectivity. In a recent essay on socialism, David Ruccio (1992) talks about notions of "community without unity" and "a community at loose ends," as well as decentered and complex ideas of collectivity emerging within various Left discourses of the 1990s.

REFERENCES

Cullenberg, S. 1992, Summer. "Socialism's Burden: Toward a Thin Definition of Socialism." *Rethinking Marxism* 5 (2): 64–83.

Folbre, N. 1994. *Who Pays for the Kids? Gender and the Structures of Constraint.* New York: Routledge.

Foucault, M. 1973. *The Order of Things.* New York: Vintage Books.

Fraad, H., Resnick, S., and Wolff, R. 1989, Winter. "For Every Knight in Shining Armor, There's a Castle Waiting to be Cleaned: A Marxist–Feminist Analysis of the Household." *Rethinking Marxism* 2 (4): 10–69.

Gibson-Graham, J. K. 1993, Summer. "Waiting for the Revolution, or How to Smash Capitalism While Working at Home in Your Spare Time." *Rethinking Marxism* 6 (2): 10–24.

Graham, J. 1992. "Post-Fordism as Politics: The Political Consequences of Narratives on the Left." *Environment and Planning D: Society and Space* 10 (4): 393–410.

Resnick, S. and Wolff, R. 1987. *Knowledge and Class.* Chicago: University of Chicago Press.

Ruccio, D. 1992, Summer. "Failure of Socialism, Future of Socialists?" *Rethinking Marxism* 5 (2): 7–22.

Situating the Capitalist State

MICHAEL A. LEBOWITZ

hen, theoretically, can Marxists talk about
the capitalist state? In the original conception of his "Economics," Marx
placed the "State" as the fourth of his six intended books (Lebowitz 1992a,
12). "The concentration of bourgeois society in the form of the state,"
"the concentration of the whole," was to follow the book on wage labor
which itself would complete "the inner totality" (Marx 1973, 264, 108,
227). Thus, as revealed by its placement, the concept of the capitalist state
would be developed out of the consideration (in a dialectical manner)
of capital, landed property, and wage labor—the subjects of the first three
books. Only when that "inner totality" is completed can we examine the
state as "the concentration of the whole."[1]

The problem, of course, is that Marx never went beyond *Capital* in
his original plan. Some of the implications of this (and, in particular, of
the missing book on wage labor) have been explored in *Beyond Capital*
(Lebowitz 1992a). Not only was *Capital* one-sided with respect to its examination of capitalism (presenting the side of capital but *not* "the completed bourgeois system"), but also in particular, the treatment of workers as subjects—as they struggle for their own goals and as they produce
themselves through their own activities—is revealed to be both essential
to the understanding of capitalism and missing from *Capital*.

None of this, however, has stopped Marxists from theorizing about
the capitalist state based upon *Capital* alone. Central to the extensive state
debates of the 1970s was the contribution of the "state derivationist" or

"capital logic" school, which attempted to avoid the eclecticism characteristic of so many Marxian treatments by logically deriving the category of the state directly from the concept of capital (cf. Holloway and Picciotto 1978). Yet, as Simon Clarke (1991) has indicated in his fine survey, these efforts were simply a variant of a structural-functionalist orthodoxy that considers the state in terms of its functional necessity for capital; the determining role of class struggle was necessarily displaced. And, this judgment cannot come as a surprise, when we understand that *Capital* has only capital as its subject and considers only capital's needs and tendencies but not those of workers (Lebowitz 1992a).

It doesn't mean, however, that the project of state derivation is inherently flawed. By explicitly considering the "intermediate link" omitted by the capital logic school (i.e., the side of wage labor), it is possible to reconstruct Marx's concept of the capitalist state as the object and result of class struggle. Further, the resulting understanding of the capitalist state as the "concentration of bourgeois society in the form of the state" (Marx 1973, 108) is the link to Marx's view of the form of state necessary to go *beyond* capital.

WAGE LABOR'S LATENT STATE

There is a concept of the state implicit in the concept of capital. Since this is, however, ground well covered in the earlier state derivation discussions (cf. Holloway and Picciotto 1978), it is sufficient here to note that inherent in capital's need for valorization are state activities (a) to ensure the availability of appropriate labor power at wages consistent with capital's requirements (drawing upon the power of the state wherever "the sheer force of economic relations" [Marx 1977, 382] is not adequate), (b) to ensure the existence of material conditions of production (where these are deemed "necessary without being productive in the capitalist sense" [Marx 1973, 531], i.e., profitable), and (c) to protect the fruits of capitalist exploitation through the existence of a legal system enforcing private property rights.[2]

In short, as the capital logic school demonstrated, it is possible within Marx's framework to develop aspects of a state latent in the concept of capital. Yet, precisely the same can be done by starting from the concept of wage labor (both within *Capital* and as developed in *Beyond Capital*).[3] Just as consideration of the concept of the capitalist state implicit in capital begins with the understanding of capital's drive for surplus value, examination of wage labor's latent state begins with a focus upon the impulse of workers to satisfy their needs—their needs for use values, for time and energy for their own production process and, ultimately, "the worker's own need for development" (Marx 1977, 772). Yet, insofar as we speak of wage labor, we are not considering abstract producers; rather, we mean workers who exist within the capital/wage labor relation and are thus dependent upon capital to realize those needs. In this respect, like other commodity sellers, wage laborers have the need for contract enforcement, a standard measure of prices and the determination of a circulating medium (as well the provision of stable conditions of exchange), which are attributes "proper to the state" (Marx 1977, 221–222) in a commodity exchanging society.

Yet, there are specific aspects of a state, if it is to serve as an agency for wage laborers as sellers of labor power. Since capital is able to capture the fruits of cooperation because of the separation among wage laborers—a disunion "created and perpetuated by their *unavoidable competition amongst themselves*" (Marx n.d., 347, emphasis in original), the condition for being able to achieve a quantitative participation in the general growth of wealth is the ability of wage laborers to combine in trade unions. In this respect, the state is central; for, the state has the power either to prevent (or restrict) such combinations of workers or to permit (and facilitate) them. There is, thus, an inherent logic to the struggle of workers to make the state serve their interests by legalizing and supporting the existence of trade unions.

To keep up and raise their wages, however, more is required than the ability to form trade unions. Inherent in the wage labor relation is the dependence of the worker upon the willingness of capital to purchase labor power (which itself depends upon capital's ability to realize the surplus value produced by workers). If that requirement is not met, then labor power "exists without the conditions of its existence, and is therefore a mere encumbrance; needs without the means to satisfy them" (Marx 1973, 609). Further, since the existence of unemployment clearly weakens workers, the state latent in the needs of wage laborers is one that will foster conditions of full employment.

While wage increases will permit workers to purchase more means of subsistence, the use values that correspond to their social needs are not limited to those that take a commodity form. A state acting as an agency of wage laborers would expand the provision for workers of "*that which is needed for common satisfaction of needs*, such as schools, health services, etc." (Marx 1962, 22, emphasis in original). Similarly, insofar as qualities of nature (such as clean air and sunlight) are part of the worker's set of needs and correspond to the "worker's own need for development," latent in the state are activities to protect and repair natural conditions impaired by capitalist production.[4]

Further, the moment of production that *Capital* does not consider, the worker's own process of production, requires labor power as well as the use-values that are inputs into that labor process. Implied, accordingly, is the struggle of wage laborers over the length and intensity of the capitalist work day in order to have time and energy for themselves. It is a victory for "the political economy of the working class" (Marx 1985a, 10–11) when the state legislates restrictions on the work day.

Thus, considered from the side of wage labor, we see that, acting as an agency of wage labor, the state will restrict the work day, support increases in real wages, assist in the realization of other social needs and, in general, foster the expanded reproduction of wage laborers. In this respect, the state latent in the concept of wage labor functions much like trade unions. However, although trade unions act in opposition to specific and particular capitals, in themselves they cannot confront the power of capital as a whole.

For that reason, Marx stressed not merely the *possibility* of moving beyond purely economic struggles in order to use the power of the state on behalf of workers but, rather, the *necessity*. The real victory of the political economy of the working class in the case of the Ten Hours' Bill was the demonstration that wage labor required political struggle and the use of the state. The Ten Hours' Bill, after all, was a legislative act—which it *had* to be. As Marx argued (1985b, 146), the limitation of the working day "was not to be attained by private settlement between the working men and the capitalists. This very necessity of *general political action* affords the proof that in its merely economic action capital is the stronger side" (emphasis in original). Only by going beyond "a purely economic movement" to act as a class *politically* could the working class enforce "its interests in a general form, in a form possessing general, socially coercive force" (Marx and Engels 1965, 270–271). Here we see immediately a stark contrast between the requirements of capital and wage labor that Marx identified with respect to the state. Whereas capital may be able (through the regular reproduction of a reserve army) to dispense with the power of the state and rely upon "the sheer force of economic relations" to secure its goals (1977, 899, 935, 382), workers *require* the social force of the state.

This is especially true because of the particular contradiction between wage labor as a whole and individual wage laborers. Whereas the competition of individual capitals manifests the inner laws of capital, when individual wage laborers compete, they do not manifest and execute the inner tendencies of wage labor in general. Rather, by competing with each other, workers press not in the opposite direction to capital but in the *same* direction. For this reason, the socially coercive force of the state is necessary to bind not only capital but *also wage laborers as individual self-seekers*. As Marx noted (1977, 416) in the case of the work day, "The workers have to put their heads together and, as a class, compel the passing of a law, an all-powerful social barrier by which they can be prevented from selling themselves and their families into slavery and death by voluntary contract with capital." In such cases, he commented (n.d., 344–345), "The working class do not fortify governmental power. On the contrary, they transform that power, now used against them, into their own agency."

The logical necessity of the state from the side of wage labor is clear (and, indeed, is stronger than that from the side of capital—given capital's relative strength in "merely economic action"). In this respect, it cannot be considered surprising that, in practice, workers have looked upon the state as a means of enforcing their interests within capitalism. Nevertheless, like trade unions, the state latent in the concept of wage labor does not go beyond the capital/wage labor relation. Nor can it avoid (any more than trade unions) any limits given by capital's need for valorization. In short, to consider the capitalist state, we need to situate it within the totality that is capitalism as a whole, as "the concentration of bourgeois society."

THE CAPITALIST STATE AS CONCENTRATION OF THE WHOLE

Between two conceptions of right, force decides. Inherent in capital and wage labor are two concepts of the capitalist state in struggle—whether the state will be a mediator for capital or whether it will be a mediator for wage labor. On matters such as restrictions on the length of the workday, the legalization and fostering of trade unions, the orientation to full employment, and the provision of use-values to permit the common satisfaction of needs, capital and wage labor push the state in opposite directions. The fixation of the actual practices of the state "resolves itself into a question of the respective powers of the combatants."

But, is this an indeterminacy between specific limits? Are there any "laws" that determine those limits? Consider the case of a state under the complete domination of capital, where capital is able to use the power of the state without check. In this case, capital will be successful in reducing wages to a minimum and extending the workday to a maximum; as long, indeed, as capital is able to find substitutes for specific labor or material conditions of production, the tendency will be one of non-reproduction of particular workers and natural conditions. In this respect, there is no immediate limit to capital's ability to use the state on its behalf. Yet, at the same time, to the extent that capital has been successful in using the power of the state to break down the resistance of workers, the expanded reproduction of capital does not require a state.[5]

Consider the other extreme: a capitalist state completely dominated by wage labor. Here, we would expect to find workers using the state to foster increases in wages and the reduction of the workday—thus, a tendency toward the reduction of the rate of surplus value, toward the inability of capital to engage in expanded reproduction. Is there a limit here? Clearly, capital may respond by ceasing accumulation, which (within the framework of capitalist relations) will produce a crisis—a reduced demand for labor power and the weakening of the position of wage labor. Or, there may be an accelerated increase in the technical composition of capital (and an accompanying displacement of workers). Between these two cases, the differences are significant; yet, they have in common the implication of limits to the ability to use the state on behalf of wage labor within capitalism. The prospect is one of the balance of forces shifting to favor capital both in the economic sphere and with respect to control of the state.

Recall, however, the scenario of the *Communist Manifesto*, where wage labor uses the power of the state to make "despotic inroads" on capitalist property—that is, to introduce measures "which appear economically insufficient and untenable, but which, in the course of the movement, outstrip themselves, necessitate further inroads upon the old social order" (Marx and Engels 1976, 504). In this case, the combination of restrictions upon capital (which limit the possibility of its reproduction) and the development of state sectors would be part of a process of displacing capital as the mediator for wage labor and substituting the state. To the extent that *this* outcome is possible, there would appear to be no limit to the state as an agency of workers.

And, yet, there is a critical premise for this last potential case. It presupposes workers who do not look upon capital as a *necessary* mediator. However, everything about capitalist production fosters not merely the relation of dependence but also that "feeling of dependence" (Marx 1977, 936) upon capital. Having surrendered the right to his "*creative power*, like Esau his birthright for a mess of pottage," capital becomes "a very mystical being" for the worker because it appears as the source of all productivity (Marx 1973, 307, 694; 1977, 1058; 1981, 966). Considering as well the effect of the regular reproduction of the reserve army, Marx concluded that the very process of capitalist production produces and reproduces workers who consider the necessity for capital to be self-evident:

> The advance of capitalist production develops a working class which by education, tradition and habit looks upon the requirements of that mode as self-evident natural laws. The organization of the capitalist process of production, once it is fully developed, breaks down all resistance. (1977, 899)

Even, accordingly, if wage laborers succeed in turning the state into their own agency, *so long as they remain conscious of their dependence upon capital* that state must act to facilitate conditions for the expanded reproduction of capital. That is the necessary result of functioning within the bounds of a relation in which the reproduction of wage labor as such requires the reproduction of capital.

Thus, even though there may be considerable variation based upon the "respective powers of the combatants," the capitalist state remains within the bounds of the capitalist relation and supports its continued existence. Not because a state within capitalist society *must* support the reproduction of capital. Nor because the gains workers can make through the state create illusions and sap their otherwise revolutionary spirit. Rather, capital *itself* spontaneously produces illusions—illusions that tend to dissuade a challenge to capitalism as such. Ultimately, it is precisely insofar as workers look upon the requirements of capitalism "as self-evident natural laws" that makes the capitalist state the guarantor of the reproduction of capital.

BEYOND THE CAPITALIST STATE

There is, of course, more to the story. Marx, after all, believed that workers would succeed in going *beyond* capital. And that would be the result not of some automatic crisis of capitalism but, rather, as the result of that process (not considered in *Capital*) by which workers produce themselves through their own activities. Nothing is more central to Marx's entire conception than the coincidence of the changing of circumstances and self-change—that is, the concept of "revolutionary practice" set out in his Third Thesis on Feuerbach (Marx 1976, 4). When workers struggle for higher wages, struggle against capital in the workplace and for the satisfaction of their social needs in general, that very process is one of transforming them into people with a new conception of themselves—as subjects capable of altering their world.

The same is true of the struggle to make the state the workers' agency. Not only is this struggle necessary (because "in its merely economic action capital is the stronger side"), it is also an essential part of the process by which workers transcend their local interests and take shape as a class against capital as a whole. Thus, for example, the struggle to make the state expand its provision of use-values "*needed for common satisfaction of needs* such as schools, health services, etc." not only is an effort to substitute the state for capital as a mediator for workers but also unifies workers (skilled and unskilled, waged and unwaged). In this respect, the struggle for the state is an essential moment in the process of producing the working class as a class for itself, an essential moment in the process of going beyond capital.

And, yet, all of this refers only to the very process of struggle. Past victories are incorporated—just as are the results (e.g., increased wages) of past trade union victories. Fixated within existing state practices, the transformative effects of their achievement are constantly undermined by that spontaneous process by which the dependence of wage laborers upon capital is reproduced as common sense. Accordingly, the struggle to make the state an agency of workers must be continuous; only the constant effort to compel the state to satisfy (directly or indirectly) the social needs of workers can change both circumstances and people. This emphasis upon the centrality of revolutionary practice, however, points as well to specific characteristics of a state that will be *other* than the "concentration of bourgeois society."

In short, as Marx concluded, we cannot be indifferent to the *form* of the state as an agency of workers. Only insofar as state functions are "wrested from an authority usurping pre-eminence over society itself, and restored to the responsible agents of society" are the activities of the state those by which workers produce themselves as capable of governing. Only where the state as mediator for (and power over) workers gives way to the "self-government of the producers" is there a continuous process whereby workers can change both circumstances and themselves (Marx 1971b, 72–73).

Implicit in the concept of revolutionary practice is, then, a form of state in which workers themselves determine their needs and the means of satisfying them, in which capital's position as mediator between producers and their needs is transcended—that is, a state of the Paris Commune type. "The working class," Marx commented, "can not simply lay hold of the ready-made state machinery, and wield it for its own purposes." This was because the very nature of the existing state was inherent in "the historical genesis of capitalist production," where "the rising bourgeoisie needs the power of the state"—a state infected because its very institutions involve a "systematic and hierarchic division of labour," because it assumes the character of "a public force organized for social enslavement, of an engine of class despotism"(Marx 1971b, 68–69).

For the state to be "the political form . . . under which to work out the economical emancipation of Labour," Marx argued, requires "the reabsorption of the state power by society as its own living forces instead of as forces controlling and subduing it, by the popular masses themselves, forming their own force instead of the organized force of their suppression" (Marx 1971a, 153; 1971b, 75). For the struggle to make the state the agency of workers to produce more than the representation of workers' interests in the capitalist state, the conversion of "the state from an organ standing above society into one completely subordinate to it" (Marx 1962, 30) is required.

One thing, then, is certain. When we proceed from the vantage point of the self-production of workers, the shift in perspective reveals the inadequacy of attempts to use the capitalist state ("the concentration of bourgeois society in the form of the state") to go beyond capital. For Marx, it was clear that what was called for was a struggle to transform "the ready-made state machinery" into a political form that insures a continuous process of revolutionary practice.

ACKNOWLEDGMENTS

In revising the paper from its original form, I am indebted to Harry Cleaver, Martha Gimenez, and Jim O'Connor for their comments and to Simon Clarke for his gift of *The State Debate* (Clark 1991). They will not agree with all arguments retained.

NOTES

1. By the same logic, the concept of the state itself as initially developed in Book IV must be incomplete. The full and adequate development of the concept of the capitalist state occurs only when the state is considered in the context of the world market (the subject matter of the concluding book), "in which production is posited as a totality together with all its moments" (Marx 1973, 264, 273). That is, the aspect that the state takes on in the context of competing national capitals and nation-states is essential to understanding the capitalist state. See the strong argument to this effect in von Braunmuhl (1978). This side of the capitalist state, however, is not explored here.

2. We cannot concern ourselves here with the capital logic discussions of the inherent necessity for the "autonomy" of the state or of the state as "ideal" total capitalist acting against individual capitals. On the former, see Clarke (1991, 186); regarding the latter, my position is implicit in Lebowitz (1992b).

3. Except where otherwise noted, supporting arguments and textual evidence may be found in Lebowitz (1992a).

4. For discussions of capital's tendency to impair the conditions of production, see O'Connor (1988) and the recent symposium in *Capitalism, Nature, Socialism* on "the second contradiction of capitalism" (September 1992), which includes Lebowitz (1992b).

5. Clarke notes that in the strictest sense for Marx the state is not necessary for the reproduction of capital. Indeed, "if there were no class struggle, if the working class were willing to submit passively to their subordination to capitalist social relations, there would be no state" (Clarke 1991, 190).

REFERENCES

Clarke, S., ed. 1991. *The State Debate*. New York: St. Martin's Press.

Holloway, J. and Picciotto, S. 1978. *State and Capital: A Marxist Debate*. London: Edward Arnold.

Lebowitz, M. A. 1992a. *Beyond Capital: Marx's Political Economy of the Working Class*. New York: St. Martin's Press.

———. 1992b, September. "Capitalism: How Many Contradictions?" *Capitalism, Nature, Socialism* 3 (3): 92–94.

Marx, K. n.d. "Instructions for the Delegates of the Provisional General Council. The Different Questions." In *Minutes of the General Council of the First International, 1866–8*. Moscow: Progress Publishers.

———. 1962. *Critique of the Gotha Programme*. In *Selected Works*, Vol. 2, K. Marx and F. Engels. Moscow: Foreign Languages Publishing House.

———. 1971a. "First Outline of *The Civil War in France*." In *On the Paris Commune*, K. Marx and F. Engels. Moscow: Progress Publishers.

———. 1971b. *The Civil War in France*. In *On the Paris Commune*, K. Marx and F. Engels. Moscow: Progress Publishers.

———. 1973. *Grundrisse*. New York: Vintage Books.

———. 1976. "Theses on Feuerbach." In *Collected Works*, Vol. 5, K. Marx and F. Engels. New York: International Publishers.

———. 1977. *Capital*, Vol. 1. New York: Vintage Books.

———. 1981. *Capital*. Vol. 3. New York: Vintage Books.

———. 1985a. "Inaugural Address of the Working Men's Association." In *Collected Works*, Vol. 20, K. Marx and F. Engels. New York: International Publishers.

——— 1985b. *Value, Price and Profit*. In *Collected Works*, Vol. 20, K. Marx and F. Engels. New York: International Publishers.

Marx, K. and Engels, F. 1965. *Selected Correspondence*. Moscow: Progress Publishers.

———. 1976. "Communist Manifesto." In *Collected Works*, Vol. 6. New York: International Publishers.

O'Connor, J. 1988, Fall. "Capitalism, Nature, Socialism: A Theoretical Introduction." *Capitalism, Nature, Socialism* 1 (1): 11–38.

von Braunmuhl, C. 1978. "On the Analysis of the Bourgeois Nation State within the World Market Context. An Attempt to Develop a Methodological and Theoretical Approach." In Holloway and Picciotto (1978): 160–177.

Beyond Democracy:
The Politics of Empowerment

RICHARD LEVINS

The struggle for empowerment should and will be a central political theme when the Left returns to the offensive after the disorientation of the late 1980s and early 1990s.[1] By empowerment I mean the all around capacity, resources, information and knowledge, self-confidence, skills, understanding, organization, and formal rights people can use to determine individually and collectively what happens to them. I also include the mobilization of the collective imagination, intelligence, creativity, enthusiasm, courage, and energy of the people in a liberating enterprise. As such this struggle has a much more profound aim than democracy.

My arguments in support of empowerment are both empirical and theoretical. My starting point is the observation that empowering practice is spreading in the world through many popular and nongovernmental local and regional movements of the sort the Left would usually have ignored. The first step is to appreciate the significance of these movements in their evolution and in their contradictory relations to governments. I can then argue that a politics of empowerment such as these movements are creating meets several short- and long-range needs for revolutionary politics. The potential for such a politics exists in the accumulated experience of the feminist, socialist, national liberation and other movements. I draw on such diverse sources as Gramscian analysis of ideology, Freirean pedagogy, and feminist consciousness raising.

Finally, I would like to call attention to some implications of this thesis for our political and theoretical agendas.

A SPECTRUM OF NON-GOVERNMENTAL ORGANIZATIONS

In the last few years we have seen a worldwide disillusionment with traditional political parties as the appropriate vehicles for the oppressed to use to protect their interests. In the face of the world recession and the demands of the World Bank and International Monetary Fund for "structural adjustment" programs, political movements have been unable to provide viable alternatives. Two major reactionary alternatives to the traditional politics have emerged: religious fundamentalism and nationalism. A new and growing progressive alternative is the NGO (Non-Governmental Organization) movement.

NGOs have a diverse origin. Many were organized at a grassroots community level to meet particular needs that the state refused or could not meet. Others came from the urban middle-class intellectuals who retained some links to their communities of origin, or simply perceived the urgent needs for health services or education, environmental protection or the care of homeless children. As such they were usually ignored by the Left, which tended to see self-help as merely palliative, even helping the rulers to rule at lower cost, and to see the NGOs as apolitical pacifiers. Left politics, in contrast to the strategy of self-help, either made demands of the state or sought to seize state power so that social changes could be initiated.

Governments have shown an ambivalent attitude toward these organizations. On the one hand the organizations have provided services the governments could not or would not provide. But they have also been independent and therefore potentially subversive. Governments have ambivalently licensed and encouraged them, tried to coopt them, suppressed them and sometimes even killed their leaders. USAID (the State Department's Agency for International Development) has encouraged the formation of other organizations that could compete with these NGOs and act as vehicles of control.

Generally but not uniformly the evolution of these NGOs has been toward a broadening of their vision, toward asking questions about the roots of the problems they try to ameliorate, expanding from self-help to advocacy, and networking among themselves to present a joint front to donors from Europe and North America in determining how development should proceed. The Arusha Conference in 1990 was a major step in the consolidation of an African NGO sector calling for an African pathway of development.

A second type of organization arose in the context of armed conflict in places such as Eritrea and El Salvador. Here organizations were often sponsored or stimulated by political movements in order to meet people's needs in zones over which the government had lost control. But they have developed their own constituencies and programs, ranging from direct organizing to meet people's basic needs to making demands on the state.[2]

Following is a sample of organizations that are worthy of note.

Eritrea. During the long war, many organs of local self-government were set up, including village councils, regional and national bodies, the Union of Eritrean Women and the Eritrean Relief Association. Local political organizations are now taking on government roles.They have moved from struggling to seize power to directly organizing people to meet their basic needs and taking over government function.

Sudan. The NGO sector includes such diverse groups as the Inter-Africa Committee against Traditional Practices Harmful to Women and the Babiker Badri Scientific Association for Women. The present fundamentalist government sees them as going beyond a legitimate service role toward the empowering of disadvantaged groups and looks at them with suspicion.

Guinea Bissau. ALTERNAG (Guinean Association for the Search for Alternatives) was set up in 1991 by local grassroots groups and people in and out of the civil service to confront the clearing of the forests, toxic dumping on the outer islands, and the opening of the economy to private capital. It is now in the stage of promoting discussions on social, economic, and political options, land issues and environmental impacts of projects and policies.

Senegal. The Association for the Promotion of Senegalese Women grew out of the women's branch of the sports and cultural association in Kaolack, one of thousands of such associations that emerged in the 1970s in that country. At its general assembly in 1987 the women's section decided to get involved directly in development work, and is seeking ways of development other then those being imposed under the heading of "structural adjustment."

Africa. FAVDO (Forum of African Voluntary Development Organizations). An international organization with some 200 affiliated African NGOs, FAVDO was organized about four years ago. It was an active participant in the Arusha Conference in February 1990, which drew up the

Charter on Popular Participation in Development. It has been embroiled in struggle since the beginning, resented by some in government and the international (European–North American) development circles for its readiness to challenge the status quo and to debunk received notions of what development and development cooperation should be about.

India. Sankalp is a program among silk embroidery workers of the Lucknow slums. It works to upgrade skills (e.g., providing new designs), teaches about marketing and prices, and "simultaneously reaffirms the traditional culture of the embroidery workers (who have been doing this work since the seventeenth century) and transforms a female workforce into a feminist one" (quoted from OXFAM internal project documents).

Eastern Caribbean. Eastern Caribbean Popular Theatre (Dominica, Grenada, St. Lucia, St. Vincent) was organized in 1983 as an umbrella for popular theater groups. "As popular educators our task is in the realm of communicating the difficulties and helping to seek out alternatives by using a cultural mode which is rooted in our own experience. Our task is to overcome the patterns and traditions of high-handed methods of education and learning and to . . . use non-formal means to challenge old patterns and to allow people to speak out, and to come up with their own choices" (quoted from OXFAM internal project documents).

El Salvador. With the new "peace" agreement, Left strategy aims to build a strong civil society capable of thwarting the oligarchy. There are many organizations for land rights, health, alternative development, communication, and education, loosely linked into an overall strategy for carrying out a peoples' program. Resettlement communities returning from wartime refuges are especially comprehensive in their programs, with committees of the village councils attending to production, health, education, security, relations with the government and all other spheres of their lives. The cooperative economy must be economically viable, ecologically sound as well as oppositional. Therefore the co-ops teach accounting and administration, agricultural methods, and machine maintenance as well as political history.

Guatemala. CPR (*Comunidades Populares en Resistencia*). Successive governments have tried to force indigenous peoples into "model villages" and to abandon their land rights and some traditions (e.g., in clothing or certain crops). Many have fled to Mexico. About 25,000 went into the forest and lead nomadic lives based on subsistence agriculture. The military is still trying to ferret them out. In one community of 257 families over the last few years, health workers were trained, education was provided up to fourth grade (including Spanish as a second language), and ways were worked out to produce and harvest crops despite indiscriminate bombing. Corn production has been stabilized and they are now expanding to beans, rice, and vegetables. All land preparation and production questions are decided by group committees, and tasks are divided among everyone capable of working.

The South American indigenous land rights movements require special attention. Coming out of a long history of resistance, they are nevertheless a recent development made urgent by a new wave of capitalist penetration of the Amazon, the discovery of oil and gold in previously unexploited areas, the impact of other popular movements, and the formation of interethnic alliances. The socialist movements have generally had a poor record of support for indigenous peoples' struggles. Although the destruction of native peoples was included in the lists of barbarities of expanding capitalism, there was rarely any mobilization in alliance with them as there was in fighting slavery. Perhaps the idea of the grand march of history through stages of progress led to the belief that indigenous peoples were doomed as societies and that their emancipation depended simply on their constituting the proletariat or converting into a modern peasantry organized in peasant associations, rural labor unions, and political parties.

The indigenous land rights movements raise the demand for recognition of their communal property, and are the most coherent force in the world today resisting privatization of the means of production because they have seen that capitalist penetration of their lands and private ownership have meant impoverishment. The indigenous movements have also taken up ecological concerns. For them, autonomy, economic development and ecological rationality are part of the same package, not conflicting goals. When viewed without the degrading seventeenth-century Romanticism, these movements can be recognized as important allies and in some respects leaders of the struggle.

Cases of indigenous rights movements can be found in Bolivia and Ecuador. In Bolivia the *Central de Pueblos Indigenas de Beni* (between the Andes and the Amazon) was organized in 1987. It played a major role in the March for Territory and Dignity in the capital, placing indigenous issues on political agenda. In Ecuador the Confederation of the Indigenous Nationalities of Ecuador links three regional federations (coast, Andes, Amazon), embracing nine major national groups. Formed in 1980, it led the Indian Uprising of June 1990, currently represents about 80% of the indigenous peoples, and has forced the government to enter into dialogue. Their program includes: land, natural resource and territorial rights based on indigenous peoples' self-determination, constitutional changes to recognize the multicultural nature of the society and to promote multicultural and multilingual education for all, respect for indigenous cultures, women's rights, and support for research on traditional medicine. It rejects the principle of private property and development concepts imposed by the capitalist market economy, which have kept the indigenous population in deep poverty, dependence, and marginalization, and calls for a stop to the colonization of Indian territories, ecological conservation, and sustainable use of natural resources based on communal labor and traditional technologies for conservation.

SOME LESSONS

The evolution of the NGO sector has not been a smooth process. NGOs form and dissolve; governments and U.S. agencies work to coopt, divide, or destroy them. They are beset by internal problems and have to deal with the same corruption and incompetence that afflicts the rest of their countries. But their mass appearance in many parts of the world and their parallel or convergent development identifies them as a force of great liberating potential. The experiences and promises of NGOs lead me to the three following theses.

1. *Empowerment is viable.* Empowerment is a viable challenge to the increasingly hollow formal democracy being trumpeted as a model for capitalist governance. In those places where formal freedoms were not tolerated until recently, the demands for "pluralism" and elections are so attractive that when combined with calls for private enterprise they seem to be equivalent to freedom, and are a rallying point for the opposition. At the same time, in those places where formal democratic rights have long been embodied in law, the mechanisms for thwarting the exercise of those rights have become pervasive and increasingly cynical, with whole new specialities arising for election management, "damage control," "plausible deniability," image making, disinformation, psychological warfare, and opinion manipulation.

While liberals have emphasized the first proposition, the Left has usually focused on the second. The traditional radical criticism of bourgeois democracy remains valid. First, the major decisions affecting people's lives are taken by the rulers of the economy outside of the elected organs of democratic government. Second, the structure of the political process has many filters in it that usually assure that public office is held by those who will accept the boundary conditions imposed by the ruling class, either out of a sense of "realism" or for more venal reasons. Third, the formation of political choice depends on information. Information is a commodity produced for and bought and sold in the marketplace. The combination of government lying and private ownership of information restricts the exercise of choice to a narrow range of the conceivable and the acceptable. Fourth and finally, the formation of consciousness in capitalism, with its divisive and disempowering ideologies of individualism, impotence, anti-intellectualism, and consumption reinforced by various social sanctions impede the critical evaluation of information and even of direct experience, so that electoral decisions are often capricious.

None of these barriers is absolute, but together they usually guarantee that the formal political process protects the system of power from large perturbations and from serious challenges. In the face of these barriers, it is unconscionable opportunism for Leftists to talk of "democracy" in the abstract, without qualifying adjectives. Of course, this criticism should not lead to contempt for even minimum formal democracy in a world where direct terrorist oppression is alive and well. But the justifiable disillusionment with bourgeois democracy should open up space for a platform of real empowerment that calls for popular determination about what affects our lives.

2. *Self-determination functions as a process.* The imbalance of world forces means that the seizure of power by the people will be a prolonged process requiring much more than majority approval. The determination of the United States to overthrow popular governments has not disappeared. The cold war is not over; only one side of it has disintegrated. A combination of economic sanctions, massive disinformation, support for legal and illegal counterrevolutionary movements, and armed intervention will make the survival of any revolutionary regime precarious. Only a people capable of mobilizing its own creative intelligence would be capable of surviving the long process of a besieged transformation. The boldness of the Salvadoran model is its envisioning of a prolonged dual power in which people's movements become *de facto* government in one social sphere after another, while their own strength and international support prevent the unleashing of the full brutal force of the state against them.

3. *Empowerment must precede revolution.* Broad empowerment must be the cornerstone of a revolutionary society. The experience of European socialism underlines the complexity of trying to build a new society with the materials of the old, including ourselves. We must cope with the complexities of planning, the menace of corruption, the pressure from various kinds of urgency to take shortcuts that disempower. We must resist the easy impatience with people who, despite analyses that revolutionaries make of their interests, persist in dealing with the world the way they learned to deal with it. This impatience often leads to intolerance of difference of opinion and ultimately to coercion.

PATHS TO EMPOWERMENT

I have claimed that empowerment is a deeper notion than democracy. It is concerned not only with rights but with opportunity and capacity to exercise rights, and not only with procedure for decision making but also with the decisions that are made. This helps define the short-term political goals. I outline below the most essential of these goals.

1. Resources for the exercise of choice imply basic economic security: Only when immediate survival needs are met can people devote their energy and imagination to long-range issues. The struggle for resources includes control over the circumstances of work, the use of space, and the nature of what is produced. This struggle is therefore implicitly anti-capitalist.

2. Information for choice implies the decommodification of the media, with the building of alternative media as an immediate demand. It also implies the broad education of people in understanding their lives so that they can imagine alternatives and select means of change. This in turn leads to the end of the exclusionary practices that limit and distort education for the oppressed sectors of society.

3. Self-confidence is not usually recognized as a right because it seems so personal. But the lack of confidence either in one's own capacity or in the expectation of being listened to that comes from growing up in a racist, sexist, hierarchical, and bigoted society is a major destroyer of human potential.

4. Discussion around empowerment should also lay to rest the notion that we are against the individual. The basic communist goal is making it possible for people to achieve their own free individual development through collectively creating the conditions that make it possible for everyone.

5. Opportunity implies solidarity, a supportive atmosphere. Again this is not something to legislate but to build in struggle.

6. Finally, we come to formal rights. In the context of empowerment we can evaluate these rights by the measure of empowerment or disempowerment. Elections, for example, are often disempowering, since they create illusions of power or of being on the edge of power. Yet they can also be empowering when they are used by a mass movement to ratify its agenda.

The goal of empowerment should inform not only the long-term strategy but also the tactics of a revolutionary movement. In the United States, progressive politics rises and falls in episodes around particular struggles such as the abolition of slavery, women's suffrage, industrial unionism, civil rights, opposition to the war in Vietnam, and so on. After months, years, or sometimes decades the struggle inevitably subsides with some gains and many unfulfilled promises. In engaging in these struggles we always have to ask, how will people come out of this struggle more empowered? Such a measure would lead us to evaluate demonstrations not by numbers of people alone, nor by how many newspapers we distributed or the press coverage we received, but by what we did to raise consciousness. What ideas did we teach or feelings mobilize? How did we as participants come out of the action changed?

Each element of an empowering politics is distinct, requiring particular practices or goals. Each of them also needs research and discussion. Revolutionary scholars should give priority to research for empowerment. Following are three elements of that agenda. First, the economics of resistance: In a world dominated by the transnational corporations, how can local economically viable efforts survive? In order to succeed do they have to behave like any other business? If they are successful, what prevents commercial interests, better financed and connected, from moving in and taking over? How can cooperatives flourish in a hostile environment? What can progressive local and municipal governments do to meet peoples' needs within the financial and legal constraints of the new world order? What could national governments do to control their own participation in the global economy, with its unequal exchange and monopoly of credit resources in ways that benefit their own people?

Second, consciousness raising: I mean this in the full sense of people questioning their unexamined beliefs and feelings about their place in the world, about why things are the way they are, about whether change is possible, about whether politics is intelligible, about self. We have to study this process to understand the role of a good argument when either new experiences contradict deeply held ideology or when contradictory aspects of one's consciousness can no longer be kept separate. These are the "educable moments" when the buffers and rationalizations that keep people accepting what is as what must be begin to melt, the unthinkable is thought, the unfeelable is felt.

Third, we must create a theory of daily political practice—meetings, leafletings, marches, rallies, resolutions, symposium lectures, canvassing, talking to people, and so on. These activities make up the nitty-gritty of Left politics—with a view toward making them empowering events for the participants.

NOTES

1. The term "empowerment" is not satisfactory. It has too many meanings, from the political self-determination of the oppressed to assertiveness training

for businessmen. It can be coopted by the World Bank to refer to ways of getting communities to "participate" and acquiesce in their own domination. Furthermore, I do not have a good Spanish equivalent, and much of my thinking about it has come from or is directed toward Latin American experience. Therefore I use the word provisionally until we have a better, generally accepted term.

2. Some of the international and national aid, development, and environmental organizations have also gone through the process of broadening their vision as the limits of single issue amelioration have became apparent. Greenpeace, for example, has expanded from the protection of baby seals to the critique of pesticide addiction and from there to the search for alternative development. The OXFAM organizations grew out of a concern for world hunger and became prominent through their symbolic fasts. They recognized the limitations of famine relief and began to explore famine prevention, moving from a relief agency to development agency and from donor to partner. OXFAM America refuses government funding. Its program is based on the inseparability of economic viability, equality, empowerment of the most exploited and powerless, ecological rationality, and advocacy. Its analysis recognizes that women are the basic support of the rural economy and gives priority to women's empowerment. It argues that economic self-help without equity and empowerment would only create new structures of exploitation; equity without economic viability merely shares misery; economic development without ecological rationality would quickly create a wasteland.

Reclaiming the Alternative

RALPH MILIBAND

The title of this paper, "Reclaiming the Alternative," raises two questions: First, what alternative is to be reclaimed? And second, from whom and from what must the alternative be reclaimed? The alternative is of course socialism—a social order altogether different from the present one, and whose main features I discuss below. I want first to concentrate on the second question: From whom and from what does the socialist alternative need to be reclaimed?

One obvious answer is that it must be reclaimed from the antisocialist ideologues who, from a wide variety of positions, have always denounced the socialist enterprise as utopian, deluded, foolish, and also dangerous and sinister, since any attempt to put into practice the fantasies spun by deluded or malevolent intellectuals of the Left must inevitably lead to economic disaster and totalitarian rule. These denunciations, accompanied by the eulogy of the virtues of capitalism, have been the stock-in-trade of conservatism (and of liberalism) for a very long time, but they have had exceptionally strong currency in recent years. Reclaiming the alternative clearly requires that this propaganda should be countered. This involves both a sustained critique of things as they are *and* a plausible affirmation that a different social order is not only desirable but possible.

Unfortunately, it is not only against the Right that this affirmation has to be made but also against much of the Left as well. The culture of the Left nowadays is pervaded by a deep, corrosive pessimism about the possibility of a radically different social order, or by an even more corrosive skepticism about whether, if change were possible, it could achieve much or any improvement on what is now available in the more socially oriented capitalist democratic regimes. At no time in the last 200 years have so many people who situate themselves on the Left been less inclined to believe that there was meaning in a socialist project, however long-term it might be conceived. An idea and a hope that had nurtured generation after generation, despite catastrophic defeats, is now widely discounted from within the ranks of the Left itself. This is not to say that the people concerned have given up the struggle for specific reforms. It means rather that the struggle, for them, is not inscribed in a larger scheme of social renewal, which is now dismissed as a naive illusion. Implicitly, and sometimes explicitly, they have accepted the claim expressed with great clarity in Francis Fukuyama's *The End of History and the Last Man* that capitalist democracy represents "the end point of mankind's ideological evolution," and "the final form of human government" (Fukuyama 1992, xiii). Another way of saying this is that the best that can now be hoped for is a capitalism with a more human face.

The demoralization and disarray that affects much or even most of the Left is not very surprising. Here is a brief catalogue of reasons for it. First and perhaps most importantly, there is the disintegration of the Soviet Union and the collapse of Communist regimes in Eastern Europe. Socialists had no cause to regret the passing of the Brezhnev regime. But the coming to power of Mikhail Gorbachev, and the inauguration of *perestroika*, did foster the belief that the Soviet Union was embarked on a program of reform that might at long last turn it into something that would begin to resemble socialist democracy. This proved to be an illusion, rendered all the more bitter by what actually did follow Gorbachev's failure: a "Thermidor" more thorough than had ever been expected by Left critics of the Soviet regime, the resurgence of ethnic and nationalist hatreds, and incipient or actual warfare between some of the constituent units of the former Soviet Union. To this may be added the "Thermidors" of Eastern Europe, and the catastrophic degeneration of Yugoslavia into the savagery of "ethnic cleansing"—this after nearly half a century of Communist rule.

Secondly, there is the manifest failure of social democracy anywhere to offer a serious alternative, either programmatically or in practice when in power, to the policies pursued by bourgeois governments. The horizons of social democratic party leaders (and this includes the leaders of ex-Communist parties as well) are now limited to managing capitalism more efficiently and, circumstances permitting, more humanely than their conservative opponents. Social democratic parties remain an arena of struggle between "moderate" leaders and their radical challengers, but the leaders are in quite firm control.

Thirdly, changes have been occurring in capitalism itself—notably changes in the composition of the working class, and the ever-greater internationalization of capital. The shrinkage of the "traditional" working class and the break-up of working-class communities has also reduced, it is believed, the base of support on which parties of the Left and trade unions once relied. In any case, the working class, it is said (and has been said generation after generation), is no longer really interested, if it ever was, in Left politics or in any politics.

For its part, the internationalization of politics has greatly accentuated the vulnerability of national economies to currency and other fluctuations, and correspondingly reduced the room a Left government, if it ever came to power, would have to undertake a radical program of legislation. As if this were not enough, there is a widespread belief that the main agencies of the Left—parties and trade unions—far from being "prefigurative" institutions, pointing to a liberating future, are themselves plagued by racism, sexism, bureaucratic centralism, top-down leadership, undemocratic practices, and so on.

Clearly, it would be foolish to deny that there is much about the developments of the last few decades that has been deeply unfavorable to socialist prospects. What is at issue, however, is not this but whether these developments justify the triumphant attitude of the Right about the demise of socialism, and the despair of the Left. I don't believe this to be the case, not on the grounds that all is bound to be well in the long run because history so ordains, but for much more solid reasons.

Most important of all is the fact that capitalism is ever more afflicted by the most fundamental of its contradictions, namely that while it is an immensely productive and expansive system it is nevertheless unable, because its organizing principle is private profit, to provide a materially secure and morally satisfying life for all. This is not simply a matter of deprived minorities in the inner cities, but of the majority who, despite access to consumer durables, live in the shadow of unemployment, insecurity, poor and worsening social and collective services, a steadily less friendly environment, and a correspondingly deteriorating "quality of life."

Capitalism remains a system based on domination and exploitation, in which a minority constitutes a power elite or ruling class, based on the ownership or control of the main means of production, the means of administration and coercion, and the means of communication and persuasion. For all its democratic pretensions, it is a system of oligarchy, only tempered by weak democratic forms. These forms, and the pressure that they permit from below may help to attenuate the worst effects of capitalist rule (though this is becoming ever more problematic), but do not in any case eliminate them.

Because of these inherent, systemic features, capitalism remains a permanent battlefield, which makes a bitter mockery of the idea of community, civic contentment, and social harmony. The system is the source of an endless stream of demands from below, for better wages, hours, and conditions, for better social and collective services, for the protection of the environment, for an end to discrimination, for an extension of the rights of citizenship. These demands are countered by a variety of entrenched interests, at the core of which are the vested interests of corporate power, with a state unable or unwilling to challenge them. The struggle this produces is now more acute, now less, but it cannot be resolved within the system.

What then is the place of socialism in this picture? An answer to that question requires us first of all to say what socialism is not. First of all, it is not Soviet-type Communism. This was perceived and proclaimed from the time of the Bolshevik Revolution onward by people on the Left of very different persuasion, from social democrats at one end to anarchists and (from the early 1920s onward) by Trotsky and his followers at the other. Whatever else these critics were wrong about, the Soviet experience proved them to have been right on this score. It is because the Soviet Union was very far removed from socialism that it is ignorant nonsense to claim, as is so often done nowadays, that its demise means "the death of socialism." However important in many different ways, the failure of Soviet-type Communism is irrelevant as a judgment on the future of socialism, and will increasingly come to be seen to be such.

It is also important to say that socialism does not hold the promise of impending redemption. The notion that it did promise a world made anew by the cleansing process of revolution, a world freed from all the ills that have beset humankind, has been a powerful strand in the socialist tradition. It is a vision that has sustained many socialists, generation after generation. Unfortunately, it needs to be said that it bears no relation to reality.

Realistically, socialism has to be seen as both an extension and a transcendence of a capitalist-dominated social order. It has to build on what has been achieved by dint of a stubborn struggle over many years in terms of political and social advance; it also seeks to push this process ever further in order to realize the basic aims of socialism. These aims, which define the meaning of socialism, encompass three interrelated and interdependent sets of policies. One of them is the democratization of life far beyond anything of which class societies are capable, or indeed can afford. The second is the achievement of an egalitarianism of condition without which the notion of citizenship turns into a more or less empty shell. The third—and the most controverted on the Left itself—is the bringing of a *predominant* part of the means of economic activity into various forms of social ownership. The emphasis is intended to suggest the persistence under socialism of a "mixed economy," but one in which the public sector is much more extensive than the private one, and includes the "commanding heights of the economy"—a reversal of what now obtains in capitalist economies.

Democratization under socialist auspices means the radical extension of citizenship rights, at work and in society at large. It means that power should be so distributed as to prevent any single group from enjoying an undue measure of it, and that wherever power is democratically bestowed, it should also be subject to effective checking and control. Socialism is a permanent struggle against the production and reproduction of oligarchies, in the state and in society. Egalitarianism means, not the striving for perfect equality, which is an absurd notion, but for a radical reduction in the inequalities of every sort—in income, wealth, life chances, and so on—that are an intrinsic part of the life of capitalist societies.

The necessity for socialization arises from the fact that to maintain most of the means of economic activity under private ownership and control is, in effect, to accept the indefinite perpetuation of a capitalist-dominated social order, with its oligarchic and exploitative features only very partially qualified. Experience both in Communist countries and in capitalist ones shows well enough that the mere transfer of means of production from the private to the public domain is no guarantee that anything much is changed in the production process. But socialization is not just public ownership: It means the extension of democracy to the economic realm and a fundamental transformation in the nature of that realm.

Socialism is a goal, the full realization of which stretches into an indefinite future. It is in this perspective a *process* to be fashioned and strengthened by successive generations. There are many things that a socialist government, backed by powerful popular support, can do immediately. Yet experience has shown that an excessive "voluntarism," which seeks to mold society without regard to the many historic forces that have previously shaped it, is a recipe for disaster. The obverse danger to "voluntarism" is accommodation to these forces and a consequent paralysis of the will for change.

The point is that the goals of socialism, as outlined here, are not in the least "utopian." On the contrary, they are solidly grounded in the concrete reality of the social order and correspond to aspirations that are not confined to socialists alone, since the discontents that the social order evokes are not confined to a small minority. They are felt by the vast majority of the population, and that majority is mainly constituted by wage earners. Contrary to a facile sociology that speaks of the "disappearance" of the working class, wage earners in industrial, clerical, service, and distributive occupations do remain a majority of the population of advanced

capitalist countries. They also remain the main (but not the only) constituency that socialists have to reach. The reason why this is so is not that
wage earners are the bearers of some kind of historical mission, but simply that, if the support of a majority of the population is necessary for
serious socialist advance, that support will in large part have to come from
wage earners—and of course from other layers of the population as well.
The pessimists tell us that to hope for such support is itself "utopian."
For is not the working class deeply divided by gender, race, ethnicity,
nationality, religion, skills, location in the process of production, and
conditions of life? And is it not the case that these divisions not only inhibit
the kind of "class consciousness" that socialist advance requires, but also
foster deformations such as racism, sexism, hypernationalism and xeno-
phobia, antisemitism, and a search for scapegoats?

To note this is indeed necessary. But to stop at that point leaves much
out of account. It leaves out of account the fact that the divisions in the
working class, real though they are, do not obliterate the fact that wage
earners share certain basic characteristics: the fact that their main source
of income is the sale of their labor power and/or state entitlements; that
their income places them in the lower and lowest levels of the income
scale; that they have little or no individual power in the process of production or in society at large, great though their potential collective power
is; that their standard of living is greatly dependent on inadequate collective and social services; and that it is they above all who are most subject to all the failings and derelictions of a system that is not run by them
or for them. They do not all experience these failings and derelictions
in the same way, but "privileged" though some may be in relation to
others, they remain part of a common subordination.

Also, the pessimists ignore the fact that all the divisions that exist
among wage earners have not prevented majorities being found again
and again in many countries in support of programs of radical reform,
offered by parties of the Left. This is all the more remarkable, given the
daily assault on consciousness from anti-Left forces, to which wage earners and everybody else is exposed. Sociological majorities *can* be transformed into political ones; and the fact that the electoral success of Left
parties has, to say the least, so often led to disappointing results cannot
be attributed to the constituencies that supported these parties. Clearly,
all experience thus far shows that no substantial number of people in
capitalist democracies will support parties committed to a project whose
realization depends on an insurrectionary upheaval, and whose rhetoric
is correspondingly unacceptable. But there are nevertheless potential
majorities in these countries to support programs of radical reform that
seriously challenge the existing structures of power and privilege.

The real problem is how potential majorities are to be turned into
actual ones. This is, or should be, the task of agencies of change; and

there is no doubt that the situation, from this point of view, is not good. Parties of the Left are in disarray, and so are social movements that, not so long ago, were widely believed to be strong sources of pressure upon the established order. Reclaiming the alternative requires, among other things, the solid implantation of socialist parties able to make their presence effectively felt on the political scene. The time is long past for indulging in a fetishism of the party, according to which building the party is the answer to all problems. But it is nevertheless a necessary task.

Another such task is the strengthening of the intellectual forces that can counter the propaganda that pours forth in the defense of capitalism and the social order it dominates. In this task, Marxism, or at least the Marxism of Marx, has an important role to play. The qualification is required in order to distinguish classical Marxism from its later accretions and deformations. Classical Marxism may be compared to a box of tools, some of which have become blunted and unusable over time; but the box also includes tools that remain indispensable to pry open contemporary reality. In particular, class analysis, which is at the core of Marxism, provides a precious clue—no more but no less—to that reality. These tools may need sharpening or modification, but they should not be discarded.

Finally, the question may well be asked: Why worry about socialism at all, since it is such a long-term and problematic prospect? What need is there for the vision that socialism represents? Why not concentrate on reform and the daily struggles it necessitates, rather than think in terms of uncertain alternatives? The answer to this is that having socialism as a point of reference orients daily struggles and locates them within a larger framework; and socialism as a point of reference also makes possible a comprehensive and systematic critique of the social order, which is by definition lost where the struggle for reform is only seen as a response to "problems" unrelated to their larger context.

I hope I have made it clear that I don't think of reclaiming socialism as an exercise in the rescue of a block of ideas set in concrete that, once rescued, simply need to be "applied." As I have suggested, socialism is a process, open, flexible, malleable, with a set of goals that lie at its core and that define it. Striving for their advancement remains the noblest of all possible tasks.

REFERENCE

Fukuyama, F. 1992. *The End of History and the Last Man*. London: Hamish Hamilton.

Revolution as Strategy and Tactics of Transformation

IMMANUEL WALLERSTEIN

id the French Revolution fail? Did the Russian Revolution fail? These are two questions that at one time might have seemed absurd. They no longer seem absurd. But how does one answer such questions?

Revolution is a strange word. Originally it was used in its etymological sense to mean a circular movement that returns to the point of origin. It can still be used to mean this, but it soon became extended to mean simply a turning and then an overturning. The Oxford English Dictionary records its usage as early as 1600 in the sense of the overthrow of a government by persons subject to it. Of course, the overthrow of a government is not necessarily inconsistent with the concept of a return to a point of origin: Many a political event called a "revolution" by its protagonists has been asserted by them to be the restoration of rights infringed, and hence a return to an earlier, better system.

In the Marxist tradition, however, revolution has been firmly ensconced within a linear theory of progress. Victor Kiernan (1991, 476) captures it best, I believe, when he asserts that it means a "cataclysmic leap" from one mode of production to another. Still, like most concepts, it is insufficient to define it; it must be placed in opposition to some alternative. And, as we know, again in the Marxist tradition (but not only), the alternative to "revolution" is "reform."

Reform versus revolution came to mean, in the debates of the late nineteenth and twentieth centuries, slow aggregative change versus swift change, small-scale changes versus large-scale change, reversible change versus irreversible change, improving change that is therefore pro-systemic versus transforming change that is therefore antisystemic, inefficacious change versus efficacious change. Of course, in each of these antinomies I have loaded the dice, giving each the characterization that revolutionary discourse utilized.

There is in addition an ambiguity within the Marxist tradition itself. Marxists often made a distinction between a political revolution (which could be a surface phenomenon) and a social revolution (the real thing). In addition, Marx and Engels themselves were not averse to using the word "revolution" for such concepts as "industrial revolution," and even to suggest that the "industrial revolution" was more important or more fundamental than the "French Revolution." This suggestion was of course quite consonant with the basic philosophical bias of historical material-ism, but it was not necessarily a great succor to voluntarist political action. Hence it was that revolution came to symbolize more and more in the tradition of the Marxism of the parties—and especially in the Bolshevik tradition—the violent overthrow of a bourgeois government by the pro-letariat, or at the very least the violent overthrow of a reactionary government by popular, progressive forces.

We are not at an end of the ambiguities. The concept of "violent overthrow" is not self-evident. Does a so-called spontaneous uprising, or a disintegration of the existing power structure, constitute a revolution, or is it only one if such an uprising is then canalized by a revolutionary party? When did the French Revolution occur—with the attack on the Bastille, or with the effective coming to power of the Jacobins? The Russian (October) Revolution was traditionally thought to have begun with the storming of the Winter Palace. Later, however, "revolutions" were thought to start before the actual seizure of state power. That is, it was thought essential to lead up to such a seizure with long guerrilla campaigns, the whole being characterized by Mao Zedong as "protracted struggle." The protracted struggle was thereupon put forward as the essential element of the revolutionary process, and not only before the seizure of the state organs but also afterwards (the "cultural revolution").

And one last ambiguity remains to be noted. After the Baku Congress, anti-imperialist struggle was given the label of "revolutionary" activity, but the theoretical relationship of such anti-imperialist revolution to socialist revolution has never been entirely clear. This is because there has been no consensus whatsoever. Was the Algerian Revolution in a category with, or quite different from, the Vietnamese Revolution? There have been many actual trajectories. In Cuba, the "revolution" was not Marxist or even socialist before the seizure of power, but Marxist and socialist afterwards. In Zimbabwe, the rhetorical road traveled was the inverse.

In any case, as we now see clearly, the results have been extraordinarily mixed. The Mexican Revolution does not seem today to have had very revolutionary results. And the Chinese? For their part, the Russian revolutionaries are now a historical memory, and at the moment not one very honored in Russia. The first question that it seems reasonable to ask, therefore, is whether the so-called revolutionary trajectory has indeed been more or less efficacious than the reform trajectory. Of course, we can do the same skeptical review of the accomplishments of social-democratic reform. How fundamentally was the Labour Party able to transform Great Britain? Or even the Swedish Social Democratic Party? In the 1990s when almost everyone from China to Sweden to Mexico is talking the language of the "market," one may wonder legitimately whether 150 to 200 years of revolutionary tradition have paid off.

One may wonder even more how great has been the distinction of revolutionary and reformist activity. Particular parties, particular social movements, particular complexes of social activity that are perceived as a long and large "revolutionary" event can all be described (probably without exception) as the locus of shifting tactics, such that they looked more revolutionary or insurrectionary or radical or transformatory at some points in time and distinctly less so at others. Real-existing revolutionary leaders have always tried to steer a middle course, often in zigzag form, between "selling out" at one end and "adventurism" at the other. Of course, one person's "adventurism" has been another's "true revolutionary commitment." One person's "sellout" has been another's "one step backward, two steps forward."

It is perhaps time to stop throwing stones at each other and to take a sober look at the objective constraints on Left political activity over the past two centuries throughout the world, and the degree of strength of the underground pressure for transformation. Let us start with the givens. We live in a capitalist world-system that is deeply inegalitarian and oppressive. It has also been successful in expanding world production, which has therefore placed considerable economic strength in the hands of those who are the chief beneficiaries of the world-system. We may assume that those who benefit wish to continue the system more or less as is, and will invest considerable political energy in maintaining the status quo. Can we assume that those who do not benefit wish with equal fervor to transform it? No we cannot, for several reasons: There exists ignorance; there exists fear; there exists apathy, and there exists the outlet for a clever minority of the oppressed of individual upward mobility. In addition, the nonbeneficiaries are weaker—economically and militarily— than the beneficiaries.

This asymmetry of political strength and sociopsychological stance is the basic dilemma that has faced the world Left since it began to organize itself consciously in the nineteenth century. It was the question what to do about this asymmetry that the reform versus revolution debate was about. It is remarkable in retrospect how similar were the answers each side gave. Collective self-education will overcome ignorance; collective self-organization will overcome fear and apathy. An organized class culture will restrain the potential deserters who are tempted by individual social mobility by offering this group leadership roles in the present movements and future governments. And the imbalance of social strength between the beneficiaries and the nonbeneficiaries can be overcome by taking away from the beneficiaries the control of the state machineries, which once done will change the balance.

This is what major movements have been doing for some 150 years now. The strategy and the tactics of the Chinese Communist Party, the African National Congress of South Africa, and the Austrian Social Democratic Party—to take three well-known examples—have been remarkably similar, given how different have been the three historical circumstances. One can label all three movements magnificently successful, or all three miserable failures. What I find difficult to accept is any analysis that gives a different success rating to each of the three. They have been magnificently successful in their ability at mass mobilization, and in achieving some significant reforms in their respective countries such that the situation today is radically different from the situation in 1900 or so; and for some persons and in some respects, radically better. They have been miserable failures in that we are still living in a capitalist world-economy that is, if anything, more inegalitarian than it was in 1900. There are still multiple forms of oppression in each of these countries, and these movements have in various ways constrained rather than facilitated current protests against some of these forms of oppression.

Is the cup half full or half empty? Perhaps we are asking the wrong questions. The first question is whether, in the nineteenth and twentieth centuries, there were historical alternative strategies for each of these movements that retrospectively seem plausible and could have achieved more. I doubt it. It is in many ways a silly exercise to rewrite history on the basis of a simulation. But it does seem to me that the alternative movements that actually presented themselves in each of these cases lost out because they were obviously less efficacious from the point of view of the nonbeneficiaries of the system, and that the sum of the reforms achieved by the dominant movements have been worth something, even if there is no postcapitalist utopia in any of the three countries. Quite the contrary.

Having said this, the sum total is very disappointing, given the incredible social energy that has been put into revolutionary activity in the twentieth (and nineteenth) centuries. I share the sense of the revolutionaries of 1968 that the Old Left in all its versions had become by that point in time "part of the problem." Since then, however, the world Left has moved on. The worldwide revolution of 1968 has had an immense impact on forces everywhere that think of themselves as antisystemic. I would say there have been six major consequences in our mode of analysis, each of which I wish to state in a restrained way.

1. The two-step strategy—first take state power, then transform society—has moved from the status of self-evident truth (for most persons) to the status of doubtful proposition.
2. The organizational assumption that political activity in each state would be most efficacious if channeled through a single cohesive party is no longer widely accepted.
3. The concept that the only conflict within capitalism that is fundamental is that between capital and labor—and that consequently other conflicts, based on gender, race, ethnicity, sexuality, and so on are all secondary, derivative, or atavistic—no longer has wide credence.
4. The idea that democracy is a bourgeois concept that blocks revolutionary activity has been giving way to an idea that democracy may be a profoundly anticapitalist and revolutionary idea.
5. The idea that an increase in productivity is the essential prerequisite of socialist construction has been replaced by a concern with the consequences of productivism in terms of ecology, in terms of the quality of life, and in terms of the consequent commodification of everything.
6. The faith in science as the foundation stone of the construction of utopia has given way to a skepticism about classical science and popular scientism in favor of a willingness to think in terms of a more complex relationship between determinism and free will, order and chaos. Progress is no longer self-evident.

None of these six revisions of our premises is totally new. But the revolution of 1968, by shaking the legitimacy of the Old Left, has transformed the doubts that a small handful of persons had into a far more widespread revisionism, a veritable "cultural revolution." Each of these six revisions of premises is complex and could be elaborated at length. I cannot do that here. I can only talk to the implications of these revisions for antisystemic political activity, and in particular for the strategy and tactics of "revolution."

The first and most fundamental implication is that "revolution"—as the word was used in Marxist–Leninist movements—is no longer a viable concept. It has no meaning, at least no meaning now. "Revolution" was supposed to describe an activity by a party, its struggle to achieve state power, its role as the standard-bearer of labor in the capital–labor struggle, its scorn for democracy as mere "bourgeois rights," its dedication to increased productivity, its self-description as scientific. Do parties meeting this description and attracting significant support still exist? I don't see very many, if any at all. What we see in their place are two things. The first are Old Left parties, often with changed names, who are struggling to survive electorally on the basis of eclectic centrist programs about which they don't seem to feel very strongly, heirs of a vague sentiment for social justice (in the manner in which the Radical Socialists in the France of the Third Republic incarnated the tradition of laicity). The second is the ever-evolving panoply of parties and movements who are the diluted heirs of the revolution of 1968: Green parties, feminist movements, movements of oppressed ethnic and racial so-called minorities, gay and lesbian movements, and what might be called base community movements.

In the United States, in the 1980s, there was talk of creating a Rainbow Coalition of such movements. But in the end nothing much came of this idea. Indeed, as we come into the 1990s, we observe two enormous political dilemmas for the world's antisystemic movements. First, the new antisystemic movements that emerged out of the revolution of 1968 were quite successful in their attack on the premises that undergirded the Old Left, but have floundered ever since in their quest for an alternative strategy. Is state power still relevant, or not? What could be the basis of any lasting alliance between movements? As time has gone on, the answers have seemed increasingly similar to that of the now highly eclectic Old Left movements. Secondly, the 1990s are seeing the spread of movements launched in the 1980s that are racist and populist. But quite often they use themes and assume tonalities that overlap partially with what the new antisystemic movements do. There is enormous risk of political confusions of multiple types.

So here we are: tired and eclectic shells of Old Left parties, no viable concept of "a revolution," new antisystemic movements that are vigorous but have no clear strategic vision, and new racist–populist movements of growing strength. Amidst all this, the besieged defenders of the existing capitalist world-system are by no means disarmed, and are pursuing a policy of the flexible postponement of contradictions, waiting as they are for the moment to pursue a radical transformation of their own away from a capitalist mode of production to some new but equally inegalitarian and undemocratic world-system.

It is time long past when we should have defined with some clarity an alternative strategy to the defunct one of "revolution." I think that such redefinition is a collective, worldwide task. I can only suggest here a few lines of action that might be elements of such a strategy, but that do not add up to a total strategy.

1. The first is a return to a traditional tactic. Everywhere, in every workplace, we should push for more, that is, that more of the surplus value be retained by the working class. This once seemed so obvious, but it came to be neglected for a variety of reasons: The parties were afraid of trade unionism and economism; protectionist tactics of workers in high wage areas; movement-dominated state structures acting with the logic of employers. Simultaneously, we must press for the full internalization of costs by every enterprise. Local level constant pressure for such internalization and for more—more in Detroit, more in Gdansk, more in Sao Paulo, more in Fiji—can deeply shake the patterns of accumulation of capital.

2. Secondly, everywhere in every political structure at every level, we must demand more democracy, that is, more popular participation and more open decision making. Again, once thought obvious, this has been restrained by a deep distrust by Left movements of mass psychology, the origin of vanguardism. Perhaps this was legitimate in the nineteenth century, but a transformation to a better world-system will not be possible without genuine, deeply motivated popular support, which has to be created and developed through more democracy now.

3. Thirdly, the world Left has to come to terms with its dilemma concerning universalism versus particularism. The Napoleonic imperial universalism affected by the Old Left has no merit, but neither does an endless glorification of smaller and smaller particularisms. We need to search for how to construct a new universalism based on a foundation of countless groups and not on the mythical atomic individual. But this requires a kind of global social liberalism that we are reluctant to accept. We need thus to give operational meaning (and not mere puffery) to Senghor's "*rendez-vous de donner et de recevoir.*" It should be tried at countless local levels.

4. Fourthly, we need to think of state power as a tactic, utilizing it whenever we can and for whatever immediate needs, without investing in it or strengthening it. Above all, we must shun managing the system, at any level. We must cease to be terrified at the political breakdown of the system.

Will this transform the system? I do not know. I see it as a strategy of "overloading" the system by taking the ideological slogans of liberalism seriously, something never intended by the liberals. What could overload the system more than the free movement of people, for example? And, along with overloading the system, it is a strategy of "preserving our options," of moving towards better things immediately, of leaving the total responsibility of managing the existing world-system to its beneficiaries, of concentrating on creating a new sociality at the local and world levels.

We must in short become practical, consequential, constant workers in the vineyard, discussing our utopias, and pushing forward. As the present world-system crashes down amidst us in the next fifty years, we must have a substantive alternative to offer that is a collective creation. Only then have we a chance of obtaining a Gramscian hegemony in world civil society, and thereby of winning the struggle with those who are seeking to change everything in order that nothing change.

REFERENCE

Kiernan, V. G. 1991. "Revolution." In *A Dictionary of Marxist Thought*, 2nd revised edition, ed. T. Bottomore. Oxford: Blackwell.

PART FOUR

FEMINISM, RACE, SEXUALITY, AND NATURE: INTERSECTIONS WITH MARXISM

Marxism and Sexuality: The Body as Battleground

ROSALYN BAXANDALL

In the past Marxists haven't been bothered with questions of sexuality. What discussion there has been on the Left took place among the utopian socialists in the 1830–1950s as well as among some of those involved in the early heady days of the Russian Revolution (1914–1921) and scattered socialist, sexually radical groups in Yorkshire, England and Germany from the 1880s to the 1920s. The beats, however, in New York City and in San Francisco in the 1950s did challenge the bourgeois conventions of sexuality and the family. Even the social movements of the 1960s and 1970s, with the exception of the women's and gay liberation movements, have had little to contribute to a sexual politics.

During the antiwar movement of these recent decades, women were told to say "yes" to men who said "no" to the draft, and to "put their bodies on the line." The slogan "the personal is political," made up by Redstockings, a radical feminist group, was transformed by movement men to mean that they dictated the forms the movement should take, while women ran the risks involved in radical political action. On the whole, the ejaculatory politics of the antiwar and civil rights movements was oppressive to women's bodies and minds. As both Tom Hayden and Todd Gitlin of Students for a Democratic Society (SDS) put it in their autobiographies, "The movement hangs together on the end of the penis" (Hayden 1988, 107; Gitlin 1987, 108). To be fair, some aspects of the "sexual revolution"—which for many constituted an essential component of the radical movements of this period—were emancipatory and empowering for women. Women acquired skills, political savvy, and confidence. As Alice Echols (1992, 20) points out, North American feminists except for Ellen Willis and Kathy Sarachild have been too one-dimensional about their approach to the New Left and the sexual revolution.

We can, however, be emphatic and unqualifying about the fact that after twenty years of the Reagan–Bush conservative assault on sexual freedom and reproductive rights, it becomes imperative to rethink and act on a liberating sexual agenda. The Clarence Thomas–Anita Hill debacle also points up the need to articulate a radical analysis that focuses on racism and sexism. Clinton and Gore are opportunists in this area, which is a positive factor only if the Left organizes a position counter to theirs. For example, both were previously on record in their states as supporting state antiabortion laws. Their recent switch shows that they can be moved by women's mass action. As No More Nice Girls, a reproductive rights activist group that has been in operation since the 1970s, put it, "Politicians read our lips, vote pro-choice or get pink slips." In fact, all the newly elected women—Democrats and Republicans alike—are pro-choice. Of course, there is a question of where these new female legislators stand on issues other than choice, and there are problems with the concept of choice itself. The manner in which abortion rights issues have been handled in public debate reveals the complexity of these issues, a complexity due at least in part to the intimate association of these issues with current notions about and attitudes toward sexuality—especially female sexuality. In order to frame a radical sexual agenda it is thus essential to examine both abortion rights per se, and the attitudes toward sexuality and eroticism that have informed the debate over those rights.

ABORTION RIGHTS: CHOICE, EQUALITY, AND REPRODUCTIVE FREEDOM

The idea of the right to choose is problematic at the same time that it is politically compelling. First, the right to choose ignores the fact that peoples' desires are often contradictory. A woman may want to be a mother, but not want to be a mother like her mother. A poor woman may desire both a child and a personal life outside of poverty that a child would prevent. The principle of free choice also evades the moral questions about when, under what conditions, and for what purposes reproductive decisions should be made. Should women get abortions on the grounds that they prefer one gender over another, which amniocentesis can now determine? Such a decision would be sexist in a society where the majority of people say that they prefer to have male children. There is another potential danger in the assertion of women's right to control over reproduction as an absolute or exclusive right: It can be turned back on women to reinforce a view of reproductive activity as the special, biologically destined province of them alone.

The right to choose also means little when women are without sufficient political and economic power to set the terms of their choices. In cultures where illegitimacy is stigmatized and female infants are devalued, often no real reproductive alternatives exist for women. Nor should the choice be that of either a job or a child. Many women would choose children over abortion if there were adequate day care and mothers' allowances. The American Cyanamid plant in West Virginia, for example, gave women an option between sterilization or losing their jobs. Is this a real choice? A Marxian redirection of the reproductive rights movement should focus less on choice and more on how to transform the social conditions of choosing, working, and reproducing. One situation that would thereby gain more attention is the fact that the conjunction of medical, corporate (especially drug and insurance companies), and state interests in the management of reproduction has defined the choices of all women, but in a way that is crucially different depending on one's class and race. It is poor and "third world" women who are more likely to be used as experimental subjects in international population control programs for testing or dumping contraceptive chemicals, or for implants whose safety may be questioned by the Federal Drug Administration.

And yet, in spite of this lack of options, it is wrong to depict women of any class as passive victims of medical, commercial, and state policies of reproductive control. Women of all classes have successfully challenged and changed laws on birth control and summoned drug companies and doctors regarding the severe health hazards of the pill, the coil, deprovera, and other synthetic hormones. Groups of Mexican American, Native American, and African American women have fought together with women's health groups against involuntary sterilization.

Such resistance notwithstanding, the phrase "the right to choose" actually constitutes a step backwards, a compromise with the growing Right, who use the more compelling slogan "the right to life." The idea of the right to choose ignores the essential feminist truth that in a male-dominated society no choice a woman makes is entirely free or entirely in her interest. Many women have had abortions they didn't want or wouldn't have wanted if they had any plausible means of caring for a child. Countless others wouldn't have gotten pregnant in the first place were it not for inadequate contraception, sexual confusion and guilt, male pressure, and other stigmata of female powerlessness. Women who have abortions are victims also of ordinary miscalculation, technological failure, or vagaries of passion, all of which are bound to exist in any society.

It was clear in the 1970s that abortion was a women's rights issue and a necessary condition for women's autonomy. In the late 1980s and early 1990s abortion began to be referred to as a human rights issue, and the life referred to became abstract. Without an emphasis on women's rights, we leave the door open for a discussion of fetal rights and parental consent. In the 1990s people seem afraid either to use the word "abortion," or to state that abortion is a women's issue. Since abortion and feminism have become dirty words, we use the word "choice" and speak of parental and human rights. This is a sign that the Left has become defensive and is losing ground to the neoconservatives.

In the women's liberation movement of the 1970s abortion rights activists asked for total repeal of all abortion laws, and free abortion on demand. During this period, activists referred to forced pregnancy as slavery. Feminist lawyers argued that criminal abortion laws imposed a formal servitude, an inequality for women that violated the Thirteenth Amendment, which ended slavery. Abortion rights should have continued to be regarded as a crucial aspect of women's equality. Women cannot participate equally in economic and social life without this ability to control their reproduction. This equal rights argument is a stronger, less ambivalent, and more compelling argument than that of the right to choose. It is also more compelling than the argument for the right to privacy, the grounds on which *Roe v. Wade*, the 1973 Supreme Court decision legalizing abortion, was ultimately made.

In *Roe v. Wade* the justices based their decision on the Fourth Amendment, which guarantees the right of people to be secure in their persons and houses. The Amendment is itself based on the right to privacy and personal liberty, a position that has two contradictory principles. Privacy was compatible with a legal tradition of noninterference in marriage, which denies women legal relief from economic and physical abuse by their husbands and enforces male dominance in the home. This tradition thus ultimately conflicts with the principle of personal freedom, insofar as it applies to the lives of women. Privacy buttresses the conservative idea that the personal is separate from the larger social structure and that the structure has no impact on private individual choice or action. A radical position on these ideas should insist that women be in control of decisions over abortion, but that noninterference by the state reinforce rather than undermine women's autonomy—autonomy being a clearer concept than privacy.

There is, however, one notion of privacy that does incorporate in an empowering manner the notion of personal freedom. The traditional liberal idea of privacy is that of the negative and qualified right to be left alone, while the more radical idea of privacy emphasizes the positive liberty of self-determination, and constitutes an aspect of equality. Thus the privacy doctrine is practically and theoretically double-edged, having the tendency to constrain as well as to expand reproductive rights. Privacy in the liberal sense makes it impossible to challenge traditional gendered reproductive and sexual norms. This negative right of privacy carries no corresponding obligation on the part of the state to facilitate reproductive rights, and obscures the public responsibility for reproductive freedom (Petchesky 1984). To avoid a narrow interpretation of privacy in regard to abortion issues, the social aspects of reproductive rights need to be emphasized (Copeland 1990).

There are two essential ideas that underlie a Marxist–feminist and activist view of reproductive freedom. The first is derived from the biological connection between women's bodies and sexuality and reproduction, which is an extension of the general principle of "bodily integrity," or "bodily self-determination." The notion that women should control their bodies—that is, their procreative capacities—derives from this materialist view (Petchesky 1984; Delphy 1977). The argument emphasizes the individual dimension of rights, individual self-determination, while its philosophical framework, that of natural rights, assumes a fixed biological person. The second philosophical idea is based on the historical, changing social position of women. This position states that in so far as women, under the existing division of labor between the sexes, are the ones most affected by pregnancy and most responsible for child rearing, it is they who must decide about conception, abortion, and child rearing. This argument implies a social arrangement that may be changed. It invokes the legitimating principle of socially determined needs, rather than natural rights. Both of these concepts are necessary for a Marxist–feminist reproductive platform (Petchesky 1984).

The nature of a radical reproductive position is therefore both individual and social, operating at the core of social life as well as within and upon women's individual bodies. The nature of these arguments is complex and confusing, and can seem contradictory in comparison to the simplistic right-to-life position, in which biology is destiny. Radical feminists think that although women control their sexuality and reproduction, they should at the same time ask men and society to take more responsibility for children and conception. Reproduction is a shared female experience transcending class division and permeating everything—work, politics, community involvement, sexuality, creativity, and dreams. Yet sexuality takes place in a particular society at a particular historical period. The sexual experience is therefore socially constructed and experienced differently by different classes and races, and by social groups in different eras. The acknowledgment of biological reality cannot be mistaken for biological determinism. Biology is a capacity as well as a limit, and can be a source of female power as well as of female confinement. Women want the right to control their bodies, but don't want to be defined or circumscribed by their reproductive capacity.

SEXUALITY AND EROTICISM: RECLAIMING PLEASURE, STIMULATING TOLERANCE

Coming to terms with the complex issues surrounding abortion rights necessarily involves an examination of the contradictions inherent in American attitudes toward sexuality and eroticism. To begin to frame a radical sexual agenda, we have first of all to be daring, and then to emphasize that sexual passion and love are also important human needs. However, in a male-dominated society female sexuality is a more complex matter than male's. For women, sex spells potential danger as well as pleasure (Vance 1984). A Marxist–feminist politics of sexuality, if it is to be credible and yet optimistic, must seek both to protect women from sexual danger and to encourage their pursuit of sexual desire and pleasure. The feminist preachers of sexual prudery such as Andrea Dworkin (1981, 1989) and Catherine MacKinnon (1987) make no distinction between rape and intercourse, marriage and prostitution, or fantasy and reality. Dworkin labels penetration in sexual intercourse rape. MacKinnon regards abortion reform as removing women's last protection from men's pressure for sex.

To focus only on the dangers of sexuality, violence, rape, and incest ignores the explorations of the body, curiosity, intimacy, sensuality, excitement, and human connection. Sex is delightful and frightening because it touches on the nonrational and the infantile. Exploring sexuality activates a host of intrapsychic anxieties: fear of merging with another, the blurring of bodily boundaries, dependency, the wish to dominate or be dominated, the loss of control, and one's own aggression and wishes to incorporate body parts, even entire persons: "Eroticism is a realm stalked by ghosts. It is a place beyond the pale, both cursed and enchanted" (Paglia 1990, 3). Having been told by Freud that pleasure threatens civilization, we wonder what will happen if there is no end to desire.

Sexuality also raises the fear of competition, as women recognize their own wishes to compete for attention and for love objects. Whether women are lesbian or heterosexual, their competitors are other women—an unsisterly prospect. Finally, female desire signals the giving up of vigilance and control—the responsibility of the proper woman—and causes profound unease about violating the boundaries of "traditional femininity." Transgressing gender boundaries raises the specter of separation from other women—from the mother and from literal and metaphorical sisters—leaving one isolated and vulnerable to attack. These subterranean pulls on women are no less powerful for the fact that they remain unnamed, so that unspoken fears are added to the sum of sexual terror. Without a better language to delineate these other sources of danger, everything is attributed to men, thereby inflating male power and impoverishing women's sense of agency. Women have to try to comprehend their own fears so that they don't project them. Otherwise, they leave the irrationality and volatility of sex open to manipulation by others, even becoming open to right-wing campaigns against sexual deviance, degeneration, and pollution.

Obscured in these debates is the fact that the hallmark of sexuality is its complexity, its multiple meanings, sensations, and connections. It is all too easy to cast sexual experiences as either wholly pleasurable or wholly dangerous. American society encourages this type of binary thinking, so that debate about sexuality tends to be couched in terms of either/or and yes/no positions. Actual sexual experience is multifaceted, difficult to grasp, and often unsettling. As the male world has overemphasized women's enjoyment of rape, in opposition the feminist community has emphasized the ubiquity of humiliation and danger. Initially useful as a consciousness-raising position, and an ideological counterpoint and leavening, this critique now shares the same undialetical and simplistic focus as its opposition. Neither position acknowledges sufficiently the interplay between power and desire, attraction and repulsion, acceptance and disavowal.

Nevertheless, it is precisely this interplay that complicates women's ability to maintain control of sexual interaction. In my experience I have often said "no" when I was really ambivalent, my mind and body in contradiction. However, in a male-dominated society a woman's "no" should be read as "no." Such definitive responses are difficult in sex and courting, since many of their rituals involve unspoken body language and marvelous expectation and mystery. Yet women and men alike do have to learn to communicate verbally, because they are socialized differently around sex: Both use different body languages and interpret the body languages of others differently.

In order to understand the rich brew of our sexuality we also have to be tolerant of difference. Women and men have a wide diversity of sexual experiences; what is pleasurable to one might be painful to another. We must dare to discuss the details of our experiences, desires, and fantasies; otherwise we fall back on myths about sexuality and texts that are prescriptive and overgeneralized. Sexuality is a particularly fluid, everchanging arena, evolving through adult life in response to internal and external vicissitudes. This constant flux in sexual experience renders it an unpromising domain for regulation. There can and should be political movements around issues of sexuality, but a radical sexual agenda should not promote rigid standards of politically correct behavior.

Gay rights advocates and "queer theorists" have emphasized that there are privileged forms of sexuality—such as heterosexuality, marriage, and procreation—that are protected and awarded by the state and subsidized through social and economic incentives. Those engaging in privileged acts, or who pretend to, enjoy good name and good fortune. To say that marriage is a privileged form of sexual relationship is not to imply that it does not involve difficulty and struggle, but merely that the married person's sexuality is affirmed by public attitudes and policy as that of the unmarried or homosexual person is not. Less privileged forms of sexuality are instead often regulated and forbidden by the state, religious and medical establishments, and public opinion. Those practicing these forms suffer stigma and invisibility, although they often attempt to resist the marginalization forced upon them by a disapproving society.

It should be obvious to say that any form of sexuality is nothing to be ashamed of, that its experience is not trivial, that all forms are very much part of the political landscape. But both the Right and the Left have often treated sexuality as either shameful or unimportant. Some people feel that sexuality is a topic of privilege, about which the intellectual and economic elite alone have sufficient leisure to be concerned. The right wing has been more vocal about its conservative sexual politics, which can be summarized as "Just say no," or as the "Three w's"—worship, war, and work. As Marxists we have to define our sexual ideology, or face being constantly caught off guard, merely reacting to the Right and retreating from radical positions to win favor from the ever-expanding middle ground of the political spectrum.

Ignoring sexuality means letting the powerful in our culture speak and leaving individual families in control, rather than forcing the state to take social responsibility and assure equality of sexual treatment. If Marxists are to be promoters of a radical agenda, we have to question this dichotomy between public and private in matters of sexuality. An insistence on the private nature of sexuality often means that women make decisions about sexual practice and that men and public institutions aren't responsible for these decisions or their outcomes. In America we have a private, for-profit, competitive health care system that makes the best care available only to the rich. The direction of research is decided by dollar amounts. Prevention is not emphasized, and research is not shared but kept secret for commercial reasons. Secrecy makes public scrutiny and informed choice difficult. Although in the United States the rhetoric of science and technology parades the neutrality of both, their practice is largely in the hands of drug corporations, physicians, and researchers who are motivated by profit, rather than social need.

Historically, women have been perceived as either madonnas (good girls) or whores (bad girls). Aborting women are associated with selfishness and immorality, while married mothers are regarded as morally pure and self-sacrificing. Women are taught by the mass media to be the objects of men's desire, rather than the subjects of their own desires. As sex objects women have been violated and used to sell products. An important part of the Marxist–feminist project must be for women to reclaim their sexuality and see themselves as desiring subjects in the full sense of the word—not only as victims of men's sexuality, but as active seekers of their own pleasure.

CONCLUSION

The conflation of sexuality with threat and violence that has marked public debate in recent years results in two related misrepresentations. On the one hand, abortion has become a moral issue, rather than a question of equality or personal freedom. On the other hand, sexuality has come to be associated with danger rather than pleasure. Our era is characterized by trials of violence and sexuality—the Lorena Bobbitt castration trial, the Amy Fisher shooting and statutory rape trials, the Mike Tyson rape conviction and all the attention paid it, including the protest of the Baptist Church—rather than by cases of political momentum like the Rosenberg, Hiss, or the Scope trials. At the same time, public assessment of politicians' capabilities has been similarly focused on sexual morality. Our potential presidents are judged not by their programs, but by their sexual infidelities: In an era of total corruption and lack of political imagination or vision, Gary Hart and Bill Clinton are raked over the coals for marital infidelities, and candidates for government appointments resign to avoid questions about their sexual proclivities. Sexual correctness has become the measure of ability and leadership.

The attitudes toward sexuality that characterize current U.S. society are in fact deeply contradictory. On the one hand, noncontact sex proliferates: telephone sex, 900 numbers, sex cable stations, mail-order porn, homemade pornographic videos, and so on. Perhaps this proliferation is in part because the fear of AIDS has made sexual contact increasingly stigmatized. At the same time, temperance, marriage, and chastity are regaining status. There is even a National Chastity Association, which has a dating service, whose beliefs include premarital sexual abstinence. Many of my female students who in dress and general appearance seem most invested in their own desirability proudly tell me that they are virgins and want to wait until marriage for sexual consummation. This confluence of chastity and eroticism is reminiscent of the Victorian era, when sex was a forbidden topic, but sex was so all-present that even chair legs had to be covered—skirted for fear of arousal. Then, as now, people lived in a highly ambiguous eroticized atmosphere.

Such an atmosphere generates a peculiar tension between prudery and prurience. Americans are obsessed with the suppression of many sexual practices that are voluntary, consensual, spontaneous, and joyful, yet have a voyeuristic fascination with the weird, violent, exploitative, and pathetic. Many state governments and television stations refuse to advertise condoms for protection against HIV infection, because it could be interpreted as promoting premarital sex. At the same time Americans have an insatiable appetite for lurid sexual detail: Witness the allure and the amount of media drama devoted to the Amy Fisher case, and the fact that the Meese report detailing what types of sexual practice should be censored became a best-seller.

These conflicted attitudes are reflected in the contradictions between explicit or sexually encoded media representation and public policies that betray a squeamish reaction to actual bodies. All around us are advertisements in which the face of a cartoon camel resembles a penis and testicles. Nearly naked buttocks stare at us from the backsides of buses. Sex, skin, and shock are used to sell us products. Yet we are a society of prudes, banning nude bathing and public breast feeding. Negative attitudes toward sexuality—which prescribe repression and Puritanism as an antidote for AIDS and teenage pregnancy, and which exist in oddly complicit conjunction with a prurient focus on sex—are part of the illness, not the cure. A measure of this is the fact that the caution, fear, and discussion of sexual practice in the newspapers have not made Americans more knowledgeable about sex. In what is billed as the "first representative survey of what people know about sex" conducted by the Kinsey Institute and Roper Organization, Americans couldn't answer ten out of eighteen questions correctly. The surveys asked elementary questions about basic physiology, like whether women can get pregnant during menstruation—which they can (*New York Times*, September 6, 1990).

These current attitudes are not only caused by the fear of AIDS. They exist also because we live in a frightening, volatile, and violent time. One cannot be sure that one will have or continue to have a job, bank savings, retirement, or home, or that one will not be shot randomly on the street or in school, or killed by carelessness in a plane or car. Safety standards have fallen and everyday existence is experienced as unregulated by corporate government policy. Perhaps the body has come to be perceived as the only remaining locus of possible control and autonomy, in an increasingly invasive and precarious society. People seem to have the idea that if they can control their physical selves through exercise, dietary measures, and restriction of sexual activity, life will be secure. Not to eat meat, smoke, drink alcohol, or engage in sex now means that one is a moral, responsible human being. America is in the midst of a major new temperance movement, the third in its history (*New York Times,* January 1, 1990).

In a world of so much flux, of shifting borders and national priorities, the physical body has thus become the site of the struggle for rights and freedom because it appears to be an entity we can harness. This is as much the case in Eastern Europe, for example, where abortion rights are being reconsidered and may be restricted, as it is in the United States. Restraining and controlling sexuality often goes with rising nationalism, since the patriot tends to regard the woman's primary role as populating the nation. Sexuality that is less controllable is therefore regarded as a danger rather than a pleasure. The body has become the nexus of our fears and aspirations alike, an object of social and political utility and a potential threat to the existing moral order. Marxist–feminists should respond to this ideological crisis with an agenda that both emphasizes state support of women's right to control their bodies, and encourages the open expression of and delight in our many sexualities.

REFERENCES

Copeland, R. 1990. "From Privacy to Autonomy: The Conditions for Sexual and Reproductive Rights." In *From Abortion to Reproductive Freedom: Transforming a Movement.*, ed. M. Fried, 27–43. Boston: South End Press.

Delphy, C. 1977. *The Main Enemy: A Materialist Analysis of Women's Oppression.* London: Womens Research and Resources Centre.

Dworkin, A. 1981. *Pornography: Men Possessing Women.* London: Women's Press.

———. 1989. *Letters from a War Zone.* New York: Dutton.

Echols, A. 1992. "We Gotta Get Out of This Place: Notes Towards a Remapping of the Sixties." *Socialist Review* 22, 2 (April–June): 9–33.

Gitlin, T. 1987. *The Sixties: Years of Hope, Days of Rage.* New York: Bantam.

Hayden, T. 1988. *Reunion: A Memoir.* New York: Random House.

MacKinnon, C. 1987. *Feminism Unmodified: Discourses on Life and Law.* Cambridge, MA: Harvard University Press.

Paglia, C. 1990. *Sexual Personae: Art and Decadence From Nefertiti to Emily Dickinson.* New Haven: Yale University Press.

Petchesky, R. 1984. *Abortion and Woman's Choice, the State Sexuality, and Reproductive Freedom.* Boston: Northeastern University Press.

Vance, C. 1984. "Pleasure and Danger: Toward a Politics of Sexuality." In *Pleasure and Danger: Exploring Female Sexuality,* ed. C. Vance, 1–27. Boston: Routledge and Kegan Paul.

Postwar Panics and the Crisis of Masculinity

BARBARA EPSTEIN

uring the 1940s and 1950s the United States was swept by an extraordinary number of fears, many of them widespread enough, and irrational enough, to deserve the term "panics." The best known of these was the fear of communism. But there were also fears of homosexuality and other forms of "sexual perversion," of juvenile delinquency and of youth culture more generally, of aliens, invaders from outer space, flying saucers. All of these fears reached their heights in the postwar years. But each of these fears (with the possible exception of flying saucers/invaders from outer space) revolved around themes that were already being expressed during the war years.

These panics tapped into many elements of the culture of these decades. I use the term "culture" rather than "popular culture" because professionals, including university intellectuals, were as caught up in most of these panics as anyone else; in fact, intellectuals, university-based and otherwise, were leading promoters of several of them. I find looking at these panics to be useful in an effort to try to understand the various overlapping mentalities that prevailed during these decades. I find it helpful to see these panics less as isolated phenomena than as specific expressions of a broad current of fear, or perhaps of linked fears, within American culture. This culture of fear flourished in the postwar years, but several of the panics of the time began to take hold during the war years.

One of the themes that ran through the panics of the 1940s and 1950s was the fear that masculinity was in crisis, that American men were ceasing to be "real men." Public expressions of concern about the state of masculinity focused around two issues: the fact that, during World War II, a much higher proportion of young men were rejected from military service for "psychoneurosis" than had been the case during World War I; and the publication in 1948 of Kinsey et al.'s *Sexual Behavior in the Human Male*, with its claim that one third of American men had had at least one homosexual experience. These two events appear to have touched off deep anxieties: Public discussion of the issue of military rejectees, and of the Kinsey report, merged with a widely expressed worry about the manliness of American men.

I find it puzzling that anxiety about masculinity took hold at this particular historical moment. The United States was on the winning side of a world war; the war was followed by a period of unprecedented domestic prosperity; many men were able to move a notch or so up the class ladder, to enjoy some degree of economic success. Military and economic success are conventional measures of masculinity. How are we to understand the public expressions of fear that masculinity was in crisis? In this paper I will briefly describe the expressions of concern touched off by the issue of military rejections, by the question of male homosexuality raised by the Kinsey report, and the broader public discourse of the 1940s and 1950s about the crisis of masculinity. I will then briefly explore the question of where these worries came from, and speculate about the implications of this history for the subsequent development of gender relations and politics in the United States.

U.S. entry into World War II raised the issue of the mental health of young American men in an acute way. The military was anxious to minimize the problem of "shell-shock" that had emerged during World War I. Though the induction process had included psychiatric screening, significant numbers of soldiers had to be removed from the battlefield due to the emotional trauma of war. As the military prepared for U.S. entry into World War II, it was seen as important to identify emotionally unstable recruits who might be susceptible to shell-shock, or otherwise cause problems.

During World War I, 2% of recruits were rejected from military service for psychiatric reasons. During World War II, this figure rose to 8–10%. The larger percentage of psychiatric rejections at the point of induction in World War II, did not reduce the incidence of psychiatric problems during the war, when discharges for psychiatric reasons were between two and three times the World War I rates. Furthermore, during World War I psychoneurosis was a relatively minor component of wartime psychiatric problems. The largest number of rejections were for mental insufficiency, the next largest for psychoses and constitutional psychopathic states. During World War II, psychoneurosis became the leading cause of psychiatric rejection at induction, and also of psychiatric dismissal during the war (Anderson 1966).

Before World War II the position of psychiatry, especially Freudian psychiatry, had been marginal in the United States. As a result of its wartime role, psychiatry was accepted as an important branch of medicine. Before the war there were fewer than 3,000 members of the American Psychiatric Association in the United States, but the war created a need for more psychiatrists. Many psychiatrists saw the war as bearing out their view that psychiatry should be accorded much more status than it had been in the past, and they hoped that wartime gains could be maintained once the war was over. Leading psychiatrists argued that the war demonstrated that their profession was crucial to the health of society, not only in the narrow sense that the military needed mentally stable soldiers, but in a broader sense. They saw both fascism and the initially uncertain response of the West as rooted in mental illness. They argued that after the war, sustaining democracy and preventing another war would require a vast expansion of the influence of psychiatry (Meyer 1941; Strecker 1941; Sullivan 1941).

The fact that large numbers of recruits were rejected from military service for psychiatric reasons provoked considerable uneasiness both inside the military and in the general public. It raised the question of whether these young men were malingerers, conning their way out of military service, and if there was anything genuinely wrong with them, why mental problems were so widespread among young men, and what that said about American society. The high level of psychiatric rejections led Chief of Staff George C. Marshall to write what was intended as an internal memorandum, in which he came close to taking the "malingering" position:

> The most important factor contributing to the spread of psychoneurotics in our Army has been the Nation's educational program and environmental background since 1920. While our enemies were teaching their youths to endure hardships, contribute to the national welfare, and to prepare for war, our young people were led to expect luxuries, to depend upon a paternal government for assistance in making a livelihood, and to look upon soldiers and war as unnecessary and hateful." (Menninger 1966, 133)

Army psychiatrist Menninger responded that the problems of military rejectees were the result of a selfish, infantile individualism, widespread in American society; psychiatrically, he wrote, this was a product of "the immature stage of development, characterized by 'I want what I want when I want it, and the hell with the rest of the world'" (Menninger 1966, 136). This debate, leaked to the press, led to a policy of refusing to release any statements on psychiatric conditions in the Army at the end of 1943.

The contrast between World War I and World War II statistics of psychiatric diagnoses was in fact not a very good measure of levels of mental health among young American men at these two points in time. Officers who had been involved in the military psychiatric process pointed out that in the early stages of mobilization psychiatrists were instructed to reject anyone who showed any signs of instability, because relatively small numbers of soldiers were needed. The resulting broad definition of psychoneurosis took on a life of its own and continued to be applied after U.S. entry into the war; it was changed only when it became clear that it had become an obstacle to recruiting sufficient numbers (Glass 1966, 740–741). Furthermore, the concept of neurosis (or "psychoneurosis" in the vocabulary of the time), of personality disorders that fell short of psychosis, was much more prominent in the Freudian-influenced psychiatry of the World War II era than had been the case during World War I. Increased diagnoses of psychoneurosis have to be seen in the context of growing psychiatric interest in this category.

During World War II and the years immediately after it, however, the high levels of military rejections and dismissals for psychiatric reasons, especially for reasons of "psychoneurosis," were seen by many as alarming; discussion of this question overlapped with suggestions that American masculinity was in trouble. Philip Wylie's book, *Generation of Vipers*, first published in 1942, introduced the term "momism" into mainstream vocabulary; Wylie argued that domineering mothers were responsible for a generation of weak, dependent, immature sons. Wylie's argument evidently resonated with existing uneasinesses about young men, masculinity, and mothers; it seems to have become a part of a widespread "common sense" very quickly. Discussions of the question of military rejections contain offhand, almost joking remarks about mothers trying to hold onto their sons, about sons seizing upon military service in order to break away from their mothers. A Captain Sol S. Grossman, for instance, stationed at an induction center in Michigan, wrote,

> Sometimes, it may be good therapeusis for the Army to effect the severance of the maternally binding "apron strings." As Col. S. C. Parter says, "There are many men who would be labeled psychoneurotics at the induction station who would thrive in the military service. It provides the particular conditions and outlets demanded by their personality disorder." (Grossman 1944)

Edward A. Strecker, a prominent (and prolific) psychiatrist, argued that momism was the leading cause of neurosis among American soldiers.

In "Psychiatry Speaks to Democracy," he cited Wylie's description of the overbearing "mom" and suggested that the difference between moms and mothers was that moms held onto their children and thus prevented them from gaining maturity. Referring to the "alarmingly large number of young men [unable] to serve [in the military] because of indefinite psychoneurotic symptoms and psychopathic behavior," he claimed that "a considerable proportion of the number is due to the fact that these rejectees had 'moms' instead of mothers" (Strecker 1945, 601). He argued that the leading characteristics of psychoneurosis were lack of morale and of will:

> In the peacetime practice of psychiatry, we encountered not too infrequently individuals trapped by life because they lacked in their personalities even the beginnings of social morale. . . . It was not difficult to retrace their social helplessness to a vacuum during their childhoods, produced by the ego-grasping immaturity of their "moms." Until we were forced to prepare for war, however, we had no idea how common these situations were. . . . In this war we have already paid a high price for the too large number of "mom"-made ineffectives. We will pay a still higher price in the years to come. (Strecker, 1945, 603–604)

In 1946, Strecker published a book, *Their Mothers' Sons: The Psychiatrist Examines an American Problem.* He opened the book by pointing to the large numbers of young men lost to the military due to psychoneurosis, and expanded upon his claim that large numbers of American men were immature and their mothers responsible for it. He claimed that mother-induced immaturity was the cause of the vast majority of rejections and dismissals from the military for reasons of psychoneurosis. Speaking from his experience as a former military psychiatrist, he told stories of mothers who had undermined their sons' ability to function in the army by writing plaintive letters begging them to come home; of sons for whom military service was a brief respite from maternal domination, but who were drawn back under their mothers' control once the war was over, and were never again able to lead lives of their own (Strecker 1946, 28–29). At the end of the book he offered a quiz for mothers among his readers, entitled "Are You a Mom?" The questions made it clear that "mothers" and "moms" had different conceptions of the family. "Moms" were old-fashioned; they took aging parents into their homes, tried to hold back their children's strivings toward independence, and continued to insert themselves into their grown children's lives. "Mothers" were modern; they put their parents in old age homes, and encouraged their children to leave home and lead their own lives (Strecker 1946, 208–209).

In 1948, Kinsey et al.'s *Sexual Behavior in the Human Male* was published, with its claim that a third of all American men had had at least one homosexual experience. There were many reviews of the Kinsey report, but little response to its claim about male homosexuality. Homosexuality was not considered a fit topic for discussion; through the 1950s the Readers' Guide to Periodical Literature lists no more than a dozen references to homosexuality per year, and most of these were relatively matter-of-fact reports of medical investigations. While the mainstream press maintained a polite silence, public anxiety found expression elsewhere—in a psychiatric literature that bridged popular and technical audiences, in the scandal magazines of the time, and, occasionally, in Congress, where the issue was raised in connection with the charge that homosexuals were taking over the government, especially the State Department, and endangering national security.

Psychiatrists and scandal magazines agreed that male homosexuality was increasing at a dangerous pace, that American manhood was in danger, and that while the problem was being magnified by homosexual men's practice of recruiting younger men, the source of the problem lay in the relation of mothers to their sons. They also agreed that the spread of male homosexuality indicated the weakening of "real" sex—that is, heterosexuality—in American society. Edmund Bergler, psychoanalyst and author of many books on psychiatric topics, published a book in 1951, *Neurotic Counterfeit Sex* (republished in 1958 as *Counterfeit-Sex: Homosexuality, Impotence, Frigidity*), in which he argued that alarming numbers of young men were being drawn into homosexuality, that male homosexuals were fundamentally passive, feminine, and weak, that homosexuals might appear to be interested in sex but that homosexuality was in fact a renunciation of "real" sex, and that male homosexuality was a flight from a possessive, intrusive mother.[1]

The question of what was wrong with American youth, especially young men, was also addressed by Robert Lindner, like Bergler a psychoanalyst and a prolific author, but politically liberal. Lindner (1944) wrote an account of his analysis of a young working-class man in prison, *Rebel without a Cause* (on which the film of the same name was very loosely based). Lindner led the young man through a classic Freudian narrative, revolving around an unresolved Oedipal conflict: Rejected by his remote, bullying father, emotionally thrown upon his overprotective mother, he expressed his hatred of authority in criminal actions, and was drawn to homosexuality as a defense against psychological merging with his mother. Lindner's concern, in this and his other books, was with what he saw as the widespread failure of young people, especially young men, to attain maturity; he focused on the twin dangers of conformity and antisocial rebellion. In his 1956 book, *Must You Conform?*, he argued that in the past adolescence had been a time of lonely brooding; he contrasted this with the "pack-running" of teenagers in his own time, which he saw as a renunciation of individuality, and identified as psychopathic. He described homosexuality as a product of what he called a sex-repressive culture, one in which great obstacles were placed in the way of real, heterosexual, sexuality, just as they were placed in the way of the attainment of genuine maturity. In the course of his discussion of homosexuality he noted his agreement with other psychoanalysts that "youth is succumbing to effemination," but, more thoughtful than Bergler and others, withheld judgment on the causes of this problem (Lindner 1956, 58–62).

Concerns about the decline of masculinity in the postwar period were not limited to the writings of psychoanalysts. The scandal magazines exploited the postwar fear of/fascination with homosexuality, especially male homosexuality, and their treatment of this theme focused on the crisis of masculinity. In spite of their lack of respectability, the scandal magazines were an important postwar genre: *Confidential*, the leading scandal magazine, had a circulation of 3.8 million in the mid-1950s, making it the most widely read magazine in the United States at the time. Others, including *Uncensored, Top Secret, Inside Story*, and *Suppressed*, enjoyed circulations of 300,000–500,000 ("The Curious Craze" 1955). The scandal magazines generally subscribed to a variety of sexual libertarianism that included anxiety about male virility, and hostility to homosexuality—which, unless noted otherwise, meant male homosexuality. Much of the text of the scandal magazines was taken up with gossip about movie stars or politicians. But "theme" articles were also published regularly by many of the magazines; these articles put forward a point of view that was remarkably similar to the perspective expressed by psychiatrists of the time, though expressed in much more lurid language.

The publication of the Kinsey report, and the existence of homosexual communities in Greenwich Village and elsewhere, provided grist for alarmist articles in the scandal magazines about the spread of male homosexuality. A few such articles appeared in the late 1940s; they became more frequent in the 1950s. In 1956 *Dare* ran an article entitled "Will 'Fruits' Take Over?" which warned that the United States was on the way to being "a nation of deviates." An article in *Revealed*, entitled "Are Homosexuals a Hidden Menace?" answered in the affirmative (Adams 1958); other articles gave advice on how to identify a homosexual (Levine 1956). The scandal magazines accepted the view that mothers were somehow at the root of male homosexuality. An article in *He*, "Do You Have the Homosexual Urge?" (1956) provided a quiz, which included the question, "Do you hate your mother?" Other articles suggested that a man's excessive love of his mother was a clue that he might be a homosexual. The scandal magazines frequently ran articles denouncing laws restricting sexual freedom, especially laws against extramarital sex and sexual relations with minors. Larson (1950) argued that the vast majority of American adults, or at least men, had violated one sex law or another, and that the laws should be revised to bring them into line with modern sexual practices. This article, and others like it, did not extend sexual libertarianism to a defense of homosexual rights; homosexuality, they argued, should be discouraged because it threatened the family and "real" sex.

The discussion of the crisis of masculinity that took place in the 1940s and 1950s was so distorted by misogyny and homophobia that it is easy to regard it as simply an instance of false consciousness. The problem, in the realm of gender, was not the excessive power of women, or the threat to male heterosexuality and the nuclear family by homosexuals. The problem was the stifling quality of domestic life and the subordination of women within it—the confinement of women and men, but especially women, to narrow and repressive roles. But I think that it would be a mistake to dismiss the postwar concern with the crisis of masculinity. The cultural and political dissent that began to emerge in the late 1950s was shaped by the belief that social order and sexual repression were female—specifically, enforced by mothers—and that rebellion against these was male, that it expressed the spirit of young men. Beat literature promoted these attitudes; there was virtually no place for women in beat culture, except as providers of sex for men. The view of rebellion as male (and, implicitly, of oppression as female) also influenced the student movement of the 1960s. The New Left gave young men a chance to be male in a way that was unhampered by social conventions, and by women's claims.[2] By the latter part of the 1960s, the problems posed by this version of masculinity were driving women to form their own separate movement. Anxieties about masculinity, and the need to assert it, have been a powerful force in the postwar era.

One can understand such anxieties in the present: The roles of men and women are in turmoil, the traditional family, based on the male wage, has become a minority form, homosexuality has become a major force in U.S. culture and politics. But why was there concern about masculinity in the 1940s and 1950s, when the middle-class nuclear family held sway, and men could point to military victories and economic success? The only answer that I can give is that the traditional organization of the family does give women a great deal of power over the lives of children. It also makes it easy for women to become targets for anger when family life feels suffocating. There was of course nothing new in the 1940s and 1950s about women having the primary responsibility for child care. But women's power may have seemed particularly overwhelming because many men were gone during the war, and after it, the suburbs especially became largely communities of women and children much of the time. Perhaps the anger that some mothers felt about their isolation in the home seemed threatening. These factors might help to explain the sense of uncertainty that surrounded masculinity, and the tide of rebellion against maternal power as the closest available representative of the social order.

NOTES

1. Bergler was also the author of *Homosexuality: Disease or Way of Life?* (1957), in which he rejected the view that homosexuality and heterosexuality were different points on the same spectrum; homosexuality, he argued, was neurotic, a "spurious" form of sexuality, and was rooted in infantile fears of the mother.

2. Alice Echols (1992), makes a similar analysis. She quotes Todd Gitlin's point that the fact that C. Wright Mills rode a motorcycle had a good deal to do with his hero status in the New Left (1989, 34).

REFERENCES

Adams, J. "Are Homosexuals a Hidden Menace?" 1958, April. *Revealed*, 2 (3): 34–35, 49.

Anderson, R. S. 1966. *Neuropsychiatry in World War Two: Vol. I. Zone of Interior*. Washington, D.C.: Medical Department, United States Army. Office of the Surgeon General, Department of the Army.

Bergler, E. 1957. *Homosexuality: Disease or Way of Life?* New York: Hill and Wang.

———. 1958. *Counterfeit-Sex: Homosexuality, Impotence, Frigidity*. New York: Grune and Stratton. (First published as *Neurotic Counterfeit-Sex*. New York: Grune and Stratton, 1951.)

"Do You Have the Homosexual Urge?" 1956, October. *He*, pp. 8–9.

Echols, A. 1992, April–June. "We Gotta Get out of This Place: Notes Toward a Remapping of the Sixties." *Socialist Review* 92: 9–34.

Gillin, T. 1987. *The Sixties: Years of Hope, Days of Rage*. New York: Bantam.

Glass, A. J. 1966. "Lessons Learned." *Neuropsychiatry in World War Two: Vol. I, Zone of Interior*, 735–761. Washington, D.C.: Medical Department, United States Army. Office of the Surgeon General, Department of the Army.

Grossman, S. S. 1944. "The Psychiatric Screening Process for Selectees: Some Observations Made at U.S. Armed Forces Induction Station, Kalamazoo, Michigan." *Mental Hygiene* 28, 2: 237–238.

Kinsey, A. C.; Pomeroy, W. B.; and Martin, C. E. 1948. *Sexual Behavior in the Human Male*. Philadelphia: W. B. Sanders.

Larson, N. 1950, March. "You're Probably a Sex Criminal," *Whisper* 3 (6): 8–9.

Levine, W. 1956, August. "Ten Ways to Spot a Homosexual," *Whisper* 10 (7): 25, 59–60.

Lindner, R. M. 1944. *Rebel Without a Cause: The Hypnoanalysis of a Criminal Psychopath*. New York: Grune and Stratton.

——. 1956. *Must You Conform?* New York: Rinehart and Company.

Menninger, W. C. 1966. "Public Relations." In *Neuropsychiatry in World War Two: Vol. I. Zone of the Interior,* 129–152. Washington, D.C.: Medical Department, United States Army, Office of the Surgeon General, Department of the Army.

Meyer, A. 1941. "Mental Hygiene in the Emergency; Introduction." *Mental Hygiene* 25 (1): 1–2.

Strecker, E. A. 1941. "Mental Hygiene and Mass Man." *Mental Hygiene* 25 (1): 3–5.

——. 1945. "Psychiatry Speaks to Democracy." *Mental Hygiene* 29 (4): 591–605.

——. 1946. *Their Mothers' Sons: The Psychiatrist Examines an American Problem.* Philadelphia: Lippincott.

Sullivan, H. S. 1941. "Psychiatry in the Emergency." *Mental Hygiene* 25 (1): 5–10.

"The Curious Craze for 'Confidential' Magazines.'" 1955. *Newsweek* (July 11): 50.

"Will 'Fruits' Take Over?" 1956. *Dare* (April): 28–29, 60–62.

Wylie, P. 1942. *Generation of Vipers.* New York: Rinehart and Company.

The Production of Divisions:
Gender Struggles under Capitalism

MARTHA E. GIMENEZ

ccording to Lebowitz (1992), *Capital* was one-sided and incomplete because it dealt with the side of capital and excluded, among other things, the consideration of the side of wage labor. From his standpoint, to consider the side of wage labor requires the treatment of workers as subjects and this, in turn, requires the examination of the process of reproduction of labor power and of the living owners of labor power: the workers themselves. In the process of self-reproduction, workers consume use values to which they have access through a variety of channels, among which domestic or private production is the most important. The examination of domestic relations yields the concept of a domestic mode of production where male workers exploit/oppress women and children, and females are, for all practical purposes, domestic servants. These domestic relations, in turn, are part of the material basis for the different interests dividing male and female workers and one of the main contexts in which they become political subjects. The identities workers develop in the process of reproducing themselves daily and generationally are enormously important to an understanding of the forms and directions taken by political struggles.

I agree with the need to examine workers not only as objects for capital but also as subjects. I also agree with the importance of the domestic setting in the formation of political subjects. The focus of my discussion is the examination of the capitalist determinants of gender and other divisions within the working class, and the implications of these divisions for political struggles and the reproduction of capitalism.

Some of the assumptions underlying my arguments are the following:

1. The absence of a book on wage labor may make Marx's work one-sided (in the dialectical sense) but not "deterministic." Marx's theory cannot be appropriately characterized as a theory that leaves no room for agency, for people do make history, though they do not choose the circumstances or the elements with which they make it. Marx's work captures both the recalcitrance of social structures that constrain actions and ideas and, at the same time, the contradictory and changeable nature of those structures that open up the space for the emergence of subjects aiming not only to reproduce them but to transform them.

2. In the *Critique of the Gotha Programme*, Marx (1970, 3) reminds us that nature, besides labor, is also a source of use value, thus stressing the material foundations of the capital–labor relation. Likewise, in the analysis of the reproduction of wage labor, it is important to acknowledge the mediating role of biology, which cannot be reduced to its "social construction." Hunger, sexuality, childbirth, dependency during childhood and old age, vulnerability to disease and death are irreducible to thought. These material aspects of the human condition are the basis for fundamental political demands as well as for the emergence of social relations and forms of consciousness whose power resides precisely in the immediacy and materiality of their foundations (Timpanaro 1975).

3. We don't construct reality, we transform it, and in the process there is both transcendence and preservation of that which is transformed. This is another way of stating Marx's point about the conditions under which people make history. Current intellectual fashions (i.e., social constructionism and the tendency to privilege agency over structure) neglect, in my view, the extent to which conditions not of people's choosing permeate their active involvement in processes aimed at times at reproducing the *status quo*, and at other times at challenging it and changing it (Bhaskar 1989, 66–88).

4. My standpoint is critical of universal patriarchy theories and of dualisms positing an independent patriarchal or gender system "interacting" with capitalism. In my view, gender and other politically relevant social divisions are "universal concretes"—that is, phenomena with specifically capitalist origins and conditions of reproduction (Gimenez 1982).

5. My standpoint is also critical of the politics of identity if isolated from class politics. There is a positive side to the emergence of the so-called new social movements, for they challenge long-standing practices of economic exploitation, social oppression, political domination, and

environmental degradation. The negative side is the strengthening of divisions among workers. These divisions are reinforced by government policies of racial classification and data collection and dissemination, and by the labeling of these groups as interest groups, each in conflict with the others. The ideology of civil rights also reinforces these divisions, due to the belief that the worse effects of class exploitation and oppression—which fall disproportionately upon women workers and populations classified as nonwhite, so that they are perceived primarily as the effects of sexism and racism—can be fully redressed through civil rights legislation and litigation. This encourages the formation and maintenance of victimized identities seeking redress through new laws and the courts (Bumiller 1988). It also encourages the resurgence of white supremacist movements and the self-perception of "majority" workers as "whites," thus strengthening the divisions that weaken even further the American working class.

THE CAPITALIST PRODUCTION OF GENDER DIVISIONS

Outside their relationship to capital, wage workers differ in many ways. Among those differences, gender is perhaps the most pervasive and important. It would also seem to be the most concrete, the most real. Once gender, as a category of analysis, penetrates one's consciousness, it is difficult to think about gender inequality without focusing on male/female differences (biological, psychological, physical, social, etc.) and male/female intentions, goals, interests, and so on. This mode of thought compels us to think in terms of men versus women, patriarchy, domestic exploitation, and similar dichotomous dynamics. But to attain a fuller grasp of the relevance of gender divisions and struggles for the political future of the working class, it is necessary to leave behind the notion of gender as being primarily an individual attribute and to examine it, instead, as the observable effect of underlying social relations of physical and social reproduction. Given that, dialectically, production and reproduction are two moments of the same process (Engels 1970, 5), it follows that the material basis of the phenomenon conceptualized as gender divisions is inextricably historical and specific to the mode of production.

These social relations, like class relations, are not forms of social interaction or intersubjective relations; they are structures independent from individuals' consciousness; they set boundaries to their opportunity structures and interaction, thus affecting their forms of consciousness. The sexual division of labor within and outside households, differences in men's and women's socioeconomic status and relative social and political power, and so on, are the observable and measurable effects of underlying relations of reproduction that are neither visible nor intersubjective, because they are mediated by men's and women's relationship to the means of production and to the conditions of biological, physical, and social reproduction. I am referring to the network of social relations within which social classes are reproduced daily and generationally, namely, relations of procreation and of physical and social reproduction (Gimenez 1992).

Under capitalist conditions, the organization of production determines the organization of reproduction. To postulate only interaction, giving equal causal weight to production and reproduction would, in my view, overlook the fact that the driving force of capitalism is capital accumulation, rather than the satisfaction of needs. While under socialism the goals of reproduction would have causal primacy, because production would be organized to satisfy needs, it is the case that we live under capitalism, where production for profit comes first and people's material and spiritual needs are satisfied only in so far as their satisfaction is profitable. The subordination of the satisfaction of needs to profit maximization is an aspect of the subordination of reproduction (which is part of the material basis for gender relations) to commodity production and the maintenance of capitalist class relations.

In advanced capitalist societies, the biological, physical, and social reproduction of wage and salary earners takes place through relations that vary within the limits set by the effects of almost universalized commodity production, advanced proletarianization, unemployment, and underemployment. At any given time, a substantial proportion of the population can only have access to the material conditions for reproduction either through claims upon the resources of wage/salary earners, state provision, private charity, petty commodity production of goods and services for local markets, or some combination thereof.

The "genderization" of biological males and females is constantly produced and reproduced through the survival strategies propertyless people develop under these circumstances and through the corresponding sexual division of labor. It is through marriage and kinship bonds that a large proportion of women and those too young or too old to work, the sick, the disabled, and the unemployed can have access to the conditions necessary for their physical and social reproduction. In the sphere of production, male and female workers compete for employment, a competition that is real, though tempered by occupational sex-typing. In the sphere of reproduction, men and women establish contradictory relations of cooperation and domination within the "family," the most widespread survival strategy, which allows women and children to have access to goods and services through their connection to an employed male. The dynamics of production both set the basis for family formation as a desirable strategy and, at the same time, undermine it; depending on socioeconomic status, levels of employment, and wages, family formation becomes increasingly undesirable, unstable, or unattainable for growing proportions of the population.

But a focus on "the family" is unproductive because other strategies can then be perceived either as deviations from it or as successful challenges. Arguments for or against "diversity in family forms" cloud the issue and keep discourse within the confines of the relationships between "the family" and other institutions. The focus should be on the organization of social reproduction and the changing networks of relations between the sexes and the generations that the development of the forces of production and reproduction make possible at a given time. The methodological, ideological and political implications of this theoretical standpoint are the following.

Methodologically, gender inequality as a principle of social stratification is irreducible to micro foundations; that is, it cannot be explained on the basis of men's physiology, psychology, or intentionality because it is the structural effect of a complex network of macrolevel processes that have to do with the articulation between the spheres of production and reproduction. This network establishes parameters for the relations between men and women that allocate the latter primarily to the sphere of domestic/reproductive labor and only secondarily to waged or salaried labor, thus creating the material basis for differences in the relative economic, social, and political power of the sexes. It is true, on the other hand, that *specific* manifestations of gender inequality within firms, households, institutions, and so on are not only amenable to reduction to micro foundations but require it.

Ideologically, the social organization of reproduction produces the "genderization" of males and females. It establishes the conditions for the effectivity of preexisting ideologies and practices about the proper attributes and behavior of men and women, as well as of the emergence of new ones.

Politically, given that consciousness reflects, in fundamental ways, our direct experiences and that we experience only the effects of the relations of reproduction, what we experience and observe are concrete instances of men's economic, political, and sexual dominance, in both the so-called public and private spheres. The theoretical and political effect has been that of reinforcing a problematic of men versus women, the critique of the family, the elaboration of theories of patriarchy, and the conceptualization of women's oppression as something all women share, as the basis for sisterhood.

This understanding of the effects of the relations of reproduction has been divisive because it overlooks the existence of privileged women and underprivileged men. Theories about what is and is not in the interest of all "women" are vulnerable to critiques indicating that women's experiences, interests, and power vary according to social class, socioeconomic status, ethnicity, and race. These are objective differences that do not disappear with changes in women's consciousness. While women undoubtedly share some common interests around issues of sexuality and procreation, even these cannot be taken for granted as a basis for shared political objectives (see, e.g., Luker 1984). Individual women may have more in common with men and women of their own class, race, ethnicity, than with all other women. And it is in the interest of privileged women and capitalist/corporate class women that the status quo remain unchanged; otherwise, who would do their housework, mind their children, and manage their households? Today feminists rejoice at the increase in the number of women who reach top places in the professional, corporate, and political structures. Their ability to do so rests upon their extensive use of domestic help and ability to purchase high quality child care. But the use of domestic servants is not limited to the very wealthy. Most working women who can afford to do so hire domestic workers on a part- or full-time basis. Civil rights victories are not sufficient to eradicate the existence of class, racial, and ethnic divisions among women, nor the fact that some women are oppressed and exploited by other women.

Racial and ethnic divisions enter into the process of domestic reproduction of wage labor but they are not generated by it. The racial and ethnic heterogeneity of the population of advanced capitalist countries is the result of past processes of colonization, enslavement, and international migration generated by the exploitation of semiperiphery and periphery countries by core states and transnational capital. Changing practices of racial and ethnic classification as well as processes of assimilation periodically change the racial/ethnic composition of the population (Gimenez 1988). What remains is the heritage of racism, second-class citizenship, economic exploitation, and social exclusion. Racial and ethnic populations are in turn divided in terms of class and gender. The process of the reproduction of wage labor takes place along the lines of processes that perpetuate gender, racial, and ethnic divisions as integral components of individual workers' identities.

There is a contradiction between capitalist ideologies about political, legal, civil equality, and equality of opportunity, and capitalism's inherent tendency to reproduce and deepen socioeconomic inequality over time. The genderization of the population, like its racialization and ethnicization, are processes that legitimate capitalist inequalities and obscure the contradiction between chronic inequality and universalistic and egalitarian hegemonic ideologies. Gender, race, and ethnicity serve as criteria for the allocation, often through processes of "free" self-selection, of certain workers to less desirable jobs. Their presence there can thus be legitimated on the grounds of their gender (or racial/ethnic) characteristics. These characteristics are reproduced over time, across the generations, through practices protected by abstract political and civil rights (e.g., parents' right to socialize their children as they see fit and the right of racial/ethnic groups to preserve their culture). The private reproduction of gender (and other) differences is an integral part of the reproduction of social inequality in a context that ideologically extols the virtues of equal rights and equality of opportunity (Wallerstein 1991).

In the long term, the political implications of these divisions are detrimental for the well-being of most workers, though in the short term they may yield some benefits and advantages, especially to those in the middle and upper middle strata. The tendency among some in the Left to dismiss gender, racial, and ethnic politics as forms of false consciousness has been met with the tendency to see these politics of identity as more genuine and effective than the politics of class. To make matters more complicated, gender divisions are supported and reproduced over time by the unyielding organization of reproduction. Racial and ethnic divisions, particularly the latter, are more amenable to change. On the other hand, the attainment of racial and ethnic equality both legally and in practice, so that white and nonwhite workers have the same probability of being poor, would not undermine the capitalist organization of social reproduction and, consequently, gender inequality.

CONCLUSION

No challenges to the politics of identity are likely to be successful as long as people continue to believe that all that is needed to solve their problems is effective legislation. Gender, racial, and ethnic grievances are also forms in which people become conscious of "the hidden injuries of class" and it is therefore important to go beyond political standpoints that view class, gender, race, and ethnicity as discrete, mutually exclusive phenomena. The alternative, that everything is "gendered" or "raced" or "ethnicized" is a play on words rather than a substantive advance in one's understanding of the connections among these levels of analysis. Economic restructuring has radically altered the prospects and opportunities of the American working class, exacerbating the competition for well-paid jobs while sinking a larger proportion of the population into poverty and near poverty. In this context, gender and racial/ethnic conflicts are intensified while the real grievances of white workers remain invisible within the dominant political discourse, something that strengthens racism and sexism and often generates self-destructive and violent behavior.

The political and legal abolition of gender, racial, and ethnic barriers to full admission to citizenship, employment opportunities, and the "heavenly life" of the political community does not abolish them as continuing dimensions of social life, for they are ongoing effects of material practices rooted in the capitalist mode of production (Marx 1975, 149–156). Consequently, political struggles designed to push to the limits the expansion of civil rights legislation might have important political effects because the limits of political emancipation could, to some degree, become obvious to people not just in theory but in their own experiences.

I know that in reasoning in this way I leave myself open to charges of "class reductionism" and worse. It is my view that political efforts to avoid the straw man of "class reductionism" have led to fragmented theoretical and political analyses of class experiences and the forms in which people experience their class situation. This is reinforced by the state-sponsored production, though the Bureau of the Census and other official sources of data, of statistics that classify people primarily in terms of race, ethnicity, age, and gender. These categories have acquired a facticity that pervades contemporary consciousness. The power of these reifications is evident in the difficulties involved in trying to overcome them theoretically and in practice. In the growing literature on diversity, the sources of diversity are kept separate from class and are linked to class and the mode of production through contingent or external, rather than internal or necessary, relations (Ollman 1993; Sayer 1984, 82–87). We need educational, research, and political practices that endeavor to transcend these reifications by bringing up the commonality of interests among people who appear to have irreconcilable opposing interests. I am not minimizing nor denying the reality of gender, racial, and ethnic divisions nor their effects on people's lives; but, in isolation from the other fundamental relations that affect people's opportunity structures, gender, race, and ethnicity become, in my view, one-sided, reified categories of analysis that identify taxonomic collectives rather than theoretically significant and politically effective groups.

Vicente Navarro once wrote that we need statistics that unite people, not statistics that divide people. We also need scholarship that unites people, highlighting the common class determinants of the opportunity structures and changing fates of the poor, the near poor, the "new poor," single mothers, "nonwhite" workers, poor children, poor elderly people, the downwardly mobile, the employed, the unemployed, the "middle class," and the growing numbers of temporary, disposable workers.

To consider the side of wage labor entails, therefore, not just the intellectual goal of elucidating the structural determinants of the existing divisions among workers but the political goal of using our intellectual skills to elaborate the badly needed theoretical/political discourse that overcomes the so-called postmodern fragmentation of the subject by bringing clearly and to the fore the commonalities all these populations share. By elaborating a politics of reproduction, concerned with the need of all workers for jobs, for decent wages, for stable and safe working conditions, for housing, health care, education, and an old age without indignities, we can begin to overcome in thought the divisions that need to be overcome in practice.

REFERENCES

Bhaskar, R. 1989. *Reclaiming Reality. A Critical Introduction to Contemporary Philosophy*. London: Verso.

Bumiller, K. 1988. *The Civil Rights Society. The Social Construction of Victims*. Baltimore: The Johns Hopkins University Press.

Engels, F. 1970. *The Origin of the Family, Private Property, and the State*. New York: International Publishers.

Gimenez, M. E. 1982. "The Oppression of Women. A Structuralist Marxist View." In *Structural Sociology*, ed. I. Rossi, 292–324. New York: Columbia University Press.

———. 1992. "The Mode of Reproduction in Transition: A Marxist-Feminist Analysis of the Effects of Reproductive Technologies." *Gender and Society* 5 (3): 334–350.

———. 1988. "Minorities and the World-System. The Theoretical and Political Implications of the Internationalization of Minorities." In *Racism, Sexism, and the World-System*, ed. J. Smith, J. Collins, T. K. Hopkins, and A. Muhammad, 39–56. Westport, CT: Greenwood Press.

Lebowitz, M. A. 1992. *Beyond Capital: Marx's Political Economy of the Working Class*. New York: St. Martin's Press.

Luker, K. 1984. *Abortion & the Politics of Motherhood*. Berkeley: University of California Press.

Marx, K. 1970. *Critique of the Gotha Programme*. New York: International Publishers.

———. 1975. "On the Jewish Question." In *Collected Works*, Vol. 3, K. Marx and F. Engels, 146–174. New York: International Publishers.

Ollman, B. 1993. *Dialectical Investigations*. New York: Routledge.

Sayer, A. 1984. *Method in Social Science: A Realist Approach*. London: Hutchingson & Co.

Timpanaro, S. 1975. *On Materialism*. London: NLB.

Wallerstein, I. 1991. "The Construction of Peoplehood: Racism, Nationalism, Ethnicity." In *Race, Nation, Class, Ambiguous Identities*, ed. E. Balibar and I. Wallerstein, 71–85. London: Verso.

Incorporating Queer Theory on the Left

ROSEMARY HENNESSY

istorically, sex has been a compelling issue for the Left. In the past twenty years alone there has been an enormous outpouring of theoretical, scholarly, and activist work on sexual difference, sexual identity, and sexuality. Many of the leading thinkers of radical social theory for the past century have addressed sexuality as a field of power, a category of identity, or a site of critique. But until very recently, heterosexuality as a regulatory social practice has been all but ignored in progressive political agendas and the critical frameworks of social theory. There are indications that things are changing. I would like to think that they really are.

Under the rubric of "queer theory" a critique of heterosexuality has recently begun to circulate on the Left. One of the defining features of queer theory is its effort to rewrite a cultural politics founded on the categories "gay" and "lesbian" in order to produce "another discursive horizon, another way of thinking the sexual" (de Lauretis 1991, iv). In academic theory, invoking the signifier "queer" parallels the fairly recent shift among activists from the terms "lesbian" and "gay" to "queer." Claiming a queer identity is an effort to speak from and to the differences that have been suppressed by the monolithic identities "lesbian" and "gay," including the complex ways lesbian and gay sexualities are inflected by heterosexuality, race, gender, and ethnicity. Embracing the category used to shame and cast out sexual deviants, queer theory and politics defiantly refuse the terms of the dominant discourse. Touting queerness is a gesture of rebellion against the pressure to be invisible or apologetically abnormal. It is an "in your face" rejection of the "proper" response to heteronormativity, a strategy both antiassimilationist and antiseparatist.

A growing number of conference panels and special issues of Left-leaning journals hint that queer theory is a hot new topic in cultural critique. But does the showcasing of this new knowledge on the Left signal that political priorities and frames of intelligibility are being radically challenged and rewritten, or are we simply to conclude, in the words of a recent T-shirt slogan, that "Out Is In"? I want to approach this question by inquiring into some of the strategies of incorporation that permeate and enable hegemonic reconfigurations of sexuality and identity, strategies that queer theory itself utilizes.

If the Left is noticing queers now, in this regard it is not very far out of step with the cultural mainstream. Lesbian and gay issues—whether formulated in terms of civil rights, alternative lifestyles, or family values—have entered public debates in unprecedented ways. Much of the insurgent force propelling lesbian and gay political representation into the national news has, of course, been driven by the life-and-death urgency of the AIDS crisis. For all the publicity that lesbians and gays have gained in the wake of AIDS activism, it is clear that the normative status of heterosexuality remains an intense cultural battlefield. Testimonies abound. The new multicultural curriculum in New York City's schools has sparked intense opposition because it requires that children in the primary grades be taught respect for lesbian and gay families. In Oregon, Colorado, Florida, and Maine citizens voted in November 1992 to revoke the civil rights of homosexuals. Yet, at the same time that queer bashing is escalating and homosexuals are being threatened with state-enforced exclusion from civic life and work, lesbians and gays are becoming more visible and to some degree "allowed"—appearing on television shows, in advertising, video, and film. This new level of gay "visibility" in the United States now is made possible in part by shifts in the historical forces defining family, gender, and sexuality under advanced capitalism. But despite these shifts, or perhaps more accurately *across* them, the public remains deeply ambivalent about gay and lesbian aspirations. In the words of *Newsweek*'s report on "Gays Under Fire," Americans are "torn between a basic impulse to be tolerant and a visceral discomfort with gay culture" (Turque et al. 1992, 36).

That the limits of tolerance in mainstream discourses on homosexuality are set by the body—that is, by appeal to a visceral, gut reaction—indicates the ways in which this strategy of incorporation does the work of ideology by naturalizing and thus legitimizing the heterosexual norm as the way things should be. As the supreme ideological regulator, the visceral serves as a body of evidence that speaks for itself, closing off the meaning-making process from social struggles over the limits of democratic representation and civic identity. At the same time that heterosexuality is naturalized as what "feels right in the gut," tolerance makes a wedge for some flexibility in a symbolic order organized according to cognitive maps demarcating prescribed and forbidden practices. Forbidden practices threaten to display the arbitrariness of the social real. But tolerance smoothes over the irruption of the forbidden, incorporating it as the "allowable" by delimiting it as a minority discourse. In this sense, tolerance is crisis management in action.

Full democracy, of course, makes tolerance of minorities unnecessary. When practices that disturb the coherence of the social imaginary or that test the limits of intelligibility are tolerated as "minority deviations," the threatened propriety of the prevailing symbolic order is restored. Tolerant incorporation of homosexuals into the social body manages the contradictions that these forbidden practices disclose. The effect is to leave intact the status quo, since the appeal both to the visceral and to tolerance help shore up notions of the natural and of representation that the bourgeois subject and the liberal democratic state presuppose.

A similar stance, torn between diplomacy and discomfort, also shapes the views of many progressives. As Carole Vance once put it, invariably "sexual liberals are caught between a reluctance to lose privileges attendant upon their being members of the majority and a fear of losing their claims to political savvy if they do not side with the newly vocal, emerging minorities" (1984, 19). If this sort of crisis management underlies the Left's silence on heterosexuality, in what ways have queer politics and theory interrupted or at least begun to address it? To what extent does queer theory intervene in and reconfigure our collective political agendas?

Queer theory's critique of heterosexuality is not a monolithic body of work but rather itself a terrain of struggle whose genealogy delineates many of the tensions between materialism and idealism that have shaped (post)modernity. This history is absent in many current analyses of queer theory, however, and, unfortunately, falls outside the scope of this essay. It is a very telling limit, nonetheless, and marks an important horizon for future work. For now I only want to draw attention to one facet of this history—an all-but-suppressed materialist critique of heterosexuality that queer theory is often presented as displacing. Almost twenty years ago lesbian feminists in the West—among them, Charlotte Bunch, The Furies, The Purple September Staff, Monique Wittig—argued that feminism, including discussions of lesbianism among cultural feminists, dealt with sexuality as a personal or civil rights issue in order to avoid a deeper materialist critique of the normative status of heterosexuality. Although their systemic analysis has been contested by a postmodern cultural politics fixated on local strategies and proliferating identities, it seems to me that these knowledges offer a rich radical tradition for developing postmodern materialist queer theory. What I am calling "avant-garde" queer theory, however, is the more widely circulating discourse now. And it too, of course, offers a critique of heterosexuality. Emerging out of a decade of cultural work on several fronts, avant-garde queer theory is the critical framework currently redefining the "cutting edge" of lesbian and gay studies and cultural critique in general.

Both materialist and avant-garde queer theory call into question obvious categories (man, woman, butch, femme, Latina, Jew, etc.) oppositions (man vs. woman; heterosexual vs. homosexual), or equations (gender = sex) upon which conventional notions of sexuality and identity rely. Both contest traditional notions of sexuality as a personal or civil rights issue. Both challenge an identity politics in which identity is understood to be represented in a self-evident way through one's body, and collectivity is reduced to group affiliation defined according to the standard of authentic embodiment. Avant-garde queer theory often acknowledges its indebtedness to materialist feminism; Monique Wittig's work, for example, has been claimed and rearticulated by several prominent queer theorists. But the theory of the social and the modes of critical practice offered in avant-garde and materialist queer theory are quite at odds. I want to explore some of the features of this difference, for it points to what is at stake in the incorporation of queer theory on the Left now.

Without a doubt the diva of avant-garde queer theory is Judith Butler. Her work is cited frequently at conferences and in journals, features prominently in new collections, and is conspicuously discussed in more popular cosmopolitan venues like the *Voice Literary Supplement*. Butler's book *Gender Trouble* is an incisive counter-narrative, a critique of the relation between bourgeois subjectivity and the "heterosexualization" of desire. Butler argues that identity based on features of the person prior to representation or on appeals to self-evident bodies or group affiliations is necessarily "troubled" once we recognize the distinction between sex and gender. If gender is understood to be a culturally constructed regulatory practice, the "coherence" and "continuity" of the person can be seen to be "socially instituted and maintained norms of intelligibility" rather than empirical givens (Butler 1990, 17). "'Intelligible' genders," she writes, "are those which in some sense institute and maintain relations of coherence and continuity among sex, gender, sexual practice, and desire" (1990, 17). One of the crucial regimes for maintaining this coherence, Butler contends, is the heterosexualization of desire, the discrete and asymmetrical opposition between masculine and feminine, where these are understood to be expressive attributes of males and females (1990, 17). For Butler, the fiction of heterosexuality ensures the stability that so-called "expressions" of gender and sexuality rely on by forestalling the recognition that gender and sexuality are in fact performative, a matter of repeated stylizations inscribed on the body (1990, 32).

One of the most notable and trenchant features of Butler's work is her extension of feminism's critique of gender as culturally constructed to the more radical argument that the internal coherence of *either* gender—man or woman—relies on institutional heterosexuality. Much of the oppositional force of her critique lies in its insistent claim that heteronormativity is absolutely central to the bourgeois ideology of expressive and coherent self-hood. This imaginary representation, Butler argues, "conceals the gender discontinuities that run rampant within heterosexual, bisexual, gay, and lesbian contexts where gender does not necessarily follow from sex, and desire or sexuality generally does not seem to follow from gender" (1990, 135–136). From this perspective, heterosexuality, usually assumed to be an expression of the core of oneself, is exposed as a precarious fabrication always potentially at risk and always vulnerable to betrayal by an excess, an other, that it is compelled to keep at bay by continual repeated narrativization.

Butler's performative theory of identity presupposes a narrative of social life that equates the social with signification or textuality. Like Derrida, Lacan, Laclau, and Mouffe, Butler understands the indeterminacy at the heart of identity formation as the effect of an instability of signification that is the very condition of meaning and by extension of identity. But by emphasizing the *difference within* identity and positing it as so exclusively textual, Butler erases both the history and the materiality of meaning and identity, as well as its continued social structuring in terms of *difference between*. If meaning-making practices are understood in a historical and materialist sense, the indeterminacy of signification can be seen as the textual mark of social contradictions, the effect of struggles over the categories that shape social life.

Butler acknowledges that her argument against claiming the identity "lesbian" or "gay" might suppress this struggle or even worse be complicitous with those political forces that would obliterate any challenge to the heterosexual social order, but (echoing Laclau and Mouffe) she counters that avowing the sign's strategic provisionality safeguards the "openness" of its possible uses in the future (1991, 19). The problem with this argument, however, is that the sign and identity for Butler are always open: "I would like to have it permanently unclear," she writes, "precisely what that sign (lesbian) signifies" (1991, 14). But what Butler "would like" is not necessarily what is. Her homotextual critique does not—indeed cannot—acknowledge that social practices rely upon and help secure meanings by way of the hierarchical fixing of signifieds. For all of its potential plurality, the hegemonic construction of social reality by relations of ruling that structure prescribed, allowed, and forbidden practices *is still organized in terms of differences between* (between white and colored, man and woman, normal and pervert, have and have-not)—with profound consequences for people's lives.

Understanding sexuality—and by extension the social—as primarily or even exclusively textual or cultural is not of course unique to Judith Butler's work. A quick look through the pages of some of the latest academic queer theory will confirm that her example is only one of many. The essays of Diana Fuss, Teresa de Lauretis, Wayne Koestenbaum, Ed Cohen, and Sue Ellen Case (to name but a few avant-garde queer theorists), consistently conceptualize the social as primarily a matter of representation, of discursive, or symbolic relations. When social life is explained as thoroughly textual or cultural, the *stakes* in the struggle over meaning—over what sexualities and subjectivities are allowed or forbidden—get suppressed. As testimonies from Oregon to Maine assert, not every lesbian or gay man in the United States has the luxury of reveling in the play of gender indeterminacy, especially when the significance of sexuality and identity is often legitimized with such brutal consequences. The stories of people like Hattie Mae Cohens and Brian Mock, the lesbian and gay man murdered by skinheads in Oregon, illustrate quite pointedly that the normative status of heterosexuality has *effects* that are more than discursive. In varied and complex ways heteronormativity has served historically to sustain state power and access to social resources, such as a place to live and work and thrive.

In a time when Madison Avenue so lucratively employs an increasingly plural eroticism to recruit consumers, and when persons with AIDS around the globe are held hostage by profit-driven corporate–state alliances, we need to be wary of analyses that present sexuality only in terms of textual indeterminacy. Framed exclusively as an issue of cultural representation—discursive shifts, tropes, rhetorical axes, narrative strategies—difference loses its punch. One effect is that the political dimension of the construction of sexuality in all of its varied and complex formations threatens to become thematized, isolating preoccupation with erotic remappings of the body in the West from a global political economy. At what cost to the emancipatory aims of a queer politics is this other narrative of sexuality suppressed?

One possible cost is the assimilation of queer critique into hegemonic postmodern culture. As postmodernism is fast becoming the cultural common sense of postindustrial capitalism, it brings in its wake more porous, gender-flexible, and playful subjects, subjects more adequate to the complexities of high-tech multinational commodity exchange, where the expressive self and transcendent morality of liberal humanism have become embarrassingly inadequate (Zavarzadeh 1992, 8). Performative play with cultural codes is a postmodern fashion statement, of which Madison Avenue's promotion of cross-dressing is only one example. These popular challenges to naturalized gender difference share a certain ideological affiliation with avant-garde queer theory. In fact, I would go so far as to suggest that both indicate the ways in which under late capitalism the liberal stance on homosexuality is being transcoded from the moral and determinate axes of tolerance and disgust to the more postmodern, indeterminate terms of signifying play and pleasure, and in the process helping to consolidate a new hegemonic postmodern culture. Postmodern incorporations of sexuality displace the binary logic of liberal moralism's vacillation with the logic of the supplement. Here identities are fluid, open to resignification and recontextualization. The fixed polarities of liberal morality dissolve into engenderings of incoherence as pleasure-full erotic indeterminacy. For Diana Fuss, as for many other avant-garde queer theorists, the new cultural and sexual arrangements "occasioned by the movements and transmutations of pleasure in the social field" will serve as the ground for political organization (1991, 5). Indeed pleasure *has* served as a rallying cry for gay activism. To cite one example: On the back cover of the special issue on queer theory of *Social Text*, a photo/manifesto by the art collective GANG boldly asserted, "Our Bodies Should Be Playgrounds/Not Just Battlefields." Echoing and qualifying Barbara Kruger's now famous "Your Body Is a Battleground" poster for the 1989 march on Washington, this slogan acknowledges that bodies and sexualities are indeed battlefields. But it also claims them as sites of pleasure and play. What does it mean in this historical moment for a queer politics to claim play and pleasure as its primary political stakes in such an equivocal relation to struggle? To what extent does the simple affirmation of pleasure in queer politics participate in the consolidation of postmodern hegemony?

Accompanying post-Fordist information technologies and the more flexible, decentered divisions of labor in consumer capitalism has been an emphasis on understanding subjectivities in terms of lifestyle, taste, and culture rather than in terms of social class (Hall 1991, 58). But this does not mean that the divisions of labor that the category "class" describes have disappeared, even though theoretical articulations of more porous, textualized subjectivities and the gender flexibility of postmodern chic invite us to think so. So long as gender flexibility is understood as just a matter of signification, of style, or of consumer pleasure, the connections between new gender formations, public patriarchy, and the international division of labor make it possible, even necessary, for the untraditional family, the new professional woman, and marginally legitimate gay lifestyles to remain as obscure as ever. When queer theory's critique of a naturalized and invisible heterosexuality is restricted to analysis of textual play, cultural discourse, or eroticized bodies, it fails to connect the reengendering of sexual identities in postindustrial culture and the increased visibility of lesbians and gays with new but nonetheless unequal divisions of labor and work in capital's global political economy. As a result, it risks reenacting the ideological effects of the discourses of liberal tolerance it purportedly disputes.

A materialist queer critique endorses postmodernism's challenge to the bourgeois subject, but it also maintains that the function of sexuality in the formation of complex, unstable, and multiple subjectivities cannot be theorized very effectively for any sort of fundamental social change without coming to terms with the systematic operations of capitalism and patriarchy. In other words, for a materialist queer critique, sexuality, along with those features that often accompany its construction in the postindustrial West—pleasure, consumption, diversity—is part of a given global reality in which these terms have a very specific and privileged address. In the wake of poststructuralism's inroads into academic feminism and as a result of the firm grip deconstruction and Foucauldian analysis hold on the imagination of a lesbian and gay academic avant-garde, this systemic alter-narrative has often been dismissed as totalizing theory. I want to argue, however, that it is precisely this systemic analysis of the social that makes a materialist critique of heterosexuality politically urgent.

A materialist queer critique is materialist because it starts with the assumption that social production takes place in a variety of intersecting material ways—through divisions of labor and power, and through systems of value and meaning making. Like other human capacities—for work or consciousness, for example—the human capacities for reproduction and for pleasure are always historicized or organized under certain specific conditions across a complex ensemble of social relations—economic, political, ideological. Sexuality is one way these capacities have been named and regulated, and this process has in turn mediated and traversed other facets of social reproduction.

Understanding sexuality from a systemic social perspective has several implications for a queer political project. First of all, while it acknowledges that sexuality is always discursively constructed, it simultaneously insists that the materiality of sexuality is not *just* discursive. This perspective shift encourages us to address how the normative discursive construction of sexuality as heterosexuality has been imbricated in divisions of wealth and has helped organize state relations and formations of citizenship. But such a systemic materialist analysis also exerts critical pressure on lesbian, gay, and queer politics as well, raising questions about the relationship between the view of social life in most queer theory as so thoroughly and exclusively stylized, textual, and performative, and the increasing commodification of homosexuality as a new market niche, (life)style, or fashion statement. It questions as well the loosening of heterosexual gender codes among the professional/consumer class in "postindustrial" economies and the invisible laborers elsewhere on which they depend.

Certainly in the intervening years since the 1970s we have come to understand that sexuality disciplines bodies and knowledges in more complicated ways than the materialist analyses of two decades ago acknowledged. Recognizing this does not require the displacement of historical materialism's systemic framework with postmodern cultural theories, however, but rather should inspire the development of more rigorous and specific analyses that allow us to explain the many dense and uneven ways sexuality serves as a transfer point in capitalist expansion, both in its dominant heterosexual configurations and in its counterdominant forms. Such a standpoint invites us, even requires us, to make connections between the proliferating discourses of sexuality in industrialized social formations and the international division of labor, between sexy commodity images and sexual citizenship, spectacles and sweatshops, style and class. In so doing, a materialist queer theory can refuse to be incorporated in a Left cultural politics that has all but abandoned historical materialism's defining theoretical premises. Instead, materialist queer theory can both provoke the Left to confront its blindness to heterosexuality and further develop a radical oppositional politics that speaks out not only for urban middle-class queers but also to those lesbians, gays, and queers in prisons and shelters, in factories and migrant camps, for whom the playful subversion of sexual identities is a much more limited option.

REFERENCES

Butler, J. 1990. *Gender Trouble*. New York: Routledge.
———. 1991. "Imitation and Gender Insubordination." In *Inside/Out: Lesbian Theories, Gay Theories*, ed. D. Fuss, 13–31. New York: Routledge.
De Lauretis, T. 1991. "Queer Theory: Lesbian and Gay Sexualities: An Introduction." *differences* 3: iii–xviii.
Fuss, D. 1991. "Inside/Out." In *Inside/Out: Lesbian Theories, Gay Theories*, ed. D. Fuss, 1–12. New York: Routledge.
Hall, S. 1991. "Brave New World." *Socialist Review* 24 (1): 57–64.

Social Text. 1991. 9 (4): 3–56.

Turque, B. et al. 1992. "Gays Under Fire." *Newsweek* (14 September): 35–40.

Vance, C. S. 1984. "Pleasure and Danger: Toward a Politics of Sexuality." In *Pleasure and Danger: Exploring Female Sexuality*, ed. C. Vance, 1–28. London: Pandora.

Zavarzadeh, M. 1992, Fall. "Pun(k)deconstruction and the Postmodern Political Imaginary." *Cultural Critique* 22: 5–46.

Under the Falling Sky: Apocalyptic Environmentalism and the Production of Nature

CINDI KATZ

pocalypticism is suddenly fashionable again in North American and European constructions of nature and society. For anyone with the merest connection to the media, it is difficult to avoid prognostications hailing the end of nature, the death of the oceans, global warming, mass ecocide, an ozone hole growing faster than the national debt, or the end of history. More scholarly authors are in on the doomsaying as well (e.g., Ehrlich and Holdren 1988; Fukuyama 1989; Gordon and Suzuki 1990; McKibben 1989). Crackpot reactionaries, without a trace of modesty, tout the "end of evolution." Increases in hospital births, television watching by young people, and day care attendance are to blame. As a remedy they offer a thinly veiled environmental determinism to justify keeping women barefoot, pregnant, and at home. Environmental apocalypticism is in fact widely tied to the control of women. Paul Ehrlich, Donella Meadows, and Garrett Hardin (in Ehrlich and Holdren 1988), to name a few, have begun to find new audiences for old clichés about "the limits to growth," despite acknowledged evidence to confound their neo-Malthusian prophecies: Food production, income, and life expectancy in Asia, Africa, and South and Central America have all increased (cf. Kates 1993). While some of these authors acknowledge that inequalities in social and economic distribution are key to environmental resource problems, their solutions focus on limiting population and technology rather than attacking the social sources of resource inequality. Biocentrists, such as the "Earth Firsters," see

"humans" as the essential problem. Thus some deep ecologists have argued against famine relief despite their recognition of the uneven social and economic relations that create conditions of famine. Even the more moderate Sierra Club endorses immigration control for the United States. Finally, various Greens and homegrown environmentalists point constantly to the crises of biodiversity, ozone, global climate change, and the loss of the rain forests, recognizing the social and political-economic roots of environmental crises but extending the dismal logic of the Frankfurt School to treat the domination of nature as a transhistorical form. Chicken Little has run amok.

This paper is a polemic against environmental apocalypticism, and for a Marxist feminist environmental politics. Millennial jitters have adversely affected environmental politics and yet, quite simply, apocalypticism is politically disabling. It is also contradictory. On the one hand the "human species" is blamed for taking us to the brink of environmental disaster, brought on, often as not, by the inevitability of human "greed" vis-à-vis nature. Infinitely capable of wrong, "human beings" are paradoxically incapable of transformative action; greed after all is human nature. Until the apocalyptic moment human action drives history, but history-become-apocalypse renders human agency moot. In apocalyptic readings of crisis, conscious beings become spectators, shrill exhortations to action notwithstanding. This historical contradiction is simultaneously geographical: A given past and voluntarist future are refracted as a congeries of global problems with strictly local, individual solutions. Recycling, for example, has become a moral imperative, and families now argue over disposable versus washable diapers. Meanwhile, military and industrial waste from Siberia to New Hampshire rots the air, water, and earth in often irreversible ways. Our visits to the recycling center may save our individual souls but will not release the world from its purported damnation.

Apocalypse promises one of two results: devastation or salvation. Insofar as devastation is unacceptable, salvation is posited as the answer. Redemption can come, the doors of Paradise can open, only if human beings have a massive species-wide conversion from their erstwhile evil ways. Further, the religiosity of apocalyptic visions is closely intertwined with their masculinism: An omniscient I narrates the present danger and arbitrates the behavior of salvation.[1] As such, apocalypticism may be the totalizing narrative to end all totalizing narratives. Its purpose, of course, is to wield the threat of devastation in hopes of assuring conversion, but it does not always work that way. As environmental geographers are well aware, a common response to actual disasters is to disassemble them—to deconstruct their totality—as a way of making them manageable. "Decalamitizing" the event is a related response. Thus, within only a few weeks of its happening in 1992, Hurricane Andrew became a "storm" in the national press; and the 1906 San Francisco earthquake quickly became a "fire." This process is double-edged: While treating it as simply a fire might have made the disaster easier to cope with, it also facilitated business interests in encouraging a building code more attentive to fire than seismic activity. Many "third world" disasters, from floods in Bangladesh to famine in East Africa, are decalamitized more simply; either they are not reported in any detail at all to European or American audiences, or else they are reported in full apocalyptic mode.

When apocalyptic scenarios offer any politics at all, it is a dreary politics of self-sacrifice and self-denial, focused on the individual acts of consumers. The production process is at best underplayed, if not entirely ignored. Consumption-oriented politics are necessarily reactive, and in a "first world" context where consumption is the central payoff for tolerating the depredations of capitalism, it is not likely to succeed. In the so-called third world, a consumption-based politics of denial are an obscenity. Made poor or kept poor in part through the economic power of the developed countries, the majority of third world residents are now being asked to forego technological innovation, resource use, and other means of economic development for sake of "the environment." Luddism should not underwrite survivable productions of nature. Appropriate technology, by the same token, is only a gentler denial of the means of development. The point here is not that Western technology is good and represents the way forward. Rather, environmental destruction is not a question of technology per se, and cannot be addressed at the level of technology, "appropriate" or otherwise. Environmental assumptions are already embedded in the form and direction of technological development.

More creative strategies will require attention not only to production *and* reproduction, but to the production of new political ecologies that embody altered social relations of production and reproduction. The voluntarism that has become a mainstay of the environmental movement will hardly save the world, but it may perpetuate the social practices of predation that are the hallmark of advanced capitalism. And, in part, it is an apocalyptic reading of the problem that underwrites this redemptive reform.

It should go without saying that I do not mean to efface the existence of environmental crises. Quite the reverse. Contemporary problems are so serious that rendering them apocalyptic *obscures* their political ecology—their sources, their political, economic, and social dimensions. Pollution; famine; ozone depletion; putative declines in biodiversity; human, plant, and animal epidemics; and staggering inequalities in wealth are local, global, and transterritorial. They are endemic not to "human nature" but to a specific mode of organizing social production and consumption: global capitalism. They reflect particular productions and reproductions of nature that can only be transformed.

Global capitalism is premised on a series of socially constructed differences that, in apocalyptic visions, take a universal character: man/woman; culture/nature; first world/third world; bourgeoisie/working class. These binaries, according to Donna Haraway, elicit "a dialectic of the apocalypse." The first of the pair is "the One who is not dominated, who knows that by the service of the other," the second "the one who holds the future, who knows that by the experience of domination, which gives the lie to the autonomy of the (first)" (Haraway 1991, 177).

As Neil Smith (1990) forcefully argues, nature is produced materially and metaphorically in historically and geographically specific ways. Its conceptualization as something external to society (rather than produced) is itself a thoroughly social construction. Any contemporary politics of nature must therefore be rooted in the specifics of capitalism and society. A revolutionary politics of nature cannot emerge from transhistorical or binary treatments of nature, such as those of the Frankfurt School, much modern natural science, and many parts of the environmental movement.

The question remains, what does the recrudescence of apocalyptic constructions of nature tell us about the contemporary world. What social norms and practices are "we" naturalizing with such narratives? For alongside the apocalypticism of nature written by Western theorists and activists, we find equally irresolvable, calamitous, and suffocatingly total texts of *social* disaster. From the popular press to the scholarly, at least in the United States, there has been a barrage of social crises: urban decline; abysmal failures in education, health, social welfare; spiraling debt; the democratization/capitalization of the Soviet empire gone awry; genocide in Bosnia; famine in Somalia; Islamic fundamentalism everywhere. As old orders come under attack from so many quarters, and the ruling class in the United States feels an acute loss of global control (of which the Gulf War may have been one symptom), the apocalypse talk seems to make sense. The apocalypse of nature is entwined with the apocalypse of social control. It is perhaps not coincidental that this talk arises under the conditions of postmodernity when white, Western, masculinist ruling classes stand increasingly on shifting ground; a world coming apart feels like less to lose. Although it might make sense from this ruling-class perspective, apocalypticism makes no sense for the Left.

To paraphrase Margaret FitzSimmons,[2] nature made apocalyptic gives rise to a politics of hopelessness from which the means of social and environmental transformation are unlikely to emerge. However reenergized it has become, the environmental movement has few workable visions of transformation. Nor, it has to be said, has the Left. And yet the profound political–economic shifts of the past five years—albeit largely within the assumptions of capitalism—surely give a glimmer of the kind of social change that *can* be realized.

To develop a new politics of nature it will be crucial to move away from what might be called a politics of domination and antidomination. The "domination of nature" is a central theme in the Frankfurt School and has come to dominate socialist politics of the environment. Yet this perspective tends to reaffirm as much as erode the dualisms of culture and nature, woman and man, and so forth; suppresses the importance of class; and posits "man" as locked in a universal struggle with nature (Smith 1990, 28–30).[3]

A new politics of nature requires that we get off the high horse of the apocalypse. Marxism too has been given to apocalyptic interpretation, but there is nothing inevitable about revolutionary change, and no guarantee that political organization will translate into such change. A politics of nature requires a keener sense of the dialectic of nature and human society—neither Engels's dialectics of nature nor a politics of antidomination. Human beings are simultaneously different from and of a piece with bees. Marx was right: Our consciousness both implicates and privileges us.

A new politics of nature will not conflate human beings and other fauna as biocentrists tend to do, will not refuse to differentiate between spotted owls and Somalis, or worse, treat the starvation of African peasants as Gaia's balancing act while spotted owls are something "we" can fight to save. Rather, a usable environmental politics takes seriously the political responsibility implied by the difference between people and bees. Marx did not deal with this, and yet his conceptualization of society–nature relationships provides parts of a vital framework for developing a politics of nature. This is grasped in parallel ways in Smith's (1990) "production and reproduction of nature," and in Haraway's (1991) "reinvention of nature."

A vital, creative, and promising politics of nature must have serious regard for Jackson's "in-between," for the produced natures that fall between dense urbanism on one side and "wilderness" on the other. Environmentalists' focus on the extremes invites an apocalypticism; the "in-between" rehumanizes the extremes, reincorporates them into everyday life. As Jackson (1991, 51) puts it, "the wilderness of the Sierra will disappear unless little pieces of nonwilderness become intensely loved by lots of people. . . . Harlem and East Saint Louis and Iowa and Kansas and the rest of the world where wilderness has been destroyed will have to be loved by enough of us, or wilderness is doomed." More than anything, Jackson seeks a politics where "[p]eople who struggle for social justice by working with the poor in cities and people out to prevent soil erosion and save the family farm are suddenly on the same side as the wilderness advocate" (Jackson 1991, 51). If Jackson fails to see wilderness as itself socially constructed, this political vision still has much to recommend it. It holds out promise of an integrated, imbricated political ecology, rooted in the in-betweens of nature and society, and in social structures and practices.

Jackson's invocation of the "in-between" resonates with the provocations and possibilities of many oppositional theories—among them, postcolonial, feminist, queer, and antiracist theories. The in-between offers the possibility of privileging neither nature nor society in political practice; of working against the interconnected structures of dominance from a position that respects the transformative potential in everyday practices; and of interweaving wild, agricultural, and urban concerns with one another and with biospheric and global political-economic issues. In this way, we might, in Donna Haraway's words, "seize the tools to mark the world." The social movements would be marked green while the environmental movement would be marked as an inevitably social project.

NOTES

1. The myth of Paradise, and its counterpoised Eden, are also connected to the loss of human agency. Such constructions posit places outside of history and geography, outside of social relations. Admission to both is controlled externally by the omniscient I-God.

2. In one of the most lucid analyses of nature written in recent years, Margaret FitzSimmons (1989) noted, "Nature-made-primordial provides a source of authority to a whole language of domination." My recasting of this phrase is meant to build on this insight.

3. On the dismalness of the Frankfurt School, see also Gilmore (1993), who begins a recent article with, "I am not of the Frankfurt School. One must live a life of relative privilege these days to be so dour about domination, so suspicious of resistance, so enchained by commodification, so helpless before the ideological state apparatuses to conclude there is no conceivable end to late capitalism's daily sacrifice of human life to the singular freedom of the market."

REFERENCES

Ehrlich, P. R. and Holdren, J. P. 1988. *The Cassandra Conference: Resources and the Human Predicament.* College Station, TX: Texas A & M University Press.

FitzSimmons, M. 1989. "The Matter of Nature." *Antipode* 21: 106–120.

Fukuyama, F. 1989, Summer. "The End of History?" *National Interest* 16: 3–18.

Gilmore, R. W. 1993. "Public Enemies and Private Intellectuals: Apartheid USA." *Race and Class* 35 (1): 69–78.

Gordon, A. and Suzuki, D. 1990. *It's a Matter of Survival*. Cambridge, MA: Harvard University Press.

Haraway, D. J. 1991. *Simians, Cyborgs, and Women: The Reinvention of Nature*. New York: Routledge.

Jackson, W. 1991. "Nature as the Measure for Sustainable Agriculture." In *Ecology, Economics, Ethics: The Broken Circle*, eds. F. H. Bormann and S. R. Kellert, 43-58. New Haven, CT: Yale University Press.

Kates, R. W. 1993. *Credible Scientist, Effective Advocate: The Divided Self*. Paper presented at the Meetings of the American Association for the Advancement of Science. Boston, Massachusetts, 12 February.

McKibben, B. 1989. *The End of Nature*. New York: Random House.

Smith, N. 1990. *Uneven Development: Nature, Capital and the Production of Space*, 2nd edition. Oxford: Basil Blackwell.

Feminism Without Guarantees: The Misalliances and Missed Alliances of Postmodernist Social Theory

CAROL A. STABILE

In this essay, I sketch an argument about the practices and perceptions of feminism in the new world order. I am concerned with intellectual vision—not as Donna Haraway (1988, 1989, 1990, 1991a, 1991b) theorizes it, for I believe her to be myopic around the very issues that are central to my concerns, but more in keeping with Pierre Bourdieu's insistence on the identification of "the point from which you can see what you see" (1990, 131). I focus on the politically interested nature of feminist visions—more specifically, on how the point from which we see what we see is structured and often limited by unacknowledged yet specific class interests.

This essay is in part a dystopic rendering of the misalliances and missed alliances effected by postmodernist social theory during the conservative restoration. By "postmodernist social theory," I mean the work of those theorists who believe that, in the late twentieth century, politics can exist only in the necessarily fragmented, divided, and contentious identities through which subjects conceive of themselves; and that the only similarity among such groups is their struggle—from very different positions and in isolation from one another—against an amorphous and ill-defined object known as "power" (e.g., Foucault 1977, 216). I also use the designation to refer to forms of critical theory that rely on an uncritical emphasis on the discursive constitution of the "real," a positivistic approach to the notion of "difference," and a marked lack of concern about the context of multinational capitalism and their own locations within that process of production (see Lazarus 1991; Norris 1990, 1992).

Within the global context of a worsening economic scenario, and from my location in academia, it seems that multinational capitalism depends upon the very mystifications that postmodernist social theorists reproduce around the category of "class." To try to unpack the implications of such mystifications, I begin by summarizing one of the more influential postmodernist arguments. Then I discuss concrete examples of how certain inadequacies operate in feminist theory and mainstream feminist activism. Since the social theory espoused by Laclau and Mouffe bears more than a passing resemblance to many feminist arguments in the United States, I begin with their notion of "radical democratic politics."

Central to the argument of Laclau and Mouffe (1990) is the claim that the Marxist concept of "class" is essentialist and impedes a truly "radical democratic politics." In place of the alleged fixity and "essentialist apriorism" of the working class, and in opposition to any conceptualization of a social totality, Laclau and Mouffe (1990, 113, 140) argue for a practice of articulations that "take place not only *within* given social and political spaces, but *between* them," and replace alliances previously forged through class struggle.

Laclau and Mouffe are consistent in their argument that Marxism "privileges" class in ways that marginalize or ignore the oppression of social groups not constituted economically (n. b., however, that the oppression of lesbians and gay men, to take one example, is expressed legally and violently through denial of employment, housing, and health care). But, one is obliged to ask who it is, precisely, that Laclau and Mouffe's argument privileges as the agents of social change—a change whose *telos* is, for them, reformist rather than revolutionary. Or, in slightly more pointed terms, whose political interests are served by their theory of nonfixity and discursive equivalences?

Laclau and Mouffe (1990, 186) conclude:

> To the extent that the resistance of traditional systems of difference is broken, and indeterminacy and ambiguity turn more elements of society into 'floating signifiers', the possibility arises of attempting to institute a center which radically eliminates the logic of autonomy and reconstitutes around itself the totality of the social body.

Although they insist that the centrality of class in Marxist analyses is essentialist, Laclau and Mouffe recognize the need for some form of centrality, some "new" center. What is the nature of this new "center"? Around what new "totality" will it converge? From what place, what now invisible class positions, does it emanate? Within the scope of their argument, it seems clear that—however tacit the claim—articulation and articulatory practices can best be done by those trained in the nuances of discourse and discursivity, namely, intellectuals: "Synonymy, metonymy, metaphor are not forms of thought that add a second sense to a primary, constitutive literality of social relations, instead, they are part of the primary terrain itself in which the social is constituted" (110). That being the case, who other than intellectuals could better form this new center for political struggle? In place of the so-called privileging of class, we find the privileging of intellectuals. This is, of course, a fine thing for intellectuals since it means that (1) we needn't invoke the notion of class at all since the concept is intrinsically essentialist; and (2) nor do we need to concern ourselves with the class privilege enjoyed by intellectuals, since oppressions are, within the discursive field, necessarily unfixed and somehow equivalent.

I turn now to a discussion of the connections between the problems of postmodernist social theory in the academy and problems in mainstream activism, especially in the form of mainstream feminism. I want to use as an example an event that garnered an enormous amount of media attention during the 1992 presidential campaign: Dan Quayle's speech on "family values" (1992). Quayle's speech was made in response to the L.A. uprising and played a part in Republicans' attempts to efface problems of racism and economic injustice (a move to which the Democrats implicitly consented). Quayle's speech deflected attention from the current economic crisis to another, more discursive and abstract crisis. In the conservative cause, Quayle (1992, A1) rendered the crisis in these terms:

> Right now the failure of our families is hurting America deeply. When families fail, society fails. The anarchy and lack of structure in our inner cities are testament to how quickly civilization falls apart when the family foundation cracks.

The discourse that Quayle mobilized has a lengthy racist history. The speech began by referring to the "terrible problem" of racism in the United States, but claimed, "The landmark civil rights bill of the 1960s removed legal barriers to allow full participation by blacks in the economic, social, and political life of the nation." According to Quayle, "By any measure the America of 1992 is more egalitarian, more integrated and offers more opportunities to black Americans and all other minority group members than the America of 1964." Despite his claim that substantial change has occurred, Quayle resorted to a traditional conservative rhetoric dating back to Daniel Moynihan's 1965 report, *The Negro Family*. In that report, Moynihan claimed that the problems plaguing inner-city residents could be reduced to a single, isolated factor: a family structure "which, because it is so out of line with the rest of American society, seriously retards the progress of the group as a whole."(For discussions of the deployment of this argument by the New Right, see *The Nation* [1989] and Lavin [1988].)

In 1986, CBS aired a Bill Moyers's special, *The Vanishing Family: Crisis in Black America*, that reworked the message contained in Moynihan's earlier report: Economic problems in America's inner cities have been solely caused by single mothers and absent or otherwise irresponsible fathers. Moyers's purpose resembles both Moynihan's and Quayle's: to duck the question of how people can support themselves and their communities in the absence of an economic base. In 1992, Quayle's appeal to this discursive crisis neatly removed attention from the material circumstances in which such families struggle to survive. Families, he tells us, have failed. It is never a matter of how—in terms of health care, day care, employment, housing—the system has abandoned and failed its constituents. In the aftermath of the L.A. uprising, this is precisely the sort of diversionary tactic so urgently sought by conservatives and liberals to disguise their incapacity and lack of will concerning race politics.

The logic that links the L.A. uprising, Dan Quayle's speech, and *Murphy Brown* has profound importance for those of us who call ourselves feminists, since feminist ideologies played a major role in erasing the context for Quayle's accusations. Both television and newspaper coverage of Quayle's speech originally contextualized the speech, quoting Quayle as claiming that a "poverty of values" caused the L.A. uprising. The day after Quayle's speech, in fact, the *New York Times* ran a front page story entitled "Quayle Says Riots Sprang from Lack of Family Values." On the following day, the *New York Times* began an article with,

> Thailand is in turmoil, the Federal deficit is ballooning and hot embers of racial resentment still smolder in the ruins of inner-city Los Angeles. But today the high councils of government were preoccupied with a truly vexing question: Is Murphy Brown a tramp? (Wines 1992)

Why did subsequent attention to Quayle's argument center around this single sentence referring to a fictional television character? "It doesn't help matters when prime-time TV has Murphy Brown—a character who supposedly epitomizes today's intelligent, highly paid, professional woman—mocking the importance of fathers by bearing a child alone and calling it just another 'life style choice'" (Quayle 1992).

Because liberal feminists are those with the education and class position to have access to the media and the government, the terms of what counts as feminist politics in popular culture are usually set by them. Without the quip about the television show, it seems doubtful that there would have been a feminist response. It is not surprising, then, that feminists were outraged not by Quayle's racism, but by his critique of Murphy

Brown. As a highly paid, liberal, aggressive, articulate, and indisputably successful anchorwoman, Murphy Brown embodies the goals and lifestyle choices of many feminists. *Time Magazine* has called her "feminism's point guard, schmoozing with the big boys" (Corliss 1992, 48).

If feminism has been represented as a class specific, single-issue affair, representations such as *Murphy Brown* have contributed to this problem: that the circumstances under which the television character labored bore no resemblance to the circumstances under which poor women labor seemed beside the point. Indeed, I think it fair to say that many feminists have increasingly invested in dematerialized campaigns. Since the late 1970s, feminists have translated their political energies into symbolic actions and debates that have only a distant relationship to the lived experience of many women in the United States. For example, in 1977 the Hyde Amendment, prohibiting the use of Medicaid funds for abortions, rendered abortion rights a moot point for poor women. Directly after passage of this amendment, as antiabortion forces were massively mobilizing for their concerted assault on *Roe v. Wade*, the National Organization for Women invested most of its time, energy, and funding in the ill-fated Equal Rights Amendment campaign. And during the mid-1980s, when cutbacks in health and welfare were drastically affecting huge numbers of women, men, and their children, feminists like Catherine MacKinnon and Andrea Dworkin were pursuing antipornography legislation as the solution to violence against women. Finally, in the aftermath of Quayle's speech, which conjoined racism and sexism (and class, if only through its glaring absence), and might have provided enormous impetus for a feminist campaign against racism, far too many feminists instead took on the task of defending a fictitious woman's right to parent, winding up in a much-publicized squabble over definitions of what counts as a family.

In the last case, feminist politics seem to function dangerously like trickle-down economics, since how these representations of family values affect women in socioeconomic positions other than those of the more privileged and educated middle classes was ignored in the *Murphy Brown* controversy. When writer/producer Diane English accepted an Emmy award for the show, she thanked "all the single parents out there who, either by choice or necessity, are raising their kids alone. Don't let anybody tell you you're not a family." On the season premiere of *Murphy Brown*, Murphy paraphrases English's earlier remark. Surrounded by "families," she says: "Perhaps it's time for the Vice President to expand his definition and recognize that whether by choice or circumstance families come in all shapes and sizes."

Two points are worth drawing attention to in these statements. First, there's the underlying belief in a particularly American form of pluralism, which is not all that dissimilar from arguments made by postmodern social theorists. Here, Laclau and Mouffe's argument about pluralism has followed a politically reactionary trajectory, for—as Elizabeth Spelman (1988) has pointed out—pluralism always has a defining center, a center defined by dominant economic interests. Thus, the solution to conservative appeals to "traditional" family values is merely to expand the definition of what constitutes a family, without addressing the manner in which this highly particularized and racist version of "family" is being used as a scapegoat for the economic crisis. In this way, feminism fights battles on a terrain owned and defined by the Right.

The second point concerns the equivalence between the terms "choice" and "circumstance," and the underlying notion that those who can afford to choose single parenthood and those who have no such choice confront the same or similar problems. The rhetoric of choice, as in "whether by choice or necessity," further works to imply that such choices are uniformly available to women. All the choices afforded Murphy and the constituency she represents are choices enabled by economic advantage and cultural capital. The reality is that a vast majority of single parents in the United States—most of them are women—raise their children in a society that has in effect abandoned them. Unlike many liberal feminists, these women cannot afford in-home day care; nor can most afford health care.[1] The belief that the solution to the problem is to adjust or expand the definition of what counts as a "family" without working toward institutional changes as well, operates through a very abstract and ultimately ineffectual form of politics.

By not discussing the intertwined contexts of race and economics, the feminist response to Quayle's speech further ceded any discussion of class privilege to the Right. The program and its producers, Quayle could claim (with some legitimacy) are "out there in the world of comfort. They ought to come with me out to where the real America is." White House spokesman Marlin Fitzwater endorsed Quayle's comments about the "poverty of values," saying that "The glorification of the life of an unwed mother does not do good service to most unwed mothers who are not highly paid, glamorous anchorwomen." The claim that liberal feminists were "glamorizing" single parenthood is not far from the mark, given the economic circumstances enjoyed by the fictitious Murphy Brown. It is distinctly ironic that the discourse of essentialism should be interrupted by the New Right.

Why has this particular context been erased? Why should it matter to feminism? When feminism works in concert with a conservative agenda to gloss over an issue of urgent political necessity such as the L.A. uprising, then as feminists we need to rethink the strategies being employed. The fragmentation celebrated by postmodern social theorists and the retreat from any understanding of the economic structuring of various discourses continue to work in specifically hegemonic ways. For example, the erasure of the L.A. uprising in the *Murphy Brown* incident moved the debate away from issues of race, from the condition of inner cities, and from the deteriorating economic base in the United States, to a much safer, symbolic ground. By shifting the debate from the material conditions of inner cities to the discursive field of "family values," both parties occupied a much more comfortable terrain for debate. Here indeed we can see the material effects of the replacement of the "economics of untruth" with "the politics of truth."

These are the political legacies that feminism must come to terms with in preparation for the struggles ahead. To repeat a now familiar litany, the point from which feminists see what they see, and ultimately construct claims about feminist political interests, is determined by race, gender, and class. While recently feminists have been attentive to the first two categories, the long-standing antipathy between Marxism and feminism in the United States has rendered attention to class relations and divisions an empty genuflection, despite its inclusion in the trinity. Attempts to disentangle these strands or pursue a single, linear model of analysis can only consolidate and privilege certain forms of oppression to the exclusion of other oppressive structures and practices. Establishing class as a central category of analysis for feminism emphasizes the relationality of structures of oppression in politically powerful ways. Furthermore, this move does not mean relinquishing the theoretical and practical gains following from feminist analyses of gender and race; instead, it provides a much more nuanced and complicated understanding of the manner in which oppressions are structurally intertwined.

Perhaps most importantly, this emphasis would enable feminists to produce feminist theories and actions that are meaningful to those who do not enjoy "the institutional privileges of power" (Spivak 1988, 280) that are so frequently taken for granted. In order to identify the particular class perspectives that structure feminist visions, we need to be scrupulously honest about the fact that for many African American, Latina, and Asian American women working within the academy, "feminism" only signifies white privilege, while for most women outside the academy, it seems remote from the concerns and problems of their everyday existences. We live in a country where 1% of the population owns 37% of the wealth. In university settings where feminism has become institutionalized, multiculturalism has become standard fare in the academic diet, while fewer and fewer poor people and fewer and fewer people of color can hope to acquire a college education. If feminism is to regain any integrity and momentum as a progressive political force, then it has to acknowledge and move beyond the confines of its existing, narrow class interests.

At the same time, this does not entail a return to a strict economism, or a willed ignorance of social relations not explicitly linked to class formations. We should hope that both feminists and Marxists have learned some lessons during the conservative restoration. I want quite explicitly to resist the assimilation of my argument to an antifeminist tendency that conflates feminism with reformism and blames the former entirely for the latter. In place of an antifeminist Marxism or an anti-Marxist feminism, I am arguing for feminist Marxism. In view of the fact that over 60% of the United States working class is female, neither feminism nor Marxism alone can offer an adequate framework for political struggles. Previous objections to Marxian theory, such as the belief that, as Joan Scott puts it, "the explanation for the origins of and changes in gender systems is found outside the sexual division of labor" (1988, 35), hold less purchase within the context of multinational capitalism. No longer can "families, households, and sexuality" (35) be seen as autonomous, or cut off from the mode of production; in fact, Scott herself comments upon the problems arising when families, households, and sexualities are accorded such autonomy. It seems reasonable to suggest that such formulations depend on the mythic nuclear family. Instead, as women increasingly constitute a greater percentage of the labor force both locally and globally, shifts in gender ideology need to be understood in terms of their context within the capitalist mode of production. As feminists and intellectuals, we might keep in mind the words of Rosa Luxemburg (1976, 253): "In order to exist or develop, this society not only needs certain relationships of production, exchange, and communication, but it also creates a certain set of intellectual relations within the framework of contradictory class interests." Before we can envision a more just future, we need to be able to assess more systematically from what point it is that we see what we see and what has been habitually, and is once again, excluded from that perspective.

NOTE

1. An example of this occurred during the debates over President Clinton's appointment of Zoe Baird for Attorney General and the revelations about the hiring of illegal aliens. Many claimed that such scrutiny only applied because of Baird's gender. There was, however, absolutely no attention in the mainstream media as to why privileged women and men hire illegal aliens—namely, the issue of wages. Barbara Katz Rothman (1989) offers an excellent analysis of the entry of women's unpaid labor into the market place and its implications for feminist theory.

REFERENCES

Bourdieu, P. 1990. *In Other Words: Essays Towards a Reflective Sociology*. Stanford, CA: University of Stanford Press.

Corliss, R. 1992. "Having It All." *Time Magazine* (September 21): 48.

Foucault, M. 1977. *Language, Counter-Memory, Practice: Selected Essays and Interviews*, trans. D. F. Bouchard and S. Simon. Ithaca: Cornell University Press.

Haraway, D. 1988. "Situated Knowledges: The Science Question in Feminism as a Site of Discourse on the Privilege of Partial Perspective." *Feminist Studies* 14 (3): 575–599.

——. 1989. *Primate Visions: Gender, Race, and Nature in the World of Modern Science*. New York: Routledge.

——. 1990. *Simians, Cyborgs and Women*. New York: Routledge.

——. 1991. "Cyborgs at Large: Interview with Donna Haraway," by C. Penley and A. Ross. *Social Text* 25/26: 8–23.

——. 1991. "The Promises of Monsters: A Regenerative Politics for Inappropriate/d Others." In *Cultural Studies*, eds. L. Grossberg, C. Nelson, and P. Treichler, 295–337. New York: Routledge.

Laclau, E. and C. Mouffe. 1990. *Hegemony and Socialist Strategy: Towards a Radical Democratic Politics*. New York: Verso.

Lavin, M. 1988. "The Feminization of Poverty and the Media." In *Global Television*, eds. C. Schneider and B. Wallis, 237–253. New York: Wedge Press.

Lazarus, N. 1991. "Doubting the New World Order: Marxism, Realism, and the Claims of Postmodernist Social Theory." *Differences* 3 (3): 94–138.

Luxemburg, R. 1976. *The National Question*, ed. H. B. Davis. New York: Monthly Review Press.

Moynihan, D. P. 1965. *The Negro Family: The Case for National Action*. Washington, D.C.: U.S. Department of Labor, Office of Policy Research.

The Nation. 1989. "Scapegoating the Black Family." Special Issue (July 24): 31.

Norris, C. 1990. *What's Wrong With Postmodernism: Critical Theory and the Ends of Philosophy*. Baltimore: Johns Hopkins University Press.

——. 1992. *Uncritical Theory: Postmodernism, Intellectuals, and the Gulf War*. Amherst: University of Massachusetts Press.

Quayle, D. 1992. "Speech on Cities and Poverty." *New York Times* (May 20): A1.

Rothman, B. K. 1989. *Recreating Motherhood: Ideology and Technology in a Patriarchal Society*. New York: W. W. Norton.

Scott, J. 1988. *Gender and the Politics of History*. New York: Columbia University Press.

Spelman, E. 1988. *Inessential Woman: Problems of Exclusion in Feminist Thought*. Boston: Beacon Press.

Spivak, G. 1988. "Can the Subaltern Speak?" In *Marxism and the Interpretation of Culture*, ed. C. Nelson and L. Grossberg, 271–316. Urbana: University of Illinois Press.

Wines, M. 1992. "Views on Single Motherhood are Multiple at White House." *New York Times* (May 21): A1.

Wood, E. M. 1986. *The Retreat from Class: A New "True" Socialism*. London: Verso.

Feminist Standpoint Theories and the Return of Labor

KATHI WEEKS

ne reason why the modernist–postmodernist debate has not been more productive is that each side tends to adhere to a partial and distorted understanding of the other. For their part, postmodernists often fail to appreciate the place of Marxism within the modern tradition. It is as if in order to establish postmodernism's credibility as a radical alternative and coherent challenge to modernism, some postmodernists simplify the image of their opponent. As a result, in many cases, the complexity of and variety within modernism is eclipsed as the tradition of modernist thought is reduced to a particular version of the Enlightenment that can be negatively contrasted to postmodernism. This tendency to dismiss or underestimate the specificity and potential force of Marxism is apparent in many of the postmodernist critiques of feminist standpoint theories.

In the pages that follow I attempt to reconstruct the links between certain feminist standpoint theories—specifically, the versions developed by Nancy Hartsock, Hilary Rose, and Dorothy Smith—and a particular strand of Marxist interpretation. This effort is centered around a rearticulation of the concept of labor that emphasizes the immanent and critical dimensions of this key Marxist category and a formulation of the concept of a standpoint as the affirmation of an achieved, selective, and strategic essentialism. Marxism is often identified as a "bad influence" on feminism—the abusive spouse in an unhappy marriage. While this may be true in many cases, it is not necessarily true in every case; there are more creative appropriations of Marxism within feminism, as well as many more possibilities for interesting alliances that cannot be adequately captured by this formula. My project involves a selective reading of standpoint theories that emphasizes what I see to be their most productive elements and in some cases pushes these insights further. I hope that this will contribute to our understanding of the potential value of Marxism for feminism.

FEMINIST STANDPOINT THEORIES: THE EPISTEMOLOGICAL AND ETHICAL CONSEQUENCES OF THE GENDER DIVISION OF LABOR

The fundamental assumption of standpoint theories is that what we do can have consequences for who we are and what we think, and that what we do is determined in part by our gender.[1] Feminist standpoint theories thus begin with an account of women's labor as it is organized within the gender division of labor, and then explore its potential epistemological and ethical consequences.

Women's labor is presented in a number of different ways in these accounts. Hilary Rose describes women's traditional work as "emotionally demanding labor," or "caring labor." As Rose explains it, "Whether menial or requiring the sophisticated skills involved in child care, it always involves personal service" (1983, 83). Dorothy Smith describes women's labor as labor in the concrete bodily mode, pointing out that women

> do those things that give concrete form to the conceptual activities. They do the clerical work . . . the routine computer work, the interviewing for the survey, the nursing, the secretarial work. At almost every point women mediate for men the relation between the conceptual mode of action and the actual concrete forms on which it depends. (1987, 83)

Not only is this labor made invisible, the skills women develop in and through this socially necessary caring labor, or labor in the concrete bodily mode, are typically naturalized and undervalued (Rose 1986, 165). The crucial point here is, as Nancy Hartsock puts it, that "whether or not all of us do both, women as a sex are institutionally responsible for producing both goods and human beings and all women are forced to become the kinds of people who can do both" (1983a, 291).

This gender division of labor, which structures two fields of practice, carries important implications. Standpoint theorists point to the possibilities for developing different ways of thinking about and being in the world on the basis of women's practices. Feminist standpoint theories posit a model of the self that is the product of a complex relational network. This model of subjectivity in turn grounds an epistemology that eschews dualistic, either/or thinking and revalues the material, concrete, everyday, and bodily dimensions of existence. Standpoint theories thus suggest the potential for developing both powerful critiques of and compelling alternatives to existing social relations.

TWO CRITIQUES OF ESSENTIALISM

Postmodernist feminists challenge feminist standpoint theories on many fronts. However, one of the most consistently levelled critiques is that of essentialism. Yet while the critique of essentialism is a nearly universal feature of the postmodernist feminist indictment of modernism, it is not always clear exactly what is meant by it. There are, in fact, at least two different critiques included under this heading: first, a critique of claims about the "true nature" of subjects, that is, a critique of naturalized models of subjectivity; and second, a critique of centered models of subjectivity, that is, of models that privilege a single, fundamental feature of the subject. Let me address each of these critiques in turn.

According to some of its critics, standpoint theories are founded upon a philosophical or scientific claim about what women are. By this reading, the feminist (or rather, the woman's) standpoint rests upon a naturalized essentialism, or a claim about woman's essential nature. Many of these critics are suspicious of the significance that is placed on attributes that are so closely associated with women's specific biological capacities. The model of the subject employed by standpoint theorists is, they argue, organized around a biological core that is supposedly constitutive of the genuinely authentic, "true nature" of woman.

Clearly, however, this critique is based on a misrepresentation of the project of standpoint theory. The laboring subject of feminist standpoint theories is an historically specific subject involved in a culturally specific set of practices. Caring labor and labor in the concrete bodily mode have no necessary or natural connection to sex-specific biology. When they speak of essence, standpoint theorists refer to the more essential (deeper, more intractable) attributes of gender, not to the more natural attributes of sex. Gender is privileged in these accounts as one deeply constitutive feature of subjective identity, not as a natural consequence of sex specificity. In other words, this model of the subject does not extend down to some core of unsocialized human nature shared universally by women.

In arguing that standpoint theories are grounded in a philosophical or scientific claim about what women are, the Marxist dimensions of the project are rendered invisible. In particular, the creative role, the constitutive force of labor is negated in these accounts of feminist stand-point theories. So how is labor conceived and what function does it serve in these theories? First of all, I would argue that labor is not best described as a claim about what we are. Rather, labor is an immanent category that serves as a principle of historical movement and social production. As a creative force in a theory that rejects teleology, it can be described as an ontological dynamic or as a principle of ontological self-assertion. In other words, labor is a causal principle that propels life into history, or rather, to be more accurate, it is a principle by which we can make sense of and intervene in this movement.

There are some suggestive parallels between the role of labor in Marxist thought and the role of the will to power in Nietzschean thought. By reading labor through the lens of recent interpretations of the will to power we can highlight the immanent and materialist dimensions of this fundamental category. Like the will to power, labor functions as a prin-ciple of internal genesis or as an ontology of practice.[2] Like the will to power, labor is a claim about existence, about the constitutive force of practices, rather than a claim about the essence of things. By this read-ing, then, labor serves as an immanent creative principle in the service of a materialist analysis of the present.

We can observe this same understanding of labor as a principle of ontological self-assertion in feminist standpoint theories. For example, Dorothy Smith explains that she turns to Marxism to find an ontology that affirms that "our world is continually being brought into being as it is and as it is becoming, in the daily practices of actual individuals" (1987, 125). This originary principle constitutes an ontology that puts things into historical motion such that then, as Smith explains, "questions of what become less significant than questions of how—how it gets done, how it works" (1987, 126–127). It is this dimension of standpoint theo-ries, the continually dynamic quality of labor, its constitutive force, that this first group of critics fails to account for.

A second group of critics agree that standpoint theories are grounded not in a claim about what women are; rather, they argue that the project is based on an equally problematic claim about what women do. The second version of the postmodernist critique of essentialism claims that standpoint theories center their model of gendered subjec-tivity around labor and, in doing so, posit a kind of cultural essential-ism. Donna Haraway, unlike the first group of critics, does not accuse standpoint theorists of naturalizing gender unity. Instead, "the essentializing move," she argues, "is in the ontological structure of labor or of its analogue, women's activity" (1985, 76). Haraway argues that labor is "an ontological category permitting the knowledge of a subject, and so the knowledge of subjugation and alienation" (1985, 76). In a similar vein, Irene Diamond and Lee Quinby argue that even though Marxist feminists have been critical of natural essences, "that critique remains problematic because, to the extent that their definitions of power grant primacy to the category of labor, their arguments about the social constructions of self retain a centering that may be understood as a type of cultural essentialism" (1988, xii–xiii). Labor is not rendered invisible in these readings of standpoint theory. On the contrary, labor is identified as the problem with the project. Labor, they argue, functions essentially by ontologizing women's experiences; it fixes what women are around an account of what (only some) women do. According to these critics, this privileging of labor, this generalization about women's practices and the standpoint it supposedly makes possible, renders certain differences among women invisible.

Whereas the critique of a naturalizing essentialism misses its mark, this critique of a centering essentialism is based on a more accurate rendition of the project it criticizes. However, I want to contest some of the assumptions about the role of labor that inform this analysis. Labor, I argue, can be seen to play a somewhat different role than the one these critics describe. Rather than "an ontological category permitting the knowledge of a subject and so the knowledge of subjugation and alienation," labor is best conceived as an ontological category permitting the contestation of a fixed subjectivity and the resistance to subjugation and alienation. Standpoint theory, as I propose conceiving it, is not a philosophical or scientific project grounded in a claim about what women are, not a sociological project grounded in a claim about what women do, but a political project grounded in a claim about what women *can* do.

To respond to this second version of the essentialist critique we need to continue our exploration of the category of labor and then reconsider its relationship to standpoint theories' account of subjectivity. So far, I have argued that labor in standpoint theories serves not as a claim about what women are, but rather, as a specific claim about what women do. But this is not yet an adequate description. In its strongest, most compelling formulation, labor is a category designed to raise questions about what we can do. This should be clearer once we examine how the traditional scope of labor is expanded in standpoint theories and how that expansion forces a shift in the focus of the category.

Standpoint theorists fault nonfeminist Marxism for its narrow conception of production, which fails to recognize an alternative standpoint grounded in women's laboring activity. To remedy this, feminist standpoint theorists expand the traditional focus of Marxist analyses in order to include the kinds of work that women traditionally do. This expansion of labor involves more than any simple addition of reproduction to traditional analyses of production. Clearly, the addition of emotional work, caring labor, and labor in the concrete bodily mode to the list of laboring activities substantially broadens and complicates this key Marxist category.

The problem, however, is that the concept of labor would now seem to be construed too broadly. Some claim that by expanding the category in this way it loses its specificity and becomes synonymous with activity: Labor is whatever we do. I want to suggest that rather than a simple expansion of the category to include the "reproductive" work that women do, we can locate within this project a shift in the focus of the category from production and/or reproduction to value-creating activity.[3] That is, by including activities not traditionally classified as "work," standpoint theorists help to move our focus to a more contested terrain.

More specifically, by reading labor not in terms of world-creating activity but in terms of value-creating activity we shift our attention from the sociological question of what women do to the political question of how it is valued. By focusing on value-creating activity we concentrate more clearly on judgments about these activities; we bring to the foreground the question of how or if these activities are or should be valued in society. Labor conceived as value-creating activity thus serves to affirm our abilities to (re)construct the world, to focus our attention on the ways in which these abilities and activities are limited or restrained, and to encourage struggle over which constituting activities are valued in society. The point is to open up fields of contestation over the organization and valorization of specific activities. In this way, the activities in question and the terms of debate arise as political issues. In short, the concept of labor lacks a practical thrust unless it is accompanied by the question of value.

What are the advantages of this formulation? By emphasizing the political dimensions of this analysis, we can see the ways that labor can animate specific problematics and sites of struggle; labor as value-creating activity is contested, not presupposed. By shifting our focus in this way we can extract labor from the discourse of alienation: conflicts over value need not be mediated through claims about what we are, what we lose, and how we are estranged from the self. To repeat my earlier proposition, I believe that in its strongest conception, labor in these analyses is not central to the construction of a philosophy of what we are or a sociology of what we do; rather, labor is best conceived in these analyses as part of a politics of what we can do.

Laboring processes are also productive of subjectivities. At their best, standpoint theories construct a dynamic model of the social construction of subjectivity as a process wherein always already gendered subjects continually renegotiate the daily act of "en-gendering" in and through their everyday activities. Labor serves thus as a key to a structurally determined site of practices within which choices are made and the will is exercised. Through our laboring activity we are constituted by and constitutive of the power relations that organize our world. As a mediating practice linking human beings to social forces, labor is one key to the (re)production of the self as agent: the (re)producer as opposed to the consumer of the ideals, values, and images that constitute identity. Labor, then, as both a predetermined and a potentially self-creating set of practices, organizes standpoint theories' accounts of subjective agency. In centering their models of the subject around labor, standpoint theories do not search for the voluntary origin of "determined" identity, but rather attempt to valorize a moment in the process of subjectification or exploitation that carries with it the potential for social critique and oppositional activity. With this model of a situated agency, these accounts affirm both the determined character of social existence and the constitutive force of the subjective will, a will that is neither free nor determined, or rather, a will that is both free and determined.

FROM THE ONTOLOGY OF LABOR TO THE POLITICS OF A STANDPOINT

The goal of standpoint theories, as they are delimited in this account, is to transform this capacity for agency into political projects, in this case, to transform the subject position of women into one or many feminist standpoints. There are three dimensions of this version of the standpoint that we must make clear. First, it is crucial that we are discussing a feminist rather than a women's standpoint: It is a collective interpretation of a particular subject position rather than an immediate perspective automatically acquired by an individual who inhabits that position. A standpoint must be derived from political practice, from a collective effort to revalue and reconstitute women's activities. As a product of critical engagement with practical intent, a standpoint is, then, a position to be achieved rather than a preexisting consciousness to be recognized (see Hartsock 1983a, 288, 303). In short, a feminist standpoint is willed (it affirms what we can do) rather than presupposed (on the basis of what we do). Second, a standpoint is selective. As Hartsock explains it, a standpoint "picks out and amplifies the liberatory possibilities" of women's social location and life experience (1983b, 232). A feminist standpoint is not predicated on the unqualified affirmation of what we are and what we do. Instead, it is constructed around a *selective* valorization of what we have done and what we have become as an ongoing achievement. This becomes the ground for what we can do, can become, and can know. Third, a standpoint is strategic. Feminist standpoint theories propose that we transform the subject positions of women constituted by the structures and ideas that organize women's collective practices into feminist standpoints—collective and politically engaged endeavors. It is the project's transformative potential that is the ultimate measure of its value. In sum, a standpoint is achieved, selective, and strategic and the goal is, finally, to construct "effective selections."

Earlier I made some comparisons between labor and the will to power in order to clarify certain aspects of the reading I am proposing. There are some similarly suggestive parallels between a feminist standpoint and recent interpretations of the Nietzschean idea of the eternal return. In Nietzsche's very enigmatic formulation, the eternal return is a "cultivating idea" that teaches us that whatever we will, we should will that it return eternally. The eternal return teaches us to affirm selectively the past as an ongoing achievement and a basis for action, as opposed to a necessary fact and a source of resignation. As Gilles Deleuze describes it, the eternal return teaches "not affirmation as acceptance, but as creation" (1983, 185). With this thought Nietzsche reformulates the notion of being by uprooting it from its transcendental foundations.[4] What we can do, what we can be, what we affirm in practice becomes being, becomes necessary, becomes essential. Being does not preexist becoming as its directing force or telos. Rather, being serves as both the (contingent) product and the (changing) ground of social practice. We are that which we selectively and actively affirm.

Like the eternal return, a standpoint is an ethic that teaches, rather than a metaphysic that is presupposed. More specifically, like the eternal return, a feminist standpoint is an ethic that teaches us to select and affirm the "being" of becoming, or, in this case, the "essence" of collective activities, as the ground of our future practices. This sense of commonality, this "we" that coalesces around any particular standpoint, is a dynamic achievement rather than a static fact. A standpoint thus represents an attempt to locate a ground around which we can generate collectivities without relying on some transcendental, natural, or otherwise pregiven essence.

Now I am in the position to respond to the second critique of essentialism. While it is accurate to claim that standpoint theories offer a centered and, in that sense, essentialized subject, it is important to understand this as an achieved, selective, and strategic essentialism based on the creative force of labor.[5] That is, standpoint theory, as it is reconstructed here, should be read as a political project that builds on the capacity for agency valorized through labor. The feminist standpoint as a project serves as *one* means by which we can bring differences together on the basis of an affirmation of what women can do, be, and know, rather than on the basis of a claim about what women are, or what some women do or know. By conceiving the concept of labor as political rather than metaphysical and by reading a standpoint as an open horizon, both the subject and the project of standpoint theories can be seen to be more contingent, fluid, and contested than these critics suggest.

NOTES

1. For good descriptions of the project of standpoint theory, see Harding (1986, 141–161; 1991, 119–137) and Hartsock (in press).
2. I owe these descriptions of the will to power to Deleuze (1983, 91) and Warren (1988, 111), respectively.
3. For an elaboration of this notion of labor as value-creating activity, see Antonio Negri and Michael Hardt (1994).
4. See also Warren's reading of the eternal return (1988, 196–206).
5. The term strategic essentialism is from Spivak (1988).

REFERENCES

Deleuze, G. 1983. *Nietzsche and Philosophy*, trans. H. Tomlinson. New York: Columbia University Press.

Diamond, I. and Quinby, L. 1988. "Introduction." In *Feminism and Foucault: Reflections on Resistance*, ed. I. Diamond and L. Quinby, ix–xx. Boston: Northeastern University Press.

Haraway, D. 1985. "A Manifesto for Cyborgs: Science, Technology, and Socialist Feminism in the 1980's." *Socialist Review* 80: 65–107.

Harding, S. 1986. *The Science Question in Feminism*. Ithaca: Cornell University Press.

———. 1991. *Whose Science? Whose Knowledge? Thinking from Women's Lives*. Ithaca: Cornell University Press.

Hartsock, N. 1983a. "The Feminist Standpoint: Developing the Ground for a Specifically Feminist Historical Materialism." In *Discovering Reality*, ed. S. Harding and M. Hintikka, 283–310. Dordrecht: Reidel.

———. 1983b. *Money, Sex, and Power: Toward a Feminist Historical Materialism*. Boston: Northeastern University Press.

———. In press. "The Feminist Standpoint Revisited." In *The Feminist Standpoint Revisited and Other Essays*, ed. Boulder: Westview Press.

Negri, A. and Hardt, M. 1994. *Labor of Dionysus*. Minneapolis: University of Minnesota Press.

Rose, H. 1983. "Hand, Brain, and Heart: A Feminist Epistemology for the Natural Sciences." *Signs: Journal of Women in Culture and Society* 9 (1): 73–90.

———. 1986. "Women's Work: Women's Knowledge." In *What is Feminism?*, ed. J. Mitchell and A. Oakley, 161–183. Oxford: Basil Blackwell.

Smith, D. 1987. *The Everyday World as Problematic: A Feminist Sociology*. Boston: Northeastern University Press.

Spivak, G. 1988. *In Other Worlds: Essays in Cultural Politics*. New York: Routledge.

Warren, M. 1988. *Nietzsche and Political Thought*. Cambridge, MA: MIT Press.

Consenting to Whiteness: Reflections on Race and Marxian Theories of Discrimination

RHONDA M. WILLIAMS

arxists and non-Marxists alike are rethinking race. Theoreticians of the past dozen years increasingly refuse either to reduce race to class or to insist on conceptualizing race as an historically invariant social practice. As an alternative to reductionist and essentialist thinking, these new projects explore the social production of racial meanings, race formations, and racial identities (Gooding-Williams 1993; Hall 1989; hooks 1992; Omi and Winant 1986; Roediger 1991).

This essay critiques recent Marxist economic discourse on discrimination. I argue that, our substantive differences notwithstanding, Marxian economists share a common tendency to undertheorize race. Neither side has accorded sufficient significance either to the economic and extra-economic practices that create gendered, race-conscious workers or to the historical specificity of those practices. Hence our understanding of discrimination remains incomplete, our antiracist politics contorted. I suggest that both poststructuralist and feminist theories provide analytic means to the end of developing a richer theory of race and gender subjectification, agency, and "class interests."

WINNERS AND LOSERS: CALCULATING THE COSTS AND BENEFITS OF DISCRIMINATION

Marxian economists agree that racial discrimination is a persistent feature of the daily operation of capitalist labor markets. However, we disagree as to the practices that reproduce racial inequality. The radical mainstream presents two forms of class-based models. The "divide and conquer" tradition argues that discrimination divides the working class, lowers workers' bargaining power relative to capitalists, increases profits, and is consistent with perfect competition (Reich 1981). For example, mainstream theorists explain that divisions in the working class made possible capitalists' employment of black workers as strikebreakers between World Wars I and II. Strikebreaking increases capitalist profits, since the new workers sell their labor power for less than the strikers, and reduces all workers' wages, since divisions reduce bargaining power.

Cherry (1988, 1989a) amends the class-based model by noting that in the post-World War II era of segmented labor markets, capitalists rarely hire only African American strikebreakers. Moreover, gender-based occupational segregation limits the extent to which employers threaten their male workers with the specter of mass hirings of women. Still, contemporary capitalists use global wage hierarchies to reduce costs via the subcontracting of work to firms in secondary labor markets locally, nationally, and internationally. Cherry (1989a, 53) also observes that technologically backward firms depend on women and men of color's labor power to maintain competitive rates of profit.

Supporters of the divide and conquer tradition supplement their analysis with empirical and historical evidence. Reich (1981) demonstrates a positive correlation between black–white family income inequality on the one hand, and income and schooling inequality among whites on the other. He reads this correlation as an affirmation of the hypothesis that racial inequality lowers workers' bargaining power and therefore their ability to shift income from profits to wages and community development. Cherry (1991) uses an analysis of corporate manufacturer's "Southern strategy" in the late 1950s and early 1960s to demonstrate how white men's collaboration with racism and sexism undermined their class interests. In an effort to avoid the high cost of unionized, predominantly white male labor in the late 1940s, capitalists shifted productive investment to the antiunion South and hired thousands of white and black women. Because they failed to organize the South, accomodationist union leaders set the stage for their undoing (as measured by declining rates of wage and employment growth), and guaranteed the short-lived nature of their gains. Meanwhile, capitalists increased profits by hiring Southern women at lower wages.

At least two explanations of white working-class racism persist in the radical mainstream. Sherman (1987, 118–122) espouses a functionalism that posits racism as something capitalists "do" to workers because it facilitates the preservation and expansion of capital. Cherry (1989a) argues that whites cling to "discriminatory attitudes" because of the *percep-*

tion that they benefit from racism. He explains a resurgence of white discriminatory attitudes in the post-World War II period as the fault of an opportunistic union leadership that supported capitalist-led foreign policy objectives, eschewed formation of a labor party, and convinced white male union members to act against their class interest.

Challengers to the Marxian mainstream include both neo- and classical Marxists. Whereas neo-Marxists tend to reject value theory and accord primacy to the analysis of segmented labor markets and social structures of accumulation (Shulman 1984, 1990, 1991), the classical camp employs Marxian theories of competition to conceptualize discrimination (Darity 1989; Mason 1992; Williams 1987, 1991). Both schools of thought agree with the traditionalists that discrimination persists in capitalist economies. However, neo- and classical Marxists posit different mechanisms for the continuation of discrimination and challenge the notion that white workers always lose when they collaborate with or pursue racist practice.

Darity, Mason, and Williams ground their models of discrimination in Marx's analysis of competition and new theoretical work on non-compensating wage differentials (Botwinick 1993). They argue that the competitive structure of capitals is consistent with recurring inter- and intraindustry wage differentials between comparable workers. The reserve army, job-specific labor queues, and the wage hierarchies shape inter- and intraclass conflicts over the allocation of workers to jobs. Moreover, the classical school argues that labor market activities are a site for the construction, reproduction, and disruption of race/gender subjects who define their interests in race and/or gendered terms.

To accept the classical premise of race/gender subjectification interrupts the mainstream thesis that race and gender inequality are intrinsically contrary to white (male) workers' interests, and reinterprets white male workers' racism and sexism. Even when racial divisions reduce workers' bargaining power and lower labor's income relative to capital, dominant groups may still increase their absolute standard of living by controlling preferred industries, firms, and occupations. To the extent that white workers are concerned with absolute income levels, their losses relative to capital are insufficient to render irrational the pursuit of racial inequality. We cannot take for granted the notion that white workers define their well-being and status relative to capitalist or upper-income whites. Other interpretations of "interest" and the meaning and value of particular economic outcomes to workers are both plausible and historically observed.

Because discrimination's outcomes are complex, contradictory, and contingent, challengers to the mainstream remain skeptical that there exists a set of economic outcomes that proves white workers lose from discriminations. The outcomes are complex because both continuing and ending discrimination are costly. They are contingent because these costs are mediated by political and aggregate economic conditions. Discrimination's outcomes are contradictory, in that occupational, wage, and employment discrimination need not necessarily increase or decrease in tandem (Shulman 1991).

Heckman and Paynor (1989) document the complexity of racialized inter- and intraclass conflicts. They observe that for many years, and in keeping with Jim Crow traditions and generalized white racism, manufacturers in South Carolina maintained the factories as all-white enclaves. Here, the costs of discriminating were low due to ample white labor reserves. Two phenomena increased the costs of discrimination in the 1960s: White labor supplies began to diminish, and the federal government passed antidiscrimination legislation. The passage of antidiscrimination legislation both provided a legitimate reason to break the industrial segregation barrier and reduced the bargaining power of white workers.

There is a symmetry to the new theories of discrimination. Neo- and classical Marxist challengers to the traditionalists reject the notion that racism is something that capitalists impose on workers even though employers sometimes benefit from racist practice, yet they also resist the thesis that white workers are the only obstacle to ending discrimination. The challengers' proposition is rather more modest: White worker agency warrants inclusion in the social practices that reproduce discrimination.

OMISSIONS AND OBLITERATION: ON DISCRIMINATING SUBJECTS

Traditional Marxist theories of discrimination construct white workers as the possessors of objective class interests determined by their relations to the imposition and appropriation of surplus value. In other words, white workers are the bearers of a stable and noncontradictory class identity, grounded in the social relations of production. Radicals know what those interests are, and discrimination is antithetical thereto. Mainstream radical theory yields a clear political strategy: Radicals must convince working-class whites that they suffer from discrimination. If radicals can change white perceptions as to the benefits derived from discriminatory behavior, they will have achieved a necessary (but perhaps not sufficient?) step along the path toward ending racist behaviors and attitudes.

The challengers argue to the contrary: discrimination's cost-benefit calculus is complex and contingent. One of the reasons white workers discriminate is because of the absolute or relative benefits as "white people" from so doing. Neo- and classical Marxists are loath to reduce racism and discrimination's persistence to false perceptions. On the contrary, we begin with the historically located and racially identified white workers for whom whiteness mediates notions of self, gender, community, and class interest. Racial discrimination presupposes racial identity, and the creation of racial identities requires "racializing" sociocultural relations. Thus neo- and classical Marxists argue from a perspective that "whiteness" is constitutive of identity, gender, community, and interests.

In expanding conceptualizations of race, the new theorists of discrimination open a door to dialogues with a wide range of social theorists exploring the social and discursive construction of meaning and culture. This community of scholars includes feminists, ethnic studies scholars, poststructuralists, historians, literary critics, and philosophers (to name but a few) who are thinking about the social construction of race and racial representations, but do not take discrimination as their entry point (Butler 1993; hooks 1990; San Juan 1989).

In their important discussion of the formation of the racial state in the United States, Omi and Winant argue that individuals and groups contest the meaning of race, and that these struggles are not limited to the macrostructural world of state politics or the economic realm. In other words, we make racialized meanings and identities in the everyday action contexts (workplaces, families, political organizations, etc.) wherein we engage one another on the basis of an intersubjective consensus about community, values, and objectives. In a similar spirit, San Juan urges us to conceptualize racism as part of a totality wherein the bourgeoisie constructs its domination via the "production of subjects inscribed in racist discourse and institutional practice" (San Juan 1989, 74).

Feminists continue to theorize the gendering of race and class in capitalist social formations. The experience and meaning of race and class within families, workplaces, kinship systems, migratory communities, settler colonies, unions, clubs, and political movements is deeply gendered. To paraphrase Stuart Hall, if race is the modality in which class is lived, it is a gendered and multivalent modality as well. Many feminists now call for and conduct critical readings of class, gender, race, ethnicity, and sexuality that historically, culturally, and materially locate the subjects and communities under investigation (Brown 1992; Hewitt 1992; hooks 1990). Lastly, a new generation of Marxist economists has begun a dialogue between Marxist and postmodern theories of subject formation. Economists Milberg and Pietrykowski argue that Marxists can benefit from the conceptual contributions of poststructuralists and phenomenology:

> The melding of poststructuralism and phenomenology gives a "trans-subjective" conception [of] meaning and understanding, focusing on the

social construction of the subject as a process of mediation between self and "lifeworld." Subjectivity is a process, an ongoing one of interaction among individuals in which power . . . is inherent and within which interpretation is the only access to meaning. The individual is determined by social relations but these relations themselves are a function of individual and social interpretation. (1991, 16)

IMPLICATIONS

Much work remains to be done. Although we have problematized white racial identity, challengers to the radical mainstream have barely begun to detail the racializing processes relevant to theorizing discrimination. I close with a final example that affirms the importance of postmodern insights for Marxist economists. Both mainstream theorist Cherry (1989a) and challenger Shulman (1991) have presented analyses of Congress of Industrial Organizations (CIO) organizing drives from the 1930s through the 1950s. Cherry affirms communist efficacy in organizing multiracial unions in Alabama mines and the textile mills of North Carolina. He argues that CIO-inspired antiracist sentiment generated rising black–white income ratios in the 1940s. Indeed, it was the very success of multiracial organizing that generated a host of liberal responses intended to divert mass attention from the fundamentally economic nature of racism in the 1940s and 1950s. Liberal success culminated in purges of communists from the CIO, a retreat to business unionism, and the ultimate merger of an accomodationist CIO with the AFL.

Shulman offers a dramatically different account, premised on white male workers' race identification with management. White male managers consented to unions (at least in principle) but also cooperated with white workers in preserving a racial division of labor that privileged white men. Whites benefited because occupational segregation replaced the old method of paying blacks less for the same work; black workers no longer threatened white job security. Shulman argues that race consciousness displaced class consciousness and that white workers participated in the establishment of a racial system of identification.

Each account presumes the existence of rather stable and coherent race/class agents. Yet neither narrative explores nor makes explicit the sociocultural practices and conventions that informed and transformed the (gendered) meanings of race and class embraced by those involved in this historic struggle. Shulman references long-standing white supremacy as a linchpin in managerial strategies to establish hegemonic control over white workers. Yet the sociocultural practices that made possible a gendered cross-class alliance remain unexplored. Cherry's account of the shifting saliency of race and class is equally mysterious. He argues that white workers consented to multiracial unions because they realized they could not win their struggles as workers in the face of capitalists using blacks as strikebreakers. We are left wondering what prompted this realization at this particular juncture, since capitalists started using blacks as strikebreakers as early as 1855. What's missing from both accounts is a richer discussion of transformed mappings of racialized and gendered class identities and ways of life that characterize this era.

To date Marxists economists have eschewed serious consideration of the social construction of discriminating subjects. Most of us have neither generated accounts that penetrate racialized and gendered self-understandings nor examined how such understandings inform the meaning of class interests and political possibilities. Yet these accounts are a necessary component of a fuller Marxist theory of discrimination. Without them, our discussions of discrimination all too easily dissolve into cost–benefit calculations only partially linked to the self-understanding of workers creating and consenting to whiteness as a culture and political economy of domination.

REFERENCES

Brown, E. B. 1992. "'What Has Happened Here': The Politics of Difference in Women's History and Feminist Politics." *Feminist Studies* 18 (2).

Butler, J. 1993. "Endangered/Endangering: Schematic Racism and White Paranoia." In *Reading Rodney King, Reading Urban Uprising*, ed. R. Gooding-Williams. New York: Routledge.

Botwinick, H. 1993. *Persistent Inequalities: Wage Disparity under Capitalist Competition*. Princeton: Princeton University Press.

Cherry, R. 1988. "Shifts in Radical Theories of Inequality." *Review of Radical Political Economics* 20 (2–3): 33–57.

———. 1989. *Discrimination: Its Impact on Blacks, Women, and Jews*. Lexington, MA: Lexington Books.

———. 1991. "Race and Gender Aspects of Marxian Economic Models." *Science and Society* 55 (1): 60–78.

Darity, W. A., Jr. 1989. "What's Left of the Economic Theory of Discrimination?" In *The Question of Discrimination: Racial Inequality in the U.S. Labor Market*, ed. W. A. Darity, Jr. and S. Shulman. Middletown, CT: Wesleyan University Press.

Goldberg, D. ed. 1990. *The Anatomy of Racism*. Minneapolis: University of Minnesota Press.

Gooding Williams, R. 1993. "Look, A Negro!" In *Reading Rodney King, Reading Urban Uprising*, ed. R. Gooding-Williams. New York: Routledge.

Hall, S. 1989. "Ethnicity: Identity and Difference." *Radical America* 23 (4): 9–22.

Heckman, J. and Paynor, B. 1989. "Determining the Impact of Government Policy on the Economic Status of Blacks: A Case Study of South Carolina." *American Economic Review* 79.

Hewitt, N. 1992. "Compounding Difference." *Feminist Studies* 18 (2): 313–326.

hooks, b. 1990. *Yearning: Race, Gender, and Cultural Politics.* Boston: South End Press.

———. 1992. *Black Looks: Race and Representation.* Boston: South End Press.

Mason, P. 1992. "The Divide-and-Conquer and Employer/Employee Models of Discrimination: Neoclassical Competition as a Familial Defect." *The Review of Black Political Economy* 20 (4): 73–89.

Milberg, W. and Pietrykowski, B. 1991. *Objectivism, Relativism, and the Importance of Rhetoric for Marxist Economics.* Unpublished manuscript.

Omi, M. and Winant, H. 1986. *Racial Formation in the United States From the 1960's to the 1980's.* New York: Routledge and Kegan Paul.

Reich, M. 1981. *Racial Inequality: A Political-Economic Analysis.* Princeton: Princeton University Press.

Roediger, D. 1991. *The Wages of Whiteness: Race and the Making of the American Working Class.* London: Verso.

San Juan, E., Jr. 1989. "Problems in the Marxist Project of Theorizing Race." *Rethinking Marxism* 2 (2): 58–82.

Sherman, H. 1987. *Foundations of Radical Political Economy.* Armonk, NY: M. E. Sharpe.

Shulman, S. 1984. "Competition and Racial Discrimination: The Employment Effects of Reagan's Labor Market Policies." *Review of Radical Political Economics* 16 (4): 111–128.

———. 1990. "Racial Inequality and White Employment: An Interpretation and Test of the Bargaining Power Hypothesis." *The Review of Black Political Economy* 18 (3): 5–20.

———. 1991. "Why Is the Black Unemployment Rate Always Twice as High as the White Unemployment Rate?" In *New Approaches to Economic and Social Analyses of Discrimination,* ed. R. Cornwall and P. Wunnava. New York: Praeger.

Williams, R. M. 1987. "Capital, Competition, and Discrimination: A Reconsideration of Racial Earnings Inequality." *Review of Radical Political Economy* 19 (2): 1–15.

———. 1991. "Competition, Discrimination, and Differential Wage Rates: On the Continued Relevance of Marxian Theory to the Analysis of Earnings and Employment Inequality." In *New Approaches to Economic and Social Analyses of Discrimination,* ed. Cornwall and Wunnava. New York: Praeger.

———. 1993. "Racial Inequality and Racial Conflict: Recent Developments in Radical Theory." In *Labor Economics: Problems in Analyzing Labor Markets,* ed. W. A. Darity, Jr. Boston: Kluwer.

PART FIVE

SOCIALISMS/CAPITALISMS

The Political Economy of Reform in South Africa

LAURENCE HARRIS

n 1976 Joe Slovo, a leader of the African National Congress (ANC) and the South African Communist Party (SACP) and the intellectual force behind many of those movements' modern positions, published a remarkable essay, "South Africa—No Middle Road." Laying out a reasoned argument for the revolutionary struggle in South Africa, it is one of the classics of international communism. The argument it advanced, that there was no middle road for the oppressed of South Africa except a left-wing revolutionary road, was a double argument: Instead of a middle road of peaceful pressure to achieve only national liberation the only road was armed liberation struggle, and instead of a middle road between capitalism and socialism, national liberation was inseparable from *socialist* revolution.

The national liberation struggle reached a turning point in 1990 when the ANC and its allies were legalized, Nelson Mandela was released, and the government of South Africa committed itself to negotiating the end of the apartheid polity. Since that turning point, signaling the end of apartheid, is widely viewed as a victory for national liberation, the question is posed of whether it places socialism on the agenda, for Slovo's classic position was that national liberation would unleash socialist revolution as well as being incomplete without it.

At first sight that prognosis appears to be accurate; proletarian political forces—which classical Marxism identifies as leading socialist struggles—have grown. The trade union confederation COSATU (Congress of South African Trade Unions), which has espoused socialism as a goal, has articulated the claims of organized workers and more general claims of the poor. Similarly, the South African Communist Party (SACP) has grown since its legalization, and at times the requests to join have outstripped the organization's ability to process applications. The SACP has links with COSATU unions and trade unionists are a large proportion of its membership. In this paper, I argue that this view is false; socialist forces in South Africa are weak because, in the absence of an effective socialist strategy or a "socialist idea" that represents an alternative to capitalist logic, socialism is not on the agenda. Instead of the socialist imperative associated with the idea that "there is no middle way," the watchword in South Africa today is effectively that "there is no alternative" to capitalism.

RADICAL REFORM

It would be a mistake to imagine that a socialist strategy or socialist idea is completely absent, for the success of the national liberation movement has been accompanied by active socialist attempts to define appropriate strategy. The following paragraphs outline their main direction in the field of political economy,[1] but in the later sections of the paper I argue that the new perspective does not amount to an effective socialist strategy.

In the decades before the 1990 turning point, "socialism" was an important ingredient in the ideology of the national liberation movement. Although the main organizations, the African National Congress, the constituent parts of the United Democratic Front (UDF), and the black consciousness organizations generally rejected the "socialist" label given them by the regime's anticommunist crusade, their ideology of national liberation was one in which socialist ideas mixed with ideals of Christian justice, nationhood, historic irredentism, and liberal human rights. The notion that apartheid was inseparable from capitalism and benefited big business promoted socialist ideas to an almost hegemonic position within that national liberation ideology, especially within the ANC and UDF, and that identification of apartheid with capitalism became a focus of debate between the organized movement and its critics such as Merle Lipton. The fact that the South African Communist Party was a cornerstone of the ANC and UDF was one sign of the socialist ideological hegemony.

However, the socialist ideology that played such an important role in the construction of national consciousness was relatively undeveloped. South African Marxist scholarship had great strengths in specific areas such as history and sociology (see Wolpe 1976, 1980), but for several reasons that academic work did not provide a basis for the socialist ideology that could inform a movement for transformation. For most of the period, the implicit framework for the movement's understanding of how to achieve social transformation was the "reform versus revolution" perspective inherited from the classics of a century ago. As Slovo's "No Middle Road" exemplifies, the reform of capitalism was considered impossible; to the Leninist rejection of reform was added the specific view that since South African capitalism was inseparable from apartheid, liberation was inconceivable without the overthrow of capitalism. That blunt dichotomy was not conducive to discussions of how a liberated South Africa would set about transforming society, for the idea of a revolutionary capture of state power was associated, by default, with a conception that centralized control of the state would confer the ability to control economic and social change.

The climate of socialist thinking underwent significant change in the popular upheavals of 1985, for the new grassroots organizations grouped within the UDF created political structures at a level beneath the formal, centrally controlled political institutions, while the COSATU trade unions similarly won new power and space at the base. The need to understand this new political balance and to appraise the policy issues posed by local situations of power, was partly filled by the appropriation of the Gramscian concepts of "civil society" and "dual power" and, at the practical level, by the development of fine negotiating and organizing skills by socialists. Nevertheless, the 1990 turning point found the South African Left without a coherent socialist strategy. The defeat of the centrally planned systems of the Communist bloc and the fact that 1990 was the beginning of a process of negotiation rather than a revolutionary seizure of power, meant that the reform versus revolution paradigm offered no model on which to build, while socialist ideas forged in local popular struggles against severe repression had not led to a consciousness of how to build socialism in the context of negotiated national power.

The South African debate that has developed in the new circumstances of the 1990s starts from the premise that the Left's old dichotomy of "reform versus revolution" is not useful; instead of reform being a dirty word, it is argued that "structural reform" or "radical reform" is a step on the road toward socialism that should be firmly adopted (Saul 1991, 1992; Webster and von Holdt 1992).[2] Structural reform is envisaged as quite different from the reformism that was advanced by Bernstein and, since the beginning of this century, has been attacked by Leninists. John Saul, Eddie Webster, Karl von Holdt, and its other proponents define it in terms of two key characteristics: First, structural reforms have an inbuilt dynamic that carries them forward toward a socialist society; and, second, instead of being handed down they must be rooted in popular initiatives that increase the empowerment of the masses.

The potential for such structural reform lies in the fact that the breaking of the old forms of apartheid was achieved by precisely the popular initiatives of trade unionists and communities that are a defining feature of the strategy. The growth of powerful black unions from shop floor struggles in the 1970s to the creation in 1985 of the trade union federation COSATU, which is today the principal national body with a defined socialist strategy, is well documented (Fine and Webster 1989; Webster and von Holdt 1992), and, despite the inevitable problems that weaken trade union democracy, the socialist commitment of COSATU continues to be founded on its shop floor and community roots. At the same time, the rise of community power groups, the "civics," in urban struggles over education, housing, and infrastructure achieved real gains and formed the basis of the ANC-linked United Democratic Front, whose campaigns destroyed the legitimation of the old regime.

Since popular initiatives brought down the old system, can they not be harnessed for reconstruction, to create a new society that is moving toward socialist ends? Webster and von Holdt (1992), focusing on the role of trade unions, argue that they can achieve such radical reform, for COSATU has already transformed itself into a major player in determining economic policy on a wider front than traditional trade union issues. For example, in 1991 it initiated an impressive, broad-based campaign and strong general strike against the imposition of a new tax, the Value Added Tax, and, although it did not achieve more than marginal changes in the tax, it

> brought together a wide range of trade unions, consumer and welfare organizations, political organizations, medical associations and small business. Probably a broader coalition than any seen in South Africa before . . . It brought mass action and mass participation back into the arena of negotiations. (Webster and von Holdt 1992, 15–16)

Going beyond that, these authors point to the commitment COSATU has to formulating an economic strategy for the country, and to its rapid strides toward being accepted in tripartite bodies negotiating over industrial strategy and broad macroeconomic policies.

CRITIQUE OF "RADICAL REFORM"

Does structural or radical reform amount to a socialist path forward that would justify the optimism some European and North American Leftists have about the prospects for socialism in South Africa? The answer has to be no for two reasons: The concept is weak in principle, and, in any case, the South African reality does not match up to the concept.

The principle embedded in the notion of structural reform can be seen as a constructed determinism; reform strategies can be constructed in such a way that they necessarily carry the movement forward to further reform, and they build on popular initiatives in such a way that they "*leave a residue of further empowerment*" that automatically strengthens future struggles.[3] The principle suffers from the weakness of all forms of determinism, for we know that there is no such thing as a set of changes that necessarily flow from changes already achieved, and we also know that while mass struggles can increase empowerment in the sense of heightened consciousness and the space in which to act, it is a "residue" that is easily erased by the high-powered cleaning fluid (or dark paint) of reaction.

Underlying the weakness of the principle of structural reform is the circularity introduced in an attempt to bolster its forward direction. To give meaning to the idea that successful reform struggles impose a logic from which further reforms must follow, Saul (1992, 6) places them in the context where "the popular movement cum party attempting a program of structural reform must constantly articulate to itself and to its broadest potential constituency the goal of structural transformation/ socialism." But at the same time this context begs the question that should be the starting point for the concept, "What is the socialism that is the goal of structural reform?"

In practice, the reality of South Africa does not live up to the claim that the country is moving along a path of radical reform towards socialism. On the important question of popular participation, grassroots initiatives and organization did achieve the great political victories of the past decade or more, including the legalization of the new trade unions, the 1990 agreement to improve labor relations law, and the legalization of the ANC and SACP. But the ability of popular bodies to achieve further gains is thrown in doubt by their weakness. The civics, which effectively took power in the townships and administered them as popular bodies in 1985, are fragmented, weak, and no longer have the same popular support. They have been weakened by the whole process of national negotiations and, above all, by the terror unleashed in the townships through Inkatha.[4] The trade unions retain their shop floor structures and extensive shop steward system, but, as in any country, acute economic crisis has forced them into defensive struggles instead of forward looking campaigns and, as unemployment has worsened, has weakened their power base and strengthened the employers' hand.[5] And, of course, there are large numbers of poor and oppressed South Africans whom the civics and trade unions do not represent and who are outside any significant radical popular initiative: The largest and arguably most hegemonic organization with roots deep in every community is the reactionary Church of Zion.

On the other important principle of structural reform, that reforms lead on from one to another in a long-term direction of socialist transformation, the reality of economic and social reform in South Africa consists of a progress measured by increased tripartism—forums for discussion or negotiation between the state, business, and trade unions (or civic associations)—but it is a collaboration that involves no challenge to the agenda of business. Several intellectuals of the South African Left, like Webster and von Holdt, have presented that as the core of a new socialist strategy, so that success in achieving a place at the negotiating table is itself seen as a positive step, but socialists with experience of corporatism in other countries have to take a view that is at least equivocal. One problem is determining the agenda the popular forces are to follow, while another is whether tripartite arrangements enable them to pursue this agenda instead of being coopted.

Within COSATU, the SACP, and the ANC, an economic agenda or "growth path" has been formulated under the slogan "Growth Through Redistribution," which Alec Erwin contrasts with "growth and redistribution" (the notorious right-wing concept of trickle down from increased profits) and "growth with distribution" (the Chenery concept of development policy formerly pursued by the World Bank) (Erwin 1992). For Erwin, the leading economist of the SACP and COSATU, a strategy of "growth through redistribution" achieves growth through altering the distribution of resources. In its original formulation this strategy took a form that would have been familiar to left-wing Latin American followers of Prebisch in the 1950s and 1960s, emphasizing that the state should take a strong role in redistributing income and wealth toward the masses, simultaneously developing domestic industry's production to meet the demand for increased living standards, and essentially growing on the basis of that domestic market while seeking simultaneously to increase the competitiveness of export industries.[6] However, Erwin's (1992) proposal is broader, for he rejects the concept of redistribution as "simple income transfers" and defines it to include all elements of economic restructuring. As a result, in his main presentation of his strategy it appears, as he says, "to be a very sweeping approach with no content to it" (6).

The narrower version of "growth through redistribution" is itself far from having a socialist orientation, for we know from other countries' experience that it frequently degenerates into a mechanism for protecting sections of domestic capital while delivering few working-class gains; in South Africa large sections of business advocated such a policy (calling it "inward industrialization") for a long time before democracy came onto the horizon. We also know that even from the point of view of capital it has a poor record, for it has frequently protected stagnation and managerial backwardness. Bearing that in mind, the economic strategy of COSATU emphasizes the importance of export competitiveness as well as domestic markets and is based on the view that the backwardness of South African management can only be overcome by the trade unions themselves forcing modernization and the adoption of high productivity techniques (Joffe 1991).

Since the agendas to be pursued in tripartite bodies are, therefore, no different from a rational capitalist agenda, the structural reform idea that the greater voice of trade unions at the negotiating table represents a dynamic of progress, leading from popular democratic victories to gains which are more socialist, has no basis in reality. Equally as important, however, is the political question of whether the business–union arrangements themselves do leave room for the Left to avoid cooption. Webster and von Holdt pin their hopes on constructing a new kind of unionism, "strategic unionism," but their definition of it is the same as the corporatist forms of unionism under which the labor movements in Britain, France, and Germany were secured as allies of capital. "Strategic unionism calls for conscious intervention at the macro-economic level, and the setting of goals such as low unemployment, low inflation, and social development" (1992, 3; see Hall 1986; Middlemas 1979).

Erwin, following the same lines but seeking to address the problem that the unions represent only one section of the people, proposes that such a corporatist strategy should be backed by a broad coalition, traversing the whole of "civil society," and united behind a Reconstruction Accord. In the past year these concepts have led COSATU into a National Economic Forum embracing itself and business.

Arguably corporatist solutions do have much to recommend them and can bring strong gains to the working class and wider sections of the population as well as to capital, but they do not warrant the claim that structural reform is a strategy toward socialism unless it is believed that corporatist Britain, France, and Germany were socialist societies. If it is a mistake to believe that the current growth of negotiating forums and strategies agreed between the state, business, and popular organizations represents moves in a socialist direction, can they nevertheless succeed in their own terms and deliver the benefits associated with corporatism? That question is considered in the next section.

PROSPECTS

If corporatism is to bring strong gains several conditions are required, but none seem to hold in South Africa. First, the coalitions involved must be capable of holding together. In simple models of corporatism the coalitions can hold because all classes and groups gain, and that idea is embodied in South African discussions of the strategy, for they predicate a narrowing of South Africa's extreme income inequality on achieving growth that can benefit all. But the idea that the whole country will gain from the construction of a new South Africa is a serious weakness in the politics of the ANC and the Left. If coalitions are built on that Panglossian assumption they will fall to pieces in the face of the reality that reconstruction involves severe social dislocation, producing losers as well as winners, and as the coalition for change degenerates into conflicting interests corporatism will be unable even to deliver the wide gains and working-class gains achieved in other countries and other circumstances.

Second, when, as in post-war Europe, corporatism has been accompanied by sustained high growth, capital accumulation, and improvements in working-class conditions, that growth is not attributable to the "settlement" or "compact" itself. In that European experience, international conditions were as important or more important, since that growth was accompanied by an initially huge transfer of resources in the form of Marshall Aid (now recognized as having itself been designed to buy off workers' militancy); international regulation and stabilization of financial markets; a regulated steady expansion of world markets for trade; and the driving force of strong growth in the United States' hegemonic economy (Marglin and Schor 1990). A corporatist treaty in South Africa would exist in a much changed world; the world's financial system is volatile and fragile; the growth of world trade has slowed; conflict between trading blocs is unlikely to benefit South Africa; and there will be no inflows into South Africa comparable to Marshall Aid in Europe.

Third, since those conditions are likely to prevent high-flown compacts between South Africa's capital and labor from delivering the fruits associated with social democracy, a further condition for the success of corporatism—success itself, or the materialization of results—will not be present. As a result, either conflict over control of production and the distribution of resources will intensify and undermine any arrangements, or corporatist arrangements will persist as a shell under which old and new business elites operate without opposition.

Fourth, in the present era reconstruction in all except the most powerful countries is monitored and steered by the powerful international forces of the International Monetary Fund, the World Bank, and other institutions. Their weight on the side of capital ensures that when corporatist arrangements weaken in the face of economic crisis, the perceived interests of capital prevail. Webster and von Holdt (1992, 7) envisage that "radical reform" will enable unions to intervene at the macroeconomic level and set goals "such as low unemployment, low inflation, and social development." But who can doubt that when choices have to be made the multilateral institutions will put their power behind low inflation at the cost of social development or employment?

ECONOMIC STRATEGY AND POLITICAL FORCES

In sum, therefore, the organized Left in South Africa has given up any hope of socialist economic reconstruction in the foreseeable future and is settling for a corporatism that is, itself, likely to fail in its own terms. Why this should have occurred is an interesting problem. A paper by Joe Slovo published toward the end of 1991 suggests one explanation for the conscious shift of the Left towards reforms with no perspective of socialism: The democratic rights associated with national liberation have not been achieved. Therefore, the goal for the foreseeable future must be some share of power, while full political democracy is postponed and socialist reconstruction delayed to an unspecified future.

Those views that Slovo (1992) sets out in an article "Negotiations: What Room for Compromise?" and elaborates on in comments reported by Carlin (1992) are designed as conjunctural interventions concerned with details in the negotiating process that had sparked political dissent.[7] As such, most of his views were subsequently adopted by the ANC as the basis for negotiations (ANC, 1992). It was decided to negotiate for entrenchment of power sharing after elections. But despite its immediacy the paper also presents an explicit underlying analysis. Slovo's rationale is that South Africa is not even at the stage of a national democratic revolution; the ANC has not won the liberation struggle. In this bleak situation, a historic compromise is seen as necessary, under which the machinery of state will remain in the hands of the conservative Afrikaners that have held it since 1948. Its logic, according to Slovo, is that although power would be winnable in the election booths it should be eschewed in order to ensure that frightened right-wing forces do not put a total block on democracy.[8]

Slovo's arguments for power sharing have been vigorously contested and are subject to several criticisms,[9] but they offer one explanation of the intellectuals' retreat from hopes of rapidly moving toward socialism in South Africa, while at the same time being part of that retreat.

Two years after the legalization of the ANC and the South African Communist Party, South Africa is unique in the modern world, for it is in a process of being transformed from a rigid cold war tyranny to some type of post-cold war democracy, with socialists, underpinned by a large, militant, and organized working-class base, having leading roles in that transformation. Moreover, that socialist movement is close to the apparatus of power in a country with an industrial base and an infrastructure historically far stronger than most of today's new industrial giants (South Korea, Taiwan, Singapore, or China, for example) had twenty or thirty years ago. Paradoxically, however, those strong preconditions for a socialist future are accompanied by the dissolution of any effective commitment to a serious socialist strategy.

The "big issues" that were for so long the touchstones of socialists in South Africa—nationalization of banks, mines, and factories; nationalization and redistribution of the land; universal health care and universal, equal education—have effectively been abandoned. Although the country is dominated by a handful of conglomerates with a stranglehold on every sphere of economic and political activity, and although the economy is in an alarming state of decline, the democratic movement's leadership rejects nationalization of any enterprises (while it only retains a vestigial presence as a possibility in ANC conference documents and the SACP program).[10] Despite the historic injustice at the root of apartheid, under which the black majority had rights on only one eighth of the land mass, the ANC and SACP leaders do not have plans to expropriate white farms in order to effect a large-scale land redistribution. It is right that received ideas, formulated (but rarely analyzed and discussed) in an earlier period, should have been critically evaluated and appraised, and it is healthy that the simple slogans of the past have been superseded. But the "big ideas" have been dropped under pressure from capital, without an informed socialist debate, and without the elaboration of effective new socialist perspectives. While the movement's intellectuals find left-wing meaning in corporatist tripartite councils under a "radical reform" perspective, the ineffectiveness of that direction is signaled by the fact that the movement has not devoted resources to planning how to finance a universal health care system or universal secondary education system in the way that Britain's social democrats did during and after World War II.

It is clear that, regarding social and economic reconstruction, South Africa's democratic and Left politicians do not have a socialist strategy and are not developing one. At present they are hoping for some share of power in order to administer an existing structure into which they can introduce some marginal reforms—reforms agreed to, if not promoted by, capital. They will be in a similar position to that of Robert Mugabe who, after winning a real victory over the Rhodesian regime, has presided over largely unchanged structures of social and economic apartheid. A South Africa following the Zimbabwe option would be one where, in Slovo's (1976) words, "the national struggle is stopped in its tracks and is satisfied with the cooption of a small black elite into the presently forbidden areas of economic and political power."

NOTES

1. In this paper I am only concerned with some issues of political economy; I neglect other areas such as socialists' active discussion of the concept of "civil society," of the concept and role of nation, of law, gender, and community action. This paper concerns the situation in 1992 and does not take subsequent changes into account.

2. Saul uses the term "structural reform," while Webster and von Holdt refer to "radical reform"; since the latter identify their perspective with John Saul's, I use the terms interchangeably. However, as becomes evident in this text, there is a difference between the two approaches in that Saul's is linked in principle to a conception of a long-run transformation that is revolutionary in character, while Webster and von Holdt explicitly opt for a goal of traditional social democracy.

3. "Any reform, to be structural, must not be comfortably self contained . . . but must, instead, be allowed self consciously to implicate other 'necessary' reforms that flow from it" (Saul 1992, 6).

4. That comparative weakness should not, however, be interpreted as a complete destruction of the civics, for they have continuing significance in certain areas, although their character has changed everywhere since 1985.

5. Webster and von Holdt (1992, 20) detail the efforts made at the national level to force employers in mining and textiles to agree to a union role in restructuring industry to meet the economic crisis. Far from being steps in a socialist direction, the 1991 mining talks gave unions a voice in redundancies and reductions in real wages in return for productivity gains; moreover, under pressure from grassroots regional delegates the union rejected such deals in future. As the authors note, the experience "shows that most South African managers, for all their talk of a new era of social contracts and co-determination is [sic] responding to the crisis in its [sic] traditional way, i.e. with unilateral authority and attempts to force workers to work harder without conceding any real participation."

6. Such a strategy was named Growth Through Redistribution by Raphie Kaplinsky at a conference of ANC and COSATU economists at Harare in 1990, and subsequently formed the basis of a Harare Document on economic policy.

7. This dissent concerned especially the size of required majorities and the definition of regional entities and powers.

8. In a private communication with the author, Joe Slovo makes clear that a formally agreed compromise on minority political privileges for the precise time period of a decade is not envisaged.

9. A number of criticisms are set out in Harris 1993.

10. South African Communist Party 1992, Section 4.

REFERENCES

African National Congress. 1992. *Negotiations, a Strategic Perspective as adopted by the National Working Committee on 18 November 1992*. Unpublished manuscript.

Carlin, J. 1992. "ANC Radical Softens His Line." *The Independent*, 30 October: 11.

Erwin, A. 1992. "Economic Reconstruction." In South African Communist Party, *African Communist*, Discussion Paper.

Fine, A. and Webster, E. 1989. "Transcending Traditions: Trade Union Unity and Politics." In *South African Review*, Vol. 5. Johannesburg: Ravan Press.

Hall, P. 1986. *Governing the Economy*. Cambridge, England: Polity Press.

Harris, L. 1993. *South Africa's Economic and Social Transformation: From "No Middle Road" to "No Alternative."* School of Oriental and African Studies Economics Department, Working Papers.

Joffe, A. 1991. "COSATU Economic Policy Conference." *South African Labour Bulletin* 15(8).

Marglin, S. A and Schor, J. B. eds. 1990. *The Golden Age of Capitalism: Reinterpreting the Post War Experience*. Oxford, England: Clarendon Press.

Middlemas, K. 1979. *Politics in Industrial Society*. London: Andre Deutsch.

Saul, J. 1991. "South Africa Between Barbarism and Structural Reform." *New Left Review* 188: 3–44.

——. 1992. *Structural Reform: A Model for the Revolutionary Transformation of South Africa?* Ruth First Memorial Colloquium, University of the Western Cape.

Slovo, J. 1976. "South Africa—No Middle Road." In *Southern Africa, The New Politics of Revolution*, eds. B. Davidson, J. Slovo, and A. Wilkinson, 103–210. Harmondsworth, England: Penguin.

——. 1992. "Negotiations: What Room for Compromise?" *African Communist* 3: 36–40.

South African Communist Party. 1992. *SACP Manifesto: Building Workers' Power for Democratic Change*. Johannesburg: Umsebenzi Publications.

Webster, E. and von Holdt, K. 1992. *Towards a Socialist Theory of Radical Reform: From Resistance to Reconstruction in the Labour Movement*. Ruth First Memorial Colloquium, University of the Western Cape.

Wolpe, H. 1976. "The White Working Class in South Africa." *Economy and Society* 5 (2).

——. 1980. "Towards an Analysis of the South African State." *International Journal of the Sociology of Law* 8.

The End of the USSR:
A Marxian Class Analysis

STEPHEN RESNICK
RICHARD D. WOLFF

With the demise of the USSR, modern history's most enduring and globally influential upsurge of workers against capitalism has ended. Marx analyzed earlier upsurges (the revolts of 1848, the Paris Commune, etc) in order to learn from their mistakes how to do it better next time. Marxists must do likewise for the USSR. This time, the analysis needs to include a Marxist self-critique focused on how the interpretation of Marxism dominant there contributed to the mistakes. Our goal here is to outline such a self-critique and its implications for a Marxist assessment of the USSR's recent history that is different from other recent analyses.

In our view, the interpretation of Marxism that came to prevail in the USSR failed to distinguish between a state form of capitalism and communism. This failure was signaled by attaching the name "socialism" to the state capitalism established in the USSR after 1917 and banishing a transition to communism to a vague and ever-receding future. While many other factors contributed to the USSR's inability to go beyond replacing a private with a state capitalism, Marxism's contribution was to fail theoretically and practically to distinguish among private capitalism, state capitalism, and communism.

The rages against war, poverty, autocracy, and religion that fueled 1917's explosion matured quickly into anticapitalism partly because of the interventions by Marxists. They relied, understandably, upon the Second International's tradition of anticapitalist criticism. That tradition focused its attack on private property and markets and their social consequences (Diskin 1990). Thus, the Soviet revolution substituted state for private property and state planning for markets. One group of state officials thus became the surplus appropriators; together with other state officials they decided and managed how those surpluses were distributed.

Conceiving the USSR as a state capitalism enables a new, concrete analysis of its rise and fall.[1] First, we may apply Marxian analyses of *capitalist* crises to the particular state form of capitalism in the USSR. Second, we may recommence analysis of the USSR's *class structure* in terms of its multiple organizations of the production and distribution of surplus. On this basis we find that (1) a crisis in state capitalism provoked a restoration of private capitalism, and (2) because Marxists had joined in calling this state capitalism a "socialism en route to communism," the restoration was understood as a transition from socialism/communism to capitalism.

Many labels—"command economy," "bureaucratic regime," "communism," "socialism," "state-capitalism," and so on—have been used to describe the USSR. They typically reflect a power theory approach: The social distribution of power determines which label to use. Thus, traditional (non-Marxian) economics views the USSR as socialist or communist because power was not decentralized into the hands of individual agents of supply, demand, and ownership. Similarly (and remarkably) traditional Marxism labels the USSR as socialist or communist because the state owns the means of production and commands their products' allocations.

Even dissenting Marxian approaches use power as the ultimate criterion. Thus Bettelheim (1975, 1978) labels the USSR capitalist because autonomous state managers rather than the collective of workers actually control the means and procedures of production. Sweezy (1985) disagrees: The USSR is not capitalist because state planning eliminates competition and hence capitalist accumulation. Sweezy rejects the communist label too because state bureaucrats rather than workers control the state and enterprises (Sweezy and Bettelheim 1971). Parallel differences can be found in Lenin's, Trotsky's, and others' preoccupations with the distribution of power within the USSR to determine who (proletariat versus state bureaucrats) ultimately controlled the economy, and hence what to call the USSR—socialist, state capitalist, or bureaucratic regime (Resnick and Wolff 1993).

Because we differ from all of these approaches, making the process of class rather than power the conceptual entry point of analysis, old labels take on new meanings (Resnick and Wolff 1988). For example, to label the USSR as communist should mean quite precisely that those who produced and those who collectively received and distributed surplus labor in Soviet enterprises were the exact same people. In contrast, within the currently prevalent traditions of analysis, which concentrate on power, the precise question of who produced and appropriated the surplus either disappears, or, if present, is made derivative of power. With rare exceptions, the USSR itself did not organize its enterprises by reference to this surplus production and distribution criterion.

THE SOVIET UNION AS A STATE CAPITALIST CLASS STRUCTURE

Deploying our approach to research histories, management studies, and factory reports, we conclude that members of the Council of Industrial Ministers (hereafter COM) received and distributed the fruits of the surplus labor performed by productive laborers in Soviet industrial enterprises.[2] We label this state (as opposed to private) exploitation because the COM was located within the state apparatus. Soviet state exploitation was capitalist because its specific social context put the COM in the position of receiving surplus value in a manner parallel to that of private capitalist corporations' boards of directors.

The COM helped to secure this social context by distributing the surplus values it appropriated to its own subagencies, to other state agencies (Gosplan, Gosbank, and Gosnab), to the Communist Party, to the military, police, and educational establishments, and so on. For example, the COM distributed portions of the surplus to legislatures and courts. This enabled the passage and adjudication of laws making the COM function quite like the members of private corporate boards of directors. Thus the COM was placed in the (class) position of being the first receiver of workers' surplus value. In terms of our Marxian class analysis, the COM's specific exploitative position as surplus value appropriator warrants our labeling the USSR state capitalist.

The COM distributed some of its surpluses to enterprise managers (as salaries and operating budgets) to supervise the labor process and make it yield surplus value. COM also distributed surpluses to the Communist Party and to the state educational apparatus. These institutions persuaded workers that performing surplus labor constituted their patriotic duty, their personal contribution to the building of communism, and so on.

Gosplan obtained distributed surplus to finance its allocation of labor power and means of production to the enterprises under COM. Various state agencies also established the length of the workday, the portion of total output to be returned to the workers as wages for their consumption (Marx's "necessary labor"), and the portion used to replace the means of production used up in production.

The COM also secured from Gosplan a set of accounting rules that assigned state-administered values to all inputs and outputs based on the labor time estimated as necessary to produce them. These state-administered values—given state-set working days and wage rates—yielded state-administered surplus values produced in each enterprise and received and distributed by COM. The state-administered values and surplus values were the overdetermined results of multiple determinations emanating from planners' calculations; bureaucracies' economic, ethnic, regional, and military aims; managers' maximizing-output goals; Communist Party officials' ideological and political objectives; and union and factory organizations' interests.

Once these values were established, profits rates could also be calculated and used to shape the allocation of resources and the accumulation of capital. Since economic growth was considered a prime necessity for the continuation of the Soviet class structure (and of Soviet society generally), the COM distributed much of its appropriated surplus values to expand (accumulate) the means of production and labor power in state enterprises.

In summary, the COM exploited the labor of Soviet industrial workers. Within a state capitalist fundamental class process, it functioned to appropriate their surplus labor in a state-administered value form.[3] As such, COM was then also in the position to distribute that surplus—a state capitalist subsumed class process—so as to secure the diverse economic, political, and cultural processes that comprised the conditions of its continued existence. We may elaborate this analysis by considering the class aspects of the relation between the COM and the Communist Party.

The COM financed the Party's activities by its subsumed class distributions of portions of its appropriated surplus to the Party. Yet the Party was not a passive recipient. Through its Politburo, it exercised power over the decisions of the COM. Thus, while it was alone in the *class* position of state capitalist appropriating and distributing surplus value, the COM was not alone in wielding power over the size or distribution of its appropriated surplus. For example, the Politburo also influenced the decisions over how much surplus to distribute to Gosplan, capital accumulation, the Communist Party itself, the security apparatus, and so forth.

But the Party's participation in power processes was not equivalent to it becoming the first appropriator and distributor of that surplus. That capitalist class position was occupied by the COM alone. Power over the way in which the COM distributed the surplus was the object of struggle among the COM, the Party, workers through their trade unions, regions through their republic bureaucracies, intellectuals through educational and media activities, and so on. The capitalist class processes—producing, receiving, and distributing surplus values—interacted with the processes of distributing and wielding power, but the two kinds of processes are not identical.[4] The COM and the Party had very different relationships to Soviet state capitalism.

SOVIET STATE CAPITALISM AND ITS CRISIS

After 1917 the Soviet state established state capitalist industrial and farm enterprises across the USSR.[5] It also extolled such state capitalism as achieving the revolution's goal, as socialism or sometimes even communism. This was not just a matter of seeking revolutionary legitimacy. It also reflected the theoretical hegemony among Marxists of notions of class unconcerned with surplus labor. Most Marxists focused on the distribution of power (over property, management, and political decisions generally) as *the* essential quality distinguishing capitalism from socialism or communism. Class was, for them, a matter of power: who controlled the property and the decision making, the worker–peasant alliance of formerly powerless classes or the formerly powerful "ruling class" of capitalists. Thus, what were state *capitalist* enterprises spread across the USSR with no debate or criticism focused on the issue of their internal organization of surplus labor per se. Instead, *the* issues—framed as "class" issues—were ownership, income equality, and political democracy.[6] The "socialist" nature of the USSR was defined and debated on the basis of collective ownership, income equality, and popular democracy exercised through the Communist Party. On the issue of surplus labor there was complete silence.

This silence solidified, at least on the Left, a conceptualization of socialism as a "happy medium" between capitalism and communism. Capitalism was the evil past defined as private ownership, markets, and the inequalities pejoratively associated with them. Communism, "realistically" viewed as a distant goal, was defined by vague gestures toward "full equality and democracy" and distribution according to "needs." Socialism was what radicals could achieve in the twentieth century. Socialism thus became the name for particular kinds of capitalism, those with "a human face," that managed to provide workers with job security, adequate income, a generous array of public services and supports, and political democracy. The USSR was defended as socialist by some because its state capitalism conformed to this definition. Others criticized the USSR's claim to be socialist, likewise on the basis of these criteria with special attention to political democracy. In the twentieth century, many other nations were designated socialist in very similar ways.[7] While they mostly left capitalist class structures in private enterprises, they greatly expanded state controls and taxation of privately appropriated surpluses. They thereby provided high employment levels and generous public services. Such private capitalisms were regularly called socialist, social democratic, or welfare statist.

The pro- and anti-Soviet socialists clashed over which socialism (i.e., which kinds and mixes of private and state capitalism) provided the more generous public services, enabled the more rapid economic growth and rising consumption levels, and promoted the more democratic polity. Even when each side denounced the other as not genuinely socialist, their conceptualizations of socialism shared the same silence on how the production and appropriation of surplus was organized (exploitative or not) and on the social effects of that organization. The relevance of alternative, noncapitalist organizations of surplus labor evaporated from the debate and from the view of most socialists.

The irony here runs deep. In the USSR, the public ideology of socialism operated as a legitimating veneer over the economic reality of a state capitalism. Before the 1970s, Soviet state capitalism had seemed an unqualified *socialist* success because it (1) rebuilt rapidly from the traumas of World War I, foreign invasions, civil war, and World War II; (2) guaranteed employment and previously unavailable basic public services (housing, medical care, education, etc.); and (3) raised standards of living for all. The looming but unrecognized question became: would the population turn against "socialism" if and when Soviet state capitalism encountered an economic crisis that contributed to a broader social crisis?[8]

In capitalist class structures, one period's success generates the next period's failures: Conditions enabling an economic upswing are changed by that upswing into conditions for a downswing or crisis. The USSR's stunning recovery and growth records from 1917 to the 1960s achieved not only great-power status, a basic industrial infrastructure, and a relatively advanced level of consumption. The USSR also acquired costly global obligations and a détente with the West that acquainted its own populations with levels of individual consumption and political democracy they had not enjoyed. Moreover, the ideology of socialism mentioned above had trained the people's sights on "overtaking" the West in every respect, economically and eventually politically as well.

A crisis emerged when state capitalist enterprises could no longer appropriate enough surplus and distribute it in the ways needed to sustain the Soviet economy in these new post-1960s conditions. Wage levels simply could not then be reduced to generate more surplus because workers would not tolerate it. For the same reason, it was impossible to tighten low-productivity working conditions. These constraints combined with the relatively backward technology (results of war, shortages of investment, bureaucratically distorted distributions of productive resources, etc.) to generate too small a total surplus. It was "too small" in relation to the demands of (1) great-power status and competition;

(2) improving collectively consumed services; (3) catching up techno-logically; (4) the ideological, political, and economic bureaucracies; and (5) the popular hunger for individual consumption levels similar to those of the West. During the 1970s and 1980s, successive Soviet leaderships made decisions that erupted in the current crisis. They could not extract much more surplus and so they left unmet the demands on the surplus for technical progress and for rapid consumer goods development.

What happened next was the final act of a predictable drama. The failure to distribute surplus in the requisite amounts and directions re-acted back upon the production of the surplus to lessen it, which in turn reduced distributions in a downward spiral. The exhortations to work harder fell on increasingly deaf and angry ears. In a declining economic situation, state capitalist enterprises, then whole industries, and eventu-ally ministries departed increasingly from central plan arrangements to secure their own individual and increasingly precarious conditions of existence privately, outside of and thereby further undermining the cen-tral plans.

Workers and those to whom ever less surplus was distributed increas-ingly resented those who still got their surplus distributions. Popular anger mounted against the Party apparatus, favored state officials, cer-tain industries, and so forth. Political repression once tolerated as the price of national security and rapid economic growth became unbear-able in the face of global détente and deepening economic inequality and decline. The situation boiled over. In a society that had not debated alternative notions of capitalism, socialism, and communism, no move-ment to resolve the state capitalist crisis by instituting communism de-veloped. Instead, the widening crisis of Soviet state capitalism—under-stood as "socialism"—provoked an oscillation from state back to private capitalism, reversing what was achieved after 1917. Replacing planning with private markets and privatizing state capitalist enterprises became *the* solutions: necessary, obvious, and exclusively appropriate.[9] A hun-dred years of criticism, elaborated in different ways by *both* Marxist and non-Marxist critics, are being swept away in an orgy of wholly uncritical celebration of private capitalism. The mood of the 1950s in the United States repeats in the USSR, this time as tragedy and farce together.

From a Marxian class perspective, a century of hot debate over socialism/communism versus capitalism ignored and thus masked a set of oscillations from private to state to private capitalism. The socialists and Marxists who led the revolution against private capitalism could not yet go beyond state capitalism. This has meant, at least for the moment, that the rise and fall of one region's state capitalism could be ideologi-cally recast in the popular imagination—especially by those who prefer private capitalism—as the rise and fall of socialism or communism per se.[10]

Will the oscillation back to private capitalism resolve, even temporarily, the state capitalist crisis in the former USSR? On the one hand, the demands on the surplus from the Communist Party will be eliminated and those from the military reduced; an influx of wealth lent or invested from abroad will also help, as may an inflow of consumer goods. On the other hand, how will productive workers react to the surpluses now demanded by private appropriators? Likewise, republic governments may make greater demands on the surplus than the central government did, total military demands may yet rise, a revived Church apparatus may be a new drain on surpluses, and the complex unifying, motivating, and disciplining functions performed by the Communist Party may not be accomplished otherwise without yet other massive drains on the surplus. And if no other institutions replace the Party's functions, the negative impacts on surplus production could be as devastating to the upcoming private capitalist period as anything that operated during the state capitalist period.

We are, it seems, still at an early stage in the realization of the positive side of Marxism's critiques of capitalism. That side entails discursive explorations of and concrete practical experiments in the alternative class structure of communism. The point for Marxists now is to show how transitions to various possible communisms might resolve the crises of private or state capitalisms *better* than oscillations between them. Marx's dramatic vision and ethic remain: The problems and contradictions peculiar to communisms are preferable to those of capitalisms.

ACKNOWLEDGMENTS

We thank Allan MacNeil for his invaluable research assistance in identifying the appropriators and distributors of surplus labor in the USSR.

NOTES

1. For basic differences between our concept of state capitalism, defined in terms of surplus labor, and the concepts defined instead in terms of power by the few other writers who have used the term, see Resnick and Wolff (1993). A book-length analysis of Soviet state capitalism is forthcoming.

2. See also Berliner (1957, 1976), Gorlin (1985), Granick (1954, 1960), Gregory (1990), Hough and Fainsod (1979), Lane (1985a, 1985b), and Millar (1981, 1990).

3. The terms "fundamental" class processes, used to designate the production/appropriation of surplus labor, and "subsumed" class process, used to designate its distribution, are fully defined and elaborated in Resnick and Wolff (1987, Chapters 3–5).

4. Of course, occupants of specific class and power positions could be the same individuals. For example, most texts underscore the overlap in membership between the COM and top Party leaders (Gregory 1990, 30; Hough and Fainsod 1979, Chapters 10 and 11; Kerblay 1983, 250–252).

5. Our focus is on the dominant feature of the history of the Soviet social formation: state capitalism. However, that formation exhibited class structures as well. For example, an ancient class structure (producers who appropriate their own surplus labor as individuals) repeatedly expanded and contracted across Soviet history. Private capitalism first declined, then revived in the NEP period, and then nearly vanished. A few scattered communist class structures existed in the 1920s, flourished briefly on the collective farms in the 1930s, and then vanished.

6. For example, a vice president of the USSR Academy of Sciences introduced a popular text on the political economy of communism with the argument that because "one of the co-owners of the public means of production enters into comradely co-operation with another co-owner . . . hence, there is not and cannot be any exploitation" (Rumyantsev 1969, 19).

7. Before World War II, German, Italian, and other fascisms also used the term socialist ("national socialist") to describe their mixes of state and private capitalist class structures. They too funneled private and state capitalist surpluses partly to finance the delivery of public services. However, their rejection of democracy as decadence gave their mixes of the two kinds of capitalism a very different quality from the nonfascist "socialisms" of their adversaries.

8. The presumption here is that a "social" crisis—Russia in 1917 or the USSR in 1990—can never be reduced to merely one of its contributory or component factors, such as the economic. We focus on the economic dimension—and within that on the class aspects—not because they determined the crisis, but because those aspects have never been theorized via the Marxist framework utilized here and because the insights yielded enable a new and different interpretation of Soviet history.

9. It is worth noting that these oscillations, in both directions, are always celebrated by their proponents as means to economic renewal and efficiency and to democracy. That is how Marxists characterized their goals and achievements in 1917 and how Yeltsin and his supporters define theirs today.

10. The stories on Eastern Europe published almost daily in the *New York Times* since 1989 demonstrate such formulations in popular discourse. Richard Rorty (1992, 1–3) does likewise in academic discourse, equating Marxism and socialism with nationalized property and the absence of markets.

REFERENCES

Berliner, J. 1957. *Factory and Manager in the USSR*. Cambridge, MA: Harvard University Press.

———. 1970. *The Innovation Decision in Soviet Industry*. Cambridge, MA: MIT Press.

Bettelheim, C. 1975. *Class Struggles in the USSR First Period: 1917–1923*. New York: Monthly Review Press.

———. 1978. *Class Struggles in the USSR Second Period: 1923–1930*. New York: Monthly Review Press.

Diskin, J. 1990. *Classical Marxian Economic Theory and the Concept of Socialism*. Ph.D. dissertation. University of Massachusetts, Amherst.

Gorlin, A. 1985. "The Power of Soviet Industrial Ministers." *Soviet Studies*, 37(3): 353–370.

Granick, D. 1954. *Management of the Industrial Firm in the USSR*. New York: Columbia University Press.

———. 1960. *The Red Executive*. Garden City: Doubleday.

Gregory, P. 1990. *Restructuring the Soviet Economic Bureaucracy*. Cambridge, England: Cambridge University Press.

Hough, J. and Fainsod, M. 1979. *How the Soviet Union is Governed*. Cambridge, MA: Harvard University Press.

Kerblay, B. 1983. *Modern Soviet Society*. New York: Pantheon.

Lane, D. 1985a. *Soviet Economy and Society*. Oxford, England: Blackwell.

———. 1985b. *State and Politics in the USSR*. New York: New York University Press.

Resnick, S. and Wolff, R. 1987. *Knowledge and Class: A Marxian Critique of Political Economy*. Chicago: University of Chicago Press.

———. 1988, Spring. "Communism: Between Class and Classless." *Rethinking Marxism* 1(1): 14–48.

———. 1993, Summer. "State Capitalism in the USSR: A High Stakes Debate." *Rethinking Marxism* 6(2): 46–68.

Rorty, R. 1992, April. "The Intellectuals and the End of Socialism." *Yale Review* 80(1 & 2): 1–16.

Rumyantsev, A. 1969. *Categories and Laws of the Political Economy of Communism*, trans. by D. Danemanis. Moscow: Progress Publishers.

Sweezy, P. M. 1985, July–August. "After Capitalism—What?" *Monthly Review* 37(3): 98–111.

Sweezy, P. M. and Bettelheim, C. 1971. *On the Transition to Socialism*. New York: Monthly Review Press.

Was the Soviet Union Socialist?

FRANK ROSENGARTEN

The collapse of the Soviet Union as a political entity and the overthrow of the Communist governments that had been in power in Eastern Europe since the late 1940s have raised many questions concerning "really existing socialism." One of the main questions is whether these regimes and the societies they engendered were really socialist at all. What I offer in the following pages is a tentative answer to this question as it concerns the Soviet Union. Evidence to substantiate my point of view will be drawn from recent articles in the *New York Times*. Obviously, these articles reflect limited and scattered experiences in the former USSR, and as such cannot form the basis for any broader generalized notions about socialism in that country. Nevertheless, I think that they do suggest the possibility of a view of Soviet society quite different from the one in vogue at present. In any event, it is a pleasure for me to use the "newspaper of record," long the legitimate target of anger provoked by skewed and one-sided reporting, as a source of balanced commentary about the former USSR.

I would like to confront in particular certain positions concerning the Soviet Union that embrace a mélange of political and moral considerations. From a political point of view, a recent article by Ralph Miliband (1992) will serve to illustrate the kind of position that I think calls for a reasoned political critique. The moral issue involved in assessing Soviet history has been cogently articulated by Mark Naison (1993) in an essay on the Popular Front.

Miliband's article, originally a talk given in April 1992 at a symposium on Joseph Schumpeter's *Capitalism, Socialism and Democracy*, is an altogether praiseworthy effort both to expose the historical and political deficiencies of Francis Fukuyama's book *The End of History and the Last Man*, and to advance a series of propositions concerning the feasibility and desirability of socialist democracy. In the course of his discussion, Miliband stops twice to repudiate in the most decisive manner the notion that socialist democracy has anything to do whatever with Soviet Communism. "I wish to argue," he says early on in his intervention, "that there does indeed exist a radical alternative on the Left to capitalist democracy, which has nothing whatever to do with Soviet Communism" (Miliband 1992, 108). At a later point, in considering the socialist alternative to capitalism, he observes: "At the outset, it must be emphasized that socialist democracy has nothing to do with the 'model', or rather the anti-model, represented by Soviet Communism" (112). He then lists some of the features of the Soviet model, such as all-embracing and imperative central planning, and the monopoly of power by the leaders of a single party, that in his view have nothing to do with socialism.

Now, I have no intention of disputing Miliband's arguments concerning the characteristic features and merits of socialist democracy, which he presents as an alternative to capitalist democracy. I wish to point out several things, however. First, while it is true that democracy has certain dynamics of its own, and has an autonomous history that goes back at least 2,500 years to the ancient Athenian republic, it is also true that democracy can develop in different economic frameworks. Democracy exists in certain capitalist states and not in others, and can exist in certain socialist states and not in others. Just as there is no necessary and intrinsic connection between capitalism and democracy, so, I wish to argue, there is none between socialism and democracy. Moreover, as crucial as the Bill of Rights is to democracy, these rights are often defined and practiced in a formalistic manner. Socialist theory is based on the proposition that the principles inherent in formal political rights must be extended to the organization of society, of the economy, and of culture in such a way as to safeguard the effective equality of worker-citizens.

By focusing on economy, society, and culture, it becomes possible to introduce the issue of democracy into the discussion of Soviet socialism in ways that are precluded by Miliband's arguments. To do so is not, to be sure, to accomplish the impossible, namely to hold up the former USSR as a model for any kind of formal democratic practice, but rather to expose precisely the formalistic aspects of Western-style democracy and to argue that, in some respects, Soviet socialism made it possible for people to exert their collective capacities and decision-making abilities in a variety of ways. In order to document this point one would have to study everyday life in the Soviet Union, something most of us in the United States know very little about, since we have tended to focus much more intensively on power as it is exerted on the level of the state and its agencies, and, in the case of the Soviet Union, on the level of party-dominated activity. We have denied even that "really existing" socialist states can be said to possess something called "civil society" independent of, or at any rate distinguishable from, state-generated and state-authorized enterprise. The existence of a civil society in Eastern Europe and the USSR was made evident, I think, by the remarkable convergence of political and moral energy expressed by the populations of all these countries, as soon as it became clear in 1989 that Soviet tanks would not be rolling to put down their movement for change. What I am driving at is that, if the alternative to capitalist democracy is socialist democracy, the alternative to capitalism is socialism. If we exclude from our concern the issue of democracy understood as a political system guaranteeing the freedoms enshrined in the Bill of Rights, it is possible to argue that the Soviet Union *was* socialist—that, indeed, the system that Boris Yeltsin and his supporters are trying very hard to dismantle is in some basic respects a socialist economic and social system.

Readers may find it strange that an editor of the journal *Socialism and Democracy* would assert that socialism is separable from democracy. Ideally it is not, but practically and historically speaking, I think that one must come around to the view that socialism can and does exist as a defining term for the dominant system of property and social relations existing in certain countries, independently of the cluster of ideals and procedures we call political democracy. There is little in Soviet history to which we can look with pride as exemplifying the realization of democractic practices in the areas of free speech, free press, free assembly, and so on. For over seventy years, Soviet life was marked much more emphatically by the absence of these freedoms than by their presence. As far as I am concerned, it is a terrible mistake for socialists to become caught up in defending the often brutal and tyrannical methods of the Soviet state as aiming at a form of democratic polity. But on the question of socialism, limited as I wish it to be to the realms of economy, social organization, and culture in some of its expressions and purposes, it seems to me that there is room for a reasonable argument to be made in defense of the socialist character of Soviet society.

Coming back to Miliband's article, if we pose socialism as the alternative to capitalism, and if we concede that socialism and capitalism can exist both with and without the forms and institutional guarantees of political democracy as they are understood in this country, then I think that it is not necessary to treat Soviet socialism as the misbegotten child of fever-ridden Bolshevik revolutionaries with whom we have nothing whatever in common.

As I understand it, capitalism is characterized primarily by a system of production for profit, whose requirements tend to eclipse those of production for use, and by a predominantly market-based and market-oriented conception of life, resulting in the commodification not only of things but also of human relations and even of abstract notions such as that of time. Since Ben Franklin, we have been made conscious that "time is money." Capitalism is also marked by the political ascendancy of the class of people who own and/or control the principal means of production, and by gross disparities in wealth and in ease of access to the sources of wealth, including education, which are appropriated by the ruling capitalist class and its professional and technical adepts. The profit motive of production, the commodification of human relations, the political dominance of the capitalist class, and gross inequality in income and access to wealth, are among the distinguishing features of the capitalist system, no matter how modified and modernized they are to cope with the pressing needs of the masses of citizens and producers.

Over the past ten years, I have given serious consideration to critiques of Soviet socialism, some of which have been published in *Socialism and Democracy*, critiques that undermine my argument that there is something in Soviet history to which socialists can connect themselves in a useful manner. Hillel Ticktin's analysis (1986), for example, is based on the assumption that Soviet society under Stalinist rule was even more fragmented and atomized than the typical capitalist society. In his overview of what went wrong in Soviet planning, Patrick Flaherty depicts an economy hopelessly mired in top-down decision making not at all determined by the needs of the society as a whole but instead by the need of ministers, factory bosses, and party organizers to grab what each could of a militarily dominated state budget (Flaherty 1988, 1991). One could go on with other similar critiques and analyses, the thrust of which is to build a case for saying that the Soviet Union reproduced and in some ways exacerbated some of the worst aspects of the capitalist state. Nevertheless, as some of the *New York Times* reporters seem to think in their coverage of developments in post-Communist Russia, there is a case to be made on the other side. Here, for example, is what Louis Uchitelle had to say on "profits" and "costs" in Russia:

> Call on a store or a factory in Russia today and no matter how rundown it looks or how desperate its circumstances, the manager will probably declare that the enterprise is very profitable. By all the rules of Russian accounting, that is the truth. But that is largely because those rules encourage

managers to spend their profits on housing, food, day care, holiday retreats and numerous other amenities for workers. When an American company spends its money like that, the outlays are listed as costs. Those costs cause profits to shrink, owners to suffer, and chief executives sometimes to be dismissed. But in a land where every state enterprise belonged in theory to the people, spending on benefits was—in the logic of Russian accounting—a distribution of profits to the worker-owners. This accounting standard persists, even as Russia makes the transition to private enterprise. (Uchitelle 1992a, D2)

On June 26, 1992 the *Times* published a dispatch by Celestine Bohlen on summer camps for children before and after the Yeltsin revolution. She gives an evenhanded description of summer camps before and after, emphasizing that the newly won emphasis on the bottom line has caused some difficulties:

In more ways than one, the Green Pine Forest camp is stuck between two worlds. Its very existence is testimony to a system that tightly bonded workers and their families to their factories or organizations. Salaries are only one way employees are compensated for their work in Russia. They also have access to day-care centers and an annual 24-day trip to the countryside or seaside, often at a sanitarium built and maintained by their factory and their trade union.

For most Russians, these perquisites are as much a part of life as mosquitoes are part of summer. Now, with the coming of capitalism, institutions like the Green Pine Forest are in danger, threatened by the new attention paid to the bottom line. (Bohlen 1992, A1, A7)

The dilemma facing educators in Russia today hinges on a previous set of assumptions about what could be taken for granted as far as rights and entitlements are concerned. I submit that these rights and entitlements are part of what socialism is all about. Poor planning and the undemocratic, somewhat militaristic features of summer camping in the former USSR do not, in my view, vitiate the socialist nature of the commitment made to young people in that country. The same holds for medical care. We now know that the quality of medical care given the Soviet population was often grievously inadequate at many clinics and hospitals. But does that fact in itself constitute an indictment of the effort to provide free, tax-supported medical care to everyone who needed it? Perhaps we should be looking at some of the problematic aspects of socialized medicine, but that it was socialized, and made available to all members of society in the former USSR, remains something that we should think about in a serious fashion.

Another article by Uchitelle from July 2, 1992 is a report on the 64,000 steelworkers at the Magnitogorsk Metallurgical Complex. He comments on the forces at play in determining how fast executives at a steelworks in this country and in contemporary Russia can close down their plants, if economic conditions so require.

> While the executives who closed Lackawanna and Homestead responded to pressure from stockholders, Mr. Starikov [the general manager of the Russian steelworks] will not have shareholders until the steel works are privatized, which is not expected for at least a year and could take much longer. His constituents remain the townspeople he would have to lay off. They and their families make up half the population in this company town of 450,000 people.
>
> "The workers have the power, and the managers try to satisfy them so that they can hold on to their own positions, and keep alive their hopes of some day becoming owners," said Aleksei Titkov, a Russian economist and sociologist. "These managers are operating in a middle ground between the old socialist state and the markets." (Uchitelle 1992b, A1, A8)

Here again, one senses something different in the mentality of ordinary Russians in relation to the fundamental issues and forces at work in their everyday lives as producers and as members of a town dominated by a large economic enterprise.

As for the collective farms, Serge Schmemann, a fervent, Russian-born standard-bearer of the capitalist-democratic way of life, surveyed the situation at Russian collective farms in an article published on October 6, 1992.

> Ask about the "free market" or "reform," and people out on these fertile South Russian plains still begin to snarl. . . . Last year, when the first decrees came down proclaiming the new era of the free market, virtually every member of the huge Rossiya collective here—1,900 workers on 55,000 rich, black acres in the wheat belt between Krasnodar and Stavropol—signed a petition to the regional administration saying, in effect, "Leave us alone." . . . The debate is far from over, of course. Kolkhoz members still argue vehemently against parceling out collective land for private farms, and Parliament has not yet crossed the hurdle of private land ownership. But what is already clear is that the Rossiya kolkhoz, much like the country it is named after, is learning to look to the bottom line.
>
> For one thing, it has become a real cooperative, in which all the workers and pensioners have a formal share. Even the fields look better, because workers have been far more careful harvesting. (Schmemann 1992, A1, A10)

Can this attachment to the Kolkhoz, this expectation of low-cost summer camping, this close link between factory and town, this mistrust of speculative, profit-driven economics, be attributed entirely to some atavistic strain of collectivism in the Russian soul? Are these attitudes a holdover from the world of the Russian *mir*, the village collectivism so venerated by Leo Tolstoy? Far be it from me to deny such an influence. But I think that we should also give some thought to the possible influence of a system that, in important respects, was built on a socialist scaffolding of institutions and habitual ways of carrying on the ordinary business of life.

Let's look briefly now at the moral question as it affects one's assessment of the history of the Soviet Union. My point of reference is Ronald Reagan's famous phrase, "the evil empire," the general assumptions of which have long guided the thinking of this country's political, diplomatic, and foreign policy leaders. The tendency to brand societies and regimes we don't like as evil, as morally repugnant and therefore beyond the pale of the civilized world community, is an ancient one, deeply rooted in the psyche of political man and woman. In ancient times, during the Renaissance, and on into our own day, there has never been a scarcity of moralists ready to depict their ideological foes not as incompetent or wrong-headed, but as wicked, as morally tainted. Such judgments were made with respect to the Soviet Union from the very inception of the Soviet state.

I believe there is a need for moral consideration of political and social institutions, beginning with our own, since we know them best, but extending to all regimes, perhaps especially to those that lay claim to some form of representative and socially beneficial polity. But I also believe that moral judgment can often prevent us from distinguishing adequately between what regimes attempt to do and what they are constrained to do under specific sets of circumstances. That there were evil, morally repugnant aspects of Soviet society is evident to me, and I would not try to deny that I have that attitude. Yet to use a sweeping moral judgment in order to condemn and therefore dismiss everything that occurred or was attempted in that society is not, it seems to me, an appropriate or helpful thing to do. Such moralism does not advance the cause of understanding, and it drives a wedge between observer and observed that becomes virtually impossible to dislodge once it is set in place. The political climate created by such moralism also has seriously negative consequences for the ability of the Left to organize its own struggles.

In the course of his analysis of the Popular Front and of the role played in the Front by the U.S. Communist Party, Mark Naison expresses the kind of sweeping moral judgment to which I have just referred. After asserting that the 1936 trials highlighted the brutality of Soviet society, Naison writes:

> The "confessions" of those accused did little to reassure observers of the trials; at best, they revealed a society traumatized by divisions among its founding generation. For those who chose to look deeper, a more devastating picture emerged; Soviet Communism had evolved into something truly evil, a society in which paranoia, thought control, and murder had become institutionalized. (Naison 1993, 65)

I am certainly not arguing that the Soviet Union put an end to the nightmare of history. It added new chapters to the harrowing tale. At the same time, in a spirit of fairness, we need to gain a perspective on the history of the Soviet Union that allows us to perceive efforts and accomplishments, be they ever so tarnished in their execution, that were part of the first attempt in human history to construct a socialist society on a large scale. The scale was truly enormous, and involved changing a society shaped by centuries of what most agree were backward and extraordinarily oppressive conditions. I submit that the *New York Times* reporters quoted above were on to something that we should ponder as we make our way through the debris of recent events and try to make sense out of a confusing array of data in many sectors.

A concluding word on the question of whether the Soviet Union was socialist, and whether such a question is worth asking in the first place. The question is an important one, because unless we can answer it in the affirmative we face a rather desolate situation: a history almost devoid of resources for socialism—a history not only of failures and defeats, of abortive experiments and false starts, but of initiatives so misshapen and distorted as to lose the name socialism entirely. Let's remember that almost all of the previous and currently existing socialist countries have been influenced heavily by the Soviet example, and have depended on the Soviet Union for crucial assistance. Cuba, Vietnam, North Korea, Angola, even China in some areas, were branches that grew from a common trunk. Many of the Left parties of Europe, Latin America, and elsewhere fought for socialism in ways influenced to one degree or another by the Soviet Union. So unless we are willing to recognize as legitimate only those socialists and social democrats who have made their peace with a predominantly capitalist society, we do not have very much to rely upon in building for the future.

REFERENCES

Bohlen, C. 1992. "Disco, Not Marching, at Russian Summer Camp." *New York Times* (June 26): A1, A7.

Flaherty, P. 1988. "A Political Economy of the Soviet Union." *Socialism and Democracy* 7 (Fall/Winter): 31–74.

———. 1991. "Perestroika and the Soviet National-Security Complex." *Socialism and Democracy* 14 (Fall): 141–156.

Fukuyama, F. 1992. *The End of History and the Last Man.* New York: Free Press.

Miliband, R. 1992. "Fukuyama and the Socialist Alternative." *New Left Review* 193 (May/June): 108–113.

Naison, M. 1993. "The CPUSA and the Popular Front." In *New Studies in the Politics and Culture of U.S. Communism,* ed. M. E. Brown, R. Martin, F. Rosengarten, and G. Snedeker, 45–73. New York: Monthly Review Press.

Schmemann, S. 1992. "Free Market Ideas Grow on Russian Farm." *New York Times* (October 6): A1, A10.

Schumpeter, J. 1950. *Capitalism, Socialism, and Democracy.* New York: Harper.

Ticktin, H. 1986. "Summary by F. Rosengarten of Ticktin lecture." *Socialism and Democracy* 2 (Spring/Summer): 90–92.

Uchitelle, L. 1992a. "Figuring Profits the Russian Way." *New York Times* (June 16): D2.

———. 1992b. "On the Path to an Open Economy, a Decrepit Steel Plant in the Urals." *New York Times* (July 2): A1, A8.

Chinese Socialism and the Transition to Capitalism

GORDON WHITE

China is in transition to some form of capitalist economy and can no longer offer any significant prospect of an alternative system of political economy that is radically different from those already available in the world today. However, while the future of a distinctive form of Chinese socialism is decidedly dim, it is not entirely hopeless if one is willing to revise one's definition of "socialism" and to consider what elements of socialist values and institutions can be salvaged from the wreckage of Marxist–Leninism. While capitalism has its central inherent logic, it can take a variety of forms and thus the transition to capitalism in China can take different paths to different systemic destinations.

The future of Chinese political economy depends heavily on the specific character of the transition process itself. We need to ground our predictions in an analysis of two levels of historical causation. The first level is that of the more glacial socioeconomic movements that determine the distribution of economic power and the configuration of classes in society, factors that define the dynamics of economic accumulation and distribution and heavily influence the institutional character and ideological content of political life. The second is the more fluid and volatile level of politics itself, which can countenance changes of bewildering rapidity and scale (as witnessed in Eastern Europe) and contains a high degree of indeterminacy. Here chance and short-run conjunctures can play a cardinal role in shaping the longer-term political trajectory as

342

a whole and influencing the speed and shape of movements at the socio-economic level. These two levels are thus mutually determinant, often in highly unpredictable ways. Given the limits of this paper, I shall concentrate on the former—the socioeconomic—level of analysis; I have tackled the complex area of alternative scenarios of political transition elsewhere (White 1993, Chapter 8).

I begin by identifying the factors behind the weakening of the previous system of state socialism. Then I put forward several alternative scenarios for the economic transition and an analysis of the conditions that might make one more likely than another.

THE EROSION OF THE PREVIOUS MODEL OF CHINESE SOCIALISM

The impact of market-oriented economic reforms that began in 1978 has had a profound influence in undermining the rhetoric and reality of the Chinese version of Marxist–Leninist socialism. However, this should be seen as just the latest stage in a process of cumulative political decline, set in train by the disasters following the Great Leap Forward in the late 1950s and early 1960s and the internecine political struggles and economic disruptions of the Cultural Revolution decade between 1966 and 1976 (White 1993, Chapter 1). The determinants of decline are at three levels—political-ideological, economic, social—and operate both domestically and internationally.

At the political–ideological level, the credibility of the official ideology (Marxism–Leninism–Mao Zedong Thought) has lost much of its credibility as a legitimating rationale for the regime and as a system of public morality. The ideological framework has itself been radically revised to drop the revolutionary elements of the past, to replace the Maoist notion of "politics in command" with the primacy of economic modernization, to legitimate the incorporation of markets (instead of planning) as the fundamental element of a "socialist" economy, and to place any idea of "transition" to a hypothetically "higher" level of socialism on the historical backburner.

While damaging the motivations of older generations of political activists, these changes have failed to generate political conviction among a newer generation growing up in an increasingly market-oriented economy. The Dengist regime has consciously fostered the depoliticization of society by drastically reducing the amount of ideological education and political mobilization characteristic of earlier days. Political apathy has been reinforced by a highly successful record of economic growth over the past fifteen years that, having raised popular aspirations for consumption, has gone a considerable way towards satisfying them.

Increasingly, the credibility of the regime has come to rest on its developmental performance and not on a separate appeal to Marxist–Leninist principles, a trend that makes it politically vulnerable to economic fluctuations. To the extent that conviction politics survives, it largely embodies Western political values and models that the regime has vainly tried to repress as "bourgeois liberalization."

Since ideology provided much of the motivational glue that kept this Communist Party together, morale within this still hegemonic political institution has deteriorated, and it has increasingly become a mere aid towards upward mobility—in some cases, personal enrichment through corruption. While some of this is illegal venality, by far the larger portion is the exploitation of personal power and connections to take advantage of legal (or at least not illegal) opportunities offered by the market. This has contributed to a further decline in the Party's standing among the general population, but despite repeated efforts by the central leadership, official corruption has so far resisted correction. The political force of anticorruption drives is blunted by the fact that the relatives and friends of Party–government leaders themselves are heavily involved in these entrepreneurial activities.

The Party aside, the principle and practice of collective organization has been undermined by the *de facto* privatization of agriculture in the countryside. It is true that the expansion of the "collective" sector of the nonagricultural economy has far outpaced that of the state sector over the past decade, particularly in the countryside in the form of "township and village enterprises" (TVEs). Yet these are hybrid institutions and seem in large part to reflect a productive synergy between local state and private entrepreneurship, rather than any genuine principle of cooperative or collective organization. (For a more optimistic view of TVEs, see Huang 1992.)

The reason for this secular process of political decay has been the lack of a new conception of "socialism" that could provide the intellectual and political basis for an alternative form of political and economic organization. Official descriptions of the "socialist market economy" are hazy to say the least, and it is difficult to resist the conclusion that the principles of marketization and *de facto* privatization that the reforms embody cannot culminate in anything other than some form of capitalism—that is, private appropriation of the means of production, commodification of the main factors of production (capital, labor power, and land), and a high level of integration with the global capitalist economy. There are current efforts to come up with some "third path," involving, for example, an attempt to redefine state ownership through the formation of publicly owned joint-stock companies as an alternative to privatization. But such innovations are proving difficult to implement in practice and their success depends a great deal on support from a particular section of the Party leadership and on the continuation of the current system of Party–government institutions.

On the political side, the regime has little to offer in the way of significant reform. Despite much talk about the expansion of "socialist democracy," it remains unwilling to share power with other political institutions, to allow checks on the power of the Party–state (for example, by a more independent and critical mass media), to open up new channels of political participation for the general population, or to allow greater space for the organization of autonomous social groups (any genuine "civil society" still poses a threat). No "third way" to political reform is on offer, either from the political elite or the opposition, and there appears to be little visible confidence in the feasibility of an alternative system of "socialist" democracy that would be superior to liberal democracy.

Small wonder, therefore, that those advocating political change turn towards foreign, particularly North American, models of liberal democracy, and advocate root and branch transformation of the existing political system. Certain elements among the political elite, led by the children of older generation Communist leaders, are aware of the potentially explosive contradiction between economic transformation and politico-ideological sclerosis, and are willing to innovate. However, rather than leading towards a new and more democratic conception of socialist political economy, this takes the form of a "new conservatism" and tends towards reducing the "socialist" component of official ideology in favor of a mixture of neotraditional authoritarianism, nationalism, and developmentalism comparable with their earlier East Asian counterparts in Japan, South Korea, and Taiwan (Gu and Kelly 1992).

At the economic level, the changes brought about by the reforms have been far-reaching, resulting in a significant redistribution of economic power and resources between the state-owned and other sectors of the economy and between economically more sluggish and economically more dynamic regions of the country. The role of the state-owned sector in the economy has declined and increasing shares have been taken by collective and private enterprises. These changes in the domestic economy have been reinforced by trends in China's relations with the international economy. Wholly owned, joint, and cooperative Chinese–foreign ventures have proliferated, particularly in the coastal and southeastern regions, expedited by the establishment of "special economic zones" and "open areas" offering favorable conditions for foreign investors. Foreign trade has also expanded rapidly and Chinese companies have themselves begun to invest abroad. For example, according to Washington sources, not only was China the largest foreign supplier of small arms to the U.S. market in 1991, but Chinese interests (apparently linked with the armed forces) were buying companies and operating in the arms trade in seven states (*The San Jose Mercury News*, March 4, 1993, reported by *China News Digest* [*News Global*]).

These economic changes have set in train potentially fundamental changes in China's class structure. First, one can detect the gradual (and, in the early 1990s, accelerating) emergence of a new bourgeoisie. We can identify two chronological stages here. The first, which began in the early 1980s with the liberalization and consequent flourishing of small-scale private and quasi-private (albeit labeled "collective") businesses led to the growth of a petty bourgeois stratum. In the urban areas, they were heavily concentrated in services and commerce, but in the rural areas they were also involved in specialized agriculture and small-scale industry. In the second stage, which began in the late 1980s and gathered pace in the early 1990s, economic conditions and reform policies have fostered the growth of a larger bourgeoisie, exploiting the lucrative, perhaps once-in-a-lifetime opportunities offered by the expansion of real estate business, the growth in foreign trade and investment, the spread of shareholding and the growth in attractive business ventures in rapidly expanding sectors such as finance, commerce, and knowledge-intensive, high-tech industries. This latter phase requires larger accumulations of capital and higher levels of skills than the former, so it is not surprising that an increasing number of China's intelligentsia, either by themselves or in alliance with domestic and foreign holders of capital, are increasingly leaving their jobs for private business; this is called "plunging into the sea," "*xia hai*."

Since this transformation requires not only capital and skills but influence, another major trend is for state officials—whether remaining in or moving out of their official position—to establish companies either on their own or in alliance with domestic or foreign entrepreneurs. (This phenomenon has been called "nomenklatura capitalism.") Official efforts to slim down the bureaucracy have reinforced this. From the point of view of central reformers, this is a convenient way to get surplus administrative personnel off the books; such ventures are thus winked at if not actively encouraged.

While these trends are nurturing a lower and higher order bourgeoisie, they are also generating elements of a new and diversifying "middle class": accountants, lawyers, economists, linguists, managers, technicians, engineers, and the like. Some of these are moving from the public into the collective, private, or foreign/joint sectors (e.g., university economics lecturers or researchers getting jobs in securities companies at five to ten times their previous salaries); others are reducing risk or biding their time by moonlighting in both sectors. Either way, the divide between professionals and skilled personnel in the state and nonstate sectors is becoming less clear-cut and the balance between them is gradually shifting.

As for the general working population, the effort to create a labor market is exerting ambiguous effects. For rural workers, economic liberalization has opened up more opportunities for occupational and geographical mobility. A large and indeterminate number have moved into the big cities or the richer provinces in the southeast such as Guangdong, constituting an ever increasing "floating population" that lives in cities illegally or on a short-term legal basis doing contract work or living hand to mouth through petty hawking, casual labor, or crime. Other rural residents have entered business in the countryside by setting up household enterprises and TVEs, or have become workers in these enterprises. Though the small-scale rural enterprise economy is more market dependent and therefore more volatile than the urban state sector, these workers still have a cushion to fall back on if they are made redundant, since they and their families in the village retain the right to a piece of "collective" land.

In the cities, workers in state enterprises, who previously constituted a labor aristocracy because they had relatively good wages, welfare benefits, and working conditions, and security of job tenure, have been a consistent target of the economic reforms. Reform economists have criticized overstaffing in state enterprises and the practice of lifetime tenure (dubbed the "iron rice bowl") as prime causes of poor productivity in the state sector. There has thus been an attempt to introduce a labor market and weaken the status of state workers by putting them on a term-contract basis. The trade unions, albeit still within the grip of the Party, have resisted these inroads on the interests of their members, with some success. However, the trade unions are mainly based in the state sector and run the risk of being accused of protecting the interests of a relatively privileged and unproductive sector of the workforce. Their success in organizing the collective, private, and foreign/joint venture sectors has been partial and patchy so far, and their influence in these sectors is far weaker than in the state sector. A process of proletarianization is well under way. The specific social character of this process depends partly on the ability of the Chinese trade unions to organize workers in the new economic sectors and to exert political pressure for legislation to provide a new system of basic social protections and guarantees for Chinese workers.

Given these three sets of trends—political, economic and social—a transition towards some form of capitalism is well advanced in China. But what type of capitalism?

THE FUTURE OF CHINESE CAPITALISM: SOME SCENARIOS

The factors conditioning the evolution of the Chinese economic system are complex, including changes in economic institutions, processes of class formation, political events, and diverse international pressures (political, economic, and sociocultural). I cannot deal with these satisfactorily within the scope of this paper, so I shall concentrate on outlining four types of capitalism that represent alternative futures for the Chinese economy. These should be seen as analytical constructs that are not mutually exclusive in the real world.

1. *Chaotic, Hobbesian capitalism.* This form of capitalism, "red in tooth and claw," could follow upon a breakdown of political and social order in China, comparable to what has happened in certain parts of the former Soviet Union. Accumulation could continue under such conditions, particularly in certain regions with more extensive external links, but would operate without any degree of regulation or institutionalization. It would be oriented towards short-term or speculative returns, operate on a dog-eat-dog basis, and be accompanied by a high degree of coercion, instability, insecurity, and exploitation, unmitigated either by the action of the state, the presence of self-regulatory institutions (such as business and trade associations), or countervailing forces such as a strong union movement. Sectors such as prostitution and drug trafficking would flourish, as they already do in certain provinces, notably in the South and Southeast. Socioeconomic cohesion would be maintained largely through kinship, localism, and personal networks rather than through state institutions or formal social institutions. Moreover, as in the former Soviet Union, part of the economy could be occupied by mafia-type organizations such as the secret societies that were powerful before the revolution in 1949, which retained their influence thereafter in overseas Chinese communities and are already spreading into southeastern China. One might also expect there to be a proliferation of local "economic bosses" (already apparent in China as recent incidents in Hubei and Yunnan province testify), who rule the local economy through a mixture of economic inducement and force. Though this is a Doomsday scenario, it is one that many Chinese fear as a possible consequence of a collapse of the Chinese Communist political system along Soviet lines.

2. *Crony capitalism.* In this form a bourgeoisie is nurtured by, and remains dependent on and interlocking with, the state apparatus, based on networks of personal relations between individual state officials/politicians and business people. This alliance, which—*pace* the theory of "rent-seeking"—can be economically dynamic and productive, is based on a systematically penetrated (and some might say "corrupt") political

system and state machine and a "symbiotic" bourgeoisie. These alliances form either as a consequence of the need of independent entrepreneurs to secure resources or protection from a still-powerful state, or from the process whereby state officials move out into private business but retain their previous official contacts. While one would expect labor in this system to be politically demobilized and excluded, unions also could be brought into this logic of state dependence and personalistic networks. Within enterprises, moreover, there would be an attempt to extend the principle of personalistic ties, often quasi-familial, to relations between capital, management, and labor. The formation of this symbiosis has been documented by David Wank (1992) in his study of the southern commercial city of Xiamen in Fujian province (opposite Taiwan). He sees this not as a transitional phenomenon but as a potentially long-term process of private sector development in which the expansion of the "private" bourgeoisie is dependent on and supportive of the maintenance of a powerful state presence in the economy (cf. Solinger 1992).

   3. *New industrial country (NIC)-style state-led capitalism.* In this model, a strong, coherent, and probably still authoritarian state would retain a powerful role in steering and organizing the accumulation process, both directly through the retention of a large state sector and indirectly through various controls over private business. Like its South Korean and Taiwanese counterparts, the state would act in pursuit of certain strategic national economic interests in its relations with the international economy. Domestically, it would retain a good deal of autonomy from private interests and the political leadership would be able thereby to enforce its will over them. The state would also be able to shape the evolution of private business through various forms of direct and indirect regulation—not merely through policy and law, but also through corporatist manipulation of intermediate organizations, or a form of "administrative guidance" through informal methods of consultation and coordination akin to that of Japan. Unlike its other East Asian counterparts, however, which excluded labor from its "inclusive corporatist" arrangements, the political complexion of the regime and the continuing strength of the trade unions might guarantee a more central role for organized labor in this scenario. Like its East Asian counterparts, however, this system would be subject to growing pressures, both domestic and international, for a reduction in the state's economic role, an undermining of corporatist structures, and democratization of the political regime. (For an instructive analysis of such a process in South Korea's financial system, see Woo 1991).

   4. *Socialized capitalism.* This is a form of capitalism that develops within a political and social framework that embodies certain elements of the preceding socialist system, thereby not "throwing out the baby with

the bath water." This would involve (1) a mixed economy with a significant state sector and encouragement of a relatively wide range of ownership forms in the nonstate economy, including cooperative and local/
community as well as private capitalist firms, perhaps building on the
"community sphere" in local enterprise identified by Huang (1992);
(2) the continued hegemony of some kind of "socialist" party emerging
out of a reformed Chinese Communist Party and playing a historical role
comparable to that of the Swedish Social Democratic Party, the Institutionalized Revolutionary Party (PRI) in Mexico, or (albeit with different
political principles) the Japanese Liberal Democratic Party; (3) institutionalized guarantees of certain social rights and protections both for
the population as a whole and for particularly vulnerable groups such as
women, poor people, the aged, the unemployed, and so on; and (4) the
existence of a civil society in which mass organizations such as trade
unions, farmers associations, and women's organizations were encouraged to develop freely and play a significant role in political and economic
events. In its weakest form, this system would be in effect an East Asian
version of Western European social democracy, with its attempt to produce a complementary combination between capitalist and socialist
political economy.

SOME TENTATIVE CONCLUDING REMARKS

The only thing we can say for certain about the form of capitalism that
will emerge in China is that it will be distinctively Chinese, both at the
macrolevel of its overall political economy and at the microlevel of relations of production within the enterprise. Like its Japanese counterpart,
it will be a "national" phenomenon rooted in China's specific cultural
context and historical antecedents, and embodying a conception of the
Chinese national interest and of the Chinese way of doing things. Unlike Japan, China's national capitalism will take an international form in
the context of its relations with Chinese communities outside China's
borders in Southeast Asia and elsewhere (Jones et al. 1992).

The distinctive character and "spirit" of Chinese capitalism will derive
elements from each of the above four models. The particular form of
that fusion depends heavily on *political* trends: the extent to which political
order can be maintained during the transition (if not, then model 1 becomes more likely); the extent to which the autonomy and coherence of
the state can be maintained (if not, then model 2 becomes more and
model 3 less likely); the extent to which the hegemonic political institution or constellation of political forces overseeing the transition is willing to retain certain socialist principles in the new society (if so, then

model 4 becomes more likely); and the extent to which the existing regime is transformed through a process of political reform to allow scope for the development of a strong civil society and the emergence of diverse forms of economic life (thereby providing the democratization and participation necessary for model 4 or evolving from model 3).

Given the crucial importance of these political factors, the specific character of the future Chinese version of capitalism will be shaped heavily by the evolving balance of political forces and the upcoming political struggles of the *fin de siècle*. There are still political forces in China that could throw their weight behind the struggle for a socialized version of capitalism (reformist elements inside and outside the Party, local communities in the countryside, and mass organizations such as the trade unions or the women's federation). But these potentially progressive forces face an unenviable battle on two fronts: on one side against the conservative forces of a repudiated Leninist status quo, on the other side against the rising new forces of private profit and the market, aided by their allies overseas. The power equation does not look encouraging.

REFERENCES

Gu Xin and Kelly, D. A. 1992. *New Conservatism: Ideological Program of the "New Elite"?* Paper presented at the conference, "Socio-economic Trends and Consequences in China," January 29–31, Fremantle, Australia.

Huang, P. C. 1992. "The rural 'community sphere' in China's modern development." Mimeograph, UCLA.

Jones, R.; King, R.; and Klein, M. 1992. *The Chinese Economic Area: Economic Integration without a Free Trade Agreement.* Paris: Economics Department Working Papers, No.124, OECD.

Solinger, D. J. 1992. "Urban Entrepreneurs and the State: The Merger of State and Society." In *State and Society in China: The Consequences of Reform,* ed. A. L. Rosenbaum, 121–142. Oxford: Westview Press.

Wank, D. L. 1992. *Symbiotic Alliance of Entrepreneurs and Officials: The Logics of Private Sector Expansion in a South China City.* Paper presented at the conference "The Political Consequences of Departures from Central Planning," August 25–30, Arden House, Harriman, New York.

White, G. 1993. *Riding the Tiger: The Politics of Economic Reform in China.* London: Macmillan.

Woo, J. 1991. *Race to the Swift: State and Finance in Korean Industrialization.* New York: Columbia University Press.

PART SIX

DIMENSIONS OF CLASS ANALYSIS

Importing History into Trade Theory:
A Class Perspective

THOMAS DELGIUDICE

It has become fashionable to speak of a "new international economics" in which trade is said to reflect "national advantages created by historical circumstances" rather than solely exogenous underlying national differences (Krugman 1990, 109). We can be encouraged by this recognition that history matters and by the movement away from the static propositions that have so long dominated neoclassical trade theory. However, acknowledging history is an empty move if it is not accompanied by a further recognition that how one conceptualizes history is also important. The history of the new international economists is devoid of class relationships. Therefore, the pursuit of government policies based on it can leave peoples as vulnerable to processes of exploitation and wealth redistribution as prior analyses and policies.

It has been a dominant proposition of economists that countries trade because of inherent differences in their physical and human nature. In the more formal neoclassical competitive model, the conventional wisdom (known as comparative costs theory) reduces a country's inherent differences to human preferences, physical endowments and technology. Trade based on these *given* differences would mean greater utilization of global resources and mutual benefits (greater national wealth) for all trading countries. This understanding of international trade became the theoretical backbone for proponents of free trade and the opening of markets.

The success of some countries' interventionist trading strategies and the growing proportion of trade dominated by large (imperfectly competitive) firms created new challenges for trade theorists. Over the past decade, some international economists have reconceptualized international trade within a new dynamic theory of comparative advantage that recognizes the importance of change over time. They have begun to conceptualize trading advantages as the result of strategic actions by firms and governments. For some this emphasis on "historical circumstances" opens the theoretical door to "government policies that can *in principle* shape the pattern (of international trade and specialization) to benefit their domestic economies" (Krugman 1990, 109).

These ideas are reminiscent of an earlier time when, in the post-war era, many economists tried to theorize the conditions required to develop the countries of the Southern Hemisphere and Asia. They found that developing these countries meant altering the "historical circumstances" of their insertion into the international trading network. They advised multilateral institutions, governments, and multinational and domestic enterprises to implement various policies designed to alter countries' resources and technologies in order to change patterns of exports and imports. With the implementation of the appropriate commercial and industrial policies, developing countries could alter enough of their historical circumstances to turn trade from a shackle on development into an engine of growth.

The new international economists share with their earlier development counterparts a willingness to go beyond the assumption that the determinants of economic activity are exogenous givens. However, both remain faithful to mainstream economics in their blindness to the same thing: the importance of class relationships and class struggle to understanding historical circumstances. Their neglect of class relationships leaves no place for theorizing how tensions and struggles over exploitative production processes shape economic phenomena. Struggles and conflicts of the kind that characterized many developing countries in the 1960s and 1970s were seen as external to economic analysis, as military or political matters not crucial to economic analysis.

In this paper, I use the case of a country (Nicaragua) to illustrate the importance of considering history from a class perspective. Nicaragua's development path of export diversification in the 1950s and 1960s was deemed quite successful at stimulating economic growth. However, during this period, Nicaragua also experienced growing social unrest and political instability, which contributed to the undermining of the very capitalist institutions upon which the economic "success" was built. Understanding the relationship between these events requires a class analysis of the circumstances surrounding Nicaragua's export diversification program. Our example can provide insights into the danger of economic theories that fail to consider class effects in developing international trade strategies.

DEVELOPMENT, CLASS, AND TRADE

The problem facing many developing countries in the 1950s and 1960s was too much reliance on the export of a single primary product to earn foreign exchange. Dramatic swings in prices have long characterized the market for primary goods, leaving many developing countries vulnerable to declines in export earnings and foreign exchange reserves. To remedy the situation, development economists of the 1950s recommended a policy of export diversification. The agroexport diversification programs undertaken by the small countries of Central America in the post-war period represent good examples of the strategies prescribed by development economists to increase export earnings and stimulate growth. They were initially successful.

The promotion of new exports was still informed by the propositions of comparative advantage. However, development economists also recognized the importance of mobilizing a variety of economic conditions beyond a country's given resources. For example, Nicaragua's promotion of cotton exports can be attributed to infusions of capital in the form of loans and grants for public investment in infrastructure, new technologies and machinery, and advisers to teach new techniques of production. Government officials intervened to *develop* a comparative advantage in cotton by augmenting the country's resources, transferring technology, and getting producers started down the learning curve. As a result, and as promised by the theory of comparative advantage, the production and export of cotton stimulated a rising national product for Nicaragua.

But, if the economics of cotton export promotion was a "success," how can we understand the social conflicts that accompanied it? Is there a reading of the circumstances that can explain the linkage between economic "success" and social unrest? The answer is found in the role capitalist class relations can play in promoting the production of a commodity.

A country may engage in a variety of strategies to promote the production and export of particular commodities. Two strategies for increasing the profitability of a commodity's production are, first, lowering the costs of production and, second, altering the level of the revenues realized by the producer. From a class perspective, the first strategy involves increasing the amount of unpaid labor relative to paid labor, while the second involves securing access to/control over important conditions of production. The former represents an increase in the rate of exploitation, the quantitative dimension of the capitalist *fundamental class process*, and the latter the capitalist *subsumed class process*. Both strategies are often at the center of tensions and struggles.

TRADE AND EXPLOITATION

The first strategy can effect the international competitiveness of a producer. Any increase in the labor for which the capitalist does not have to pay represents a condition for a fall in unit costs. Assuming the international price of cotton is equal to its unit value, which, in turn, is governed by the normal conditions of production prevalent among world capitalist cotton producers, the lower a producer's unit productive costs the greater the surplus value realized. The return to the low cost capitalist will be composed of his or her own appropriated surplus value *and* an extra share of the industry's surplus value. According to Marx, producers with unit costs lower than the average in the industry realize surplus value transferred from producers with unit costs higher than the industry's average. Thus the reward at this level of analysis for being a low unit cost producer is greater realized surplus value or a surplus profit (Roberts 1988).

In Nicaragua, the promotion of cotton production included the introduction of agricultural technologies that lowered costs but also created class tensions. The introduction of agrochemicals—pesticide and fertilizers—and tractors led to higher productivity, lower unit costs and opportunities to realize surplus profits.[1] However, the effects of the new technology did not end with greater profitability. The improved profitability of cotton cultivation led to the expropriation of many noncapitalist food producers from the land by means of higher rents, or by force, and to a decline in food production. Forced to seek wage employment, displaced food producers found few opportunities for year-round employment in the cotton sector due to the labor-saving bias of the new agricultural technology. Adding to their misery, the drop off in food production pushed food prices higher. The combination of these circumstances led to a decline in real wages for year-round agricultural laborers (Biderman 1986, Appendix).[2] For cotton workers, technological change resulted not only in a rise in their productivity but also in a loss of bargaining power in favor of capitalist growers, and this resulted in a prolonged decline in real wages and a deterioration in living standards. While the initial effect of technological change was a rise in labor productivity and lower costs, its interaction with a variety of other social processes resulted in a rise in worker exploitation, which contributed to still lower costs at the expense of the workers' living conditions (DelGiudice 1991, 95).

By facilitating the acquisition and use of new technologies by cotton growers, government policies shaped the historical circumstances to create a trading advantage in cotton. The rise in labor productivity and rate of exploitation led to lower costs and improved profitability for the cotton growers, contributing to Nicaragua's comparative advantage in cotton. However, lower costs became associated with an increase in the relative poverty of cotton laborers, resulting in an increase in class tensions between productive laborers and capitalist cotton growers (Williams 1986, 167).

CLASS MOBILITY AND UNEVEN DEVELOPMENT

We can turn now to the second strategy for export promotion, the strategy of facilitating access to/control over natural and social conditions for the production and realization of profit (surplus value). Expenditures to secure conditions of production are no less important than the form of exploitation to understanding the distinctive class character of an industrial policy. For example, Nicaraguan cotton capitalists had to distribute surplus value, in the form of rents, to secure access to land; as interest, to secure credit; as payments to monopoly input distributors; and in other subsumed class payments. Individuals receiving a portion of the surplus value occupy subsumed class positions, and the distributions by the capitalist are subsumed class expenditures. Both the level of these distributions and the various arrangements made for their payment represent additional factors shaping the "historic circumstances" surrounding a comparative advantage.

In the early 1950s, Nicaragua's comparative advantage in cotton was built on the fertile land of its Pacific coastal plains, generous supplies of government-backed credit, new cultivation techniques, and the acquisition of new agrochemicals and tractors. Taken collectively, these "historic circumstances" provided the new capitalist grower the basis for low costs and relatively low subsumed class payments at a time when international prices for cotton were at historic highs. Nicaragua seemed to be enjoying the kind of export success that the theory of comparative advantage would predict. Yet, this success was not without class and nonclass consequences that threatened its continued existence. Each of the above conditions was subject to a myriad of effects from both economic and noneconomic processes, effecting the level of subsumed class payments and the growers' competitiveness. For example, the cotton growers' increased dependence on pesticides to ward off resistant strains of cotton pests and on fertilizers to curb the effects of erosion (changes in natural processes) led to rising subsumed class payments to monopoly chemical distributors. Infrastructure development in the Pacific plains region (a nonclass condition of existence) resulted in a rise in subsumed class rental payments. Falling international prices (an exchange process) contributed to many growers defaulting on loans, and in turn, higher subsumed class interest payments. Each of these occurrences shaped both the provision and the cost of important conditions for Nicaragua's trading advantage in cotton.

These examples represent a narrow though important range of effects arising from the effects of nonclass processes on subsumed class processes. The response of Nicaragua's cotton growers to these and other changes is an example of how class processes shape a country's ability to sustain a trading advantage. During the 1950s and 1960s Nicaragua's cotton growers responded differently to their cost (subsumed class payments) changes. *Some* growers sought control over the conditions of existence for which they had formerly paid: *They moved to occupy those class positions themselves.* Other growers were forced into new, more informal class relationships to acquire their land, credit, and various inputs.

Thus, in the case of Nicaragua's cotton growers, changes in nonclass processes led to changes in the structure of subsumed class relationships. Specifically, some growers adapted by becoming "class mobile." By occupying various class positions, these producers were able to obtain some degree of control over conditions important to their production processes while also realizing new sources of revenues. The class mobile growers obtained distinct advantages over producers unable to engage in such a strategy. The strategy of diversifying one's class position afforded the cotton grower opportunities to improve both their cost and revenue positions. By virtue of occupying subsumed class positions as landowners, shareholders of input and ginning firms and nonclass positions in financial and merchant enterprises, class mobile cotton growers were able to gain cheaper and preferential access to arable land, raw material inputs, and credit (Strachan 1976, 115). This often translated into lower costs and greater realized surplus value for the class mobile grower. On the revenue side, class mobile growers received revenues not just from sale of their cotton output but also from the multiple class positions they held. The class mobile grower might receive subsumed class revenues such as rents, dividends, and interest payments from productive enterprises and other revenues, such as dividends, from ownership shares in nonproductive enterprises (e.g., export houses and banks).

For the small and medium growers changing economic and non-economic processes gradually meant greater dependence on their larger competitors. In the late 1950s, low cotton prices and higher productive costs left many small- and medium-sized producers with insufficient revenues to meet loan and interest payments. As the number of defaults mounted, credit eligibility in the formal markets became stricter. The small- and medium-sized producers were increasingly forced out of formal credit arrangements. The need for start-up capital forced smaller growers into informal credit arrangements with providers of their land, inputs, and purchasers of their output. These providers were increasingly the class mobile larger growers, the new owners of much of the land, input producing and processing firms, as well as the export houses. The vulnerability of the smaller growers to the class mobile capitalist often translated into higher subsumed class expenditures for the small growers. Their subsumed class payments included higher interest payments in the informal credit market, interest payments on supplier credits, and large discounts on the advanced sale of cotton to ginning companies, to name only a few. The new structure of subsumed class payments represents yet another factor contributing to the class tensions emanating from Nicaragua's cotton sector.

Changing cotton prices was one factor contributing to the changing class relationships in the cotton sector. The price of cotton in the 1950s and 1960s, as is characteristic of the prices of many primary goods, was subject to dramatic swings. These price fluctuations combined with changes in the natural and social processes shaping costs and subsumed class relationships to bring about an uneven development in the cotton sector. During periods of high prices and favorable natural conditions, class mobile growers were in the best position to realize high earnings and in turn expand production. Between the mid-1950s and the 1960s the largest 1% of the growers—those cultivating in excess of 500 manzanas (1 manzana = 1.73 acres)—increased their proportion of the total cotton area planted from 7% to 19% (Biderman 1986, 76). Breaking down the size of farms even more reveals that the list of cotton growers with more than 346 acres of cotton planted accounted for 60% of the cotton area cultivated in 1963 (Williams 1986, 32). It appears that cotton production became increasingly concentrated and centralized during the 1960s. In addition, by occupying multiple class positions these growers also benefited from the class and nonclass payments other growers were forced to pay them (or the firms in which they owned shares) for access to needed conditions of production. When cotton prices declined, these additional sources of revenues buffered the effects from a decline in the surplus value realized by their cotton enterprises.

For the smaller cotton growers, cotton became a profitable invest-ment when costs were low and cotton prices were high, as was the case in the early 1950s. However, fluctuating cotton prices and changing natu-ral and social conditions shaping their costs translated into a stagnant and at times even declining ability to maintain production levels. Fur-thermore, changing credit eligibility forced the smaller growers to be-come increasingly dependent on the providers of their land, inputs, and credit. One consequence was a transfer of surplus value, in the form of subsumed class expenditures, from smaller to larger growers who increas-ingly owned and controlled the provision of credit, inputs, and process-ing operations. Thus large growers realized a growing relative advantage over the smaller growers over time.

In the early and mid-1950s, the large growers were able to turn high profits from growing cotton into class mobile strategies. Increasingly, large growers used earnings from cotton production to obtain control over more conditions of cotton production and export, enabling them to better withstand the pressures of falling prices in the late 1950s. Many smaller producers were unable to earn profits during periods of low prices and were forced either into bankruptcy or greater dependence on the class mobile producers. With each succeeding cycle of high and low prices, the class mobile capitalists were able to expand their cotton enterprises and consolidate their control over the conditions of existence necessary to the other capitalists. The interlocking of costs and revenues among the small and large cotton capitalist growers was an important contributor to a centralizing of wealth in the cotton sector. It was the large class mobile growers who maintained their competitiveness and reaped the largest benefits from Nicaragua's comparative advantage in cotton production.

Throughout this period the seeds of class conflict between the large class mobile growers and the smaller growers were sown. The divisions created among these different appropriators of surplus value and the eventual receivers of the surplus value were an additional factor contrib-uting to the eventual collapse of the coalition of capitalists supporting the Somoza regime in Nicaragua.

CONCLUSION

For the student of development economics or the "new" international economics, the promotion of new technologies, increased utilization of natural endowments, and the use of government policy to increase the availability of credit represent a prescription for the enhancement of an export sector's competitiveness. Nicaragua would appear to be a good example of how historical circumstances can be mobilized to create an international trading advantage. In a Marxist depiction, the success of Nicaragua's cotton growers was built on relationships of class, resulting in rising exploitation of the cotton laborers and centralization of the cotton sector's wealth into the hands of large cotton growers occupying multiple class positions. These latter factors created tensions that threatened the very continuance of capitalist development in Nicaragua.

Nicaragua's experience, like that of so many other countries implementing policies based on development economics, offers us a warning regarding the relevance of economic theory. While the new international economists trumpet the importance of history and lay the groundwork for a new round of government intervention, their blindness to class leaves untheorized the social implications of their recommendations for relationships of exploitation and the distribution of wealth. Class, as is shown in the case of Nicaragua, has as much to do with the development of a trading advantage and the prosperity (or lack thereof) derived from international trade as do any of the engineering relationships that economists focus on, between factors of production and technology or learning and scale of operation.

The failure of development economists to consider the class consequences of their policy recommendations is one historical lesson that the new international economists seem content to ignore. The continued absence of class considerations from the new economic theories and policies guiding advanced capitalist countries will leave many of their citizens vulnerable to the same unforeseen suffering and hardship experienced by so many in the developing countries.

NOTES

1. The government supported the introduction of such technology through generous supplies of credit and overvalued exchange rates on imported inputs to new cotton producers (Williams 1986, 19).

2. Many of the displaced laborers were left with no alternative than to become migrant laborers earning wages for only a few months a year and subject to wide fluctuations in wages depending on the harvest.

REFERENCES

Biderman, J. 1986. *Class Structure, the State and Capitalist Development in Nicaraguan Agriculture.* Ph.D. dissertation, University of California—Berkeley.
DelGiudice, T. 1991. *A Marxist Theory of Costs: The Case of Nicaraguan Cotton Growers.* Ph.D. dissertation, University of Massachusetts, Amherst.

Krugman, P. R. 1990. "Is Free Trade Passé?" In *International Economics and International Economic Policy*, ed. P. King, 109–114. New York: McGraw Hill.

Roberts, B. 1988. "What is Profit?" *Rethinking Marxism* 1 (Spring): 136–151.

Strachan, H. W. 1976. *Family and Other Business Groups in Economic Development: The Case of Nicaragua*. New York: Praeger.

Williams, R. 1986. *Export Agriculture and the Crisis in Central America*. Chapel Hill: University of North Carolina Press.

A Farm under a Class Lens

MARY A. ENGELMEYER

Although fewer farms are experiencing severe distress, "family farming" is far from secure, and perhaps even in danger of becoming an historical relic (Davidson 1990; Heffernan 1989). The importance of "family farming" begins with its historical role of providing "Old World" immigrants with economic independence from feudal lords and industrialists. Thus, images of family farming portray a family working together in a communal fashion with minimal interference from outsiders and, in this sense, a lack of exploitation.[1] Farm families are presumed to reside in communities of relative equals who frequently help each other out (Goldschmidt 1978). These images are perpetuated by movies produced during the 1980s "farm crisis." In "Country," for example, the neighbors of the Ivy family gather at the FMHA (Farmer's Home Administration) foreclosure sale of their farm to shout down the auctioneer with a chorus of "No Sale." The sale is postponed and eventually canceled due to a moratorium (federal court order) on FMHA foreclosures. In "The River," the Garveys' neighbors help build a levee that protects their corn crop from flood waters. In both cases, devotion to "family farming" calls all of the community together to resolve immediate crises that threaten neighbors' farms.

Yet, these images omit much of farm family life. Issues of whether existing farms measure up to images of "family farms" as safe havens are largely disregarded.[2] In "Country," for example, when, in order to help pay farm debts, Jewel decides to sell produce she has raised and canned

365

for home consumption, her husband orders the children to return it to the pantry. The scene, although meant to demonstrate Jewel's willingness to makes sacrifices for the farm, can be read as an illustration of Gil's authority over the products of Jewel's labor. These class relations (exploitation) are overshadowed by the theme of working together. Again, in "The River," Tom Garvey expects his young teenaged son to work around the clock to build the levee. This young child is expected to perform labor beyond that of a wage laborer in an industrial factory. Yet, the scene presents everyone working together to save the farm while it neglects issues of possible exploitation. The son is finally allowed to work shorter hours when neighbors are called in to help. Class relations are largely ignored as a result of the emphasis on communal images.

Theoretical analyses also largely neglect class relations within and between farm families by focusing on relations between farms and a broader system (prices and interest rates). There is, therefore, a need to theorize these class relations. An analysis of these class relations can show that existing farm families deviate from an ideal version of family farms in which surplus labor is performed, appropriated, and redistributed in a communal fashion (for a discussion of such class processes, see Resnick and Wolff 1987, 109–124). Farm policy discussions could then add considerations about social (class and gender) relations to traditional concerns about external conditions of farming. As a result of this enriched discourse, policies could be seen as a way to participate in the ongoing transformation of class processes on farms, rather than simply as a reaction to crises that save existing farms (and the class relations they contain).

TRADITIONAL ANALYSES OF EXTERNAL CONDITIONS OF FARMING

Since economic analyses generally see social change as directed by systems (a competitive market system, a market system dominated by big business, or a capitalist system), the "farm problem" has been defined in terms of relations between farms and these systems. Thus, the pertinent policy goal has been the mediation of these relations to eliminate domination of farm families by these systems. But, by theorizing the class processes in which particular individuals (farm family members and nonfarm persons) participate, policy can go further and begin to affect changes that might move toward more communal class relations.

Conservative economic analyses, which focus on exchange in the market place, generally define the "farm problem" as one of finding optimal prices (Paarlberg 1987; Tweeten 1988). When these so-called optimal prices prevail, goods are understood to exchange at their (equilibrium) value. When conditions change, some farmers may be forced out of business (via bankruptcy or insufficient profits) when prices adjust in order to restore equilibrium. The central policy question, then, is whether prices are too volatile, causing inefficiency in the farm sector. Congress and the United States Department of Agriculture spend long hours debating "optimal" target price levels for commodities. Once these prices are determined, rural development policies can create jobs for exfarmers.

For these analyses, class relations are a nonissue. Since this analysis focuses on market exchange, relations between persons who produce goods (and perhaps perform surplus labor) and those who bring them to market (and perhaps appropriate the surplus labor of others) are considered to be beyond the realm of economics. Since discourse regarding cultural processes (e.g., producing the meaning of the role of women within society) and political processes (e.g., controlling the behavior of individuals within society) is also unexplored, the question of whether class relations exist between husband and wife, and whether they are communal or feudal, are not formulated. Likewise, the discussion of whether the product was produced by a nonfamily member, perhaps a wage laborer, is also left unasked. Transformation of the class processes in which family members or other farm workers participate are not pertinent policy objectives for these analyses.

Liberals, unlike conservatives, argue that the market will not deliver "optimal" prices since agribusinesses, via the exercise of power, charge excessively high prices for farm input goods and pay excessively low prices for farm produce (Marion 1986). They argue that farmers would thrive more on a level playing field. Periodically, agribusiness acquires greater power, inducing a "crisis" that condemns many farmers to bankruptcy. Despite these insights into commodity exchange, liberals, like conservatives, focus on issues of market exchange and prices. Since they also neglect class, their policies also often promote changes that are antithetical to securing a way of life akin to an ideal image of family farms. Policies that promote higher farm prices, for example, increase incomes of large farms relative to "family-sized" farms, enabling large farms (which are more likely to use wage labor) to acquire "family-sized" farms. Thus the policy serves to destroy those farms that it presumably aspires to save.[3]

Traditional radical analyses argue that farmers not only engage in market exchange on an unfair basis but also have a disadvantage in gaining access to the means of production controlled by "capitalists" (Carvalho and Holland 1985, Mooney 1986; Wilson 1986). Although capitalists allow farm families to gain access to means of production, they appropriate surplus value via rental payments for use of land, interest payments for access to credit, and direct confiscation of products through contract production. Furthermore, when capitalism is in "crisis," it sucks more surplus from the farm sector, forces farmers into bankruptcy and produces a declared farm crisis.

Since these analyses focus on the capitalist system and its dynamic, they explore only the relations between farmers and "capitalists" while presuming that farm family members are all equally exploited by outside capitalists. In reality, however, there are class processes within the farming sector. Members of some farm families appropriate the surplus of neighbors via land rental payments, interest payments or direct confiscation of output in contract production; some farm families may also use members of other farm families as wage laborers; and some adult males may appropriate the surplus produced by their wives and children. Attempts to rectify injustices between "capitalists" and "farmers," perhaps via price supports, can lead to increased exploitation among and between farm families, in terms of increased rental and interest payment exchanges between farmers, more usage of wage labor, or more intense exploitation of family members.

NEGLECTED CLASS ASPECTS

The exploitative side effects of policy have become grist for conservatives, such as Bovard (1989), who argue that government "intervention" can only serve to further interests of the powerful. This criticism could be answered by arguing that new policies, informed by an analysis of the particular ways in which individuals participate in class processes, can help build a farm sector in which surplus labor is communally produced, appropriated, and distributed. The remainder of this paper will begin to sketch such a class analysis of farm families.[4]

While members of farm families may be exploited (as wage laborers or contract producers) by capitalists, some "family farm" members may hire wage laborers or contract out production and occupy the class position of capitalist. Furthermore, farm family members may participate in a multitude of noncapitalist class relations that are not communal. The adult male member of a farm family, for example, may appropriate surplus labor produced by himself (ancient class process) and/or by his family members (feudal class process) on the "family farm." This individual may also occupy subsumed class positions, such as supervising the labor of others and making payments to access means of production.[5] The adult female in this same family is exploited as a feudal serf, although she may also receive a distribution of surplus labor by occupying subsumed class positions such as supervisor of laborers (children, hired labor, or herself), bookkeeper, or errand runner. All or some of the family members may also work off the farm in "capitalist" enterprises and either produce surplus labor for capitalists or provide conditions of existence for its production and appropriation.

In order to transform the class relations in which farm families participate, policy can address a plethora of nonclass processes that provide the conditions of existence for these class processes.[6] In order to transform the feudal class process, for example, policy can attempt to effect changes in cultural processes (production of meanings regarding women's roles in society) and political processes (ways of controlling behavior). Policy might establish community property laws giving women and men equal legal rights over farm family property and implement child labor laws regarding farm family production. Attempts to transform subsumed class processes of rental and interest payments for land might include establishment of a community land trust for farm land that gives usage rights to farm families.

I will use data from the 1987 Census of Agriculture (COA), a 1980 farm women's survey (FWS) (Rosenfeld 1985), and farm women's life experiences—drawn from Sachs's (1983) theoretical sampling, Pelton's (1984) personal experiences (as narrated in her book), and my experience of living in and visiting my home town farm community—to show that many noncommunal class processes do, in fact, exist in farming.[7] There is evidence, for example, that some farm family members occupy capitalist class positions. Of COA farms 60% use wage laborers and 11% use contract labor in farm production. Of FWS families 30% have at least one full-time hired hand (Rosenfeld 1985, 45). Furthermore, many members "work" in capitalist enterprises. Of COA farm operators 30% worked off the farm, while 15% worked off the farm at least 100 days.[8] The FWS findings showed that 49% of the husbands and 38% of the wives worked off the farm. In only 37% of FWS families neither husband nor wife worked off the farm, while in 18% of these families both spouses worked off the farm (Rosenfeld 1985, 173). It is likely that these individuals occupied a fundamental capitalist class position, as producers of surplus value, or a subsumed capitalist class position, such as bookkeeper or supervisor, in these enterprises.

In many farm families almost all members, except very small children, participate in the performance of surplus labor. Children over the age of ten, for example, work an average of 35 hours per week on the farm (cited in Rosenfeld 1985, 31). Some FWS women *regularly* perform farm labor, such as operating farm equipment (12%), doing field work without machinery (19%), harvesting crops (18%), and caring for farm animals (32%), in addition to raising animals and vegetables for family consumption (76%) and performing housework (98%). Another 20–30% perform these farm tasks occasionally and an additional 11% occasionally raise food for family consumption (Rosenfeld 1985, 66–68). One time-budget study showed that farm women spent 58 hours per week on domestic tasks and another 41 hours per week on farm tasks for a 99-hour work week (cited in Rosenfeld 1985, 52). These statistics provide evidence that many farm children and almost all farm women perform labor beyond what is necessary to reproduce themselves.

Although it seems clear that most family members participate in the performance of surplus labor, this does not mean that surplus labor is communally produced, appropriated, and distributed. In fact, there is evidence that some men appropriate and redistribute surplus labor that is performed by women and children. Fraad, Resnick, and Wolff (1989) argue that women who perform household chores are exploited as feudal serfs by their husbands as a result of political, cultural, and economic processes through which women are convinced that these class relations are best for them, or that largely prevent women from participating in alternative lifestyles as a way to maintain their standard of living. Farm women, like women in general, participate in these nonclass processes that provide conditions of existence for noncommunal class processes within farm families.

The cultural process of gendering, for example, fosters beliefs that men should dominate women and children. Some religions bid wives to obey their husbands, children to obey their fathers, and fathers to beat disobedient children. Men who do not dominate their wives are considered to be "hen-pecked." Although in 52% of FWS families men *alone* make final decisions concerning purchase of farm equipment (while, by contrast, women alone make final decisions regarding household appliance purchases in only 25% of these families), most women are found to be satisfied with these decisions (Rosenfeld 1985, 104). Satisfaction, however, occurs in cases where the spouses share the same sex-role attitudes. Women who are dissatisfied generally want a greater role, women who have more education are more likely to be involved in farm decision making, and women who work off the farm are more likely to make household decisions jointly or alone (Rosenfeld 1985, 110–135). Some women believe that it is the role of men to appropriate and distribute, as they see fit, the surplus labor performed by women. These women accept a class position of feudal serf in return for protection by their husbands, the feudal lords. Furthermore, the FWS indicated that many women are willing to provide some of the conditions of existence of their exploitation by occupying subsumed class positions (or nonclass positions, if they receive no distribution of surplus for doing these tasks), such as bookkeeping (74%), running errands (83%), making purchases upon which men have decided (33%), and marketing products (29%).

This belief that men should dominate women and children is reinforced in the political arena. Government regulations that limit the hours of work individuals can be required to perform in industrial factories do not apply to family farms. Extension staff do not encourage women to become equal partners in the farm enterprise. Women are given information about becoming "better" farm wives, such as picture-framing classes, and are ridiculed if they want to take classes providing information on farming (Sachs 1983, 90). Politics within farm organizations have discouraged women from joining. Some farm organizations have auxiliaries for farm wives where these women serve coffee to and prepare food for men's meetings. Half as many FWS women as FWS men belong to farm organizations, marketing cooperatives, farm supply cooperatives, or commodity producers' associations (Rosenfeld 1985, 193). Excluding women from these information networks keeps from them knowledge that could be used to divest men of dominating behavior. Within the politics of the family, women are also second-class citizens. Although 60% of FWS women participated regularly in farm tasks, only 35% helped make final decisions (Rosenfeld 1985, 66–68, 104). Furthermore, men attempt to control the behavior of women by humiliating them (Pelton 1984, 59–63), including holding their performance of surplus labor up to the standards of other farm women.

These effects are further reinforced via economic processes. The lack of women's opportunities to obtain credit for the purchase of farm land and equipment discourages them from trying to farm on their own (Sachs 1983, 90–91). Women who are farming without a man are more likely to be overcharged for farm input goods and underpaid for their products, since they are generally excluded from information networks. Furthermore, the ability to obtain a satisfactory standard of living from off-farm employment is limited since women are paid much less than men. Escaping from feudal exploitation on a "family farm" is often not a viable alternative for women.

COA data also support the claim made by traditional radical analyses that surplus produced by those who work the land often accrues to others. Almost 60% of farms make rental payments and 80% make interest payments in order to access means of production. Some of these payments accrue to other farm families. About 10% of "family" farms receive land rental income from other farms. Furthermore, 10% of "large" farms and 16% of "small" farms receive such payments. Class processes other than communal occur between men within the farm community.

The farm family and farm community falls short of an ideal situation where a communal class process prevails. By neglecting class relations among and between farm families, policies seem to be securing farm life that is a far cry from an ideal notion of family farming. If farm policy is indeed concerned with securing a communal way of life on family farms, the debate regarding the "farm problem" would do well to focus on class relations among and between farm families as well as the relations between farm families and some broader system.[9] This would allow policy to attempt to move class relations toward a communal entity.

ACKNOWLEDGMENTS

Thanks to David Ruccio, Suzanne Bergeron, and Carole Biewener for their support of the research for and writing of this paper.

NOTES

1. Thomas Jefferson (1903, 228–230) lauded these virtues of agrarianism.

2. Issues of farm life are skirted in Washington, for example, by redefining the concept of the family farm to include a broader range of farms (Brewster 1979) and by assuming that farms in a mid-range size category somehow have the characteristics of an ideal "family farm" (USDA 1981).

3. Bovard (1989) argues that farm policies often promote inequality.

4. Stormes (1988) uses a similar framework to question prevailing conceptions of poverty and opens up new policy options.

5. Subsumed class processes are those that provide conditions of existence for (i.e., overdetermine) fundamental class processes (Resnick and Wolff 1987, 117–122)

6. For more on overdetermination and class as process, see McIntyre (1992) and Resnick and Wolff (1987).

7. Census of Agriculture data include only farms in the Midwest (Illinois, Indiana, Iowa, Kansas, Michigan, Minnesota, Missouri, Nebraska, North Dakota, Ohio, South Dakota, and Wisconsin) that have annual sales between $39,999 and $250,000.

8. Although the concept "family farm" is often used to support many farm policies, the Census of Agriculture collects data on *farmers* rather than farm families omitting information regarding women and children who are not *the* farmer.

9. Strange (1988) argues for striving toward an ideal although it may not be achieved in the near future.

REFERENCES

Bovard, J. 1989. *The Farm Fiasco*. San Francisco: ICS Press.

Brewster, D. E. 1979. "The Family Farm: A Changing Concept." In *Farm Structure: A Historical Perspective on Changes in the Number and Size of Farms*, U.S. Congress, 74–79. Washington, DC: 96th Congress, 2nd Session, Senate Committee on Agriculture, Nutrition, and Forestry.

Carvalho, J. and Holland, D. 1985. "The Changing Mode of Production in American Agriculture: Emerging Conflicts in Agriculture's Role in the Reproduction of Advanced Capitalism." *Review of Radical Political Economics* 17 (4): 1–27.

Davidson, O. G. 1990. *Broken Heartland: The Rise of America's Rural Ghetto*. New York: Free Press.

Fraad, H., Resnick, S., and Wolff, R. 1989, Winter. "For Every Knight in Shining Armor, There's a Castle Waiting to Be Cleaned: A Marxist–Feminist Analysis of the Household." *Rethinking Marxism* 2 (4): 9–69.

Gabriel, S. 1990, Spring. "Ancients: A Marxian Theory of Self-Exploitation." *Rethinking Marxism* 3 (1): 85–106.

Goldschmidt, W. 1978. *As You Sow: Three Studies in the Social Consequences of Agribusiness*. Montclair, NJ: Allanheld, Osmun.

Heffernan, W. D. 1989. "Confidence and Courage in the Next 50 Years." *Rural Sociology* 54 (2): 149–168.

Jefferson, T. 1903. "Notes on Virginia." In *The Writings of Thomas Jefferson*, ed. The Thomas Jefferson Memorial Association, 1–334. Washington, DC: The Thomas Jefferson Memorial Association.

Marion, B. W. ed. 1986. *The Organization and Performance of the U.S. Food System*. Lexington, MA: D. C. Heath and Company.

McIntyre, R. 1992, Fall. "Theories of Uneven Development and Social Change." *Rethinking Marxism* 5 (3): 75–105.

Mooney, P. H. 1986. "The Political Economy of Credit in American Agriculture." *Rural Sociology* 51 (4): 449–470.

Paarlberg, D. 1987. "Tarnished Gold: Fifty Years of New Deal Farm Programs." *Imprimis*. Hillsdale, MI: Hillsdale College.

Pelton, B. M. 1984. *We Belong to the Land: Memories of a Midwesterner*. Ames: Iowa State University Press.

Resnick, S. and Wolff, R. 1987. *Knowledge and Class: A Marxian Critique of Political Economy*. Chicago: University of Chicago Press.

Rosenfeld, R. A. 1985. *Farm Women: Work, Farm and Family in the United States*. Chapel Hill: University of North Carolina Press.

Sachs, C. E. 1983. *The Invisible Farmers: Women in Agricultural Production*. Totowa, NJ: Rowman and Allanheld.

Stormes, J. R. 1988, Summer. "The Poor in the United States: A Class-Analytic Approach." *Rethinking Marxism* 1 (2): 76–102.

Strange, M. 1988. *Family Farming: A New Economic Vision*. Lincoln: University of Nebraska Press.

Tweeten, L. 1988. "Domestic Food and Agricultural Policy Research Directions." In *Agriculture and Rural Areas Approaching the Twenty-first Century: Challenges for Agricultural Economics*, eds. R. J. Hildreth, Kathryn L. Lipton, Kenneth C. Clayton, Carl C. O'Connor, 122–144. Ames: Iowa State University Press.

United States Department of Agriculture. 1981. *A Time to Choose: Summary Report on the Structure of Agriculture*. Washington, DC: U.S. Government Printing Office.

United States Department of Commerce, Bureau of the Census. 1989. *1987 Census of Agriculture*. Washington, DC: U.S. Government Printing Office.

Wilson, J. 1986. "The Political Economy of Contract Farming." *Review of Radical Political Economics* 18 (4): 47–70.

Children as an Exploited Class

HARRIET FRAAD

The Victorian period was the height of the Religious Right's family nostalgia: the stay-at-home mom and the out-to-work dad. This ideal has dominated family ideology from the 1800s to the 1980s. Reality, however, has been different from the projected ideal. Mothers and children of the Victorian poor worked as servants, separated from their own families, maintaining the households of the wealthy. However, it was not only the labor of poor U.S. women and children that diverged from the ideal of the patriarchal family: Rampant child and wife abuse of all kinds, child labor, and the Victorian penchant for child sexual abuse were of course contradictory to the family ideology of the period. Moreover, as this paper indicates, strongly posited and sentimentalized ideologies of benevolent families are often a smoke screen for systematic oppression and exploitation.

In the United States today, the ideology and the reality of the patriarchal family are weakened. A slow transformation of the patriarchal family probably began with the end of the household as a production unit and, not coincidentally, with Freud's writings, which revealed the family as the cradle of neurosis and psychosis. The results are now starkly visible. Three quarters of the mothers of young children are not at home but in the labor force. Of mothers whose children are under two years old, fully 52% work outside of the home (Berry 1993). One quarter of mothers have never been married. Others are divorced or separated. Realities of wife battering, rampant child abuse and neglect are now revealed as part of family life. The myth of the nurturant patriarchal family is dying while the Religious Right mobilizes to resuscitate its corpse. Rather than joining the necrophiliac Right we may take this opportunity to explore the position of children in the United States and intercede in their lives by providing them and their parents with alternatives to isolated family units.

Our search for different ways to organize domestic life may be eased by reexamining the work of communitarian socialists and materialist feminists who saw the need for alternatives when Victorian family ideology was at its height. They considered the private dwelling to be the greatest obstacle to women's social and economic equality. Although their emphasis was on the liberation of women rather than children, they fought for social responsibility for child rearing and created a multiplicity of alternatives to isolated patriarchal family units (Hayden 1985). The demands of the materialist feminists and communitarian socialists such as industrialized house work, communal dining rooms and kitchens, and free quality child and infant care remain unrealized.

Although the Victorian ideal family is presented as natural, optimal, and constant, parents in private homes have never been reliable guardians for children. From the beginning of time parents have not only routinely abandoned and neglected their children, but also sexually abused and battered them (de Mause 1974, 1990, 1991; Rush 1980). The ideal of the protective parent masks household oppression and exploitation. Currently, some of the parameters of that exploitation have changed. The rape and battery of one's children that were previously legal, are now formally illegal, although rarely prosecuted.

There are still the flimsiest of safety nets for children. Protection barely exists where it is most needed. Children need to be protected from their most dangerous predators, their parents. In the most extensive incest study to date, Diana Russell (1986) found that 16–21% of girls are victims of incest before the age of eighteen. Across the United States every year an estimated 2,000–5,000 children die from child abuse. Between 25% and 50% of those deaths occur in families that are not only known to authorities but have already been singled out as high risk cases (Duger 1992; Ulig 1987). In 1992 a U.S. child was reported abused or neglected every thirteen seconds. Every three hours a U.S. child is murdered (Children's Defense Fund 1992). These murders result from the abandonment of children to their families. Most of the murders were committed at home by fathers, mothers, relatives, or family friends babysitting at the parents' request. Children are almost twice as likely to be abused at home as they are in day-care centers (Faludi 1988).

The case of missing children is yet another example of a safety net in the wrong place that permits children to plunge. Ubiquitous photos of missing children convey warnings: "Marauding, stranger–kidnappers may abduct your children." However, here again, parents pose the greatest threat. Every year between 200 and 300 children are abducted by strangers, while 350,000 are abducted by family members. Another 127,000, usually referred to as "throw-aways," are evicted annually from their homes by parents who provide their children with no alternative care. Fully 1 million children run away from home. The majority of these runaways flee from parents who abuse them (Forst and Blomquist 1991; Lee 1993; Merkel-Holguin 1993).

How can our society ignore these now well-documented statistics on parent to child abuse? There are many threads tangled in the knot of childhood injury. That knot would come untied if adults were not so distanced from children and from our own childhood memories. There is an "othering" of children that allows us to imagine that children are not at all like adults. Adults often imagine that children do not have the need to be spared pain, or to be respected. For adults, being physically struck is an assault rather than a learning experience, but many adults advise physical force as a method of teaching children how to behave (Greven 1990; Pleck 1987). Would these biblical quotations ever apply to teaching adults? "Chasten [beat] thy son while there is hope and let not thy soul spare for his crying" (Proverbs 19:18); "Withhold not correction from the child: for if thou beatest him with the rod, he shall not die. Thou shalt beat him with the rod, and shalt deliver his soul from hell" (Proverbs 23:13–14).

Although for adults it is important to be respected, it is routine for well-meaning adults to trivialize children's passionately experienced truths (Miller 1982). It is similarly important for adults to know what is happening to them. However, few adults imagine that for children, who have little control over their own lives, it is crucial to know what to expect or what has happened to them. Few parents think that children deserve explanations.

Children need the right to acknowledge their own childhood feelings and needs in order to be able to recognize themselves as they are. They learn who they are by observing their reflections in a kind of hall of mirrors of other people's reactions, which reflect to children what the children are. Parental reflections are those that children constantly see. They therefore have a powerful impact on children's developing self-conceptions. When they are not recognized as the complex, passionate people that they are, children learn to enact what the adults in their lives project or reflect back to them. If the dominant adults react to children as if their feelings and needs are a nuisance, a burden, or an imposition, children base their own assessment of the import of their feelings, ideas and needs on those parents' reactions. A child will feel anger and pain at the rejection of self that she feels she needs to make in order to be valued by her parents.

Children correctly perceive that they will not survive without caretaking adults. Therefore, if the caretaking adults reflect a child's desires as unacceptable, the child will do likewise and smother his own desires, leaving a residue of pain, rage, and frustration. Expressions of the latter are likewise unacceptable. They will enter the child's unconscious with other "unspeakable" feelings, only to emerge later in symptomatic behavior. Thus, when children become adults they may experience rage at their own children's demands for just the kind of attention that the adult's repressed child-self never had. These adults, having sealed off as "other" their emotional experiences of childhood, now project them onto their own children. Repression permits these adults to abuse children and deny the pain they cause. Adults thwarted in their childhood emotions may vent them on a convenient target. Who can be more helpless, dependent, and convenient than one's children? Repressed adults transmit the curse of cruelty to their children, who pass it to their own children, and so on.

CHILDREN AS AN EXPLOITED CLASS

If we do not assume that family means nurturance, we may be able to answer a puzzling question. Because a couple is capable of conceiving, does that mean they will be capable of the endless labor involved in protecting a totally vulnerable young life? That continuous demanding twenty-four-hour labor can be performed most consistently and well by a carefully organized, collective labor effort. If family is to mean continuous care, support, and protection, it does not make sense to assume that anyone who can get pregnant can also automatically support, nurture, and protect a child. Why would we make that assumption?

An analysis of the household that is the product of right-wing nostalgia may yield some answers to our question. In this particular kind of household, the wife labors in a home with means of production (stove, vacuum cleaner, etc.) provided by her husband. She performs both necessary labor (cooking, cleaning, etc. for herself) and surplus labor (also cooking, cleaning, etc. for her husband (Fraad, Resnick, and Wolff 1989, 1994). In addition, she tries to please the lord of the manor with sexual and emotional services. Like a feudal serf, the wife produces surplus for another and hopes for love and protection. Within the ideology that helps to perpetuate this kind of family, the wife is not viewed as a laborer. Instead she is "nest making," or expressing love as part of a genetic emotional destiny quite parallel to the religious destiny that converted the labor of the medieval serf into a mission ordained by God. The knowledges and skills the wife acquires through housework and caring intimately for her family are unspoken, unrecognized, and unpaid. The invisibility of the homemaker's labor facilitates her household exploitation.

In the early nineteenth century U.S. law permitted the father to exercise authority over a wife and child as he would over his other property. What happened in the family was considered a private matter under paternal jurisdiction, not a concern of the state. Thus feudalism, though abolished by the state, could flourish in the family. It is this family, free from state interference, that right-wing "family values" institutions promote.

In feudal-type households, children may also be serfs, producing surplus for their fathers alongside their mothers, or they may be exempted for all or part of their childhood from such surplus production. In either case they are expected to "serve" both parents; a servitude that is primarily emotional. Children cannot help but try to be what their parents want. In Lacanian terms children strive to be the desire of their parents (Lacan 1968, 1982). They toil to satisfy the often contradictory and changing desires of their parents. Their survival in fact depends on their pleasing the adults in charge, or they come to feel that it does. Often children in feudal households feel that the desire of their parents is to have created the parents *they themselves* had wanted when they were children, instead of focusing on children who now require their care. Children may spend a lifetime straining to compensate their parents for the burdensome crime of being children and therefore needful of care. They often withhold that which they most desire out of the wish to be adequate in the eyes of parents they can never please enough.

Many child–parent emotional arrangements parallel other classic feudal obligations between serfs and lords as well. Both feudal serfs and their lords swore to love each other. Lords usually protected their serfs from danger from other lords, leaving their serfs little protection from their ostensible protectors, the lords themselves. Feudal parents demand love and obedience and often claim to protect their children from the predations of strangers, while the children have little protection from those same parents. Although there are some legal protections against child abuse, child murder, sexual abuse, and incest, the legal system is not directly available to children. Parents and their children, like feudal lords and their serfs, are bound by mutual obligations. Like feudal serfs with lords, the power to enforce these bonds is overwhelmingly in the hands of the parents.

Many children sustain themselves emotionally while toiling to produce happiness for their parents. Their own pressing emotional concerns may be ignored, and their hard emotional labors may be unrecognized in the same way that their mother's domestic labor may be unacknowledged. They are reported to be as congenitally "happy" as the happy housewives in 1950s television commercials. In a Marxian analogy, children provide their own emotionally necessary labor and a surplus for their parents.

Children are legally tied to their parents as feudal serfs were tied to the land. If they run away, those that shelter them may be prosecuted for "harboring runaways." When runaway children are found they are returned unless they are legally "emancipated." It is telling that the legal release of children from parental custody is referred to in the legal vocabulary for releasing slaves from bondage: It is called the "emancipation of minors."

In many families, parents want and need their children to be whatever it is that the parents need, rather than what may be best for the children. Parents unconsciously school their children in emotional servitude and parental needs. They rear their children within their own neurotic limitations while they often provide some physical safety, some support, some protection from outsiders, some form of love, and some concern for what they feel lies in the child's best interest, however tainted with self-serving that may be.

Children may be involved in exploitative relationships as exploiters. The "spoiled" child who commands ever more material possessions and parental services mirrors the feudal lord in exploiting the labor of his parents. Yet, these children are still fulfilling their parents' desire for children who can have everything. Parents, like all other humans, have conflicting desires. They may overindulge their children's demands, while at the same time these parents may also need their children to be undemanding. Children's oppressive behavior may simultaneously fulfill some of their parents' needs while it frustrates others. Children navigate the contradictions, doing their best to please.

Some parents' greatest desire is to see their children grow up to become independent, fulfilled people. It is possible for these parents to strive to provide encompassing support to their children. They labor to recognize and appreciate their children as separate people. In this case the children will strain to fulfill the desires of their parents by straining to achieve independence, self-acknowledgment, and happiness for themselves since those are the desires of their parents. In such families *both* parents and children emotionally labor to provide fulfillment of their own and each others' affective needs. No one is alone in creating emotional surplus for another who appropriates it; both individuals involved toil communally for themselves and each other. This type of family participates in a kind of Marxian communal class process, in which family members jointly produce and together appropriate emotional services.

CHILDREN AND THE STRUGGLE OVER FAMILY VALUES

At different points in U.S. history there have been struggles concerning the exclusive authority of parents, and particularly fathers, over children. One such struggle was over state mandated, regulated public education. Today, the Religious Right leads a similar battle over public child care, after-school care, and state protection against child abuse and sexual violation. Conflicts over so-called "family values" are in fact partly class struggles over the household serfdom of women and children. Public child care, after-school programs, and protections against child abuse and sexual violation are conditions of existence for women's and children's emancipation from feudal class exploitation and emotional oppression in households. The Right's agenda of suppressing abortion and birth control, denying women's independence of family roles, and opposing children's rights and public child care, reinforces conditions of existence for the maintenance of the feudal family.

Children in the United States are in crisis. Their educational attainment levels are at record lows while their poverty, crime, and suicide rates are at record highs (Select Committee on Children Youth and Families 1989; Children's Defense Fund 1991, 1992, 1994; Children's Defense Fund and the Black Community Crusade for Children, 1993; Merkel-Holguin 1993). Children's care is increasingly provided by overworked, over-stressed mothers. While both the career aspirations and the wage-earning needs of mothers have increased markedly, responsibilities for housework, child rearing, and jobs combine to keep mothers exhausted and to prevent them from being equal to fathers in the workplace. More than 50% of women in top management positions are childless; while women with large families have the lowest wages of all (Hewlett 1986). Although 90% of U.S. women have children (Hewlett 1986), there is evidence to suggest that a growing number regret it. In a poll inviting response from her readers, presumed to be average Americans, Ann Landers found that 70% of the parents reported anonymously that if they could do it all over again they would not have children (Sommerville 1990). Notwithstanding the many biases that attend such surveys, the widespread regrets at parenting are testimony to both the strain of parenting and a change in family ideology that would allow parents to admit their regrets.

The crisis of child care and the necessity for women to enter the job market helps to create an environment in which social responsibility for (i.e., mass provision of) child care is urgent. However, there are significant ideological barriers to thinking and moving in this direction. Right-wing ideology has in the last twelve years successfully achieved a kind of displacement (Resnick and Wolff 1994). Peoples' sense of being exploited is projected from the capitalist sector (and everywhere else it occurs) exclusively onto the public sector. The government is presented as the victimizer while corporations join individuals as victims. The feeling that if our government systematically fails to provide us with what we need, we should radically transform it, is repressed. Instead the dominant view is that if our government systematically fails us, then the public sector should be gutted.

Transformation of our system of private child rearing to a system of public services would be costly and require governmental action. It could address some of the problems of inequity between men and women while providing top quality child care. It is precisely because social responsibility for child rearing could accomplish these goals that it encounters right-wing opposition. Although Americans generally cringe when discussing collective kitchens, they readily embrace the collective kitchens of McDonalds and the rest of the monumentally profitable fast-food industry. Although the idea of collective noncommodity child care is anathema to many, quality child care centers are so attractive that they must turn away many of their applicants.

COLLECTIVE, COMMUNAL CHILD CARE

What would collective child care mean? It would mean a different organization of society with children's care shifted from the individual shoulders of parents to collectively shared public child care facilities. Ingenious and varied possibilities for communal child rearing have been developing since the nineteenth century (Hayden 1985). To implement these kinds of child rearing strategies on a national scale would require a revolutionary transformation of our society, which does not seem immanent. However, at this moment there are transitional forms such as parenting centers, group homes, after-school, weekend, and summer camps, and neighborhood family counseling centers. None of these services would have to be mandatory. They are so desperately needed that I am convinced they would be sought after and fiercely defended once established on a voluntary basis.

For children this could mean the beginning of a change from being a serf, isolated and dependent on the care of whomever bore them, to full personhood. In class terms, it could mean a transition from household serfdom to full citizenship in a communal household setting. At present, the only possibility for children's liberation from oppressive homes occurs if their parents recognize their own inability to care for their children and voluntarily bear the social stigma of relinquishing them to what are often inadequate state agencies or inadequate relatives. Otherwise, if the children's neglect and/or abuse is sufficiently dramatic and if it is frequently reported, it might get the attention of overworked child care bureaucrats who could initiate custody proceedings. When public agencies finally remove children from abusive and/or neglectful homes, these agencies often place the children in equally neglectful or abusive foster homes (Armstrong 1989).

We can now combine the newly developed tools of Marxian class analysis of households with innovative psychoanalytic understandings of the intimate arena and with communitarian and materialist feminist understandings of domestic life. We need to apply this combination of powerful tools to a deeply exploited, oppressed, and neglected group: the children of the United States. Socially responsible child care will be one step towards freeing both our children and the child within each of us.

ACKNOWLEDGMENTS

In this paper I am indebted to the work of Richard Wolff and Stephen Resnick in Marxian class theory, and Lloyd de Mause and Florence Rush on child abuse. My thanks to Richard Wolff, Julie Graham, Stephen Resnick, and Antonio Callari for careful readings of previous versions of the paper.

REFERENCES

Armstrong, L. 1989. *Solomon Says*. New York: Simon and Schuster.
Berry, M. 1993. *The Politics of Parenthood*. New York: Penguin.
Children's Defense Fund. 1991. *The State of America's Children 1991*. Washington, DC: Children's Defense Fund.
——. 1992. *The State of America's Children 1992*. Washington, DC: Children's Defense Fund.
——. 1994. *The State of America's Children 1994*. Washington, DC: Children's Defense Fund.
Children's Defense Fund and the Black Community Crusade for Children. 1993. *Progress and Peril: Black Children in America*. Washington, DC: Children's Defense Fund.
de Mause, L. 1974. "The Evolution of Childhood." In *The History of Childhood*, ed. L. de Mause. New York: Harper.
——. 1990. "The History of Child Assault." *The Journal of Psychohistory* 18 (2): 11–29.
——. 1991. "The Universality of Incest." *The Journal of Psychohistory*. 19 (2): 123–164.
Duger, C. 1992. "Shortage of Trained Caseworkers Imperils Young Victims of Abuse." *New York Times* (December 28): A1.
Faludi, S. 1988. "Are the Kids Alright?" *Mother Jones* (November): 16–19.

Forst, M. and Blomquist, M. 1991. *Missing Children*. New York: Macmillan.

Fraad, H.; Resnick, S.; and Wolff, R. 1989, Winter. "For Every Knight in Shining Armor, There's a Castle Waiting to Be Cleaned: A Marxist-Feminist Analysis of the Household." *Rethinking Marxism* 2 (4): 9–69.

——. 1994. *Bringing It All Back Home*. London: Pluto.

Greven, P. 1990. *Spare the Child*. New York: Random House.

Hayden, D. 1985. *The Grand Domestic Revolution*. Cambridge, MA: MIT Press.

Hewlett, S. A. 1986. *A Lesser Life*. New York: William Morrow.

Lacan, J. 1968. *The Language of the Self*, trans. A. Wilden. New York: Delta (Dell).

——. 1982. *Feminine Sexuality*, eds. J. Mitchell and J. Rose, trans. J. Rose. New York: W. W. Norton.

Lee, F. 1993. "Tracking Leads When the Young Disappear." *New York Times* (February 9): B1–2.

Merkel-Holguin, L. 1993. *The Child Welfare Stat Book*. Washington, DC: Child Welfare League of America.

Miller, A. 1982. *The Drama of the Gifted Child*, trans. R. Ward. New York: Basic Books.

Pleck, E. 1987. *Domestic Tyranny*. New York: Oxford University Press.

Resnick, S. and Wolff, R. 1987. *Knowledge and Class*. Chicago: University of Chicago Press.

——. 1994. "A Tale of Two Crises." In *Bringing It All Back Home*, eds. Fraad, Resnick and Wolff.

Rush, F. 1980. *The Best Kept Secret*. New York: McGraw Hill.

Russell, D. 1986. *The Secret Trauma*. New York: Basic Books.

Select Committee on Children Youth and Families. 1989. *Current Conditions and Recent Trends 1989*. Washington DC: U.S. Government Printing Office.

Sommerville, J. 1990. *The Rise and Fall of Childhood*. New York: Vintage Books.

Ulig, M. 1987. "Many Child Abuse Deaths Come in Cases Where Risk Is Known." *New York Times* (November 9): B1.

Marxism and Archaeology

DEAN J. SAITTA

hat does archaeology have to do with the challenges facing Marxism in the "new world order"? Archaeology is, after all, a science of the past: its subject societies are extinct, its human subjects are dead and mute. Of what possible consequence is archaeological knowledge in a modern world facing unique historical crises? How can archaeology possibly serve a critical Marxist theory looking to nudge this world in a particular direction? Archaeology cannot, by itself, have a dramatic reconstructive effect on contemporary capitalism or other global problems (McGuire 1992; Tilley 1989). But archaeology is not without a radical, emancipatory potential. Two features of archaeology strike me as especially relevant in this regard.

The first directly relates to this volume's theme of possibilities, and has to do with the "otherness" of the remote past. That is, archaeology can tell us about alternative arrangements for organizing social life that existed before the dawn of written history and the age of capitalism. Archaeology is, in fact, the only social science that can study variation in social form over the entirety of humankind's existence on the planet. Further, it is the only social science that can provide access into the everyday lives of all members of society, be they elites, peasants, merchants, craftspeople, slaves, or nomads. Archaeology is thus well positioned to examine the struggles and strategies of a full spectrum of social agents in diverse social circumstances over the long sweep of history. Understanding why various social strategies and alliances succeed or fail in different historical circumstances should be relevant to any science concerned with imagining and creating alternative forms of social life.

The second potentially emancipatory feature of archaeology relates to the subject's enormous popular appeal in cultures here and abroad. In the last couple of years every major American newsweekly has featured a cover story on one archaeological subject or another. Favorite topics have been the origins of modern humans in Africa about 150,000 years ago and, most recently, the Native American world before 1492. The Public Broadcasting System and various cable channels (e.g., "The Learning Channel") regularly feature programs dealing with archaeological subjects. Finally, museums of natural and cultural history infuse archaeological knowledge into the public consciousness on a constant, everyday basis. The museum has been viewed, with reason, as a prime example of Althusser's "Ideological State Apparatus" (e.g., Meltzer 1981). It powerfully shapes public perceptions of society and history, reinforces mainstream social norms and values, and helps legitimize dominant political interests. There is, however, always room for subversion of these dominant interests. Archaeological information about alternative organizational possibilities and histories, when critically contextualized and communicated via narratives and exhibits, can be a powerful means for creating *different* subjectivities that can help the cause of a Marxian critical project. I return to this point below.

The intellectual content and wider social context of archaeology thus should make it of more than passing interest to Marxian thinkers. In the remainder of this paper I want to reaffirm the naturalness of a relationship between Marxian theory and archaeological inquiry. I focus on how each can and has enriched the other, and discuss what this means for intervening in the new world order.

Marx himself may have been first to recognize the importance of archaeological remains to a revolutionary social project. In *Capital* (Marx 1977, 286) Marx notes how ancient tools can be used to investigate extinct forms of society, specifically the social conditions under which labor was produced (see also Kohl 1983). The great British archaeologist V. Gordon Childe furthered the historical materialist project in the West between the 1930s and 1950s (e.g., Childe 1942, 1951). He showed how material objects tell us not only about ways of capturing energy from the environment, but also about the ideas and cultural meanings through which people engage the natural world. Today archaeologists are pushing new frontiers in material culture studies, assisted in part by Marxian theory's unique understanding of social differences. We recognize today that objects, architecture, and socially created landscapes—even the most nondescript and mundane—actively articulate with *all* aspects of social life. Material culture actively structures and constrains human action and interaction, and is routinely used to create, reproduce, and challenge existing social arrangements.

Some of the best examples of this dialectic between people and objects come out of historical archaeology and especially studies of emergent capitalism in North America. Robert Paynter's (1982) use of David Harvey's (1973) ideas about the "space economy" to study colonial settlement patterns in New England shows how space was used by colonial elites to accumulate and control social surplus. Mark Leone and coworkers (Leone and Shackel 1987), in a manner reminiscent of Braverman's (1974) work on technology and the degradation of labor, have shown how everyday domestic objects including forks and clocks served to segment and standardize daily behaviors in ways that naturalized and legitimized the rhythms of industrial capitalism. In so doing, these objects helped to create in their users the distinctively *individualist* subjectivities upon which industrial capitalism depends. Finally, other historical archaeologists have explored how subordinate groups such as African slaves used material culture to build ideologies of resistance to exploitative social relations (e.g., Ferguson 1992).

The more we understand the dialectical relationship between material culture and social reality in well-controlled historical contexts the more complicated and interesting the *prehistoric* past becomes. Studies of prehistory can make two contributions to Marxian thought. First, they can correct simple views of precapitalist social formations that are still commonplace in Marxian theory. Marxian scholars tend to underestimate the variability that exists in precapitalist social formations or "modes of production" (Hindess and Hirst 1975). Marxian models of precapitalist society are largely based on ethnographic information gathered from societies in the process of being transformed by expanding global capitalism. Thus, these models are not the best guides for exploring the enormous organizational diversity that existed prior to and independently of capitalism. Alternatively, interpretive models constructed out of general social theory and informed by the substantive empirical detail of specific archaeological cases can facilitate more interesting and meaningful comparisons of social arrangements across time, space, and environmental context.

Second, prehistory can teach us something significant about the possibilities for variation within, and characteristic tension points of, specifically *communal* social arrangements. It's my hunch that the vast majority of prehistoric, precapitalist societies known thus far were variants on a communal theme. What Steve Cullenberg (1992) might call a "thin" definition of communalism has been especially useful in exploring these prehistoric variants. On a thin definition of communalism— and here I also draw on the work of Amariglio (1984), Jensen (1982), and Resnick and Wolff (1988)—there is no necessary correlation between communal relations of surplus labor appropriation (i.e., communal class processes) and the various other social conditions that sustain communalism. That is, there is no requirement that communalism be attended by consensual decision making, equal access to property, or an egalitarian distribution of wealth. The only stipulation is that surplus labor be collectively produced and distributed. A thin definition is appealing because it allows for variation and complexity in *all* the social processes that organize communal life.

I have found a thin definition of communalism very helpful in interpreting the archaeological record of prehistoric North America (Saitta 1988). Like data in other disciplines, archaeological data can be remarkably ill behaved. In certain times and places the North American data on human settlement, production, and exchange behavior are at best ambiguous and at worse contradictory. Observable material patterns often do not square with the archaeological expectations of mainstream interpretive models, models that stipulate a close correlation between the political, economic, and cultural processes that structure social life. Thus there is a deep uncertainty within contemporary archaeology about whether specific empirical patterns reflect communal or noncommunal labor relations, accumulationist or redistributionalist political economies, individualist or collectivist ideologies, and so on. However, the longer I work back and forth between a thin Marxian definition of communalism and the North American data, the more the empirical ambiguities and contradictions begin to make sense.

In some places these ambiguities suggest communal landscapes of unprecedented geographical scale and complexity. Foremost among these landscapes is the so-called Chaco Phenomenon in the Four Corners area of the American Southwest. (See Sebastian 1992 for a review of thinking about this archaeological case.) The Chaco Phenomenon refers to a set of distinctive styles in public architecture and ceramic decoration shared by small agricultural communities across the Four Corners area between AD 900–1100. These shared styles cover an area of 60,000 square miles, and they overlay other, distinctively local patterns of variation in domestic architecture and ceramics. The center of the Chaco Phenomenon was a group of large, multistoried, labor-intensive masonry "towns" located in Chaco Canyon in northwestern New Mexico. The largest of these towns average almost 500 rooms in size. The towns are especially striking in light of their environmental context, a desolate, treeless setting characterized by thin soils and precious little rainfall. The most distant communities exhibiting the Chacoan architectural style lie 200 miles from the rim of Chaco Canyon. Tying these communities together—and further indicating the complexity of the Chacoan social

system—is an extensive network of formally constructed and labor-intensive avenues or "roads." At least seven major road systems emanate from
Chaco Canyon and reach into Arizona, Colorado, and Utah. The roads
collectively run up to 1500 miles in length (Stein 1989).

For some scholars the unprecedented scale and labor-intensive nature of the Chacoan system implies the existence of a tributary chiefdom,
with the tribute takers residing at the Chaco Canyon towns. The notion
of tributary chiefdom implies social class divisions if, as is usually the case,
one defines tribute relations as inherently exploitative (i.e., primary producers have no say over the terms of surplus appropriation nor the
amounts of surplus appropriated; see Wessman 1981). Other scholars
postulate the existence of a Chacoan tributary state maintained through
coercive force (Wilcox 1993). In short, mainstream theory looks at Chaco
and discovers us—individualism, monopolies of power, class divisions, and
exploitation. If not exactly "us," then certainly a variety of familiar, middle
class anxieties having to do with population size, resource availability,
and so on.

A thin definition of communalism, however, allows for a more egalitarian alternative. This alternative strikes me as equally consistent with
the available data. In fact, it may even be more consistent, given new
information about Chacoan towns and roads. Recent studies suggest that
the large towns at the Chaco core were, despite their massiveness, *vacant*
for most of the year, save for a small caretaker population (Lekson,
Windes, Stein, and Judge 1988). Moreover, some of these towns display
trash mounds whose contents (broken pots, animal bone) are out of
proportion with the number of estimated full-time inhabitants. It is thus
plausible that the core towns bustled only during seasonal, ceremonial
aggregations of "pilgrims" who brought resources, marriageable offspring, and ideas from outlying areas. Further, the roads along which
these pilgrims would have travelled make little sense from a strictly utilitarian or economic standpoint. The roads (1) do not consistently run to
economically important resource areas, (2) do not show the greatest labor
investments in expected areas (e.g., where topography is most difficult,
(3) lack evidence of associated construction materials and campsites, and
(4) often connect settlements not occupied at the same time (Stein 1989;
Roney 1992; Fowler and Stein 1992). They are thus difficult to square
with the movement of tribute-extracting armies or labor-bearing client
populations as stipulated by class division models. Instead, the archaeological context of these roads suggests a highly structured, ceremonial
use (Stein 1989) which would be consistent with the inference of collective pilgrimage festivals in Chaco Canyon. Such festivals may have provided a context for communal religious observances as well as the communal appropriation of social labor for town and road construction. The

Chaco roads may have functioned as "symbolic umbilicals" or, as the modern Navaho suggest, "sacred tubes" for the transfer of people as well as spiritual essences critical to the reproduction of communal life (Fowler and Stein 1992). Another especially striking aspect of the Chaco Phenomenon is its apparent multiethnic and multilinguistic character, as inferred from its impressive geographical scale and the existence of significant formal variation in material culture at local levels. This conclusion is strengthened by the fact that Chaco Canyon is claimed as ancestral territory by a diverse group of modern Pueblo Indians (e.g., the residents of Hopi, Zuni, and Acoma).

In light of all this, I'm tempted to interpret Chaco as a form of community recently discussed in the abstract by David Ruccio (1992). That is, I see it as a communal enterprise "conceived in multiplicity and difference in an open social reality" (Ruccio 1992, 19), and held together by a sense of community (a "being in common"; see Nancy 1991) that thrived on and celebrated social difference rather than subordinating difference to strict regulation and control. If these ideas about the Chaco Phenomenon are reasonable, then the Chaco case challenges mainstream theoretical expectations that increases in societal scale, labor investment in monumental construction, and specialized forms of production are inevitably and necessarily attended by the erosion of communality and the rise of class divisions. It also provides a concrete historical example of just the kind of complex communality that can be useful in critically rethinking communalism's forms, limitations, and potentialities.

Other examples of complex communality likely await reconstruction in prehistory. The challenge for archaeology is to build interpretive theory to grasp these communal alternatives. I think it is important to preserve the Marxian focus on surplus labor—that is, class relations of surplus extraction and distribution—in building such theory, given the theoretical productivity of thin definitions of communalism. A theoretical interest in labor is still undeveloped in archaeology, however, and Marxian categories for capturing formal variation in labor flows are still a minor part of everyday archaeological discourse. Paynter (1989) notes that it has only been recently that the word "capitalism" has been admitted into polite company among historical archaeologists. Concepts for studying noncapitalist labor relations are entering the company of prehistoric archaeologists just as slowly. This situation needs to be remedied if archaeologists are serious about sorting through the empirical ambiguity that confounds mainstream models, and about understanding the novel and complex relationships between flows of labor, power, and meaning likely implied by such ambiguity.

Another challenge for archaeology is how to press insights about the "otherness" of the past into the service of a critical Marxian project.

This returns us to the popular narratives and exhibitions that draw people to archaeology and that simultaneously shape their thinking about the nature of society and history. It is through such cultural processes that different forms of subjectivity and consciousness are created in society, and it is in this arena that archaeology can perhaps best realize its radical potential in the new world order. Some of the ways in which archaeology can help bring about a new subjectivity—a distinctively *collective* subjectivity or a consciousness of "being in common"—include the following:

1. Archaeologists can emphasize that competition and other forms of capitalist rationality are historically contingent rather than timeless phenomena, and that the vast bulk of human existence has in fact been communally organized in ways we are only now beginning to comprehend.
2. Archaeological study can reveal the darker side of the economic rationality written into and celebrated by mainstream stories of human history—the drudgery, monotony, isolation, anxiety, and alienation that often attend conditions of capitalist production— as contrasted with the richness of the collective economic and cultural life evident at Chaco Canyon and elsewhere.
3. Via the common denominator of human labor, archaeologists can stress the common existential problems that tie people of all historical epochs together (Chaco folk and colonial New Englanders alike), and also the enormous variety of ways in which people solved these problems. Such a perspective seems desperately needed in order to create a new consciousness of class to go along with, and perhaps serve as an antidote to, those already formed around race, gender, and nationality.

This challenge to reach the wider public will not be easily met. Stories of a critical archaeology are inherently less entertaining than those of a "cult" archaeology that invokes alien space invaders and/or lost tribes of Atlanteans to explain the past. They are also less comforting than stories from a mainstream archaeology that looks into the past and rediscovers the present, or at least an unbroken evolutionary trajectory leading from Stone Age "primitive communism" to democratic capitalism and culminating today with what some see as the "end of history."

Happily, however, gains are being made. Historical archaeology is actively contributing to a critical project by showing the historical origins of capitalism and the forms of economic rationality and consciousness associated with it. Prehistoric archaeology, for its part, is providing the raw material for rethinking and perhaps even reconstructing communal social forms. Clearly, Marxism and archaeology have much to offer each other. An archaeology informed by Marxian theory and a Marxian theory informed by archaeology should allow each enterprise better to meet its scientific and emancipatory goals.

REFERENCES

Amariglio, J. 1984. "Forms of the Commune and Primitive Communal Class Processes." *Association for Economic and Social Analysis*, Discussion Paper No. 19. Amherst: Department of Economics, University of Massachusetts.

Braverman, H. 1974. *Labor and Monopoly Capital*. New York: Monthly Review Press.

Childe, V. G. 1942. *What Happened in History*. Harmondsworth, England: Penguin.

———. 1951. *Social Evolution*. New York: Schuman.

Cullenberg, S. 1992, Summer. "Socialism's Burden: Toward a 'Thin' Definition of Socialism." *Rethinking Marxism* 5: 64–83.

Ferguson, L. 1992. *Uncommon Ground: Archaeology and Early African America 1650–1800*. Washington, DC: Smithsonian Institution Press.

Fowler, A. and J. Stein. 1992. "The Anasazi Great House in Space, Time, and Paradigm." In *Anasazi Regional Organization and the Chaco System*, ed. D. Doyel, 101–122. Albuquerque, NM: Maxwell Museum of Anthropology.

Harvey, D. 1973. *Social Justice and the City*. London: Arnold.

Hindess, B. and Hirst, P. 1975. *Pre-Capitalist Modes of Production*. London: Routledge and Kegan Paul.

Jensen, R. 1982. "The Transition from Primitive Communism: The Wolof Social Formation." *Journal of Economic History* 42: 69–78.

Kohl, P. 1983. "Archaeology and Prehistory." In *A Dictionary of Marxist Thought*, ed. T. Bottomore, 25–28. Cambridge, MA: Harvard University Press.

Lekson, S.; Windes, T.; Stein J.; and Judge, W. J. 1988. "The Chaco Canyon Community." *Scientific American* 259: 100–109.

Leone, M. and Shackel, P. 1987. "Forks, Clocks and Power." In *Mirror and Metaphor*, ed. D. Ingersoll and G. Bronitsky, 45–61. Lanham, MD: University Press of America.

Marx, K. 1977. *Capital*, Vol. 1. New York: Vintage Books.

McGuire, R. 1992. *A Marxist Archaeology*. Orlando: Academic Press.

Meltzer, D. 1981. "Ideology and Material Culture." In *Modern Material Culture: The Archaeology of Us*, ed. R. Gould and M. Schiffer, 113–125. New York: Academic Press.

Nancy, J. 1991. *The Inoperative Community*. Minneapolis: University of Minnesota Press.

Paynter, R. 1982. *Models of Spatial Inequality*. New York: Academic Press.

———. 1989 "Steps to an Archaeology of Capitalism." In *The Recovery of Meaning*, ed. M. Leone and P. Potter, 407–433. Washington, DC: Smithsonian Institution Press.

Resnick, S. and Wolff, R. 1988, Spring. "Communism: Between Class and Class-less." *Rethinking Marxism* 1: 14–42.

Roney, J. 1992. "Prehistoric Roads and Regional Integration in the Chacoan System." In *Anasazi Regional Organization and the Chaco System*, ed. D. Doyel, 123–131. Albuquerque, NM: Maxwell Museum of Anthropology.

Ruccio, D. 1992, Summer. "Failure of Socialism, Future of Socialists?" *Rethinking Marxism* 5: 9–22.

Saitta, D. J. 1988, Winter. "Marxism, Prehistory, and Primitive Communism." *Rethinking Marxism* 1: 146–169.

Sebastian, L. 1992 *The Chaco Anasazi: Sociopolitical Evolution in the Prehistoric American Southwest*. Cambridge, England: Cambridge University Press.

Stein, J. 1989. "The Chaco Roads: Clues to an Ancient Riddle?" *El Palacio* 94: 4–17.

Tilley, C. 1989. "Archaeology as Socio-political Action in the Present." In *Critical Traditions in Contemporary Archaeology*, ed. V. Pinsky and A. Wylie, 104–115. Cambridge, England: Cambridge University Press.

Wessman, J. 1981. *Anthropology and Marxism*. Cambridge, MA: Schenkman.

Wilcox, D. 1993. "The Evolution of the Chacoan Polity." In *The Chimney Rock Archaeological Symposium*, ed. J. Malville and G. Matlock, 76–90. Fort Collins, CO: USDA Forest Service.

Markets Do Not a Class Structure Make

arkets are one thing, class structures something else. Marxism does contain (1) a critical analysis of markets, (2) a critical analysis of class structures, and (3) explorations of the different ways they can relate to one another in different societies. However, Marxism does *not* conflate, merge, or collapse these two different things into an identity. It does *not* define markets in terms of class structures, nor class structures in terms of markets. Yet, Marxism's systematic and analytically productive distinction and differentiation of markets from class structures now risks being lost in the avalanche of postmortems on the USSR from both the Left and the Right.

For example, many critics of the Soviet system ascribe its difficulties to "socialism," which they define in terms of the *absence* there of markets and their precondition, namely private, alienable property in resources and products. Such critics applaud the post-Soviet "transition to capitalism," the latter defined as privatization plus markets. Critics from the Left denounce privatization and markets, which they likewise understand as the return of capitalism. They urge instead that workers and others inside the former USSR and other Eastern European countries fight to "retain socialism," meaning thereby the planned allocation of resources and products, and state or collective property in means of production. Such uses of "socialism," by conflating class and market, miss Marx's differentiation of these concepts and the insights it yields.

Markets have historically been one alternative arrangement for the *distribution of resources and products.* Planned state allocations of state-owned objects have been another. In contrast, capitalist class structures are one kind of arrangement for the *production and appropriation of surplus labor*; communism is another. In capitalist class structures, the workers who perform surplus labor *do not* also appropriate its fruits; hence, they are exploited. It is rather different people, capitalists, who appropriate the surplus and then decide how, to whom, and for what purposes to distribute the fruits of that surplus labor. In communism, the workers who perform surplus labor also appropriate it collectively and then decide collectively how, to whom, and for what purposes to distribute it.[1] The definitional difference between capitalism and communism, for Marx, hinges on these different class structures—the presence of exploitation in one, its absence in the other—and their social consequences.

Thus, for Marxian theory, the following conclusions flow from these premises: (1) markets may be present or absent in either capitalism or communism, and (2) capitalism may be present or absent when planned allocations of resources and products is the prevalent mode of distributing them. In short, markets are one thing and capitalism is something else. Keeping them separate enables an interpretation of current transitions in Eastern Europe that is sharply different from the interpretation shared by most observers on virtually all sides. Indeed, keeping them separate yields, as argued below, a systematic Marxian alternative viewpoint on the whole set of issues comprising transitions between communism and capitalism and transitions among forms of each class structure.

Marx explicitly recognized that commodity markets and capitalism are not the same thing (1967, 1, 714; 1973, 465–467). Moreover, a few additional examples can illustrate the point conclusively. The products of feudal manors in medieval Europe were sometimes distributed according to the plans of feudal lords, whereas at other times, such products were rather sold as commodities on markets: feudal class structures with and without markets. The products of slave class structures exhibit the same variations across time and region. Likewise, the products of individually self-employed producers may be distributed by plan or by markets; history offers examples of both.

Capitalist class structures have existed with market exchange as the mode of distribution—what is usually taken as the "normal" arrangement—and also without markets. Vertical integrations among firms, after all, represent the abolition of their market exchanges in favor of planned distributions within the integrated enterprises. Such nonmarket distributions have surely not meant that capitalist class structures have ceased to exist in such firms. Examples of economy-wide coexistence of capitalist class structures and nonmarket modes of distribution include "emergencies" of varying durations, such as wars or natural disasters necessitating state controls, rationing, and outright planned distributions. However, there have also been long-lasting partial or complete state-planned distributions among private capitalist enterprises and between them and individual consumers, undertaken in the interests of "economic development" or "social justice" or other objectives.

An especially important twentieth-century example of capitalist class structures coexisting without commodity markets concerns the issue of "state capitalisms." Private capitalism has historically given way repeatedly to state capitalism.[2] This means quite simply that the capitalist exploitation of workers—having nonworkers appropriate their surplus labor in the Marxian sense—has altered from a private to a state form. Instead of private individuals, operating outside of any official or bureaucratic status in or relation to the state and functioning as surplus-appropriating boards of corporate directors, their surplus-appropriating places in the same class structure have been taken by state officials.

In the case of the USSR, notwithstanding the communist goals and rhetorics of many Soviet leaders, what happened in its industries was a transition from pre-1917 private capitalism to Soviet state capitalism.[3] Among the factors that functioned to preclude the establishment of communist class structures in Soviet industry were successive emergency conditions (world war, revolution, foreign invasion, civil war, collectivization of agriculture, and a second world war) and the drive to develop an industrial base quickly. Moreover, the Marxian tradition's deep hostility to markets as modes of distribution led successive Soviet leaderships to combine their particular kind of state capitalist class structure in industry with state-owned means of production and with state-planned allocations of resources and products. The USSR thus represented a (state) capitalist industrial class structure existing largely (but never completely) without commodity markets.

Of course, to argue that markets and class structures are different things is not the same as arguing that they have no impacts upon one another. Depending on the class structure of production, markets will function differently. Depending on the presence or absence of market exchanges as the mode of distribution, specific class structures will function differently. Modes of production and modes of distribution affect one another, in ways depending on the broad social contexts in which they coexist. Yet, that is no warrant for failing to keep their differences in theoretical view. The logic of Marxian theory does not permit inferring the existence of a particular class structure from the presence or absence of markets. Oscillations between market and nonmarket modes of distribution are different from oscillations between capitalist and noncapitalist class structures of production.

Markets, where and when found, have always had complex and contradictory relationships to the class structures with which they coexisted. They have always both enhanced and undermined those class structures. For example, in the history of capitalism, markets have facilitated growth and development in the usually celebrated ways (deepening the division of labor, diffusing new technologies, etc.). However, markets have also provoked those recurring disjunctures between supplies and demands known as recessions, depressions, inflations, and so on. This has prompted similarly recurring demands for controls on markets (chiefly state interventions of varying kinds and degrees) to, in effect, secure their positive impacts on existing class structures while at least constraining their negative impacts.[4]

Every national capitalism displays a unique pattern of ceaselessly shifting qualities and quantities of controls exercised over markets. Their histories demonstrate the contradictory relation between markets and capitalist class structures. Indeed, an enduring feature of twentieth-century economic debates in societies with predominantly capitalist class structures has been a dispute over the positive versus negative impacts of markets on economic activity and over the positive versus negative impacts of controlling markets.

It follows that in considering communist class structures, their possible coexistence with and without markets must be included among their possible forms. That is, workers' collective appropriation and distribution of their own surplus labor may occur with commodity markets in which communist enterprises buy and sell resources and products. Alternatively, centralized or decentralized planning systems may accomplish such distributions. Moreover, a Marxian perspective would anticipate that markets would have contradictory impacts on communist class structures as they have for all other class structures. Societies with markets and predominantly communist class structures would presumably generate comparable calls for controls over or even the suppression of markets, and debates over the wisdom of doing so.

However, one of the many differences between capitalist and communist class-structured economies emerges from the deep hostility to markets per se within both the Marxist and other socialist traditions. They have offered powerful and widely persuasive critiques of markets as institutions that have often undermined community, equality, cooperation, creativity, and democracy. They have also typically viewed them as especially closely associated with the capitalist class structures they oppose. This suggests that they would, if capable of establishing communist class structures, likely also replace markets with planned distribution systems governed by different rules and norms. This leaves, of course, all sorts of possible intermediate situations for shorter or longer periods, such as, for example, allowing markets for some resources, products, and regions, while abolishing them for others.

It seems reasonable to suppose that societies in which communist class structures prevail would likely experiment with and debate the virtues and vices of a range of mixes of "free" and controlled markets and nonmarket distribution systems. The ever-changing cultural, political, economic, and natural contexts of each of such experiments would overdetermine their specific histories. No a priori forecast about them is warranted.

This sort of Marxian analysis, then, differentiates the social organization of distribution by means of markets and private property or otherwise from the social organization of surplus labor—that is, class structure. Because the Soviet experiment of 1917 to 1990 offers a paradigmatic case study of the importance of this differentiation, I will conclude by applying the differentiation to that experiment.

Marxists led the 1917 revolution in Russia. They generally advocated (1) the abolition of private in favor of collective or state property, (2) the abolition of the "anarchy" of markets in favor of the rationally planned state allocation of resources and products, and (3) the institution of "workers' control" (as against capitalists' control) culturally, politically, and economically. They spoke constantly in terms of a communist society as the goal of their transitional situation, labeling the latter as socialism. They did succeed in socializing property in means of production and they did largely suppress markets in favor of centralized economic planning. The political control exercised by the Communist Party represented, to them, the substantial achievement of workers' control in politics and planning. The powers of trade unions, factory committees, and Party committees in industrial enterprises represented, to them, the substantial achievement of workers' control within enterprises.

The question is, did successive Soviet leaderships achieve or even try to achieve a specifically *class* transition within industrial enterprises? That is, was the pre-1917, largely private capitalist exploitation abolished by establishing the productive workers as the collective appropriators and distributors of their own surplus labor? A Marxian analysis premised on the difference between abolishing markets and private property and abolishing capitalist exploitation must answer no.

For a variety of reasons, as noted, Soviet authorities did not establish communist class structures. They established instead state capitalist enterprises with the hope, as Lenin stated explicitly, that state capitalism would provide an intermediate stage leading to communism (Lenin 1932, 37). However, as time passed and establishing communist class structures became a dimmer and more distantly future possibility, Lenin's

admission of a "state capitalist" phase faded away. Soviet discourse increasingly stressed socialism, not communism. And socialism came to
mean state capitalism in industry coupled with state property in means
of production, and centralized state planning instead of markets. Indeed,
the great "class struggle" of the twentieth century came to be fought in
terms of capitalism, defined as private property and markets, versus
socialism, defined as state property and centrally planned distribution
of resources and products.

The issue of class structure was more than merely subordinated to
the issues of markets and property. The issue of class, as the structure of
production, appropriation, and distribution of surplus, largely vanished
from discourse altogether.[5] In a peculiar convergence, supporters as well
as critics of the USSR thus left the terrain of class analysis behind. They
focused their sights and criticisms instead on property and markets and
on what they viewed as their consequences for output, efficiency, income,
and wealth distributions. If they talked of class at all, it was class *defined*
also in terms of property, markets, planning, and so on, rather than class
defined in terms of surplus labor.

From the viewpoint of this paper, the Soviet revolution displaced
private capitalism in favor of state capitalism accompanied by conver-
sions of private to state property and markets to central state planning.
Soviet state capitalism also distributed portions of the surplus it appropriated from industrial workers for levels of mass, collective consumption very different from what existed in most private capitalisms. However, these changes did not reflect or constitute or initiate a transition
to communism. The Soviet experiment never got to that point in its
industrial development.[6]

The crisis of the 1980s and 1990s was, in its class dimension, a state
capitalist crisis. It might thus have been resolved by either a shift back to
private capitalism or a shift forward to a communist or indeed other
noncapitalist class structures. However, in part because class-focused
analysis had given way to property and market-focused analyses, the Soviet
system was seen as socialism or communism, whose only possible alternative was capitalism. Supporters and critics alike had accepted these
parameters of discourse. Both had entered a contest understood as capitalism, private property and markets, versus socialism/communism, state
property and planned distributions. If the latter was in crisis, it made
sense to many on all sides that the appropriate response or resolution
would be transition to the former.

In this way, the conflation—by Marxists—of class structures with distributional structures itself contributed to the recent developments in
Eastern Europe. The lessons for Marxists to draw, then, include some
important self-critical components. Marxists need to reaffirm and reap-

ply the central differentiation of class from distributional structures. Whatever the term "socialism" is to mean, communist refers to a class structure that has yet to be tried on a systematic basis in any industrial economy. The twentieth-century experiments have been made with various combinations of different kinds of capitalism, private and state, coupled with varying mixtures of private and state property, market and nonmarket distribution systems, collective and individual consumption patterns, and so on. While Marxists can and should analyze, criticize, and express preferences among these different kinds of capitalism, the Marxian project remains inseparable from the critique of capitalism in the name and with the goal of transition to a fundamentally different class structure, communism.

NOTES

1. Our interpretation of Marxian theory holds that Marx defined class in a new way, making it a matter of the social arrangement for the production, appropriation, and distribution of surplus labor. He did not simply recirculate the long-existing pre-Marxian definitions of class, which made them matters of ownership of property (haves vs. have-nots) and/or wielding of power (ruling vs. ruled): see Resnick and Wolff (1987, especially Chapters 3–5; 1988).

2. This has sometimes happened partially—for example, as a result of the great depression of the 1930s, when several European capitalisms supplanted private with state capitalist enterprises in particular industries. It also has been nearly total, as in the case of German and Italian fascism, where private capitalist appropriators were merged with state-appointed official appropriators under one national administration. History displays varying mixtures of private and state capitalist class structures coexisting with various mixtures of market and nonmarket distribution systems. The case of the USSR's state capitalism is treated in this paper.

3. Of course, in countless important ways, Soviet state capitalism differed from other state capitalisms, and especially from the fascist forms of state capitalism. The Marxist and socialist traditions always played significant roles in shaping how Soviet state capitalism organized production and used its surpluses for collective consumption, cultural activities, and so on. By contrast, for example, in German and Italian state capitalisms, the early connections of fascism to the socialist tradition were totally eliminated and their organizations of production and use of state capitalist surplus yielded a very different social life. Indeed, Soviet state capitalism became the ultimate evil and enemy for German and Italian state capitalism, even more hated than the private capitalisms in such countries as France and England. However, it is not a Marxian analysis to infer from such differences and enmities what their respective class structures were. Class analysis looks rather at how surplus labor was produced, appropriated, and distributed to determine whether social differences were connected to dif-

ferent class structures (e.g., capitalist vs. communist) or to different forms of one class structure (e.g., state vs. private capitalist).

4. As noted above, such calls can escalate, when serious social crises are attributed to market mechanisms, to the point of demanding the total suppression of markets in favor of other systems of resource and product allocation.

5. In the words of a former vice president of the USSR Academy of Sciences, the economist A.M. Rumyantsev, "There is not and cannot be any exploitation [because] one of the co-owners of the public means of production enters into comradely co-operation with another similar co-owner" (1969, 19). Lenin perhaps encouraged this line of thinking when he wrote in 1917, "Socialism is nothing but state capitalist monopoly *made to benefit the whole people*; by this token it ceases to be capitalist monopoly" (1932, 37, italics in original). From a Marxist perspective, *who benefits* might be an appropriate criterion for determining whether and when a capitalist class structure is to be labelled "socialist," but it cannot serve to distinguish a capitalist from a noncapitalist, let alone a communist class structure. That is a matter of how surplus labor is produced, appropriated, and distributed, not the important, but quite different, issue of who benefits.

6. It did, after the collectivization of agriculture in the early 1930s, establish collective farms with more or less communist class structures. However, it also established state farms with state capitalist class structures. In the subsequent decades, the latter partly displaced the former while the remaining collective farms evolved increasingly capitalist class structures coupled with collective ownership.

REFERENCES

Lenin, V. I. 1932. *The Threatening Catastrophe and How to Fight It*. New York: International Publishers.

Marx, Karl. 1967. *Capital*, Vol. 1. New York: International Publishers.

———. 1973. *Grundrisse*, trans. by M. Nicolaus. Baltimore: Penguin Books.

Resnick, S. and Wolff, R. 1987. *Knowledge and Class: A Marxian Critique of Political Economy*. Chicago: University of Chicago Press.

———. 1988, Spring. "Communism: Between Class and Classless." *Rethinking Marxism* 1: 14–48.

Rumyantsev, A. M. 1969. *Categories and Laws of the Political Economy of Communism*. Moscow: Progress Publishers.

PART SEVEN

BORDERS OF THE
NEW WORLD

Has "the World" Changed?

ETIENNE BALIBAR

T he important thing in my title is the quotation marks. Initially, I chose this formulation in reaction to the title that the journal *Actuel Marx* had selected for its own conference, "Le nouveau système du monde" (The New World System), which had such subdivisions as : "The Collapse of the Soviet World," "The Nature of East/West Historical Confrontation," "The New Division of the World," and "Social Structures in the Center." Similar formulations are to be found almost everywhere these days: Witness the title of this conference, "Marxism in the New World Order." Taken literally or with some irony, they echo not only well-known mottoes of the Marxist/Socialist tradition (e.g., the famous verse in the *Internationale*: "*Le monde va changer de base*"[1]), but also older, sometimes very ancient cosmological representations. To what extent do our judgments on current history, our very way of questioning the significance of seemingly decisive events, depend on such representations?

No doubt, the world has changed. It has changed considerably since yesterday and the day before, when such Marxist or socialist concepts as "bourgeoisie" and "proletariat," "development of productive forces" and "socialization of labor," "falling rate of profit," "reformist" and "revolutionary" strategies, "imperialism" and the "transition phase," and so on

An earlier version of this paper was presented at that conference "Le nouveau système du monde," Paris, Sorbonne, May 29–30, 1992.

were coined and developed. We may want, even need, to measure the degree of that change, locate it in space and time, discuss its consequences on our theoretical and political practices. For example—although this is certainly a very rough way of stating the alternatives—should this considerable change lead us to reform Marxism, to transform piecemeal this or that component of its traditional body, or to reject boldly its unitarian/singular/totalitarian worldview in a single, unique, and total move?

I do not address this last question directly. Instead I discuss the fact that a statement like "The World (or World Order, or World System) has changed," involves two different questions. One is, did the World actually *change* (and therefore: to what extent? why? in which direction? etc.)? The other is, did *the World* change? What do we mean by the word "world"? As soon as we think of a radical change (or become aware or are told that the undergoing change is radical), this second question becomes inevitable. The question of whether *the World* has changed would then mean, did our image, view, idea, conception, notion of "the World" change? We may even be forced to push the critical question one step further: Is it not perhaps the very possibility of relating structures, forces, events, tendencies, movements, "changes" to something like "a" world that has changed?[2]

There is a political or a set of political concerns underlying this kind of speculation. In our representation of the radical novelty of a "new world order" coexist strikingly contrasting phenomena: *irreversible* processes, as the collapse of so-called really existing socialism, but also *repetitive* processes, as the recreation (yet another) of German Unity according to the people-nation-state model. According to this model—and it seems very hard to decide whether it is an obsolete or triumphant model—something like "the USSR" (not to speak of Yugoslavia) did not exist, whereas something like "Germany" did exist. These contradictory manifestations make us realize that "change" had perhaps already taken place long before its official date and, foremost, that what we regarded as "the world" probably was not what we believed it to be. This realization implies that the transformation of "the world" probably does not have exactly the meaning often announced.

Let me now introduce a very formal but also very rough hypothesis. Thinking of "the World" or "World History," whether in Marxist terms or within other paradigms (including "the World Market" or "the World Environment") was never primarily a *conceptual* operation. It was always a *metaphorical* thought process governed by space–time patterns or schemes that date to much earlier stages of "civilization." What is conceptual is not the scheme itself, but the practical and theoretical critique of the metaphor, which by its nature is never over. Let me be precise: since the beginnings of Western civilization, and possibly of others as well, schemes of "the world" and schemes of "history"—whether finite or infinite, circular or progressive—have never really differed. To speak of the world has always also immediately been to speak of history, to temporalize space, and to spatialize time in a given manner.[3]

Let me add a second hypothesis, equally formal and rough. For at least two centuries—that is, since the so-called bourgeois revolutions[4]—*ideology* (in the sense of political representations and discourse) has been dominated by one great dualistic scheme or, better, a *doubly dualistic* scheme that relies on the correspondence between two couples of opposites: the opposition between progression and regression (or transition and obstacle, revolution, and counterrevolution, etc.); and the opposition of two "classes," or more generally "camps" or "systems" (which can become nations, races, genders, etc.).

This doubly dualistic scheme (or reduplicated pattern of opposition) itself has many translations or variations. A particularly typical and powerful case is Marx's well-known "Preface" to the *Critique of Political Economy*, whose few lines have produced thousands of pages of commentaries by the best minds of this century, displaying all its internal combinatory possibilities.[5] It is mainly structured by the juxtaposition of two oppositions, one—directly derived from the discourses of the 1848 Revolutions—between "order" and "movement," and the other between the "ruling" and the "ruled" class. A slightly different presentation, found in much of the Marxist tradition as well as elsewhere, appears as the juxtaposition of, on the one hand, order and anarchy (or chaos, which can be a positive notion), and "society" (or civil society) and "the state" (or government, or "statism") on the other.

I simply conclude this: What we traditionally consider as typically modern thought—in order to apply it, continue it, or in order to criticize or dismiss it—is actually governed by very archaic schemes, or mental structures (as any speculative thought probably is).[6] When we discuss, elaborate on, in short, think about the world and world history, we undoubtedly refer to and make use of very ancient, if not transhistorical, *cosmological* or, better, *cosmo-political* schemes. Historians of mythologies, anthropologists, and so on—I am especially thinking of the analyses of Jean-Pierre Vernant (1980)—have shown that geometric visions of the universe and patterns of political organization are reciprocal prerequisites.

Now, admittedly, there does not exist in our "world culture" only *one* cosmological scheme. The dualistic or reduplicated antagonistic pattern is not the only one. At least one other has continuously challenged its hegemony—by substituting it, combining with it, or trying to absorb it—from Aristotle onwards and up to the recent theorizations of Braudel (1973), Wallerstein (1988), and others: This is the pattern of center and periphery, the pattern of a "system" that can be stable or unstable, fixed or mobile (a constant presence, the result of its self-reproduction in new conditions, according to new relations of forces). I might note in passing here that the great difficulty with Aristotelian/Braudelian schemes is not so much to understand why the unstable region *par excellence* should be the intermediary region, the so-called semi-periphery, which, located between the core and the outer boundaries of "the world," offers the maximum possibilities for politics in the active sense, that is, open confrontation between antagonistic forces.[7] This is instead a clear implication of the pattern. The difficulty is rather what I would call the problem of historical inertia: I mean the question of how the "center" could be "decentered," how, for example, social formations that are located at the center could ever be pushed to the margins, become "peripheral," and with what kind of effects. This is, no doubt, more than just a speculative question today. If we think of a "crisis" of the world order, of which the collapse of the "socialist" semiperiphery could be the signal, is it not because, among other things, we are faced with the disturbing impression that most "peripheries" remain desperately peripheral, while the "central" position of the traditional "centers" is not so secure?

But, returning to the formal aspects of the question, I will now add some critical reflections of a very mixed nature.

Remark 1. Although dualistic (antagonistic) and systemic (center/periphery) cosmological patterns have undoubtedly played a major role in the history of Marxist and neo-Marxist or post-Marxist theories—as they did in most "modern" ideologies—they have certainly not been the only significant and active ones. There is, in addition to the "dualistic" and to the center/periphery patterns, at least a third pattern, a *triadic pattern* to be precise. It is the one which, notably, Claude Lévi-Strauss elaborated in a famous chapter of *L'Anthropologie structurale* (1973) entitled: "Do Dualistic Organizations Really Exist?" He was borrowing from American Indian cosmological myths based on a representation of "the World" as consisting of three elements/regions: heaven, earth, and water. Such patterns initially were projected upon kinship relations in order to symbolize the possibilities of alliances between exogamic groups within a globally endogamic society. But there is no doubt in my mind that there are also *modern* applications of them. An obvious one concerns the very representation of political regimes and ideologies: the tripartition of ideologies as "conservative," "liberal," or "socialist," according to the perception of their different relation to the "direction of history."[8] Another one, I would suggest, which from the nineteenth century onwards has never ceased to challenge the dualistic picture of politics as an opposition of masters and slaves, dominant and dominated, exploiters and exploited, has been the introduction of the gender relationship, with

women constituting a "third camp," beside capitalists and workers, bourgeoisie and proletarians, and irreducible to them.[9] And since the possibilities of application of such a formal scheme are always multiple (which
means that the same formal constraints are imported in a variety of different domains), we are also reminded here of the fact that most great
representations of the difference (or conflict) of "civilizations" are triadic: for example, the East, the West, and the South. They are likely to
play a crucial role in political discourse again, now that the scheme of
the "two camps" has faded away (although it is still haunted by "catastrophic" pictures of the "North/South" antagonism), and "cultural"
oppositions in a world of "unified communications" become crucial.[10]

Remark 2. Mimicking great philosophers of the past,[11] some minor
ideologues have recently claimed that we have reached the end of history. Now, if something has to resemble an "end of history"—in the sense
of a collapse of possibilities of real transformations—that would more
likely be the previous pattern of a World divided into two camps, each
one led and controlled by one "superpower." That situation practically
blocked any attempt to really "transform the world," since there was no
option for any force that wanted to challenge the existing order other
than to "exit" from one camp and to "enter" (and be absorbed) into the
opposite camp. (This has occurred in both directions: Witness the case
of Cuba and the case of the German Democratic Republic.) In any case,
good Leninists should have known in advance that history could not end
as a struggle between two camps, be they social and/or geographical,
since Lenin repeatedly criticized this "reductionist" presentation of the
class struggles.

Remark 3. The most interesting property of systemic or center/
periphery patterns, in their modern versions (now leaving Aristotelian
cosmology aside), is that they are not representations of the world as a
given structure so much as representations of the process of globalization
(the becoming-a-world of the World). And the most interesting property
of a metaphorical pattern that leads to picturing this process of World-
Becoming is that it forcibly raises the question of limits or boundaries in
a crucial and "dialectical" way. First, what constraints does the existence
of a periphery and the necessity of ruling over it impose on the core itself? How much do these constraints influence the nature and the evolution, or transformation, of the core itself, that is to say, its "politics"?[12]
Second, how is a completely "globalized" world—a world that has really
become a totality, a saturated world—possible? What we observe but do
not fully understand, certainly not with the help of Marxist concepts (even
such concepts as "relative overpopulation," or "industrial reserve army"
etc.), is that in such a world there are regions (and populations) that, having
been historically incorporated, must be excluded again, violently rejected

outside the "system" or World itself—although, of course, this is physically impossible. It is perhaps not by chance that these are the same regions into which a good deal of the garbage and residues of the world tend to be dumped. This is a very violent process indeed, which can be symbolized by one single name: Africa. (I would even dare to suggest the combination of the two "damned" names *"Africa"* and *"Aids"*: *"Africaids."*)

Remark 4. A fundamental element of "change" in the current "new world order" undoubtedly arises from the fact that we are simultaneously leaving the dualistic representation of social antagonisms (mainly in the form of "class struggles") *and* the possibility of viewing world politics as consisting mainly of conflicts between nation–states and national–statist forces. This results from the fact that "really existing socialism" and the "cold war" (which probably involved something like a "really existing liberalism") had actually meant a fusion of these two patterns. The confrontation between the two camps had become an extension, a generalized form of the conflict between national state powers; each camp in the social confrontation was, willingly or not, organized around one superstate or superpower. We can indeed see this as a degeneration of class struggle—and that is certainly what most Marxist intellectuals, or critical Marxist intellectuals would say, recalling all the forms of popular and moral resistance to this statist degeneration of the genuine concept of class struggle. But the fact that it was a degeneration does not mean that it was not *real*, really existing, producing irreversible effects. To the contrary. Class struggle is not likely simply to vanish, and we may have to describe new forms for it. But it will never again be the same. Nevertheless, since this "historical" class struggle has come to an end—which is *not* a return to the "starting point"—we have irreversibly entered the era in which problems of emancipation in "the world" are multilateral. (I like this term more than "pluralist," which seems to beg the question of how "peaceful" or "convergent" this multiplicity of different struggles can be.)

Again here, a more serious treatment of the question would deserve establishing careful distinctions. To juxtapose the picture of different "processes of emancipation," "social movements," or "liberation struggles" in which the "dominated" and the "dominant" are not the same (since they refer to structures of economic exploitation, or racial discrimination, or gender oppression, etc., which are never identical, but can cross and overdetermine each other), is already a recognition of the actual complexity of the world. But it does not go beyond representing them in accordance with the dualistic model, which refers back to an old moral and political picture of "subjection." To differentiate the notion of "subjection" itself, therefore the very idea of "emancipation," is a crucial philosophical prerequisite of any transcendence of the dualistic model.[13]

Let me conclude, or simply reformulate the speculative questions with which I wanted to draw attention to that often "unconscious" level where concepts interfere with metaphors. When Marxism thought that it was dealing only with "real" processes (or even returning from the abstractions of "ideology" to the realities of history: economic conditions, the state, the class struggles between capital and labor), it was indeed (like all other theories) submitted to imaginary pictures of the "real world," themselves commanded by the formal constraints of some fixed "symbolic schemes," particularly the dualistic, or reduplicated dualistic scheme of "progress through antagonism."[14]

Now I would conclude not by asserting that we need to abandon "grand narratives,"[15] but rather by saying that we should learn how to play with the various schemes of cosmology, politics, and history. This is a very serious game, because it is an essential part of that unraveling of the "theoretical unconscious" of the concepts—or, as we once used to say, in the Heideggerian/Lacanian/Althusserian "jargon" of the 1960s, "*le retour aux impensés de la théorie*"—without which there is no proper critique of what Canguilhem calls the "scientific ideologies." It is serious also because it could be the key to actually learning, that is, to creating a *new* mode of political and philosophical thought.

But this is indeed already an old story. In fact, there is nothing completely new in this necessity; it is only becoming more obvious and more compulsory. The traditional picture of politics as a process that is essentially structured by the opposition of classes, camps, or ideologies ("friends and foes"), was already challenged in a more or recent past by three main events: (1) the emergence of the "third world," which already amounted to relativizing the capitalism-versus-socialism confrontation (while paradoxically providing it with a new field for its antagonism); (2) the discovery (or better, rediscovery) that "class struggle" is not the *only* radical or "fundamental" social antagonism or polarization (another one, equally determining, being the sexual difference and the hierarchy of genders[16]), which poses the problem of how to "articulate" different forms of emancipation; and (3) the discovery that a generalized condition of violence (especially in the form of growing militarization of the world and of societies, both before and after the fading away of the "camps") makes it a vital necessity to invent forms of political activism that transcend the classical alternatives of revolutionary and legal change, counterviolence and nonviolence, and elaborate practical forms of collective political action against violence as such, or "antiviolence" (Balibar 1994b). However, it was not my aim here to recall this story. I just wanted to draw attention to the formal aspects of our debates—which, in passing, is also a way of showing that "structuralism" still could retain a certain use for "Marxists," not to speak of others.

NOTES

1. From the "utopian" motto of "the world turned upside down." This, in turn, echoes the old tradition of *carnaval* or *charivari*, in which social hierarchies were transgressed and inverted—as can be seen in a famous painting by Breughel, "The Fight Between Carnival and Lent" (1559).

2. The question was already asked by Heidegger in 1938. See Heidegger 1980.

3. Georges Canguilhem understood this infinite process of creation and conceptual critique of metaphors—"ideologization" and "de-ideologization"—as the very essence of knowledge. See Balibar (1993).

4. This is itself a "bourgeois" concept, combining the "infrastructural" notion of an industrial revolution with the "superstructural" notion of political or constitutional change. See Wallerstein (1988) for a discussion of the relationships between the two kinds of "revolution," which are closely associated in "Whig" historiography and in the Marxist tradition.

5. The first and most influential of these interpretations was proposed by none other than Engels in *Anti-Dühring*. It would explain the class struggle of the capitalist class and the working class as an "expression" of the underlying contradiction between the "socialized" productive forces and the "private" character of appropriation and market relations.

6. Most "histories of ideas" (including those that use such notions as "modernity" and "postmodernity," etc.) still ignore the structural condition that no thinking activity or practice can be its own contemporary.

7. An illuminating but also problematic aspect of the "Wallersteinian" structure seems to me to be the following. On the one hand, it explains why the "sensitive" area in the world system—where political activity becomes organized, finds cogent ideological formulations, and expresses the contradictions of the whole system in an antagonistic form—is the semiperiphery. But at the same time it explains very well why the determining economic factors, in the long run, must escape the scope and practical possibilities of this "politics," since they reside mainly in the relationship and balance of forces between the "core" proper and the "periphery" proper. This is one reason, among others, why I always doubted the optimism with which Wallerstein foresees the coming role of "antisystemic movements" in his pattern. I have never been sure that the "ambiguous identities" of the "antisystemic movements" rooted in the social conditions of the core and the periphery would reach a *political* clarification. Leninism, which is a great example of a political construction of an "overdetermined" language allowing this clarification (by means of a combination of the ideas of "class struggle" and "imperialism"), is typically a semiperipheral doctrine.

8. See the contributions by Immanuel Wallerstein, Pierre Macherey, Eric Hobsbawm, and Domenico Losurdo in Dossier (1992). The "modern" tripartition of political ideologies bears an "obvious" (hence also obscure) resemblance to the "classical" tripartition of political regimes: monarchy, aristocracy, democracy. To my knowledge, this sequence in the history of ideas has never been extensively studied. It would be highly interesting for Marxists, especially because it is a question of understanding the formal reasons why, in his political

analyses and in his economic definitions of the "mode of production," Marx never ceases to oscillate between dualistic and triadic patterns of *class differences*. (Usually the triadic pattern of classes is derived from the "trinitarian formula": landlords/rent, capitalists/profit, workers/wages). Another triadic model (which was very influential in Saint-Simon) is the "Indoeuropean" system of the "three social functions." In Marx it emerges mainly in the form of the three "instances" of the social formation (the "economic," the "political," and the "ideological"), which become incorporated into the pattern of base/superstructure.

9. "Rediscovered" by contemporary feminists, for reasons which are easy to understand, this pattern had been familiar to Romantic philosophers and political theorists: See particularly the doctrine of Auguste Comte (1858).

10. Notice that although this very ancient pattern is extremely cogent, its level of application is not predetermined. Not only does the World as such have its three great "areas" of civilization (or *Weltanschauung*), but so does each particular "region" (e.g., the "European" religious legacy, typically divided among "Eastern" Orthodoxy, "Western" Protestantism, and "Southern" Catholicism). This example is also particularly interesting because it shows clearly that a formal property of such "triadic" patterns is to leave an empty place, outside the World it pictures, which is the place of the absolute "Other." In the case of the "world civilizations," this is the place of the *noncivilized* Other, of "cultures" that are supposed not to reach the level of civilization (mainly through the art of writing)—notably the "black" cultures. In the case of the European religious tradition, it is the place of the "semitic" Other: Judaism and Islam. These are structural places much more than substantial determinations, hence the possibility of substituting other terms: The Yugoslavian conflict would not appear as a "concentrate" of European history—which shows us our own face in the guise of a lethal Medusa and therefore paralyzes us—if it did not display the same pattern in reduction, with the "Serbs" representing the East, the "Croats" representing the West, and the "Muslims" representing the South, all of them speaking the same language.

11. This is not the case with Perry Anderson (1992). Any serious treatment of the question should now take this very impressive argument into account.

12. For our generation, this question came to the fore and became crucial with the experience of colonial and postcolonial wars. Its inescapable character is now mainly connected with the conflicting requisites of "citizenship" and "migrations" in "developed" countries.

13. It is very striking indeed that, in *Three Guineas*, Virginia Woolf (1977, 21) systematically applies the term "class" when dealing with sexual difference, in order to provide a "class analysis" of the oppressive inequality of gender and the corresponding ideology. The paradoxical result is to relativize and, at the same time, to emphasize the Marxist "class criterion": "Take the fact of property. Your class possesses in its own right and not through marriage practically all the capital, all the land, all the valuables, and all the patronage in England. Our class possesses in its own right and not through marriage practically none of the capital, none of the land, none of the valuables, and none of the patronage in England."

14. Since this terminology ("real," "imaginary," "symbolic") refers to Lacan, this is a good place to point out one of the main difficulties of his work. According to him, the "symbolic" is essentially triadic, whereas "dualistic" patterns (and especially antagonistic patterns) are typical of the "imaginary" (since they display the ambivalence, the love/hatred oscillation of the specular relationships). It seems to me that there is nothing indisputable in this view. Not only does there indeed exist a "triadic" (and especially a trinitarian) imaginary, but there also exists a "symbolic" level or use of the notion of "antagonism." The whole question of symmetries and dissymetries between such historical and political representations as "class struggles," "race struggles," and even "gender struggles" turns on this.

15. A motto that, surprisingly, "postmodernists" share with the most classical positivistic tradition. Could this explain why they are simultaneously so successful in some countries (like the United States)?

16. To which I would personally add, as an equally important element, the "intellectual difference." See the essay "'Rights of Man' and 'Rights of the Citizen,' The Dialectics of Modern Politics" in Balibar (1994a).

REFERENCES

Anderson, P. 1992. "The Ends of History." In *A Zone of Engagement*, 279–375. London: Verso

Balibar, E. 1993. "Science et vérité dans la philosophie de Georges Canguilhem." In *Georges Canguilhem, Philosophe, historien des sciences*, 58–76. Paris: Albin Michel.

———. 1994a. *Masses, Classes, Ideas: Studies on Politics and Philosophy before and after Marx*. London: Routledge.

———. 1994b. "Violence et politique: Quelques questions." In *Le passage des frontières* (*Autour du travail de Jacques Derrida*) direction de Marie Louise Mallet. Paris: Editions Galilée.

Braudel, F. 1973. *Capitalism and Material Life*. New York: Harper and Row.

Comte, A. 1858. *The Catechism of Positive Religion*. London: J. Chapman.

Dossier. 1992, October. "Conservatisme, Libéralisme, socialisme" *Genèses* 9: 7–91.

Heidegger, M. 1980. "Die Zeit des Weltbildes." In *Holzwege*, 73–110. Frankfurt: Klostermann.

Lévi-Strauss, C. 1973. *Anthropologie structurale*. Paris: Plon

Vernant, J. P. 1980. *Myth and Society in Ancient Greece*. Atlantic Highlands, NJ: Humanities Press.

Wallerstein, I. 1988. *The Modern World System*, Vol. III. New York: Academic Press

Woolf, V. 1977. *Three Guineas*. Harmondsworth, England: Penguin Books.

Intimations of Mortality: On Historical Communism and the "End of History"

GREGORY ELLIOTT

The contemporary *topos* of the "end of history" has a distinguished pedigree, rendering it a virtual cliché of intellectual culture. Eschatological and soteriological doctrines of the Final End have been around since the very beginning. Ends come and go; or, as they used to say in Eastern Europe, "the future is certain; the past is unpredictable."

In the twentieth century, the immediate precedent for current sightings of a cessation or culmination of history is to be found in cold war liberalism—in particular, Daniel Bell's *End of Ideology* (1960). The latter revolved around the postulate of a convergence between East and West: the tranquil conclusion of the contest between capitalism and socialism as a result of the post-war "democratic social revolution," which had solved the riddle of modern history with the reconciliation of liberty and equality, efficiency and humanity, in regulated capitalism. A bleakly pessimistic left-wing version of the thesis was advanced concurrently, in Herbert Marcuse's *One-Dimensional Man* (1964), which counterposed an impotent "Great Refusal" to the omnipotence of the ubiquitous "technocratic society."

For an elaboration of the ideas presented in this paper, see Elliott (1993). Copyright 1993 by Gregory Elliott. Adapted by permission.

FOR TO END YET AGAIN AND OTHER FIZZLES

The intervening turbulence of the 1960s and 1970s having passed without undue perturbation of the OECD order, another variation upon the theme has emerged in the 1980s. To characterize today's cultural climate as one in which "endism" is pandemic would doubtless be an exaggeration. And yet the efflorescence of what might be called the p-word is surely an index of something: postmodernism, poststructuralism, post-Fordism, postindustrialism. The prefix is neither fortuitous nor innocent. The final decade of the second millennium A.D. signals, according to a certain apocalyptic litany, the death of communism and socialism, the passing of the working class, the termination of the cold war, the waning of industrial society, and—most portentously of all—the end of history. *Fin de siècle, aube de siècle*—except that the contours of the new dawn are only dimly discerned, the future invariably being depicted as the eternal repetition of the transitional, untranscendable present: a future of no future, so to speak.

Considerations of time and tact prevent me from saying anything much about the cultural complex known as postmodernism. But I do want to indicate two things. Firstly, propositions to the effect that the West is in passage to a postindustrial society, a post-Fordist economy, a postsocialist politics, and a postideological culture, wherein postmetaphysical philosophy comes into its own: these are half-truths, where not outright falsehoods, symptoms of a late twentieth-century reality systematically misrecognized, not adequately conceptualized. Secondly, the class of '68 that articulates or recognizes itself in them coincides, albeit inadvertently and in a distinct idiom, with cold war liberalism in its assessment of the socialist legacy. What Richard Rorty calls "North Atlantic postmodern bourgeois liberal democracy" and North Atlantic modern bourgeois liberal democracy have more in common than the self-images of the age, infused with the "narcissism of small differences" (Freud), care to acknowledge.

As critics have demonstrated, postmodernist affirmations of an end of history succumb to a series of crippling performative contradictions, which prevent them from grasping their indicated object. The reconfiguration of avant-garde Anglophone theory leaves much of the Left intelligentsia caroling the virtues of a meretricious miscellany that would shake all metaphysics (Marxism included) to the superflux, while leaving material structures intact (therewith replicating metaphysics in the very gesture of repudiating it). The intrinsic problem with this sub-Maoism of the signifier is that it flouts its own protocols. It employs reason as an instrument of illumination to denounce reason as an arm of oppression. It deploys a metanarrative—and one of the tallest, if not greatest, stories ever told—to deliver metanarrative its quietus. It constructs an expressive social totality, the entirety of whose phenomena would be exfoliations of the postmodern essence. Disposing of history historically, of theory theoretically, of ethics ethically, of politics politically, this intellectual recidivism drafts its own indictment: *de te fabula magna narratur*.

Viewed in the twilight of the idles, what is striking about Francis Fukuyama's essay, "The End of History?" is its avoidance of such performative contradictions (Fukuyama 1989). Fukuyama reverts to the French Hegelianism—metanarratives of speculation and emancipation, *par excellence*—against which (post)structuralism was largely directed. Fukuyama, I want to argue—borrowing Blake's verdict on Milton—is "of the Devil's party without knowing it," a circumstance that may account for the hostility or suspicion with which his original article of 1989 was greeted on the Right.

Fukuyama is of the Devil's party *analytically*, insofar as he has resurrected totalizing theory as an indispensable mode of conceptualization of the "One World" impending on the threshold of the twenty-first century. His work displays the arresting paradox of a (post-) cold war liberal political individualism whose historicist philosophical framework, with its holism and teleologism, was anathematized by his Anglo-American predecessors as the royal "road to serfdom." For them, moral-political individualism entailed methodological individualism, while teleological prospects dictated "totalitarian" results. By the norms of mainstream Anglophone philosophy Fukuyama is culpable of the kind of dialectical metaphysics extirpated by the interwar "analytical" (counter-) revolution.

Fukuyama is of the Devil's party *politically*, insofar as he has punctured some of the historical amnesia induced by the Right during the 1980s. For Fukuyama reminds us what was at stake in the second cold war: a comprehensive reversal of the consequences of World War II in the first world (Keynesian welfare capitalism); in the second (the existence and performance of Stalinism); and in the third (the defeat of colonialism). As Fred Halliday (1986, 243) has written, "The actions of the Reagan Administration and its allies in Europe sought to reverse these consequences, using the recession, anticommunism, and historical amnesia to impose a new set of values and policies on the world." They have largely succeeded; and Fukuyama's is one, especially ambitious endeavor to prospect the "new world order" arising upon the ruins of formerly existing socialism: the only actual socialism, alas, that we have known.

AFTER THE DELUGE

"A specter is haunting Europe—the specter of Communism." Historically overly optimistic, at the moment of its composition, the opening line of the *Communist Manifesto* was, by its centennial in 1948, unduly pessimistic geographically, as accomplished or imminent revolutions in Asia compounded the postwar transplantation of Stalinism from one country to a whole geographical zone, occasioning the cold war in concerted Western response. Some four decades (and a second cold war) further on, the ghost has been exorcised. The specter haunting the world today is not the end of *prehistory* envisaged by Marx, but the end of *history* envisioned by Fukuyama: the global apotheosis—as opposed to the global abolition—of capitalism. The main premise of the *Manifesto* might be thought to have been vindicated, close to a century and a half later, while its consequent has been infirmed en route. The predicted global expansion of capitalism has finally transpired, but in such a way as to eliminate its principal twentieth-century impediment. This was "historical Communism," tributary to the Bolshevik Revolution—"the moment when," according to Edmund Wilson (1991, 546), "for the first time in the human exploit the key of a philosophy of history was to fit an historical lock."

For another, *right*-Hegelian philosophy of history capitalism has vanquished its secular antagonist—actually existing socialism—in the East, and dug the grave of its appointed gravedigger—the proletariat—in the West, allegedly rendering socialism utopian (for lack of agency and rationality as a goal), and Marxism redundant (for want of explanatory or normative purchase). The knell of socialized public property has sounded: The expropriators are expropriating. Satirizing a "scientific socialism" that certified the inevitability of the classless future, the French Communist Paul Nizan had written in 1938 of a "world destined for great metamorphoses."[1] Great metamorphoses, the reverse of those foreseen, have supervened. What, for Fukuyama, do they consist of?

In sum, the "epic of transition" heralded by Lenin amid the "highest stage of capitalism," has proved to be a mere *divertimento* (Fukuyama 1989). Sundown having fallen on the Union, Minerva's owl spreads its wings and espies the materialization of Kant's "Universal History": "an unabashed victory of economic and political liberalism" over its "world-historical" competitors, portending a "Common Marketization" of world politics, or "liberal democracy in the political sphere combined with easy access to VCRs and stereos in the economic." Following Hegel, then, for Fukuyama "the History of the World is none other than the progress of the consciousness of Freedom"; and that consciousness has prevailed. The "triumph of the West"—or of the Western *idea*, at any rate—has concluded history, not in the sense of bringing empirical events to an abrupt halt (these will continue), but in the sense of realizing a goal: "Freedom" as "the end point of mankind's ideological evolution." The end of history is the end of ideology, for the consummation of one universal ideology. History with a capital "H"—construed as a *Kampfplatz* between competing universal ideologies, "embodied" (so Fukuyama stipulates) "in important social or political forces and movements . . . which are therefore part of world history"—has arrived at its terminus. The train of history has terminated not at the Finland Station, but at the nearest hypermarket.

Given Fukuyama's construction of "History," the myriad malcontents of posthistorical civilization represent no challenge to his basic thesis. The "strange thoughts occur[ring] to people in Albania or Burkina Faso" (we should now have to substitute the former Yugoslavia or India) are impotent before the march of history (Fukuyama 1989). The "past" is unpredictable; the future is certain: an Americanization of the planet—a "universal homogeneous state" of liberal capitalist democracy—from which system-threatening antagonisms (or contradictions) have been eliminated.

Not that this triumph prompts a triumphalist tone. Indeed, Fukuyama's article strikes an elegiac note in conclusion: "The end of history will be a very sad time," bereft of the "struggle for recognition" and the audacity it elicited from human beings. To conjugate the terms that provide the title of Fukuyama's book-length expansion of the prospectus, the Hegelian End of History will be inhabited by Nietzschean Last Men. A narcissistic culture of conspicuous self-consumption is condemned to the spiritual vices of its material benefits.

MYSTICAL SHELL AND RATIONAL KERNEL

When, in a postface to the second edition of Volume I of *Capital*, Marx sought to specify his relationship to the Hegelian dialectic, he famously contended that via its "inversion" he "discover[ed] the rational kernel within the mystical shell" (Marx 1976, 103). I want to attempt an analogous operation with the *ersatz* Hegelian dialectic of Fukuyama.

A first—and pervasive—objection to the thesis has been its apparent irrefutability. What evidence, if any, could refute it? Or is it, consequent upon the definition of "History," a vacuity, immune to contradiction? This, to backtrack, is the gravamen of the critique of metanarratives *stricto sensu*. Lest anyone think that I am now praising what I had earlier damned, it should be noted that the single most influential contemporary form of Marxism, Althusserianism, was precisely based upon dissent from orthodox historical materialism, with its epic tale of the forward march of the productive forces towards an ineluctable communism, on the grounds that it was a "materialist" inversion of Hegel's philosophy of history—starring the ruse of economic reason—which secreted a mystical kernel within a technological shell.

The first dimension to Fukuyama's mystical shell, then, is what Althusser identified as the mystical kernel of Hegelian Marxism (and which is preserved intact in this inversion of the inversion): the very notion that History harbors goals and progressively realizes them—be they the Soviet Communism indicated by Kojève in the aftermath of Stalingrad (comrade history), or the Western liberalism identified by Fukuyama after the deluge (citizen—or is it sovereign consumer?—history).

A second area of contention concerns Fukuyama's quite non-Hegelian understanding of "contradictions." For him contradictions are exogenous to systems, not endogenous to them. The relevant contradictions are *inter*systemic (between systems), as opposed to *intra*systemic (within systems). Hence the transition from a bipolar world system, principally structured by the antagonism between capitalism and historical Communism, to a multipolar world system, comprising competing capitalisms—a restoration, in other words, of the prewar primacy of intrasystemic contradictions—is read as an elimination of significant contradictions. A certain historical myopia construes the exception—the post-World War II composition of capitalist differences for the pursuit of the "great contest"—as the norm. Yet historical Communism was one product of—a response to—a capitalist ascendancy riven by antagonisms so acute as to plunge the world into two cataclysmic wars in the span of a mere quarter century. Communism was given its chance in 1917 by liberalism (not to mention social democracy). It came into existence promising to resolve the chronic problems generated by the "combined and uneven development" of capitalism. It manifestly bequeaths those problems to liberal capitalism, which, if its immediate horizons stretch no further than "ready access to VCRs and stereos" on a planetary scale, is doomed to exacerbate them.

If Fukuyama is able to exclude systemic intracapitalist contradictions from his panorama, it is as a result of the sleight of hand whereby fascism is assimilated to Communism—a standard cold war move—and both are counterposed to capitalism. This conveniently dissimulates the historical reality that, since the parliamentary road to fascism proved considerably more fecund than that to socialism, fascism was a general tendency of prewar capitalism. Horkheimer's dictum assumes a new urgency: Those who do not wish to speak of capitalism should keep silent about fascism—just as, I would argue, anyone who has nothing to say on the subject of imperialism is disqualified from pronouncing on Stalinism.

One would not guess it from Fukuyama's presentation, but on the fiftieth anniversary of Stalingrad there is less excuse for neglecting an uncomfortable fact: namely, that Stalinism vanquished European fascism, therewith, paradoxically, laying the foundations for the revival of liberalism after 1945.

Fukuyama may be an unreliable guide to the past; most criticisms of his work center on the present, however. And it is here—in Fukuyama's reading of contemporary history—that the rational kernel of his thesis is to be found. Setting aside the discursive alchemy whereby, capitalism supposedly no longer being capitalism, it cannot be said to have triumphed, we may attend to the converse consolation: that since formerly existing socialism was not socialism, the latter cannot be claimed to have suffered a setback—indeed, can only benefit from the termination of a travesty and tragedy in the East.

Regrettably, this line of critique seems to me seriously misplaced. It is true that the second world was not socialist, and that contemporary capitalism might appear to furnish—in the classical Marxist schema—the material and social preconditions for international socialism. It may also be true that the vision of a global socialist order is the new realism dictated by the immense challenges besetting humanity. In these respects, the collapse of historical Communism removes the Stalinist incubus—the calamitous descent of socialism into barbarism in the twentieth century—which has functioned as one of the main impediments to the struggle for human emancipation. Nevertheless, in the current conjuncture that collapse constitutes a decisive defeat for socialism, which may be the abstract order of the day, but which is nowhere on the concrete agenda. Why?

First we may note the efficacious propagation of the cold war equation: Socialism = Stalinism = (optimally) Penury + Tyranny—an imposture sufficiently credible, for the foreseeable future, to inoculate not only those recently liberated from the "prison of peoples," but many more besides, against the socialist plague. Its prosperity derives not solely from the depredations of Stalinism, but from the palpable absence of any feasible and desirable alternative to it as a noncapitalist societal future. For the disappearance of the international Communist movement has not redounded to the benefit of social democracy, whose own crisis has rather been accentuated by it. What has occurred in the 1980s is the extinction or exhaustion of the two central traditions of socialist politics in the twentieth century—without anything plausible emerging to fill the vacuum. And capitalist nature adores a vacuum.

Alternatives to Communism and social democracy—futures for socialism that could clear its name, rehabilitate its reputation—have come and gone with alarming regularity. Restricting the focus to contemporary history, the spectacular promise of "1968" was flagrantly breached. A conjuncture marked by the triple crisis of imperialism in the third world (the Vietnamese Tet), of Stalinism in the second (the Prague Spring), and of capitalism in the first (the Parisian May), seemingly resynchronized dialectical theory and the historical dialectic. The harvest of May severed them once more. In the East the Soviet invasion of Czechoslovakia brutally arrested de-Stalinization. In the West an unexpectedly resilient liberal capitalism surmounted yet another "terminal" crisis. Among the bitterest fruits for the revolutionary class of '68 was the failure of elective third-worldist alternatives to the Soviet model: the exposure of the Chinese Cultural Revolution as a virulent Oriental compound of *Zhdanovschina* and *Yezhovschina*; the involution of the Cuban regime; the murderous dispensation of the Khmer Rouge in Kampuchea's Year Zero; Vietnam's embroilment in wars with two "fraternal countries" within years of the liberation of Saigon.

The imitation, rather than the supersession, of the Soviet experience could, in every instance, only discredit (as well as demoralize) those who had hitched their socialism to the red star over Beijing, Havana, or Hanoi. With the passing of such reveries, the Soviet experience appeared exemplary, not aberrant—the "totalitarian" corollary of "totalizing politics." In any event, what cannot be gainsaid is the record of failure of socialism, West and East, North and South, in the twentieth century, prompting perception of it as utopian (unviable) or dystopian (undesirable). Writing in *Le Monde* in October 1991, the Spanish ex-Communist Jorge Semprun suggested, "Today we are confronted with this reality: the society in which we live is an untranscendable horizon." Wittingly or not, his terms echoed a slogan with which the 1960s had opened—Sartre's celebrated characterization of Marxism as "the untranscendable philosophy for our time"—while reversing its verdict: the adventures of the dialectic vindicate "dialectical" theory *à la* Fukuyama, not *à la* Sartre.

What, however, of the post-Marxist intelligentsia who would point to the "new social movements," rather than the old socialist movement, as the bearer(s) of an emancipatory politics? Granted, it might be said, socialism as traditionally conceived is dead, but what of its recasting, for example, as one moment of a more capacious project for a "radical and plural democracy?" The answer is simple: Lacking the requisite agency, organization, and strategy, the "new social movements" are not—and are not set to become—(counter-) hegemonic forces of the kind required to refute the Fukuyama thesis. In the absence of articulation and mobilization of the anticapitalist "general interest" to which their concerns ultimately point, hegemony will be endured, not forged. Moreover, those on the Left who detect a silver lining in acid rain clouds, drawing solace from the putative fatality inscribed in capitalist accumulation, overlook the fact that "environmentalism" precisely possesses no necessary class belonging. In and through its very "universalism," it is *socially* indeterminate—compatible, in the medium term at any rate, with a grotesquely inegalitarian and authoritarian global capitalist order.

Not least among the reasons for a certain skepticism about the "new social movements" as a contestant of the new order is their own manifest crisis and eclipse by some very old social movements: the furies of communalism, fundamentalism, nationalism, and so on. And yet, if the prominence of regressive social movements on the current world scene contributes to the disconsolation of socialists, does it not simultaneously discountenance Fukuyama's prospectus—the beneficent global diffusion of liberal commerce? The answer must be both yes and no: yes, because the "Common Marketization" of global politics is a fanciful projection, but no, because, almost by definition, they are not of the requisite "universal" character. Furthermore, they are scarcely anticapitalist, offering no alternative to the economic "modernization" of whose contradictions and dislocations they are a symptom, rather than a solvent. The dialectic of Enlightenment qualifies, but does not contradict, the Fukuyama thesis.

RESULTS AND PROSPECTS

With the destruction of actually existing socialism, we are witnessing the elimination, possibly only temporary, of socialism as a world-historical movement. "*Die Weltgeschichte ist das Weltgericht*: world history is the final arbiter of right," Fukuyama, invoking Kojève, proclaims in his book (1991, 212). We need not accept that economic might is political right. But it would be paradoxical, to say the least, were professed historical materialists to evade the reality that world history is the final arbiter of might—or the conclusion that, relative to the projections of classical Marxism, socialism is utopian once again: a desirable future confronting an unamenable present.

And yet there is more to be said about the failure of revolution in the East. For if much of the Left consistently underestimated the durability and vitality of capitalism, as a result of its disastrous record from 1914–1945, it similarly discounted the significance of historical Communism—not to the extent that it constituted an obstacle to socialism in the West, given its dire record in numerous respects, but insofar as it possessed, in addition to much that was simply deplorable and unforgivable, what Lucio Magri (1991) has called "another side."

To speak thus, controverting a certain anti-Communist commonsense on the Left, is to court the charge of "closet Stalinism." For is it not to identify a socialism deserving of the name with formerly existing socialism; to accept the sometime Soviet Union and its satellites at their own mendacious self-valuation; to deny the reality of an odious system whose crimes have besmirched the reputation of socialism the world over? One might as well come out of the closet: The unequivocal response is "no." It is to insist that whereas social democracy had already sold the pass at the outbreak of World War I and again at its conclusion; had proved unequal to the test of the Second World War, was restricted to the advanced capitalist world, and had matched its accommodations to capitalism at home by collusion with imperialism abroad, by contrast, the record of Communism was significantly different.

Crudely inventoried, the existence and performance of historical Communism were positive in three crucial respects. First and foremost, in the resistance to, and defeat of, European fascism: a fact accounting for the prestige in which the Soviet model was held after 1945. Second, in the subsequent emergence of the third world and its protection thereafter. As Noam Chomsky (1991, 60) has argued, the rational kernel of "deterrence theory" is to be found here—that is, in the Soviet deterrent to imperialist designs on the South. Where that deterrence failed to avert U.S. intervention, the forces confronting it prevailed only when sustained by the second world. A third—and final—merit of historical Communism was its role in precipitating the postwar compromise in the first world itself; the presence, within and without, of the "red menace" weighed decisively in the meliorist reconstruction of Europe after Liberation.

Considerations such as these explain why it was rational, given the dilemma of *les mains sales*, to opt for Communism or, in the manner of Sartre and Merleau-Ponty, for "anti-anti-Communism." To wash one's hands of the Communist movement was to risk dirtying them with something else—the implacable dominion of capital—or to elect for political innocence at the cost of historical impotence. To the predictably adverse impact upon the reputation of socialism of any collapse of historical Communism must be added, then, a second fundamental reason for looking to a regeneration of the revolution *where* it had degenerated: the contradictory character, internally and externally, of Communism as a historical phenomenon.

The last rites and ceremonies of the cold war disclosed its systemic character: a great, but unequal, contest between opposed socioeconomic and political systems, initiated by the Bolshevik Revolution. That contest has concluded, as predicted by Fukuyama, in the unqualified victory of capitalism, bringing an era—the era opened by 1917—to a close. In his "Theses on History," completed in the unrelieved gloom of spring 1940, Benjamin (1973, 257) wrote: "*Even the dead* will not be safe from the enemy if he wins; and this enemy has not ceased to be victorious" (italics in original). In the intervening half century, the enemy ceased to be victorious: but only when and where the forces contesting capitalism and imperialism mustered under, or subsequently rallied to, the banners of the international Communist movement. In winding up the cold war journal *Problems of Communism* last year, the U.S. State Department filed an affidavit for the counterhegemonic role of historical Communism. It would be paradoxical, to say the least, were the post-Communist Left, by traducing its memory, to sacrifice some of the dead to the enemy.

NOTES

1. "Thank God, in November [1929], the Wall Street crash was to reassure them: they welcomed it like news of a victory. Since they tended to confuse capitalism with important people, when they saw their fathers' faces they convinced themselves that they had been quite right to stake their lives on the cards of confusion, and that they could indubitably count upon a world destined for great metamorphoses" (Nizan 1988, 49).

REFERENCES

Bell, D. 1960. *The End of Ideology*. New York: Collier.

Benjamin, W. 1973. *Illuminations*. London: Fontana.

Chomsky, N. 1991. *Deterring Democracy*. London: Verso

Elliott, G. 1993. "The Cards of Confusion: Reflections on Historical Communism and the 'End of History.'" *Radical Philosophy* 64 (Summer).

Fukuyama, F. 1989. "The End of History?" *The National Interest* (Summer). Reprinted in *A Look at the End of History*, ed. M. K. Jensen. Washington DC: U.S. Institute Peace, 1990.

Fukuyama, F. 1991. *The End of History and the Last Man*. London: Hamish Hamilton.

Halliday, F. 1986. *The Making of the Second World War*. London: Verso.

Magri, L. 1991, September–October. "The European Left between Crisis and Refoundation." *New Left Review* 189.

Marcuse, H. 1964. *One-Dimensional Man*. London: Routledge and Kegan Paul.

Marx, K. 1976. *Capital*, Vol. 1. Harmondsworth, England: Penguin.

Nizan, P. 1988. *The Conspiracy*. London: Verso.

Wilson, E. 1991. *To the Finland Station*. Harmondsworth, England: Penguin.

Capitalism, Socialism, and Historical Materialism

M. C. HOWARD

J. E. KING

CLASSICAL MARXISM AND SOCIALISM

The central methodological contribution of Marx and Engels in their analysis of postcapitalist society was the idea of "scientific socialism." Socialism was conceived not simply as the ideal of a free, egalitarian, planned, and marketless society, but also as inevitable (and thus feasible) because it arose embryonically within capitalism as a result of its own maturation. Bourgeois individualism, private property, and market organization, Marx and Engels argued, were increasingly becoming a fetter on the productive forces, and were therefore destined to wither away or be replaced.[1]

The expanding socialization of production—the eradication of the isolation, independence and separateness of different productive activities—led to a growing interdependence that made bourgeois individualism anachronistic. At the same time the concentration and centralization of capital progressively replaced market organization with planning, while the separation of ownership and control inherent in the joint stock company reduced the positive functions of private property. Associated with these phenomena, an extensive social intervention in civil society proved necessary as the collective catastrophes arising from the interaction of *particular* interests became ever more evident. These developments were, in turn, reflected in severe crises of various kinds as capitalist social relations came increasingly into conflict with the functional need of the productive forces for new socialist relations of production (Howard and King 1985, Part IV; Marx 1970, Chapters 10 and 25; 1971b, 437–438; 1973, 163f.).

Before considering the limitations of these arguments, it is advisable to acknowledge the strength of the perspective of scientific socialism from which they derive. Central here is the attempt to marry ideals and practicalities—in Marx and Engels's own terminology, to be non-utopian. This is the enduring merit of their approach to the assessment of socialism, quite aside from the validity of the specific arguments they employed to make their case. The materialist conception of history relates the feasibility of socialism to the question of efficiency, measured by the ability to operate the productive forces optimally.[2] For Marx and Engels, socialist relations of production would be sustained only if they could on this criterion out-compete those of capitalism. And because they saw socialist forms arising within capitalism, Marx and Engels reasonably took this as evidence that capitalism was beginning to fetter the productive forces, and that the balance of advantage had begun to swing in favor of socialism. If they were incorrect on these factual issues—and, as we will argue in a moment, they appear to have been wrong in some crucial respects—the way in which they approached the issue nevertheless remains robust. In other words, on the perspective of historical materialism, to argue for the feasibility of socialism requires an argument for the efficiency of socialism.

Until the 1920s, socialists had little need to employ dogmatism in defending their position because the Marxian narrative did not appear obviously at variance with the facts (Howard and King 1989, Chapters 5, 13, and 14; and Howard and King 1992, Chapter 18). Nevertheless, with hindsight, it is now possible to see crucially important flaws.

Note first that part of Marx's original argument may be irrelevant to the feasibility of socialism. Even if it were true that capitalism was ever more crisis prone, as Marx maintained—with secular tendencies to rising unemployment, falling rates of profit and increasingly severe problems of underconsumption—this would not preclude capitalist relations of production from being reestablished on the morrow of any anticapitalist revolution. These crises are systemic; they arise from the whole matrix of socioeconomic relations of capitalism and do not directly bear upon the efficiency of the capital–labor relation that constitutes their microfoundation. Thus, unless socialism proved to be more efficient in each and every activity, only coercion or self-restraint could prevent the reemergence of "capitalist acts between consenting adults" (Nozick 1974). But coercion conflicts with the enhanced freedom that socialists have usually supposed socialism would provide, while the relevant kind of self-restraint would seem to presume the prior existence of a fully formed socialist culture, and hence to be utopian.

This explains the pivotal importance of Marx and Engels's argument that capitalist economic development ultimately makes a planned, socialized, and marketless economy everywhere more efficient than relations of commodity production and commodity circulation. At the heart of this claim is the belief that technical change under capitalism concentrates and centralizes the means of production. Some indices do indeed show that this has occurred over the long run. But Marx and Engels presumed, and necessarily had to presume, that concentration and centralization went hand in hand with vertical integration. In other words, their argument required innovations to have a market-eradication bias. This is much less evident: Concentration and centralization of capital coupled to a more pronounced density of market relations is possible, and appears actually to be occurring. The increasing commodification of production and the tendency for economic activity to be organized in larger and fewer units do not exclude each other, and both have occurred simultaneously in important sectors of advanced economies. Furthermore, the internal organization of the largest corporations is often founded on quasi-market principles, as is that of so-called nonmarket institutions: Relations between subdivisions within large firms and other institutions frequently involve a cash nexus, as well as elements of hierarchy and cooperation.

SOCIALISM AND NEOCLASSICAL ECONOMICS

Some of these considerations were alluded to by Marxian revisionists at the turn of the century (Howard and King 1989, Chapter 4). But what proved to be a more influential line of criticism took a very different form. Neoclassical economists treated the issue of socialism in a rationalist, nonempirical and ahistorical manner, and one reason why this approach eventually predominated was that socialist economists themselves began to respond in the same terms. In other words, socialists started to accept the frame of reference, if not the specific propositions, of their critics. Moreover, this was no accident. Not only did neoclassical economists make some telling arguments against Marx's conception of socialism, but, as we shall see below, neoclassical theory has a perspective and an analytic structure that facilitates a positive answer to the question of the feasibility of a different type of socialism, when judged by its own (Paretian) conception of what constitutes efficiency.

The argument of Ludwig von Mises (1971), first presented in 1920, is now widely regarded as crucial to this intellectual development. In fact, his discussion was poorly structured and has been the object of diverse interpretations. At the time, and for many years thereafter, it was understood in neoclassical terms. More recently it has been read in ways that bring it in line with contemporary Austrian ideas. However, irrespective of the exact construction put upon Mises' text, the bare bones of his polemic can be outlined as follows. Mises claimed that without private property there could be no exchange, and, in the absence of exchange, the rational valuation of different resources would be impossible, so that they could not be used economically, and only chaos would result from the establishment of socialism.

Beginning in the interwar years, the dominant response among socialist economists involved two fundamental changes in their approach to the problem of the feasibility of postcapitalist society. First, they accepted allocation through markets. Second, they acknowledged neoclassical theory as the appropriate conceptualization of how markets could function under socialism, and as providing the most relevant criterion of efficiency in terms of which they should be judged. The first sentiment was more widespread than the second, but both became very evident among Western socialist academics. Separately or together, however, they represented a major break with the theory of socialism as it had been previously understood.[3]

The acceptance of markets was bound to cause problems for the integrity of socialist values. Even when it is recognized that there is no such thing as the "market," and that all markets are institutionally dependent, market organization per se must be in tension with socialist ideals. All markets require the existence of property rights that are particularistic and possessive, and promise the continuation of a connection between reward and performance. More generally—and in the terms of Marx—markets necessarily involve bourgeois right, and thereby entail that alienation cannot be transcended. A socialism that retains markets, therefore, cannot be regarded as the complete solution to the problems of social philosophy that the young Marx had proposed.

The limitations inherent in the notion of market socialism were, however, disguised by the simultaneous acceptance of neoclassical theory, especially as employed by Oscar Lange in the 1930s. Lange's essential insight was his recognition that neoclassical theory allowed the use of the price mechanism to plan the economy in the context of public ownership of the means of production. His blueprint permits the private ownership of consumption goods, over which there is free-market choice. Workers also have choice of occupation, but all other property is socially owned. A central planning board fixes prices, and guarantees production units that they can buy and sell as much as they choose at these prices. Managements are instructed to maximize profits, taking prices as given. If there are excess demands or excess supplies, the central planners alter the prices in a manner similar to that of a Walrasian auctioneer until markets clear. Since external effects and the provision of public goods can be easily incorporated into the process, Lange was thus able to claim that prices would be "rational" and resource allocation efficient. No "real world" capitalism could ensure this, he argued, because of the existence of disequilibrium, market power, and inadequate policies with respect to externalities. Moreover, Lange pointed out that planners could also fix the interest rate to bring about any desired rate of accumulation, which would be financed from renting public property to producing units, and from taxes. In addition, these resources might be used to offset income inequalities arising from the operation of a free labor market (Lange 1971).

Lange's scheme had great strengths. It provided a refutation of Mises, since private property was not needed for exchange, and there was no obvious reason to suppose that coercion would increase. Further-more, Lange's system is not utopian; it does not require an elevation of tastes and motivations. Yet it clearly realizes the important socialist values of equality, rationality, planning, and the elimination of waste. Since Lange left unspecified the exact nature of socialist management, his model could also incorporate workers' participation, or even workers' self-management. Both liberation and efficiency were served.

Not surprisingly, Lange's ideas have become the prototype for all subsequent versions of market socialism. However, he was able to bring about this revitalization of socialist ideals only by making three major breaks with the tenets of historical materialism. First, he treated ownership as a set of powers, or rights, the elements of which could be separately varied and allocated. Marx, like Mises, took a different view, regarding the ideal-typical property relations of capitalism as highly interdependent, and not amenable to radical recombination.[4] Second, in Lange's framework socialism ceased to be a postcapitalist society, in the sense that it arose from the contradictory development of capitalism; instead, market socialism was viewed as an ever-present alternative form of economic organization. Third, socialism was to be judged by a new standard of efficiency to which historical materialism makes no reference: Resource allocation in relation to consumer preferences, not the development of productive power, took center stage.

None of these qualities of Lange's work was arbitrary; each follow from his neoclassicism. Neoclassical economics is universalistic. It makes no concession to the principle of historical specificity, according to which all the principal elements of a socioeconomic system are joined together in noncontingent ways. Furthermore, the elements of the analysis developed by neoclassicals are separated into two categories—exogenous and endogenous—and it is presumed that the exogenous elements are separable, so that "one at a time" comparative static thought experiments are legitimate. At the same time strong assumptions are made about the "noneconomic" areas of social life, while the institutional structures that might underpin them are unspecified. Neutral, honest, and efficient administrations facilitate the exercise of political power; cultural values accommodate individualism without threatening communal order; rationalism pervades human consciousness, while economic agents maximize as passive automatons within the prevailing rules of the game.

Of special importance for the question of market socialism is the neoclassical conception of endowments as exogenous, and the treatment of equilibrium prices as the principal explanandum. On this perspective the key neoclassical theorems are insensitive to what is assumed about asset distribution, and endogenous variables are not systematically related to different class structures (see, e.g., Arrow and Hahn 1971; Debreu 1959). Thus neoclassical theory attaches no significance to the existence of a capital–labor relation. It does not matter whether "workers rent capital" or "capital hires workers." Consequently, while the theory can make a case for market allocation, this case does not extend to capitalist markets.[5] It was precisely Lange's recognition of this, together with the dominance of neoclassical thought patterns within orthodox economics, which explains why he won the day during the 1930s.

THE AUSTRIAN COUNTERREVOLUTION AND THE RETURN OF HISTORICAL MATERIALISM

Austrian theorists, notably Friedrich von Hayek, conceded virtually nothing to the socialists. Instead they reformulated and extended Mises's original argument. In the process they broke with neoclassical theory and emphasized that capitalist property rights form an integral whole, which is especially conducive to the development of the productive forces. At the same time, the Austrian theorists reasserted other basic themes of historical materialism, themes which had been long forgotten because of the dominance of neoclassicism as the discourse in terms of which the economics of socialism was assessed. In short, while it would be too strong to claim that Lange and the market socialists had to abandon Marxism to defend socialism, and Hayek and the Austrians embraced Marx to attack it, to say this is to emphasize an ironic quality in the intellectual history of the socialist project. It has often been from the opponents of socialism that the arguments of historical materialism have been heard, and these are of crucial importance for assessing the feasibility of socialism.[6]

Disregarding the differences in language, Marx and Hayek are in agreement on two fundamental matters concerning the nature of capitalist social relations. First, the strength of capitalism lies in its dynamic transformative power, not in its ability to engender allocations that satisfy static utilitarian welfare criteria. Second, capitalism is especially effective in raising productivity, and this is so for three reasons. Capitalist relations provide relatively open access to the means of production for those willing to undertake innovation; they permit great flexibility in implementing technical change through the institutionalization of contractual freedom and wage labor; this in turn removes constraints on competing against those attached to existing technologies. Taken together, these three qualities ensure a tendency for technology to change, and also that this tendency is one of technical *progress*.

This last point is crucial to the question of the feasibility of socialism, including market socialism, and has been spelled out more fully by the Austrians than by Marxian exponents of historical materialism. Technical change induced by capitalism will have a pronounced bias to be genuinely productive, because production is for the market, and the receipt of profit and the costs of loss ensure that competence is rewarded and that mistakes are penalized. Frequently denounced as no more than a statement of bourgeois prejudice, this argument is generally misunderstood. Its force lies as much in the negative as in the positive. Outside the context of capitalist social relations the issue may not be one of an insufficient supply of innovations due to an absence of incentives, but of an inordinate demand for resources to implement new ideas, which arises from the reduced penalties for making mistakes.[7] And how can socialism implement penalties on the scale of capitalism, because part of the socialists' case is that these penalties are too severe? In other words, even if socialist relations of production encouraged inventiveness, this would not ensure more rapid technical progress. Unless those who erred bore the costs, the demand for resources to experiment could outstrip supplies, and, by the very nature of the case, any mechanism used to allocate resources would find it difficult to discover in advance what would prove to be genuinely productive. Concentrating the costs of failure on those responsible, however, conflicts with socialist values of equity and is impossible if property is socialized.

POST-LANGEAN ARGUMENTS FOR SOCIALISM

There are those who still proclaim the integrity of the classical Marxian conception of postcapitalist society (e.g., Mandel 1986). More typical, however, has been the view that the feasibility of any socialism requires the acceptance of markets, hard budget constraints, and some private property in the means of production. From the perspective of historical materialism, to be convincing these arguments must hinge on the claim that a socialization of markets will accelerate the development of productive power. Applied to specific activities such as health care, insurance, and informational services the logic is often compelling. As dissertations on the feasibility of a postcapitalist mode of production, however, these arguments are inadequate. In this section we examine a sample of the literature.

Michael Harrington (1989), and many others, claim that tendencies toward crises remain endemic in capitalism. In addition to the traditional forms of economic malfunctioning, new catastrophes also threaten, notably environmental destruction and the extermination of the species in a nuclear holocaust. Thus, it is maintained, humanity as a whole has a collective interest in transcending the status quo. As an argument for the feasibility of socialism, however, it is flawed when judged by the criterion of historical materialism. It confuses the irrationalities of a social system with the contradictions of a mode of production. Prevailing cultural norms may condemn real developments as dehumanizing and dangerous, but by the standards of historical materialism it is the contradictions that inhibit extended reproduction that ultimately count. Moreover, Harrington's argument does not touch upon the efficiency of the capital–labor relation in any particular branch of production, but relates only to the overall effects that he associates with capitalism as a system. For the reasons outlined in the first section above, crises that are purely systemic may carry little force with regard to the viability of sustainable socioeconomic transformations.

One might expect the argument of Gerry Cohen (1978, Chapter XI) to be more robust, since it appears in the final chapter of *Karl Marx's Theory of History*, which is widely regarded as the Magna Carta of exact thought in the field of historical materialism. But appearances are deceptive. Despite the claim that his argument for the feasibility of socialism hinges on the "distinctive contradiction" of advanced capitalism, Cohen in fact identifies no contradiction in the sense employed by historical materialists. Instead, the core of his analysis is the charge that capitalist relations of production preclude the fulfillment of people's needs for self-realization, as a result of the artificial bias that these relations lend to consumerism and routinized work. Cohen's argument thus focuses upon a maldistribution of the productive forces, not a fettering of their development, and, moreover, it is a misallocation only when judged by a hypothetical set of preferences. Thus, like Harrington, Cohen's concern is really with the irrationalities of capitalism, not with the contradictions as understood by historical materialists. And, judged by this latter standard, he accepts that capitalist relations do indeed develop productive power most rapidly. On the criteria set by his own work, then, Cohen's argument fails.

By the very same token, the thesis of Samuel Bowles and Herbert Gintis (1987) is much superior. Socialist forms, they argue, are both immanent and efficient. Since the eighteenth century there has been a discernible trend for political mobilization to center on the "rights of persons" rather than the "rights of property." In particular, the extension of the franchise has involved recognizing rights of citizenship that conflict with those of property, and property owners have had limitations placed on their legal title to use their assets as they deem appropriate. Moreover, Bowles and Gintis argue, economic development has now reached a stage where participatory organizational structures can increase labor productivity.

But there are two grave weaknesses in this argument. The "rights of persons" are not *ipso facto* anticapitalist; they have often purified and strengthened capitalist relations by weakening forms of oppression and patriarchy, as in the case of extending civil rights to minorities and women. Of course, if this "tendency" now involves the democratization of the economy, and the new relations of production can out-compete authoritarian forms of organization, historical materialism suggests that this version of socialism does offer a viable postcapitalist society. The doubt arises from the fact that such new forms of participatory organization are not much in evidence.[8] After all, capitalism is founded on contract, with both incentives and compulsions to develop the productive forces. Thus, if participatory forms proved effective, they should have developed endogenously *within* capitalism.[9] Furthermore, democratization must be constrained if the "creative destruction" of innovation is to be allowed to do its work. Those whose lives are disrupted can hardly be expected to refrain from the rent-seeking potentialities that their political power provides.

Not surprisingly, other modern-day socialist economists take a position that is almost the direct opposite to that of Bowles and Gintis: If socialism is to be feasible, it must confine democracy in much the same way as capitalism does. This, for example, is the view of Bardhan and Roemer (1992) who, in addition to recognizing possible conflicts between popular control and economic efficiency,[10] also attempt to provide a model of market socialism that takes account of the information and incentive problems inherent in principal–agent relationships. Their work seeks to incorporate the "informational revolution" of neoclassical theory, and in consequence their "blueprint" is very much more complex than that of Lange. The heart of their scheme might reasonably be summarized by saying that it represents "Japanese capitalism without private property." This, they claim, can be expected to combine efficiency with equity by rendering the distribution of profits less unequal. The overriding deficiency of this argument stems from a failure to recognize that innovations affect institutions as much as production processes. This means that organizational arrangements must be regarded as transient, as can be seen from the very Japanese example from which Bardhan and Roemer draw their inspiration. It appears that the *keiretsu* system has been unraveling in recent years, due largely to the financial innovations originating in Anglo-American capitalism that have made securitization more efficient than bank-centered finance (*The Economist* 1992). Thus any model of socialism designed in the detailed manner of Bardhan and Roemer must fail on the grounds that, whatever its efficiency at any specific date, the probability is that, relative to capitalism, it will ultimately fetter the productive forces because it lacks the flexibility of institutional adaptation.

CONCLUSION

Marx's economics provides a convincing explanation as to why capitalist modes of production thrive, and an unconvincing explanation as to why this will be temporary. He recognized that the capital–labor relation is highly functional for the development of the productive forces by comparison with precapitalist economic formations. And, because his argument hinges on the absence of conscious social control, its continued acceptance need imply nothing Panglossian.[11] However, Marx's belief that capitalism would be superseded by socialism is flawed, since there is no foundation for the view that a qualitative leap in social control will facilitate a more rapid advance of the productive forces. Moreover, political economy since Marx has provided nothing to subvert this conclusion. Whatever solace there is for socialists lies only in the realm of analysis: it is socialist theory, in the form of historical materialism, that provides a powerful account of why this is so.

NOTES

1. There are many interpretations of historical materialism. We take the summary provided by the Preface in Marx (1971a, 20–22) as definitive.

2. Admittedly, there is some ambiguity in this concept. See, for example, G. A. Cohen (1988, 109–133).

3. This applies to many non-Marxian socialists as well as Marxians: See Beilharz (1992).

4. See, for example, Marx (1971c), where he attacks Proudhon for failing to recognize this.

5. More specifically, this statement is true of neoclassical economics before the "informational revolution" of the last thirty years, which has substantially modified traditional neoclassical propositions. See, for example, Stiglitz (1975; 1986), Putterman (1986), and Alt and Shepsle (1990).

6. Hayek can be criticized for failing to recognize the historical significance of very different forms of capitalism, which reflect institutional substitutions resulting from uneven development, alternative methods of labor control, varying positions within the world economy, and diverse cultural heritages. But much the same can be said of Marx, despite the attention given to these issues by Marxian political economy in the twentieth century. We are concerned here only with the similarity between Hayek's and Marx's ideas on the productivity effect of "ideal-typical" capitalist relations, and not their views as to how far particular concrete manifestations of these relations are sustainable.

7. The evidence from what were then "actually existing socialisms" in Eastern Europe is fully in accord with this: See Kornai (1980).

8. There are other grounds for doubt, which have been highlighted by the literature on worker-owned firms. Equity problems aside, employee owners would have a tendency to undervalue the revenues that accrue beyond their term of employment, thus generating suboptimal investments and a proclivity to cannibalize assets. At the same time, the concentration of workers' assets in the firm that they own will bias their choices owing to risk aversion, and, insofar as profits are maximized, they will favor those projects with the highest profits per worker. Again, this can result in nonoptimal patterns of resource allocation.

9. Bowles and Gintis do address this issue, suggesting that imperfections in capital and labor markets, and opposition by property owners, may inhibit the development of participatory forms of economic organization. However, from the viewpoint of historical materialism the effect can only be temporary if economic democratization does indeed bring about productivity gains. According to the materialist conception of history, neither the form of productive relations, nor ideologies, are independent variables; insofar as they have economic significance, each is ultimately determined by the requirements of the productive forces. Nevertheless, there is a problem for historical materialism here, since the time dimension involved is unspecified.

10. Bardhan and Roemer's treatment of democracy affirms it as a value, but their discussion of its role approximates the view of Woodrow Wilson, who, it is alleged, once remarked, "If this thing is to be democratically run, I must have complete control."

11. In this respect it is sobering to remember Schumpeter's depiction of capitalism as summarized by Joan Robinson (1964, 130): the "system is cruel, unjust, turbulent, but it does deliver the goods, and damn it all, it's goods . . . [that people] . . . want."

REFERENCES

Alt, J. E. and Shepsle, K. eds. 1990. *Perspectives on Positive Political Economy*. Cambridge, England: Cambridge University Press.

Arrow, K. J. and Hahn, F. H. 1971. *General Competitive Analysis*. Edinburgh: Oliver and Boyd.

Bardhan, P. and Roemer, J. E. 1992. "Market Socialism: A Case for Rejuvenation." *Journal of Economic Perspectives* 6: 101–116.

Beilharz , P. 1992. *Labor's Utopias*. London: Routledge.

Bowles, S. and Gintis, H. 1987. *Democracy and Capitalism*. New York: Basic Books.

Cohen, G. A. 1978. *Karl Marx's Theory of History*. Oxford, England: Oxford University Press.

——. 1988. *History, Labour and Freedom*. Oxford, England: Clarendon Press.

Debreu, G. 1959. *Theory of Value*. New Haven, CT: Yale University Press.

Harrington, M. 1989. *Socialism: Past and Future*. New York: Arcade.

Howard, M. C. and King, J. E. 1985. *The Political Economy of Marx*. Harlow: Longman.

——. 1989. *A History of Marxian Economics, Volume I, 1883–1929*. London: Macmillan.

——. 1992. *A History of Marxian Economics, Volume II, 1929–1990*. London: Macmillan.

Kornai, J. 1980. *Economics of Shortage*. Amsterdam: North Holland.

Lange, O. 1971. "On the Economic Theory of Socialism." In *Socialist Economics*, eds. A. Nove and D. Nuti, 92–110. Harmondsworth, England: Penguin.

Mandel, E. 1986. "In Defense of Socialist Planning." *New Left Review* 159: 5–37.

Marx, K. 1970. *Capital*, Vol. I. London: Lawrence and Wishart.

——. 1971a. *A Contribution to the Critique of Political Economy*. London: Lawrence and Wishart.

——. 1971b. *Capital*, Vol. III. London: Lawrence and Wishart.

——. 1971c. *The Poverty of Philosophy*. New York: International Publishers.

——. 1973. *Grundrisse*. Harmondsworth, England: Penguin.

Nozick, R. 1974. *Anarchy, State and Utopia*. New York: Basic Books.

Putterman, L. ed. 1986. *The Economic Nature of the Firm: A Reader*. Cambridge, England: Cambridge University Press.

Robinson, J. 1964. *Economic Philosophy*. Harmondsworth, England: Penguin.

Stiglitz, J. 1975. "Information and Economic Analysis." In *Current Economic Problems*, ed. M. Parkin and A. Nobay, 27–52. Cambridge, England: Cambridge University Press.

——. 1986. "The New Development Economics." *World Development* 14: 257–265.

The Economist. 1992. "A Survey of World Banking." May 22: 1–52.

von Mises, L. 1971. "Economic Calculation in the Socialist Commonwealth." In *Socialist Economics*, ed. A. Nove and D. Nuti, 75–91. Harmondsworth, England: Penguin.

The Relevance of Marxist Theory for Understanding the Present World Crisis

ERNEST MANDEL

THE CAPITALIST ECONOMIC CRISIS

The present crisis of the international capitalist economy is a classical business cycle crisis, the twenty-third one since the inception of the world market for industrial goods (the early 1820s). As such, it is both a crisis of overaccumulation of capital and a crisis of overproduction of commodities, triggered by a decline of the average rate of profit. But it is a classical business cycle crisis within the framework of a long depressive wave, which started in the early 1970s and which is characterized by a constant rise in unemployment (in the imperialist countries from around 10 to more than 50 million, in the third world countries at least 500 million), as well as by a reduction of the long-term average rate of growth to less than half of what it had been in the previous long expansive wave (the so-called postwar boom).

All business cycles and "long waves" in the nineteenth and twentieth centuries combine basic general characteristics with specific features. During a long depressive wave, the capitalist class tries to produce new general conditions of accumulation that permit a rise of the average rate of profit. This does not imply only a series of technological innovations enabling vanguard firms to gain surplus profits. It also implies a general increase in the average rate of surplus value (the rate of exploitation of wage labor), and attempts to erode, or break, wage labor's resistance to this drive.

Today this drive centers around the attempts to introduce a "dual society," to break up the collective solidarity of the working class, to hit especially weaker sectors of the class: "third world" wage earners, the unemployed, youth, ethnic minorities, immigrant workers, women, and so on. In addition, attempts at transferring production locations and reorganizing the work process tend to weaken or even destroy collective solidarity and the unions at the workplace.

However, all these attempts, while putting the working class on the defensive, do not automatically lead to full success. The class relationship of forces plays a key role in that respect. That relationship of forces is more a cumulative result of the previous, partially autonomous, class struggle cycle, than of the current economic "long wave." From that point of view, a basic difference with the previous long depression is obvious. In no major country has the working class suffered a crushing defeat as it did in the 1920s and 1930s, with the exception of the United States.

But as there has been a significant lowering of the class consciousness of the working class, a general crisis of credibility of the socialist goal (socialist project) at least for broad masses, a historical stalemate has emerged. Neither of the two basic classes, the capitalist class or the working class, is able to impose its overall solution to the crisis. The capitalist class cannot, because of the relative strength (capacity of resistance) of the working class. The working class cannot because of its crisis of consciousness and mass leadership. So the crisis will be a prolonged one. No radical outcome will occur in the coming years, in one way or another.

One cannot challenge this analysis and its conclusions by just stating that it is "dogmatic" or "old-fashioned." One can only challenge it by proving that there is strong empirical evidence that contradicts it, and that it is internally incoherent. We haven't seen any such demonstration. Those who continue nevertheless to challenge us therefore are themselves guilty of unscientific dogmatic prejudice.

THE CRISIS OF THE "THIRD WORLD"

In the "third world," the socioeconomic crisis of underdevelopment is fundamentally a crisis of quantitative and qualitative underemployment—qualitative underemployment meaning average employment at a level of productivity of labor radically lower than that of industrialized countries. Again, there is no possibility of overcoming that crisis in the foreseeable future. The stranglehold of imperialist Big Business, aided and abetted by the "local" ruling classes, prevents this.

But within the framework of the long depression, traditional third world misery, at least as it was during the previous long wave, has dramatically increased. Hunger and poverty have risen to the point where U.N. officials speak about one billion people living below the poverty line, very conservatively defined. Sixteen million children die every year from hunger and curable diseases. This means that every four years the same number of children die as the total number of victims during the whole of World War II, Auschwitz, Hiroshima, and the Bengal famine included. Every four years a world war against third world children: There you have the reality of today's imperialism/capitalism with all its barbaric implications.

That misery has already acquired a biological dimension. In the Northeast of Brazil, a new "race" of pygmies has arisen, as the cumulative result of several generations of hunger and malnutrition. Their average body height is around thirty-five centimeters lower than that of the average Brazilian. The ruling class—its hangers-on and ideologues—calls them "rat people." As in the case of the Nazis, "dehumanization" in language and ideology opens the road to inhuman practices. The Ralph Nader group of investigators has discovered similar biological/genetic disorders right at the U.S.–Mexican border.

It is an absolute illusion to believe that the effects of rising barbarism in the third world on the metropolitan countries themselves will remain insignificant. The low income of the great majority of the third world already severely limits a further expansion of world trade and is therefore one of the causes preventing a new "expansive long wave" to occur. The "pay back your foreign debt" offensive of the International Monetary Fund (IMF) and the World Bank towards the third world countries is economically counterproductive, causing loss of jobs and increasing poverty in the West as well. It is likewise morally repugnant, because it means that the poor of the poor countries are subsidizing the rich of the rich countries.

But the gravest effects of rising barbarism in the third world are those upon the overall world health situation. Poverty-related epidemics like cholera and tuberculosis are on the rise again, worldwide. The total inadequacy of AIDS prevention measures in the third world, where for the time being the great majority of AIDS infections occur, will strongly increase the number of AIDS-related deaths in the West too.

To summarize: The spread of barbarism in the third world will lead to a growing "third worldization" of an increasing number of "Northern" countries too, including the bureaucratized postcapitalist countries.

THE CRISIS IN THE BUREAUCRATIZED POSTCAPITALIST SOCIETIES

The collapse of the Stalinist and post-Stalinist dictatorships in Eastern Europe and the former USSR can be explained with the tools of Marxist analysis of historical materialism. Indeed , we have not come across any more sophisticated explanation of that collapse than the Marxist one. For orthodox Marxists, "really existing socialism" never was socialism. They don't say this only today; they have been saying it for nearly seventy years, since Stalin launched his ill-fated theory of achieving the building of socialism in one country. There was no way in which the USSR or the "socialist camp" could in the long run escape the pressure of the arms race with imperialism and the pressure of the capitalist world market, the undeniable partial success it achieved in both respects notwithstanding. Nor can the collapse of the Stalinist/post-Stalinist dictatorships be viewed as a failure of central planning. Central planning means proportional development of the main branches of the economy and of social expenditure, at least as proportional as possible. Bureaucratically centralized planning was from the beginning characterized by tremendous disproportions, bordering on the irrational.

The consequences were inevitable. The laws of reproduction being what they are, the average rate of growth was doomed to decline, to the point where it became impossible to realize simultaneously the continuation of the call for arms parity with the United States, the further modernization of the economy, and a modest but regular increase in the masses' standard of living. The rest is recent history.

Of course, this is only part of the picture. Bureaucratic central planning made possible several striking achievements. The most important one was in the field of cultural-scientific progress, including first-rate technological advances in several limited sectors. Within one generation, the USSR was transformed from a relatively backward country into the second industrial power of the world. This was achieved at tremendous costs and under a bureaucratic stranglehold that more and more impeded further progress.

This was not the only road open for the USSR. There was a concrete alternative, as developed by the Left Opposition and Trotsky's and Rakovsky's writings from 1930 (Mandel 1992b). More generally, the idea that there exists only a choice between an economy ruled by the market and a bureaucratically ruled command economy—"*tertium non datur*," in the words of Alec Nove—is unproven and incorrect. There is a third alternative: the economic system of democratic socialism, in which the priorities in the allocation of scarce resource are to an important extent determined a priori by the mass of the toilers/consumers/citizens themselves, in a democratic way, with a pluriparty system and full political democracy, enabling the masses to choose between coherent alternative central plans. This implies necessary corrections through a limited use of market mechanisms, but without these determining the general trends of socioeconomic development. The feasibility of this third model hinges above all upon a radical reduction of work time, and the sovereignty of the direct producers freely to determine what to produce, how to produce it, and how to distribute the major component of current production. Any progress in the direction of socialism can be measured by the results achieved in that respect.

I say, "in the direction of socialism." A fully developed socialist society is unrealizable in a single country, or a small number of countries, even when this optimal economic/political model is successfully applied. It will still be a society in transition between capitalism and socialism. But it will mean important economic and especially social progress toward emancipation. And it will unleash a process of dialectical interaction (successive feedbacks) between these emancipatory processes on the one hand, and the development of challenges toward the capitalist system in the metropolitan countries on the other hand, on the basis of maturing class consciousness and class organization/vanguard organization inside these countries. Only when a key number of industrially leading nations will have broken with capitalism will the realization of a fully developed socialist society be put on the agenda.

THE WORLDWIDE CRISIS OF CREDIBILITY OF THE SOCIALIST PROJECT

From the collapse of the Stalinist/post-Stalinist dictatorships in Eastern Europe and the USSR, large masses, in these countries as well as in the rest of the world, conclude that socialism as a model of a qualitatively better society has failed. As a result of the parallel indoctrination of the Stalinists/post-Stalinists, and the bourgeois/pro-Western ideologues, the bureaucratic dictatorship became identified with communism/socialism. As the masses resolutely rejected that dictatorship, they also reject communism, Marxism, and socialism, at least for the time being.

This identification is of course completely unfounded. Stalin and the Soviet *Nomenklatura* were not "utopians" dedicated to building a classless society. They were cynical Realpoliticians, bent upon consolidating and expanding their power and material privileges. For adherents to historical materialism these processes were a function of the struggle between specific social forces. If Stalinism claimed to be "Marxist–Leninist," while negating in theory and practice key aspects of Marx's and Lenin's theories and projections, this had a very concrete function. Stalinism arose as a political counterrevolution (the Soviet Thermidor) in a country that had gone through a profound social revolution, in a party that had been fully dedicated to socialism. Claiming a historical continuity with these traditions made the consolidation of bureaucratic power easier.

But the crisis of credibility of socialism is not primarily the result of that claimed continuity. If the masses reject the Stalinist/post-Stalinist "model," it is in the first place because that "model" went against their elementary interests. It did not fulfill their material expectations. It negated their basic human rights. It committed terrible crimes, caused the death of millions, among them one million Communists. It violated the masses' elementary thirst for justice and equality. No bourgeois propaganda was necessary to make them hostile to the system; their daily experience was sufficient to produce that hostility.

There is a second source of the worldwide crisis of credibility of the socialist project: the historical failure of social democracy, although it is true that this failure has to be more clearly circumscribed. The social democratic labor movement (later in conjunction with mass Communist Parties (CPs) in a process of *de facto* social democratization), largely in periods of impetuous mass mobilizations and mass struggles, had wrenched important concessions from the capitalist class. The most important of them were the reduction of the work week from seventy-two to an average of thirty-eight hours, universal equal franchise, and various degrees of protection against the greatest hazards of the proletarian condition. The sum total of these reforms has substantially changed the world compared to what it had been in 1800, 1850, or 1914. In that sense, we can be proud of the achievements of the socialist struggle, in which Marxists played a key role.

But nowhere did the accumulation of these reforms lead to a qualitative change of society. Nowhere did they eliminate the basic nature of the social (dis)order. This is not a purely semantic dispute; it has imminently practical implications. To say that these reforms have not transcended the capitalist nature of economy and society implies that they have not prevented periodic economic crises, periodic bursts of mass unemployment and mass poverty, periodic restrictions or abolitions of democratic freedoms and human rights, and periodic wars and other catastrophes. It implies that the reforms themselves are periodically threatened as long as the bourgeois class has the power to try to do so. And it also implies that the extent of the reforms is at least correlated with a certain level of economic development, and therefore limited to a large degree to a given number of countries.

Now, it is a historical fact that millions of wage earners throughout the world were deeply convinced that these partial conquests would eventually lead to a new, just society—to socialism. Today, in their eyes, it is clear that they didn't. This negative side of the balance sheet of social democracy and neo-social democracy is strengthened by the record of the crimes committed by the social democratic leaders: colonial wars and the spearheading of the austerity policy-type attacks against the workers' living conditions, to cite the most important examples. This means that the two main historical projects of realizing socialism have failed in the eyes of masses. Since the revolutionary socialists operating on the left of the CPs and the social democrats are both still much too weak to represent a political alternative, there exists no such credible project anymore for the working class. This does not mean that the masses accept capitalism with all its evils or that they don't fight to defend their interests as they see them. On the contrary, some of the mass struggles unfolding today are broader than ever before. But they are single-issue struggles, not embedded in an orientation towards an overall social and political alternative to capitalism. Therefore, they tend to be discontinuous and fragmented.

In order to overcome this crisis of credibility of the socialist project, it is necessary to eliminate any form of substitutionism from socialist practice and theory, and to return to Marx's main contribution to the doctrine of socialism: to wit, that the emancipation of the toilers can only be the work of the toilers themselves. While Stalinists and post-Stalinists (today above all, Maoists) have been guilty of the most extreme forms of substitutionism, they are by no means the only culprits. Social Democrats, reformists of all shades, extreme ecologists, belong to the same current. In the name of all kinds of priorities, like economic efficiency, an "open" economy, the protection of the environment, a stop to demographic "explosion," they want to impose policies that the masses do not accept, and that can only be implemented by institutions and organizations that want to substitute themselves to the self-activity and self-organization of the masses as the main tools of progress and emancipation.

This substitutionism is based on the technocratic arrogance that "experts" and ideologues know better, if not that they are infallible. Substitutionism is the ideology of the labor bureaucracy, as I have tried to prove in my book *Power and Money* (1992a). It is alien to Marxism and to the interests of the working class, and is fundamentally ineffective in the long run. If there is one lesson to be drawn from the collapse of Stalinism and the crisis of social democracy it is this: You can't make the masses happy against their will. You can't ram a "radiant future" down their throats; sooner or later, they will throw it back to your face.

This recuperation of the practice and theory of self-activity and self-organization of the working class as the main motor of emancipation—trade unions, parties, governments, states being indispensable tools, but remaining subordinate to self-activity and self-organization of the proletariat[1]—has to go hand in hand with full support to mass struggles throughout the world, regardless of any "superior priority" like "defending the socialist camp," anti-imperialism, protecting a "competitive edge of 'national' economy on the world market," and so on.

It has likewise to go hand in hand with an unlimited defense of democratic freedom and human rights. It is not the smallest of the crimes of Stalinists, Maoists and Social Democrats that they have broken the original unity between socialism and freedom. This unity was symbolically expressed by the classical song of the Italian labor movement, "Bandiera Rossa," when, after Mussolini's coming to power, Italian Communist workers and intellectuals added to it as final words: "*Evviva il comunismo e la libertà*": Long live communism and freedom.

Today and tomorrow, socialism will only recover its credibility in the eyes of the broad masses if experience teaches them that socialists stand more radically for freedom than bourgeois liberals, that the socialist goal towards which we strive will guarantee much more freedom than bourgeois society.

AN INITIAL AGENDA FOR A NEW FLOWERING OF CREATIVE, OPEN MARXISM

A thousand books and magazine and newspaper articles are proclaiming, "Marx is dead," and "Marxism is dead." You do not need to be an adherent of the dialectical way of thinking to understand that this campaign proves exactly the opposite of what it intends to prove. One does not see hundreds of medical doctors gathering day after day at the cemetery, to prove that a given casket contains a corpse. In fact, if the uninterrupted assault proves anything, it is that Marx and Marxism are alive and kicking. But Marxism can stay alive only if it does not become dogmatically petrified, only if it is open and creative. The crisis of Stalinism/post-Stalinism since the Hungarian Revolution of 1956 has already stimulated a first flowering of creative Marxism, away from sterile scholasticism, neo-positivism, and vulgar pragmatism. Today the floodgates can open.

Marxists have to integrate into their basic theories—which are working hypothesis and not axioms or definitively revealed truths—the accumulated results of current scientific research. They have to examine to what extent these results can be integrated into the theories without challenging their inner coherence. Marxists are especially under the pressure of new objective realities, which did not exist or existed only marginally in earlier decades, and of a new subjective awareness of them.

Without pretending to be exhaustive, I would tentatively list the following agenda of priorities for "theoretical practice":

1. To explain the basic trend towards "globalization" of key economic and social developments, obviously tied in with the growing internalization of the productive forces of capital, and draw-

ing the necessary conclusions therefrom regarding the growing internationalization of the class struggle.

2. To integrate into the struggle for socialism and our model of socialism the main aspects of the ecological crisis, to discover a way to quantify ecological costs and combine them with labor costs.

3. To deepen our understanding of the dialectics of work, leisure, and (re)education, while combining it with a broadened understanding of the hierarchy of human needs. Nothing can justify any vision of the world and world's future in which the need to feed the hungry, to house the homeless, to cure the sick, to eliminate torture, and to fight against the main forms of discrimination, inequality, and injustice are not considered as immediate urgent priorities.

4. To develop the theory of political institutions necessary for radical emancipation, involving direct and representative democracy, using as stepping stones Marx and Engels's writings on the Paris Commune, Rosa Luxemburg's writings of 1918, Gramsci's writings of *Ordine Nuovo*, Trotsky's writings of the 1930s, and later contributions as those of the Fourth International.[2]

5. To broaden our understanding of the dialectical impact of the media revolution (the culture of images as different from the culture of printed texts) on cultural consumption and cultural production. To analyze the crisis of proletarian counterculture in that light, its impact on the relative decline of class consciousness, and the ways to overcome them.

6. To further develop our understanding of the origins of women's oppression, the ways to overcome it, the dialectics of the crisis of the nuclear family, the integration of an understanding of that crisis with an understanding of the crisis of broader human communities.

7. To deepen our understanding of the dialectics of social and individual emancipation and freedom.

This tentative agenda of "theoretical practice" cannot, for epistemological reasons, be divorced from practical endeavors to build a better world. There is no other way than through practice finally to test the validity of any theory. And it cannot be so divorced for moral objectives. Marxism has two roots that are independent from each other, in spite of all their obvious intertwinings. It has a scientific basis, which obeys only the laws of science, and these cannot be subordinated to any political purpose. It has also a moral basis, clearly formulated by the young Marx and restated by him towards the end of his life: the categorical imperative to strive to overthrow all social conditions in which human beings are exploited, oppressed, humiliated, and alienated.

This categorical imperative remains as valid today as it ever was. In letting our actions and our lives be guided by it, we are the heirs of a proud tradition of more than 3,500 years of rebellion, revolt, and revolution. Let our enemies shout "dangerous utopians" at us. History speaks against them. We have by and large overcome slavery, overcome serfdom, overcome the Inquisition and the burning of heretics at the stake. We have stormed the Bastilles. We shall overcome wage labor too. But we shall only succeed if our own political/social practice strictly conforms to our principles, if we do not approve or condone any policy contrary to them, even when it is applied in the name of socialism or progress, by self-styled socialists. If we succeed in convincing broader and broader masses of our real and honest resolution in that sense, we shall achieve a moral superiority over all other political/social forces, which will make us truly invincible.

NOTES

1. I use the concept "proletariat" in the classical Marxist sense: all those who are under an economic compulsion to sell their labor power.

2. More precisely, I refer to the Fourth International's programmatic documents on women's oppression and on socialist democracy, to the programmatic Manifesto emanating of its latest World Congress, and to the document "Ecology and Socialism" prepared for its next World Congress.

REFERENCES

Mandel, E. 1992a. *Power and Money*. London: Verso.
Mandel, E. 1992b. *Trotzki als Alternative*. Berlin: Dietz.

Columbus, Paradise, and the Theory of Capitalist Development

RICHARD MCINTYRE

In the Preface to the second edition of *Marxist Theories of Imperialism*, published in 1990, Anthony Brewer writes: "In revising the book for the second edition, I found few major new ideas to incorporate; the last decade has been one of consolidation and reassessment" (1990, ix). The last great reassessment of the theory of imperialism, which began in the 1950s with the work of Paul Baran (1957), had largely exhausted itself by the late 1970s. Since then specific issues in the history of imperialism have received new attention, but the sense of imperialism as provoking new and important work in Marxian theory is absent, despite general dissatisfaction with the received wisdom. Simultaneously, there has been a flowering of studies of European cultural domination and of the ecological dilemmas posed by European expansion. While some of this work has been carried out by Marxists, much of it is by authors for whom Marxism is part of the problem or completely irrelevant. In addition, there is a general sense that the time and spatial characteristics of late twentieth-century social and natural life are profoundly different from what has preceded it. "New world order," "the end of history," "the global economy," and "multiculturalism" are only some of the trendy phrases trotted out to describe a vaguely understood difference.

The exhaustion of the theory of imperialism, the rise of cultural and ecological studies, the new world order and the end of history, the global economy and multiculturalism: Into this theoretical and polemical maelstrom walked the shade of Christopher Columbus. The end of history seemed, for some, to be a good time to reflect upon the beginning of modern history, with Columbus's "enterprise" as its leading edge. Grand celebrations were planned to commemorate the man who began the process of global unification and played such a critical role in establishing the first European world order five hundred years ago.

What was in the end most impressive about the official quincentenary was its *absence*. Many of the most conspicuous events were canceled, those that did occur either ignored Columbus, the supposed reason for the event in the first place, were quite defensive in tone, or balanced whatever celebration that could be mustered with a critical eye towards the negative impacts of Columbus's invasion of the Americas. Shortly after the feeble commemoration of Columbus, Rigoberta Menchu won the Nobel peace prize for her work defending indigenous peoples in Guatemala. The contest over Columbus was a sign of the strength of the multicultural critique of imperialism. It was a remarkable teaching opportunity, since it was obvious that the discussion of Columbus was also a dialogue on today's world. It also demonstrated, I believe, the contradictory effects of a purely cultural critique. The seamless story of a decadent West descended directly from Columbus misreads the diverse history of European expansion, creates an untenable continuity between Columbus and the present day, and reinforces negative aspects of identity politics.

THE CONQUEST OF PARADISE

Kirkpatrick Sale's *The Conquest of Paradise* (1990) is the most accessible of the various revisionist accounts of Columbus and his legacy. For Sale, the "modern age" begins with the voyages of Christopher Columbus. The legacy of Columbus's "discovery" is clear to Sale: European global dominance; "modern" civilization; extinction, alteration, and creation of species; and, "most significant," human domination over and potential destruction of nature. It is notable that two of the four aspects of Columbus's legacy are ecological, and that human domination and potential destruction of nature is the "most significant" for Sale. His is an ecological critique of European expansion, which finds the cause of new world ecological destruction in aspects of European culture that were prevalent in Columbus's time and have been conserved to the present. Studying Columbus's character gives clues to the forces that shaped the origins of the modern age and that "still for the most part shape it" (1990, 5). Directly, and by example, Columbus is responsible for the implantation of European culture in and domination of the Americas. Thus Sale emphasizes the continuities between the sixteenth century and the present, and claims that the character of the modern age—both in its beginnings and today—can be read off from the shadowy figure of Columbus.

Sale's treatment of the European crisis at the time of Columbus is consistent with his general thesis. Disease and famine were both widespread and the Dance of Death was a recurrent cultural theme. The possibility of the imminent end of the world was taken seriously. Estrangement from nature, the death cult of late medieval decay, and rising "capitalism": This is what invaded the Americas, according to Sale. The European reaction to the native peoples was a confused and shifting combination of the *noble savage* and the *savage beast*. Descriptions of the natural life and egalitarian societies of the Americas sharply struck the "morose and troubled European soul." More's *Utopia* was inspired by Vespucci's lavish descriptions of the new world. But the noble savage is always intertwined with the savage beast. The latter image gradually dominated, particularly when something of real value was discovered in lands occupied by non-Europeans. What was a tension in Columbus was a one-sided story for Cortez and Pizarro. Bestial themes, tales of cannibalism, and figures of wild men increasingly dominated the literature. According to Sale, "The only way the people of Christian Europe ultimately could live with the reality of the noble savage in the Golden World was to transform it progressively into the savage beast in the Hideous Wilderness— and to progressively destroy it" (1990, 203).

This cautionary tale seems to me highly appropriate and one Sale himself might have paid more attention to. The savage beast lurks in every tale of the noble savage. Yet Sale himself goes to great lengths to establish the nobility of the native peoples. The world Columbus found "was, in fact, as close to Paradise as non celestial existence has" (1990, 177). For Sale, the native Americans were the "first ecologists," consciously limiting their numbers to prevent environmental destruction. Because of their own prejudices, the Europeans could not grasp the egalitarian nature of these societies. The native peoples had no idea of progress, and lacked both humanism and a utilitarian view of nature. According to Sale, European historians, particularly Marxian materialists, fail to understand this biological and ecological thought-world. The new world could have been Europe's salvation. The sick society that was sixteenth-century Europe could have been soothed by the new world societies' communitarian values, biological rather than humanist outlook, antiprogressive culture, and sacred rather than material approach to the land.

This tendency to glorify native society is, I believe, increasingly prevalent on the Left. It is founded on an uncritical acceptance of the myth of the noble savage, and a failure to deconstruct the noble savage/savage beast couplet. Sale's rejection of all that is "Europe" leaves him with a rather naive and mystical celebration of pre-European North American culture. Sale castigates "Europe," rather than seeing in Europe a complex, contradictory set of social and natural practices that must be deconstructed. Despite some statements to the contrary, Sale seems to believe that the critical aspects of English expansion were those that mirrored Spanish colonialism. This contention is crucial for Sale since he wants to argue for the essential continuity of history from Columbus's time to the present, despite his awareness that English imperialism differed from Spanish imperialism in critical ways. Thus the transfer from Spain to England must not involve any *essential* rupture, just as the later, and mostly presumed transfer from England to the United States must also involve continuity rather than change.

But whereas Spanish expansion was a continuation of the attempt to solve the crisis of feudalism, English expansion was a commercial, political, and social enterprise spurred by international struggle with Spain and a search for greater self-sufficiency. Spain attempted to solve its feudal crisis by locating, seizing, and distributing booty. England solved its crisis internally through intensified cultivation, the development of manufactures, and cooperation among the Crown, merchants, and landowners. English and Spanish attitudes toward the nature of wealth, the land, and the rights of indigenous peoples differed dramatically. The later differences in English and Latin American development are related to these quite different modes of colonial conquest. Sale's collapse of Spain into England, and England into America abstracts from all of these differences (Martland 1992).

By 1620, the Virginia planters were completely absorbed with tobacco production, ensuring that the minimum number of people would have the maximum impact on the soil. The Tidewater region still exhibits the ecological effects of this form of agriculture. Sale finds it instructive that the first colony of what was to become the United States was saved by and constructed around a cancer causing, environmentally destructive crop.

A comparative handful of Europeans had done more to alter the environment in a century than the native Americans had accomplished in 1,500 years. According to Sale,

> It took a special kind of mind to see that impact as beneficial, as "progress," indeed as "civilization." But the European (and the American successor) possessed just such a mind: those English who clear-cut their way through ancient primordial forests actually spoke of "making land." (1990, 291–292)

Sale's *Conquest of Paradise* is a splendidly angry and beautifully written book. It makes a substantial contribution to history and to our understanding of contemporary North American society. From a Marxian perspective, however, several of its themes are troubling. These are its equation of capitalism with the market, the presumption of continuity rather than discontinuity in the history of imperialism, a drift toward cultural determinism, and glorification of the noble savage. Sale's story dovetails not only with prevalent themes in cultural studies, but with the still influential world systems theory. Indeed, Sale draws heavily from Braudel, in some ways the grandfather of the world systems approach. According to world systems theory, the place of any society in the world today was more or less established in the initial European division of the world in the sixteenth century; capitalism is a system of production for the market; and different modes of labor exploitation are determined simply by efficiency considerations. Sale is antagonistic to Marxism, but he is also more attuned to the ecological and cultural considerations that increasingly dominate discussions of imperialism than are most writers in the world systems approach. Each of the themes common to Sale and to world systems theory has, I believe, unfortunate political effects. Before elaborating these effects, I present an alternative Marxian approach to European expansion.

EUROPE AND THE PEOPLE WITHOUT HISTORY

Eric Wolf's *Europe and the People without History* (1982) is not about Columbus. Rather, it is an attempt to rethink anthropology in light of the revival of Marxian theory—particularly what Wolf calls historically oriented political economy—of the 1960s and 1970s. For Wolf, societies differ according to their mode of production, or the combination of modes of production of which they are constituted. The *capitalist* mode, for Wolf, possesses an ability to develop internally as well as to branch out and to enter into symbiotic and competitive relations with other modes. Capitalism's "internal dynamic" more or less implies expansion.

Wolf defines the *tributary* mode as one in which the primary producer has access to the means of production, but tribute is exacted politically or militarily. Ideology plays a central organizing role in tributary societies, and the most successful societies have been those that have effectively provided supernatural origins and validation for surplus takers. There are a variety of ways in which tribute is gathered, circulated, and distributed. Most often, merchants play a crucial role in exchange and transfer of surplus.

While the rise of merchants, and joint ventures between merchants and sovereigns, such as Columbus's enterprise, were critical aspects of European development and expansion, Wolf denies a smooth continuity between merchanting and capitalism. He follows Marx in arguing that mercantile wealth was not capital so long as production was dominated by kin-ordered or tributary relations. The expansion of Europe beginning in the early fifteenth century extended the scope and scale of the market but did not lead to the installation of the capitalist mode of production. The tributary mode remained dominant until attacked from within by capitalism in the eighteenth century. Merchants opened up channels of exchange, profiting from price differentials and plunder. They sought political protection of markets and relied on political and military power to gain access to suppliers, bar competitors, and reap monopoly profits. But they did not create a wage labor force. Rather, they remained wedded to the tributary mode.

In *kin-ordered*, or primitive communist modes, there is no division of society into surplus takers and producers. Whereas other modes require the coercive apparatus of the state to ensure surplus appropriation, kin-ordered modes do not. Contact with foreign formations often stimulates class formation in kin-ordered modes, based on distinctions between elder and junior individuals. A shift from self-sustenance to production for the market brings "a radical transformation, if not the social destruction of the communities" (Meillassoux 1980, 197). Contact with markets often engenders transition to a tributary mode. Chiefs can now mobilize resources to escape the kinship order.

> This is why chiefs have proved to be notorious collaborators of European fur traders and slave hunters on two continents. Connections with Europeans afforded chiefs access to arms and valuables and hence to a following outside of kinship and unencumbered by it. (Wolf 1982, 96)[1]

Thus Wolf's book is about the articulation of modes of production on a world scale. We are separated from Columbus by a radical break—the transition from feudalism to capitalism. Culture is understood not as higher or lower on some scale of global wisdom, but as complexly tied to modes of surplus appropriation and distribution. Wolf's different theoretical approach produces a correspondingly different story of European expansion. The worsening of the climate and the epidemics of the fourteenth century were, for Wolf, part of a larger European crisis—the crisis of feudalism. Whereas Sale essentializes an environmentally destructive "Europe," for Wolf, the ecological crisis was part of a much broader picture. Tribute takers stepped up extraction, producing resistance and rebellion. New frontiers provided a solution: "Economically, the crisis of feudalism was solved by locating, seizing, and distributing resources available beyond the European frontiers" (1982, 109). Expansion then was not only or mainly part of the rising capitalist spirit, but a solution to the crisis of a distinctly noncapitalist mode of production. Primitive accumulation involved the seizure of wealth by state organizations embodying a coalition between centralizing royalty and merchants. For Spain in particular, overseas conquest represented a continuation of old rather than the establishment of new behaviors.

The demise of Iberian hegemony in the early seventeenth century precipitated the expansion of the North American fur trade. This trade, carried on in the context of interstate competition, changed the character and scope of warfare among Amerind peoples, displacing some while destroying others. In the Northeast, there was a precipitous population decrease as well as a shift in the mix of indigenous group economic activities, with resulting changes in social relations. For instance, hunting territory held and defended exclusively by small family groups was a consequence of new individualized exchange relations between trapper and trader. The forms of kinship affiliation sometimes remained, but their meaning and function changed. Among the Iroquois, existing kinship processes (including matrilineage) were challenged by warriors and traders, whose strength grew with the spread of hostilities. Alteration in kinship procedures and their limitation were part of a social transformation conditioned not just by the market but by new forms of subjectification such as individualism and patriarchal families (Amariglio 1983).

The fur trade spurred the transition from kinship to tributary modes. So long as kin relations dominated, fur hunting was a supplement to traditional activities. Inter-European conflict and access to European goods, however, soon led to the rise of big men and war leaders. "Tribes" and "nations" took shape in response to the changes associated with the fur trade. New cultural forms developed to bind new ethnic identities. It was English hegemony that finally destroyed Amerind independence. As the English consolidated their position, warfare declined. Amerinds increasingly relied on the trading post for their subsistence, necessitating ever more labor committed to commodity production. Amerinds became specialized laborers in what was essentially a putting-out system. In other words, the social changes set off by inter-European conflict and the fur trade created new formations whose viability could not be sustained once the wars ended.

Sale's is a moralistic tale of the first ecologists being wiped out by a sick and ignorant "Europe." Wolf's story concerns a variety of intertwined cultural, economic, and political changes set off in kin-ordered societies by contact with the tributary, expansive Europeans. The internal changes in Amerind groups are as much a part of the story as the oppression visited on them by Europeans. This difference in the treatment of the native North American peoples provides a clear illustration of the difference between the cultural/ecological and Marxian perspectives. While Sale's discussion of natural processes is a welcome antidote to Marxists' tendency to ignore these issues, cultural essentialism and glorification of the underdog tend to cloud the variety of interactive social processes by which societies are transformed.

CAPITALISM AND IMPERIALISM

European mercantile activity was strengthened and enhanced by state protection, but it remained largely within state-defined channels and was hedged in by tributary privileges. Merchants delegated the risks of production while reaping the profits of commodity circulation. It was only when merchants transformed their capital into wealth in production, and the state was transformed from a tributary structure to a supporter of capitalist enterprise, that the limits and contradictions of mercantile circulation were overcome.

The industrial revolution marked a qualitative change, a new world order that built on and rearranged the world created by the interaction of expanding European merchant capital and the tributary and kin-ordered societies of Africa, America, and Asia. The "really revolutionary road" taken by English merchants allowed capital to call up machines and labor power as required, to organize and rearrange them, through a continuous process of internal and international capital migration, drawing ever more people into its orbit. Extensive regions of the world were reorganized to supply the English mills, destroying peasant production in Egypt, substituting cotton for food crops in India, and reinforcing North American slavery. By the end of the nineteenth century, virtually the entire planet had passed through the sequence of incorporation, specialization, and dependence, that was typical of contact with expanding Europe, and these transformed populations were subjected to the peculiar rhythms of capital accumulation.

The successive restructuring crises in the industrialized countries have created and recreated "peripheries within the core." Former leading areas become subsidiary or dependent regions, providing cheap labor and agricultural and craft goods in a variety of capitalist and noncapitalist modes for new leading areas. This leads Wolf to accept Mandel's characterization of the nineteenth- and twentieth-century world economy as "an articulated system of capitalist, semi-capitalist, and pre-capitalist relations of production, linked to each other by capitalist relations of exchange and dominated by the capitalist world market" (Wolf 1982, 297). These definitions are particularly useful, since they distinguish between the market and the mode of production, open the question of the continuing articulation of various modes, and raise the problem of articulation in both the "core" and the "periphery." Capitalism is not simply the search for wealth, nor is it simply production for the market. Thus we develop a story of a complex and changing process of uneven development and domination, rather than the unfolding of a singular political–economic essence, as in world systems theory, or cultural essence, as in Sale's formulation.

It was after the industrial revolution that Europe in general, and England especially, left the rest of the world behind in terms of its material standard of living (Bairoch 1982). The onset of English hegemony and the industrial revolution indicate a break, both in class relations and patterns of uneven development. The industrial revolution did not, however, create a *unified, capitalist* economy. Noncapitalist elements were sustained in some cases and newly created in others. The different and uneven combination of capitalist and noncapitalist elements in various countries was seized on by parts of the emerging international labor movement as the key to political strategy. In other words, the various societies of the twentieth century remained articulated combinations of capitalist and noncapitalist elements, although capitalism now, at least for Wolf, dominated the other modes in new and critical ways.[2]

THE END OF HISTORY, THE NEW WORLD ORDER, AND THE WORLD ECONOMY

Rather than questioning all metanarratives, and developing a decentered concept of imperialism, ecocultural critiques like Sale's construct a new essence, "Europe," which is the root of all evil. Thus can be recouped notions of continuity rather than discontinuity, that all is capitalism, that the exploited peoples have an essential goodness. The discredited (but only consciously) political–economic determinisms of dependency theory can be replaced by an equally comforting cultural determinism.

Wolf, in his focus on articulation, discontinuity, and connection, provides, I believe, a superior path for a critical theory of changing global processes of exploitation and oppression. This is not to say that ecocultural criticism has nothing to offer, or that there are no continuities in the history of European expansion. We live today amidst the multiple layers of imperialist history. Marxists' fetish with the stages of European capitalism and the various imperialisms that can be read off from them has been and needs to be criticized.

The unifying practice of the now not so new social movements seems to be a rejection of the European enlightenment and its attending parables of development and progress, in favor of a faith in the multiplicity of civilizations and cultural nationalisms. While this has been profoundly liberating at the personal level, there is absolutely no guarantee that it will be socially liberating. The ruling classes depend increasingly on the current appropriation of surplus rather than the protection of accumulated wealth (Wallerstein 1991). Thus we might see the rise of a flexible and vicious meritocracy, in which representatives of non-European cultures are displayed as totems of formal equality and access. This seems to be very much the current liberal tendency. Thus multiculturalism is neither reactionary nor oppositional—the key is its content. The argument of this paper is that the Left would be best served if that content were articulation, discontinuity, and connection, rather than the eco-cultural determinism so popular today. Columbus does speak to us, but the translation requirements are stringent indeed.

NOTES

1. That chiefs were not *always* the problem is amply illustrated in Bodley (1982).
2. The question of the "dominance" of one mode of production over another in the case of the case of the United States is addressed in McIntyre (1993). A general discussion of concepts of uneven development appears in McIntyre (1992).

REFERENCES

Amariglio, J. 1983. *"Primitive Communism" and the Economic Development of Iroquois Society*. Unpublished Ph.D. Dissertation, University of Massachusetts, Amherst.

Bairoch, P. 1982. "International Industrialization Levels from 1750 to 1980." *Journal of European Economic History* 11: 269–332.

Baran, P. 1957. *The Political Economy of Growth*. New York: Monthly Review Press.

Bodley, J. 1982. *Victims of Progress: Tribal Peoples and Development Issues*. Palo Alto, CA: Mayfield.

Brewer, A. 1990. *Marxist Theories of Imperialism: A Critical Survey*. London: Routledge.

Martland, D. 1992. "A Comparison of Spanish and English Imperialisms." Mimeograph, University of Rhode Island.

McIntyre, R. 1993. "Is there Capitalism in America?" Mimeograph, University of Rhode Island.

———. 1992, Fall. "Theories of Uneven Development and Social Change." *Rethinking Marxism* 5: 75–105.

Meillassoux, C. 1980. "From Reproduction to Production: A Marxist Approach to Economic Anthropology." In *The Articulation of Modes of Production*, ed. H. Wolpe, 189–201. London: Routledge Kegan and Paul.

Sale, K. 1990. *The Conquest of Paradise: Christopher Columbus and the Columbian Legacy*. New York: Penguin.

Wallerstein, I. 1991, Spring. "Post-America and the Collapse of Leninism." *Rethinking Marxism* 5: 93–100.

Wolf, E. 1982. *Europe and the People without History*. Berkeley: University of California Press.

Changing Borders, Changing Cartography: Possibilities for Intervening in the New World Order

KEVIN ST. MARTIN

The "changing borders" in the title of this paper refers to the recent geopolitical changes that have occurred in the last few years: the establishment or decomposition of countries and autonomous territories that are literally changing the appearances of the globes we use. Border changes mark changes in social, cultural, political, and economic practices, and their existence over time is used to point to eras of stability or transition. Border changes act as significant indicators of one or another world order.

Currently, the borders of the world are being established or reestablished in new ways with new meanings that are thought by many to correspond to a new world order. I assume that there are, in fact, world orders and that we are now witnessing the birth of a new one. I take this position not because all the data is available and we can now plot the demise of an old world order and predict a new one, but because thinking in terms of a new world order has the effect of letting us imagine more spaces in which to intervene.

Given the strong conceptual link between world orders and their representation on maps, it is curious that cartography is seldom seen as a method or discipline of intervention. Cartographers have drawn and redrawn the world for centuries, always distancing themselves from any responsibility for the borders they draw. They have never examined the effects of their maps in the larger social context; they have never seen the world order as constituted by their practice.

However, cartography is changing. While the discipline is in many ways continuous with its past approaches and applications, we can currently document major changes in the tools, methods, and theories that cartographers use. The set of processes that make up this discipline are at this time loosing their coherence. The accepted approaches are being challenged by both new developments in technology and theory.

Both cartography and a given world order might be thought of as sets of processes, however complicated and extensive. There is one set of rules, tools, methods, and theories that we call cartography and there is another that we can refer to as the world order. I propose that these two spheres of processes, the world order and cartography, are perhaps more closely interconnected than we usually think. That is, a slowly changing and rather small academic discipline might be seen to constitute and be constituted by a rapidly changing and quite large world order. It is not a matter of the ability (or lack thereof) of cartography to "keep up" with the documentation of territorial changes (cf. Powers 1993). I am addressing, rather, the question of cartography's implication in those changes, in the way it produces them and is produced by them.

This thesis about the interconnectedness of these two bundles of processes (cartography and a given world order) is informed by a particular ontological and epistemological position that sees all processes (social, cultural, political, and economic) as mutually constitutive, as overdetermined (Resnick and Wolff 1987). Other conceptions of ontology and epistemology (akin to, but not necessarily the same as mine) have inspired a handful of cartographers to produce what they call "alternative cartographies" (Crampton 1992). These are new stories that challenge traditional concepts of the study and practice of cartography. They criticize the objective and scientist status of cartography historically, by focusing on the ways that cartography has served the politically powerful and has fostered economic exploitation. While these new voices are few within the discipline, they are extremely refreshing and getting much attention—as shown by the popularity of "alternative cartography" sessions at the Association of American Geographers meetings in 1991, 1992, and 1993.

It is perhaps useful to categorize these approaches (and mine) as postmodern. That is, they are partially the result of postmodern theoretical approaches. What is relevant here, and in cartography more generally, is the postmodern critique of traditional notions of representation—particularly, a focus on the inability of different forms of representation (paintings, knowledge, texts, maps) to mirror reality. Knowledge/representation according to this postmodern theory is at best a partial perspective on its object: Maps can no longer be said to simply mirror reality, a claim that they, perhaps more than other forms of representation, maintained. Within cartography, alternative positions on representation undermine the theoretical pillars of the last forty years of the discipline and, I would argue, expand the ways cartographers can relate maps and their meanings to other processes within society. Put simply, if maps are no longer just about the reflection of the landscape, then the door is open to theorize how they may be about culture, politics, and economics.

CHANGING CARTOGRAPHY: THE NEW WORLD OF THE SIXTEENTH AND SEVENTEENTH CENTURIES

Any discussion of cartography and postmodern ideas of representation cannot be complete without at least briefly discussing the work of the late Brian Harley. Harley consistently confronted traditional cartographic thinking by pursuing and promoting an alternative approach of post-modern inspiration (e.g., Harley 1988a, 1989). The metaphor of map as mirror, according to Harley, is no longer appropriate and should be replaced by the metaphor of map as text. Text, as opposed to the unfeeling surface of the mirror, implies a subjective author, a cultural artifact, and a tool of ideology. It would appear that the text is the product of many processes, whereas the mirror is by definition devoid of such interference. The innocent mirror is replaced by Harley with a "richer" interpretation that sees the map as embroiled in the social processes of power, morality, and ideology.

Harley's approach opened the door to theorizing maps as connected to a variety of social processes, something unheard of within "sound" cartographic science. He must be given credit for being the most outspoken advocate of analyzing maps within a wider social, political, and economic context. Harley has laid much of the groundwork that lets us think about the relationships that exist between cartography and the world order (Harley 1988b). However, Harley's work was cut short, and he did not have the opportunity to extend his ideas beyond an analysis of cartography and the changing world order of the sixteenth and seventeenth centuries—the golden age of European expansion and cartographic practice.

Harley showed us how maps were variously implicated in this transitional period of early modern Europe and has given us new interpretations of maps that help us better understand that time of internal political and economic expansion and external colonization. Throughout his work he strove to show how in Europe "cartography was primarily a form of political discourse concerned with the acquisition and maintenance of power" (Harley 1988b, 57). In addition, he was very much concerned with the role of maps in the "discovery" and subsequent exploitation of new world peoples and resources (Harley 1992). This very different approach to the history of cartography shows maps not as the successive revelation of spatial truth but as instruments of European powers. Maps aided economic and imperial expansion by masking the rich societal diversity that existed in both the old and new worlds; they produced a structured matrix of space that could be known and controlled. The sweeping changes in Europe and the advent of colonization meant the production by cartographers of gridded and homogeneous (often empty) spaces that could be filled by new cultural identities, new forms of government, and new systems of production. Harley is not alone in this story of maps; others have also exposed the alternative relationships that exist or existed between maps and society at this time (e.g., Mukerji 1983). The alleged noncontroversial golden age of cartography seems to be particularly rich ground for critical analysis.

David Harvey has incorporated a telling story of maps into his thesis concerning the rise of modernism/capitalism in western society (Harvey 1990). Harvey highlights the relationship that existed between maps and the expansion of capitalism that played itself out at a time when "geographical knowledge became a valued commodity . . . the accumulation of wealth, power, and capital became linked to personalized knowledge of, and individual command over, space" (244). Maps and mapping technology changed along with the economy and politics of renaissance Europe. They no longer portrayed the "sensuous" aspects of places prevalent in medieval maps; instead they focused on "objectivity in spatial representation . . . because accuracy of navigation, the determination of property rights in land . . . , political boundaries, rights of passage and of transportation, and the like, became economically as well as politically imperative" (245).

In a similar vein but more directly about cultural rather than economic domination is the parallel between cartographic and colonial discourse noted by Graham Huggan (1989). Huggan states that the "reinscription, enclosure, and hierarchization of space . . . provide[s] an analogue for the acquisition, management and reinforcement of colonial power" (115). This reinterpretation and resituation of cartography seems to hint at the liberating capacity of postcolonial theory aimed at cartography. Struggles of decolonization are clearly linked by Huggan with the struggles against inscription and homogenization of landscape from above or outside, largely the practice of cartography.

William Boelhower (1988) has also connected the flourishing of cartographic practice in the sixteenth and seventeenth centuries to the inscription of space at the expense of place, a technique clearly used to the benefit of those making the maps. Boelhower relates advances in cartography to the "invention" of America. Cartography evolved to legitimate state formation and to mask the diversity of a continent. Boelhower writes, "So interwoven is their relationship that the following research matrix naturally proposes itself: 'America' is a cartographic revolution; the cartographic revolution is 'America.'" Similarly, Harley (1992, 532) points out in his essay on the Columbian Encounter: "In America, cartography is part of the process by which territory becomes. The paper disposition and anticipation of the map often preceded the 'real' geography which we seek so earnestly to triangulate."

These authors have broken from traditional histories of cartography. They no longer limit their stories to just the techniques and personalities that have been given credit (perhaps rightly so) for a seemingly linear progression of ever more accurate spatial representations. Rather, they have worked hard to point to the interconnectedness of cartography to the larger society and not just its practitioners. Their examples have clearly demonstrated that cartography constituted and was constituted by a particular world order that formed in the sixteenth and seventeenth centuries—one focused on the cultural, political, and economic domination and exploitation of the new world made accessible by the new technology of cartography.

Common to the work of the above authors, is a shift away from the map as only (or ideally) a mirror of the landscape. While each author does it differently, there is a concerted rethinking of what maps represent and the limits to representation itself. I would argue that it is this rethinking of maps and representation that allows for an analysis of colonial era cartography in terms of other social processes traditionally seen as external to cartographic practice. With these theoretical tools we can think of maps as not just reflections of an increasingly known world but as constituent parts of processes of ideology, power, possession, and exploitation.

CHANGING CARTOGRAPHY: THE COLD WAR

While colonial era cartographic practice seems easily deconstructed, and while such reassessment seems even an appropriate thing for cartographers and geographers to do, the insights of postmodern theories that allowed that type of analysis can be applied to other eras, other periods of world order. There appears to be little work done on other historical moments in these terms; in particular, I have found very little attempt to analyze the underlying premises of the cartographic practice of the cold war (with the exception of Pickles 1992). However, such an analysis would be very helpful to current rethinkings of cartography because it is only now that cartography is struggling with the set of rules, methods, and theories that it inherited from the post-World War II era. And it is only now that cartographers have the social theoretical tools to criticize cold war cartography, a set of processes whose hegemonic position is not yet completely lost.

Academic cartography became a thoroughly modernist pursuit after World War II. That is, it solidified into an objective, positivist science concerned with perfecting cartographic communication. The conveyance of cartographic information to a reader, the ability to understand and get meaning from the map, was not a function of the larger society or any external processes. It was a psychophysical and/or cognitive process of an individual reading. The objective of cartography was to eliminate the noise that interfered with the communication between map and reader. This research started to falter by the end of the 1980s. Cartographers became disillusioned that the approach had not succeeded in its mission to isolate a universal graphic language that would solve issues of misperception. As a result, cartographers increasingly turned their attention to new technical innovations, such as automated cartography and geographic information systems, made possible by the computer. While technique and accuracy have always been part of cartographic practice, it is only now that they have become the legitimating interests of cartographers.

Cartography, then, was about two general interests. First it was a technical field with an obsession for accuracy in spatial data representation. And secondly it strove to understand the human barriers to the accurate perception of that data. The best maps were those that were the most technically accurate and that contained elements of design that made reading unambiguous. Those maps that contained inaccuracies or ambiguity were relegated to certain subfields of cartography that dealt with primitive maps, mental maps, and propaganda maps. It was a system that worked hard to maintain the map's status as a mirror of reality and cartography's mission to perfect that mirror.

At the same time that data accuracy and communication models reigned supreme in cartography, the world order consisted of a globe geographically and cartographically divided between two superpowers—East and West separated by iron and bamboo curtains. There were lines of division (perhaps not unlike that which split the world into Portuguese and Spanish spheres of influence in the sixteenth century) that represented two different political systems, ideologies, and economic forms of exploitation. I am proposing that cartography invented and was invented by this world order as surely as it invented and was invented by the world order of the sixteenth century. It is thoroughly implicated in the constitution of the cold war world.

To examine this point further, I turn to our understanding of economic systems over space: what do or did economies look like in particular places? It's here that cartography has served to mask the diversity of the world during the cold war. The East was portrayed as homogeneous in almost every respect, but particularly in terms of its economy. While specific map examples are helpful, all that we have to do as children of the cold war is to examine our cartographic imaginations—to try and imagine what the economies of Eastern Europe might look like from place to place, to try and imagine them as heterogeneous. It's more difficult to visualize the difference between St. Petersburg and Warsaw than it is to visualize the difference between Liverpool and Paris in terms of the cities' main industries, their labor composition, and their relation to the larger economy. Likewise it would be hard for us to map the variety of class processes that might exist in a given territory of the former USSR.

During the cold war a sense of diversity within power blocks was stifled. The western economies were clearly about capitalist production processes; other class processes were seen as secondary or archaic and purged from the center of our economic theories on both the Right and the Left (on this theoretical point, see Gibson-Graham in Part Three of this volume). Eastern economies suffered a similar representational fate. They were seen as alternatively totalitarian, communist, or state socialist, but almost always as economically homogeneous. This view of the economic landscape was, in part, the fault of a static, atheoretical, and apolitical cartography. While cartographers were drawing the lines of division that represented the cold war world order, academic cartographers were interested in only the ability of design to communicate the reality captured by the map; they were not, could not be, interested in questioning that reality and how maps constituted it. The form of science that cartographers worked at preserving and furthering was unable to make the connections between cartographic practice and the larger society. It did not question the connections between the technical advances in cartography and their potential uses in the cold war, nor did it question the possible effects of the maps it was producing in building society's perceptions of other places and distant processes. Like the maps of the sixteenth century, cartographers produced specific maps with specific effects that went unexamined.

CHANGING CARTOGRAPHY: THE NEW WORLD ORDER

I have tried to make the point that postmodern theories, in particular the crisis of representation, have been partially responsible for the current rethinking of the relationships that exist between maps and society, between cartography and the world order. While several people have very convincingly done this for the golden age of cartography in the sixteenth century, positing that the new world and classic cartography invented each other, I've tried to offer some ideas on how a similar analysis could be possible in the cold war era. However, the second half of this paper's title is "possibilities for intervening in the new world order." It would appear that we must now step beyond an alternative history of cartography toward a rethinking of the practice of cartography within academia.

Clearly, cartography is implicated in the constitution of world orders in at least two historical moments, the discovery and exploitation of the new world and the cold war era. These were two periods when cartography found coherence around a set of standardized practices that, in retrospect, we can see had some relationship with a larger also coherent world order. However, I prefer to construct the current world order as yet unsettled and current cartography as in a state of theoretical and technological change. I am not at this point interested in new periods of coherence and correspondence between cartography and a new world order. I don't have in mind a plan that would pull together in non-contradictory ways either set of processes. Rather, I am at this time only interested in opening up the spaces for cartographic discovery and representation. I am interested in exposing the relationships, complex and contradictory, that exist between the two sets of processes.

I believe that it is possible to work towards a reformulated cartography that would be aware of its potential relationships with some larger world order. Starting from the premise that cartography overdetermines and is overdetermined by the world order (or any other set of social processes for that matter) greatly expands the opportunities for intervention and potential change. It is time to develop a cartography that actively theorizes its contradictory position relative to societal processes of cultural domination and economic exploitation currently as well as historically. Cartography can no longer be excused from the effects that the maps it makes have, nor can it deny the effects of society upon it. The celebration of "alternative cartographies" in the spirit of Brian Harley's approach is clearly in order if cartography is to develop beyond its slide into a field of only technical expertise.

My own preference, and it is only one of many potential alternative cartographies, would be to formulate a cartography that would work to discover the many forms of economic activity that are scattered across our landscapes, rather than just the ones that have filled our national territorial spaces during the cold war. That is, it is difficult to imagine that either the West or the East could possibly be as economically homogeneous as our maps would suggest (or suggested). The spaces of capitalism and communism, I believe, are interspersed with spaces occupied by feudalism, ancient production processes, and a variety of other forms of surplus expropriation and redistribution. That these processes are unimaginable when we cartographically delineate the landscape into economic activities is partly the fault of modern cartography's inability to question the reality that it maps, its inability to see itself constituting that reality while it draws it. I can imagine, for example, urban city maps that divide the city into sectors of dominant types of surplus expropriation and redistribution in an effort to see if they correspond to the urban maps we traditionally make of wealth, race, and industry. I would be eager to discover the landscapes masked by our big stories of capitalism and communism, and to inquire as to their potential for alternative economic formations.

In addition, I would also prefer an alternative cartography that recognizes maps as very powerful rhetorical instruments. Maps, particularly with their new-found alliance with computers and their historic insistence on being simple mirrors of reality, are extraordinarily persuasive devices. It is time that cartographers recognized their responsibility in this process beyond design elements to the actual data that they are choosing to portray. For example, I can imagine an automated mapping system designed with a set of alternative assumptions that would locate new economic investment in abandoned and decaying city centers rather than greenfield sites. The persuasive computer display showing the new locations would also indicate the set of assumptions that went into its production, a simple form of immediate documentation that is not yet standard practice.

I think that it is through this sort of rethinking of cartography that we can find new ways to represent the changing world, ways that establish particular processes previously masked by the homogeneity of our landscapes. Huggan (1989, 124) notes a reassessment of cartography that accepts diversity and interprets maps "not as a means of spatial containment or systematic organization, but as a medium of spatial perception." Maps should be devices for spatial exploration and for deliberate intervention in the new world order.

REFERENCES

Boelhower, W. 1988. "Inventing America: A Model of Cartographic Semiosis." *Word and Image* 4 (2): 475–497.

Crampton, J. 1992. *Alternative Cartographies: Exploring New Frontiers*. Unpublished Ph.D. dissertation, Pennsylvania State University.

Harley, J. B. 1988a. "Maps, Knowledge, and Power." In *The Iconography of Landscape*, eds. D. Cosgrove and S. Daniels. Cambridge, England: Cambridge University Press.

———. 1988b. "Silences and Secrecy: The Hidden Agenda of Cartography in Early Modern Europe." *Imago Mundi* (40): 57–76.

———. 1989. "Deconstructing the Map." *Cartographica* 26 (2): 1–20.

———. 1992. "Rereading the Maps of the Columbian Encounter." *Annal of the Association of American Geographers* 82 (3): 522–535.

Harvey, D. 1989. *The Condition of Postmodernity*. New York: Blackwell.

Huggan, G. 1989. "Decolonizing the Map: Post-Colonialism, Post-Structuralism and the Cartographic Connection." *Ariel* 20 (4): 115–131.

Mukerji, C. 1983. *From Graven Images*. New York: Columbia University Press.

Pickles, J. 1992. "Texts, Hermeneutics and Propaganda Maps." In *Writing Worlds*, eds. T. J. Barnes and J. S. Duncan. New York: Routledge.

Powers, J. 1993. "New World Borders." *The Globe Magazine* (February 21): 16.

Resnick, S. and Wolff, R. 1987. *Knowledge and Class*. Chicago: University of Chicago Press.

PART EIGHT

POLITICAL STRUGGLES OVER THE NORTH AMERICAN ORDER

Mexico's Integration into the North American Economy

DAVID BARKIN

exico is becoming a major player in the global marketplace. For decades, successive administrations have tried to restructure the productive apparatus so that it resembles more closely those in the more advanced countries. Implementing a vast array of seemingly disparate policies, successive administrations have modified the sectoral, regional, and even class basis of their investment programs. In spite of profound differences among regimes, the cumulative effect has been to move Mexico inexorably toward greater integration into the world economy.

In the early 1970s, Europe and Japan were challenging the United States' claim to global leadership. New strategies were needed to strengthen capital in North America as part of a program to reassert U.S. dominance in the world economy. The United States attempted to defend its leadership by broadening the scope of international agreements that defined the rules for the unimpaired operation of capital. The Uruguay round of negotiations to modify the General Agreement on Tariffs and Trade (GATT) was a crucial arena in which to advance this agenda; the United States wanted to extend the rules for free trade to encompass agricultural products and services and to protect intellectual property.

This article offers an extension of the analysis in Barkin (1990), based on a detailed reading of the Mexican economy during the 1990–1992 period. Unfortunately, because of the very same problems that are mentioned as a serious cause for concern in the present analysis, virtually no critical academic literature is available.

New initiatives were also necessary to consolidate and extend U.S. hegemony in the Western hemisphere. The Caribbean Basin Initiative and the Enterprise for the Americas were proposed to modernize U.S. control over the various economies of the South. In the North, an alliance of U.S. and Canadian groups spearheaded the negotiation of a Free Trade Agreement (FTA) between the two countries that went into effect in 1989. The election of a committed neoliberal regime in Mexico in 1988 set the stage for its extension to Mexico.

This article offers an analysis of the socioeconomic effects of international integration and neoliberal restructuring in Mexico. It then proceeds to examine some likely impacts of the North American Free Trade Agreement (NAFTA) on Mexican society. This is an essay opposing NAFTA, not integration per se. It focuses on the way in which this process is proceeding and its effects on society. The agreement was negotiated in secret to accelerate the rate of integration, and contains few provisions for protecting society and our environment from the most opportunistic behavior of profit-maximizing enterprises. The financial and administrative resources available to civil society are insufficient in all three countries to confront successfully the threats posed by the faster growth of capitalist production. Even more troublesome is the profound social disintegration that the unfettered expansion of the market will impose on unprepared societies. Can we afford to permit ourselves to experiment with the kinds of irreversible changes that accelerating integration will wreak?

SALINASTROIKA

Attempting to throw off the cloud tainting his claim to electoral victory, Carlos Salinas de Gortari galvanized Mexican society. He unseated several despotic leaders of Mexico's most corrupt industrial unions and ordered important business leaders jailed for fraud. A new social pact sparked a precipitous decline of living standards for Mexico's workers and its middle class, although consumerism continues to be bolstered. After a disappointing negotiation to restructure the foreign debt, the regime jumped headlong to the free trade agreement. The structural adjustment program controlled inflation with direct intervention to limit the devaluation of the peso, curb government spending, and lower real wages. Vibrant consumer demand from the upper layers of society created a larger market than in many developed countries: Perhaps as many as 18 million big spenders came from an elite segment of the industrial labor force, established merchants, commercial farmers, professional groups, and financial interests. Export-oriented foreign investment and industrial modernization further stimulated the domestic market, while the automobile industry thrives on its privileged position in policy circles. But most Mexicans still cannot participate: Real wages for the majority are still declining and absolute poverty is spreading, official spending on education, medical care, and other social services is woefully inadequate, while formal employment opportunities are scarce.

To overcome the political debacle of the 1988 elections, Salinas embarked on a program of democratization. "*Salinastroika*," as some baptized the new program, was short lived. The political battles of the next four years proved that the mere emplacement of the trappings does not guarantee the substance of democracy. The Mexican state, and its system of overlapping provincial elites, staunchly defended its control of the nation's wealth and power. Economic reorganization and integration offer too many opportunities for existing groups to share voluntarily their privileged access to the nation's vaults and resources. On rare occasions, the state begrudgingly ceded control to the moderate opposition. To protect its hegemony, the official party, PRI (Partido Revolucionario Institutional), strategically heaped bountiful rewards on selected marginal groups in return for their support on the ballot, winning many key gubernatorial elections in 1992.

THE LEGACY OF SUCCESSFUL CAPITALIST DEVELOPMENT

Mexico's current crisis dates from 1976, when the peso was sharply devalued for the first time since 1954. Although ostensibly the result of a rapid increase in foreign debt, a cursory examination of social struggle reveals its true origins: a 350% rise in the purchasing power of minimum wages in Mexico City along with an increase in the share of labor in national income from 25% to 37% in the period from 1950 to 1976. Throughout Mexican society, every group enjoyed substantial improvements in living standards as industrial output and peasant production rose, social services became more available, and the middle class burgeoned. Constrained by an oligarchy unwilling to pay taxes and organizing to oppose these improvements, the government resorted to deficit finance and foreign loans and investments to ease social tensions that had caused so much bloodshed at the end of the 1960s.

The crisis was postponed, however, by the discovery of petroleum. The country embarked on a spending spree, fueled by the dream of unlimited wealth and financed by debt. Although the purchasing power of wages began its prolonged decline, the ready availability of jobs and high government spending created a false sense of prosperity. The sharp devaluation of the peso in 1982 rudely burst the dream after the price of petroleum fell precipitously. Unfortunate investment decisions and poorly conceived economic policies aggravated the country's problems, forcing it to declare a debt moratorium, precipitating the world debt crisis. The apparent signs of successful correction—an early surplus on current account and retrenchment in the public sector—proved inadequate. The crisis gave Salinas an opportunity to impose draconian stabilization programs that would have been unthinkable less than a decade earlier. The ascendent neoliberal forces were demanding a thorough realignment of power.

The midterm (1985) change in public policy firmly positioned the country on the path of neoliberal reconstruction. Rather than reviewing the complex array of policies adopted to implement this new strategy, I will examine some salient features of the new society.

1. *A changing incomes policy.* The dramatic decline in the real purchasing power of wages was slowed somewhat with the imposition of a series of Economic Stabilization Pacts, beginning in 1987. By mid-1992, however, the minimum wage had lost about 65% of its 1960 purchasing power, to some 25% of its 1976 zenith. Of course, in the formal economy, wage settlements were higher: The Social Security Institute reported that entry level wages in the industrial sector during the early 1990s averaged about 1.8 minimum wages. The basic market basket of consumption goods required for a typical worker's family cost about 4.78 times this bench mark in 1988, while a total family income of about 3 times the minimum (2.72) was required to not be classified as living in extreme poverty. The 1990 census reports that 60% of the households in Mexico received less than this standard; 72.4% earned monetary incomes below 4 times the minimum.[1] The share of labor in national income is now less than one quarter.

2. *Differential industrial growth.* With wages plummeting, the internal market contracted dramatically. The new policy promotes export production rather than goods for the local market. The major beneficiaries of this new approach were the automobile and computer industries. The assembly plants or *maquiladoras* also grew rapidly from 1982 to 1992, taking advantage of special legislation bestowing privileged tax treatment on certain exports to the United States. By 1992, more than 2,000 plants with about 500,000 employees were in operation. The automobile industry regained its role as the mainstay of Mexican industry, reorienting production to the U.S. market. Existing assembly operations were modernized and new automated plants were built. An easy credit policy encouraged Mexicans to purchase new vehicles. Foreign investment and the spread of new marketing systems contributed to increased demand. The electronic equipment industry in general, and computers in particu-

lar, also enjoyed dynamic growth. After the onset of the crisis, support was offered for transforming and extending maquila production to supply domestic markets. Full foreign ownership of enterprises was permitted. Credit and training plans offered easier access to new equipment and encouraged businesses to use electronic data processing and production systems. In contrast, traditional manufacturing industries declined. With the drastic fall in purchasing power of the middle and working classes and the opening of consumer markets to imports, many producers of nondurable consumer goods and some durables were forced to close; inexpensive imports from lower-cost producers flooded the mass consumption markets, while upscale shopping centers offered their affluent consumers the opportunity to acquire in Mexico goods for which they formerly made pilgrimages to the elite malls of California or Texas. On balance, the industrial sector employs fewer people now than it did a decade ago. Although about one million new jobs were created in the growth sectors during the 1980s, almost an equal number became redundant in declining industries.

3. *A balance of payments crisis.* Long-term foreign claims on domestic resources auger ill for the ability of the Mexican economy to finance its foreign sector without further foreign indebtedness, peso devaluations, domestic inflation, and depressed living standards. Official reassurances notwithstanding, the overvaluation of the peso and the growing trade deficit are a measure of the high price the regime is exacting from Mexican workers for international support. Massive inflows of speculative private foreign capital are temporarily financing the trade deficit and bolstering the central bank's reserves. This outside assistance is very costly: Real returns on foreign financial investments in Mexico are more than three times those paid in the United States. But capital is needed for new productive investments. Up to now, Mexican financiers have been reluctant to reduce their imports and transfer resources to domestic investments. These objectives would require profound changes that are contrary to the strategy embodied in the NAFTA.

4. *Unemployment.* Official unemployment rates are less than 3%. In a country where poverty is increasing, nutritional standards are declining, and migration is a permanent feature of the labor market, such reports seem unrealistic. These low rates reflect a social system that offers no welfare or unemployment insurance system: The unemployed must fend for themselves to survive. The data show that more than one quarter of the labor force works less than thirty-five hours a week, and a surprising 5% of the employed reports that it labored without spending any time on the job. In Mexico, people are eking out an existence in the burgeoning service and commercial sectors, where poor and unproductive rejects from the rest of the economy must compete. In rural areas,

migratory and off-farm employment grows as traditional planting of basic food crops is officially discouraged, offering a precarious existence and exposing themselves and their families to the worst horrors of agrochemical and gastrointestinal poisoning. Each year, millions of Mexicans cross the U.S. border in search of work. Although almost three million Mexicans tried to legalize their residence in the United States under the Immigration Reform and Control Act of 1986, the flow of undocumented workers continued. As many as five million Mexicans seek temporary employment in the United States each year. This outlet provides an escape valve and an important supplement to individual incomes; for the country it contributes about five billion dollars a year in foreign exchange. Although a continuing source of irritation in bilateral relations, this labor market has become an essential ingredient in the Mexican government's domestic economic stabilization planning process.

5. *Privatization and the concentration of capital.* The international financial community joined its Mexican counterparts to redistribute public sector holdings among themselves. Privatization touches almost every aspect of life in Mexico, reflecting the pervasiveness of government intervention in the economy on the eve of the crisis. The public subsidies to productive activities permitted substantial profits as private businesses bought inexpensive goods and services from public enterprises. With privatization, the prices of many goods rose and some inexpensive goods disappeared. The Mexican beneficiaries of this development and international integration strategy were handsomely rewarded. The data from the Mexican Stock Exchange offer a vivid picture: Less than 8,000 accounts, including about 1,500 owned by foreigners, control more than 94% of the total value of shares in public hands. This centralization of wealth aroused the envy of the international press. *Business Week* (July 29, 1991) identified five members of a "protected plutocracy" who benefited handsomely from the neoliberal reform package. More recently, *Forbes* (July 20, 1992) placed them and two other Mexicans among the 289 richest people in the world, whose family worth is greater than $1 billion each. Increasingly, however, questions are being raised both at home and abroad about growing social and economic polarization in Mexico.

6. *The restructuring of the public sector.* The government has forcefully reoriented its entire program to benefit the rich and shelter their incomes from taxation. The cutbacks in the bureaucracy and in public services for the working class and peasantry seriously reduced service levels and quality. The changes were so profound that privileged employees throughout the economy (including some bureaucrats) now enjoy supplementary private sector health insurance, and educational and other fringe benefits. In spite of charges of "fiscal terrorism" from the middle sectors, taxes as a proportion of gross domestic product have not varied

substantially over the past decade because the government is still unable to impose taxes on capital gains, an important source of personal enrichment since the policy changes of the 1980s.

7. *The reorganization of rural Mexico.* Rural Mexico is an important part of the modernization program. At first, the administration channeled resources to producers of export crops, abandoning its commitment to food self-sufficiency. It later modified its position as food imports rose to an alarming $5 billion and the popular outcry became widespread. Supports for maize and bean production now go to the nation's richest farmers in the irrigation districts and the fertile plains of the north, rather than to the peasant farmers who traditionally sowed these crops on rain-fed lands. In early 1992, a constitutional reform was promulgated that paved the way for a reorganization of land tenure and the introduction of corporate capital into farming. Its goal was to modernize rural production in a way that a corrupt and underfinanced bureaucracy could not do. By freeing recipients of land under the agrarian reform legislation to enter into a wide variety of commercial contracts, the private sector is expected to finance the land improvements and cultivation. The new program probably will be very effective in pushing a select group of farmers into export production and facilitating urban expansion. The remaining millions of farmers, whose plots are too small and/or whose land is of marginal quality, will be isolated from the institutional and financial supports that allowed them to continue in the face of unfavorable market conditions (including heavy export subsidies for grains by the advanced countries). The Undersecretary of Agriculture predicts that more than 13 million people will be forced to emigrate from poor farming communities during the next decade. To many thoughtful critics, the country can ill afford the effects of a narrowly defined program like the one presently being implemented.[2] The environmental and social problems that another massive rural–urban migration would occasion are beyond the capabilities of the system to manage in either economic, political, or environmental terms. It also seems particularly unfortunate that at the very moment when Mexico is beginning to negotiate more equitable terms for the export of its fruits and vegetables, the government is forcing these farmers to cultivate grains.[3]

8. *The antipoverty program.* Mexico's antipoverty program, *Solidaridad*, offers a case study in the use of public largesse for political goals. It helps finance local groups who channel their collective energies into local improvement projects for collective infrastructure projects, such as schools, water and sewage systems, paving streets, park development, and beautification. In an environment of marginality and hostility or mistrust, it creates a window of opportunity for people desperately struggling to survive or opportunistically resigned to accept whatever crumbs

they can glean from the federal budget. *Solidaridad* does not fool many into believing that the present economic strategy offers real opportunities for "*Los de abajo*."[4] It is internationally celebrated, however, as an effective instrument of political control and mobilization.

AN INTEGRATED FUTURE

Both George Bush and Carlos Salinas staked a great deal of their political future on the free trade negotiations.[5] In Mexico, the NAFTA assumes even greater importance because the government hopes that it will make its policies irreversible. As long as NAFTA is not ratified by the legislatures in the three countries, Salinas correctly fears, there will be pressure to modify profoundly present policy. In all three countries, opposition is spreading from human rights, labor, and environmental groups to broad segments of the business community. There is a clear divergence between the promised benefits to consumers and the forecasts of declining employment and/or incomes for broad segments of the population.

As the negotiations draw to a conclusion, a new phenomenon has emerged in Mexico: the beginning of broad-based coalition politics that transcends national boundaries, individual issues, and sectarian positions. The Mexican coalition is forcing the government to reveal more about the negotiating process than it would have liked (but still not much), and to listen seriously to the concerns of grassroots constituencies (although not to modify its strategy). The NAFTA negotiations transformed multinational collaboration into a respectable tool for a formerly nationalistic political opposition. These modifications are creating a basis for broader civil participation in the political process.

The economies of North America are integrating. The FTA will accelerate this process, but is not addressing the fundamental problems of any of the three. For Mexico, integration will mean more trade and new jobs; production will continue to increase in certain privileged sectors, but will also accelerate the displacement of large groups of workers. Productive imbalances and social polarization are exacerbating, while environmental problems become more serious. The present strategy is betting that foreign investors will bring sufficient resources to Mexico to pay to correct the problems. This seems like a hazardous gamble.

DALE TIEMPO AL TIEMPO (GIVE TIME A CHANCE)

Mexico's economy will become even more distorted in the coming years, if the present development strategy has time to mature. Important segments of the population are being excluded; resources under peasant control are being devalued while those in the hands of the rich are becoming more important. No thought is given to preserving the country's rich heritage for posterity; Mexico policy pundits assign little value to the natural cornucopia, the country's indigenous past, its anticolonial struggle, and the brilliant and abundant storehouse of cultural and artistic creativity. These resources are apparently devoid of any intrinsic value for them, and they will be treasured only if they can be sold on international markets or to fickle tourists.

A different strategy is needed for the people who are excluded from the new integrated economy. As an alternative to the current narrow model of industrial modernization, there is a clamor for a more diversified productive base, taking advantage of abundant and varied natural resources and the enormous reserve of inherited knowledge stemming from treasured cultural differences. Such an approach offers a way to employ productively those who get left behind.[6]

Today's "*científicos*"[7] want to eradicate this shameful and obsolete native heritage. The culinary wealth and diversity is no more cherished than the enormous treasure of biodiversity that is being annihilated by transnational hybrid seeds and other tools of progress. Both are themes for poetic discourse, but like the paintings of its famous artists, or the musings of its writers and poets, they are appreciated more for their marketability than their intrinsic worth. Their contribution to the earth's integrity or society's enjoyment is recognized by very few.

These technocrats are unwilling "to give time a chance," as the popular Mexican expression might be translated, to permit Mexico to adjust gradually as integration links nations and cultures. They are blind to the lesson of another popular saying: "Simply by waking up earlier, the sun won't rise sooner."[8] That is, Mexico—the country, its people, its culture—will not magically change its course, its very essence, simply because the President orders its industrial structure modified, its resources sold or leased out, or foreign goods imported on a massive scale. This official myopia distorts history: Mexico's extraordinarily diverse but impoverished peoples will force unpredictable changes that will disintegrate today's neoliberal dreams.

NOTES

1. Teresa Rendon and Carlos Salas, of the Faculty of Economics at the Universidad Nacional Autónoma de México (UNAM) are among the most insightful analysts of the employment and wage data in Mexico. For a short discussion of recent trends see Rendon and Salas (1993).

2. For an informed discussion of this policy direction, see the relevant articles in Hewitt (1994).

3. Production controls are imposed by allocation of water use permits in irrigation districts. If farmers in selected areas wish to receive water to cultivate export crops, they must also agree to produce basic grains for the internal market; high internal prices also guarantee attractive profits for mechanized production.

4. This is the title of a popular and universally acclaimed novel of the revolutionary period by Mariano Azuela (1912) celebrating the ideals and victories of those who joined the struggle.

5. Although the Canadian ex-Prime Minister, Brian Mulroney, also strongly supports the NAFTA, he was forced to resign because of his unpopularity, caused by the country's serious economic problems—which are due, in large measure, to the problems created by the FTA.

6. This short paragraph owes a great deal to Guillermo Bonfil's insightful argument that a recognition of the vitality of Mexico's indigenous past is essential for a solution to the country's present problems. The search for these solutions is the basis for our present research agenda. Bonfil (1987) deals with the importance of Mexico's indigenous heritage for the country's present-day vitality. His recent death leaves us with the message of the urgency of preserving and enriching our society by assuring a cultural and economic diversity for the future. One of his last articles (Bonfil 1992) vividly expresses the problems created by the confrontation between the trend towards neoliberal globalization and the possibility, indeed the necessity, of a different more plural world, if humanity and the earth itself are to survive. This current of thought has become increasingly pervasive in Mexico and elsewhere in the third world, where people of many different persuasions and approaches are developing these ideas as analysis, programs, and political platforms.

7. These are a group of technocrats at the highest levels of policy making who are mechanically applying the precepts of neoliberal restructuring to all dimensions of life in Mexico. They are broadly criticized by sensitive analysts throughout Mexican society for their lack of consideration of many important facets of national life and their apparent disregard for the welfare of the mass of poor people who comprise more than 75% of the population. They are named after a similar group who dominated high policy positions during the lengthy period (1876–1910) before the Revolution when President Porfirio Diaz imposed a dictatorial regime. For more on this period, and a general introduction to the profound problems that presently beset the country, see Hellman (1983.)

8. In Spanish: "*No por mucho madrugar, amanece más temprano.*"

REFERENCES

Azuela, M. 1912. *The Underdogs.* (English edition 1992, Pittsburgh: University of Pittsburgh Press.)

Barkin, D. 1990. *Distorted Development: Mexico in the World Economy.* Boulder, CO: Westview Press.

Bonfil, G. 1987. *México Profundo: Una civilización negada*. México: Grijalbo.
——. 1992, April. "Por la diversidad del futuro." *Ojarasca* 7.
Hellman, J. 1983. *Mexico in Crisis*, 2nd ed. New York: Holmes & Meier.
Hewitt de Alcántara, C. ed. 1994. *Economic Restructuring and Rural Subsistence in Mexico: Corn and the Crisis of the 1980s*. LaJolla, CA: Center for U.S.-Mexican Studies, University of California.
Rendon, T. and Salas, C. 1993, December. "The probable impact of NAFTA on non-agricultural employment in Mexico." *Review of Radical Political Economics*, 25 (4): 109–119.

The Competitiveness Debate: Toward an Internationalist Critique

STEPHEN CULLENBERG
GEORGE DEMARTINO

Concern over the relative position of the United States in the global economy has reached fever pitch in recent years. This concern underlies the most recent installment in the recurrent competitiveness debate, which has been joined by analysts from liberal and Left persuasions. The liberal position is best represented by Labor Secretary Robert Reich (1991a), who argues that renewed competitiveness will require U.S. workers to work *smart* in order to encourage firms to locate their high-skilled, high-waged jobs here. A Left view, as developed by William Lazonick (1991), claims that workers must be convinced to work *hard* in order to facilitate the introduction of productivity-enhancing innovations. It follows that Reich targets education and worker training for reform, while Lazonick encourages managers to revamp their internal structure of corporate governance in a manner that will envelop labor within the corporate community.

We find both types of proposals problematic. Reich and Lazonick fail to question the conditions under which countries and corporations are allowed to compete. Corporations (and nation–states) seek advantage today on the basis of all manner of conditions: wages, taxes, environmental standards, health care provision, and so on. For Reich and Lazonick, the rules of the game in the global capitalist economy that allow such forms of competition are a (perhaps unpleasant) reality that must be respected. The problem, as they see it, is that the U.S. government

(Reich) and firms (Lazonick) have responded unwisely to the competitive pressures. The progressive content of their proposals is to achieve renewed competitiveness through enhanced skills and innovation, which facilitates a high standard of living. The alternative is for competition to be based on low wages, lax environmental standards, and an overall anti-worker/citizen economic climate.

But need these rules be taken as immutable? If the goal is to have a high standard of living, then should we really foreclose *ex ante* on institutional reforms that might achieve this goal directly? In our view, before we sign on to competitiveness-enhancing strategies, we must first pose a difficult theoretical question: What can be taken out of global capitalist competition while still capturing whatever progressive innovative force competition is seen to induce? We believe that (at a minimum) those aspects of social, political, and economic life that are integral to a decent standard of living and basic human welfare must be removed from the terrain of competition. We argue below that international agreements must be negotiated that delineate precisely the permissible contours of competition. We suggest a social-index tariff structure (SITS) that can be incorporated into international negotiations, which would serve to enhance the standard of living for workers across the global economy.

The next sections summarize briefly the recent work of Reich and Lazonick. The following section develops our critique and outlines a progressive alternative to the competitiveness-enhancing perspective. The final section develops briefly our tariff proposal, SITS.

REICH AND THE RISE OF THE SYMBOLIC ANALYST

In a series of articles in the *Harvard Business Review* (1990, 1991b) and his recent book *The Work of Nations* (1991a), Reich has developed a provocative analysis concerning the competitiveness crisis facing the United States. Reich's central claim is that the interests of U.S.-owned corporations no longer coincide with the interests of U.S. citizens. Today's corporation no longer sinks deep roots into a community and ties its fate to the resources and productivity of its home base. Instead, modern corporations are global enterprise webs, joining diverse functions that are dispersed across the globe. Speaking of the twenty-first century, Reich argues, "There will be no *national* products or technologies, no national corporations, no national industries" (1991a, 3). Instead, American-owned multinationals will increasingly "employ large numbers of foreigners relative to their American work forces," and "rely on foreign facilities to do many of their most technologically complex activities" (1990, 54).

A new international division of labor is developing alongside the spread of the global web of production. Reich identifies three classes of jobs: routine production workers, in-person servers, and symbolic analysts. Routine production workers include assembly line workers, data entry personnel, and clerical workers, among others. Their low level of skill elicits low remuneration, in part because the supply of such workers is nearly inexhaustible in the poorest regions of the world. Hence, the United States cannot hope to restore its standard of living by competing for such jobs. In-person servers, such as waiters, janitors, secretaries, and real estate agents do not face international wage competition directly, but their pay depends in part on the generalized level of income in the economy. It is instead the symbolic analysts who are of particular importance in the emerging world economy. Symbolic analysts design and manage the production systems of the global factory. More generally, they identify and solve problems and broker the skills needed to run the global web. Symbolic analysts undertake the tasks of research and development (R&D), market the goods and services produced, and manage the flow of finance and information within and between corporate entities. These jobs require high levels of skill and education, they add high levels of value to production, and hence they command high wages.

From this analysis follows Reich's policy proposals, which are designed to inaugurate a "virtuous circle":

> Well-trained workers attract global corporations, which invest and give workers good jobs; the good jobs, in turn, generate additional training and experience. As skills move upward and experience accumulates, a nation's citizens add greater and greater value to the world—and command greater and greater compensation from the world, improving the country's standard of living. (1990, 59)

The real economic challenge for the United States, then, is to invest in the skills of its citizens in order to enhance the potential value they can add to the global economy. No longer is it "the profitability of a nation's corporations nor the successes of its investors" (Reich 1991a, 8) that will necessarily improve the standard of living of most of the nation's citizens. Rather, "the competitiveness of American workers is a more important definition of 'American competitiveness' than the competitiveness of American companies" (1990, 55–56). Consequently, Reich calls for a number of new policies that will attract or keep high-value global corporate activity to the United States. His policy recommendations emphasize publicly supported R&D, antitrust legislation, foreign direct investment, and especially public and private investment in education and infrastructure (1990, 60–64).

LAZONICK AND CORPORATE GOVERNANCE

Lazonick has criticized Reich recently on the grounds that Reich overlooks the issues of corporate governance and ownership: "One role of the national government is to provide, where necessary, the infrastructure to support such enterprises." "But," he continues, "the national government must also be concerned with how business corporations within its boundaries allocate the often considerable surpluses they control" (in press, 35). At the heart of Lazonick's critique of Reich is the distinction Lazonick makes between those progressive firms that emphasize value creation and those exploitative firms that rely on value extraction of already produced surplus. Only an economy comprising the former type of firm can remain globally competitive and provide an increasing standard of living for its citizens.

For Lazonick, a firm's long-term competitive success requires constant technological innovation that reduces the unit costs of production (Lazonick 1991). But there is a dilemma facing the innovating firm: To realize the potential cost savings that the new technology promises, the firm must secure the willing cooperation and good faith effort of its workforce. Fundamental to this line of argument is the assumption that new technologies often yield higher per unit costs of production at low levels of effort, but lower per unit costs (and higher levels of new value created) when workers provide higher levels of work effort. This results, in part, from the higher fixed costs that attend new technologies, and partly from the process of learning by doing (i e , the introduction of a new technology requires that new skills be developed, and these can only be acquired through experimentation)—a process that is facilitated by greater work effort. Greater work effort in this context has quantitative and qualitative dimensions: Workers must be motivated to master new technology, and to contribute to its ultimate success. Passive or active acts of sabotage, on the other hand, prevent the new technology from yielding lower per unit costs.

Cooperative labor–management relations provide the organizational framework for a win-win strategy of technological innovation, which generates a net gain in value created that can be shared between the two parties. On this basis Lazonick concludes that workers must be included in the corporate community, as stake sharers if not stake holders (worker–owners). This must entail high and rising pay, long-term employment protection, skill enhancement, and, presumably, some say in workplace decisions (although this last is not emphasized). Renewed prosperity requires as a precondition that managers realize that they can get more with the carrot than the stick—that by integrating production workers into the corporate community, they can gain the cooperation they need to innovate and compete.

AN INTERNATIONALIST CRITIQUE

Both Reich and Lazonick seek solutions to the competitiveness problem of the United States, first and foremost, and therefore abstract from the international implications of their respective analyses. We see two fundamental problems with this approach: First, the policy prescriptions are unlikely to yield a solution to the competitiveness problem; and second, the proposals are founded on a thoroughly regressive nationalism.

With respect to the former, Reich and Lazonick both search for a magic bullet that will ensure a permanent solution to the problem of capitalist competition.[1] The goal is not simply to secure a high rate of productivity and/or innovation per se, but to secure a *perpetual* competitive *advantage*. Only if a nation can create a better environment for producing symbolic analysts or new innovations than its competitors, can it expect to reap the intended benefits. Only under such circumstances can it continually expect to win the competitive race. But what evidence is there to support the conclusion that a country *can* gain a *permanent* advantage in these or any other respects? No answer is forthcoming in the work of Reich or Lazonick, and we doubt that a compelling answer could be devised. Neither history nor theory provides justification for the view that any nation can secure the ability to perpetually out-compete others in terms of innovations in its social, organizational and educational infrastructure. Instead, we view capitalist competition as an exceedingly dynamic, uneven and contradictory process, in which today's innovations often become tomorrow's fetters.

It is worth emphasizing that the social reforms on offer are proposed as a means to the end of enhanced competitiveness. But so long as competitiveness remains the goal, the progressive content of these reforms remains hostage to a daunting test—not of whether they stand to improve the living conditions of workers, but of whether they yield the promised perpetual competitive advantage. If our view of the impossibility of perpetual advantage is correct, then by the Reich/Lazonick standard of adjudication we must conclude that this progressive content will have to be sacrificed as soon as some competitor devises a successful response, one that may not be as socially benevolent. Progressive industrial policy requires an inversion in which the attainment of a decent life becomes the end rather than the means.

If, on the other hand, these proposals were to achieve their intended effects, we must still inquire whether they represent merely a prescription for renewed U.S. hegemony. Both proposals would reshuffle the international deck, with the United States holding aces and the rest of the world holding decidedly inferior hands. Third world countries would be dealt low-wage routine work, which they "win" via the competitive advantage that poverty affords. Regrettably, there is simply no mechanism here—in Reich's or Lazonick's vision—to deliver an upward harmonization in the conditions of working people the world over. Rather, the vision on offer is one in which the gains of the United States come at the expense of other nations. The reason why Reich's and Lazonick's analyses fail, in part, is because they accept the logic of capitalist competition and seek ways for the United States to win the competitive battle with other countries. At the heart of both analyses is the need to raise the rate of exploitation through productivity-enhancing innovations, which will attract global corporations (and their high skill tasks).

FILLING IN THE "X"

We view the competitiveness crisis of the United States to be as much a political crisis as an economic one, one that need not be overcome so much as displaced. A progressive response to the crisis must begin by challenging the nature and prerogatives of capitalist competition. Building upon the founding principles that have joined workers in labor unions since the dawn of capitalism, we must ask which aspects of society can be *taken out of competition* without inhibiting progressive technological innovation. While unions have sought to insulate wages and working conditions, we see the need to expand the scope of such demands to encompass other aspects of social, political, and economic life. We are arguing here not for central planning, but for a redefinition of the rules of the game of competition in order to ensure that high standards of living are universalized.

We see no a priori limits to this demand.[2] A partial list of demands might include the recognition and enforcement of a basic set of human, political, and economic rights, the right to organize trade unions, protection of basic environmental standards, and so on. In an ideal world, of course, the burden of proof would rest on those who take the pro-market view, to prove that innovation requires that an aspect of social life be subjected to competition, before it would be so exposed.

An equalization of such social conditions cannot be implemented immediately or by fiat. But we view this obvious fact as a benefit, not a cost, of this approach. Even were abrupt equalization possible, it would place an egregious burden on citizens in developing and developed countries alike. Rather, equalization must occur gradually through international negotiations that balance the disruptions and hardships that such equalization might entail against the ultimate benefits that it might be hoped to deliver, and that weigh carefully and respectfully the contending perspectives that are brought to the table by the members of societies from very different positions in the global economy.

We are cognizant of the objections that may be raised against the proposal to take "X" out of competition. Mainstream economists will argue that to do so would be to remove all incentives for innovation, and hence, for economic growth and development. We disagree. Surely, not even the most ardent neoclassical economist contends today that all aspects of social life must be subjected to unmitigated market forces if innovations are to occur (consider child labor and the ownership and sale of human beings). But, then, *where do the limits lie*? Even neoclassical theory provides no definitive answer. We believe that the incentive structure that will suffice to induce innovation (or, for that matter, willing labor) is socially created and historically variable. The task, then, must be to explore in theory and enact in practice a process that continually reduces the magnitude of these incentives, thereby minimizing the contact between social life and global capitalist competition.

Others may object that such a proposal is hardly workable. Again, we disagree. Every trade arrangement that arises between countries of necessity establishes, rearranges, and codifies certain rules of the game. Typically, today, most resulting provisions are not oriented toward removing aspects of social life from competition, to be sure. But there are cases where wages and other aspects of "worker rights" are taken out of competition by international agreement. In 1984, the Generalized System of Preferences (GSP) was amended to require the United States to rescind preferential trading privileges to any nation not taking steps to adopt recognized worker rights. Similar provisions were incorporated in the Caribbean Basin Initiative (CBI) in 1983, and the Overseas Investment Corporation (OPIC) rules in 1985. Currently, efforts to secure the now stalled Social Charter in the European Community, and the pressure that has been brought to bear on President Clinton to include environmental and labor protections in NAFTA are further examples of taking onerous aspects of social life out of competition.

A progressive way forward, then, might entail new social movements joining with labor and other traditional political movements to articulate and struggle to attain the goal of limiting the contours of global capitalist competition. These parties would militate for a "leveling up" of the conditions of social life, not in order to impose a homogeneous social, political, and economic order across nations, but to ensure an extension and deepening of entitlements and capabilities (Sen 1983). Put simply, the challenge would be to fill in the "X" as we seek to expand the terrain of a cooperative, internationalist industrial policy.

THE SOCIAL INDEX TARIFF STRUCTURE

This discussion has been perforce rather abstract, given the early stages of this project. But let us close with a simple proposal that indicates how these concerns might be concretized. Today, the threat of capital flight and international competition present formidable obstacles to unions and other social movements that seek to limit the terrain of competition. The onus in such struggles is squarely on those who promote social advancement to demonstrate that its demands will not jeopardize the international competitiveness of its domestic capital. As this century closes, it is apparent that this burden has become heavier to bear than several decades ago, in developed and developing economies alike. We can expect that the current rush to liberalize trade, if it succeeds, will exacerbate this pressure.

But it is not difficult to imagine certain rules of the game that use competitive pressures to promote rather than stifle social progress. Consider, for example, what we will call a "social index tariff structure" (SITS) to govern the terms of trade between any two countries.[3] In such an arrangement, each country would be assigned a social index number, reflecting some measure of the capabilities and entitlements of its inhabitants. Preliminarily, we might consider the Human Development Index (HDI) as developed by the United Nations Development Program as an appropriate candidate. This index seeks to provide an international ranking of human welfare that reaches beyond the traditional economic measure of per capita Gross Domestic Product (GDP): It derives a composite measure from income, life expectancy, and educational attainment data. On the basis of this index, it is able to rank countries; based on 1990 data, Canada ranked first, the United States sixth, and Guinea last.

If we take GDP per capita as a very loose measure of a society's *ability* to provide human welfare, then by combining these two indexes we can reach some tentative conclusions about a nation's performance relative to its means. We can further adjust this index to account for differences in wage costs across countries which do not reflect productivity differences. This is the international analog of the traditional trade union demand to take wages out of competition. By making this final class correction, we now have what can be called the *class–means adjusted HDI index*.[4]

With this new index in hand, we can design a social, world tariff structure that would reward and penalize countries based on effort relative to means. The terms of trade between any two countries would be determined by their relative index values: if the United States has a higher index number than France, France would face a tariff in its sales to the U.S. market, the magnitude of which would reflect the difference in their respective index numbers; if, on the other hand, France's number exceeds that of Britain, it would win tariff protection on British imports.

The logic is straightforward: Countries would be rewarded for making improvements in the conditions of social life measured and codified in the index. Hence, rather than being penalized with diminished competitiveness and capital flight for increasing worker rights or instituting progressive taxation, it would win improved access in its trading arrangements. Critically, such a trading regime would help to shift the burden in domestic political struggles: For example, environmentalists would be able to seek new regulations without having to confront the objection that such regulations would necessarily imperil the survival of domestic firms. A well-structured social index tariff, at a minimum, would mitigate the effects of the increasing costs attending the new environmental protections. Moreover, a composite index would grant maximum latitude for the progressive elements in each society to define for themselves the content of their demands; one might champion improved worker rights, another, enhanced environmental protections, a third, gender equality—each would be rewarded in terms of its terms of trade while pursuing objectives that reflect its own cultural, economic, and social priorities.

CONCLUSION

For a social index tariff structure to win support, of course, it must not carry a bias either in favor of nor against the less developed countries (LDCs). Moreover, it must reward efforts at improvement heavily, especially those improvements made by the lagging countries, so that it does not become a new means for cementing existing international economic disparities. But these technical problems are minor by comparison with the more troublesome theoretical questions posed earlier. To translate those problems into this context, what is especially problematic is the specification of the indicators of human welfare and development that the index would comprise. If we want to reward effort, we need still to define what the terms of this effort are in ways that minimize biased cultural baggage. This, again, is by no means simply an economic question: it falls within the purview of political economy and political philosophy, most broadly defined.

The theoretical and political project to take "X" out of competition is and must be, then, a rigorous interdisciplinary, international, and multicultural endeavor. If this project seems daunting, we should keep in view the tremendous social and economic costs of our failure to embrace it.

ACKNOWLEDGMENTS

We would like to acknowledge the research assistance of Vanessa Conti and the financial support of the Dana Internship Program of Dickinson College.

NOTES

1. See in particular Lazonick (1991, 4–5) where he emphasizes the need for a country to retain leadership in technology and social organization in order to avoid decreases in its standard of living.

2. See Brecher and Costello (1991a, 1991b), Lebowitz (1988), and Dorman (1988) for similar views.

3. See Chapman (1987, 1991) and Dorman (1992) for related, albeit different, concepts of a social tariff.

4. For alternative detailed constructions of the class–means adjust HDI index see DeMartino and Cullenberg (1993) and Cullenberg and DeMartino (1994).

REFERENCES

Best, M. 1990. *The New Competition*. Cambridge, MA: Harvard University Press.

Brecher, J. and Costello, T. 1991a. "Labor Goes Global: I." *Z Magazine* (January): 90–97.

———. 1991b. "Labor Goes Global: II." *Z Magazine* (March): 88–97.

Chapman, D. 1991. "Environmental Standards and International Trade in Automobiles and Copper: The Case for a Social Tariff." *Natural Resources Journal* (Summer): 449–461.

———. 1987. *The Economic Significance of Pollution Control and Worker Safety Costs for World Trade*. Cornell Agricultural Economics Staff Paper, No. 87-25, November.

Cullenberg, S. and DeMartino, G. 1994. *The Social Index Tariff Structure: An Internationalist Response to Economic Integration*. Mimeograph, Department of Economics, University of California, Riverside.

DeMartino, G. and Cullenberg, S. 1993. *Taking 'X' Out of Competition: An Internationalist Alternative to Competitive-Enhancing Industrial Strategies*. Mimeograph, Department of Economics, University of California, Riverside.

Dorman, P. 1992. "The Social Tariff Approach to International Disparities in

Environmental and Worker Rights Standards: History, Theory and Some Initial Evidence." In *Multinational Culture: Social Impacts of a Global Economy*, eds. by C. R. Lehman and R. M. Moore, 203–223. Westport, CT: Greenwood Press.

———. 1988. "Worker Rights and International Trade: A Case for Intervention." *Review of Radical Political Economics* (Summer and Fall): 241–246.

Lazonick, W. In press. "Industry Clusters versus Global Webs: Organizational Capabilities in the U.S. Economy." *Industrial and Corporate Change.*

———. 1991. *Business Organization and the Myth of the Market Economy.* New York: Cambridge University Press.

Lebowitz, M. 1988. "Trade and Class: Labour Strategies in a World of Strong Capital." *Studies in Political Economy* (Autumn): 137–148.

Reich, R. 1991a. *The Work of Nations.* New York: Alfred A.Knopf.

———. 1991b. "Who Is Them?" *Harvard Business Review* (March–April): 77–88.

———. 1990. "Who Is Us?" *Harvard Business Review* (January–February): 53–64.

Sen, A. 1983. "Development: Which Way Now?" *Economic Journal* (December): 745–762.

Clintonism, Welfare, and the Antisocial Wage: The Emergence of a Neoliberal Political Imaginary

NANCY FRASER

Important political–cultural shifts are underway in the United States, as a new, neoliberal hegemony is being constructed. In this essay I try to determine what these changes are, and what they mean, by examining the political culture surrounding social welfare. I interrogate the new "national common sense" that is emerging in talk about "welfare reform" and "family policy," as these intersect with talk about "taxes." My aim is to determine whether and how "Clintonism" is transforming the discursive space in which such issues appear, and what might be the political consequences.

To this end, I analyze what I call the *political imaginary of social welfare.* I examine a public sphere that is saturated with, indeed structured by, various taken-for-granted assumptions about people's needs and entitlements. These assumptions inform the ways in which social problems are named and debated in the United States, and they delimit the range of solutions that are thinkable (Fraser 1989). They are often distilled in catch phrases and stereotypical images, which dominate public discourse. Taken together, such catch phrases, images, and assumptions constitute the political imaginary of social welfare.

This paper is an abridged version of Fraser (1993). Copyright 1993 by the Association for Economic and Social Analysis. Adapted by permission. It was delivered as a plenary lecture at the conference on "Marxism in the New World Order," Amherst, MA, November 1992 and was revised for publication in late January and early February, 1993.

493

To analyze the political imaginary of social welfare is simultaneously to shed light on the construction of social identities. It is to examine the terms in which people formulate their sense of who they are, what they deserve, and what they hope for. These in turn are bound up with assumptions about identity and difference: Who is like me and who is not, who is my ally and who is my enemy? The analysis I am proposing thus illuminates the discursive construction of affinities and animosities. It lets us see how social solidarities and social antagonisms are elaborated (Fraser 1992).[1]

What then is the impact of Clintonism on the political imaginary of social welfare? To what extent and in what ways is the national common sense being reconfigured? How might lines of solidarity and antagonism be redrawn? My response is divided into two parts. First, I identify the main elements of the *neoconservative* political imaginary of "welfare" during the era of Reagan and Bush. Then I examine the *neoliberal* common sense that is emerging under Clinton.

THE NEOCONSERVATIVE POLITICAL IMAGINARY OF WELFARE

Under Reagan and Bush, a neoconservative political imaginary of "welfare" held sway. For analytical purposes, we can identify six salient sentiments and assumptions, which underpinned this neoconservative common sense.

1. *The antisocial wage*. U.S. political culture under Reagan and Bush exalted a reductive, economistic, commodified view of the standard of living as (merely) one's personal and/or familial cash income. This view omitted such essential elements of a decent life as a clean, safe, and sustainable environment; a vibrant public culture; and the entire gamut of public goods and services that have been included along with income in the idea of *the social wage*. This latter idea had no place in the national common sense under Reagan and Bush. Rather, the dominant response to declining standards of living was opposition to taxes and to "government spending." Many people narrowed their horizons to concentrate on protecting "their own." They viewed their wages as exclusive personal-familial property, while jettisoning their stake in public goods and services, which were increasingly viewed as benefiting "others." The result was the eclipse of the social wage by a possessive–individualist–familialist construction, the antisocial wage.

2. *Commodities of choice versus public goods of last resort*. Common sense under Reagan and Bush disdained tax-financed, state-provided goods and services, while extolling their commodity equivalents. As public services

deteriorated, the word "public" itself became more pejorative. The term's primary association in social welfare contexts was not the commons but the stigmatized poor, as in "public hospitals" and "public housing" (Fraser and Gordon 1992). The flip side was the valorization of commodities. Common sense held commodities to be superior to public goods, not just contingently but in principle. Commodities, it was claimed, permit "choice." The result was a raft of initiatives to recommodify public functions, whether through subcontracting, as in the case of prison management, or through vouchers, as in the case of schools. The school proposals were especially significant, given the long-standing historical association of public schools with U.S. citizenship.

3. *Contract versus charity.* Reagan–Bush era common sense resurrected a sharp, apparently exhaustive, binary opposition between "contract" and "charity." It approved transactions thought to resemble exchanges of equivalents, while disdaining those viewed as unreciprocated gifts. In the social welfare context, this opposition informed an ideological contrast between "social insurance" programs, such as Social Security retirement pensions, and "public assistance" programs, such as Aid to Families with Dependent Children (AFDC or, more popularly, "welfare").[2] Common sense held the insurance programs to be "contributory," hence legitimate; since people seemed merely to "get back what they put in," the transaction was considered a contractual exchange, and claimants' entitlements were secure. Public assistance programs, in contrast, were labeled "noncontributory," hence of dubious legitimacy; since recipients seemed to "get something for nothing," the transaction was deemed a unilateral gift, undeserved, socially deviant, and possibly harmful. The contract-versus-charity opposition mystified the true character of both kinds of government programs.[3] In addition, it imposed narrow limits on what sorts of social welfare arrangements were conceivable. By classifying *all* relations as *either* contractual *or* charitable, it appeared to exhaust all available alternatives. Forms of mutual aid that were reciprocal but noncontractual were purged from the universe of public discourse (Fraser and Gordon 1992).

4. *Independence versus dependence.* Reagan–Bush era common sense sharpened an old ideological opposition between "independence" and "dependence." This opposition informed a spate of new attacks on "welfare dependency." Receipt of "welfare" (AFDC) was identified with "dependence," while wage earning was assumed to confer "independence." The subtext of this opposition, like that of the contract-versus-charity opposition, was an androcentric conception of work: Waged labor was recognized and rewarded, whereas women's unwaged domestic and child rearing labor was not. That conception was hardly new, of course, but it took on new meaning in a post-Fordist, postindustrial context.

During this period the family wage ideal was increasingly contested and the "working mother" was becoming the norm. Pressure to be "self-supporting" through wage work intensified. "Taxpayers'" antagonism toward "welfare dependents" increased, consequently, as poor single mothers on AFDC were perceived as "not working" (Fraser and Gordon 1994).

5. *From entitlement to obligation.* During the Reagan–Bush era, the meaning of "welfare reform" changed dramatically. In the 1960s and 1970s, its principal sense was strengthening recipients' entitlement: broadening eligibility, increasing benefits, removing strings and administrative discretion, and eliminating stigma—in short, making "welfare" a right. During the Reagan–Bush era, in contrast, "welfare reform" meant curtailing entitlement and cutting costs: conditioning benefits on recipient "obligations," restricting eligibility, decreasing allowances, imposing work requirements, or even abolishing support for poor women and children altogether. "Reforms" like workfare, learnfare, and wedfare hedged grants with strings and conditions, eroding the idea of an unconditional right. Lawrence Mead's influential (1986) book distilled this common sense in its title: *Beyond Entitlement: The Social Obligations of Citizenship.* Entitlement came under attack in two senses: first, in the sense of a right to receive help from others without loss of dignity; second, in the sense of an "uncontrolled" government expenditure triggered without any new legislative appropriation.

6. *Personal responsibility.* Common sense under Reagan and Bush seemed to hold individuals responsible for their fates, although alleged group-based characteristics were insinuated as well. Structural explanations of poverty receded from the political culture, and moral explanations moved to center stage. Journalists discovered "the underclass," and social "scientists" located the causes of its misery in its own behaviors and culture. The ghetto poor were said to lack commitment to "mainstream values," including (female) sexual self-restraint and the work ethic. Opportunity was there, it was said, but the culture of the poor prevented them from grasping it. Liberal social welfare programs were partly to blame, as well, since they had rewarded and encouraged such "dysfunctional" behaviors as "out-of-wedlock" childbearing and "work avoidance." The remedy was "personal responsibility."[4]

Together, these six elements constituted the neoconservative political imaginary of "welfare." They were vividly condensed in the image of "the welfare mother." She was imagined in the national mind's eye as a black, unmarried, inner-city teenager. This image condensed stereotypes of parasitism and passivity, female sexual license and racial primitivism, laziness and unchecked fertility, cultural and familial disorganization, everything, in short, that stands opposed to the reigning normative images of social order: work discipline, heterosexual nuclear family organization, female chastity, law abidingness, "paying one's way," and paying one's taxes (Fraser and Gordon 1994).

The neoconservative political imaginary of "welfare" was coded by gender, "race," and class. It privileged waged work and the commodity form, casting the wage-worker-cum-taxpayer as the ideal typical citizen, entitled to benefits under the rubric of social insurance. Claims to help, then, were firmly tied to primary labor force participation. This was a capitalist construction, to be sure, but also an androcentric one, since it occluded socially necessary unwaged domestic work, disproportionately performed by women—including work performed by "welfare mothers." It also had a racist subtext, since not even all wage earners enjoyed the entitlements reserved for "workers." Excluded from social insurance benefits were many agricultural workers, domestic workers, part-time workers, undocumented workers, and others whose work was seen as menial and/or servile, and hence dissonant with "independence." These workers were disproportionately people of color.

The neoconservative political imaginary of "welfare" also organized social antagonisms and social solidarities. It reinforced a series of long-standing oppositions, including the "dependent" versus the "independent"; "workers" versus "work avoiders"; "taxpayers" versus "tax-eating parasites"; social insurance recipients versus public assistance recipients; the "sexually and reproductively irresponsible classes" versus the "responsible and respectable classes"; "the middle class" versus "the underclass" (supposedly the only two classes in the society). These multiple oppositions often seemed to reduce to the single master opposition of "black" versus "white," even as they invited "respectable" blacks to identify as "socially white."

Why did the neoconservative political imaginary prove so widely resonant in the 1980s? This period continued the transition to a post-Fordist phase of capitalism. The relative deindustrialization of the United States brought economic dislocation and increased impoverishment. It also brought the loss of higher paid, traditionally male manufacturing jobs; increased female labor-force participation in the burgeoning new "service" sector; and, consequently, the decentering of the ideal of the family wage. Family structure, too, underwent major structural shifts, and gender norms became increasingly contested. The result was a set of new stresses on norms of work, sexuality, and reproduction. During the 1980s in the United States "welfare" increasingly served as a vehicle for expressing such stresses, while also encoding antagonisms of gender, "race," and class.

CLINTONISM: THE EMERGING NEOLIBERAL POLITICAL IMAGINARY

Will the neoconservative political imaginary persist during the Clinton presidency? Or will the discourse on "welfare" be reconfigured? Let us consider each of the previous six assumptions in turn.

1. *The quasi-social wage.* Will the common sense of the Clinton era assume the antisocial wage? Both in his campaign and in his presidency, Clinton has projected a somewhat broader, less economistic conception. By stressing health care and the environment, he has broken with the extreme view that all that is required for a decent standard of living is an adequate cash income, low taxes, and a full-time wife and homemaker. The new common sense in formation seems to hold that goods and services provided by government are also essential. This certainly modifies Reagan-Bush era common sense. But Clintonism also aims to accommodate continuing hostility to taxes. Most important, it leaves open crucial questions about what public goods and services will be provided, and in what forms, and to whom, and at whose expense. Those questions are in the process of being answered in ways not consonant with the ideal of the social wage. The likely result will be a new, neoliberal conception, the "quasi-social wage," in which provision is stratified by class.

The ambiguities of the emerging new common sense can be read in Clinton's take on "family values." In response to an increasingly shrill conservative defense of the traditional male breadwinner–female homemaker family, he sponsored "family-friendly" social welfare policies such as family leave and national health insurance. These proposals seemed to recognize needs arising from women's participation in wage labor, while broadening what could count as a respectable family. Clinton thus broke with the neoconservative assumption that the ideal-typical worker has a nonemployed wife at home. He recognized, in contrast, that workers may also be primary parents in need of social services. Thus "family values" discourse was recast in a form that could support expanded government involvement in social welfare.

This represents an important discursive shift, but not necessarily one to a social wage. Clinton's rhetoric is susceptible to programmatic interpretations that would enforce social inequalities and antagonisms. The form of health insurance he supports, for example, is not genuinely universalist; although "managed competition" provides coverage to the "working poor," it perpetuates class differences in health care, reserving high-quality medicine for the wealthy and high profits for insurance companies. Likewise, Clinton signed a law mandating *unpaid* family leave and never contemplated universal family allowances; his approach is not particularly "friendly" to the families of low-income workers; and it is of no value whatever to those without paying jobs.

The class-specific character of the Clinton Administration's "family friendliness" was especially clear in its handling of the controversy over the employment of undocumented domestic and child care workers by two (failed) female nominees for Attorney General. Clinton did not take an approach adequate to the structural complexity of the problem in a context where child care is a "private" (i.e., individual *female*) responsibility, where the organization of paid employment does not accommodate parents' needs, and where there exists a "racial [and class] division of paid reproductive labor" (Glenn 1992). Instead, he responded opportunistically and *punitively*, by punishing the female employers instead of expanding the social entitlements of paid domestic workers.

The sorts of policies likely to represent the new common sense under Clinton, then, will consolidate class stratification. They entail a quasi-social wage.

2. *Between commodities and public goods.* Will common sense in the era of Clinton revalue public goods in relation to commodities? We have already seen evidence of a political culture more friendly to public provision, albeit one fraught with ambiguities. In general, Clinton has changed the tone of public discourse by refraining from praise of commodities and from attacks on public goods in the name of "choice." He has stressed that "government can help," thereby breaking with the anti-government, pro-business discourse of Reagan and Bush. But he has nevertheless sent mixed messages. On the one hand, Clinton joined the attack on "entitlements," implying a pejorative view of public provision. On the other hand, he has sponsored a publicly funded program of immunization for children over the opposition of drug manufacturers. Finally, he has rejected the privatization of public schools while simultaneously "choosing" a private school for his daughter. The upshot, however, is not simply ambivalence. It is, rather, an emerging neoliberal approach that allies government more directly with capital. That alliance will yield hybrid fruits—neither pure commodities nor pure public goods, but new intermediate strains that combine certain features of both.

Health insurance neatly illustrates this approach. Clinton has rejected a truly public "single-payer" model in favor of "managed competition." The latter publicly organizes and partly funds the purchase of group coverage from private insurance companies. It therefore blurs the distinction between commodities and public goods.

This hybrid neoliberal approach was also apparent in the campaign rhetoric of "infrastructural investment." This expression was intended to distinguish Clinton's "pro-government" stance from traditional post-

New Deal liberalism; it implicitly accepted the conservative critique of the latter's "tax and spend" orientation. "Investment" may look like a rhetorically clever substitute for "spending," but its extension is not the same. "Infrastructural investment" means building bridges, roads, high-speed trains, and high-tech fiber-optic communications systems. It also means subsidizing corporations by helping to fund their high-tech research and development. What it does *not* encompass is spending on public day care, public housing, or public health. This rhetoric thus incorporates a gender bias in favor of "production" at the expense of "reproduction." It translates programmatically, moreover, into a bias in favor of creating the sorts of technical, professional, and skilled blue-collar jobs that are traditionally reserved for white men, as opposed to the sorts of jobs likely to be held by women and/or people of color.

The theme of a "partnership" between government and business is the hallmark of neoliberalism. The models usually cited in Clintonist discourse are Germany and Japan. Sweden, in contrast, is virtually never invoked, since it would require the presence of a third "partner"—the labor unions—as well as generous, solidaristic provision of public goods. Neoliberalism in the United States, on the contrary, seems committed to blurring the distinction between commodities and public goods.

3. *Contract versus charity redux.* Will the emerging common sense under Clinton soften the contract-versus-charity opposition? We can expect some decline in the sort of moralistic cant that was so central to neoconservative political culture. But the underlying ideological structure appears intact. Certainly, Clinton's rhetorical stress on "investment" as opposed to "spending" reinforces the logic of contract. It suggests an invidious contrast between those expenditures that generate a return in the form of further revenues versus those that merely disburse cash to feed and house needy human beings.

Programmatically, moreover, Clinton's proposals would preserve invidious divisions between "contract" and "charity" in social welfare. Campaign promises to "end welfare as we know it" never contemplated eliminating the division between social insurance and public assistance. They never envisioned the sorts of genuinely universal programs that would break down the contract-versus-charity dichotomy: a guaranteed annual income, a single-payer health care system, universal public day care, a national child support insurance system. "Welfare reform" à la Clinton continues to "target" and stigmatize the poor. Although it promises (targeted) child care, child-support collection, and job training, it does not guarantee jobs. Most importantly, the "reform" would impose a two-year time limit on the receipt of AFDC, to be followed by mandatory "community service" (a.k.a. workfare). *That* implies that recipients are shirkers who stay on the rolls longer than necessary in order to avoid work. The effect is to exacerbate common sense disdain for poor solo-mother families who need help. On this point neoliberalism and neoconservatism converge.

4. *Independence versus dependence redux.* Here, too, neoliberal common sense seems to echo its neoconservative predecessor. Neither in his campaign nor in his presidency has Clinton challenged the dependence-versus-independence dichotomy. He has joined, rather, in the conservative attacks on "welfare dependency," accepting the view that receipt of help must reduce one's "independence," that support for the poor should be minimized, that recipients should be moved off the welfare rolls and into "work" as soon as possible, and that child raising does not count as "work." Those assumptions informed his campaign slogan that "welfare" should be "a second chance, not a way of life." That slogan echoed, while appearing to modify, Bush's claim that "welfare was never meant to be a lifestyle." The offer of a "second chance" seemed compassionate, but it insinuated (often counterfactually) that AFDC claimants had already had, and blown, a first chance (Williams 1993). The condemnation of a welfare "way of life," moreover, implied that women were misusing the system to free ride. Help, apparently, should be administered in small doses; otherwise it will induce "dependency."

Rhetorically, then, both neoliberalism and neoconservatism condemn "dependency."

5. *From entitlement to obligation redux.* The emerging neoliberal common sense will continue to support an obligation, as opposed to an entitlement, view of welfare. We have already seen that Clinton's campaign rhetoric included attacks on "entitlements"—that is, on the idea that people have a right to help. We saw, likewise, that he has proposed a two-year limit on the receipt of AFDC with compulsory workfare thereafter. While governor of Arkansas, moreover, he sponsored "reforms" requiring mandatory Parent–Teacher Association (PTA) attendance for poor women as a condition of receiving their grants. He has also supported the New Jersey "reform" that denies support to poor children born after their mothers have qualified for AFDC. All these "reforms" hedge assistance with conditions; all are punitive, victim blaming, and discriminatory. Neoliberalism thus rejects an entitlement view of "welfare reform," which would aim to make "welfare" a right. It converges instead with the neoconservative view that "welfare" should entail "obligations."

6. *Mutual responsibility.* Finally, does the Clinton era portend any shift from moral to structural explanations of poverty? Here the signs are mixed. Rhetorically, Clinton has alternated between two formulations, which suggest two somewhat different approaches to poverty. At times he has spoken of "personal responsibility," which reprises the neoconservative common sense. At other times, however, he has preferred the

expression "mutual responsibility," suggesting a division of labor between structural and moral factors in the causation of poverty. The new, neoliberal common sense, apparently, is that it is not *only* poor people's "bad behaviors" and "bad values" that are at the root of their troubles; there are macroeconomic causes as well.

The crucial question here is whether or not the "mutual responsibility" formulation implies a substantially different poverty policy. The rhetoric insinuates that it does: "Government should help the poor *and* the poor should do more to help themselves" (*The New York Times*, February 3, 1993, A9, emphasis added). That suggests an evenhanded balance between the carrot and the stick: more funds for day care and job training *and* mandatory "community service." Notice, however, that the focus is still the "supply side," that is, changing the characteristics of the poor, while the "demand side," that is, jobs, is left vague. In the absence of guaranteed jobs, of course, the carrot is no match for the stick. Since "infrastructural investment" is not likely to create jobs for "welfare mothers," moreover, neoliberal "evenhandedness" is more rhetorical than real.

Perhaps the best one can say about neoliberal talk about "mutual responsibility" is that it opens some new space for discussing structural causes of poverty, while leaving plenty of space for continued victim blaming. We can expect more debate on the causes of, and remedies for, poverty.

Such, then, are some basic elements of the emerging neoliberal political imaginary of social welfare. What do they imply for the discursive construction of solidarities and antagonisms? Will the Clinton era see any alteration of current social animosities along lines of gender, "race," and class?

Clinton's winning electoral strategy involved muting the so-called special claims of so-called special interests, especially blacks and organized labor. This strategy got its principled (as opposed to its purely strategic) rationale from social democrats like William J. Wilson and Theda Skocpol, who linked it to a defense of universal, as opposed to "targeted," social policies. The idea was to talk about helping the middle class while slipping in help for the poor under the rubric of universal programs. In theory, this aligns wage earners and their families with the poor against the wealthy and the corporations. We saw, however, that most of Clinton's programmatic proposals are not genuinely universalist. They are still very wage centered and obligation oriented. They tend thus to reinforce the old alignment of "workers" against "nonworkers" and the poor.

There is one further twist, however. The Clinton Administration is pro-reproductive choice, pro-affirmative action, and pro-civil rights for lesbians and gays. We thus face the novel prospect of a public culture that combines equal-opportunity liberalism in relation to gender, "race," and sexual orientation with a class realignment that further marginalizes the poor. This prospect is deeply ironic. The poor, after all, are dispro-portionately young, female, and racially marked. Yet the neoliberal com-mon sense incorporates versions of feminism and antiracism.

A recent set of developments highlights this irony. In his early days in office Clinton showed no interest in making "welfare reform" a prior-ity, preferring to pursue national health insurance instead. For a while, then, attention turned away from "welfare mothers" toward what had been cast as a broader, cross-class concern. In early February 1993, how-ever, Clinton revived talk about "welfare reform." He used the occasion of a major speech to repeat victim-blaming proposals to limit AFDC to two years and to impose mandatory "community service" thereafter. He did not, however, propose legislation. The aim of the speech was rhetorical, and the point lay entirely in the timing. "Welfare" discourse was revived at the moment of greatest furor over announced plans to end the ban on gays and lesbians in the military. All signs indicated an attempt to mollify homophobic suburbanites by evoking an alternative scapegoat.

This incident may prove to set the precedent for a more general neoliberal political logic of sacrificial substitutions. If so, equal-opportu-nity gains won by progressive social movements will be paid for out of the hide of the poor. That logic would cohere with an emerging pattern of granting formal rights while denying the material supports that would enable poor and working-class people to enjoy them. We have already seen this kind of class-division strategy at work in Clinton's stand on family leave, which guarantees unpaid leave for employees of large- and me-dium-sized corporations, but nothing for unemployed and underem-ployed parents. If this pattern were to continue to hold, then feminists might secure some formal reproductive rights, for example, but fail to win programs that would meet the substantive reproductive health needs of many women. Analogously, gay-rights advocates might secure some formal rights for healthy gays and lesbians, including the right to serve in the military, while the needs of people with AIDS and HIV continue to go unmet. Or, to take yet another example, antiracists might win im-proved enforcement of affirmative action procedures in the hiring of skilled and professional workers, while the ghetto poor become increas-ingly marginal to the official system of social labor.

If realized, this scenario would represent a significant new, neoliberal realignment. Class stratification would be exacerbated, including *within* formations defined by gender, sexual orientation, and "race." The most chilling prospect of all is the possible cooptation of significant elements of progressive social movements in such a post-Fordist, neoliberal hegemony.

ACKNOWLEDGMENTS

The revisions for this chapter were greatly helped by suggestions from Carole Biewener, Linda Gordon, David Ruccio, Brackette Williams, and Eli Zaretsky. Some of the ideas were developed jointly with Linda Gordon and are elaborated in our coauthored papers (Fraser and Gordon 1992, 1994). I am grateful, finally, for research support from the Center for Urban Affairs and Policy Research, Northwestern University, the NEH/Newberry Library, and the American Council of Learned Societies.

NOTES

1. Methodologically, I draw simultaneously on several different theoretical traditions. From Juergen Habermas (1989) I borrow the idea of "the political public sphere" in the sense of an institutionalized discursive space in which political issues are formulated and disputed. But I give that idea a Gramscian spin, stressing that it is a power-laden space for the construction and contestation of hegemony (Fraser 1991). To analyze discursive processes, moreover, I coopt some poststructuralist techniques, especially the interrogation of dichotomies. For substantive insights, finally, I draw on socialist–feminist analyses of family–state–market intersections.

2. This contrast did not originate in the Reagan–Bush era; it goes back at least to the New Deal. But it was sharpened and exacerbated during the period under discussion here, becoming a salient underlying feature of political culture. For a genealogy of the contract-versus-charity opposition, see Fraser and Gordon (1992).

3. All government programs are financed by "contributions" in the form of taxation. Public assistance programs are financed from general revenues, both federal and state. Welfare recipients, like others, "contribute" to these funds, for example, through payment of sales taxes (Fraser and Gordon 1992).

4. The idea of "personal responsibility" was not new; rather, the discovery of "the underclass" in effect recycled earlier notions of the "culture of poverty." But the vehemence of the victim blaming was aggravated.

REFERENCES

Fraser, N. 1989. "Struggle over Needs: Outline of a Socialist-Feminist Critical Theory of Late-Capitalist Political Culture," In *Unruly Practices: Power, Discourse and Gender in Contemporary Social Theory.* Minneapolis: University of Minnesota Press.

———. 1991. "Rethinking the Public Sphere: A Contribution to the Critique of Actually Existing Democracy." In *Habermas and the Public Sphere*, ed. Craig Calhoun. Cambridge MA: MIT Press.

———. 1992. "The Uses and Abuses of French Discourse Theories for Feminist Politics. " In *Revaluing French Feminism*, ed. N. Fraser and S. Bartky. Bloomington, IN: Indiana University Press.

———. 1993. "Clintonism, Welfare, and the Antisocial Wage: The Emergence of Neoliberal Political Imaginary." *Rethinking Marxism* 6: 9–23.

Fraser, N. and Gordon, L. 1992, July–September. "Contract versus Charity: Why Is There No Social Citizenship in the United States?" *Socialist Review* 92: 45–68.

———. 1994, Winter. "A Genealogy of 'Dependency': Tracing A Keyword of the U.S. Welfare State." *Signs: Journal of Women in Culture and Society* 19(2): 309– 336.

Glenn, E. N. 1992, Autumn. "From Servitude to Service Work: Historical Continuities in the Racial Division of Paid Reproductive Labor." *Signs: Journal of Women in Culture and Society* 18(1): 1–43.

Habermas, J. 1989. *Structural Transformation of the Public Sphere: An Inquiry into a Category of Bourgeois Society*, trans. T. Burger with F. Lawrence. Cambridge MA: MIT Press.

Mead, L. 1986. *Beyond Entitlement: The Social Obligations of Citizenship*. New York: Free Press.

Williams, B. 1993. Oral response to this paper, presented at the conference "Intellectuals," Rutgers University, February 13.

Negotiating Treaties: Maastricht and NAFTA

BARBARA HARLOW

ast wrecked" was the epithet traced on the hulk of a half-sunk fishing boat in Galway harbor—visited once, according to an apocryphal claim, by Columbus before his more celebrated voyage to the Americas. The graffiti slogan, "mast wrecked," was painted in spring 1992, like other such inscriptions as "mass tricked" that appeared on posters and fliers affixed to street posts and public walls, by volunteers in the Irish anti-Maastricht campaign prior to the June 18, 1992 popular referendum on Ireland's participation in the terms of the Maastricht agreement toward European unity.

In the meantime, 1992 was a year of retrospective celebrations, commemorations, and contestations waged in both parts of the world that had figured as part of Columbus's crusading itinerary: Five hundred years, five centuries of "discovery" of the "Americas" provided one occasion for such pageantry and historic recollection that, in the end, was more thwarted than not by the cumulative five hundred years of "resistance" to the consequences of that discovery. More prospectively, however, 1992 was also to have been the year of the "unification of Europe"—Europe, that continental space that lies between Palestine and the "Americas" and from which Columbus had set out westward on his journey east, hoping eventually to retake Jerusalem for his religious and political sponsors. It was to have been the year as well of untrammelled free trade up, down, and across North America. At midnight, December 31, 1992, if all had gone according to plan and the ratifications as-

sumed at its signing had indeed been seen through, the Maastricht Treaty
was scheduled to go into effect. But Denmark was still planning another
referendum in the hope of reversing its previous nay vote, and the English parliament was debating its own approval.[1] Yet on December 17,
1992, representatives from the U.S., Canadian, and Mexican governments
did sign into effect the North American Free Trade Agreement (NAFTA),
preparatory to that agreement's own ratification—without referendum—
by the congresses and parliaments of those countries. The Maastricht
Treaty and the North American Free Trade Agreement, in other words,
are two texts amongst others designed and written to reconfigure hemispheric arrangements and rearrange global alignments.

MAST WRECKED/MASS TRICKED; NAFTA, YOU DON'T HAFTA/NAFTA, IT'LL SHAFTYA

The practical implementations of these two documents, however,
Maastricht and NAFTA—deriving even as they do from the disciplining
and disciplinary arenas of diplomacy, bureaucracy, and, more academi-
cally, political science—will not be without their literary consequences on
the kinds of the stories that will be available for the telling in their aftermath. The consequences of these governmental negotiations for literary scenarios and histories of self, and constructions of identity around
categories of class, gender, and ethnicity apply not only to citizens of the
signatory states, but to other nationals and nonnationals as well. Will the
women of Ireland, for example, be allowed to seek pregnancy counseling and abortion information in the European community? Will the
immigration story of illegalizing aliens that has underwritten U.S. development policy and political fabrications of progress be ratified once again
by the agreement? What of refugees and political asylum applicants in
Europe? The question of states and their privilege of granting "status"—
political identity—focuses the reading and writing of these documents in
terms of their implications for alternative historical narratives that contest the imposition of treaty agreements.

Ireland, both the Six and the Twenty-Six Counties, north and south
of the partitioning border drawn by England in 1920s, and southwest
United States/northern Mexico delineate territorial and political perspectives for critically reformulating the very terms—sociocultural, economic,
and political—proposed by the mappings of Maastricht and NAFTA. Ireland, England's longest held colony, stands geographically both on and
off the European continent. Its history, too, since the first settler planta-
tions were established in the thirteenth century and continuing through
England's occupation of Northern Ireland today, similarly dislocates it

from a mainstream and mainland European agenda. And since the Treaty of Guadalupe Hidalgo in 1848 that annexed northern Mexico to the continental United States, that region has remained demographically and topographically contested. As Susan Mika, from the Coalition for Justice in the Maquiladoras, expressed it in a presentation in December 1992 in Canada sponsored by the Act for Disarmament Coalition and the Canadian Auto Workers Social Justice Fund: "South Texas is a Third World country already. . . . If the borders were redrawn today, all of that would be a Third World country. People in Texas would be very upset with me saying some of this, but it's true." More recently, however, than the last century's treaty arrangements, Mexico's 1964 Border Industrialization Program, allowing for the development of the maquiladoras, "redrafted the southern border of the United States to include northern Mexico" (Sinclair 1992, 55). But, "while this is called free trade in 1992, a century ago, when foreign capital dominated every aspect of Mexican life, it was called colonialism" (63). The offshore island of Ireland and the U.S.–Mexican border demarcate spaces, at once peripheral and interstitial, for reexamining two of the new and central charter documents of world order.

"WOULD YOU KILL FOR THE EC?"

"Is Ireland a Third World Country?" was the interrogatory title of a conference held in 1991 in Dublin and sponsored by the Belfast-based Centre for Research and Documentation. That conference was followed in 1992 by a second conference in Cork, entitled by the next question, "Where in the World Is Ireland?" These two titular questions were of singular consequence for the debate over Ireland's participation in the terms of the Maastricht Treaty, a debate that entailed a contest over the placement of Ireland within the political map of the global alignments. Would Ireland be conscripted by Europe, or would it identify with the "South"? On the one hand, there were those who insisted on Ireland's history as a former and present colony and who, for example, participated in the Irish Choctaw march for Somalia in autumn 1992, a journey whose itinerary retraced the Trail of Tears in order to solicit support to alleviate the famine in Somalia. The Irish travelers well remembered the donation of some $700 made by the Choctaw people in 1850 for the relief of famine victims in Ireland. On the other hand, the current school of Irish revisionist historiography, "Dublin 4,"[2] argues that there was no conquest of Ireland, no colonization, even no famine at all—and that to the extent that Irish people were hungry in 1847, their need for food translated into a modernizing narrative of agricultural *development* for the island, a development that has now earned Ireland a place, even if a dependent one, within the European community.

On June 18, 1992, the people of Ireland—or at least those who live in the twenty-six counties south of the border that partitions the island into its current two parts—voted in a referendum on whether to accept the terms of the Maastricht Treaty and membership in the new European Union. Only Ireland and Denmark, unlike the ten other member states whose ratification of the treaty was to be decided in parliaments by government officials, were to have made their participation in the European community contingent on the democratic approval of their populations. Nonetheless, public debate in Ireland was only minimal and delayed, and the expression of public opposition even more constrained, with all but one of the major political parties, the trade unions, businessmen's associations, farmers' groupings, and other professional organizations supporting a "Yes" vote in Ireland's Maastricht referendum, and with copies of the treaty text largely uncirculated for voters' independent scrutiny and inquiry. Such opposition as there was centered around three main foci: (1) most notoriously, and perhaps, as some have argued, distractingly, the by now infamous Protocol attached to the Treaty in December 1991 protecting the Irish constitutional ban on abortion and information on abortion; (2) economic determinations; and (3) political and military obligations. What will become now of Ireland's once principled and historical tradition of neutrality?

"Would you kill for the EC?" Joe Noonan and John Maguire (1992) in their study of "Maastricht and neutrality" asked eligible draft-age Irish voters, a question that provocatively rephrases the proverbial query that was posed in the 1984 film *Cal*. Young Cal was asked by the wife of the British soldier in whose execution he had collaborated, the woman with whom he is now having an affair: "Would you die for me?" *Cal*, like other films of the same genre—from John Ford's *The Informer* (1935) to *A Prayer for the Dying* (1987) by Mike Hodges, and now Neil Jordan's *The Crying Game* (1992)—narrates the story of a lone, indeed lonely, and isolated man who would, fleeing the coercive and obsessive "terrorist violence" of the Irish Republican Army (IRA) die instead for the love of a woman. Whereas these popular feature films, through their deployment of the gendered paradigms of sentimentality and sacrifice, consistently represent the political and military struggle against the continued British occupation of Ireland as "sectarian violence" to be redeemed only in the purer and more honorable fold of the feminine embrace (the European community?), Maguire and Noonan translate that gendered reduction "Would you die for me?" back into a political analysis of a more primary state terrorism whose relegitimization, they argue, is written into the text of the Maastricht Treaty: "Would you kill for the EC?"

Seventy years previously, similar objections had been raised in the not dissimilar debate that took place around the treaty that partitioned Ireland and established the Free State in the Twenty-Six Counties. Constance Markievicz, for example, is quoted as reporting more than a caricatured observation in her objections to the treaty. "I saw a picture the other day of India, Ireland and Egypt, fighting England, and Ireland crawling out with hands up. Do you like that?" she asked members of the Dáil debating the issue. She went on, "Now, if we pledge ourselves to this thing, whether you call it Empire or Commonwealth, that is treading down the people of Egypt and India" (cited in Greaves 1988, 276). In her objections to the treaty, Markievicz spoke in unison with all the other women deputies to the Dáil (Macardle 1937, 644). Liam Mellows likewise argued that he was not "prepared to participate in the crucifixion of India and the degradation of Egypt and that the Free State would be like the colonial administration at Dublin Castle" (Foley 1992, 21). The Maastricht referendum asked, *inter alia*, whether Ireland, even in the changed circumstances of the "new world order," would relocate its colonial past and its postcolonial future on the side of the North and its military adventures carried out in the name of a putative national security, or take its stand with the South against the continuing legacy of colonialism in the persistent form of military, economic, and political territorial occupations.

But even as women and political prisoners had contested the treaty in 1921–1922, republican POWs challenge the dominant determinations of the Maastricht document. According to Brian Campbell (1992, 22), writing from Long Kesh,

> We have a clear task, as political activists, to understand this issue. It is not impossibly complex, despite the confusion of media analysis and academic commentators. They have helped to present EC membership and its Maastricht future as inevitable. The underlying message—that There Is No Alternative—is shouted from all sections of the established media, even by many who have established misgivings about what it will mean for Ireland. But are we really caught up in a tide of history from which we can't escape and over which we have no control?

"Men of violence," they are called, the republican prisoners, male and female, in Long Kesh and Maghaberry jails. "Men of violence," as the repetitive formula goes, is one of the rhetorical devices deployed by the Westminster and Dublin governments alike to exclude Sinn Féin from negotiations concerning a combined political fate for the Six and the Twenty-Six Counties. In Texas, for its part, along the Mexican border, the demographic challenge to the maintenance of the state's status within the reigning political agenda of the country is contained as the undue threat of "illegal aliens."

"ILLEGAL ALIENS"/UNDOCUMENTED WORKERS

"Free trade" in goods and services is the principle and the practice to which the United States, Canada, and Mexico have agreed in their endorsement of the NAFTA. Unlike the Maastricht Treaty, which organizes allegedly the twelve presently participating nations into a European Union, a "community," and thus explicitly speaks as well to social, political, and cultural issues, ranging from education to cuisine, the NAFTA purports to be an exclusively economic arrangement. The specifications of that arrangement, however, detailed in the more than one thousand pages of the agreement's text, outline the distinguishing features of a reinforced North American demography and topography. The objectives of the Maastricht Treaty are described as the following:

- To promote economic and social progress that is balanced and sustainable, in particular through the creation of an area without internal frontiers, through the strengthening of economic and social cohesion and through the establishment of economic and monetary union, ultimately including a single currency in accordance with the provisions of this Treaty
- To assert its identity on the international scene, in particular through the implementation of a common foreign and security policy, including the eventual framing of a common defense policy, which might in time lead to a common defense
- To strengthen the protection of the rights and interests of the nationals of its Member States through the introduction of a citizenship of the Union
- To develop close cooperation on justice and home affairs

NAFTA differently identifies its own priorities as the following:

- Eliminate barriers to trade in, and facilitate the cross border movement of goods and services between the territories of the Parties
- Promote conditions of fair competition in the free trade area
- Increase substantially investment opportunities in their territories
- Provide adequate and effective protection and enforcement of intellectual property rights in each party's territory

- Create effective procedures for the implementation and application of this agreement, and for its joint administration and the resolution of disputes
- Establish a framework for further trilateral, regional, and multilateral cooperation to expand and enhance the benefits of this agreement

Although the difference between the rhetorics of "community" (albeit a closed and exclusive one) and "free trade" is critical to the negotiation of these two treaty projects for hemispheric rearrangement, it is the rhetoric of difference, the maintenance and management of the distinctions of insider and outsider, of center and periphery, of ethnic and class divisions, of the unequal distribution, that is, of power and control, that underwrites both projects alike.

Whereas the Maastricht Treaty—with its accompanying Social Charter—guarantees and promotes the free movement of workers, their rights to travel and to employment, that protection is restricted to citizens of EC member states alone. The sections of the Social Charter, for example, addressing the "free movement of workers" are immediately followed by the directives formulated to secure "external borders and immigration policy." Indeed, Amnesty International and other human rights organizations have repeatedly expressed concern that this "harmonization" of the tightening of external borders against refugees and asylum seekers threatens a reinterpretation, if not a rewriting, of international refugee law, and an infringement on the established processes for claiming political asylum. The boundaries thus drawn around the new Europe, however, are drawn by the NAFTA across North America, along class—and, by extension, ethnic—lines. Chapter 16 of the agreement, for example, on the "temporary entry for business persons," explicitly does not include in its provisos the movement of labor. According to elaborately defined "rules of origin," automobiles, foodstuffs, wearing apparel, telecommunications, intellectual property, even natural resources and toxic waste, as well as their purveyors, are traded "freely" across the borders between Canada, the United States, and Mexico, but workers, unless otherwise registered, remain "undocumented" in the terms of this document.

According to an ascendant linear narrative of development, one that locates necessarily the *terminus ad quem* of progress within the territorial borders and political ideology of the United States, the historical trajectory of participants in and aspirants to that modernization narrative must lead always across those nonetheless well-defended borders. Whether for migrant workers or political refugees, jobs and freedom are always to be sought "on the other side," in the United States. That is, the U.S.-Mexican border functions critically in maintaining and patroling the literary and social emplotments, character development, and settings of that political narrative, against incursive attempts in theory or in practice to intrude on its premises or to rewrite its managed alignments.

> They arrived in the secrecy of night, as displaced people often do, stopping over for a week, a month, eventually staying a lifetime. The plan was simple. Mother would work too until they saved enough to move into a finer future where the toilet was one's own and the children didn't need to be frightened. In the meantime, they played in the back allies, among the broken glass, wise to the ways of the streets. Rule one: never talk to strangers, not even the neighbor who paced up and down the hallways talking to himself. Rule two: the police, or "polie" as Sonya's popi pronounced the word, was La Migra in disguise and thus should always be avoided. Rule three: keep your key with you at all times–the four walls of the apartment were the only protection against the streets until Popi returned home. (Viramontes 1985, 61)

But the ways of the street are not responsive to wisdom. "The Cariboo Cafe" is the fifth of the eight stories, all set in a major southwestern metropolis, included in Helena Maria Viramontes' collection *The Moths*. Sonya and Macky, despite their father's instructions, have, at the story's opening, lost their latchkey. Locked out of their home, even such a threatened one, they make their own perilous way through the streets of a still more inhospitable haven, only to be found by a Salvadoran "mother of the disappeared" who mistakes—and takes—Macky for her only son Geraldo, lost to a U.S.-financed military in the country from which she has fled. The unnamed mother is killed at the story's end by those agents who police the national security of the country to which she has fled. Viramontes's story, textually and politically, effaces in its writing the very border that serves from a U.S. position territorially to displace violence to the other side, by way of a rhetoric of difference and identity. But death squads, despite the official screening, operate on both sides of the border, and the narrative continuities and conflations literarily effected in the text of the short story function just as they do literally in the Rodney King trials, in "solutions" like the Federal Weed and Seed Program in Los Angeles, and in letters dispatched by Salvadoran death squads in that same city.

> *Los Angeles, CA*
> *This letter goes toward all who work there–because you are part of a list that we have with all your names, and who one by one soon will be disappeared.*
> *All of you are parasites of the F.M.L.N., so ignorant and cynical–you are part of the death squads on the F.M.L.N.'s behalf because you just as much as those of the F.M.L.N. are savage assassins, because you kill innocent people and violate human rights too.*

> *F.M.L.N. out of El Salvador!*
> *CARECEN and El Rescate get out of the U.S., go to the USSR or Cuba.*
> *Assassins: assassins–Father Olivarez, Kennedy, all of you will die, one way or*
> *another!* (Siems 1992, 79)

Rather than the obliteration of the border discourse that takes place in "The Cariboo Cafe," "Woman Hollering Creek," the title story of Sandra Cisneros' second collection placed along the Texas-Mexican border, contests the cultural and gendered politics of the dominant linear narrative of development by a directed and transgressive reversal and expose of that narrative's fraudulent promises. Cleófilas has been given in marriage by her father to one Juan Pedro Martínez Sanchez from *el otro lado*–the other side–a space that the daughter associates with the life that the "books and songs and *telenovelas* describe" (Cisneros, 1991, 44). In Seguin, Texas, though, Cleófilas finds only the life of a battered wife in a town "built so that you have to depend on husbands. Or you stay home. Or you drive. If you're rich enough to own, allowed to drive, your own car" (50–51). But where have the parts of that car been made? Where assembled? The extensive appendix to NAFTA dealing with automotives is very specific on these terms. In the end, though, the wife and mother, pregnant now with her second child, returns to her home in Mexico. Will Cleófilas's children, however, be "Mexican"–or "Merican"–as the children in another of the stories from the same collection identify themselves to extraneous sightseers to their town?

NAFTA's "rules of origin" refer only to goods. According to the summary of NAFTA issued in August 1992 by the Office of the U.S. Trade Representative, "The rules of origin specify that goods originate in North America if they are wholly North American. Goods containing non-regional materials are also considered to be North American if the non-regional materials are sufficiently transformed in the NAFTA region so as to undergo a specified change in tariff classification." And so on. The text of the agreement itself provides more explicit formulas for determining exactly the "origin" of the various goods to be traded freely. But these equations do not calculate the origin–and thus the equality of freedoms, rights, and privileges–of Cleófilas's children, one born and the other conceived *en el otro lado*.

Other documents, however, attest to and protest the persistent denials of those rights negotiated between government representatives and written into their agreements, documents such as those included in *Between the Lines* (Siems 1992), an anthology of "letters between undocumented Mexican and Central American immigrants and their families and friends" collected in the late 1980s and early 1990s in Los Angeles:

> *Well though you won't believe this, I've never run so fast, now I laugh but in those moments I didn't feel my saliva, the blows, nothing, everything was worse than in*

the movies. I believe that we traveled like 7 to 10 kilometers, but in short I won't cross like this again, seriously, listen, follow the arrows that I put down here for you and what I tell you in each one of them. (7) (Crossing the border from L.A. to Oaxaca, Mexico, June 1990).

Get this, today we are in the most critical phase of the negotiations, since the health management wants to measure its strength against the union's and they put in a clause they invented, and we crossed it out and had to suspend negotiations for that day, and we had thought of moving them to San Salvador but they gave up and we went on negotiating at the office, Mazariego forgive me for telling you all this but since I know that everything that's happening to us interests you, even though you are away you don't stop being our work companion, much less my friend who some day by the grace of Almighty God I'll get to see again. (15) (Labor organizing in El Salvador from Sonsonate, El Salvador to L.A., May 1988)

Because I personally have noted that life there is hard and that it wears one out, all the more for someone who doesn't have the advantage of working in his own field, because there may be work available there but many are degrading jobs like cleaning the bathrooms of offices or other public places, there are those who accept them in order not to die of hunger or cold, with the exception of one who can manage a little English or who has diplomatic connections, because without a professional career one can't prosper there, at least as a laborer or cook or cleaning houses. (75) (The class structure of free trade from San Salvador to L.A., December 1990)

The stories told in the written and recorded correspondence between "illegal aliens," undocumented workers, migrant labor, and political asylum seekers and their relations, families, and friends in their countries of origin are not covered in the wording of NAFTA's text. That correspondence, however, challenges on other terms the very premises of the NAFTA project, drafted as it has been to resecure the hemisphere in the hierarchical interests of the development narrative. As David Campbell (1992b, vii, 85) has pointed out, there is a critically important correlation to be drawn between the "ethical borders of identity" and the "territorial boundaries of states," such that the "paradigm of sovereignty . . . exceeds a simple geographical partitioning: it results in a conception of divergent moral spaces." Much as the Maastricht Treaty on European union conceals within its very rhetoric of "community" the reinforcement of unequal relations of power among and between its member states, and their relation to the outside, the NAFTA needs to be reread against the grain of its discourse of "freedom": The "free" in "free trade," for example, belies the exclusivity of its remapping of those other, dominant, North American continental divides—class, gender, and ethnicity.

Already in 1972, on the eve of the finalization of the European Economic Community (EEC), one economist had argued against Ireland's participation in that consortium: "The accession of Ireland to the EEC will recreate the same kind of economic disadvantages from which Ireland suffered under the Union [with England], and from which it sought escape through independence" (Kaldor 1972, 1). The alternative to NAFTA, however, suggested by AFL-CIO president Lane Kirkland only identifies all the more aggressively the hegemonic interests at stake in the negotiated draftings of the Agreement. According to Kirkland, "If broader access to markets is to be a priority, then it would make sense to me that instead of putting Mexico first in our order of priorities, that we should seek to enter the European community and make the Atlantic Alliance economically meaningful" (*Trade News Bulletin*, February 18, 1993, 2, 31). But again, as Hurst Hannum (1989, 7) has argued in his contribution to the discussion of "new directions in human rights,"

> As an artifical legal creation, the state continues to serve a purpose as the primary interlocutor among those who possess organized military power in the world. Other actors, however—whether international organizations, transnational corporations, or individuals asserting rights against all of the above—are also making their influence felt at the international level.

International organizations, transnational corporations—or, differently, individuals and peoples asserting rights: The oppositional view from Ireland, the offshore island of an offshore island of Europe, like the critical perspectives drawn up along the U.S.–Mexican border, propose alternative, even resistant, scenarios to the narratives underwritten by the Maastricht Treaty and the North American Free Trade Agreement. It is, after all, precisely those other scenarios and their actors that the treaties are designed to write off.

NOTES

1. Denmark did reverse its position in a second referendum in April 1993. Shortly thereafter the British parliament also ratified the treaty.

2. The revisionist historians, such as R. F. Foster or Conor Cruise O'Brien, represent one position, antirepublican and English-oriented, in the cultural and intellectual debates in Irish historiography. The designation "Dublin 4" refers to the section of Dublin in which University College Dublin is located. For a useful critique of this position, see Bradshaw (1989).

REFERENCES

Bradshaw, B. 1989. "Nationalism and Historical Scholarship in Modern Ireland." *Irish Historical Studies* XXVI, 104: 329–351.

Campbell, B. 1992a, Spring. "Voices from the Edge." *The Captive Voice* 4 (1): 22–24.

Campbell, D. 1992b. *Writing Security: United States Foreign Policy and the Politics of Identity*. Minneapolis: University of Minnesota Press.

Cisneros, S. 1991. *Woman Hollering Creek and Other Stories*. New York: Random House.

Foley, C. 1992. *Legion of the Rearguard: The IRA and the Modern Irish State*. London: Pluto Press.

Greaves, C. D. 1988. *Liam Mellows and the Irish Revolution*. London: London and Wishart.

Hannum, H. 1989. "The Limits of Sovereignty and Majority Rule: Minorities, Indigenous Peoples and the Right to Autonomy." In *New Directions in Human Rights*, eds. E. Lutz, H. Hannum, and K. Burkes. Philadelphia: University of Pennsylvania Press.

Kaldor, N. 1972. Introduction. *Ireland and the Common Market: Alternatives to Membership*, by Anthony Coughlan. Dublin: Common Market Study Group.

Macardle, D. 1937. *The Irish Republic*. London: Victor Gollancz.

Noonan, J. and Maguire, J. 1992. *Maastricht and Neutrality: Ireland's Neutrality and the Future of Europe*. Cork: People First/Meitheal.

Siems, L. ed. and trans. 1992. *Between the Lines: Letters Between Undocumented Mexican and Central American Immigrants and their Friends and Families*. Hopewell, NJ: Ecco Press.

Sinclair, J. 1992. "Cheap Labour, Cheap Lives." In *Crossing the Line: Canada and Free Trade with Mexico*, ed. J. Sinclair. Vancouver: New Star Books.

Viramontes, H. M. 1985. *The Moths and Other Stories*. Houston: Arte Publico Press.

The Gulf War: Participation in Modernity

RICHARD LICHTMAN

> All our invention and progress seem to result in endowing
> material forces with intellectual life and in stultifying hu-
> man life into a material force.
>
> —*Marx (1980, 656)*

> Yes, suddenly I saw it all clearly: most people willingly de-
> ceive themselves with a doubly false faith; they believe in
> *eternal memory* (of men, things, deeds, peoples) and in *recti-
> fication* (of deeds, errors, sins, injustice). Both are sham.
> The truth lies at the opposite end of the scale: everything
> will be forgotten and nothing will be rectified. All rectifica-
> tion will be taken over by oblivion. No one will rectify
> wrongs; all wrongs will be forgotten.
>
> —*Kundera (1983, 245)*

The Gulf War was a moral catastrophe.[1] But after Korea, Vietnam, the
Dominican Republic, Grenada, Panama, and the entire range of instances
in which the United States supported the mass murder carried out by
client states from Chile to Indonesia, there should be no surprise in this.
What was so particularly repugnant was the nakedness of the procedure:
the geopolitics of energy that determined U.S. policy in the Middle East;
the struggle with Germany and Japan for international control over oil
and its consequent petrodollars; our previous alliance with Saddam Hussein as a counter to Iran and the encouragement of Iraq's transgression;
our thinly veiled corruption of the U.N.; the transparently hypocritical
claim to defense of Kuwaiti freedom. Add to these the craven subordination of the press, which openly announced the censorship of its reports
without comment or protest while providing the government an apparently neutral medium for its official policy pronouncements, and the
helpless futility of Congress, which was forced to react after the fact to
such executive initiative as the November 1990 increase in troop deployment, which took place immediately after the congressional elections.

The manipulation of the Iraqi "threat" served to resuscitate the military budget and maintain the imperial presidency, while the attempt to exorcise the "Vietnam syndrome" represented a calculated effort at reconstructing national character and memory that surpassed in its Orwellian implications anything previously initiated in recent American military propaganda. The Gulf War was paradigmatic American international oppression.

Domestically, the war continued the destruction of functioning democracy, which has been accelerating since the beginning of the cold war. It was, in fact, the immediate practical equivalent of the disappearing cold war in thinly veiled disguise. Successful wars support command rather than democratic participation, violence rather than reflection, obedience rather than agreement, hierarchy rather than equality, secrecy rather than candor, propaganda rather than information, uniformity rather than diversity and exuberance, enthusiasm and vitality rather than despair and national hopelessness. The destructive scope of the Gulf War was incomprehensible—consider the massive bombing tonnage, the insanely inappropriate means employed, and the totally precluded search for alternatives. The construction of time was disjointed and capriciously mandated (e.g., the announcement of an arbitrary date at which mass destruction would begin), the stated objective was wholly beyond credibility, and the consequences for the victims were unjustifiable and morally abhorrent. In short, the Gulf War was a totalitarian abomination.

What was unique about the war was the utter brutality with which it promoted the technocratic ideology of liberal "modernism," central to whose view is the adoration of technical rationality. This position, whose theoretical foundation can be traced back to the work of Weber, received its first real military elaboration during the World War I, at which point the introduction of tanks, airplanes, and chemical weaponry served specifically to break the protracted stalemate of trench warfare. Winston Churchill, when asked by the Royal Air Force for permission to use chemical weapons "against recalcitrant Arabs as an experiment" replied, "I do not understand the squeamishness about the use of gas. . . . I am strongly in favor of using poisoned gas against uncivilized tribes. . . . It is not necessary to use only the most deadly gasses; gasses can be used which would cause great inconvenience and would spread a lively terror and yet leave no serious permanent effect on most of those affected." Chemical weapons, according to Churchill, represent the "application of Western science to modern warfare. . . . We cannot in any circumstances acquiesce in the non-utilisation of any weapons which are available to procure a speedy termination of the disorder which prevails on the frontier" (cited in Cockburn 1991, 181).

How easily technically rational brutality and morality coalesce. And how insidiously Western science is utilized to "procure a speedy termination of . . . disorder." George Will introduced a variant of this theme in his contention that "this is in part, a didactic war," since Iraq's crime lay precisely in "transgressing values most clearly enunciated by the United States, the symbol of modern political values and cultural modernity" (cited in Cockburn 1991, 186). In fact, Will's beneficent hope was that the war will "pry parts of Arabia into participation in the modernity that is capable of such technological prowess and moral purpose. Both that prowess and that purpose derive from freedom" (186). Or, as Charles Krauthammer maintained in a *Time Magazine* essay: "A month ago, conventional wisdom had the U.S. being overtaken as a great power by Japan. Perhaps. But is making a superior Walkman a better index of technological sophistication than making laser bombs that enter through the front door?" (cited in Macarthur 1992, 102).

The general theme of these apologetics is the identification of "modern political values," particularly moral purpose and freedom with technological sophistication defined primarily as military power. This reflection emerges both from capitalist social reality and liberal ideology, which I will reflect on briefly in turn. American technological dominance had been growing in the world since the end of the nineteenth century. By World War II it seemed invincible, as our wartime allies had been decimated and our enemies destroyed. Of course, the period immediately prior to the war had been one of crisis and despair as the depression stretched from 1929 until December 7, 1941, when the onset of the war began our recovery from economic failure.[2]

Roosevelt's economic policy during the depression humanized welfare for the most needy but was incapable of altering economic decline. Unemployment levels in 1940 were close to those in 1932. The war changed everything. As the state acted vigorously to procure military goods and services and finance production facilities and the cost of labor, it brought significant central control to the previously decentralized economy. In 1940, 175,000 firms produced 70% of all manufactured goods and the largest 100, 30%. By 1944 the largest 100 companies produced 70% of manufactured goods and the remainder, only 30% (Gibson 1986, 13). Central to this transformation from "free market" to managed economy was the government's support of centralized science. Thousands of scientists were hired as "the universities transformed themselves into vast weapons laboratories. Theoretical physicists became engineers, and engineers forced solutions at the frontiers of knowledge" (Gerald Piel, cited in Gibson 1986, 14). Science was actively recruited into the process of destruction. Since the war was generally considered a grim but necessary event and its justification was unquestioned, scientists were accorded affluence, power, and national respect.

But it was not only the "hard sciences" that were so courted. "Scientific management" was also engaged. This ruling class "discipline" can trace its American lineage back to Taylor and Gilbreth, both of whom aided the corporate dissolution of workers' control over the process of labor. (The theoretical practices of "scientific management," as well as organizational psychology and sociology, can only be defined from the perspective of the ruling class's interest in increasing efficiency through controlling costs, particularly labor.) But it is the career of Robert McNamara that best illustrates the development of the military–industrial–scientific complex. At the Harvard Business School he "developed statistical techniques of systems analysis for the War Department as management tools for controlling large organizations" (Gibson, 14); during the war he developed flight patterns for bombing runs over Germany; after the war he became general manager of Ford Motor Company; in 1960 he served the Kennedy administration as secretary of defense. Economics, science, and politics were now integrated, as the role of the state expanded on behalf of capitalist interests, transforming in turn the relations of American foreign policy. As Gibson has noted:

> Politics, economics, and science were now united in a new way. Just as the state changed capitalism and changed the practice of science, so too did the now vastly expanded economy and scientific apparatus change the nature and practice of politics, particularly the conduct of foreign policy. As the possessor of an advanced technological system of war production, the United States began to view political relationships with other countries in terms of concepts that have their origin in physical science, economics, and management. A deeply mechanistic world view emerged among the political and economic elite and their intellectual advisers. (Gibson 1986, 14)

This was precisely the position of Henry Kissinger, who maintained that since the end of World War II, American foreign policy had been based "on the assumption that *technology plus managerial skills* gave us the ability to reshape the international system and to bring domestic transformations in 'emerging countries'" (Kissinger 1974, 57, emphasis added). Kissinger (54) was brutally clear: "A scientific revolution has, for all practical purposes, removed technical limits from the exercise of power in foreign policy." But if no technical limits to power exist, what does constrain America's use of power in the world? To begin to understand Kissinger's perspective it is necessary to say a word about his philosophy of the technological construction of reality, for it is in this realm of obscure theorizing that the foundation of Kissinger's "realpolitik" appears to lie. Briefly, his argument is as follows. There are three styles of leadership: the bureaucratic–pragmatic, the ideological, and the revolutionary-charismatic. The main example of the first type is the American elite, shaped "by a society without social schisms (at least until the race problem became visible) and the product of an environment in which most recognized problems have proved soluble, its approach to policy is *ad hoc*, pragmatic, and somewhat mechanical" (Kissinger, 29). Problems are broken down in constituent elements and dealt with by corresponding experts. Technical issues receive more sophisticated treatment than political issues. "Things are done because one knows how to do them and not because one ought to do them. . . . Pragmatism . . . is more concerned with method than with judgment; or rather it seeks to reduce judgment to methodology and value to knowledge" (Kissinger, 29).

Although the spread of technology and rational administration may produce "common criteria of rationality" and so bring the nations of the world closer together, a basic cleavage persists "between two styles of policy and two philosophical perspectives. The two styles can be defined as the political as against the revolutionary approach to order or, reduced to personalities, as the distinction between the statesman and the prophet" (Kissinger, 46). The statesman manipulates reality for the sake of survival; feels responsible for outcomes; holds a skeptical view of human nature; is aware of "the fragility of structures dependent on individuals";(46) and regards gradualism as the essence of stability. The prophet, by contrast, does not manipulate reality but constructs it; is less interested in the possible than the "right;" cares less for methodology than in total solutions; is less concerned with circumstances than timeless truths; is willing to risk everything because his vision is his primary reality; is both more optimistic and more intolerant of others. The prophet represents an era of enormous accomplishments and disasters. The reader may recognize in this distinction between the statesman and the prophet Kissinger's attempt to render Weber's distinction between two types of rationality; *Zweckrationalität*, in which means are oriented toward a multiplicity of values that so limit each other that the choice of one entails the sacrifice of others, and *Wertrationalität*, in which the choice of means is directed toward a single ultimate value without consideration of consequences.

Ultimately, the difference in philosophical perspective reflects "the divergence of the two lines of thought which since the Renaissance have distinguished the West from the part of the world now called underdeveloped" (Kissinger, 48). The West is committed to a real world external to the observer and to the view that knowledge consists in "recording and classifying" data; its view is Newtonian. However, cultures that do not share the Newtonian view regard reality as internal to the observer, a view that proved a great liability for centuries, since it prevented the development of technology, but that now provides significant flexibility in the current revolutionary turmoil precisely because it makes possible the transformation of reality by the sheer device of altering

> the perspective of the observer. . . . And this can be accomplished under contemporary conditions without sacrificing technological progress. Technology comes as a gift; acquiring it in its advanced form does not presuppose the philosophical commitment that discovering it imposed on the West. . . . The instability of the contemporary world order may thus have at its core a philosophical schism which makes the issues producing most political debates seem largely tangential. (Kissinger, 49)

It is easy enough to ridicule and reject these fantasies for the ideological rationalizations they are. But in their articulation of a commitment to mechanism, positivism, science, and power they express something of the view that has dominated Western forms of legitimation since the origin of the national power state. The claim to knowledge of reality defined as the acquisition of science confers power to transform the world and even to bring the "gift" of technology to the more backward nations of the world. That is Kissinger's ideological position, the position of American liberalism. The truth, of course, was that Iraq's movement toward modernization was suddenly fixed and viciously reversed.

Kissinger's philosophical reflections are the largely incoherent ramblings of one particular individual. However, the sense that technological superiority confers the ultimate means and justification of national dominance has a long history stretching back hundreds of years in the West. Ideologically, its most prominent advocate was probably Weber, whose ostensible view of the value neutrality of the social sciences only made his advocacy of the power of the nation–state all the more influential. Weber viewed the development of formal, technical rationality as the unique contribution of Western culture and counterpoised it to the realm of the "irrational," which included value judgments and the personal authority of charisma. Science, in other words, was opposed to politics. And although "pure reason" could not advocate policy, Weber unsurprisingly supported German expansion:

> Our children will make us primarily responsible—not for the kind of economic organization . . . but for the measure of "elbowroom" which we have obtained for them in the world. . . . The power interests of the nation are . . . the ultimate and decisive interests, which economic policy has to pursue. Economics is a political science. It is the servant of politics, not of the everyday interests of the ruling classes, but of the lasting interests of the nation. (Cited in Blum 1959, 5)

The formal reason that makes Western economic activity possible is ultimately at the service of the power interests of the state.

We are now in a better position to understand exactly how crucial it was to the American ruling class to expunge the memory of Vietnam through predominant reliance on technological superiority and the technological representation and idolization of that technological superiority. Chomsky has argued that the United States won the war in Vietnam, since the price imposed on the Vietnamese totally discouraged any other attempts at independence in Southeast Asia. That proposition seems arguable. But what cannot be denied is that the expectations of the American military-technological establishment were profoundly frustrated and disoriented by the capacity of a poor, third world nation to thwart the aspirations of the most technically sophisticated nation in the world.

The integration of multinational capitalism, science, technology, and the state has produced a new form of fetishism in which the expansion of capitalist accumulation appears a matter of technical imperative. Of course, this is a form of ideology. The root of the matter remains the self-conscious power interests of the ruling capitalist class. But the function of reification is precisely to present oppressive social relations as an imperative of sheer progress, one of whose mandates is the continued creation and use of technological achievement. So say Wills, Krauthammer, Kissinger, and Weber, and so also say the extraordinary media presentation of the war, which reduced it as much as possible to pure technological spectacle: chart, graph, map, military expertise, sporting event, entertainment, and video performance. In the inversions that alienation, fetishism, and reification produce, as Marx (1980, 656) noted, "All our invention and progress seem to result in endowing material forces with intellectual life and in stultifying human life into a material force." Could there be a more acute account of the obscenity of "smart bombs" and "collateral damage" or of the underlying horror of this self-righteous slaughter?

NOTES

1. This argument is a small part of a much longer discussion of the ideology of the Gulf War which I am preparing. In addition to the technological modernism of the war there are also strands of the following mystifications and legitimations: the "universal human rights" argument used to condemn Iraq as the violator or Kuwait freedom; the appeal to patriotism as the surrogate for a nonexistent lost community—the war as the embodiment of "negative unity"; the role of the media in the construction of depersonalized "video game" spec-

tacle; and the development of public participation not as active engagement, but as passive acquiescence.

2. For the material which follows I am indebted to Gibson (1986).

REFERENCES

Blum, F. H. 1959, October. "Max Weber: The Man of Politics and the Man Dedicated to Objectivity and Rationality." *Ethics* LXX. 1.

Cockburn, A. 1991. "The Press and the Just War." *The Nation* 252 (February 18).

Gibson, J. W. 1986. *The Perfect War: Technowar in Vietnam*. Boston: Atlantic Monthly Press.

Kissinger, H. A. 1974. *American Foreign Policy*. New York: W. W. Norton.

Kundera, M. 1983. *The Joke*, trans. M. H. Heim. New York: Penguin Books.

Macarthur, J. R. 1992. *Second Front: Censorship and Propaganda in the Gulf War*. New York: Hill and Wang.

Marx, K. and Engels, F. 1980. *Collected Works*, Vol. 14. New York: International Publishers.

Manufacturing the Attack on Liberalized Higher Education

ELLEN MESSER-DAVIDOW

o far as the general reading public knew, the "political correctness" debate burst suddenly onto the American scene toward the end of 1990, but liberalized higher education had been under attack throughout the 1980s. NEH Chairmen William J. Bennett (1984) and Lynne V. Cheney (1987, 1988, 1989, 1990) had issued a series of reports on the decline of humanities teaching and research, and the Heritage Foundation had drawn up an agenda for education (Gardiner 1985). By 1991, mass-market books attacking higher education (e.g., by Allan Bloom, Charles Sykes, Page Smith, Roger Kimball, and Dinesh D'Souza) had appeared at the impressive rate of two per year, the *New Republic*, *Commentary*, and *Academic Questions* had printed forums, George Will had fired salvos in syndicated columns, and D'Souza had published in a half-dozen venues, including the *Atlantic Monthly*, *Forbes*, and the *American Scholar*.

Responding to the attack, progressive academics made the proverbial mistake of too little too late. They replied to arguments, ignoring the issue of how so many of these arguments had suddenly appeared in print, and they focused on textual features (rhetoric, validity of claims), not realizing that by the time the attack was so widely textualized it had become a *fait accompli*. They also failed to notice that the strategy for the attack had percolated in right-wing periodicals during the 1980s: Conservative writers had demonized a new academic "gang of four" (feminists, Marxists, theorists, multiculturalists), an anticommunist technique

used by the Old Right in the 1950s, and targeted their criticisms to particular audiences, a direct-mail technique developed by the New Right
in the late 1970s. Already by the mid-1980s the Right had laid out the
argument that "tenured radicals" had begun a wholesale demolition of
Western culture and of the universities entrusted with preserving it.

In the mid-1980s, a group of conservatives associated with Paul
Weyrich's Free Congress Foundation (FCF) launched "cultural conservatism" as the template for renewing the movement. Turning away from
the conservative preoccupation with economics, FCF recognized that the
"activist movements built around values, life-styles, and other non-economic issues" were "the vanguards of a profound political change" and
predicted that "the politics that carry us into the twenty-first century will
be based not on economics, but on culture" (Institute for Cultural Conservatism 1987, 1). FCF's agenda called for citizens and government to
reform the mediating institutions that transmit culture (families, schools,
churches, labor unions, businesses, media, and professions) by exemplifying, preaching, and in some cases enforcing Western culture (Lind
1986, 7; Institute for Cultural Conservatism 1987, 25). Following Weyrich's *dictum* that ideas have consequences *only when* they are connected
to action, cultural conservatism supplied the ideas that conservatives are
to implement through their movement (M. Schwartz and W. Lind, personal communication, June 11, 1992).

BREAKING THE HIGHER-EDUCATION MONOPOLY

To break what they perceive as a liberal monopoly of higher education,
conservatives needed to establish a conservative presence in the academy (see, e.g., Cribb 1989, 7). They knew they could not depend only on
outsiders to force change upon an academy whose independence from
external political interference is widely acknowledged, though not always
observed. Rather, they had to attack the academy from both within and
without.

The organization most successful in moving the attack into the academy is the Madison Center for Educational Affairs (MCEA), formed from
a 1990 merger of the Institute for Educational Affairs and the Madison
Center, and headquartered in Washington, DC. It has done so largely
by developing the Collegiate Network of seventy conservative student
newspapers on sixty-six campuses across the country (Madison Center
1991, 4). To support the Network, MCEA provides grants to the newspapers (nearly $200,000 in 1991); editorial and technical assistance; a toll-
free hotline for advice; a monthly newsletter and publications from more
than eighty conservative organizations; monthly cash awards for news-

paper writing; regional conferences for newspaper staff; referrals to legal centers; and internships at federal offices, conservative organizations, and conservative publications (Madison Center 1990, 4–8, 9–10; Madison Center 1991, 6–9, 16–17; P. Pyott [Vice President, MCEA], personal communication, April 2, 1992; R. L. Lukefahr [Senior Program Officer, MCEA], personal communication, April 2, 1992).

Most of the debates on race, gender, sexuality, and Leftism in the academy were catalyzed by these newspapers, as the particularly virulent example of the *Dartmouth Review* attests. Curriculum surveys and attacks on curricular innovation have been published in virtually all of them (R. L. Lukefahr, personal communication, April 2, 1992; D. S. Bernstein [Program Officer, MCEA], personal communication, April 2, 1992). Fueling the debates, the MCEA *Common-Sense Guide to American Colleges* (Pyott 1991) evaluates the academic and political climate at colleges and universities. It is based on questionnaires asking administrators, faculty, and students about affirmative action programs, abortion counseling, organizations for women and homosexuals, political indoctrination in courses, speech and behavior codes, and speakers' ideologies (P. Pyott, personal communication, March 18, 1992). In short, MCEA publications reformulate and distribute the vanguard-movement issues that FCF believes conservatives must appropriate.

By attacking liberalized higher education from without and within, while strengthening conservative colleges and universities, the Right hopes to transform higher education into a free-market economy of competing institutions: public and private, Christian and secular, conservative and liberal. If institutions must compete, their viability can be determined by those consumers of education who, through their choices, can reorient the market. Conservatives have reasonable hopes that they can both create and reorient a higher-education market. Given its cultural agenda and free-market strategy, we should see conservatism not merely as a reticulated movement, but as a massive apparatus consisting of several systems articulated to produce cultural change. These systems are think tanks, training programs, foundations, grassroots organizations, and legal centers.

THE THINK-TANK SYSTEM

While some conservative national think tanks existed before 1975, notably the Hoover Institution (1919), the American Enterprise Institute (AEI) (1943), and the Heritage Foundation (1973), dozens were established by the mid-1980s and have been augmented more recently by some fifty-five state-level think tanks. National think tanks were originally conceived as "planning and advisory institutions" on government policy that would influence the "nation's formal political processes" (Smith 1991, xiii). The most influential during the Reagan and Bush administrations were AEI and Heritage. Although AEI was retrenched because its right-wing backers judged it too centrist (Blumenthal 1986a, D1), Heritage continued to expand. In 1991, it had 160 people on staff, 22 fellows and scholars, more than 50 adjunct scholars, and a budget of $19.3 million remarkable for its wide base of support: 50% of its income was contributed by 170,000 individual donors solicited through direct mail, 25% by foundations, 13% by corporations, and the remaining 12% derived from investments and sales. Among the foundations supporting it are Bradley, Coors, Noble, Olin, Reader's Digest, and Scaife (Heritage 1991, 28–29, 34–37).

To produce and deliver its ideas, Heritage draws on 2,000 scholars listed in its *Annual Guide to Public Policy Experts* (1992) and its nearly 200 publications per year. As Edwin J. Feulner, the president, makes explicit, "We stress an efficient, effective delivery system. Production is one side; marketing is equally important" (Blumenthal 1986b, 49). Four divisions market ideas: Public Relations to the media and the public; Government Relations to Congress, the administration, and agencies; Academic Relations to the academy and international conservative network; and Corporate Relations to businesses and trades. Division marketing is driven by policy research and coordinated at twice-weekly meetings of the senior management (C. A. Rubin [Director of Public Relations, Heritage Foundation], personal communication, June 11, 1992 and July 2, 1992).

How marketing works, Feulner explains, is that "every congressional staffer is in the Heritage computer. So are about 3,500 journalists, organized by specialty. Every Heritage study goes out with a synopsis to those who might be interested; every study is turned into an op-ed piece, distributed by the Heritage Features Syndicate to newspapers that publish them" (Blumenthal 1986b, 49). The goal is to get the message to the media and the public, who in turn get it to policymakers. Feulner's comments are not fanciful capitalist rhetoric. Through the Heritage marketing model, adopted by other right-wing organizations, the Right has developed an "ideas industry" (Smith 1991, 7), in which a cadre of professionals use think tanks, interest groups, and media to produce and distribute conservative ideas.

Although Heritage originally focused on foreign and economic policy, it launched several cultural projects during the late 1980s at the behest and through the funding of conservative foundations (J. M. Slye [Research Assistant, Cultural Policy Studies Program, Heritage Foundation], personal communication, June 11, 1992): notably, the Bradley Fellows, Salvatori Center for Academic Leadership, Conservative Curriculum, and the Cultural Policy Studies Program. The latter program, headed by William Bennett, brings "cultural issues into the mainstream of political debate" and advocates "the traditional values that should more fully influence American culture" (Heritage 1991, 25). Its Working Group, whose members represent conservative organizations and federal offices, provided former Vice President Quayle with materials on Murphy Brown's single motherhood and the Los Angeles riots, helped to raise the Congressional debate on campus speech codes, and was instrumental in Justice Clarence Thomas's confirmation (J. M. Slye, personal communication, June 11, 1992).

As this brief summary suggests, cultural conservatives use think tanks to produce the "scholarly" knowledge they cannot generate from within the academy. By conflating knowledge produced by scholarly methods with the aura of authority surrounding those who produce this knowledge, think tanks provide a "scholarly" aura of authority upon which cultural conservatives capitalize to advance their political agenda. In actuality, as Smith (1991, xv–xvi) remarks, most national think tanks grew from "the ideological combat and policy confusion of the past two decades" and "are geared toward political activism and propaganda, rather than toward scholarship." But they market ideas through a scholarly apparatus of journals and seminars as if they were the products of scholarship. Such misrepresentation allows think-tank ideas to compete with scholarly knowledge in policy making and public arenas. Although think tanks produce what passes for "scholarly" knowledge, they cannot produce scholars and professionals because they do not control the training and credentialing practices that early in this century moved within the purview of the higher-education system. Consequently, conservatives have appropriated these practices by establishing training institutes.

THE TRAINING-PROGRAM SYSTEM

Two such training institutes, the Leadership Institute and the National Journalism Center, overlap in their ideologies, goals, and programs. The purpose of the Leadership Institute (LI), founded by Morton Blackwell in 1979, is to increase the number and effectiveness of conservative activists, which it does through nine schools that offer training in youth leadership, grassroots activism, organization building, direct-mail fundraising, foreign service, Capital Hill staffing, legislative management, broadcast journalism, and student publications. Notice that four train conservatives for the movement and five train them for the professions. LI deploys the double strategy of strengthening the conservative movement by putting *professionals* into it and weakening the liberal professions by putting *conservatives* into them. Can this strategy succeed? LI offered thirty-three training programs in 1992 and graduated a record 1,002 students in 1991, for a total of 3,950 from 1987 through 1991 (Armey 1991, 5; Leadership Institute 1992, 1, 5). Its 1990 estimated income was $1,119,180, and its wide base of support resembles that of the Heritage Foundation (W. Forrest [Vice President for Programs, LI], personal communication, June 9, 1992; Leadership Institute n.d., 22–23).

The National Journalism Center (NJC), founded in 1976–1977, helps "talented young people break into the media" by providing six weeks of training in journalism and "common-sense economics," followed by six weeks of interning at its four dozen outlets (C. Warden [Editor, NJC], personal communication, April 3, 1992). NJC aims to give college graduates the experience they need to apply for entry-level journalism jobs and to correct what it sees as the liberal bias of journalism as taught in universities and practiced in the media (C. Warden, personal communication, April 3, 1992; M. Klein [Associate Editor, NJC], personal communication, April 3, 1992). Offering its program four times a year to sixty to eighty students, NJC estimated in 1990 that "500 of our alumni are working in media and media-related posts" at AP, UPI, ABC, CBS, CNN, C-SPAN, Copely News Service, the *Washington Post, Washington Times, Wall Street Journal, Detroit News, Los Angeles Times, San Francisco Chronicle, Seattle Times, Phoenix Gazette*, numerous magazines, and virtually every conservative periodical (Education and Research Institute 1990, 1, 6–9; NJC n.d.).

LI and NJC are not educational organizations but political ones engaged in political contest. As William Forrest, an LI vice president, put it, "The outcome of political contest over time is determined by the number and effectiveness of the activists on either side. . . . To some extent, what we do at this Institute is to try to increase the number and effectiveness of the activists who are conservative." That's what the fight is about, he added (W. Forrest, personal communication, July 13, 1992).

LI and NJC are also professionalizing institutions intent on breaking the academic monopoly on professionalization. By describing journalism as an easily learned craft and thus deprofessionalizing it, they delegitimate university training and legitimate their own: no need for universities to train students in technical skills that can be learned in a few weeks. Paradoxically, at the same time that they use antiprofessional critique to attack academic professionalization they are professionalizing cadres of young conservatives by giving them credentials to move into the professions. Their attack on professions articulates to the attack on higher education, and both are enabled by the flow of money from right-wing foundations.

THE FOUNDATION SYSTEM

In the mid-1980s, conservative foundations put their resources behind the shift to cultural conservatism. Elsewhere I have examined this shift in terms of the range of foundation grantors and grantees, the grants of a single foundation over time, and the cultural programs at a single organization supported by a range of foundations (Messer-Davidow 1993). Here I give only a few examples of each pattern. First, for 1989, conservative foundations awarded $115,000 to the Center for Individual Rights, $710,000 to the Free Congress Foundation, $411,902 to the Institute for Educational Affairs and $555,000 to the Madison Center (before the MCEA merger in 1990), $115,000 to the Leadership Institute, and $110,000 to the National Journalism Center. Second, for 1989, Olin awarded $817,352 to Boston University (some to Peter L. Berger), $1,261,745 to Harvard University (some to Harvey C. Mansfield and Samuel P. Huntington), $2,118,598 as four 3-year grants to Yale University; and $1,190,533 to Stanford University (Kovacs 1990, 524–528). Over the years, Olin funded numerous professorships, postdoctoral fellowships, institutes, and lecture series for conservative academics. For instance, "between 1986 and 1989," Allan Bloom "received from Olin over $3 million in mostly unrestricted gifts" (Gottfried 1991–1992, 186). Third, conservative foundations fund the new academic programs at the Heritage Foundation—for instance, the Bradley Resident Scholars Program, established in 1987 to teach young scholars about the policy process (Heritage 1992–1993, 2); and the Salvatori Center for Academic Leadership, established in 1991 to train conservatives as academic leaders and define higher-education issues (Heritage, 1991, 19).

The obvious conclusion, which I draw from a larger sampling, is that a handful of foundations—particularly Bradley, Coors, JM, Noble, Olin, Scaife, and Smith Richardson—have supported the organizations that attack liberalized higher education. These foundations, originally established by conservative families, have been taken over by neoconservative staff who are using them "to influence culture and in turn shape politics. Observing the Left's 'long march through institutions,' neoconservatives have begun their own march, producing official positions on educational, religious, and aesthetic questions and hiring or coopting advocates to publicize their stands" (Gottfried 1993, 125).

THE GRASSROOTS SYSTEM

Foundations support the institutionalization of cultural conservatism, but the work of legitimating it is done by academics themselves, primarily through the National Association of Scholars (NAS). The NAS, which took its scholarly name in 1987, evolved from a predecessor organization called the Coalition for Campus Democracy, founded in 1982 under the auspices of the neoconservative Committee for the Free World and the IEA, whose associates were Irving Kristol, Midge Decter, Elliott Abrams, and William Simon, president of Olin. The NAS, like the Coalition, is led by Stephen Balch and Herbert London and funded by right-wing foundations (Diamond 1991a, 1991b). For Fiscal Year 1991–1992, it estimated revenues of $682,830 from Bradley, Coors, Olin, Scaife, Smith Richardson, Joyce, Madison Center, and anonymous donors (National Association of Scholars 1991).

The complex structure of the NAS—a national organization with 3000 members, some thirty-five state and campus chapters, caucuses within the disciplines, and international affiliates—performs several functions (S. H. Balch [President and Executive Director, NAS], personal communication, April 1, 1992; Leatherman 1993, A15–16). In its scholarly guise, it sponsors conferences and publishes *Academic Questions*. Meanwhile, its political activities are wide-reaching. Its research center assembles the stories of alleged conservative victims of Left academic abuses and also is rumored to compile data on Left academics. National headquarters mobilizes the membership to lobby government officials and churn out writings on the excesses of "tenured radicals." State chapters establish a conservative faculty presence on campuses. Through these activities, the NAS gives legislators and the public the impression that a substantial number of faculty oppose the liberalizing trends in higher education. More insidiously, its scholarly trappings legitimate the products of the "ideas industry," thereby advancing cultural conservatism's agenda.

THE JUDICIAL REGULATORY SYSTEM

Increasingly using the conservative legal centers that have sprung up across the country, conservatives are turning to the courts to change higher education. For instance, the Center for Individual Rights (CIR), founded in 1989, differs from other legal centers by specializing in academic cases and entering them in the early stages. By the time a case reaches the appeals level, a CIR counsel explained, it has been crafted and the mistakes made. The CIR helps to craft conservative cases before litigation (J. A. Shea, Jr. [Associate Counsel, CIR], personal communication, June 8, 1992; CIR 1992). Many of its clients, described "as 'live white males'" who have been victimized by the Left (Magner 1991, A5), are referred by the NAS and MCEA.

The CIR has an annual income of $450,000, mostly supplied by the

Bradley, JM, Olin, Scaife, Smith Richardson, and Wiegand foundations, and a staff of five (Kornhauser 1991, 15; Magner 1991, A5). However, its reach is more extensive than these numbers suggest, because it arranges for attorneys, many from prestigious law firms, to represent its clients *pro bono* and obtains *amicus curiae* briefs from prominent organizations, such as the American Association of University Professors and the New York Civil Liberties Union (CIR 1992). The CIR strategy of establishing judicial precedents for cultural conservatism is likely to be successful in a federal court system now substantially packed with Reagan and Bush appointees.

To reframe the attack on liberalized higher education, I draw on a traditional model of production. Cultural conservatism may be seen as the template of the attack. The articulated systems—think tanks, training institutes, grassroots organizations, legal centers, foundations—are the manufacturing apparatus. The many writings and actions are the individual products. Conservative publications, seminars, and lobbying, together with the mainstream media, are the distribution system. The Right's use of this apparatus exemplifies a vertical articulatory practice—constructing institutional nodal points to leverage change in national and local institutions, which in turn are used to make cultural and political change.

THE FUTURE OF CULTURAL CONSERVATISM

My fieldwork in conservative organizations suggests how the Right will intensify its attack on liberalized higher education. First, it will continue to manufacture conservative victim stories such as those that already have appeared in NAS publications, Collegiate Network newspapers, *Heterodoxy*, and columns of conservative journalists. From print, the victim stories will progress to legal centers and conservative courts, not only constituting a media reality but also changing case law. Secondly, the Right will continue to support conservative colleges, scholars, and students and attempt to reinstate conservative curricula. Finally, long before the 1992 presidential election, the Right began to shift its attention away from Washington and to states, counties, and cities. It is expanding its organizations through local chapters linked by three powerful grassroots technologies: direct mail, a new national computer subscription network, and national television networks. With these technologies, the Right can diffuse conservative consciousness and circulate plans for local interventions.

The election of President Clinton may slow conservatives but it will not stop them, because they can still make change through courts, state legislatures, and their own apparatus. Doing so, they use academic rhetoric and professionalizing practices to hide their politics, but their politics, make no mistake about it, consist in courses of practical action to impose a right-wing America—political, economic, and cultural—on all of us. Any effective response from those academics who are unwilling to live under the right-wing regime will also require practical actions:

- Building coalitions among progressives, liberals, and moderates
- Campaigning for progressive, liberal, and moderate candidates
- Restaffing government agencies
- Acquiring legislative, lobbying, media, and fundraising skills
- Learning how to present liberalized higher education to other communities, especially the media, policymakers, and alumni

In short, to have a hand in determining the future of cultural conservatism, progressive academics must engage less in debate, which we have been trained to believe is instrumental in academic change, and more in activism, which the Right has shown us is decisive in all arenas of change—political, economic, and cultural.

REFERENCES

Armey, D. 1991. [Direct-mail letter]. Washington, DC: Leadership Institute, June 8.

Bennett, W. J. 1984. *To Reclaim a Legacy*. Washington, DC: National Endowment for the Humanities.

Blumenthal, S. 1986a. "Hard Times at the Think Tank for American Enterprise Institute, A Crisis of Money and Conservatism." *Washington Post*, July 26: D1.

———. 1986b. *The Rise of the Counter-Establishment: From Conservative Ideology to Political Power*. New York: Times Books.

Center for Individual Rights. 1992. *Docket Report* (1st, 2nd, and 3rd quarters). Washington, DC: Center for Individual Rights.

Cheney, L. V. 1987. *The Humanities and the American Promise*. Charlottesville, VA: Colloquium on the Humanities and the American People.

———. 1988. *Humanities in America*. Washington, DC: National Endowment for the Humanities.

———. 1989. *50 Hours*. Washington, DC: National Endowment for the Humanities.

———. 1990. *Tyrannical Machines*. Washington, DC: National Endowment for the Humanities.

Cribb, T. K. 1989. "Conservatism and the American Academy: Prospects for the 1990s." *Heritage Lectures Series* (No. 226). Washington, DC: Heritage Foundation.

Diamond, S. 1991a. "Endowing the Right-Wing Academic Agenda." *Covert Action Information Bulletin* 38: 46–49.

——. 1991b. "Readin', Writin' and Repressin.'" *Z Magazine* (February): 45–49.

Education and Research Institute. 1990. *E&RI 1990 Annual Report*. Washington, DC: Education and Research Institute.

Gardiner, E. M. ed. 1985. *A New Agenda for Education*. Washington, DC: Heritage Foundation.

Gottfried, P. 1993. *The Conservative Movement*, rev. ed. New York: Twayne.

——. 1991–1992. "Populism vs. Neoconservatism." *Telos* 90: 184–188.

The Heritage Foundation. 1991. *1991 Annual Report*. Washington, DC: Heritage Foundation.

——. 1992. *The Annual Guide to Public Policy Experts, 1992*, ed. R. Huberty and B. D. Hohbach. Washington, DC: Heritage Foundation.

——. 1992–1993. *Bradley Resident Scholars Application Form, 1992–93 Academic Year*. Washington, DC: Heritage Foundation.

Institute for Cultural Conservatism/Free Congress Research and Education Foundation. 1987. *Cultural Conservatism: Toward a New National Agenda*. Washington, DC: Institute for Cultural Conservatism/Free Congress Research and Education Foundation.

Kornhauser, A. 1991. "The Right Versus the Correct." *Legal Times* (April 29): 1, 14–15.

Kovacs, R. ed. 1990. *Foundation Grants Index*, 19th ed. New York: Foundation Center.

The Leadership Institute. 1992. *Building Leadership: The Newsletter of the Leadership Institute* 6 (1).

——. n.d. *The Leadership Institute Prospectus*. Springfield, VA: Leadership Institute.

Leatherman, C. 1993. "Conservative Scholars' Group Draws Increasingly Diverse Voices to Its Cause." *Chronicle of Higher Education* (April 28): A15–A16.

Lind, W. S. 1986. "What Is Cultural Conservatism?" *Essays in Our Times* 2 (1): 1–8.

Madison Center for Educational Affairs. 1990. *1990 Annual Report*. Washington, DC: Madison Center for Educational Affairs.

——. 1991. *1991 Annual Report*. Washington, DC: Madison Center for Educational Affairs.

Magner, D. 1991. "Law Firm Goes to Bat for Campus Conservatives." *Chronicle of Higher Education* (September 25): A5.

Messer-Davidow, E. 1993, November. "Manufacturing the Attack on Liberalized Higher Education." *Social Text* 36: 40–80.

National Association of Scholars. 1991. *Revenue and expense sheets for FY 1990–91 and 1991–92*. Distributed at the NAS Convention, Minneapolis, MN, October 18–20, 1991.

National Journalism Center. n.d. [Unpublished montage of news clips].

Pyott, P. ed. 1991. *The Common-Sense Guide to American Colleges 1991–92*. Washington, DC: Madison Center for Educational Affairs/Lanham, MD: Madison Books.

——. 1992. [Administration, faculty, and student questionnaires, enclosed in letter to author, May 18, 1992].

Smith, J. A. 1991. *The Idea Brokers: Think Tanks and the Rise of the New Policy Elite*. New York: Free Press.

Index